These books were given to me, Larry Bush, and I was happy to have them reproduced.

Knoxville, Tennessee

crippledbeaglepublishing.com

Paperback ISBN 978-1-958533-93-2

Library of Congress Control Number: 2024908264

Reproduced in the United States of America

Dedication

To the individuals who inspired me and assisted me in get this book together. I had never seen the first book of minutes from 1906 to 1970 until my cousin, Elder Daniel Brantley, gave me his copy and a beginning collection of the minutes from 1971 to 2023. Others who were a help to me were Elder Lawrence Adams, Bennie Capps, Judson Palmer, and my wife Pat. Without them, I would never have been able to get these important minutes together and publish this historic book.

Thank you,

Larry Bush

In Memoriam

In Memoriam to my Dad Elder Joe C. Bush for his love of our Lord Jesus Christ and The Primitive Baptist Church. Dad was Born January 4, 1923, in Claiborne County, Tennessee, close to Little Barren Church on Highway 33. In 1934, when Norris Dam was constructed, they moved to Lone Mountain,

Tennessee, as part of the relocation program. They lived on Bear Creek Road. Dad attended Sugar Grove Missionary Baptist Church where he was saved and then joined the church when he was thirteen.

He had a tremendous love for gospel singing and was a song leader his entire life. Dad met my mother Norma Jean Brantley at Blue Springs Church in Sharps Chapel, Tennessee, when Rev. Claude Gose asked him to lead the singing for a revival. They were married February 21, 1946. Dad announced he was called to preach and was ordained February 18, 1951, by Carrs Branch Missionary Baptist Church in Claiborne County, Tennessee. He served as Pastor to several churches in Claiborne County and led singing until 1961. In 1962 we started attending Rocky Dale Primitive Baptist Church in Corryton, Tennessee, where we lived. We joined there, and Mom and Dad remained members until their deaths. In 1969, Dad was ordained at Rocky Dale and pastored several churches in the Powells Valley Primitive Baptist Association.

Now that I am older, I have a much greater appreciation for my dad's faith and beliefs in the Lord. He enjoyed attending and participating in communion services as much as anyone there. One of his favorite things to do when he was working was to sing old gospel songs. One of the ones I remember the most was "In Gethsemane Alone." I think the words of this song say more about my dad than I could ever write.

In Gethsemane Alone

Oh, what a wondrous love I see,
Freely shown for you and me.
By the one who did atone!
Just to show His matchless Grace.
Jesus suffered for the race.
In Gethsemane Alone.

"Tarry here," He told the three
"Tarry here and watch for Me."
But they heard no bitter moan,
For the three disciples slept
While my loving Savior wept
In Gethsemane Alone.

Long in anguish deep was He,
Weeping there for you and me,
For our sin to Him was known;
We should love him evermore
For the anguish that he bore
In Gethsemane Alone.
Refrain:
Oh what love, matchless love,
Oh what love for me was shown!
His forever I will be,
For the love He gave to me,
When he suffered all alone.

In getting these minutes together, I found that my dad preached the introductory sermon for the 1971 association meeting. This is the first meeting in this book. He read from the 6th chapter of Matthew and taking his text, "A Sure

Foundation". He found a foundation with the Lord early in life that took him through life's trials. Dad passed away peacefully in his sleep March 12, 1997.

In Memoriam

In loving memory of Bennie Capps, a cherished leader and dedicated servant within the Powells Valley Primitive Baptist Association. Born on February 5, 1936, Bennie has been a pivotal figure in our community, and his dedication and service have been deeply valued by all who knew him.

When I started my journey of doing a second book of minutes, I would ask friends and family different questions, and they always said to call Bennie Capps. I can remember my dad referring to him and what a fine man he was. The first time I spoke to Bennie Capps, I understood why my dad and others thought Bennie was so valuable to the Powells Valley Primitive Baptist Association. By the grace of God, Bennie faithfully served nearly fifty years as either Assistant Clerk or Clerk until his passing in 2024.

I asked Bennie to give me a little history on his service. The 155th session of the Powells Valley Association met at the sister church at Lenior City on August 16, 1974, with moderator Elder Albert Davis presiding. Elder Albert Davis called for the clerk and assistant clerk to come forward for the business session. Brother Bill Taylor was the clerk, and there was no assistant clerk as brother O.R. (Big Boy) Parrott had passed away. Elder Davis appointed Bennie Capps to help read the church letters. Afterwards, Brother Bill Taylor was reelected Clerk. Brother Bennie Capps was elected Assistant Clerk. When the Association met August 14, 1981, at Pleasant Hill Church, Brother Bill Taylor stepped down as Clerk, and Brother Bennie Capps was elected clerk. Brother Rina Johnson was elected assistant clerk. Brother Bennie has been clerk since then, with the following assisting him: Brother Don Sharp 1996-1997, Elder Glen Davis 1998-1999, Brother Don Sharp 2000-2010, Brother Chris Parton 2011-2019, no association meetings 2020-2021, Brother Gary Johnson 2022-present.

Bennie's dedication, leadership, and unwavering faith have left an indelible mark on the Powells Valley Primitive Baptist Association, and his service will be remembered for generations to come. I would like to express my heartfelt gratitude to Bennie and the others who have served alongside him. His legacy of service and commitment will continue to inspire us all.

Introduction

The Powell's Valley Association of Primitive Baptists was constituted in Grainger County, Tennessee, in 1816, with seventeen churches, 603 members, and fifteen elders (Hassel). From Elder Leonard White (Volume 1). After 202 years, the "Grand Ole Powell's Valley Association of Primitive Baptists"(this was a quote of the late Elder Albert Davis) has continued to share the Gospel of Jesus Christ. The Association today consists of eight churches, 585 members, eighteen Elders (eight Pastors, three Assistant Pastors, four in either declining health or with no church, and three licensed but not yet ordained). The main body of the original Association has continued to stand down through the years on the Articles Of Faith (found in Volume 1) as well as this volume.

The bond of Love that has prevailed among the Elders of the Association has truly been an example of is instructed by His Word. God's instruction is to "Love your neighbor as thy self." That love and harmony in the association have been passed on through the past 202 years.

The Covid-19 Pandemic of 2000-2002 took a toll on the attendance of the associational churches, and some had deaths from Covid. This disturbance encouraged the Pastors to stand and preach stronger about Jesus Christ and His crucifixion with certainty. These Men of God were and are dedicated to serving as Pastors of churches in the Association, of whom I count myself the least.

Thanks are due to Brother Larry Bush for time, work, and expense to put together this Second Volume of Association Minutes.

Elder Lawrence Adams

INDEX

Special Section

Years 1894-1908

MINUTES

OF THE

SEVENTY-SIXTH ANNUAL SESSION

OF THE

POWELL'S VALLEY ASSOCIATION

OF

PRIMITIVE BAPTISTS;

HELD WITH THE CHURCH AT

Mossy Spring, Union County, Tennessee,

August 17th, 18th and 19th, 1894.

MAYNARDVILLE, TENN.
B. T. COX, BOOK AND JOB PRINTER.
1894.

MINUTES.

Proceedings of the 76th Annual Session of the Powell's Valley Association of Primitive Baptists, held with the Church at Mossy Spring, Union County, Tenn.

Elder William West delivered the Introductory Sermon, from Philippians 2:12, 13.

Received letters from 16 Churches as the following account shows:

CHURCHES.	DELEGATES.	Rec'd by Baptism.	By Letter.	Restored.	Declaration.	Dismiss'd by Letter.	Excluded.	Deceased.	Total.	Saturday Meetings.
Browney's Creek,	Robert Wilson, N. Smith,		2			1	3		18	4
Barren,	J. J. Wood, Chris Keck, Cal Keck,		2	2		1		1	36	3
Cave Spring,	J. W. Riggs, A. Boruff. Wm. White, A. W. Brantly,	3		1			1		64	3
Cedar Spring,	W. A. Drummonds, B. F. Simmons, A. D. Simmons, E. S. Drummonds,	4	1	1		2	1		46	
Dotson's Creek,	I. C. Haynes, C. M. Cabbage, A. J. Boruff,	2	1				2		47	1
Davis' Creek,	H. Ausmus, R. Smith, Jack Owens,	1					2	2	88	1
Hamilton Grove,	E. M. Branson, Wm. Oaks, Wm. Hamilton,	6	1			3	1	3	59	1
Hind's Creek,	T. W. Baker, A. Baker, R. Graves, M. B. Warwick,				2		7		22	2
Lost Creek,	M. V. Hill, I. Bridges, H. Hill, A. G. Hill,	2			1				73	4
Mossy Spring,	S. M. Petree, M. B. Weaver, E. Weaver, G. Weaver, I. N. Hill,	32	1				3	2	110	2
Mt. Hebron,	T. Weaver, Wm. Collins, Jesse Lewis,				1				28	4
Mays' Hill,	John Mays,								13	1
Pleasant Point,	W. C. Profit.	1		1					76	2
Rose Hill,	Wm. West, G. W. Evans, J. K. Waggoner, T. G. Waggoner, C. L. Buckner, Jno. Hamilton,	17				1			87	3
Salem,	W. F. Taylor, A. L. Hopson, Geo. Cunningham, J. R. Ritter, E. Lawson,	18	1	1	1		2	1	59	2
Union,	J. Miller, D. Paton, J. Burnet, A. Browning,	5		1	6		3		141	4
		92	9	9	511		825	9	967	

2

1st—After an intermission of 10 minutes, the Messengers met in the house, and read letters from 16 Churches.

Organized by chosing Elder Henry Ausmus, Moderator; Elder E. M. Branson, Clerk,, and A. G. Hill, Ass't Clk.

2.—Read Rules of Decorum and Articles of Faith.

3.—Called for correspondence from sister Associations and received a letter from Hiwassee Association, by the hands of her Messengers, Elder I. S. Thomas and David Roberts.

4 —Called for newly constituted Churches, not belonging to our Association, which are sound in the faith. Received none.

5.—Appointed Thomas Weaver, J. Owens, John Miller, C. Keck and C. M. Cabbage, a Committee on Correspondence. Report called for, read, received and Committee discharged.

6.— Agreed to continue correspondence with our sister Associations, Hiwassee, Tennessee, Nolachucky and Mud Creek.

7.—We appoint the following delegates:

1st—To Hiwassee: Elder T. Baker, Brethren Wm. Collins, John Mayes, A. G. Hill and William Oaks. Meets with the Church at Poplar Springs, on Friday before the 4th Saturday in September, 1894.

2nd—To Tennessee, which meets with the Church at Beech Grove, on Friday before the 2nd Saturday in October, 1894, Elders Thos. Baker, E. M. Branson, and Bro. Rufus Graves.

3rd—To Nolachucky:

5th—To Mud Creek, to convene on Friday before the 4th Saturday in September, with the Church at ———, Elder Thomas Weaver.

6th—To Flint River, on Friday before the 1st Saturday in October, 1894, with the Church at ———, Elder T. Weaver.

7.—Appointed J. Burnett, Chesley Profit, R. Wilson, with the Moderator, Clerk and Correspondents, to aid a selected Committee to arrange the business for to-morrow. Report received and Committee discharged.

8.—Appointed Brethren John Miller and G. W. Evans a Committee on Finance, and reported $15.00.

SATURDAY, August 19, 1894.

Met according to appointment.

1. —Called the roll and erased names of Messengers not present. Appointed one member from each Church in the Association, with Mossy Spring Church, a Committee on Preaching, who reported for Saturday, Elders T. W. Baker, Isaac Roberts and S. M. Petree. For Sunday, Elders Thos. Weaver, Isaac Roberts, E. M. Branson and H. Ausmus.

2. —Continued the invitation to Correspondents. None responded.

3. —The report of the Committee appointed last year to visit the West Union Association, called for, received and the Committee discharged.

4. —Corresponding letters called for, read, received and ordered signed by the Moderator and Clerk,

5. —The request from Davis Creek considered. Advise sister Churches to go and visit Red Hill Church, ascertain their standing and give them advice.

6. —We agree to publish Union Meetings at Barren Creek, for the 3rd Saturday in September; Browney's Creek, the 4th Saturday in October; Cedar Spring, 1st Saturday in October.

7. —We appoint our next Association to be held wth the Church at Dotson's Creek.

8. —The Association agrees, in future, to elect officers by private ballot, including the appointee to preach the Introductory Sermon and Alternate.

9. —Elected Elder R. Wilson to preach the next Introductory Sermon, and Elder M. B. Weaver to be his Alternate.

10. —Agreed to have 1,000 copies of our Minutes printed, that the Clerk superintend the printing and distribution of the same, and have the remainder of funds for his services.

11. —Minutes read, approved and ordered signed by the Moderator and Clerk; then adjourned to time and place before stated.

ELI M. BRANSON, *Clerk*,   HENRY AUSMUS, *Moderator*,
Esco, Tenn.   *Speedwell, Tenn.*
A. G. HILL, *Ass't Cl'k, Rhodelia, Tenn.*

OBITUARIES.

Aimma Humphries, died Aug. 27, 1891.

Jane Hansard, died June 17, 1892.

Thomas Long, died December 2, 1892.

W. F. McHaffrey, died Aug. 28, 1893.

All were members of Mount Hebron Church.

Sisters Mary Alice Keller and Susan Bridges died in the fellowship of Hind's Creek Church in 1893.

Sister Victoria O. McCloud, wife of Lafayette McCloud, was born July 18, 1849, and departed this life Aug. 29, 1893, aged 44 years, 1 month and 11 days. Sister McCloud was a member of the Missionary Baptist Church about 20 years, and joined the Primitive Baptist the first Saturday in March, 1889, lived a consistent member and model Christian until her death, leaving a husband and five children, and passed away in the full triumph of faith.

Union Meetings.

There will be a Union Meeting held with Barren Church, Friday before the 3rd Saturday in September, 1894; one with the Church at Cedar Spring, Claiborne County, Tenn., Friday before the 1st Saturday in October, 1894; also, with the Church at Browney's Creek, Bell County, Ky., to commence Friday before the 4th Saturday in October, 1894.

5

ARTICLES OF FAITH.

ARTICLE 1.—We believe in one only true and living God, as he is revealed to us in the Holy Scriptures, Father, Son and Holy Ghost.

2.—We believe that the Scriptures of the Old and New Testament are the word of God and the only rule of all saving knowledge and obedience.

3.—We believe in the doctrine of election according to the foreknowledge of God.

4.—We believe in the doctrine of original sin.

5.—We believe in man's impotency to recover himself from the fallen state he is in by his own free will or ability.

6.—We believe that sinners are justified in the sight of God only by the imputed righteousness of Jesus Christ.

7.—We believe the elect, according to the foreknowledge of God, will be called, converted, regenerated and sanctified by the Holy Spirit.

8.—We believe the saints will persevere and never fall finally away.

9.— We believe that baptism and the Lord's supper are ordinances of Jesus Christ, and that true believers are the only subjects of these ordinances, and that the true mode of baptism is by immersion.

10.—We believe in the resurrection of the dead and the general judgment.

11.—We believe that the punishment of the wicked will be everlasting, and that the joys of the righteous will be eternal.

12 —We believe that no minister has the right to administer the ordinances except those who have been regularly baptized and called of God and come under the imposition of hands by the Presbytery.

ORDAINED MINISTERS.	P. O. ADDRESS.		LICENTIATES.
S. M. Petree	Lost Creek,	Tenn.	H. Packett
M. B. Weaver	Rhodelia,	"	
T. Weaver	Bayless,	"	
T. W. Baker	Bayless,	"	
H. Ausmus	Speedwell,	"	
J. M. Drummonds	Tucker,	"	
	Minkton,	"	M. M. Drummond
	Minkton,	"	B. F. Simmons,
G. A. Atkins,	Tuorn Hill,	"	
J. W. Riggs,	Esco,	"	
E. M. Branson	Esco,	"	
H. Wyrick,	Esco,	"	
	Effie,	"	G. W. Evans.
J. Suffridge	Lone Mountain,	"	
	Little Barren,	"	Calloway Keck.
Wm. West	Maynardville,	"	
	Keck's Chapel,	"	J. J. Woods.
Richard Atkins	Clear Spring,	"	
	Acuff,	"	H. Hurst
R. Wilson	Cubbage,	Ky.	N. Smith.
J. Sayler	Cubbage,	"	

6

PROCEEDINGS.

Minutes of the Seventy-ninth Annual Session of the Powell's Valley Association of Primative Order, held with the Church at M^t. Hebron, Anderson County, Tenn., on August 20, 21 and 22, 1897.

1. Introductory discourse by Elder E. M. Branson, from Mathew XVI; 18. "Whom do men say that I the Son of man am?"

2. The Association was called to order by the Mod., Thomas Weaver.

3. Letters called for and messengers names enrolled as shown in the table of statistics.

4.* The Association organized by choosing Elder T. W. Baker, Mod., Calaway Keck, Clerk,

5. Called for correspondence, the following were received; Nolachucky, Letter and minutes by Elder Drury Craig. Tennessee, letter and minutes by J. B. J. Brickey. Received no tidings from Mud Creek, Towaliga, Flint River and Hiwassee.

6. Invited corresponding messengers to seats with us.

7. Invited transient minister and bretheren to seats with us. Elder J. Hembree from the Tennessee, Eli Williamson from Nolachucky, and J.H. Ezell came forward and took seats with us.

COMMITTEES APPOINTED, VIZ:

8. On Arrangements—Wm. Oaks, J. Miller, B. F. Simmons, Bratcher Sharp, and A. J. Hopson.

9. On Correspondence—H. Ausmus, James Miller, J. Burnett, John Waggoner, and Thomas Weaver.

10. On Finance—J. B. Simmons and J. Owens.

Adjourned to meet Saturday morning at 9 o'clock.

SATURDAY MORNING.

The Association met according to appointment. Praise and prayer by the Moderator.

1. Called the roll and eraced the names of absentees.

2. Appointed a Committee on Preaching, viz: One member from each church, with Mt. Hebron church.

REPORT OF THE COMMITTEES:

8. On Preaching—For Saturday: Elders Wm. West, Richard Wilson, and Drury Craige.

For Sunday: Elders Drury Craige, J. Hembree, H. Ausmus, T. W. Baker to close.

4. On Arrangements—Report read, received, and the committee discharged.

5. On Correspondence—Report read, received with the amendment and committee discharged.

6. Appointed correspondence, viz:

Nolachucky—Mountain Rest Church at Ogle's Chapel, Coke Co., Tenn., on Friday before the 4th Saturday in September, 1897. Elders Thomas Weaver, T. W. Baker, and Brethren B. F. Simmons and J. Waggoner.

7. Tennessee—T. J. Waggoner, B. F. Simmons, Eld. T. W. Baker.

8. Hiwassee—Macedonia Church, Morgan Co., Tenn., on Friday before the 4th Saturday in September, 1897. Eld. Wm. West and Brother Collins.

9. Towaliga—Elder E. M. Branson.

10. Mud Creek—Elders S. M. Petree and J. W. Riggs.

11. Committee on Finance reported $18.75. Agreed that the Clerk have $6.00 for his services, and that we use $2.75 to assist in defraying the visiting preachers' expenses.

12. The request from Lost Creek, that the Moderator and Clerk of the Church where the Association be held be the Moderator and Clerk of the Association, considered and agreed to follow the old rule.

13. Query from Daviess Creek—"Is an organized Church of Christ an independent body to do business? Answer; it is when it acts according to the Bible.

14. Query from Dotson Creek—"Is it according to Gospel order and Baptist usage to retain members in our chuches that belong to any secret organization? Answer; (we think not,) we advise the Churches not to be to hasty in dealing with them as we think it is not a sin unto death.

15. The Association reconsidered and agreed to print obituaries.

16. We appoint our next Association to be held at Browney's Creek Church, (15 miles north-east of Middlesborough, Ky.) on Friday before the 3rd Saturday in Aug., 1898.

17. The Association agrees to have the contribution of each church stated in each letter.

18. Appointed Elder J. W. Riggs to preach the introductory and Elder Calaway Keck his alternate.

19. Agreed that the clerk have 1000 copies of the minutes printed and distributed among the Churches.

20. Resolved that we tender our thanks to Mt. Hebron Church and vicinity for their kind hospitality during our stay with them.

21. Minutes read and approved. Adjourned to meet as stated above.

T. W. BAKER, Moderator,
Calaway Keck, Clerk. Bayless, Tennessee.
Little Barren, Tennessee.

CHURCHES.	CLERKS.	P. O. ADDRESS.	
Big Barren,	W. F. Edwards,	Little Barren,	Tennessee.
Browney's Creek,	Robert Wilson,	Cubbage,	Kentucky.
Brimstone,	J. C. Henry,		
Bean Creek,	Joel Malicoat,	Bean Station,	Tennessee.
Cave Spring,	W. C. Boruff,	Phebe,	"
Cedar Spring,	W. A. Drummonds,	Minkton,	"
Dotson Creek,	C. M. Cubbage,	Haynes,	"
Davis' Creek,	James Edwards,	Speedwell,	"
Hamilton Grove,	Wm. Oaks,	Rule,	"
Hind's Creek,	R. Graves,	Hurricane Branch,	"
Lost Creek,	H. Hill,	Sill,	"
Mossy Spring,	I. N. Hill,	Rhodelie,	"
Mt. Hebron,	Jessie Lewis,	Twinville,	"
Pleasant Point,	P. F. Keck,	Goin,	"
Rose Hill,	C. L. Buckner,	Kate,	"
Red Hill,	Jeff Treece,	Oldtown,	"
Salem,	J. Idol,	Dutch,	"
Union,	John Burnett,	Sharp's Chapel,	"

9

CHURCHES.	NAMES OF MESSENGERS.	Rec'd by Ex. & Bap.	Received by Letter.	Restored.	Confession of Faith.	Dismissed by Letter	Excluded.	Dead.	Total.	Saturday Meetings.
Big Barren	Calaway Keck, J. D. Monroe.		3	1						1
Browney's Creek	R. Wilson, J. F. Huret, T. J. Miracle.	5	3	2			3			1
Bean Creek	Wm. Collins, Joel Madicoat.	3								2
Brimstone	Letter. No Messenger.									1
Caye Spring	J. W. Riggs, W. H. Brantly, Wm. White.	1								1
Cedar Spring	B. F. Simmons, A. D. Simmons.									2
Davis Creek	H. Ausmus, S. Edwards, Jas. Herald, J. Ausmus, J. Owens.									
Dotson's Creek	Wm. West, Wm. Hammack, J. A. Capps, J. Hammack.	12			2	1	2	2		
Hinds Creek	T. W. Baker, F. B. Sharp, J. B. Simmons.									1
Hamilton Grove	E. M. Branson, J. Evans, Wm. Oaks, V. L. Rally.									2
Jessey's Creek	No Intelligence.									
Lost Creek	A. G. Hill, J. M. Miller, M. V. Hill, H. Oaks, U. Hill.	4	1	1		1	2	2		1
Mossy Spring	R. M. Petree, M. R. Weaver, W. R. Petree, J. S. Heniger, G. Weaver.	5	1				2	4		2
Mt. Hebron	T. Weaver, W. R. Hoffner, I. G. Gentry, C. Vandergriff, Wm. Collins, J Lewis, E. M. Collins.					1		1		2
Mayses Hill	No Intelligence.									
Pleasant Point	A. Collins, M. Collins, M. J. Sowder.									
Red Hill	T. J. Waggoner, Esaw Hundly, J. Waggoner, C. L. Buckner.	22				1				1
	David Treece, W. F. Robertson.									
Salem	A. J. Hopson, J. R. Ritter, A. L. Hopson, J. T. Oliver.									
Union	J. Miller, E. Graves, Esaw Streveles, J. Burnett.	11	3	1			6			1

10

ARTICLES OF FAITH.

ARTICLE 1. We believe in one only true and living God, as He is revealed to us in the Holy Scriptures, Father, Son and Holy Ghost.

2. We believe that the Scriptures of the Old and New Testament are the word of God and the only rule of all saving knowledge and obedience.

3. We believe in the doctrine of election according to the foreknowledge of God.

4. We believe in the doctrine of original sin.

5. We believe in man's impotency to recover himself from the fallen state he is in by his own free will or ability.

6. We believe that sinners are justified in the sight of God only by the imputed righteousness of Jesus Christ.

7. We believe the elect, according to the foreknowledge of God, will be called, converted, regenerated and sanctified by the Holy Spirit.

8. We believe the saints will preserve and never fall finally away.

9. We believe that baptism and the Lord's supper are ordinances of Jesus Christ, and that true believers are the only subjects of these ordinances, and that the true mode of baptism is by immersion.

10. We believe in the resurrection of the dead and the general judgement.

11. We believe that the punishment of the wicked will be everlasting, and that the joys of the righteous will be eternal.

12. We believe that no minister has the right to administer the ordinances except those who have been regularly baptised and called of God and come under the imposition of hands by the Presbytery.

ELDERS.	P. O. ADDRESS.	
H. Ausmus,	Speedwell,	Tennessee.
Thomas Weaver,	Bayless,	"
T. W. Baker,	"	"
S. M. Petree,	Rhodelie,	"
M. B. Weaver,	"	"
J. M. Drummonds,	Tacket,	"
J. W. Riggs,	Pleasant,	"
E. M. Branson,	Esco,	"
Wm. West,	Maynardville,	"
R. Atkins,	Sheltons Ford,	"
J. Suffridge,	Lone Mountain,	"
G. A. Atkins,	Thorn Hill,	"
J. D. Monroe,	Goin,	"
Calaway Keck,	Little Barren,	"
R. Wilson,	Cubbage,	Kentucky.
N. Smith,	"	"
J. Saylor,	Calaway,	"
LICENTIATES.		
J. H. Packet,	Long Hollow,	Tennessee.
B. F. Simmons,	Minkton,	"
H. Hurst,	Acuff,	"
A. J. Hopson,	Clear Spring,	"
J. B. Ritter,	Liberty Hill,	"
M. V. Hill,	Sill,	"
W. R. Petree,	Rhodelie,	"
J. A. Capps,	Acuff,	"
A. J. Boruf,	"	"
John Hammock,	Ambro,	"
J. J. Woods,	Little Barren,	"

11

MINUTES

OF THE

EIGHTY-SECOND ANNUAL SESSION

OF THE

POWELL'S VALLEY ASSOCIATION

——OF——

PRIMITIVE BAPTISTS

HELD WITH THE CHURCH AT

Hamilton Grove, Union County, Tenn.,

AUGUST 17, 18 & 19, 1900.

KNOXVILLE, TENN.:
S. B. NEWMAN & CO., PRINTERS AND BOOK BINDERS.
1900.

800 copies—Printer's Fee $9.00.

12

PROCEEDINGS.

1. Introductory sermon delivered by Elder H. Ausmus from 2nd Timothy, 4:2: "Preach the word; be instant in season, out of season; reprove, rebuke, exhort, with all long suffering and doctrine."
2. The Association was called to order by the Moderator.
3. Letters called for and read by A. G. Hill, J. M. Vandergriff and M. V. Hill, and messengers names enrolled.
4. Letters were then received.
5. Elder J. S. Lewis was chosen Moderator, and M. V. Hill, Clerk.
6. Read Rules of Decorum.
7. Called for petitionary letters.
8. Called for correspondence and received a letter and minutes from Mud Creek Association by the hand of her messenger, Elder G. W. Bulman.
9. Invited transient ministers to seats with us.

COMMITTEES APPOINTED.

10. On Arrangements—Elder Thomas Weaver, John Miller, Elvin Weaver, Wm. Oaks, and Jacob Owens.
11. On Correspondence—Elders T. W. Baker, M. B. Weaver, E. M. Branson, Brethren John Simmons, A. J. Hopson, with Moderator, Clerk and Correspondents invited to aid.
12. On Finance—Manuel Sowders and M. W. Sharp.
Adjourned to meet Saturday morning at 8 a. m.

SATURDAY MORNING.

Met pursuant to adjournment. Prayer by Elder M. B. Weaver.
1. Minutes of yesterday's proceedings read an' approved.
2. Called the roll and appointed a committee on preaching, viz.: One member from each church with Hamilton Grove church.

REPORT OF COMMITTEES.

3. On Preaching—For Saturday—Elders John Suffiridge, G. W. Bulman and J. D. Monroe.
Saturday night—Oaklona—Elders J. D. Monroe and H. Ausmus.
Miller's School House—Elders Wm. West and A. Boruff.
Cedar Grove—Elders N. T. Smith and A. J. Hopson.
Buckner's School House—Elders S. M. Petree and J. W. Riggs.
Hamilton Grove—Elders M. B. Weaver and E. M. Branson.
Lost Creek—Elders G. W. Bulman and Thomas Weaver.
For Sunday—Elders G. W. Bulman, Thomas Weaver and J. S. Lewis.
4. On Arrangements—Report read, received and committee discharged.
5. On Correspondence—Report read, received and committee discharged.
Agreed to correspond with the following associations, viz.:
Mud Creek—When convened with Macedonia church, twelve miles south of Scottsboro, Ala., on Friday before the fourth Sunday in September, 1900: Elder M. B. Weaver.
Nolachuckey—Laurel Spring Church, Cocke county, Tennessee, to commence on Friday before the fourth Saturday in September, 1900: Elder Thomas Weaver.
Towaliga—Bersheba Church, Henry county, Ga., on Friday before the first Sunday in September, 1900: Elder E. M. Branson.
Tennessee— ———— Church on Friday before the second Saturday in October, 1900: Elder J. S. Lewis.
6. We recommend that all messengers appointed to sister associations feel the necessity of their attendance and not fail on frivolous excuses.
7. Committee on Finance reported $18.63. Report received and committee discharged.

8. Agreed not to make any change in the Eighth Article in the "Abstract of Principles."

9. The Association agreed to elect the Moderator and Clerk by private ballot.

10. Agreed to allow each church three votes in the election of Moderator and Clerk.

11. Agreed that the Clerk arrange the obituaries.

12. Appointed our next Association to be held with Cedar Springs Church, at Meyer's Grove, Claiborne county, Tenn., near Powell's River Switch, on Friday before the third Saturday in August, 1901.

13. Appointed Elder S. M. Petree to preach the introductory sermon; Elder Alfred Boruff, alternate.

14. Ordered that the Clerk have 800 copies of minutes printed and distributed and that he be allowed $5.00 for his services, and after paying other expenses of the association, the remainder, $2.63, to be given to corresponding ministers.

15. *Resolved,* That we tender our thanks to the church and people in the vicinity for their kindness and hospitality shown us during our stay among them.

16. Minutes read and approved. Then adjourned to meet as above stated.

M. V. HILL, Clerk, Sill, Tenn.

J. S. LEWIS, Moderator,
Biddie, Tenn.

Sunday morning a large audience gathered at the stand and were addressed by Elders G. W. Bulman and Thomas Weaver, after which much interest was manifested in the closing exercises.—Clerk.

CORRESPONDING LETTER.

We, the Powell's Valley Association of Primitive Baptist (Old School), now in session with Hamilton Grove Church, to our sister associations with whom we correspond:

VERY DEAR BRETHREN—We desire to keep up our long cherished Christian correspondence with you, for which purpose we have appointed messengers to visit you, whom we hope you will receive. Their names appear in the body of these minutes. ELDER J. S. LEWIS, Moderator.

M. V. HILL, Clerk.

OBITUARIES.

Pleasant Point—A. Biga Collins departed this life July 28th, 1900, aged 68 years, and lived a faithful member of the Primitive Baptist Church for nearly fifty years.

Browney's Creek—Elder Richard Wilson was born November 22, 1838; died April 7th, 1900; professed a hope in Christ and began preaching at the age of 29 years. He was an ardent supporter of the Baptist faith, and as we hope has fallen asleep in Jesus, there to wear a crown of life in that "Never Ending Home."

Noeton—John Long was born in 1823; died May 19th, 1900; aged 77 years; professed a hope in Christ in 1885; joined the church in 1898, and lived a faithful member until death. He leaves a wife and five children to mourn their loss; but as we trust, their loss is his eternal gain.

ABSTRACT OF PRINCIPLES.

Article 1. We believe in one true and living God, as he is revealed to us in the Holy Scriptures, Father, Son and Holy Ghost.

2. We believe that the Scriptures of the Old and New Testament are the word of God and the only rule of all saving knowledge and obedience.

3. We believe in the doctrine of election according to the foreknowledge of God.

4. We believe in the doctrine of original sin.

14

5. We believe in man's impotency to recover himself from the fallen state he is in by his own free will or ability.

6. We believe that sinners are justified in the sight of God only by the imputed righteousness of Jesus Christ.

7. We believe the elect, according to the foreknowledge of God, will be called, converted, regenerated and sanctified by the Holy Spirit.

8. We believe the saints will preserve and never fall finally away.

9. We believe that baptism and the Lord's supper are ordinances of Jesus Christ, and that true believers are the only subjects of these ordinances, and that the true mode of Baptism is by immersion.

10. We believe in the resurrection of the dead and the general judgment.

11. We believe that the punishment of the wicked will be everlasting, and the joys of the righteous will be eternal.

12. We believe that no minister has the right to administer the ordinances except those who have been regularly baptized and called of God and come under the imposition of hands by the Presbytery.

ELDERS.		P. O. ADDRESS.
H. Ausmus	Speedwell	Tennessee
Thomas Weaver	Bayless	Tennessee.
T. W. Baker	Bayless	Tennessee.
J. S. Lewis	Biddie	Tennessee.
J. W. Riggs	Kate	Tennessee.
E. M. Branson	Lost Creek	Tennessee.
S. M. Petree	Biddie	Tennessee.
M. B. Weaver	Rhodelia	Tennessee.
Wm. West	Lost Creek	Tennessee.
J. M. Drummond	Tacket	Tennessee.
Calvin Collins	Morristown	Tennessee.
Calaway Keck	Little Barren	Tennessee.
J. J. Woods	Little Barren	Tennessee.
J. D. Monroe	Ausmus	Tennessee.
R. Atkins	Shelton's Ford	Tennessee.
J. Suffiridge	Lone Mountain	Tennessee.
G. A. Atkins	Thorn Hill	Tennessee.
N. T. Smith	Oaks	Kentucky.
J. N. Saylor	Layman	Kentucky.
Alfred Boruff	Goin	Tennessee.
A. J. Hopson	Washburn	Tennessee.
Richard Atkins	Dutch	Tennessee.
Andrew Miracle	Cubbage	Kentucky.

LICENTIATES.		P. O. ADDRESS.
B. F. Simmons	Minkton	Tennessee.
Levi Hammock	Minkton	Tennessee.
B. J. Rowe	Minkton	Tennessee.
H. Hurst	Acuff	Tennessee.
M. V. Hill	Sill	Tennessee.
W. R. Petree	Little Barren	Tennessee.
I. N. Hill	Biddie	Tennessee.
J. A. Capps	Acuff	Tennessee.
Jacob Smith	Rhodelia	Tennessee.
A. J. Boruff	Acuff	Tennessee.
J. Hammock	Washburn	Tennessee.
James Evans	Effie	Tennessee.
James Hurst	Dutch	Tennessee.

CHURCHES	NAMES OF MESSENGERS	Rec'd by Ex. and Bap.	Received by Letter	Restored	Confession of Faith	Dismissed by Letter	Excluded	Dead	Total	Saturday Meeting	Contribution
Big Barren	Elders A. Boruff, C. Keck, Brethren W. R. Petree, B. H. Johnson and J. Robison	10	1			3		1	55	1	1 00
Browney's Creek	Elder N. T. Smith, Brethren John A. Miracle, J. F. Hurst and W. Thomson							1	58	4	1 00
Brimstone	Letter								39	1	
Cave Springs	Elder J. W. Riggs, J. Smith, J. Owens and W. H. Brantley	5				1		2	106	3	1 10
Cedar Spring	J. M. and W. A. Drummonds, B. F. and A. D. Simmons	14				3			61	4	1 00
Davis' Creek	Elders H. Ausmus, J. D. Monroe, Brethren Joseph Ausmus, James Harrell and J. G. Ellis	3	2						134	1	
Dotson's Creek	John Capps, A. J. Boruff and James Ragan					4			41	1	
Hinds' Creek	Elder T. W. Baker, J. B. Simmons and H. C. Warwick	2					1		43	2	1 00
Hamilton Grove	Elder E. M. Branson, Wm. Oaks, V. S. Railey and T. H. Johnson	1						1	58	1	1 00
Lost Creek	M. W. Sharp, M. V. Hill, Henry Hill and W. C. Oaks		1			2			109	4	1 30
Mt. Hebron	Elders Thomas Weaver, J. S. Lewis, Elvin Collins and J. M. Vandergriff	3		3		1	3		47	4	
Mossy Springs	Elders M. B. Weaver, S. M. Petree, Brethren Elvin Weaver and J. F. Miller	8	1			1	1	6	115	2	1 35
Mayes' Hill	P. W. Warf, Isaac Whitson and James P. Sowders	2				2			13	1	1 10
Noeton	William Collins and Joel Mallicoat	12	4		1		2	1	47	3	75
Pleasant Point	C. R. Cox, M. J. Sowders and Matthew Keck	3				1		1	75	2	
Rose Hill	J. K. and John Waggoner C. L. Buckner, John Maples and V. Packett						5		86	3	1 00
Salem	A. J. and A. L. Hopson, J. Hammock, E. S. Branson, Martin Bunch and W. Arnwine	18	4			1	3	1	105	2	1 90
Union	Jno. Miller, Christian Keck, Mitchel White and Eli Graves	17	1			7	4		214	4	1 50

CHURCHES	CLERKS	P. O. ADDRESS
Big Barren	W. P. Edwards	Little Barren, Tennessee.
Browney's Creek	Robert Wilson	Cubbage, Kentucky.
Brimstone	J. C. Henry	Hughette, Tennessee.
Cave Spring	W. C. Boruff	Phoebe, "
Cedar Springs	W. A. Drummonds	Minkton, "
Dotson's Creek	John Capps	Haynes, "
Davis' Creek	James Edwards, Jr.	Speedwell, "
Hamilton Grove	William Oaks	Rule, "
Hinds' Creek	H. C. Warwick	Warwick, "
Lost Creek	Henry Hill	Sill, "
Mossy Springs	J. F. Miller	Biddle, "
Mt. Hebron	Jessie Lewis	Twinville, "
Pleasant Point	P. F. Keck	Goin, "
Rose Hill	J. K. Waggoner	Kate, "
Salem	J. Idol	Dutch, "
Union	John Burnett	Sharp's Chapel, "
Noeton	Joel Mallicoat	Bean Station, "
Mayes' Hill	James Mays	Hall's Cross Roads. "

....MINUTES....

OF THE

EIGHTY-FIFTH ANNUAL SESSION

OF THE

POWELL'S VALLEY ASSOCIATION

...OF...

PRIMITIVE BAPTISTS,

HELD WITH THE CHURCH AT

Salem, Grainger County, Tenn.,

August 14, 15 and 16, 1903.

———

KNOXVILLE, TENN.:
GAUT-OGDEN COMPANY, PRINTERS.
1903.

Printer's Fee, $10.00.

MINUTES

of the 85th Annual Session of the Powells Valley Association of Primitive Baptists, held with the Church at Salem, Grainger Co., Tenn., on August 14, 15, 16, 1903.

FRIDAY'S PROCEEDINGS.

1. Introductory discourse by Elder Thomas Weaver, from Rom., 12: 1, 2, 3.

2. The Association was called to order by the Moderator, Elder J. D. Monroe.

3. Called for the letters from the churches, and received nineteen.

4. On motion, the letters were read by the Clerk, Eld. C. Keck, J. M. J. Vandagriff and A. G. Hill.

5. The election of officers being next in order, Elder Thomas Weaver was chosen Moderator, and A. G. Hill, Clerk.

6. Called for petitionary letters.

7. Called for correspondence, and received the following, viz.:

Letter and minutes from Nolachucky Association, by the hands of her delegates, Eld. Samuel McMillin and Brethren C. T. Jenkins and Collas Roberts.

Letter and minutes from Tennessee Association, by the hands of her messengers, Eld. J. B. J. Brickey and Brethren W. C. Lane, J. W. Hall and A. Lane.

8. Corresponding delegates were welcomed to seats with the Association, by the Moderator.

9. Invited transient ministers to seats, when the following named brethren came forward, viz: Eld, J. J. Gilbert, of Winchester, Ky., and Eld. J. N. Culton, of Richmond, Ky.

10. Elders Gilbert and Culton were welcomed to seats with the Association by the Moderator.

11. Committees Appointed, viz.:

(a) *On Arrangements*—Elders J. S. Lewis, T.W. Baker and Brother Eli Branson.

(b) *On Correspondence*—Elders M. B. Weaver, D. Craig, J. D. Monroe, and Brethren John Miller and J. M. J. Vandagriff.

(c) *On Finance*—Elder A. Boruff and Brother J. P. Sanders.

(d) *On Obituaries, Queries and Requests*—John Miller, J. M. J. Vandagriff, Martin Bunch and John Capps.

(e) *On Preaching*—Abe Hopson, James Ragan, W. A. Drummond, C. L. Buckner, B. Jones and M. J. Sowders.

12. Adjourned to meet Saturday morning at 8 o'clock.

SATURDAY MORNING.

1. The Association met pursuant to adjournment.

2. Praise and prayer by the Moderator.

3. Minutes of yesterday read and adopted.

4. The Committee on Arrangements submitted their report, and on motion said report was adopted, as follows:

We your Committee on Arrangements beg leave to submit the following order of business:

Read rules of decorum.
Call the roll.
Report of Committee on Preaching.
Report of Committee on Correspondence.
Report of Committee on Finance.
Report of Committee on Queries, etc.
Who shall preach the next introductory sermon, and who shall be his alternate?

Who shall superintend the printing of the Minutes?
Respectfully submitted,

J. S. LEWIS,
T. W. BAKER,
ELI BRANSON.

5. The Committee on Preaching submitted their report, and on motion was adopted, as follows:

For Saturday, at the Stand—Elders J. B. J. Brickey, J. N. Culton, and Drury Craig to close.

Saturday Night, at the Church—Elders Sam McMillin and M. B. Weaver.

Puncheon Camp—Elders J. W. Riggs and Drury Craig.

Dutch Valley—Elders J. D. Monroe and A. J. Boruff.

For Sunday, at the Stand—Elders J. J. Gilbert, J. N. Culton, and Moderator to close.

Respectfully submitted,

ABE HOPSON,
JAMES RAGAN,
W. A. DRUMMOND,
C. L. BUCKNER,
B. JONES,
M. J. SOWDERS.

6. Read Rules of Decorum.

7. Called the roll and erased the names of absentees.

8. The Committee on Correspondence submitted their report, and on motion the Association adopted the following report, viz.:

We your Committee on Correspondence beg leave to submit the following:

Be it Resolved, That we continue our correspondence with Nolachucky, Tennessee, Mud Creek, Flint River, Towaliga, and that the Clerk write a petitionary letter to the Sequachee Valley Association; and,

Be it Resolved, That we send corresponding delegates to as many as possible, and letters and minutes to the others.

Be it Resolved, That our corresponding letter be spread upon our minutes, and a parcel of minutes be sent to each Association.

Respectfully submitted,

M. B. WEAVER,
D. CRAIG,
J. D. MONROE,
JOHN MILLER,
J. M. J. VANDAGRIFF.

9. Corresponding Letter:

We, the Powell's Valley Association of Primitive Baptists, to our sister Associations with whom we correspond:

Very Dear Brethren: We wish to keep up our long cherished Christian correspondence with you, for which purpose we have chosen our beloved brethren, viz.:

Nolachucky—Elders Thomas Weaver, A. J. Hopson, J. D. Monroe, J. S. Lewis, T. W. Baker and John Capps.

To the Tennessee—Elders A. Boruff, M. B. Weaver, D. Craig, and Brethren John Miller, J. P. Sanders and B. F. Simmons.

To Mud Creek—Letter and Minutes.

To Towaliga—Elder J. S. Lewis.

To Flint River—Letter and Minutes.

To Sequachee Valley—Petitionary letter by the Clerk.

THOMAS WEAVER, *Moderator.*

A. G. HILL, *Clerk.*

10. The Finance Committee reported, and the report adopted, as follows:

We, your Committee on Finance, beg leave to report $18.16.

Respectfully submitted,

A. BORUFF,
J. P. SANDERS.

11. The Committee on Queries, Obituaries and Requests submitted their report, and after some little brotherly discussion, the Association unanimously adopted the following, viz.:

We, your Committee on Queries, Obituaries and Requests, beg leave to submit the following:

(a) We recommend that the Clerk have the obituaries, submitted from the various churches, made as full as is reasonably convenient and published in our Minutes of the Association.

(b) Que: Is it gospel order for any of our ministers or members to join any secret organization?

(c) Does the church endorse such a course? Will the Association please give some advice on the matter?

Answers: (a) It is not gospel order.

(b) The Primitive Baptist Church does not endorse such a course, and we consider any church holding members belonging to any secret organization, out of order.

(c) We recommend that the churches holding members belonging to secret organizations, as soon as possible reckon with such members, requiring them to repent of their wrongs by making confession to the church and abandoning the organization; and if they will not, exclude them from church fellowship.

'(d) We further advise that the churches of this Association keep themselves unspotted from the world, and not to recognize or tolerate in their midst institutions or secret organizations gotten up by men.

(e) Ans. to requests: We recommend that the Association convene with the church at Gibson Station, Lee County,—Va., on R. R., commencing on Friday before the third Saturday in August, 1904.

(f) We further recommend that you announce the Centennial Meeting of Big Barren Church, beginning on Friday before the first Saturday in November, 1903. All Primitive Baptists invited.

Respectfully submitted,

J. A. CAPPS,
JOHN MILLER,
M. V. BUNCH,
J. M. J. VANDERGRIFF.

12. On motion, Eld. J. D. Monroe was appointed to preach the next introductory sermon, and Eld. T. W. Baker to supply in case of failure.

13. On motion, agreed that the Clerk superintend the printing and distribution of 1,000 copies of Minutes, and be allowed $7.00 for his services and distribution.

14. *Resolved,* That we tender our thanks to this church and surrounding community for their kind hospitality during our stay with them.

15. Read and adopted to-day's proceedings.

16. Then adjourned.

THOMAS WEAVER, *Moderator.*

Fountain City, Tenn.,

A. G. HILL, *Clerk.*   R. F. D. No. 3.

Lost Creek, Tenn.,

R. F. D. No. 1.

On Sunday there was a large congregation assembled at the stand and addressed, first, by Elder J. J. Gilbert, from John 3: 1-3; second, by Elder J. N. Culton, from Rom., 5: 1-11; third, Elder Thomas Weaver delivered a warm exhortation to be loyal to Christ and stand by the fundamental principles of the church; after which, took the parting hand, while the congregation sung "How firm a foundation."

OBITUARIES.

Lost Creek Church.—Bro. H. G. Miller was born October 14, 1826; joined the church Saturday April 4, 1861; died September 6, 1902.

Philpenie Bridges, joined the church July 29, 1861; died May 28, 1903.

Isabella Bridges was born March 4, 1883; joined the church at the January meeting, 1898; died January 13, 1903.

Mt. Hebron Church.—W. H. Collins was born July 31, 1832, and died January 4, 1898; professed faith in Christ in 1866, and joined the church at Hind's Creek in 1868, and lived a member of the church till his death. When he died he left abundant evidence of the faith he had in Christ. He had been a member and a deacon of Mt. Hebron church a number of years before his death.

Martha Weaver was born June 3, 1870, and died July 11, 1903; professed faith in Christ in 1888, and with the exception of about four years had lived a member of Mt. Hebron church till death.

Orlena Hutchison and her daughter, Lizzie Hutchison, died at LaFollette in March, 1903. They were both members of Mt. Hebron church when they died. We trust our loss is their eternal gain.

Cedar Spring Church.—Mary Fergerson was about 36 years old when she departed this life; lived a faithful member over eighteen years. She leaves a husband and five children to mourn the loss of a companion and a dear mother.

Dotson Creek Church.—Nancy M. Capps was born November 17, 1842; died August 26, 1901; joined the church in her sixteenth year, and lived a Christian life till death. She leaves a husband and four children to mourn her loss.

SALEM CHURCH.—Hattie Atkins departed this life April, 1903, aged 22 years; lived a faithful life.

Belle Idol departed this life March 23, 1903. She was the wife of C. J. Idol. She lived a faithful member till death.

John Idol professed faith in Christ while very young. He joined the Missionary Baptists, and lived with them a number of years. Becoming dissatisfied, he joined the Primitive Baptist church at Salem, and served the church as clerk until his death, which occurred April 2, 1903. He was a wise counselor and a faithful member. He leaves a wife and eight children and a host of friends to mourn his loss. He leaves bright evidences of heaven and immortal glory. Aged 75 years, 5 months, 14 days.

Jasper Hammock joined the church and lived a Christian life. Died April 15, 1902, aged 15 years, 8 months.

Annie Arwine joined the church and lived an orderly member till death, which occurred May 24, 1903. Aged 63 years, 4 months.

Elders	Postoffice	State
Thomas Weaver	Fountain City R. F. D. No. 3	Tenn.
M. B. Weaver	Hilltonville	Tenn.
J. D. Monroe	Coda	Tenn.
J. S. Lewis	Biddie	Tenn.
T. W. Baker	Fountain City R. F. D. No. 3	Tenn.
D. Craig	Bayless	Tenn.
C. Keck	Gibson Station	Va.
Henry Ausmus	Speedwell	Tenn.
N. Smith	Cubbage	Ky.
R. Wilson	Cubbage	Ky.
S. M. Petree	Biddie	Tenn.
J. N. Saylor	Layman	Ky.
J. A. Capps	Acuff	Tenn.
J. Suffridge	Lone Mountain	Tenn.
J. M. Drummond	Tackett	Tenn.
Wm. West	Lost Creek	Tenn.
A. Boruff	Coda	Tenn.
A. J. Hopson	Washburn	Tenn.
A. J. Boruff	Acuff	Tenn.
A. Miracle	Goin	Tenn.
J. W. Riggs	Roost	Ky.
J. J. Woods	Coda	Tenn.
J. Hammock	Washburn	Tenn.
E. M. Branson	Zenda	Kans.

Churches will please give names and addresses of their licentiate preachers next year.

CHURCHES	NAMES	CLERKS' POSTOFFICE	STATE
Big Barren	Mc. Edwards	Coda	Tenn.
Browney's Creek	F. P. Miracle	Cubbage	Ky.
Cannon Creek	A. H. Crawford	Roost	Ky.
Cave Spring	W. W. Taylor	Phebe	Tenn.
Cedar Spring	W. A. Drummonds	New Tazewell	Tenn.
Davis' Creek	J. Edwards, Jr.	Speedwell	Tenn.
Dotson's Creek	D. H. Rosanbolm		Tenn.
Gibson Station	S. S. Wilson	Walnut Hill	Va.
Hamilton Grove	H. F. Hamilton		Tenn.
Hinds' Creek	T. W. Baker	Fountain City R. F. D. No. 3	Tenn.
Lost Creek	A. G. Hill	Lost Creek R. F. D. No. 1	Tenn.
Mt. Hebron	J. M. J. Vandagriff	Heiskell R. F. D. No. 1	Tenn.
Mossy Spring	Elvin Weaver	Rhodelia	Tenn.
Nœton	J. L. Oliver	Nœton	Tenn.
Pleasant Point	P. F. Keck	Goin	Tenn.
Rose Hill	J. K. Waggoner	Kate	Tenn.
Salem	H. C. Ritter	Dutch	Tenn.
Union	John Burnett	Welch	Tenn.
Mays' Hill	J. P. Sanders	Hall's X Roads	Tenn.

Church Clerks and Ministers will please give their R. F. D. numbers next year.

TABLE OF STATISTICS.

CHURCHES	NAMES OF DELEGATES	Rec'd by Ex.	Rec'd by Letter	Dis'ls'd by Letter	Restored	Rec'd by Relat'n	Excluded	Dead	Total	Sat'dy Meetings	Contribution
Browney's Creek	Elder Robt. Wilson, F. P. Miracle and J. F. Hurst	3	1	3	2			1	43	4	$1.00
Cave Spring	Franklin Boruff	1	1				4	2	104	3	
Cedar Spring	Elders J. M. Drummond, A. D. Simmons and W. A. Drummond							1	53	4	
Cannon Creek	F. M. Riggs, W. E. Wilson			3			2		20	3	
Davis' Creek	Elder J. D. Monroe	10					8		143	1	
Dotson's Creek	Elders J. Suffridge, J Capps, and A. J. Boruff										
Hamilton Grove	David Warwick	7			1			1	37	1	.75
Hiud's Creek	Elder T. W. Baker								67	2	.50
Gibson Station	Elder C. Keck, P. Beason, S. S. Wilson and Robt. Ball	1	2					1	43	1	1.00
Lost Creek	A. G. Hill		1	4					28	3	1.50
Mt. Hebron	Elders Thomas Weaver, J. S. Lewis, D. Craig, and Brethren J. M. J. Vandagriff and E. M. Collins	7						3	101		1.00
May's Hill	J. P. Sanders, statistics, same as last year								54	4	1.00
Mossy Spring	Elder M. B. Weaver, D. R. Graves	20	1		2		2	1	12	1	1.50
Neeton	J. F. Oliver, B. F. Simmons, W. T. Hipsher, J. L. Oliver and John Hipsher.	21	1				2		145	2	1.00
Pleasant Point	M. J. Sowders	1			2			1	69		
Rose Hill	C. L. Buckner, John Waggoner								99	3	
Salem	Elder A. J. Hopson, James Satterfield, Martin Bunch and Ben Jones	4			1			4	97	2	
Union	John Miller	8	1						127	3	2.00
Big Barren	Elders J. J. Woods, A. Boruff and Brother S. Edwards	1		1					57		

ARTICLES OF FAITH.

ARTICLE 1. We believe in one only true and living God, as He is revealed to us in the Holy Scriptures, Father, Son and Holy Ghost.

2. We believe that the Scriptures of the Old and New Testaments are the word of God and the only rule of all saving knowledge and obedience.

3. We believe in the doctrine of election according to the foreknowledge of God.

4. We believe in the doctrine of original sin.

5. We believe in man's impotency to recover himself from the fallen state he is in by his own free will or ability.

6. We believe that sinners are justified in the sight of God only by the imputed righteousness of Jesus Christ.

7. We believe the elect, according to the foreknowledge of God, will be called, converted, regenerated and sanctified by the Holy Spirit.

8. We believe the saints will persevere and never fall finally away.

9. We believe that baptism and the Lord's Supper are ordinances of Jesus Christ, and that true believers are the only subjects of these ordinances, and that the true mode of baptism is by immersion.

10. We believe in the resurrection of the dead and the general judgment.

11. We believe that the punishment of the wicked will be everlasting, and that the joys of the righteous will be eternal.

12. We believe that no minister has the right to administer the ordinances except those who have been regularly baptized and called of God and come under the imposition of hands by the Presbytery.

....MINUTES....

OF THE

EIGHTY-SIXTH ANNUAL SESSION

OF THE

POWELL'S VALLEY ASSOCIATION

...OF...

PRIMITIVE BAPTISTS,

HELD WITH THE CHURCH AT

Gibson's Station, Lee County, Va.,

August 19, 20, 21, 1904.

KNOXVILLE, TENN.:
GAUT-OGDEN COMPANY, PRINTERS.
1904.

Printer's Fee, $13.00 ior 1200 copies.

MINUTES

of the 86th Annual Session of the Powells Valley Association of Primitive Baptists, held with the Church of Gibson Station, Lee County, Va., on August 19, 20, 21, 1904.

FRIDAY'S PROCEEDINGS.

1. Introductory discourse by Elder J. D. Monroe, from Eph., 1: 1-3.

2. The Association was called to order by the Moderator, Elder Thomas Weaver.

3. Called for the letters from the churches, and received sixteen, which were read and the messengers' names enrolled.

4. On motion, all the letters were received except the two from Mossy Spring Church, which were referred to the Committee on Credentials.

5. The election of officers being next in order, Elder Thomas Weaver was re-elected Moderator and A. G. Hill was re-elected Clerk.

6. Called for petitionary letters.

7. Called for correspondence, and received the following, viz.:

Letters and minutes from each of Mud Creek, Tennessee, Towaliga and Nolachucky Associations.

8. Invited transient ministers to seats, when the fol-

lowing-named Elders came forward and were welcomed to seats by the Moderator, viz: Elder J. J. Gilbert, of Winchester, Ky.; Silas Miracle, of Red Bird Association, Ky.; and J. K. P. Legg, of Crab Orchard, Va.

9. Committees appointed, to report Saturday morning, viz,:

(a) *On Arrangements*—N. T. Smith, J. Owens, Chris Keck, F. P. Miracle, W. E. Wilson, and the Clerk.

(b) *On Credentials*—Robert Wilson, A. J. Hopson, J. J. Gilbert, Elvin Collins, and W. A. Drummonds.

(c) *On Correspondence*—J. Owens, Drury Craig, Jno. Waggoner, T. W. Baker, J. D. Monroe, and the Moderator.

(d) *On Finance*—Robert Wilson and W. A. Drummond.

(e) *On Preaching*—J. M. Miller, Eli Branson, and Chris Keck.

10. Adjourned to meet Saturday morning at 8:30 o'clock.

SATURDAY MORNING.

1. The Association met pursuant to adjournment.

2. Praise and prayer by Elder D. Craig.

3. The Committee on Arrangements submitted their report, and on motion said report was adopted, as follows:

We your Committee on Arrangements beg leave to submit the following order of business, viz.:

Read Rules of Decorum.
Call the roll.
Report of Committee on Preaching.
Report of Committee on Credentials.
Report of Committee on Correspondence.
Report of Committee on Finance.
Where shall our next Association be?
Who shall preach the introductory sermon, and who shall be his alternate?

Who shall superintend the printing of the Minutes, and how many copies shall be printed?

Respectfully submitted.

> F. P. MIRACLE,
> J. OWENS,
> W. E. WILSON,
> C. KECK,
> A. G. HILL,
> N. T. SMITH.

4. The Committee on Preaching submitted their report, and on motion was adopted, as follows:

(a) *For Saturday at the Stand*—Elders J. Suffridge, Silas Miracle and T. W. Baker.

(b) *Saturday Night at the Church*—Elders D. Craig and J. K. P. Legg.

(c) *For Sunday*—Jas. J. Gilbert and Thomas Weaver.

Respectfully submitted.

> J. M. MILLER,
> ELI BRANSON,
> C. KECK.

5. Read Rules of Decorum.

6. Called the roll.

7. On motion, W. B. Ausmus and J. D. Monroe, of Davis' Creek Church, and J. J. Woods and Samp. Edwards, of Big Barren Church, were seated in the Association upon their own statements of being appointed delegates by their respective churches.

8. The Committee on Credentials submitted their report, and on motion the report was adopted, as follows:

We your committee to whom was referred the matter of the two letters and messengers of the Mossy Spring Church, advise that the matter be referred back to the said church, to use all lawful means according to the gospel of Christ to settle said matter in the church.

Respectfully submitted.

> ROBT. WILSON,
> A. J. HOPSON,
> W. A. DRUMMONDS,
> E. M. COLLINS,
> J. J. GILBERT.

9. The Committee on Correspondence submitted their report, and on motion adopted the following report, viz.:

We your Committee on Correspondence beg leave to submit the following:

Be it Resolved, That we continue our correspondence with Nola-chucky, Tennessee, Mud Creek, Towaliga and Flint River, and that the Clerk send a parcel of Minutes to Sequachee Valley Association; and

Be it Resolved, That we send corresponding delegates to as many as possible, and letters and Minutes to the others; and

Be it Resolved, That our corresponding letter be spread upon our minutes.

Respectfully submitted.

> T. W. BAKER,
> DRURY CRAIG,
> JOHN WAGGONER,
> J. OWENS,
> THOMAS WEAVER.

10. Coresponding Letter:

We, the Powell's Valley Association of Primitive Baptists, to our sister Associations with whom we correspond:

Very Dear Brethren: We wish to keep up our long cherished Christian correspondence with you, for which purpose we have chosen our beloved brethren, viz.:

Nolachucky—Elders J. S. Lewis, T. W. Baker, A. J. Hopson and Brother B. F. Simmons.

Mud Creek—Elder Thomas Weaver.

Tennessee—Elders T. W. Baker, J. S. Lewis, D. Craig, Thomas Weaver.

Flint River—Letter and Minutes.

Towaliga—Letter and Minutes.

> THOMAS WEAVER, *Moderator.*

A. C. HILL, *Clerk.*

11. The Finance Committee reported, and the report was adopted, as follows:

We your Committee on Finance beg leave to report:

From the churches...$14 70
In Clerk's hands from last year............................... 1 16
Public collection from the delegates.......................... 3 14
Received from Hamilton Grove Church since the Association. 1 00

$20 00

12. On motion we appoint our next Association to be held with the church at Mt. Hebron, Anderson County, Tennessee, sixteen miles north of Knoxville, Tenn., commencing on Friday before the third Saturday in August, 1905.

13. On motion, Elder T. W. Baker was appointed to preach the introductory sermon, and Elder Drury Craig to be his alternate.

14. On motion, agreed that the Clerk superintend the printing and distribution of 1,200 copies of Minutes, and be allowed $5.00 for services and $2.00 for postage.

ADVICE.

15. On motion, we advise each church in the Union to appoint two days of fasting and prayer that the Lord would enable each member by His Holy Spirit to lay aside everything that causes an offense; submitting themselves one to another according to the Bible, by putting away all malice, evil speaking, back-biting and hypocrisy; adhering more closely to the Golden Rule: "As ye would that men should do to you, do ye also to them likewise."

16. On motion, we tender our most humble and heartfelt thanks to the brethren and many friends at Gibson Station, who have so kindly entertained us during our stay with them.

17. Minutes read and adopted.

18. Then adjourned to meet as above stated.

THOMAS WEAVER, *Moderator.*
Fountain City, Tenn.,
A. G. HILL, *Clerk.* R. F. D. No. 5.
Lost Creek, Tenn.,
R. F. D. No. 1.

SUNDAY.

On Sunday the congregation assembled at the stand, and were addressed first by Elder J. J. Gilbert, from Matt., 16: 18, and second by Elder Thomas Weaver, from I. John, iii: 1-10, after which, took the parting hand, while the congregation sung "How firm a foundation."

OBITUARY.

CEDAR SPRING CHURCH.—Sister Martha Simmons was born May 11, 1825; joined the church September, 1866; died March 10, 1904.

Elders	Postoffice	State
Thomas Weaver	Fountain City, R. F. D. No. 5	Tenn.
Drury Craig	Fountain City, R. F. D. No. 5	Tenn.
J. W. Baker	Fountain City, R. F. D. No. 5	Tenn.
Henry Ausmus	Speedwell	Tenn.
Wm. West	Lost Creek, R. F. D. No. 1	Tenn.
J. S. Lewis	Lost Creek, R. F. D. No. 1	Tenn.
S. M. Petree	Lost Creek, R. F. D. No. 1	Tenn.
M. B. Weaver	Lost Creek, R. F. D. No. 1	Tenn.
J. J. Woods	Goin	Tenn.
A. Miracle	Goin	Tenn.
A. Boruff	Goin	Tenn.
J. D. Monroe	Goin	Tenn.
A. J. Hopson	Washburn	Tenn.
J. Hammock	Washburn	Tenn.
Robt. Wilson	Cubbage	Ky.
J. N. Saylor	Layman	Ky.
N. T. Smith	Gibson Station	Va.
Callaway Keck	Gibson Station	Va.
J. W. Riggs	Coal Creek	Tenn.
J. A. Capps	Maynardville	Tenn.
A. J. Boruff	Maynardville	Tenn.
John Suffridge	Lone Mountain	Tenn.
J. M. Drummonds	Tackett	Tenn.
E. M. Branson	Zenda	Kans.

LICENTIATES.

W. R. Petree	Goin	Tenn.
M. V. Hill	Knoxville	Tenn.
James Hurst	Dutch	Tenn.

CHURCHES	CLERKS	POSTOFFICE	STATE
Browney's Creek	F. P. Miracle	Cubbage	Ky.
Cannon Creek	A. H. Crawford	Ferndale	Ky.
Cave Spring	W. W. Taylor	Stiner	Tenn.
Cedar Spring	W. A. Drummonds	New Tazewell	Tenn.
Dotson's Creek	D. H. Rosenbalm	Maynardville	Tenn.
Gibson Station	S. S. Wilson	Walnut Hill	Va.
Hinds' Creek	Brownlow Warwick	Maynardville	Tenn.
Lost Creek	A. G. Hill	Lost Creek, R. F. D. No. 1	Tenn.
Mt. Hebron	J. W. J. Vandergriff	Heiskell, R. F. D., No. 2	Tenn.
Noeton	J. L. Oliver	Noeton	Tenn.
Pleasant Point	P. F. Keck	Goin	Tenn.
Rose Hill	John Waggoner	Maynardville	Tenn.
Salem	H. C. Ritter	Dutch	Tenn.
Union	John Burnett	Sharp's Chapel	Tenn.

TABLE OF STATISTICS.

POWELLS VALLEY P. B. ASSOCIATION

CHURCHES	NAMES OF DELEGATES	Rec'd by Exper'c	Rec'd by Letter	Dis'ss'd by Letter	Restored	Excluded	Dead	Total	Sat'd'y Meetings	Contribution
Browney's Creek	F. P. Miracle, Elijah Miracle, Lazarus D. Miracle, Robert Wilson	1				1	1	42	4	$1.00
Cannon Creek	A. H. Crawford, W. E. Wilson, Nathan Smith					2		18	3	1.25
Cave Spring	Wm. Brantley, J. Owens							104	3	
Cedar Spring	W. A. Drummond, A. D. Simmons, J. M. Drummond, E. C. Simmons, J. G. Drummond, S. W. Drummond	3							4	
Dotson's Creek	John Suffridge, Jas. Ragan						1	55	1	1.00
Gibson's Station	John Webb, W. S. Collins, Mc. Hensley, S. S. Wilson, Calaway Keck	3	3	2		1		37	2	
Hind's Creek	T. W. Baker	1	2					28	3	1.00
Lost Creek	Wm. West, J. M. Miller, A. G. Hill		2	1		5	2	46	4	.60
Mt. Hebron	Thomas Weaver, Drury Craig, E. M. Collins					1	1	93	3	1.00
Noeton	B. F. Simmons	1						50	4	1.00
Pleasant Point	W. C. Prophet, J. N. Hopper, W. H. Collins							67	3	.90
Rose Hill	John Waggoner, F. M. McBee		3	3		4		99	2	
Salem	A. L. Hopson, E. S. Branson, H. C. Ritter, J. Hammock, A. J. Hopson	17				1	2	141	2	1.50
Union	A. Browning, Chris. Keck, G. A. Whited, M. Wood, J. A. Whited, John Burnett	1				6	12	1214	4	1.00

No Letters from Big Barren, Red Hill, Hamilton Grove, Brimstone, Mays Hill and Davis' Creek.

ARTICLES OF FAITH.

ARTICLE 1. We believe in one only true and living God, as He is revealed to us in the Holy Scriptures, Father, Son and Holy Ghost.

2. We believe that the Scriptures of the Old and New Testaments are the word of God and the only rule of all saving knowledge and obedience.

3. We believe in the doctrine of election according to the foreknowledge of God.

4. We believe in the doctrine of original sin.

5. We believe in man's impotency to recover himself from the fallen state he is in by his own free will or ability.

6. We believe that sinners are justified in the sight of God only by the imputed righteousness of Jesus Christ.

7. We believe the elect, according to the foreknowledge of God, will be called, converted, regenerated and sanctified by the Holy Spirit.

8. We believe the saints will persevere and never fall finally away.

9. We believe that baptism and the Lord's Supper are ordinances of Jesus Christ, and that true believers are the only subjects of these ordinances, and that the true mode of baptism is by immersion.

10. We believe in the resurrection of the dead and the general judgment.

11. We believe that the punishment of the wicked will be everlasting, and that the joys of the righteous will be eternal.

12. We believe that no minister has the right to administer the ordinances except those who have been regularly baptized and called of God and come under the imposition of hands by the Presbytery.

Seattle's Great Aunt

....MINUTES....

OF THE

EIGHTY-SEVENTH ANNUAL SESSION

OF THE

POWELL'S VALLEY ASSOCIATION

.. OF...

PRIMITIVE BAPTISTS,

HELD WITH THE CHURCH AT

Mt. Hebron, Anderson County, Tenn.,

August 18, 19, 20, 1905.

KNOXVILLE, TENN.:
GAUT-OGDEN COMPANY, PRINTERS.
1905.

Printer's fee $11.00 for 1000 copies.

37

MINUTES

of the 87th Annual Session of the Powell's Valley Association of Primitive Baptists, held with the Church at Mt. Hebron, Anderson County, Tenn., on August 18, 19, 20, 1905.

FRIDAY'S PROCEEDINGS.

1. Introductory sermon by Elder T. W. Baker, from Jer. vi, 16; "Stand ye in the ways, and see, and ask for the old paths."

2. After an intermission of fifteen minutes the Association was called to order by the Moderator, Elder Thomas Weaver.

3. Called for the letters from the churches, and fifteen were presented and read.

4. On motion, all the letters were received except the one from Cedar Springs.

5. All the churches express themselves as standing aloof from Lodgism, Secretism and "Schemes of the day," for protection, etc.

6. The election of officers being next in order, Elder Thomas Weaver was re-elected Moderator, and A. G. Hill was re-elected Clerk.

7. Called for petitionary letters.

8. Called for correspondence and received the following, viz.:

(a) *Nolachucky Association*—Letter and Minutes by the hand of her Messenger, Elder Samuel McMillan.

(b)   Letters and minutes from Towaliga and Tennessee.

(c)   Minutes from Sequachee Valley.

9.   Invited transient ministers to seats with the Association.

10.   Invited ministers of our churches to seats, who know themselves to be in good standing in their church.

COMMITTEES APPOINTED.

(a) *On Arrangements*—Drury Craig, Timothy Hill, J. M. Miller and the Moderator and Clerk.

(b)   *On Correspondence*—Henry Ausmus, A. G. Hill, J. J. Woods, J. M. J. Vandagriff and John Miller.

(c)   *On Finance*—Wm. Howerton and Hamilton Hill.

(d)   *On Preaching*—Union Hill, A. Browning, H. H. Oaks, Canister Hill, together with the church at Mt. Hebron.

11.   Appointments for preaching tonight:

At the Church—Elder Samuel McMillan.

At Twinville—Elder N. T. Smith.

At Graham School House—Elder J. S. Lewis.

12.   Adjourned to meet Saturday morning at 8:30 o'clock.

SATURDAY MORNING.

1.   The Association met pursuant to adjournment.

2.   Praise and prayer, by Elder T. W. Baker.

3   On motion, called for the report of the Committee on Arrangements, which was adpoted as follows:

We your Committee on Arrangements beg leave to submit the following order of business:

Call the roll.

Let the Association state her objections to Cedar Spring Church in the Minutes.

That we publish in our minutes the names of all excluded ministers, viz: Elders M. B. Weaver, S. M. Petree, J. D. Monroe and A. Boruff.

Will we publish the obituaries?

Report of the Committee on Preaching.

Report of the Committee on Correspondence.

Report of the Committee on Finance.

When and where shall our next Association be?

Who shall preach the Introductory Sermon, and who shall be his Alternate?

How many copies of the Minutes shall we have printed?

Respectfully submitted,

DRURY CRAIG,
TIMOTHY HILL,
J. M. MILLER,
THOMAS WEAVER,
A. G. HILL.

4. The Committee on Preaching submitted their report, and on motion was adopted as follows:

(a) *For Saturday before Noon at the Stand*—Elders Henry, Ausmus and Wm. West.

(b) *Afternoon at the Stand*—Elder Samuel McMillan.

(c) *At Night at the Church*—Elders N. T. Smith and Drury Craig.

At Twinville—Elders Wm. West and J. J. Woods.

(d) *At Hill's School House*—Elder Samuel McMillan.

(e) *For Sunday at the Stand*—Elders J. S. Lewis and Thomas Weaver.

Respectfully submitted,

UNION HILL,
A. BROWNING,
H. H. OAKS,
CANISTER HILL.

5. Called the roll, and erased the names of absentees.

6. The answer of the Association as to her objections to the receiving of Cedar Springs' letter, are these: For holding and fellowshiping members whose baptism was administered by ministers that were in disorder.

7. On motion we fully endorse the action of the churches that excluded Elders A. Boruff, J. D. Monroe, S. M. Petree and M. B. Weaver.

8. On moton we welcome Brother J. P. Sanders to a seat in the Association.

9. The Committee on Correspondence submitted their report, and on motion adopted the following:

We your Committee on Correspondence beg leave to submit the following:

Be it resolved, That we continue our correspondence with Nolachucky, Tennessee, Mud Creek, Towaliga and Sequachee Valley; and

Be it resolved, That we send messengers to as many as possible and letters and minutes to the others; and

Be it resolved, That our corresponding letter be spread upon our minutes.

Respectfully submitted,

HENRY AUSMUS,
J. J. WOODS,
J. M. J. VANDAGRIFF,
JOHN MILLER,
A. G. HILL.

10. Corresponding letter:

We, the Powell's Valley Association of Primitive Baptists, to our sister associations with whom we correspond:

VERY DEAR BRETHREN: We wish to keep up our cherished Christian correspondence with you, for which purpose we have chosen our beloved brethren, viz:

(a) *Nolachucky*—Elders Thomas Weaver, J. S. Lewis and T. W. Baker.

(b) *Tennessee*—Elders D. Craig, Thomas Weaver, N. T. Smith, J. S. Lewis and Brethren J. P. Sanders, John Waggoner and F. M. McBee.

(c) *Mud Creek*—Letter and Minutes. *Towaliga*—Letter and Minutes. *Sequachee Valley*—Letter and Minutes.

THOMAS WEAVER, *Moderator.*

A. G. HILL, *Clerk.*

11. The Finance Committee reported, and the report was adopted as follows:

We your Committee on Finance beg leave to report:

From the churches	$13.55
Public collection from the messengers	4.00
Private parties gave the clerk for minutes	45
	$18.00

Respectfully submitted,

HAMILTON HILL,
WM. HOWERTON.

12. On motion we appoint our next Association to be held with the church at Lost Creek, Union Co., Tenn., ten miles north of Maynardville, commencing, at the request of the sisters of that church, on Friday before the first Saturday in October, 1906.

13. On motion we appoint Elder J. S. Lewis to preach the introductory sermon and Elder Drury Craig be his alternate.

14. On motion we agree that the clerk have 1,000 copies of minutes printed and distributed, and be allowed $7.00, or the remainder, for postage and services.

15. On motion we tender our most humble and heartfelt thanks to the brethren and friends of Mt. Hebron church and community, who have so kindly entertained us during our stay with them.

16. Minutes read and adopted.

17. Then adjourned to meet as above stated.

THOMAS WEAVER, *Moderator.*
Fountain City, Tenn.
R. F. D. No. 5.

A. G. HILL, *Clerk.*
Lost Creek, Tenn.
R .F. D. No. 1.

SUNDAY.

The congregation was first addressed by Elder J. S. Lewis, and second by Elder Thomas Weaver, from the subject of Faith, Hope and Charity, after which took the parting hand, while the congregation sung "My Christian Friends in Bonds of Love," amid much rejoicing in a Savior's love.

UNION MEETINGS.

Mossy Spring Church: Commencing on Friday before the first Saturday in October, 1905. All "Old Baptists" invited.

OBITUARIES.

Mt. Hebron: I. C. Gentry was born December 13, 1836. He professed faith in Christ August 1866, and joined the Primitive Baptist Church at Mt. Hebron, February, 1883, and was baptized. Brother Gentry lived a faithful member of Mt. Hebron Church till death. A short time before his death he said: "Paradise is open, I am willing to go." He fell asleep February 18, 1905.

Chesley Vandagriff, Sr., was born January 25, 1823. He professed faith in Christ and shortly after, October 4th, Saturday, 1890, joined the church at Mt. Hebron, and lived a devoted and worthy member till death. He died in full triumphs of a living faith, October 27, 1903.

Davis Creek Church: Martha W. Robinson was born November 14, 1839. Died April 21, 1904. Belonged to the church about 28 years.

Hind's Creek Church: Susan Baker was born February 1, 1818. Died January 26, 1904. She professed faith in Christ in her 18th year, and joined the church at Hind's Creek in 1836, in which she lived a faithful member till death.

Elders	Postoffice	State
ELDERS.	POSTOFFICE.	STATE.
Thomas Weaver	Fountain City, R. F. D. No. 5	Tenn
Drury Craig	Fountain City, R. F. D. No. 5	Tenn
T. W. Baker	Fountain City, R. F. D. No. 5	Tenn
H. Ausmus	Speedwell	Tenn
Wm. West	Lost Creek, R. F. D. No. 1	Tenn
J. S. Lewis	Lost Creek, R. F. D. No. 1	Tenn
J. J. Woods	Goin	Tenn
A. Miracle	Goin	Tenn
A. J. Hopson	Washburn	Tenn
J. Hammock	Washburn	Tenn
Robt. Wilson	Cubbage	Ky
J. N. Saylor	Layman	Ky
N. T. Smith	Ferndale	Ky
Calaway Keck	Gibson Station	Va
J. W. Riggs	Kensee	Ky
J. A. Capps	Maynardville	Tenn
A. J. Boruff	Maynardville	Tenn
John Suffridge	Lone Mountain	Tenn
J. M. Drummond	Tackett	Tenn
E. M. Branson	Zenda	Kans

LICENTIATES.

M. V. Hill	Knoxville	Tenn
James Hurst	Dutch	Tenn
James Ausmus	Speedwell	Tenn
T. J. Miracle	Speedwell	Tenn

CHURCHES	CLERKS	POSTOFFICE	STATE
Browney's Creek	F. P. Miracle	Cubbage.	Ky.
Cannon Creek	A. H. Crawford	Ferndale	Ky.
Cave Spring	W. W. Taylor	~tiner	Tenn.
Dotson's Creek	D. H. Rosenbalm	Maynardville	Tenn.
Hind's Creek	T. W. Baker	Fountain City, R. No. 5	Tenn.
Lost Creek	A. G. Hill	Lost Creek, R. No. 1	Tenn.
Mt. Hebron	J. M. J Vandagriff	Hiskell, R. No. 2	Tenn.
Pleasant Point	W. H Collins	Goin, R. No. 11	Tenn.
Rose Hill	John Waggoner	Maynardville	Tenn.
Union	John Burnett	Sharp's Chapple	Tenn.
Red Hill	Jeff Treece	Old Town	Tenn.
Davis Creek	James Edwards	Speedwell	Tenn.
Mossy Spring	Timothy Hill	Lost Creek, R. No.1	Tenn.
Big Barren	Sampson Edwards	Goin	Tenn.

TABLE OF STATISTICS.

CHURCHES	NAMES OF MESSENGERS	Rec'd by Experience	Received by Letter	Restored	Confession of Faith	Dismissed by Letter	Excluded	Dead	Total	Saturday Meeting	Contribution
Browney's Creek	Letter but no Messenger		3			3			39	4	$1.00
Big Barren	Elder J. J. Woods, Sampson Edwards	2					11	2	28	2	
Cannon Creek	Elder N. T. Smith, F. F. Wilson and Z. T. Robbins	3						2	22	3	1.80
Cave Spring	John White and S. A. Keller						7	2	95	3	1.00
Dotson's Creek	D. H. Rosenbalm	2					4	1	34	1	
Davis' Creek	Elder H. Ausmus, T. J. Miracle and James Edwards		3				9		130	1	
Hind's Creek	Elder T. W. Baker and A. Baker							1	46	2	1.05
Lost Creek	Elder Wm. West, H. H. Oaks, A. G. Hill, Union Hill, J. M. Miller, Canister Hill and Elvin Hill					1	5	3	74	3	1.10
Mossy Spring	Timothy Hill, H. S. Wilson, J. F. Miller, H. Hill and D. R. Graves	2				1	1	2	65	1	1.10
Mt. Hebron	Elders Thomas Weaver, Drury Craig, J. S. Lewis and Brethren E. M. Collins, Jesse Lewis and J. M. J. Vandagriff		1				1		50	4	1.05
Pleasant Point	M. J. Sowder, J. K. P. Mays, W. H. Collins and W. C. Prophet							1	36	4	
Red Hill	Letter but no Messenger	4				1		1	32	2	.50
Rose Hill	John Waggoner and F. M. McBee							1	89	3	
Union	A. Browning, C. Keck and John Miller	2					20	1	122	4	

☞Note—To avoid public collections for Associational expenses, let each church send to the Association from $1.00 to $2.00, according to membership; and 25c to 50c extra for each obituary.—*Clerk.*

45

ARTICLES OF FAITH.

ARTICLE 1. We believe in one only true and living God, as he is revealed to us in the Holy Scriptures, Father, Son and Holy Ghost.

2. We believe that the Scriptures of the Old and New Testaments are the word of God and the only rule of all saving knowledge and obedience.

3. We believe in the doctrine of election according to the foreknowledge of God.

4. We believe in the doctrine of original sin.

5. We believe in man's impotency to recover himself from the fallen state he is in by his own free will or ability

6. We believe that sinners are justified in the sight of God only by the imputed righteousness of Jesus Christ.

7. We believe the elect, according to the foreknowledge of God, will be called, converted, regenerated and sanctified by the Holy Spirit.

8. We believe the saints will persevere and never fall finally away.

9. We belive that baptism and the Lord's Supper are ordinances of Jesus Christ, and that true believers are the only subjects of these ordinances, and that the true mode of baptism is by immersion.

10. We believe in the resurrection of the dead and the general judgment.

11. We believe that the punishment of the wicked will be everlasting, and that the joys of the righteous will be eternal.

12. We believe that no minister has the right to administer the ordinances except those who have been regularly baptized and called of God and come under the imposition of hands by the Presbytery.

...MINUTES....

OF THE

EIGHTY-EIGHTH ANNUAL MEETING

OF THE

POWELL'S VALLEY ASSOCIATION

OF

PRIMITIVE BAPTISTS

HELD WITH THE CHURCH AT

Lost Creek, Union County, Tenn.,

October 5, 6, and 7, 1906.

KNOXVILLE, TENN.:
GAUT-OGDEN COMPANY, PRINTERS.
1906.

Printers' Fee, $10.00 for 800 copies.

MINUTES.

Of the Eighty-Eighth Annual Meeting of the Powell's Valley
Association of Primitive Baptists, held with the
the Church at Lost Creek, Union County,
Tennessee, October 5, 6, 7, 1906.

---

1. Introductory Sermon by Elder J. S. Lewis, from Acts
13 chapter, 2, 3, 4: "So they, being sent forth by the Holy
Ghost," etc. Contexts: Acts xvi: 6-10, "Forbidden of the
Holy Ghost to preach in Asia," etc.

2. After an intermission of ten minutes the Association was
called to order by the Moderator, Elder Thomas Weaver.

3. Called for the letters from the churches, thirteen were
presented and read; and on motion, were received and messengers names enrolled as shown in table of statistics.

4. The messengers present from Salem and Mt. Hebron
churches, stated that their churches had lettered and appointed
messengers. Then, on motion, these messengers were welcomed
to seats, and gave the clerk their churches' reports, the same
as if their letters had arrived.

5. On motion Brother Squire Treece was invited to a seat.

6. The election of officers being next in order, Elder Thomas
Weaver was re-elected moderator, and A. G. Hill was re-elected
clerk.

7. Called for petitionary letters, and one was presented from
The Emerald Avenue, Primitive Baptist Church, Knoxville,
Tenn.

On motion, the letter was received and messengers welcomed to seats.

8. Called for correspondence and received the following, viz.:

(a) *Nolachucky*—Letters and Minutes by the hands of her Messengers, Elders Samuel McMillan and I. L. Ogle.

(b) *Sequatchie Valley*—Letter and Minutes by the hand of her Messenger, Elder R. O. Raulston.

9. Invited transient ministers to seats, when Elder H. C. Hogan came forward, and was welcomed to a seat by the Moderator.

10. Committees appointed:

(a) *On Arrangements*—Elders T. W. Baker, J. M. Miller, J. Owens, John Miller and John Waggoner.

(b) *On Correspondence*—Elders H. Ausmus and J. W. Riggs, Brethren J. P. Sanders and A. G. Hill.

(c) *On Finance*—H. H. Oaks and Thomas Bridges.

(d) *On Preaching*—Canister Hill, J. M. Miller, A. Browning, W. C. Prophet, together with the Church at this place.

11. Appointments for preaching today:

At the Stand—Elder Samuel McMillan.
TONIGHT—
At the Church—Elder J. W. Riggs and R. O. Raulston.
At Oaks Chapel—Elders I. L. Ogle and H. C. Hogan.
At Robert Brantley's—Elder A. D. Rutherford.

12. Adjourned to meet Saturday morning at 8:30 o'clock.

SATURDAY MORNING.

1. The Association met pursuant to adjournment.

2. Praise and prayer, by Elder R. O. Raulston.

3. Read the Rules of Decorum.

4. Called for the report of the Committee on Arrangements, which was adopted, as follows:

We your Committee on Arrangements, beg leave to submit the following order of business:.
Call the Roll.
Call for the Report of the Committee on Preaching; 2d, On Finance; 3d, On Correspondence.
When and Where shall our next Association be? Who shall preach the Introductory Sermon and who shall be his Alternate?
How many copies of minutes?
Shall we publish the Obituaries?

Respectfully submitted,
T. W. BAKER,
J. OWENS,
JOHN MILLER,
J. M. MILLER,
JOHN WAGGONER.

5. The Committee on Preaching submitted their report, and on motion was adopted, as follows:

(a) *For Saturday*—Elders A. D. Rutherford, I. L. Ogle and R. O. Raulston.

(b) *At Night at the Church*—Elders Henry Ausmus and Thomas Weaver.

(c) *At Hill's Academy*—Elders H. C. Hogan and R. O. Raulston.

(d) *White's Schoolhouse*—Elders I. L. Ogle and John Suffridge.

(e) *At D. R. Graves' Residence*—Elders Samuel McMillan and J. W. Riggs.

(f) *For Sunday*—Elders H. C. Hogan, R. O. Raulston and Thomas Weaver.

Respectfully submitted,
CANISTER HILL,
J. M. MILLER,
A. BROWNING,
W. C. PROPHET.

6. Called the roll and erased the names of absentees.

7. The Committee on Correspondence submitted their report, and on motion, adopted the following:

We, your Committee on Correspondence, beg leave to submit the following:

Be it Resolved, That we continue our correspondence with Nolachucky, Tennessee, Mud Creek, and Sequatchie Valley; and,

Be it resolved, That we send messengers to as many as possible, and letters and minutes to the others; and,

Be it Resolved, That our Corresponding letter be spread upon our minutes.

Respectfully submitted,

HENRY AUSMUS,

J. W. RIGGS,

J. P. SANDERS,

A. G. HILL.

8. Corresponding letter:

We, the original Powell's Valley Association of Primitive Baptists, assembled with the Church at Lost Creek, to our sister Associations with whom we correspond:

DEAR BRETHREN—We wish to keep up our long cherished Christian correspondence with you, for which purpose we have chosen our beloved brethren to bear this our letter to you, viz.:

Tennessee—Elders Thomas Weaver, T. W. Baker, Brethren J. P. Sanders, John Miller, and Elder Drury Craig, to write to them.

Sequatchie Valley—Elders J. S. Lewis and J. W. Riggs.

As we meet again before Nolachucky and Mud Creek meets, we defer appointing messengers till next year.

A. G. HILL,   THOMAS WEAVER,

     Clerk.   Moderator.

9. On motion we appoint Elders Drury Craig, H. C. Hogan and Brother John Miller a committee to examine and report a resolution presented to the Association by Brother J. Owen, which was adopted, as follows:

"Whereas, The Baptist family having many divisions, caused by members leaving the Church of Christ by teaching false doctrines, which lead to false practice, yet claiming the name Baptist, which called for an Appellation to distinguish the true Baptist from the false; therefore Primitive was adopted.

In later days two other divisions have come among us, by members teaching false doctrine such as "The Absolute Predestination of All Things

Whatsoever Comes to Pass, Both Good and Evil," and others, joining wordly secret institutions, contrary to the teaching of the Bible, and a practice opposed by the Church of Christ.

As those members who have gone off from us, having constituted new Associations, each claiming to be the Powell's Valley Association, and,

Be it resolved, That we, the original Powell's Valley Association, have spread upon our minutes, that we stand on the Apostolic doctrine, Salvation by Grace alone, and with the Old Kehukee Association, standing aloof from all men-made institution. (See ch. History page 706.) This done by order of the Association while in session with the Church at Lost Creek, Tenn., October 5, 6, 7, 1906.

10. The Committee on Finance reported, and the report was adopted, as follows:

We, your Committee on Finance, beg leave to report:

From the Church for Minutes $17.15
For Correspondents 2.00

$19.15

Respectfully submitted,
H. H. OAKS,
THOMAS BRIDGES.

11. On motion, by Brother J. P. Sanders, we appoint our next Association to be held with the Church on Emerald Avenue, in the City of Knoxville, Tenn., commencing on Friday before the third Saturday in August, 1907.

12. On motion we appoint Elder Thomas Weaver to preach the Introductory sermon and Elder T. W. Baker to be his alternate.

13. On motion we agree that the clerk have 800 copies of minutes printed and distributed, and be allowed $5.00 for services, and $2.15 for postage.

14. On motion we tender our most humble and heartfelt thanks to the brethren and friends of Lost Creek Church and Community, who have so kindly entertained us during our stay with them.

15. Elder Thomas Weaver, addressed the Association on the evils of covetousness, and the blessings of liberality.

The messengers present contributed as follows: To purchase a record book, $1.50; to assist the brethren at Knoxville to pay for their church property, a free-will offering, $10.10.

16. Minutes read and adopted.

17. Then adjourned to meet as above stated.

THOMAS WEAVER, Moderator.

A. G. HILL, Clerk.   Fountain City, Tenn.
Lost Creek, Tenn.   R. D. No. 5.
     R. D. No. 1, Box 6.

SUNDAY.

The congregation was first addressed by Elder H. C. Hogan, from Genesis xxxvii, 19, subject, "Dreams."

Second, by Elder R. O. Raulston, from Job ix:2, "But how should man be just with God."

Third, by Elder Thomas Weaver, subject, "Faithfulness, avoiding covetous practices," after which the congregation sung, "How Firm a Foundation, ye Saints of the Lord," amid much rejoicing in a Savior's love.

OBITUARIES.

Davis Creek: Louisa T. Hopper was born June 27, 1818; died December 5, 1903. Professed faith in Jesus about the year 1860, and lived a devoted member till death. Her last words: "Tell all my friends I am dying happy."

Rose Hill: Vincent Packet was born about 1835. Received a hope in Christ in 1873; joined the Church, and lived a faithful member till death, which came suddenly, in 1904. Last words: "I will soon be at home."

Wm. Gross was born in 1848. Professed faith in Jesus a number of years ago. Joined the Primitive Baptist Church July, 1905, and died August, 1905.

ELDERS	POST OFFICE	STATE
Thomas Weaver	Fountain City, R. No. 5	Tenn.
Drury Craig	Fountain City, R. No. 5	Tenn.
T. W. Baker	Fountain City, R. No. 5	Tenn.
Henry Ausmus	Speedwell	Tenn.
Wm. West	Lost Creek	Tenn.
J. J. Woods	Goin	Tenn.
A. Miracle	Goin	Tenn.
A. J. Hopson	Washburn	Tenn.
James Hurst	Dutch	Tenn.
Robert Wilson	Cubbage	Ky.
J. N. Saylor	Layman	Ky.
N. T. Smith	Ferndale	Ky.
J. W. Riggs	Kensee	Ky.
John Suffridge	Lone Mountain	Tenn.
J. S. Lewis	Knoxville	Tenn.
Calaway Keck	Gibson Station	Va.
A. D. Rutherford	Jacksborough	Tenn.
Eli M. Branson	Zenda	Kan.

LICENTIATES.

M. V. Hill	Knoxville	Tenn
James Ausmus	Speedwell	Tenn.
T. J. Miracle	Speedwell	Tenn.
Francis Riggs	Pineville	Ky.
A. D. Simmons	New Tazewell	Tenn
Christian Keck	Sharpe's Chapel	Tenn.
A. Baker	Maynardville	Tenn.

CHURCHES	CLERKS	POST OFFICE	STATE
Browney's Creek	F. P. Miracle	Cubbage	Ky.
Big Barron	Samp. Edwards	Goin	Tenn.
Cedar Springs	James Burk	New Tazewell	Tenn.
Cannon Creek	A. H. Crawford	Ferndale	Ky.
Cave Spring	S. A. Keller	Sharpe's Chapel	Tenn.
Davis' Creek	James Edwards	Speedwell	Tenn.
Dotson's Creek	D. H. Rosembalm	Maynardville	Tenn.
Emerald Avenue	I. M. Idol	Knoxville	Tenn.
Hind's Creek		Maynardville	Tenn.
Lost Creek	A. G. Hill	Lost Creek, R. 1, bx 6	Tenn.
Mt. Hebron	J. M. J. Vandagriff.	Heiskell, R. No. 1	Tenn.
Mossy Spring	J. F. Miller	Lost Creek, R. No. 1	Tenn.
Noeton	J. L. Oliver	Noeton	Tenn.
Pleasant Point	W. H. Collins'	Goin	Tenn.
Rose Hill	John Waggoner	Maynardville	Tenn.
Salem	Henry Ritter	Dutch	Tenn.
Union	A. Browning	Sharpe's Chapel	Tenn.

TABLE OF STATISTICS.

Churches	Messengers Names	Rec'd by Experience	Received by Letter	Restored	Confession of Faith	Dismissed by Letter	Excluded	Dead	Total	Saturday Meetings	Average Attendance on Saturdays	Contributions
Browney's Creek	F. P. Miracle and Robert Wilson	1					2		40	4		$1 00
Big Barren	J. J. Woods, Sampson Edwards and W. J. Woods						2		26	4		1 00
Cedar Springs	A. D. Simmons, James Burk and Leonard Simmons	5					20		20	1		1 00
Cannon Creek	Preston Beason and F. F. Wilson				2				28	3		1 50
Cave Spring	J. W. Riggs, J. Owens, W. H. Brantley, Wm. Taylor, John White, Mc. H. Owens, S. A. Keller and David White						3	3	87	3		1 05
Davis' Creek	Henry Ausmus, T. J. Miracle, D. F. Cain, S. B. Hopper, and James Edwards						3	3	127	1		1 00
Dotson's Creek	No Letter or Messenger...........Total last year								34			
Emerald Avenue	A. D. Rutherford, J. P. Sanders, I. M. Idol and L. L. Brantley	1			1				17	1		2 00
Hinds' Creek	T. W. Baker, W. B. Warwick and Wm. Warsham						2		46	2		1 00
Lost Creek	Wm. West, H. H. Oaks, Thomas Bridges, E. C. Hill, J. M. Miller and A. G. Hill	1			1	1		1	71	2	20	2 00
Mt. Hebron	Thomas Weaver, Drury Craig, J. S. Lewis, Wm. Howerton and E. M. Collins	3			1	7	1		46	4		2 00
Mossy Spring	Hamilton Hill, H. S. Wilson, P. L. Weaver, Jacob Bridges and J. F. Miller					3	3	1	64	1	18	1 50
Noeton	No Letter or Messenger.											
Pleasant Point	W. C. Prophet, S. M. Miracle and J. K. P. Mays	2	3				4	1	40	3		1 00
Rose Hill	John Waggoner and John Kitts	1					4		70	3		1 50
Salem	David Bunch	2					4	2	132	2		1 50
Union	Christian Keck, A. Browning and John Miller	1					2	1	120	4		2 00

ARTICLES OF FAITH.

ARTICLE 1. We believe in only one true and living God, as he is revealed to us in the Holy Scriptures — Father, Son and Holy Ghost.

2. We believe that the Scriptures of the Old and New Testaments are the Word of God and the only rule of all saving knowledge and obedience.

3. We believe in the doctrine of election according to the foreknowledge of God.

4. We believe in the doctrine of original sin.

5. We believe in man's impotency to recover himself from the fallen state he is in by his own free will or ability.

6. We believe that sinners are justified in the sight of God only by the imputed righteousness of Jesus Christ.

7. We believe the elect, according to the foreknowledge of God, will be called, converted, regenerated and sanctified by the Holy Spirit.

8. We believe the saints will persevere and never fall finally away.

9. We believe that baptism and the Lord's Supper are ordinances of Jesus Christ, and that true believers are the only subjects of these ordinances, and that the true mode of baptism is by immersion.

10. We believe in the resurrection of the dead and the general judgment.

11. We believe that the punishment of the wicked will be everlasting, and that the joys of the righteous will be eternal.

12. We believe that no minister has the right to administer the ordinances except those who have been regularly baptized and called of God and come under the imposition of hands by the Presbytery.

The printers have been unavoidably hindered in getting out the Minutes. Hope you will pardon us all.—CLERK.

Ninetieth Annual Meeting

Powell's Valley Association

OF

PRIMITIVE BAPTISTS

HELD WITH THE CHURCH AT

Mossy Spring, Union Co., Tenn

Friday, Saturday, Sunday, August 14, 15, 16, 1908

MINUTES

of the Nintieth Annual Meeting of the

Powell's Valley Association

of Primitive Baptists, held with the church at Mossy
Spring, Union County, Tenn., Aug. 14, 15, 16, 1908.

FIRST DAY—FRIDAY

1. Introductory sermon by Elder Drury Craig, from
Eph. ii. 20, "And are built upon the foundation of the
Apostles and Prophets," etc.

2. After an intermission of fifteen minutes the messengers met in the house and the association was called
to order by the moderator, Elder Thomas Weaver.

3. Elders A. D. Rutherford and L. P. Potter occupied the stand today.

4. Called for the letters from the churches, when
sixteen were presented and read by J. M. J. Vandagriff,
J. F. Miller and the clerk.

5. On motion, the letters were received, together
with a letter from Elder C. Keck and wife, who have
withdrawn from the disorder of Gibson Station church,
who have gone off after the "new movements."

6. On motion, we welcome all of the members of
Cave Spring church to seats who stand aloof from the
"new movements."

7. The election of officers being next in order, Elder
Thomas Weaver was re-elected moderator and A. G. Hill
was re-elected clerk.

8. Called for petitionary letters.

9. Called for correspondence, when the following were received:

From Nola Chucky—Letter by the hand of Elder Samuel McMillan, who was welcomed to a seat by the moderator.

Sequachie Valley—Minutes.

10. Invited transient ministers to seats, when Elders C. H. Cayce, of Martin, Tenn., L. P. Potter, of Smithville, Tenn., and Elder A. D. Rutherford came forward and were welcomed to seats by the moderator.

11. Committees appointed:

On Arrangements—Elder H. Ausmus, Brethren Elvin Collins, J. A. S. Satterfield, J. M. Miller and Andrew Suffridge. Correspondents invited to aid.

On Correspondence—Elders D. Craig, S. Miracle and Brother John Miller.

On Finance—Elder T. W. Baker and Canister Hill.

On Requests—J. M. J. Vandagriff, Timothy Hill and H. H. Oaks.

On Preaching—G. C. Bunch, J. Owens, L. L. Brantly, T. O. Whited, Wm. Howerton, together with the church at this place.

12. Appointments for preaching tonight as follows:

At the church, Elders C. H. Cayce and L. P. Potter.

At Lost Creek, Elders Samuel McMillian and T. W. Baker.

At Privey Flat, Elder Drury Craig.

At Old Mossy Spring, Elder Thomas Weaver.

At Long Hollow, Elder Calaway Keck.

13. Adjourned to meet Saturday morning at 9 o'clock.

SECOND DAY—SATURDAY

1. The association met pursuant to adjournment.

2. Praise and prayer by Elder L. P. Potter.

3. Called for the report of the Committee on Arrangements, which was adopted:

We, your Committee on Arrangements, beg leave to submit the following order of business:

Call the roll.

Call for report on preaching.

Call for report on correspondence.

Call for report on finance.

Call for report on requests.

Where shall our next association be.

Who shall preach the introductory sermon and who shall be his alternate.

How many copies of minutes shall be printed, etc.

Respectfully submitted,

H. AUSMUS,
E. M. COLLINS,
ANDREW SUFFRIDGE,
J. A. S. SATTERFIELD,
J. M. MILLER.

4. Called the roll and erased the names of absentees.

5. Committee on Preaching submitted their report, which was adopted as follows:

Today—Elders Silas Miracle and Samuel McMillan.

Tonight, at the church—Elders H. Ausmus and Drury Craig.

At Privey Flat—Elders L. P. Potter and T. W. Baker.

At Long Hollow—Elder A. D. Rutherford and Licentiate C. Keck.

At Old Mossy Spring—Elder Calaway Keck and Licentiate Francis Riggs.

At Lost Creek—Elders A. J. Hopson and J. J. Woods.

Sunday—Elders C. H. Cayce and Thomas Weaver.

Respectfully submitted,

G. C. BUNCH,
J. OWENS,
L. L. BRANTLY,
T. O. WHITED,
WM. HOWERTON.

6. The Committee on Correspondence submitted their report, which was adopted:

We, your Committee on Correspondence, beg leave to submit the following:

Be it resolved, That we continue our correspondence with Nola Chucky, Tennessee, Sequachie Valley and Mud Creek Associations, and

Be it resolved, That we send messengers to as many as possible, and letters and minutes to the others, and

Be it resolved, That our corresponding letter be spread upon our minutes.

Respectfully submitted,
SILAS MIRACLE,
JOHN MILLER,
DRURY CRAIG.

7. Corresponding letter:

We, the original Powell's Valley Association of Primitive Baptists, assembled with the church at Mossy Spring, to our Sister Associations with whom we correspond:

Dear Brethren, we wish to keep up our long cherished Christian correspondence with you, for which purpose we have chosen our beloved brethren to bear this our letter to you, viz:

Nola Chucky—Elders T. W. Baker and A. J. Hopson and Brother John Miller.

Tennessee—Elders A. D. Rutherford, T. W. Baker and C. Keck.

Mud Creek—Elders Thomas Weaver and Drury Craig.

Sequachie Valley—Letter and minutes.

THOMAS WEAVER, Moderator.

A. G. HILL, Clerk.

8. The Committee on Request submitted their report, which was adopted:

We, your Committee on Request, beg leave to submit to you the following:

We grant the request of Mt. Hebron church to make known in the minutes the exclusion of Elder J. S. Lewis from church fellowship.

We grant the request of Salem church that the Powell's Valley Association of Primitive Baptists convene with her the next session.

Respectfully submitted,
J. M. J. VANDAGRIFF,
TIMOTHY HILL,
H. H. OAKS.

9. The Committee on Finance submitted their report, which was adopted as follows:

From the churches for minutes $16.00

From Calaway Keck for minutes............................ .34
The clerk reported balance in his hands from last year....... .60
Two churches, each, reported $1.00 for correspondence...... 2.00

$18.94

Respectfully submitted,
T. W. BAKER,
CANISTER HILL.

After placing our order with Brother Cayce for the minutes, there was 94 cents left in our hands, which we turned over to the Finance Committee to help pay the visiting ministers' railroad expenses.

10.   A request:

We, the Primitive Baptist Church of Christ at Mt. Hebron, ask the Powell's Valley Association to spread upon her minutes the exclusion of Elder J. S. Lewis from church fellowship.

Done by order of the church while in session the 4th Saturday in July, 1908.

ELDER T. W. BAKER, Moderator.
J. M. J. VANDAGRIFF, Church Clerk.

11.   On motion, we appoint the next meeting of our association to be held with the church at Salem, Grainger county, Tenn., commencing on Friday before the third Sunday in August, 1909.

12.   On motion, we appoint Elder T. W. Baker to preach the introductory sermon and Elder J. E. Hurst to be his alternate.

13.   On motion, we agree that the clerk have 800 copies of minutes printed and distributed, and be allowed $5.00 for services and $3.00 for postage.

14.   Took up a collection as a free-will offering to help pay railroad expenses of the visiting ministers.

15.   On motion, we tender our thanks to the brethren and friends who have so kindly entertained us during our stay with them.

16.   Adjourned to meet as above stated.

THOMAS WEAVER, Moderator,
Fountain City, Tenn., R. 5.

A. G. HILL, Clerk,
Lost Creek, Tenn., R. 1.

THIRD DAY—SUNDAY

The congregation met at the stand and after singing several good old songs of Zion, Elder A. D. Rutherford led the congregation in prayer. It was one of the most touching invocations we ever heard.

First, Elder C. H. Cayce addressed the congregation from 2nd Cor. iv. 5, "For we preach not ourselves, but Christ Jesus the Lord; and ourselves your servants for Jesus' sake."

Second, Elder Thomas Weaver spoke from the same subject with a warm exhortation to still contend for the dear old cause, in the good old way.

There was a halo of light and a breeze from that good land over yonder that was manifestly felt and realized during the services. Many of the sisters clapped their hands for joy and it was touching to see the dear ministers embracing each other.

This ended one of the best meetings of this dear old association.

ADDRESSES OF MINISTERS

Elder Thomas Weaver, Fountain City, Tenn., R. 5.
Elder Drury Craig, Fountain City, Tenn., R. 5.
Elder T. W. Baker, Fountain City, Tenn., R. 5.
Elder Henry Ausmus, Speedwell, Tenn.
Elder Wm. West, Sharps' Chapel, Tenn.
Elder J. J. Woods, Goin, Tenn.
Elder A. J. Hopson, Washburn, Tenn.
Elder James Hurst, Noeton, Tenn.
Elder Robert Wilson, Cubbage, Ky.
Elder J. N. Saylor, Layman, Ky.
Elder J. W. Riggs, Jelico, Ky.
Elder John Suffridge, Lone Mountain, Tenn.
Elder Calaway Keck, Walnut Hill, Va.
Elder A. D. Rutherford, Jacksborough, Tenn.
Elder Eli M. Branson, Zenda, Kan.
Elder James Ausmus, Speedwell, Tenn.

LICENTIATES

M. V. Hill, Knoxville, Tenn.
T. J. Miracle, Speedwell, Tenn.

Francis Riggs, Jelico, Ky.
A. D. Simmons, New Tazewell, Tenn.
Chrisley Keck, Sharpe's Chapel, Tenn.
A. Baker, Maynardville, Tenn.
Wm. Atkins, Washburn, Tenn.

ADDRESSES OF CHURCH CLERKS

Browney's Creek—F. P. Miracle, Cubbage, Ky.
Big Barron—Samp. Edwards, Goin, Tenn.
Cedar Springs—James Burk, New Tazewell, Tenn.
Cannon Creek—A. H. Crawford, Ferndale, Ky.
Davis' Creek—S. B. Hopper, Speedwell, Tenn.
Dotson's Creek—D. H. Rosembalm, Maynardsville, Tenn.
Sander's Chapel—J. E. Johnson, Knoxville, Tenn.
Hind's Creek—W. B. Warwick, Maynardsville, Tenn.
Lost Creek—A. G. Hill, Lost Creek, Tenn., R. 1, box 6.
Mt. Hebron—J. M. J. Vandagriff, Heiskell, Tenn., R. 1.
Mossy Spring—J. F. Miller, Lost Creek, Tenn., R. No. 1.
Noeton—J. L. Oliver, Noeton, Tenn.
Pleasant Point—W. H. Collins, Goin, Tenn.
Rose Hill—John Waggoner, Maynardsville, Tenn.
Salem—Henry Ritter, Dutch, Tenn.
Thorn Hill—Sam Atkins, Washburn, Tenn.
Union—A. Browning, Sharpe's Chapel, Tenn.

ARTICLES OF FAITH

Article 1. We believe in only one true and living God, as he is revealed to us in the Holy Scriptures—Father, Son and Holy Ghost.

2. We believe that the Scriptures of the Old and New Testaments are the Word of God and the only rule of all saving knowledge and obedience.

3. We believe in the doctrine of election according to the foreknowledge of God.

4. We believe in the doctrine of original sin.

5. We believe in man's impotency to recover himself from the fallen state he is in by his own free will or ability.

6. We believe that sinners are justified in the sight of God only by the imputed righteousness of Jesus Christ.

7. We believe the elect, according to the foreknowledge of God, will be called, converted, regenerated and sanctified by the Holy Spirit.

8. We believe the saints will persevere and never fall finally away.

9. We believe that baptism and the Lord's Supper are ordinances of Jesus Christ, and that true believers are the only subjects of these ordinances, and that the true mode of baptism is by immersion.

10. We believe in the resurrection of the dead and the general judgment.

11. We believe that the punishment of the wicked will be everlasting, and that the joys of the righteous will be eternal.

12. We believe that no minister has the right to administer the ordinances except those who have been regularly baptized and called of God and come under the imposition of hands by the Presbytery.

Let every church help its pastor, according to the Bible plan, to be there every meeting. And let each pastor teach the church its duty on these lines, is the prayer of your humble clerk. See 1 Cor. ix. and xvi. together wtih the references and connections. Hope you will suffer a word of admonition from one that loves you all, and most of all our blessed cause. A. G. HILL.

Printer's Fee and Postage, $11.00 for 800 copies.

STATISTICAL TABLE

Churches	Names of Messengers	Rec'd by Experience	Received by Letter	Restored	Confession of Faith	Dismissed by Letter	Excluded	Deceased	Total Membership	Saturday of Meeting	Contributions
Union	John Miller, G A Whited, O Keck	4				8		1	118	4	$1 00
Salem	A J Hopson, James Satterfield, George Bunch	4					4	1	125	2	2 00
Hind's Creek	T W Baker, Wm. Washburn, W B Warwick								40	2	25
Mt. Hebron	Thomas Weaver, Drury Craig, Wm. Howerton, E M Collins, James Elkins, J M J Vandagriff							1	49	4	2 00
Dotson's Creek	D H Rosenbalm						2	1	16	1	35
Rose Hill	John Waggoner, John Mapies, John Kuts								69	3	1 00
Mossy Spring	Canister Hill, H S Wilson, Timothy Hill, J F Miller, Sam Brantley	1	1		1				64	3	
Cedar Spring	A D Simmons, E E Simmons								7	1	1 50
Davis' Creek	H Ausmus, S Miracle, J Owens, Jeff Miracle, S B Hopper	2	2		2						50
Big Barren	J J Woods, Samp Edwards	2					10	2	118	2	1 00
Pleasant Point	G W Miracle, M J Sowder, W C Prophet							1	37	3	95
Cannon Creek	F F Wilson	1				1			25	3	1 00
Sanders Chapel	L L Brantley, Andrew Surridge								18	1	2 10
Browney's Creek	F P Miracle, T B Pott							3	86	4	1 00
Thorn Hill	Joel Mallcoat								22	4	1 00
Lost Creek	Wm. West, H H Oaks, J M Miller, A G Hill	1						1	76	1	50
Red Hill	Looking for you next year										1 35
Norton	Looking for you next year										
Totals		14	8	0	8	17		14	829		$17 50

66

Subscribe for

THE PRIMITIVE BAPTIST

Established by Elder S. F. Cayce
Edited by Elder C. H. Cayce
Published Weekly in the Interest of
the Regular Primitive Baptists at One
Dollar a Year. Sample copies free.

THE YOUTH'S GUARDIAN FRIEND

O. F. CAYCE, Editor

Contains not only interesting matter
for the young folks, but things that
are instructive. Fifty Cents a Year.

Send for a Sample Copy

WE PRINT EVERYTHING

CAYCES & TURNER, Pulishers
Martin, Tennessee

End
of
Special Section

1971 MINUTES OF THE POWELL VALLEY ASSOCIATION

of

PRIMITIVE BAPTISTS

Black Fox Church

Held with the Sister Church at Black Fox
in Grainger County, Aug. 20, 21 and 22, 1971

MINUTES OF THE POWELLS VALLEY ASSOCIATION OF PRIMITIVE BAPTISTS

The One Hundred Fifty-Second Annual Session

of

The Powell Valley Association

of

Primitive Baptists

Held With

Black Fox Church In Grainger County

August 20, 21 and 22, 1971

Moderator	Elder Albert Davis
Assistant Moderator	Elder Hugh Brummitt
Clerk	W. H. Taylor
Assistant Clerk	O. R. Parrott

The next session will be held with the Sister Church at Oak Grove in Union County on Friday before the 3rd Saturday in August, 1972.

The Introductory Sermon will be delivered by Elder Tony Eastridge and Elder Clifford Brantley will be the alternate.

FRIDAY, AUGUST 20, 1971

The Powell Valley Association of Primitive Baptists met with the Sister Church at Black Fox in Grainger County on Friday, August 20th for the one hundred fifty-second annual session.

After singing several good spiritual songs, Elder Albert Davis read for the lesson, from the 51st chapter of Psalms and called for the opening prayer by Elder Johnnie Atkins, followed by Elder Joe Bush of Rocky Dale who preached the introductory sermon, reading from the 6th chapter of Matthew, and taking for his text, "A Sure Foundation,", and preaching a wonderful and and spiritual sermon.

The Association was then dismissed in prayer for 15 minutes recess by Elder Lenvil Meyers of Monroe Michigan Church.

ORDER OF BUSINESS

After intermission, at the sound of singing the Association reconvened and after a good song service, the moderator, Elder Albert Davis, after pleading for peace, love and unity to reign throughout the session, called on Elder Parnick Shelton, pastor of the host church for the opening prayer.

1. The moderator called for the letters from the Sister Churches to be presented for reading by the Clerks. Eleven letters were received and more were expected on Saturday.
2. Called for members who were not delegated and desire to be seated came forward. Two came, Elder Johnnie Atkins of Oak Grove and Brother Larry Bush of Rocky Dale were seated.
3. Motion carried to accept the letters and seat their delegations.
4. Call for any petitionary letters, none were received.
5. Call. for letters from corresponding associations, none were received on Friday
6. Call for the election of officers for the coming year.
7. Motion and second approved that the Association re-elect Elder Albert Davis Moderator, and Elder Hugh E. Brummitt assistant Moderator for the next year.
8. Motion carried to re-elect Brother W. H. Taylor Clerk and Brother Onnie Parrott assistant Clerk.
9. Motion approved to have the Moderator appoint all the committees.
10. The Moderator, having been authorized by the Association,

71

appointed the committees as follows:

COMMITTEE ON ARRANGEMENTS

Elder Joe Bush
Brother Donald Sharp
Brother Henry Chamberlain

COMMITTEE ON PREACHING

Brother Bennie Capps
Brother M. A. Norton
Brother Spurgeon Thompson

COMMITTEE ON CORRESPONDENCE

Elder Johnnie Atkins
Elder Alvin Graves
Elder Clifford Brantley

COMMITTEE ON REQUEST

Brother Walton Cabbage
Brother John Oliver
Elder Everett Berry

COMMITTEE ON FINANCE

Elder George Shoffner
Brother Elmer Graves
Brother Von Beason

11. The Committees all having been appointed, the Association was dismissed in prayer by Elder Leonard White, until Saturday morning at 10:30 A.M.

SATURDAY, AUGUST 21, 1971

1. The Saturday service, after a good song service, directed by Elder Charles Taylor, was introduced by Elder Hugh Brummitt., assistant Moderator who gave a very spiritual talk and read a lesson from the 111th Psalm and called for Elder William Sparks for the opening prayer.
2. The Moderator called the Association to order and called for letters from Sister Churches not received on Friday, three were received, read and their delegates were seated.
3. Moderator called for the roll call of delegates.
4. Call for letters of corresponding associations, one letter was

72

reported from original Hiwassee Association and failed to get in but the delegates were received and seated by vote of the Association. Delegates to wit:

Brother Cecil Godfrey

Sister Billy Godfrey

Sister Myrtle Cook

5. Call for anyone of the corresponding association present and not delegated who wish to be seated. None came.

6. The Moderator called for the report of Committee on arrangements who gave the following report which was accepted and the committee released.

REPORT OF COMMITTEE ON ARRANGEMENTS

a. Call for the roll call of delegates

b. Call for a report of Committee on Preaching

c. Call for report of Committee on Correspondence

d. Call for a report of Committee on Requests

e. Call for report of Committee on Finance

f. How many minutes shall we have printed, who shall supervise the printing and distributing of them, and how much shall he receive for this service. When and where shall the next Association session be held, and who will preach the introductory Sermon and who shall be the alternate.

Respectfully submitted,

Elder Parnick Shelton

Brother Henry Chamberlain

Brother Donald Sharp

7. Call for report of Committee on Preaching who gave the following report which was received and the Committee released.

REPORT OF COMMITTEE ON PREACHING

We the Committee on Preaching wish to submit the following report:

Friday Night	Elder Lenvil Meyers
	Elder Alvin Graves
Saturday	Elder Hugh Brummitt
	Elder Everett Berry

Saturday Night	Elder Charles Taylor
	Elder Walter Lyons
Sunday	Elder Leonard White
	Elder Albert Davis

Respectfully submitted,

Brother Bennie C. Capps
Brother M. A. Norton
Brother Spurgeon Thompson

8. Call for report of Committee on Correspondence who gave the report as follows which was received and the Committee released.

REPORT OF COMMITTEE ON CORRESPONDENCE

We the Committee on Correspondence wish to recommend that since the new Bethel Association has failed for the past two years to letter and delegate, that we discontinue our correspondence with them. We also wish to keep our correspondece to the original Hiwassee Association.

Respectfully submitted,

Elder Alvin Graves
Elder Clifford Brantley
Elder Johnnie Atkins

9. Call for report of Committee on Requests who gave the report. as follows, which was received and the Committe released.

REPORT OF COMMITTEE ON REQUESTS

We the Committee on Request recommend that we have 1000 copies of the minutes printed and distributed to the Sister Churches and that we authorize the clerk to supervise the the printing and distribution of same and that he receive $50 for his service. And that he have all obituaries printed in the minutes.

We also suggest that the next session be held with the Sister Church at Oak Grove in Union County, Tenn. to begin on Friday befor the third Saturday in August 1972 at 10:30 A.M.

10. Call for report of Committee on Finance , who submitted the following report, which was received and the Committee released.

REPORT OF COMMITTEE ON FINANCE

Black Fox	$ 10.00
Bradens Chapel	10.00
Brantley's Chapel	10.00
Cedar Springs	10.00
Davis Chapel	20.00
Gibson Station	10.00
Kirkwood	25.00
Lenoir City	30.00
Monroe Michigan	5.00
Oak Grove	20.00
Pleasant Hill	15.00
Pleasant Point	10.00
Rocky Dale	15.00
Noeton	5.00
Total	$195.00

Respectfully submitted,

Elder George Shoffner
Brother Elmer Graves
Brother Von Beason

11.   CLERKS FINANCIAL STATEMENT

Balance in Bank	$ 91.00
Receipts	195.00
Total	$ 286.00
Expenses for 1971	
Balance in Bank	

12. Motion and second approved that the Association authorize

75

the Clerk to have printed and distributed to the Sister Churches 1000 Copies of the minutes, and that he receive $50 for this service.

13. Motion carried that the next session of the Association be held with the sister Church at Oak Grove in Union County, Tenn. to begin on Friday before the third Saturday in August 1972 at 10:30.

14. Motion carried that Elder Tony Eastridge preach the introductory Sermon, and that Elder Clifford Brantley be the alternate.

15. The Association voted to letter and delegate to the Original Hiwassee Association, and that we send as delegates Elder George Campbell, Elder Alvin Graves, and Elder Clifford Brantley

16. Motion that the clerk prepare a letter for the delegates to present to the Original Hiwassee Association.

17. The Association voted to extend to the church at Black Fox and the entire community our heart felt thanks for the love and kindness and the welcome way we were all received. And may God bless this church, pastor and community.

18. After several testimonies and much rejoicing the Association was adjourned with prayer by Elder Charles Taylor.

Elder Albert Davis, Moderator
Eld. Hugh E. Brummitt. Assistant Moderator
Brother W. H. Taylor, Clerk

SUNDAY SERVICE

Sunday at the appointed hour, a large and well-behaved crowd that over ran the house and into the yard, listened very attentively to the song service and prayer, followed by a well delivered Sermon by Elder Leonard White who spoke from the Book of Galations. The association was then closed out by the Moderator, Elder Albert Davis.

ORDAINED MINISTERS

Elder Gilbert Atkins
Rt. # 3 Rutledge, Tenn.

Elder Johnny Atkins
Bean Station, Tenn.

Elder Everett Berry
Rt. # 27
Knoxville, Tenn. - Phone 922-7004

Elder J. H. Branscomb
Speedwell, Tenn. - Phone 869-3735

Elder Clifford Brantley
Brown School Road
Maryville, Tenn. - Phone982-3735

Elder Johnny Ayers
New Tazewell, Tenn.

Elder Albert Davis
Speedwell, Tenn. - Phone 869-3596

Elder Hugh E. Brummitt
1329 Brown Avenue.
Knoxville, Tenn. - Phone 525-3583

Elder George Campbell
Fritts Road
Concord, Tenn. - Phone 966-5340

Elder Noble Lee Clawson
Route 4 - Speedwell, Tenn.

Elder Albert Davis
Speedwell, Tenn . - Phone 869-3596

Elder Tony Eastridge
Louisville, Tenn. - Phone 983-1068

Elder Alvin Graves
Lenoir City, Tenn. - Phone 986-5548

Elder Joe Irwin
Gibson Station, Va.

Elder Walter Lyons
1400 Jourolman Ave.
Knoxville, Tenn. - Phone 525-9640

Elder Lenvil Meyers
715 Scott St.
Monroe, Mich.

Elder J. C. Monday
Speedwell, Tenn.

Elder Roy Oliver
Bean Station, Tenn.

Elder R. H. Petitt
Jacksboro Pike
Knoxville, Tenn. - Phone 689-5581

Elder Claude Rosson
New Tazewell, Tenn. - Phone 626-3168

Elder Parnick Shelton
Corryton, Tenn. - Phone 687-6142

Elder George Shoffner
Route # 2 Louisville, Tenn.

Elder W. M. Sparks
Speedwell, Tenn. - Phone 562-7997

Elder Leonard White
LaFollette, Tenn. - Phone 562-5667

Elder Clay Widner
101 W. Norris St.
Norris, Tenn.

Elder Charles Taylor
Route # 4 Lenoir City, Tenn.
Phone 986-8172

Elder Raymond Brantley

Elder Joe Bush
Corryton, Tenn. - Phone 687-7018

LICENTIATES

Brother Odell Carpenter
Maryville, Tenn.

Brother Roscoe Branscomb

LETTER TO THE ORIGINAL HIWASSEE ASSOCIATION

We the Powell Valley Association of Primitive Baptist while in regular session with the Sister Church at Black Fox, vote to keep our beloved correspondence with the Original Hiwassee Association.

We therefore letter and delegate to you our beloved ministers, Elder George Campbell, Elder Alvin Graves, and Elder Charles Taylor who we trust you will receive and seat with you.

We also covet your prayers and fellowship, and hope to see you again in our next association.

> Elder Albert Davis, Moderator
> Elder Hugh Brummitt, Assist. Moderator
> Brother W. H. Taylor, Clerk
> Brother O. N. Parrott, Assist. Clerk

ARTICLES OF FAITH

Article 1. We believe in only one true living God, as He is revealed to us in the Holy Scriptures - Father, Son, and Holy Ghost.

Article 2. We believe that the Scriptures of the old and new Testaments are the words of God and the only rule of all-saving knowledge and obedience.

Article 3. We believe in the doctrine of election according to the foreknowledge of God.

Article 4. We believe in the doctrine of original sin.

Article 5. We believe in man's impotency to rescue himself from the fallen state he is in, by his own will or ability.

Article 6. We believe that sinners are justified in the sight of God only by the imputed righteousness of Jesus Christ.

Article 7. We believe the elect, according to the foreknowledge of God will be called, converted, regenerated, and sanctified by the Holy Spirit.

Article 8. We believe the saints will persevere and never fall finally away.

Article 9. We believe that baptism and the Lord's Supper are ordinances of Jesus Christ, and that true believers are the only subject of these ordinances, and that the true mode of baptism is by immersion. We believe also that feet washing is an example of Jesus Christ and should be kept by his deciples until his second coming.

Article 10. We believe in the Resurrection of the dead and the General Judgement.

Article 11. We believe that the punishment of the wicked will be everlasting and that the joys of the righteous will be eternal.

Article 12. We believe that no minister has the right to administer the ordinances, except those who have been regularly baptized and called of God, and come under the imposition of hands of the presbytery.

RULES OF DECORUM

1. The churches composing the Powell's Valley Association shall not be confined to any set rules as to specific number of Messengers they shall have in the body, but shall have the right to name in their letters as many as they choose, and in addition all orderly members of and of the churches being present be entitled to seats in the body as Messengers of their respective churches, with all the rights and privileges of the same.

2. The Messengers thus assembled shall be denominated the Powell's Valley Primitive Baptist Association.

3. For the purpose of historical information and statistical edification, the Churches are required to state in letters, the number of members in fellowship, the number received by Baptism, by letter, by confession of Faith, the number dismissed, excluded and dead since last session; also the time of their meeting, their pastoral supply, and the amount of money contributed for ministers and other purposes together with any other information they deem appropriate for the edification of the saints and glory of God.

4. This Association shall have no power to answer queries, give advice, or dictate to the Churches in any case, or to lord it over God's heritage nor any power by which she can directly or indirectly fringe on the internal rights of the church or censure and try any church or member in reference to faith and practice and determine upon valigity of gospel ordinances. These things shall rest entirely with the churches; but henceforward our annual meetings shall be only for the purpose of hearing from each other, and for the worship of God and mutual comfort and edification of the Saints. To this end we reserve the privilege annually before the Third Saturday in August and the two following days or at such other times as may be agreed upon with any church that may invite us having to protect our own standard, while in session, from heresey and disorder to recognize and invite any primitive Baptist minister or any lay brother ot worship with us that may deem proper; to request the brethren of our body to visit other churches or bodies in our belief with whom we may desire to culture Christian fellowship; to publish in a minute of our proceedings.

5. Each session of the body shall have a Moderator and Clerk who shall hold office until re-elected.

6. Any order member of any church belonging to this body, when convened, being present shall be eligible to elect on as Moderator and Clerk or to sit on any committee appointed by the same.

7. In all election or questions that may be necessary to determine by vote, the vote shall be taken by churches, each church being entitled to three votes for and number less than one hundred, and one additional vote for every fifty or fraction thereof above the first hundred, but the Messengers of each church may divide their vote as they see proper.

8. All elections of questions coming to vote shall be determined by a majority vote cast, and it shall be the only duty of the minority to acquiesce in the decision thus reached.

9. If new churches desire to be admitted to this union they shall petition by letter and messengers and if voted for or recommended by one or more sister churches for her Presbytery constitution them, or orthox and orderly they shall be received by the voice of the body and manifested by the Moderator

giving the Messengers the right hand of fellowship.

10. Any motion or resolution clearly inconsistent with the above rules shall be promptly ruled out of order unless withdrawn by the mover.

11. Any Messenger being ruled out of order by the Moderator shall have the right to appeal to the body on the question or order, and if sustained shall be allowed to proceed, but if not take his seat.

12. Our meeting being held in the name of Christ and the worship of God; each Messenger is expected to observe due and proper therein.

13. It will not be considered good for any Messenger whose name has been enrolled as such to abruptly break off or absent himself from the Association without leave.

14. The Moderator shall be entitled to the same privilege of speech as other members provided the chair is filled.

15. The minutes of the Association shall be read and approved by the body and signed by the Moderator before adjourning.

16. The Association shall be opened and closed by prayer.

17. Amendments to these may be made at any time by a majority of the union voting by churches when they deem it necessary, provide such amendments do not compromise the sovereignty of the churches nor have tendency to give body undue power or jurisdiction over them.

In Memoriam

Osber G. Ousley

Osber G. Ousley, 69, passed away at 5:40 p.m. Sunday at Claiborne County Hospital after a lingering illness. He was a member of Oak Grove Primitive Baptist Church and was ex-sheriff of Union County for many years. Survivors, wife, Marie Ousley, Sharps Chapel; daughter, Mrs. Judy Ousley Mitchell, Sacramento, California; grandsons, Douglas and Steve Mitchell, Sacramento; sisters, Miss Delta Ousley, Mrs. Belvia Anderson, Knoxville, Mrs. Helen Edgemon, Ten Mile, Mrs. Alma Edwards, Kokomo, Ind.; Mrs. K. D. Lively, Wichita, Kan.; brothers, O. C., Maynardville, Durward Ousley, Riceville, W. T., Kokomo, Ind.; several nieces and nephews. Funeral 2 p.m. Wednesday at Ailor's Chapel, Rev. Monday Officiating. Burial in Lynnhurst Cemetery.

Sarah Elisabeth Branscomb

Mrs. Sarah Elisabeth Branscomb, Speedwell, Tennessee, departed this life April 6, 1971, being 76 years of age. Surviving relatives are her husband, Roscoe Branscomb, Speedwell; Sons, Floyd Branscomb, Dayton, Ohio, Elder James H. and William Branscomb, both of Speedwell; daughters, Mrs. Arvil Braden, and Misses Mossie Jane, Carrie and Dorothy Branscomb, all of Speedwell; brother, James Graves, Speedwell, and 10 grandchildren.

She professed a hope in Christ and joined the Primitive Baptist Church at Pleasant Hill in 1912, where she remained a faithful member until death.

James Graves

James Graves, of Speedwell, Tenn., was born April 16, 1887. He departed this life July 13, 1971 being 84 years of age. He was married in 1912 to Aggie Miracle. To this union was born one daughter, Gracie E. They both preceeded him in death. He was married to Pearl Mayes in 1950. He had two brothers, William and McKinley, and two sisters, Rachel Belle and Sarah Elisabeth. They also preceeded him in death. He professed a hope in Christ and joined the Primitive Baptist Church at Pleasant Hill in July 1912 where he remained a faithful member until death.

Mrs. Mary Emma Stanford McKinney

Mary Emma Stanford McKinney, born March 22, 1886, went home to be with the Lord on December 13, 1970. She is survived by husband, Oscar M. McKinney; four daughters, Mrs. Gleneva McFarland, Mrs. Pearl Robinson, Mrs. June Williams, Mrs. Lola Heatherly; five grandchildren, and three great-grandchildren. She joined the Davis Chapel Primitive Baptist Church on June 24, 1924, and remained a faithful member until death. She loved her Lord and her church, and this love was portrayed in her daily life to her family and all who knew her. She will be remembered by her children as a virtuous woman, and her price far above rubies. Funeral services were held on Wednesday, December 16, 1970, at Davis Chapel Primitive Baptist Church. Elder Leonard White officiated. She was laid to rest in Sunrise Cemetery.

Jess Brooks Heatherly

Jess Brooks Heatherly, Age 74, passed away suddenly at his home, Rt. 1, LaFollette, June 16, 1971. He was born on Aug. 3, 1896. He was the son of the late George E. and Cynthia Heatherly. He was married to Mary Ford and to this union six children were born. His wife, one son, and the grandson whom he raised from infancy and who was killed in Vietnam in May, 1969, preceeded him in death. His survivors are: children, Cletus Heatherly of LaFollette, James Cecil Heatherly of Powell, Mrs. Clova Dutton of Alcoa, Mrs. Alvena Sanford of Carmmac, New York, Mrs. Inez Thomas of Chathom New Jersey; 12 grandchildren, 3 great-grandchildren; sisters, Mrs. Nannie Kitts, Centerville, Ohio, and Mrs. Elsie Sutton, Dayton, Ohio; brothers, James S. Heatherly of LaFollette, Homer Heatherly of Dayton, Ohio, and Edgar Heatherly of Monroe, Michigan. He joined the Primitive Baptist Church at Davis Chapel in 1925. Funeral services were held at the church, conducted by Elder Leonard White and Rev. Paul Heatherly. Burial was in Sunrise Cemetery.

Issac Kivett

Isaac Kivett was born in Union County, Tennessee, on Oct. 24, 1902. He passed away on July 18, 1971, at the age of 67. He was the son of J. M. and Sallie Kivett. His survivors are sisters, Mrs. Ollie Welch of LaFollette, Mrs. Myrtle Guy of Clinton, and Mrs. Della J. Petree of Wartburg; brother, William Kivett of LaFollette; nieces and nephews. He was a member of Davis Chapel Primitive Baptist Church. Funeral services were held at Davis Chapel Primitive Baptist Church by Elders Everett Berry and Leonard White. Burial was in Davis Chapel Cemetery.

Mrs. Mollie Irving

Mrs. Mollie Irving passed away at 6:30 O'clock June 9, 1971 at Middlesboro, Kentucky at the home of her daughter, Mrs. Virginia Ramsey. She was 76 years old and a faithful member of the Gibson Station Primitive Baptist Church, Gibson Station, Va. She was born at Caylor, Va., daughter of William and Ellie Britton. Services were held at the Gibson Station Primitive Baptist Church with Elder Leonard White and Elder Everett Berry Officiating. Burial was in the Southern Cemetery at Gibson Station. Survivors are Joe Irving, husband; two daughters, Mrs. Oscar Miracle and Mrs. Spurgeon Ramsey and a host of friends and relatives.

Sister Maude Atkins

Sister Maude Atkins was born Jan. 20, 1895 at Wise, Virginia and passed away on Oct. 17, 1970 at Jefferson Memorial Hospital, Jefferson City, Tenn. She was united in marriage to the late Robert Atkins Sept. 19, 1919. She professed faith in Christ in 1923 and united with Noeton Primitive Baptist Church in 1931. She was a loyal companion, a true chrisitan and a devoted mother. She leaves to mourn her passing 1 daughter, Neva Dotson, Bean Station, Tenn.; 1 grandaughter, Janet J. Dotson; 1 grandson, Robert Atkins, Ohio; 2 grandchildren, Ohio. Funeral Services was held Oct. 20, at Noeton Primitive Baptist Church, Rev. Olef Atkins officiated. Her body was laid to rest in the church cemetery to await the coming of her Lord.

A place is vacant in our home, a voice we loved to hear is still; there's an empty place within our heart that no one else can ever fill.

By daughter

Mrs. Lucy Foust Boruff

Mrs. Lucy Foust Boruff, born March 29, 1893 passed away

84

July 15, 1971 at 1:25 a.m. She joined Rocky Dale Primitive Baptist Church December 16, 1922 and remained a member until death. She is survived by 7 daughters and 1 son: Miss Edith Boruff, Mrs. Moses (Opal) Norton, Mrs. Glen (Beatrice) Johnson, Corryton, Mrs. Joshuay (Ima Lee) Stapleton, Powell, Mrs. Charles (Christine) Earl, Bluff City, Mrs. Edward (Fay) Collett, Luttrell, Mrs. Clayton (Ruth) Russell, Mr. James E. Boruff, both of Knoxville; 17 grandchildren and 9 great-grandchildren. Services were on a Saturday at 3:00 p.m. at Rocky Dale Primitive Baptist Church. Elder Hugh Brummitt, Elder Leonard White, Elder Everett Berry Officiated. Internent Clapps Chapel Cemetery. Pallbearers: grandsons, honorary pallbearers, E. D. Graves, Dewey Graves, Elmer Graves, Ernest Anderson, Ralph Clapp, Elder Parnick Shelton. The family received friends 7-9 Friday at Mynatts.

Our Mother is gone from our homes, but not from our hearts.
A place that cannot be filled; A voice we cannot hear.
We cannot ask God to bring her back, but somday we can go to her.

Beulah Munsey Guy

Beulah Munsey Guy was born December 28, 1911, and passed away October 16, 1969, being 57 years, 9 months and 18 days old. She professed faith in Christ at an early age and joined the Primitive Baptist Church at Black Fox where she was still a member. She leaves to mourn her passing, her husband, one son, 4 grandchildren, 2 great-grandchildren, 3 sisters, 3 brothers and stepmother and a host of friends and relatives.

She is sadly missed by all.

Herman Moncey

Herman Moncey passed away June 13, 1971 at Jefferson City Hospital. He professed faith in Christ at an early age and joined the Primitive Baptist Church at Black Fox where he remained a member until death. He leaves to mourn his passing, wife, Mrs. Mossie Capps Moncey; 3 half-sisters and 3 half-brothers. Funeral services were conducted at Smith's Funeral Home with Elder Parnick Shelton and Rev. Loy Shelton officiating.

Sister Trula Tabler Daniels

Sister Trula Tabler Daniels, 74 years, Route 3, Emory road Corryton, Tennessee, passed away Friday, January 15, 1971, at her home. She attended Rocky Dale Primitive Baptist Church. Survivors, Mrs. Pauline Wade, Corryton, Mrs. Mary Jessee and Mrs. Peggy Sharp, Knoxville, Granddaughter, Amelia Jessee; grandsons, Ted & Ronnie Wade, Dean Sharp; 4 great-grandchildren. Funeral services were held at Gentry's Chapel on Sunday January 17, 1971 at 3:30 p.m. with Elder Hugh Brummitt and Elder Everett Berry Officiating. She was laid to rest in Lynnhurst Cemetery.

She was a most sincere christian and is sadly missed by all.
ASLEEP IN JESUS

Mrs. Oma Mae Rosson McCann

Mrs. Oma Mae Rosson McCann, 43, of Rutledge, died August 17, 1970 at Claiborne County Hospital. She was a mother and housewife.

Survivors, husband, Amon T. McCann, Rutledge; sons, Arnold and Mike McCann, Rutledge; daughter, Charlene McCann, Rutledge; One son, Ronald Lee McCann, preceeded her in death. mother, Mrs. Francis Rosson, New Tazewell; brothers, Billie, Claude and Lawrence Rosson all of New Tazewell, Carl Rosson of Fountain City; sister, Mrs. Eula Gray Cupp, New Tazewell, Tenn. Funeral services were held at 2:00 p.m. Thursday at Central Point Baptist Church with the Rev. Marvin Phillips, Elder Tony Eastridge officiating. Burial in Church Cemetery. Pallbearers, Glenn and J. C. Williams. James and Millard Stratton, Jess and Ray Morgan. She was a member at Pleasant Point Primitive Baptist Church. Coffey Mortuary, Inc. in charge.

Mrs. Menada Keck

Mrs. Menada Keck was born October 21, 1904, passed away December 7, 1970, at the age of 66. She was the daughter of the late Floyd and Mattie Watson Carry. She was united in marriage to Arlie Keck September 19, 1919, and to this union was born five children. Two sons, James Ralph and Forester Floyd Keck. They preceeded her in death. Survivors, husband, Arlis Keck of New Tazewell, Tenn.; daughters, Mrs. Daisy Lynch of New Tazewell; Mrs. Mattie Simmons of Berlin, Germany; son, Arnold Keck, New

Market, Tenn; 13 grandchildren and 2 great-grandchildren;brother, Dan Carry, Morristown, Harry Carry, Knoxville, Arden Carry, Sarasota, Florida; sisters, Mrs. Nora Mayes, New Tazewell, Miss Frankie Carry, Knoxville, Mrs. Mabel Richardson and Mrs. Lou Westbrook at Monroe Michigan. She was a member at Pleasant Point Primitive Baptist Church.

James C. Dale

Dale, James C., 62, passed away 11:15 p.m. Wednesday at Jefferson Memorial Hospital after a brief illness. He was a retired employee of TVA at Cherokee Dam and a member of Oak Grove Primitive Baptist Church of Union County. Survivors, wife, Mrs. Pauline Groseclose Dale, New Market; three sons, J. Will Anaheim, Calif., Glenn, Jefferson City, Ezra, Flint, Mich.; two daughters, Mrs. Belle Simmons, Bean Station, Mrs. Georgia Lyons, Flint, Mich.; eight grandchildren; two brothers, John and Esco, both of Maynardville. Funeral 2:30 p.m. Sunday, Pleasant Grove Hayworth Baptist Church, Rev. Donald Morgan, Rev. Ralph Gaylon officiating. Interment in Church Cemetery.

John B. Brummitt

Brummitt, John B. - 79, of Menden, Ohio, and Erie, Tenn., died at 12:45 a.m. Wednesday in a Celina, Ohio Hospital. He was a member of Oak Grove Baptist Church. Survivors, two sons, Milton E., Erie, Alonzo, Menden, Ohio; three daughters, Mrs. Mack Patton, Monroe, Mich., Mrs. Harry K. Mize, Chattanooga, Mrs. Leon Cooper, Knoxville; 19 grandchildren, 4 great-grandchildren; four brothers, Harley, Crossville, Bennie and Estel, of Speedwell, Robert, Sharps Chapel; two sisters, Mrs. Sarah Smith, Knoxville, Mrs. Mary Turner, Luttrell. Funeral Arrangements. were by Kyker Funeral Home.

Mrs. Avie Jane Keck

Mrs. Avie Jane Keck, age 69, widow of the late Callie Keck, Sharps Chapel, passed away 9:30 p.m. Wednesday April 14, 1971. She was a member of Oak Grove Primitive Baptist Church. Survivors, daughters, Mrs. Edna Greer, Mrs. Jetta Cook, Kokomo; sons, Lloyd Keck, Sharps Chapel, Charles and James Keck, Koko-

mo, Ind; nine grandchildren; five great-grandchildren; sisters,
Mrs. Clyde Roe, Maynardville, Mrs. Hattie Keck, Sharps Chapel;
brother, Alex Walker, Chattanooga. Funeral 2 p.m. Saturday at
Oak Grove Baptist Church, Rev. Johnny Robinson officiating. Interment church cemetery.

Mrs. Lassie Paul

Mrs. Lassie Paul, 64, Sharps Chapel, passed away at 12:30
a.m. Thursday at Claiborne County Hospital. She was a member
of Oak Grove Primitive Baptist Church. Survivors, husband, Jim
Paul; daughters. Mrs. Anita Ramsey, Tazewell, Mrs. Bobbie
Daniel, Harrogate; sons, Willard and J. Will, Sharps Chapel,
Vaughn, Morristown; step-daughter, Mrs. Bertha Ray, Sharps
Chapel; sisters, Mrs. Lovia Pierce, Mrs. Sarah Cupp, Mrs. Junie
Cline, New Tazewell; brothers, Bill Ray, New Tazewell, Ike Ray,
Greenville, Murphey Ray, Florida; 13 grandchildren; 1 step-grand-
daughter. Funeral 3 p.m. Saturday at Oak Grove Baptist Church
Rev. George Pierce, Rev. John Robinson officiating. Interment
in church cemetery.

Roxie Jane Cobb

Roxie Jane Cobb was born August 28, 1908. Departed this
life at the age of 62, February 14, 1971. She was the daughter
of Robert and Mary Ball. She married Hershel Cobb in 1940 and
to this union four sons were born; James, Dannie, Bill and Floyd.
She was a faithful member of the Gibson Station Primitive Baptist
Church for the past 45 years. She was laid to rest in the Southern
Cemetery 'til Jesus comes. Funeral orations was delivered by
her pastors, Elder Leonard White and Elder Everett Berry.

Robert H. Sharp

R. H. Sharp, Sr. was born April 5, 1910 and departed this
life March 8, 1971. He joined the Kirkwood Primitive Baptist
Church where he was a faithful member until he moved to Florida
in 1965. He attended the Primitive Baptist Church in St. Peters-
burg, Florida after moving there. Survivors, wife, Zelma; three
sons, R. H. Jr., Harold R. and Edward L. Sharp and one daughter,
Mrs. Sherry Ann Travis; 6 grandchildren, one brother, C. Ambrose
Sharp; two sisters, Mrs. Ida Lowe and Mrs. Alice Keck. Funeral

services were conducted at the Rose Mortuary by Elder Leonard White. Interment in Lynnhurst Cemetery.

Nelle Sharp Norris

Mrs. Nelle Sharp Norris was born May 11, 1923, departed this life April 18, 1971. She was the daughter of Ed Sharp and and the late Lassie Graves Sharp. Survivors, two sons, David and Patrick Norris; father, Ed and brother, D. O. Sharp and one granddaughter. Funeral services were conducted at the Rose Mortuary by Eld. Everett Berry. Interment, Lynnhurst Cemetery.

Mossie C. White

Mossie C., wife of Elder Leonard White, was born May 10, 1888, died September 1, 1970, at 7:55 p.m. Funeral service was conducted at Davis Chapel (her home church) by Elders W. M. Sparks, Hugh Brummitt and Everett Berry. The body was interred in Sun Rise Cemetery to await the dawn of a new day. Her going left the old home so dark.

We loved you so, dear darling. It was so hard to say good bye, but by God's grace we will meet you in that home beyond the sky.

STATISTICAL TABLE

CHURCHES	DELEGATES	RESTORED	RECEIVED BY LETTER	BY BAPTISM	RELATIONSHIP	DISMISSED	EXCLUDED	DECEASED	TOTAL MEMBERSHIP	PRINTING OF MINUTES	REGULAR MEETING	COMMUNION SERVICE
Black Fox	Elder George Cambbell, Brothers, Bennie Capps, Calvin Capps, Roy Bailey, William Thomas, Dale Capps, Arthur Terry and Walton Cabbage; sisters, Flossie Capps, Roma Bailey, Martha Thomas, Mary Ruth Capps, Sandra Capps, Mary Terry, Naomia Cabbage, Sarah Hopson and Jessee Cabbage.	0	0	0	0	0	0	1	94	$10.00	Each Sunday and Sunday Night	Sunday after 2nd Saturday In June
Bradens Chapel	Elder Noble Clawson, Elder I. C. Monday, Elder Wm. Sparks; sisters, Lucy Sparks, and Helen Clawson.	0	0	4	0	0	1	0	126	$10.00	First Saturday and Sunday each month	First Sunday In June
Brantleys Chapel	Elder Clifford Brantley, Brothers, Von Beason, Everett Brantley, and Plumer McBee; Sisters, Mildred Brantley and Barsha Brantley.	0	0	3	0	0	0	0	88	$10.00	2nd Saturday and Sunday	Sunday after 2nd Saturday In July
Cedar Springs	Elder Johnny Ayers, brothers, Clifford Robertson, Bill Good; Sisters, Ida Robertson, Maggie Robertson, Mattie Holt, Velt Munsey, Eula Good, Ellen Good and Gloria Good.	0	1	3	0	0	0	1	57	$10.00	2nd Saturday night and Sunday – 4th Saturday night and Sunday	Sunday after 4th Saturday In May
Davis Chapel	Elder Leonard White, Brothers, Onie Parrott, Orice McCarty, Hugh Hill and Gene Hobbs; Sisters, Mamie Parrott, Mollie McCarty and Ruby Hill.	0	0	1	0	0	1	4	143	$20.00	Each Sunday and Sunday Night.	Sunday after 3rd Sunday In June
Gibson Station	Elder Joe Irwin, Brothers, Harve Rhymer Spurgeon Thompson, Floyd Cobb and Sisters Mellie Thompson and Mossie Cottrell.	0	0	0	2	0	0	2	84	$10.00	First Saturday and Sunday each month	Sunday after 1st Saturday In June
Kirkwood	Elders, R. H. Pettit, Hugh Brummitt and Walter Lyons; Brothers, W. H. Taylor, M. A. Norton, J. L. Sharp, R. O. Taylor; Sisters, Ruby Brummitt, Callie Lyons, Lou Emma Taylor, Lucy Norton, Evelyn Sharp and Myrtle Taylor.	0	0	0	0	0	0	2	107	$25.00	Each Sunday in each Month	Last Sunday In April

90

Church	Members and Officers								No.	Contribution	Meeting Time	Communion
Lenoir City	Elders, Charles Taylor and Alvin Graves; Brothers, Henry Chamberlain, Hubert Spoon, Jerry Spoon, Scott Collins, Millard Wilkerson, Raymond Wilkerson; Sisters, Estie Chamberlain, Agnes Taylor, Annie Spoons, Janice Spoons, Cora Hill and Ella Fields.	0	0	1	1	0	0	0	201	$30.00	Each Sunday and Sunday night	Sunday after 3rd Saturday in May
Monroe Michigan	Elder Lenvil Meyers; Brother John Drummond; Sisters, Roxie Drummond and Marie Evans.			1		1			12	$ 5.00	3rd Saturday and Sunday	Sunday after 3rd Saturday in May and Sept.
Noeton	Brothers, John Oliver, Charlie Collins, Carroll Oliver, Sisters, Ruth Oliver, Mildred Oliver, Doshie Collins and Bessie Collins.	0	0	0	0	0	0	1	31	$ 5.00	First Saturday and Sunday each month	Sunday after 1st Sat. in May
Oak Grove	Elders, George Shoffner, Tony Eastridge; Brothers, Aaron Cole, Cillis Shoffner, Mannie Shoffner, Alford Relford, Sisters, Francis Eastridge, VedaCole, Lillie Shoffner, Ruth Shoffner, Maggie Relford and Brother Johnny Atkins.	0	0	12	0	1	0	5	302	$20.00		
Pleasant Hill	Elders, James H. Branscomb, Albert Davis; Brothers, Ralph Edwards, Kubil Edwards and Sister, Audra Davis.	0	0	4	0	0	1	2	98	$15.00	4th Saturday and Sunday	Sunday after 4th Saturday in June
Pleasant Point	Elder Claude Rosson, Brothers, George Williams, C. D. Keck; Sisters, Doris Rosson and Allie Williams.	1	0	0	0	0	0	2	120	$10.00	1st Saturday night & Sun. - 3rd Sun. & Sunday night	Sunday after 1st Saturday in July
Rocky Dale	Elders, Everett Berry, Parnick Shelton and Joe Bush; Brothers, Elmer Graves, Donald Sharp, Avrill Graves; Sisters, Trula Berry, Wilma Shelton, Norma Jean Bush and Brother Larry Bush.	1	4	2	0	3	1		116	$15.00	Every Sunday and Sunday night	Sunday after 2nd Saturday in May
Cave Creek	No Letter								41		2nd Saturday night and Sunday	2nd Saturday night in May & October

CHURCH	COUNTY	PASTOR	CLERK	ADDRESS
Black Fox	Grainger	Elder Parnick Shelton	Bennie C. Capps Flossie Capps, Asst.	P. O. Box 91 Maynardville, Tenn.
Bradens Chapel Chapel	Union	Elder Noble Lee Clawson Elder J. C. Monday, Asst.	Arvil Braden Leecy Sparks, Asst.	Speedwell, Tenn. Speedwell, Tenn.
Brantleys Chapel	Blount	Elder Clifford Brantley Elder J. C. Monday, Asst.	Rina Johnson, Sr. Daniel Brantley, Asst.	Maryville, Tenn. 1201 Brown School Rd.
Cedar Springs	Claiborne	Elder Claude Rosson Elder Johnny Ayers, Asst.	Eula Good Patricia Kettle, Asst.	New Tazewell, Tenn.
Davis Chapel	Campbell	Elder Joe Bush Elder Leonard White, Asst.	Ruth Heatherly Lassie Ellison, Asst.	LaFollette, Tenn. Rt. 1 LaFollette, Tenn. Rt. 1
Gibson Station	Lee County (Virginia)	Elder Leonard White Elder Everett Berry, Asst.	Floyd Cobb Lucille Fleeman, Asst.	Ewing, Va. Rt. 2 Ewing, Va. Rt. 2
Kirkwood	Knox	Elder Leonard White	Estelle Petree Sharp Alice Tindell Powers, Asst.	5313 Jacksboro Pike 2923 Clearview (Knoxville)
Lenoir City	Loudon	Elder Charles Taylor	Scott Collins	707 W. 5th Ave. Lenoir City, Tenn.
Monroe Michigan	Monroe	Elder Lenvil Meyers	Gertrude Zwack	1825 Spaulding Rd. Monroe, Mich. 48161
Noeton	Grainger	Elder Gilbert Atkins	John Oliver Bessie Collins, Asst.	Bean Station, Tenn. Morristown, Tenn.
Oak Grove	Union	Elder J. C. Monday Elder Noble Lee Clawson, Asst.)	Maggie Relford Ruth Shoffner, Asst.	Sharps Chapel, Tenn. Sharps Chapel, Tenn.
Pleasant Hill	Claiborne	Elder Alvin Graves Elder Albert Davis, Asst.	William Branscomb Verlin Edwards, Asst.	Speedwell, Tenn. Speedwell, Tenn.
Pleasant Point	Claiborne	Elder Walter Lyons Elder Joe Bush, Asst.	Elder Claude Rosson	New Tazewell, Tenn.
Rocky Dale	Knox	Elder Hugh E. Brummitt	Edward Collett Avrel Graves, Asst.	Rt. 1 Luttrell, Tenn. Rt. 3 Corryton, Tenn.
Cave Creek	Roane	Elder Alvin Graves,	J. C. Johnson	Route 3 Loudon, Tenn.

1972 MINUTES
OF THE
POWELL VALLEY ASSOCIATION
OF PRIMITIVE BAPTIST

OAK GROVE CHURCH

Held with the Sister Church at Oak Grove in Union County,
Tennessee - August 18, 19, 20 - 1972.

MINUTES OF THE POWELL VALLEY ASSOCIATION OF PRIMITIVE BAPTIST

The One Hundred Fifty-Third Annual Session

of

The Powell Valley Association

of

Primitive Baptist

Held With the Sister Church, Oak Grove

Union County, Tennessee - August 18, 19, 20 - 1972

Elder Albert Davis	Moderator
Elder Hugh E. Brummitt	Asst. Moderator
W. H. Taylor	Clerk
O. R. Parrott	Asst. Clerk

† † †

The next Session will be held with the Sister Church, Pleasant Hill, in Claiborne County, Tennessee, to begin on Friday before the 3rd Saturday in August 1973 at 10:30 a.m.

The Introductory Sermon will be by Elder Toni Eastridge and Elder Alvin Graves will be the Alternate.

FRIDAY AUGUST 18, 1972

The one hundred fifty-third annual session of the Powell Valley Association of Primitive Baptist convened with the sister church of Oak Grove in Union County, Tennessee, August 18th, 1972 at 10:30 A.M.

Elder Joe Bush of Rocky Dale directed a good and spiritual song service.

After singing, the Moderator, Elder Albert Davis, introduced the devotional by reading the first Psalm, then calling on Elder Charles Taylor, Pastor of the Lenoir City Church, for the opening prayer.

Elder Toni Eastridge, who was to preach the introductory sermon, was ill and unable to attend and the alternate, Elder Clifford Brantley of Brantley's Chapel, preached instead. Elder Brantley preached a very, very good sermon, preaching from the 3rd Chapter and the 9th Verse of Ephesians, using as the theme "Love and Christian fellowship through our Lord Jesus Christ."

After preaching the Association was dismissed with prayer by Elder Johnny Atkins for a 15 minute recess.

After intermission and at the sound of singing the Association reconvened with Elder Davis the Moderator presiding. After a short talk and pleading for Love, Peace and Harmony to prevail throughout the Association then entered into the business session and called for opening prayer by Elder Walter Lyons.

ORDER OF BUSINESS

1. Called for Letters of Sister Churches to be presented to the Clerk for reading. Fourteen letters were received which was every church in the Association.
2. Call for any member present and not named as delegate who wish to be seated as such to come forward. One came, Sister Edna Atkinson of Gibson Station.
3. Motion carried, after hearing the letters read and the delegates named, that we receive all the letters and seat their delegates.
4. Call for letters of corresponding Associations. It was reported by the delegation from the Original Hiawassee Association that a letter was prepared and voted but for some reason it would not be presented until Saturday. The Association voted to seat the delegation pending their letter which did arrive on Friday.

95

5. Called for petitionary letters and none were received.
6. Business of electing officers for the coming year.
7. Motion carried that the Association re-elect Elder Albert Davis as Moderator and Elder Hugh E. Brummitt Assistant Moderator for the coming year.
8. Motion carried to re-elect Bro. W. H. Taylor Clerk and Bro. Onie Parrott Assistant Clerk for the next year.
9. Motion approved that the Moderator be empowered to appoint all the Committees.
10. The Moderator, having been empowered by the Association to do so, made the following committee apointments.

COMMITTEE ON ARRANGEMENTS
Elder Clifford Brantley
Bro. Raymond Wilkerson
Bro. M. A. Norton

COMMITTEE ON PREACHING
Bro. Millard Thompson
Bro. Clifford Robertson
Elder Spurgeon Thompson

COMMITTEE ON CORRESPONDENCE
Bro. Millard Welch
Elder Joe Irwin
Elder Everett Berry

COMMITTEE ON REQUEST
Elder Johnny Atkins
Bro. Benny Capps
Elder John Oliver

COMMITTEE ON FINANCE
Bro. Aaron Cole
Bro. Jeff Ellison
Eld. Bill Berry

11. The Committees all having been appointed, the Association voted to adjourn until Saturday morning at 10:30 A.M. and was dismissed in prayer by Elder Leonard White.

SATURDAY, AUGUST 19th, 1972

1. Saturday at the appointed hour of 10:30 A.M. the Association re-convened with an over flow crowd. After the song service directed by Elder Joe Bush, the Assistant Moderator, Elder Hugh E. Brummitt, Pastor of Rocky Dale Church, made the welcome and gave a wonderful talk on the principles and doctrine of the churches of this Association, then reading a lesson of the entire 12th Chapter of Ecclesiastes and called for prayer by Elder W. M. Sparks.

2. Moderator called the Association to order and asked for letters not received Friday. .

3. Called for letters of Correspondence, the one from Hiawassee Association was received. The delegates of Bros. C. H. Godfrey, Ray Godfrey, Tom Carmichael and Clyde Abbott and Sisters Billy Godfrey, Myrtle Cook, Mary Godfrey and June Carmichael were seated and welcomed to the Association.

4. Roll Call of delegates made and approved.

5. Moderator called for report of Committee on Arrangements who gave the following report and were released.

REPORT OF COMMITTEE ON ARRANGEMENTS

a. Call roll of delegates
b. Call for report of Committee on Preaching
c. Call for report of Committee on Correspondence
d. Call for report of Committee on Request.
e. Call for report of Committee on Finance.
f. How many minutes shall we have printed and who shall supervise the printing and distributing them and how much shall he receive for his service. When and where shall the next Association be held. Who will preach the introductory sermon and who shall be his alternate.

Respectfully submitted,

Bro. Raymond Wilkerson
Bro. M. A. Norton
Elder Clifford Brantley

6. Call for report of committee on Preaching who gave the report as follows and were then released.

REPORT OF COMMITTEE ON PREACHING

We the Committee on Preaching wish to submit the following report which was accepted and the committee released.

Friday Night:	Elder Everett Berry
	Elder Parnick Shelton
Saturday:	Elder Charles Taylor
	Elder Joe Bush
Saturday Night:	Elder Hugh E Brummitt
	Elder Albert Davis
Sunday:	Elder Leonard White
	Elder Albert Davis

Respectfully submitted,

Elder Spurgeon Thompson
Bro. Clifford Robertson
Bro. Millard Thompson

7. Called for report of Committee on Correspondence which was given as follows and committee released

REPORT OF COMMITTEE ON CORRESPONDENCE

We the Committee on Correspondence recommend that we keep our good Christian relationship with the Original Hiawassee Association and that we letter and delegate to them at their next session.

Respectfully submitted,

Elder Everett Berry
Elder Joe Irwin
Bro. Millard Welch

8. Call for report of Committee on Requests who gave the following report which was adopted and the committee discharged.

REPORT OF COMMITTEE ON REQUESTS

We the Committee on Requests recommend that we have 1,000 copies of the minutes printed and distributed to the churches. And that we authorize the Clerk to supervise the printing and distribution of same. And that we have all obituaries printed in the minutes. And that the next session of the Association be held with the Sister Church at Pleasant Hill in Claiborne County, Tennessee to begin on Friday before the third Saturday in August 1973 at 10:30 A.M.

Respectfully submitted,

Elder Johnny Atkins
Elder John Oliver
Bro. Bennie C. Capps

9.   Called for report of Committee on Finance who submitted the following report which was received and committee released.

REPORT OF COMMITTEE ON FINANCE

We the Committee on Finance wish to submit the following report.

Church	Amount
Black Fox	$10.00
Bradens Chapel	$10.00
Brantleys Chapel	$10.00
Cedar Springs	$10.00
Davis Chapel	$20.00
Gibson Station	$10.00
Kirkwood	$25.00
Lenoir City	$30.00
Monroe Michigan	$10.00
Oak Grove	$20.00
Pleasant Hill	$20.00
Pleasant Point	$15.00
Rocky Dale	$20.00
Norton	$10.00

TOTAL	$220.00
Balance in Bank	$86.00
GRAND TOTAL	$306.00
Expenses for 1972	$200.00
Balance in Bank	$106.00

Respectfully submitted,

Bro. Jeff Ellison
Bro Aaron Cole
Elder Bill Berry

10. Motion carrie that we have 1,000 copies of the minutes printed and that we authorize the Clerk to supervise the printing and distribution of same and that he be given $50.00 for his service.

11. The Association voted to have the next session held with the Sister Church at Pleasant Hill in Claiborne County, Tennessee to begin on Friday before the third Saturday in

August 1973 at 10:30 A.M.

12. Motion carried that Elder Toni Eastridge preach the introductory sermon and Elder Alvin Graves shall be the Alternate.

13. Association voted to letter and delegate to the beloved Hiawassee Association and that we send as delegates to meet with them when they convene on Friday before the third Sunday in July, Elder Charles Taylor, Elder Alvin Graves, Elder Clifford Brantley, Elder John Oliver and Bro. M. A. Norton.

14. Moved and second that the Clerk prepare a letter from this Association for the delegates to have to take with them when meeting with the Hiawassee Association.

15. The Association and the entire congregation voted to extend to the Oak Grove Church and to the entire community our thanks and appreciation for every act of friendship, love and fellowship while in your community.

16. The business of the Association being completed, the Association voted to adjourn until we meet with the Sister Church at Pleasant Hill on Friday before the third Saturday in August 1973 at 10:00 A.M. Thus bringing to a close one of the best, Joyous and Harmonous Associations in History.

Elder Albert Davis, Moderator
Elder Hugh E. Brummitt, Asst. Mod.
W. H. Taylor, Clerk
Onie Parrott, Asst. Clerk

LETTER TO HIAWASSEE ASSOCIATION

We, the Powell Valley Association of Primitive Baptist, were happy to share relationship and to have a letter and delegation from the Original Hiawassee Association. We also, while in regular session, express our desire to continue our relationship with you and also to letter and delegate to your next association.

We hereby delegate Elder Charles Taylor, Elder Alvin Graves, Elder Walter Lyons, Elder Clifford Brantley and Brother M. A. Norton to sit with you in your Godly Conversation.

Hoping you will receive these our Brethern and remember us in your prayers.

Elder Albert Davis, Moderator

Brother W. H. Taylor, Clerk

SUNDAY, AUGUST 20th, 1972

Sunday at the appointed hour of 10:30 again an overflow crowd assembled at the sound of singing for the last service of the Association.

The service was introduced by the Assistant Pastor of the Oak Grove Church, Elder Noble Lee Clawson, who gave a welcome and a very inspiring talk. After a song, "Amazing Grace" and prayer by Elder James H. Branscomb, Elder Albert Davis who was to preach with Elder White gave way to let Elder White have the time.

Elder Leonard White for the first 15 or 20 minutes gave a history of the Primitive Baptist from the time of signing of the Constitution, which was very interesting. Then using as his text the 10th verse of the 19th chapter of St. Luke preached a wonderful sermon to a very attentive crowd of people. After a song and and the last testimony, the Association was closed out by the Moderator, Albert Davis and called for the closing prayer by Elder Bill Berry.

Elder Albert Davis, Moderator
W. H. Taylor, Clerk

Elder Gilbert Atkins
Route 3
Rutledge, Tennessee

Elder Johnny Atkins
Bean Station, Tennessee

Elder Everett Berry
Route 27
Knoxville, Tennessee
Phone: 922-7004

Elder Johnny Ayers
New Tazewell, Tennessee

Elder Clifford Brantley
Brown School Road
Maryville, Tennessee
Phone   982-3735

Elder J. H. Branscomb
Speedwell, Tennessee
Phone: 869-3735

Elder Albert Davis
Speedwell, Tennessee
Phone: 869-3596

Elder Hugh E. Brummitt
1329 Brown Avenue
Knoxville, Tennessee
Phone: 546-7700

Elder Noble Clawson
Speedwell, Tennessee
Route 4

Elder Toni Eastridge
Louisville, Tennessee
Phone: 983-1068

Elder Lenvil Meyers
715 Scott Street
Monroe, Michigan

Elder J. C. Monday
Speedwell, Tennessee

Elder Roy Oliver
Bean Station, Tennessee

Elder R. H. Pettit
4907 Jacksboro Pike
Knoxville, Tennessee

Elder Claude Rosson
New Tazewell, Tennessee
Phone: 626-3168

Elder Parnick Shelton
Corryton, Tennessee
Phone: 687-6142

Elder George Shoffner
Louisville, Tennessee
Route 2

Elder W. M. Sparks
Speedwell, Tennessee
Phone: 562-7997

Elder Leonard White
LaFollette, Tennessee
Phone: 562-5667

Elder Clay Widner
101 West Norris Street
Norris, Tennessee

Elder Alvin Graves
Route 3
Lenoir City, Tennessee

Elder Joe Bush
Corryton, Tennessee
Phone: 687-7018

Elder Joe Irwin
Gibson Station, Virginia

Elder Spurgeon Thompson
Gibson Station, Virginia

Elder Walter Lyons
1400 Jouralman Avenue
Knoxville, Tennessee
Phone: 525-9640

Elder Wm. (Bill) Berry
Knoxville, Tennessee Rt. 27
Phone: 922-2269

Elder Charles Taylor
204 Martel Road
Lenoir City, Tennessee
Phone: 986-8172

LICENTIATES

Bro. Odel Carpenter
Maryville, Tennessee

Bro. Roscoe Branscomb
Speedwell, Tennessee

ARTICLES OF FAITH

Article 1. We believe in only one true living God, as He is revealed to us in the Holy Scriptures - Father, Son, and Holy Ghost.

Article 2. We believe that the Scriptures of the old and new Testaments are the words of God and the only rule of all-saving knowledge and obedience.

Article 3. We believe in the doctrine of election according to the fore-knowledge of God.

Article 4. We believe in the doctrine of original sin.

Article 5. We believe in man's impotency to rescue himself from the fallen state he is in, by his own will or ability.

Article 6. We believe that sinners are justified in the sight of God only by the imputed righteousness of Jesus Christ.

Article 7. We believe the elect, according to the foreknowledge of God will be called, converted, regenerated, and sanctified by the Holy Spirit.

Article 8. We believe the saints will persevere and never fall finally away.

Article 9. We believe that baptism and the Lord's Supper are ordinances of Jesus Christ, and that true believers are the only subject of these ordinances, and that the true mode of baptism is by immersion. We believe also that feet washing is an example of Jesus Christ and should be kept by his deciples until his second coming.

Article 10. We believe in the Resurrection of the dead and the General Judgement.

Article 11. We believe that the punishment of the wicked will be everlasting and that the joys of the righteous will be eternal.

Article 12. We believe that no minister has the right to administer the ordin-ances, except those who have been regularly baptized and called of God, and come under the imposition of hands of the presbytery.

RULES OF DECORUM

1. The churches composing the Powell's Valley Association shall not be confined to any set rules as to specific number of Messengers they shall have in the body, but shall have the right to name in their letters as many as they choose, and in addition all orderly members of and of the churches being present be entitled to seats in the body as Messengers of their respective churches, with all the rights and privileges of the same.

2. The Messengers thus assembled shall be denominated the Powell's Valley Primitive Baptist Association.

3. For the purpose of historical information and statistical edification, the Churches are required to state in letters, the number of members in fellowship, the number received by Baptism, by letter, by confession of Faith, the number dismissed, excluded and dead since last session; also the time of their meeting, their pastoral supply, and the amount of money contributed for ministers and other purposes together with any other information they deem appropriate for the edification of the saints and glory of God.

4. This Association shall have no power to answer queries, give advice, or dictate to the Churches in any case, or to lord it over God's heritage nor any power by which she can directly or indirectly fringe on the internal rights of the church or censure and try any church or member in reference to faith and practice and determine upon valigity of gospel ordinances. These things shall rest entirely with the churches; but henceforward our annual meetings shall be only for the purpose of hearing from each other, and for the worship of God and mutual comfort and edification of the Saints. To this end we reserve the privilege annually before the Third Saturday in August and the two following days or at such other times as may be agreed upon with any church that may invite us having to protect our own standard, while in session, from heresey and disorder to recognize and invite any primitive Baptist minister or any lay brother ot worship with us that may deem proper; to request the brethren of our body to visit other churches or bodies in our belief with whom we may desire to culture Christian fellowship; to publish in a minute of our proceedings.

5. Each session of the body shall have a Moderator and Clerk who shall hold office until re-elected.

6. Any order member of any church belonging to this body, when convened, being present shall be eligible to elect on as Moderator and Clerk or to sit on any committee appointed by the same.

7. In all election or questions that may be necessary to determine by vote, the vote shall be taken by churches, each church being entitled to three votes for and number less than one hundred, and one additional vote for every fifty or fraction thereof above the first hundred, but the Messengers of each church may divide their vote as they see proper.

8. All elections of questions coming to vote shall be determined by a majority vote cast, and it shall be the only duty of the minority to acquiesce in the decision thus reached.

9. If new churches desire to be admitted to this union they shall petition by letter and messengers and if voted for or recommended by one or more sister churches for her Presbytery constitution them, or orthox and orderly they shall be received by the voice of the body and manifested by the Moderator

giving the Messengers the right hand of fellowship.

10. Any motion or resolution clearly inconsistent with the above rules shall be promptly ruled out of order unless withdrawn by the mover.

11. Any Messenger being ruled out of order by the Moderator shall have the right to appeal to the body on the question or order, and if sustained shall be allowed to proceed, but if not take his seat.

12. Our meeting being held in the name of Christ and the worship of God; each Messenger is expected to observe due and proper therein.

13. It will not be considered good for any Messenger whose name has been enrolled as such to abruptly break off or absent himself from the Association without leave.

14. The Moderator shall be entitled to the same privilege of speech as other members provided the chair is filled.

15. The minutes of the Association shall be read and approved by the body and signed by the Moderator before adjourning.

16. The Association shall be opened and closed by prayer.

17. Amendments to these may be made at any time by a majority of the union voting by churches when they deem it necessary, provide such amendments do not compromise the sovereignty of the churches nor have tendency to give body undue power or jurisdiction over them.

OBITUARIES

ERNEST OCONNER ANDERSON passed away September 2, 1971; age, 70 years, 6 months, at St. Mary's Hospital. Member of Rocky Dale Primitive Baptist Church and Corryton Lodge No. 321 F&AM, a retired employee of Regular Dept. at Fultons. Survivors, wife, Mrs. Faye Hill Anderson; daughter, Mrs. Gail Shields, Lebanon, Tenn.; sons, William H. and Roy Keith Anderson, both of Corryton; 7 grandchildren; sister, Mrs. Vera Stiner, Sharps Chapel, brother, Edgar (H. E.) Anderson, Knoxville. Service 2 p.m. Sunday, Gentry's Chapel, Elder Leonard White and Elder Hugh Brummitt officiated. Interment Greenwood Cemetery where masonic graveside services were held. Nephews served as pallbearers, Gentry's in charge.
"Gone but we will be together in the sweet by and by."

SILAS V. (BUD) BERRY, age 73, passed away suddenly at his home route 2. Sharps Chapel, Tennessee, January 28, 1969. He was a member of Cave Springs Primitive Baptist 'Church Union County. Survivors, wife, Helen Berry; daughters, Mrs. Ora Bridges, Miss Trula Berry, Maryville, Mrs. Marie Weaver,Clifton, Illinois; sons, Forster, Knoxville. and Lee, Sharps Chapel; Eleven grandchildren, one great grandchild; sisters, Mrs. Tishie Creech, Miss Rhoda Berry, Sharps Chapel, Mrs. Mary Herron, New Market; brother, Millard Berry, New Market. Funeral services were held at Oak Grove Primitive Baptist Church, 1:30 p.m. January 30, 1969, conducted by Elders Hugh Brummitt and W. M. Sparks. Burial in Church Cemetery.

WANDA ANN BRYANT, born July 7, 1972 and passed away July 7, 1972- Survivors, parents, Mr. and Mrs. Charles and Bryant; sister, Sheila Gale Bryant; grandparents, Mr. & Mrs. Ralph Clapp, all of Corryton, Tenn. The family attends Rocky Dale Baptist Church. Graveside services were held at Holston Memory Gardens. Elder Brummitt officiated.
" A Rosebud was added to God's garden "

ELDER GEORGE WILLIAM CAMPBELL was born May 15, 1915, passed away October 3, 1971, at Fort Sanders 'Hospital. He was married to Leona Chesney April 19, 1940. To this union were born: daughter, Julia Faye Campbell, Knoxville; sons, Tommy and Jimmy, Maynardville. He professed hope in Christ at

an early age and joined Black Fox Primitive Baptist Church where he remained faithful until death. He also leaves two grandchildren, Larry and Stanley Campbell; six half brothers, Broda Campbell, Carl, Augusta, Pat, Jim and Ioda Cabbage. He was ordained to the ministry June 8, 1957. He also was pastor of Headricks Chapel Primitive Baptist Church at the time of his death. Funeral services were held at Black Fox Primitive Baptist Church with Elder Walter Lyons, Elder Everett Berry and Eld. Parnick Shelton officiating. Interment in Boruff Cemetery.
"Gone But Not Forgotten"

NOBLE DYKES, 814, W. Anderson Ave., Knoxville, Tenn., son of Emit and Mossie Peters Dykes. He was born July 11, 1919, and died May 20, 1972 at 6:30 p.m. at his home. He professed faith in Christ and joined Oak Grove Primitive Baptist Church. Survivors, mother, Mrs. Mossie Dykes, Sharps Chapel; wife, Zella Russell Dykes, Knoxville; daughters, Mrs. Helen Scarelet, Mrs. Anna Lour Capps, Mrs. Hilda Dunaway, and Mrs. Carolyn Sue Dunaway all of Knoxville; sisters, Mrs. Rheba Moyers, Knoxville, and Mrs. Vera Sheckles, Monroe, Michigan; brothers, Charles Edward, and Willard, Knoxville, Elmo, Kokomo, Ind., Frank, Monroe, Mich., and Herbert, Sharps Chapel; 6 grandchildren. Services were held at Oak Grove Church, Elder Albert Davis and Rev. A. G. Hall officiating. Interment in Church Cemetery.

MISS DOROTHY GRAVES, 68, passed away suddenly 3 p.m. Monday at her home New Tazewell, Route 2. Survivors, brother, Wana; niece, Mrs. Ruby Johnsone, Maynardville, Route 3. Nephew, Nolan Graves, Baltimore, Md. Funeral 2 p.m. Wednesday Ailor's Chapel, Elder Leonard White officiating. Burial Graves Cemetery. Ailor's, Maynardville, in charge.

SISTER LAURA HINES, Born 1883, passed from this life February 28, 1972. Making her stay on earth 89 years. Sister Hines was a charter member of the Lenoir City Primitive Church to which she and her late husband J. F. Hines served as Deacon and Deaconess for many years. Sister Hines was a faithful member of the church she loved so well as long as health would permit. Even after she became unable to attend, she was ready to contribute in any way possible to the comfort of those she loved so well. She will be sadly missed by all who loved her. She leaves to mourn her passing, Mrs. Jack Robinson, Miss Mildred L.

Hines, Mrs. Bill Isaacs; sons, Charlie, Carl, and Kenneth, Lenoir City, and Claude, Loudon. Besides these she leaves a host of Relatives and friends. Funeral services were held at the Primitive Baptist Church with Elder Charles Taylor and Rev. Leroy Davis Officiating. Her body was laid to rest in the City Cemetery to await her awakening on the blessed Resurrection Morning.

MRS. ROBERTA MINCEY was born November 9, 1906, departed this life May 24, 1972, being 65 years, 6 months and 15 days old. She professed faith in Christ at an early age and joined Black Fox Primitive Baptist Church where she remained a faithful member until death. She leaves to mourn her passing, husband, Robert Mincey; foster daughter, Mrs. Ruth Dalton, two foster grandchildren, Wesley and Shirley Ruth Dalton; sister, Mrs. Ellen Bell, Corryton; brothers, Millard Munsey, Knoxville, Preston Munsey, Greenback and several nieces and nephews. Funeral services were conducted by Elder Albert Davis, assisted by Elder Alvin Graves. She was laid to rest in the Cabbage Cemetery.

"While we are sad, Heaven was made glad. You are not forgotten, loved one, nor will you ever be, as long as life and memory last, we will remember thee. We miss you now, our hearts are sore, as time goes by we miss you more. Your loving smile, your gentle face, no one can fill your vacant place.

Written by Husband and Foster Daughter

MRS. LOUISE HILL PETREE of Knoxville was born March 25, 1883 at Lost Creek, Tennessee and passed away October 5, 1971 at 10:15 p.m. She was united in marriage on November 16, 1906 to the late James C. Petree. She was a charter member of the Kirkwood Primitive Baptist Church. Funeral Service was conducted at Gentry Mortuary by Elder Leonard White. The body was interred at Lynnhurst Cemetery.

"We loved you so very much, Mother. Home will never be the same without you, but through the mercy of our dear Lord, we will meet you some sweet day."

MRS. KATIE PRESLEY, 86, of Sharps Chapel, died 9 p.m. Saturday at Claiborne County Hospital. Survivors, daughters, Mrs. Hazel Walker, Mrs. Mary Treece, Mrs. Ruth Breeden, all of Knoxville, sons, William C. Presley, Sharps Chapel, Troy E. Presley, Knoxville, Walter F. Presley, Middlesboro, Milton

Presley, Johnson City; 35 grandchildren; 54 great-grandchildren.
Funeral services 11 a.m. Tuesday at Oak Grove Primitive Baptist
Church, where she was a member. Elder William Sparks, Elder
Albert Davis officiating. Interment in Taylor Grove cemetery.
Pallbearers, grandsons. Cooke Mortuary, Maynardville in charge.

PORTER CHESLEY PROFFITT, 68 year old retired miner
of Rt. 2, succumbed at Cumberland Medical Center at 2:30 p.m.
Sunday, shortly after being admitted with a self-inflicted .22
calibre gunshot wound in the head. Authorities said the victim
shot himself with a rifle and that the death was from all appear-
ances a suicide. Mr Proffitt had been in ill health for some
time, they said. Funeral services were conducted Tuesday afternoon in the chapel of Bilbrey Funeral Home by the Rev. Grover
Adkinson. Interment was in Oak Hill Cemetery. Mr. Proffitt is
survived by his wife, Ottie Carey Proffitt; two daughters, Mrs.
Geraldine Sexton, Ft. Knox, Ky. and Mrs. Corean Davis, Crossville four sons, Royal, Sam and Charles of Crossville and Wendell
U. S. Army; 17 grandchildren and two great-grandchildren. Also
surviving are a brother, Theodore Proffitt, Ohio and two sisters,
Mrs. Lea Keck, Ohio and Mrs. Sadie Rouse, Tazewell, Tenn. He
was a native of Claiborne County.

MRS. OTTIE MAE PROFFITT, 64, of Route 2 Crossville,
Tennessee, widow of Porter Proffitt, passed away Sunday after-
noon, August 23, 1971. Mr. Proffitt died Sept. 6, 1970. Surviv-
ing are two daughters, Mrs. James E. (Geraldine) Sexton and Mrs.
Claude (Corean) Davis, Route 2, Crossville, Tenn.; four sons,
Charles, Royal, Douglas and Wendell Proffitt, all of Knoxville,
Tennessee; 18 grandchildren and three great-grandchildren. Mrs.
Proffitt also leaves three sisters, Mrs. Emma Cole, Mrs. Haskell
Keck and Mrs. Janie Thompson, all of Crossville and 5 brothers,
Mitchell, Walter, Milton and Sherman Carey, Crossville, Johnnie
Carey, Monroe, Mich.; one brother, Bill, preceded her in death.
Funeral services were conducted in the chapel of Bilbrey's Fun-
eral Home Tuesday afternoon, August 24, 1971, by Rev. E. D.
Mays and Rev. Jerry Randol, with burial in Oak Hill Cemetery.
Grandsons served as pallbearers. Mrs. Proffitt was born in Clai-
borne county, a daughter of John and Dora Johnson Carey.

PARIS E. ROE, 89, Sharps Chapel, passed away at 9:30
a.m. Friday at Fort Sanders Presbyterian Hospital. Survivors,

ors, daughter, Mrs. Pearl Dykes, Kokomo; sons, Clatis, Speed-well, Audd Roe, Harrogate, Clyde, Maynardville, Roy, Sharps Chapel, Vife Roe, Kokomo; sister, Mrs. Ima Clawson, Michigan; brother, Murphy Roe, Halls; 23 grandchildren. Funeral 2:30 p.m. Sunday at Oak Grove Primitive Baptist Church, Elder Hugh Brummit and Elder Albert Davis officiating. Burial in church cemetery. Grandsons served as pallbearers.

GEORGE W. SHOFFNER of 1117 East Cumberland Ave. City, passed away May 9 at a local hospital. He was the son of the late Hiram A. and Martha Seals Shoffner; a member of the Primitive Baptist Church in Gibson Station, Va., he was also a member of Lodge No. 546 F&AM of Shawnanee, Tenn. Survivors, widow, Mrs. Laverne Edwards Shoffner, City; son, Cleatis Shoffner, Monroe, Mich.; daughters, Mrs. Tom Ed White, City, Mrs. Monteray White, Newport News, Va.; sisters, Mrs. Roxie Dadle, Mrs. Blanche Ramsey and Mrs. Mossie C. Cottrell, all of Harrogate, Tenn. Mrs. Maggie Saudifer and Mrs. Edna Adkinson, Monroe, Mich.; brother, Rufus Shoffner, Monroe; four grandchildren. Funeral services were conducted at 2 p.m. Thursday at the Cawood Funeral Home Chapel. Interment in Shoffner Cemetery, Forge Ridge.

MISS FLORENA STINER, 76, of Sharps Chapel, Tenn. died September 21, 1971 at North Eastern Community Hospital, Knoxville, Tenn. Funeral Services were held at Mynatt Funeral Home at 2:00 p.m. September 24, 1971, by Rev. Robert Crumpton. Burial was in the Stiner Cemetery, Sharps Chapel, Tenn. The daughter of Henry and Florence Stiner, she was born Oct. 8, 1894. She was a member of Oak Grove Church. She is survived by one sister, Mrs. Hattie Simmons, Monroe, Mich. and a host of nieces and nephews. Pallbearers were Billy England, Theodore Stiner, Clifford Stiner, Harding England, Ines Stiner, and E. J. Stiner. The Sherritze Quartet sang at the funeral.

MRS. EMMA LOU (ETTE) SOUTHERLAND was born Oct. 14, 1891, and passed away Dec. 3, 1971, being 80 years of age. She professed faith in Christ at an early age and joined the Black Fox Primitive Baptist Church where she remained a member. She leaves to mourn her passing, husband, W. A. Southerland; sons, Lenord and Roy of Knoxville, Ed of Oak Ridge; ten grand children, twenty-eight great-grandchildren, two great-great-grandchildren. Services were held at the Washburn Street Baptist Church with Rev. Bill Romines and Rev. Howard Hust officiating. Interment, Bookwalter Cemetery. Passbearers, Ray McDaniels, Con Arnwine, Wayne Nelson, Way Key, Ed Tramel, and Bud Coburn. Mynatts was in charge.

LOU ETTA HOPPER WILLIAMS of Knoxville, formerly of Goin, passed away at St. Mary's Hospital, Knoxville on October 23, 1971. Mrs. Williams was born Dec. 5, 1902. At an early age she professed faith and joined the Pleasant Point Church of Goin. Survivors, one brother, W. M. Shipley, Speedwell, Tenn.; one half sister, Mrs. Sally Brewer of Crossville; two step-daughters, Mrs. Blanche Seal of Fremont, Ohio and Mrs. Zola Toliver of New Tazewell, Tenn.; two step sons, Mr. E. M. Williams, Jr. of Johnson City, Tenn. and Mr. B. J. Britton of Knoxville, Tenn.; seven grandchildren and a host of neices and nephews; three sisters-in-law and one brother-in-law. Grandchildren and nephews served as pallbearers. Coffey in New Tazewell, was in charge.

CHURCH	COUNTY	PASTOR	CLERK	ADDRESS
Black Fox	Grainger	Elder Alvin Graves	Bennie C. Capps Flossie Capps, Asst.	P. O. Box 91 Maynardville, Tenn. R# 3, Maynardville, Tn.
Bradens Chapel	Union	Elder, Noble Lee Clawson	Leecy Sparks Eld. J. C. Monday,	Speedwell, Tenn. Speedwell, Tenn.
Brantleys Chapel	Blount	Elder J. C. Monday	Rina Johnson Daniel Brantley, Asst.	1217 Brown School Rd. Maryville, Tenn. Rt. 10 Mint Rd., Maryvill
Cedar Springs	Claiborne	Elder Noble Lee Clawson, Elder Johnny Ayers, Asst.	Eula Good Patricia Kettle, Asst.	New Tazewell, Tenn. New Tazewell, Tenn.
Davis Chapel	Campbell	Elder Joe Bush Elder Leonard White, Asst.	Ruth Heatherly Lassie Ellison, Asst.	Rt. 1, LaFollette, Tenn. Rt. 1, LaFollette, Tenn.
Gibson Station	Lee County,	Elder Leonard, White Elder Everette Berry, Asst. Elder Joe Ir Irwin, Asst.	Mossie Cottrell Lucille Freemon, Asst.	Rt. 2, Harrogate, Tenn. Ewing, Virginia
Kirkwood	Knox	Elder Leonard White	Estelle Petree Sharp Alice Tindell Powers, Asst.	5313 Jaksboro Pk, Knoxv 2923 Clearview Avenue, Knoxville, Tenn.
Lenoir City	Loudon	Elder Chas. Taylor	Scott Collins	707 W. 5th Ave. Lenoir City, Tenn.
Monroe, Michigan	Monroe	Eld. Lenvil Meyers	Gertrude Zwack	1825 Speedway Rd., Mon- roe, Mich.
Noeton	Grainger	Eld. Gilbert Atkins	John Oliver Bessie Collins, Asst.	Bean Station, Tenn. Rt. 5, Morristown, Tenn.
Oak Grove	Union	Eld. J. C. Monday Eld. Noble Clawson, Asst.	Maggie Relford Ruth Shoffner, Asst.	Sharps Chapel, Tenn. Sharps Chapel, Tenn.
Pleasant Hill	Claiborne	Eld. Alvin Graves Eld. Albert Davis, Asst.	William Branscomb Verlin Edwards, Asst.	Speedwell, Tenn. Speedwell, Tenn.
Pleasant Point	Claiborne	Eld. Walter Lyons Eld. Parnick Shelton, Asst.	Claude Rosson	New Tazewell, Tenn.
Rocky Dale	Knox	Eld. Hugh Brummitt	Edward Collett Avrell Graves, Asst.	Rt. 1, Luttrell, Tenn. Rt. 3, Corryton, Tenn.

CHURCHES	NAMES OF DELEGATES	RESTORED	RECEIVED BY LETTER	RECEIVED BY BAPTISM	RECEIVED BY RELATIONSHIP	DISMISSED	EXCLUDED	DECEASED	TOTAL MEMBERSHIP	PRINTING OF MINUTES	REGULAR MEETING	COMMUNION SERVICE
BLACK FOX	Bros., Dale Capps, Calvin Capps, Bennie Capps, Roy Bailey, Arthur Terry, Sis., Mary Ruth Capps, Mary Terry, Roma Bailey, Sarah Hopson, Jessie Cabbage. and Naomi Cabbage.	0	0	0	0	0	1	5	88	$10.00	Second and Third Saturday night of each month	Sunday after the second Saturday in June
BRADENS CHAPEL	Elder Buster Clawson, and Elder Wm. Sparks, Bro. Bill Lambert, Sis., Helen Clawson, Winona Monday, Leecy Sparks, and Jimmy Edwards.	0	0	5	2	0	0	0	133	$10.00	First Saturday and Sunday in each month	Sunday after the First Saturday in June
BRANTLEYS CHAPEL	Elder Clifford Brantley, Bros., Jeff Ellison, Plummer McBee, Everett Brantley, Millard Welch, Sis., Lelia Ellison, Polly Ward, Barsha Brantley, Linda Brantley, Mildred Brantley.	0	0	0	0	0	0	0	88	$10.00	Second Saturday and Sunday	Second Sunday in June
CEDAR SPRINGS	Elder Johnny Ayers, Bros., Clifford Robertson, Everett Miracle, Bill Good, Isom Drummonds, Sis., Ida Robertson, Velt Munsey, Rosey Miracle, Bonnie Miracle, Katherine Miracle, Carolyn Miracle, Eula Good, Eileen Good, and Gloria Good.	0	0	4	0	0	0	0	61	10.00	Second and Fourth Saturday Night and Sunday	Sunday after the Fourth Saturday in May

STATISTICAL TABLE

Church	Members									Schedule	Annual Meeting
DAVIS CHAPEL	Elder Leonard White, Bros. Onie Parrott, Orice McCarty, Gene Hopps Sis., Mamie Parrott, Molly McCarty, Ruby Hobbs, Lassie Ellison, Debbie Hobbs.	2	0	0	0	0	1	140	$20.00	Third Sat. Night and Sunday and every Sunday Night.	Sunday after the third Saturday in June
GIBSON STATION	Elder Joe Irwin, Bros., Spurgeon Thompson, Harve Rhymer, Franklin Jones, Sis., Fannie Jones, Mellie Thompson, Evelyn Maples, Mossie Cottrell, Edna Atkinson, Lesa Ayers and Annie Willis.	0	6	2	0	0	1	91	$10.00	First Saturday and Sunday in each month	Sunday after the first Saturday in June
KIRKWOOD	Elders, R. H. Pettit, Hugh E. Brummitt, and Walter Lyons, Bros., W; H. Taylor, M. A. Norton, J. L. Sharp, R. O. Taylor, Sis., Ruby Brummitt, Callie Lyons, Lou Emma Taylor, Lucy Norton, Evelyn Sharp and Myrtle Taylor.	0	0	2	0	0	1	108	$25.00	Each Sunday Morning	Last Sunday in April
LENOIR CITY	Elders, Charles Taylor, Alvin Graves; Bros., Henry Chamberlain, Hubert Spoons, Jerry Spoons, Lee Parris, Millard Wilkerson, Raymond Wilkerson; Sis., Estie Chamberlain Annie Spoons, Cora Hill Agnes Taylor, Janice Spoons, Lois Chaney, Mary Parris, Joe Collins, Sallie Anderson, Frankie Howard & Ella Field	0	1	0	1	3	3	150	$30.00	Each Sunday and Sunday Night	Sunday after the Third Saturday in May

Church	Members								Membership	Amount	Time of Meeting	Union Meeting
MONROE MICHIGAN	Elder Lenvil Meyers, Bros., John Drummonds, Herman Ayers, Dillard Sutton, Millard Thompson, Sis., Roxie Drummonds, Flossie Sutton and Faye Thompson.	2	0	0	3	0	0	0	15	$10.00	Sunday after the third Saturday	Sunday after the Third Saturday in July
NOETON	Elder Gilbert Atkins, Elder Roy Oliver, Bros., Carroll Oliver, Charlie Collins, Sis., R t. Oliver, Mildred Oliver, Bessie Collins.	0	0	0	0	0	0	0	31	$10.00	Third Saturday and Sunday of each month	Sunday after the Third Saturday in May & Sept.
OAK GROVE	Elder George Shoffner, Elder Toni Eastridge, Bros., Aaron Cole Alfred Relford, Cillis Shoffner, Sis., Veda Cole, Tishie Creech, Lillie Shoffner, Margie Relford, Nellie Sherritze, Ruth Edwards, Genice Brantley.	0	0	7	0	2	8	3	308	$20.00	First Saturday and Sunday of each month	Sunday after the First Saturday in May
PLEASANT HILL	Elders, Albert Davis, J. H. Branscomb, Bros., Ralph Edwards, Kubil Edwards, Glenn Davis, Sis., Audry Davis.	0	0	2	2	1	2	0	99	$20.00	Fourth Saturday and Sunday of each month	
PLEASANT POINT	Elder Claude Rosson, Bros., George Williams, C. D. Keck, Sis., Allie Williams and Doris Rosson.	0	0	0	0	0	0	1	118	$15.00	Each Sunday and Sunday Night	Sunday after the First Saturday in July
ROCKY DALE	Elder Everett Berry, Elder Joe Bush, Elder Parnick Shelton, Bros., Bill Berry, Elmer Graves, Sis., Trula Berry, Lola Berry, Wilma Shelton, Norma Jean Bush.	0	0	0	0	0	0	2	114	$20.00	Sun. Night after the Second Sat. in each Month	Sunday after the Second Saturday in May

118

1973 MINUTES

of the

POWELL VALLEY
ASSOCIATION
OF PRIMITIVE BAPTIST

*Held with the Sister Church at Pleasant Hill
in Claiborne County, Tennessee*

August 17, 18, 19, 1973

THE ONE HUNDRED AND FIFTY-FOURTH
ANNUAL SESSION OF THE POWELL VALLEY ASSOCIATION
OF
PRIMITIVE BAPTIST

Held with the Sister Church at Pleasant Hill
in Claiborne County, Tennessee

AUGUST 17, 18, 19, 1973

Next Session will be held with the Sister Church at Lenoir City
in Loudon County, Tennessee
to begin
On Friday before the Third Saturday in August, 1974
At 10:30 O'clock

Elder Albert Davis . . . . Moderator
Speedwell, Tenn. - Phone 869-3596

Elder Hugh Brummitt . . . . Assistant Moderator
1329 Brown Ave., Knoxville, Tenn. - Phone 546-7700

Bro. W. H. Taylor . . . . Clerk
Rt. 27, Knoxville, Tenn. - Phone 922-2143

Bro. Onie Parrott . . . . Assistant Clerk
LaFollette, Tenn.

FRIDAY, AUGUST 17, 1973

The Powell Valley Association of Primitive Baptist met with the Sister Church of Pleasant Hill in Claiborne County, Tennessee, August 17, 1973 for the one hundred and fifty fourth session with Moderator Albert Davis presiding.

After a good song service, directed by Elder Charles Taylor, Pastor of the Lenoir City Church, the Moderator called the congregation to order and called for the opening prayer by Elder Bill Berry of the Rocky Dale Church.

Elder Toni Eastridge, who was scheduled to preach the introductory sermon was absent due to illness and Elder Alvin Graves, the alternate, preached the opening sermon using as the lesson the 1st verse of the 4th Chapter of St. Luke.

After preaching the congregation was dismissed in prayer by Elder Walter Lyons for a 15 minute recess.

At the sound of singing the Association reconvened with the Moderator presiding, pleading for peace and harmony to prevail, then reading the 1st Chapter of the Book of Titus, and called for prayer by Elder Joe Irving of Gibson Station.

BUSINESS OF THE ASSOCIATION

1. Moderator called for letters of the Sister Churches to be presented for reading. Twelve were received and read.

2. Called for members present and not delegated, who wish to be seated as such to come forward. Two came, Sister Evelyn Maples of Gibson Station and Bro. Johnny Atkins of Oak Grove Church.

3. Motion approved that we receive the letters and seat the delegates.

4. Called for letters of Corresponding Association. None received, but was reported one was to be received on Saturday.

5. Call for petitionary letters and none received.

6. Motion approved that the Association re-elect Elder Albert Davis Moderator and Elder Hugh E. Brummitt assistant Moderator for the coming year.

7. Motion carried to re-elect Bro. W.H. Taylor Clerk and Bro. Onie Parrott assistant Clerk for the coming year.

8. Motion carried that the Moderator be empowered to appoint all the committees for this session of business.

9. The Moderator, having been appointed by the Association, made the following committee appointments.

COMMITTEE ON ARRANGEMENTS
   Elder Charles Taylor
   Elder Johnny Atkins
   Bro. Alford Relford

COMMITTEE ON PREACHING   Bro. Donald Sharp
   Bro. Franklin Jones
   Bro. Verlin Edwards

COMMITTEE ON CORRESPONDENCE
   Elder Clifford Brantley
   Elder Alvin Graves

121

COMMITTEE ON REQUEST
  Bro. Bill Lambert
  Bro. Millard Thompson
  Bro. Spurgeon Thompson

COMMITTEE ON FINANCE
  Elder Bill Berry
  Bro. Ambrose Sharp
  Bro. Roscoe Branscomb

10. The Committees having been appointed, the Association voted to adjourn until 10:30 Saturday morning. Dismissed in prayer by Elder Everett Berry of Rocky Dale Church.

SATURDAY, AUGUST 18, 1973

1. At the appointed hour of 10:30 the Association reconvened at the sound of singing.

After a good spiritual song service directed by Elder Charles Taylor, assistant moderator Elder Hugh E. Brummitt gave the welcome and made a wonderful talk on the knowledge and goodness of God and read from the 23rd Chapter of the Book of Psalms and called for prayer by Elder J.C. Monday.

2. Moderator called the Association to order for the remainder of the business and called for letters not received Friday. Two were received. The letters were read and their delegates seated making all the churches of the Association.

3. Called for letters of corresponding Association not received on Friday.. One was received from the original Hiwassee Association which was received and their delegates seated.

4. Called for the roll call of delegates.

5. Moderator called for the report of Committee on Arrangements who gave the following report and were released:

REPORT OF COMMITTEE ON ARRANGEMENTS

a. Call roll of delegates
b. Call for report of Committee on Preaching
c. Call for report of Committee on Correspondence
d. Call for report of Committee on Request
e. Call for report of Committee on Finance
f. How many minutes shall we have printed, who shall supervise the printing and distribution of same. How much shall he receive for his service and where and when shall the next session of the Association be held and who shall preach the introductory sermon.

Respectfully submitted,
Elder Charles Taylor
Elder Johnny Atkins
Bro. Alfred Relford

6. Call for report of Committee on Preaching which was given as follows and the Committee released.

122

REPORT OF COMMITTEE ON PREACHING

We, the committee on Preaching, wish to submit the following report which was accepted and the committee released:

Friday Night . . . . Elder Clifford Brantley
Elder Charles Taylor
Saturday . . . . Elder Hugh E. Brummitt
Elder Bill Berry
Saturday Night . . . . Elder Everett Berry
Elder Walter Lyons
Sunday . . . . Elder Leonard White
Elder Albert Davis

Respectfully submitted,
Brother Donald Sharp
Brother Verlin Edwards
Brother Franklin Jones

7. Call for report of committee on Correspondence. We the committee on Correspondence wish to submit the following report which was accepted and the Committee released:

We the Committee on Correspondence recommend that we desire a continuation of the Love, Christian Association and Fellowship with the good people of the Hiwassee Association and that we letter and delegate to their next Association to sit with them as follows: Elder Alvin Graves, Elder Clifford Brantley and Elder Charles Taylor and we request the prayers of all of you.

Respectfully submitted,
Elder Clifford Brantley
Elder Alvin Graves
Brother Henry Chamberlain

8. Call for report of Committee on request which was read, accepted and the Committee released:

We the Committee on Request recommend and request that we order 1,000 copies of the minutes printed and distributed to the churches, and that we authorize the Clerk to supervise same and that he receive $50.00 for his services. We also recommend that he have printed in the minutes all obituaries given to him. Also, that the next session be held with the Sister Church in Lenoir City, Loudon County to begin on Friday before the third Saturday in August 1974 at 10:30 A.M. and that Elder Bill Berry preach the introductory sermon and the alternate be Elder Hugh E. Brummitt.

Submitted by,
Brother Bill Lambert
Brother Spurgeon Thompson
Brother Millard Thompson

9. Call for the report of the Committee on Finance who gave the following report which was received and the Committee released:

CHURCH	AMOUNT
Black Fox	$ 15.00
Bradens Chapel	10.00
Brantleys Chapel	20.00
Cedar Springs	10.00
Davis Chapel	20.00
Gibson Station	10.00
Kirkwood	25.00
Lenoir City	30.00
Monroe, Mich.	10.00
Norton	15.00
Oak Grove	20.00
Pleasant Hill	20.00
Pleasant Point	15.00
Rocky Dale	25.00
	$245.00
Collection	$132.00
	$377.00
Balance on Bank	$106.00
GRAND TOTAL	$483.00
Less expenses for year	_____
Balance in Bank	

Respectfully submitted,
Brother Ambrose Sharp
Brother Roscoe Branscomb
Elder Bill Berry

10. Motion approved that we honor the Committee on Request, and have the Clerk to have printed 1,000 copies of minutes and distribute them and that he receive $50.00 for this service.

11. The Association voted to hold the next session of the Association with the Sister Church at Lenoir City in Loudon County, Tennessee, to begin on Friday before the third Saturday in August 1974 at 10:30 A.M.

12. Motion approved that Elder Bill Berry deliver the introductory sermon and Elder Hugh E. Brummitt be the alternate.

13. Motion approved that we accept the recommendation of the Committee on Correspondence and that we letter and delegate to the Original Hiwassee Association.

14. Motion that we the churches of the Powell Valley Association wish to extend to the church at Pleasant Hill and the entire community our sincere thanks, appreciation, Love and prayers for the good food and the love and kindness

to us while in your community. May God bless you all.

15. After completing the business of this session and enjoying three wonderful days of Fellowship and spiritual association with the Sister Churches, the Association voted to adjourn, hoping to be blessed to meet next year with the church at Lenoir City.

> Elder Albert Davis
> Moderator
> Elder Hugh E. Brummitt
> Assistant Moderator
> Brother W. H. Taylor
> Clerk
> Brother Onie Parrott
> Assistant Clerk

SUNDAY, AUGUST 19, 1973

Sunday at the appointed hour of 10:30 A.M. another overflow crowd assembled at the sound of singing. After a good spiritual song service directed by Elder Chas. Taylor, the pastor of the Church, Elder Alvin Graves gave the opening welcome and a wonderful short talk on the marvelous grace of God. He then called for prayer by Elder Clifford Brantley.

After prayer Elder Leonard White entertained the crowd by using as his background only three words, God-Bible-Church. After several minutes of good explanation on each he then preached a wonderful spiritual sermon.

After singing and much rejoicing the Moderator closed out the service and called for dismission in prayer by Elder Leonard White.

> Elder Albert Davis
> Moderator
> W. H. Taylor
> Clerk

LETTER TO THE HIWASSEE ASSOCIATION

We the Powell Valley Association of Primitive Baptist while in session wish to share our love, fellowship and relationship with the Hiawassee Association.

We also desire to letter and delegate to your next Association to convene in July 1974 the following delegates whom we hope you will receive and seat with you to witness: Elder Alvin Graves, Elder Charles Taylor and Elder Clifford Brantley, who are sound in the Faith and in good standing.

We desire your prayers when it goes well with you.

> Elder Albert Davis, Moderator
> Elder Hugh Brummitt, Assistant Moderator
> W. H. Taylor, Clerk
> Onie Parrott, Assistant Clerk

125

ORDAINED MINISTERS

Elder Gilbert Atkins
Route 3
Rutledge, Tennessee

Elder Johnny Atkins
Bean Station, Tennessee

Elder Johnny Ayers
New Tazewell, Tennessee

Elder Everett Berry
Route 27
Knoxville, Tennessee
Phone: 922-7004

Elder Wm. (Bill) Berry
Route 27
Knoxville, Tennessee
Phone: 922-2269

Elder J. H. Branscomb
Speedwell, Tennessee
Phone: 869-3735

Elder Clifford Brantley
Brown School Road
Maryville, Tennessee
Phone: 982-3735

Elder Hugh E. Brummitt
1329 Brown Avenue
Knoxville, Tennessee
Phone: 546-7700

Elder Joe Bush
Corryton, Tennessee
Phone: 687-7018

Elder Noble Clawson
Speedwell, Tennessee
Route 4

Elder Albert Davis
Speedwell, Tennessee
Phone: 869-3596

Elder Toni Eastridge
Route 3
Louisville, Tennessee
Phone: 983-1068

Elder Alvin Graves
Route 3
Lenoir City, Tennessee

Elder Joe Irving
Gibson Station, Virginia

Elder Walter Lyons
1602 Garfield Street
Alcoa, Tennessee
Phone: 984-3207

Elder Lenvil Meyers
715 Scott Street
Monroe, Michigan

Elder J. C. Monday
Speedwell, Tennessee

Elder John Oliver
Bean Station, Tennessee

Elder R. H. Pettit
4907 Jacksboro Pike
Knoxville, Tennessee

Elder Claude Rosson
Route 4
New Tazewell, Tennessee
Phone: 626-3168

Elder Parnick Shelton
Corryton, Tennessee
Phone: 687-6142

Elder W. M. Sparks
Speedwell, Tennessee
Phone: 562-7997

Elder Charles Taylor
204 Martel Road
Lenoir City, Tennessee
Phone: 986-8172

Elder Leonard White
LaFollette, Tennessee
Phone: 562-5667

Elder Clay Widner
101 West Norris Street

LICENTIATES

Bro. Odel Carpenter
Maryville, Tennessee

Bro. Roscoe Branscomb
Speedwell, Tennessee

Bro. Spurgeon Thompson
Gibson Station, Virginia

ARTICLES OF FAITH

Article 1. We believe in only one true living God, as He is revealed to us in the Holy Scriptures - Father, Son, and Holy Ghost.

Article 2. We believe that the Scriptures of the old and new Testaments are the words of God and the only rule of all-saving knowledge and obedience.

Article 3. We believe in the doctrine of election according to the foreknowledge of God.

Article 4. We believe in the doctrine of original sin.

Article 5. We believe in man's impotency to rescue himself from the fallen state he is in, by his own will or ability.

Article 6. We believe that sinners are justified in the sight of God only by the imputed righteousness of Jesus Christ.

Article 7. We believe the elect, according to the foreknowledge of God will be called, converted, regenerated, and sanctified by the Holy Spirit.

Article 8. We believe the saints will persevere and never fall finally away.

Article 9. We believe that baptism and the Lord's Supper are ordinances of Jesus Christ, and that true believers are the only subject of these ordinances, and that the true mode of baptism is by immersion. We believe also that feet washing is an example of Jesus Christ and should be kept by his deciples until his second coming.

Article 10. We believe in the Resurrection of the dead and the General Judgement.

Article 11. We believe that the punishment of the wicked will be everlasting and that the joys of the righteous will be eternal.

Article 12. We believe that no minister has the right to administer the ordinances, except those who have been regularly baptized and called of God, and come under the imposition of hands of the presbytery.

127

RULES OF DECORUM

1. The churches composing the Powell's Valley Association shall not be confined to any set rules as to specific number of Messengers they shall have in the body, but shall have the right to name in their letters as many as they choose, and in addition all orderly members of and of the churches being present be entitled to seats in the body as Messengers of their respective churches, with all the rights and privileges of the same.

2. The Messengers thus assembled shall be denominated the Powell's Valley Primitive Baptist Association.

3. For the purpose of historical information and statistical edification, the Churches are required to state in letters, the number of members in fellowship, the number received by Baptism, by letter, by confession of Faith, the number dismissed, excluded and dead since last session; also the time of their meeting, their pastoral supply, and the amount of money contributed for ministers and other purposes together with any other information they deem appropriate for the edification of the saints and glory of God.

4. This Association shall have no power to answer queries, give advice, or dictate to the Churches in any case, or to lord it over God's heritage nor any power by which she can directly or indirectly fringe on the internal rights of the church or censure and try any church or member in reference to faith and practice and determine upon valigity of gospel ordinances. These things shall rest entirely with the churches; but henceforward our annual meetings shall be only for the purpose of hearing from each other, and for the worship of God and mutual comfort and edification of the Saints. To this end we reserve the privilege annually before the Third Saturday in August and the two following days or at such other times as may be agreed upon with any church that may invite us having to protect our own standard, while in session, from heresey and disorder to recognize and invite any primitive Baptist minister or any lay brother ot worship with us that may deem proper; to request the brethren of our body to visit other churches or bodies in our belief with whom we may desire to culture Christian fellowship; to publish in a minute of our proceedings.

5. Each session of the body shall have a Moderator and Clerk who shall hold office until re-elected.

6. Any order member of any church belonging to this body, when convened, being present shall be eligible to elect on as Moderator and Clerk or to sit on any committee appointed by the same.

7. In all election or questions that may be necessary to determine by vote, the vote shall be taken by churches, each church being entitled to three votes for and number less than one hundred, and one additional vote for every fifty or fraction thereof above the first hundred, but the Messengers of each church may divide their vote as they see proper.

8. All elections of questions coming to vote shall be determined by a majority vote cast, and it shall be the only duty of the minority to acquiesce in the decision thus reached.

9. If new churches desire to be admitted to this union they shall petition by letter and messengers and if voted for or recommended by one or more sister churches for her Presbytery constitution them, or orthox and orderly they shall be received by the voice of the body and manifested by the Moderator

giving the Messengers the right hand of fellowship.

10. Any motion or resolution clearly inconsistent with the above rules shall be promptly ruled out of order unless withdrawn by the mover.

11. Any Messenger being ruled out of order by the Moderator shall have the right to appeal to the body on the question of order, and if sustained shall be allowed to proceed, but if not take his seat.

12. Our meeting being held in the name of Christ and the worship of God; each Messenger is expected to observe due and proper therein.

13. It will not be considered good for any Messenger whose name has been enrolled as such to abruptly break off or absent himself from the Association without leave.

14. The Moderator shall be entitled to the same privilege of speech as other members provided the chair is filled.

15. The minutes of the Association shall be read and approved by the body and signed by the Moderator before adjourning.

16. The Association shall be opened and closed by prayer.

17. Amendments to these may be made at any time by a majority of the union voting by churches when they deem it necessary, provide such amendments do not compromise the sovereignty of the churches nor have tendency to give body undue power or jurisdiction over them.

ELDER GEORGE WASHINGTON SHOFFNER

Elder George Washington Shoffner was born January 14, 1888,
and departed this life at Blount
Memorial Hospital September 25,
1972, at the age of 84 years, 8
months, and 14 days.

He was married to Lillie Lawson
for 56 years and to this union nine
(9) children were born. Three of
the children preceded him in death.
Survivors were three daughters--
Mrs. Belle Moore, Kokomo, Indiana, Mrs. Nelle Sherritze, New
Tazewell, Tennessee, and Mrs.
Francis Eastridge, Louisville, Tennessee; three sons--Charlie Shoffner, Mannie Shoffner, and Cillis
Shoffner all of Sharps Chapel, Tennessee; twenty-four (24) grandchildren and thirty (30 great grandchildren and thirty (30) great
grandchildren.

He joined Oak Grove Primitive Baptist Church in 1906 and was ordained
to the full work of the Ministry in October, 1962. He was Church Treasurer
for a number of years and a true and faithful member until God called him to
rest. He loved his church so dearly and is missed by many relatives and
friends.

Funeral services were held September 27, 1972, at 11:00 a.m. at Oak Grove
Primitive Baptist Church. Elder W. M. Sparks, Elder J. C. Monday, and
Elder Clifford Brantley officiated. The interment was in Rush Strong Ceme-
tery.

We know God knows best but we miss him so much. He was such a loyal
and loving father. We know he is at rest.

His Children

CILLIS SHOFFNER

Cillis Shoffner was born March 22, 1925, and departed this life, after a three
day illness, on June 27, 1973. He was the son of Elder George and Sister Lillie
Shoffner who preceded him in death. He was married to Vella Tapp for 26 years
and to this union was born three children: Sons--Roy Lee Shoffner, Sharps
Chapel, Tennessee, and George Paul Shoffner, Knoxville, Tennessee; and a
daughter Judy Shoffner, Sharps Chapel, Tennessee.

He joined the Primitive Baptist Church at Oak Grove at an early age and was
a faithful member until death. He also leaves to mourn his loss two brothers--
Charlie Shoffner and Mannie Shoffner, both of Sharps Chapel, Tennessee;
and three sisters--Mrs. Belle Moore, Kokomo, Indiana, Mrs. Nelle Sherritze,
New Tazewell, Tennessee, and Mrs. Francis Eastridge, Louisville, Tennessee;

a host of nieces and nephews who loved him so very much, and a host of relatives and friends.

He was so kind and always wanted to be friendly with everyone. His family misses him so much but God knew best.

Funeral services were held at Oak Grove Primitive Baptist Church, June 29, 1973, at 11:00 a.m. Elder W. M. Sparks, Elder J. C. Monday, and Elder Noble Closson officiated. Interment was in Rush Strong Cemetery.

Gone but not forgotten.

ELDER ROY OLIVER

ELDER ROY OLIVER, died May 19, 1973. Age 75. He was a member of the Noeton Primitive Baptist Church in Grainger County. He is survived by his wife: Bessie Oliver, Bean Station; sons, Fred, Bean Station, Earl, Rutledge; daughters, Bonnie Akers and Frances Oliver, Bean Station, Nellie Atkins, Thorn Hill; brothers, Jim and Doyle Oliver, Thorn Hill; 16 grandchildren, 7 great-grandchildren.

Funeral services were held at the Noeton Primitive Baptist Church with burial in church cemetery. Smith's, Rutledge in charge.

MELVIN A. NORTON

MELVIN A. NORTON was born April 5, 1901 in Union County, Tennessee, died April 20, 1973. He professed faith in Christ in his boyhood, joined Kirkwood Primitive Baptist Church January 24, 1954 and lived a faithful member until death.

Funeral services were conducted by his beloved pastor, Elder Leonard White.

He leaves to mourn his loss his wife, Lucy Oakes Norton; two sons and four step-children.

I shall meet him again where sorrows will be known no more.

Lucy Oakes Norton

EUNICE WHALEY OLIVER

EUNICE WHALEY OLIVER, age 59, died August 15, 1973 at Morristown-Hamblen Hospital. She was a member of the Norton Primitive Baptist Church. She is survived by her mother, Mrs. Anna Whaley, Morristown; sisters, Mrs. Emma Toby, Miss Vaughtie Whaley, Mrs. Zeb Wilson and Mrs. W. H. Simmons all of Morristown; brother, Elbert Whaley of Mosheim.

Funeral services were held August 17, 1973 at Norton Primitive Baptist Church by Elder John Oliver and Rev. Olof Atkins. Burial was in church cemetery. Stubblefields, Morristown, in charge.

L. ODEN SHARP

L. ODEN SHARP, of Knoxville, was born March 15, 1901 at Sharps Chapel, Tennessee and passed away October 17, 1972 at 7 P.M. He was married to Estelle Petree September 7, 1928. He was a member of Kirkwood Primitive Baptist Church.

Funeral service was conducted at Gentry Mortuary by Elder Leonard White.

The body was interred at Lynnhurst Cemetery.

It was so hard to say goodbye, darling, but through the mercy of our Dear Lord I will meet you some sweet day.

MRS. PEARLIE MEYERS HOLT

MRS. PEARLIE MEYERS HOLT, 67, of New Tazewell, died Tuesday, October 17, 1972 at Claiborne County Hospital.

Suvivors: husband, Clarence T. Holt, New Tazewell; sons, Lester Holt, Kingsport, Tenn.; Leon Holt, Memphis, Tenn.; 4 grandchildren; sisters, Mrs. Ethel Hall, LaPlata, Md., Mrs. Lenora Carr, West Palm Beach, Fla.; brothers, Lawrence and Roy Meyers, Washington, D. C.; step-mother, Mrs. Lizzie Meyers.

Funeral services were held at 2 p.m. Thursday at Coffey Mortuary Chapel with Rev. Carl Ware Jr. officiating. Burial in Fairview Cemetery.

Pallbearers, Edgar Holt, Scott Mayes, Doug Holt, Rev. Charlie Meyers, Lonnie Meyers, Lloyd Drummonds.

Coffey Mortuary, Inc. in charge.

MARTHA LOU GODDARD

MARTHA LOU GODDARD, age 25, died November 27, 1972. She was a member of Kirkwood Primitive Baptist Church.

Survivors, husband, Andrew Goddard, 3 daughters, Stacey, Dottie Mae and Becky Goddard, parents: Mr. and Mrs. Jack Cook; one brother, Thomas D. Cook; grandfathers, Sam Cook and J. A. Lyons.

Funeral services were held at Berry's Funeral Home Chapel.

Elder Leonard White and Rev. James Lauderback officiating. Interment Holly Hills Memorial Gardens.

DAILY, CATHERN (Owens) BREEDING

DAILY, CATHERN (Owens) BREEDING, of Speedwell, Tennessee, who was born September 1, 1903 departed this life May 2, 1973. She is survived by six sons and four daughters, twenty-seven grandchildren, one great grandchild, one half-brother, two sisters and six half-sisters.

Very early in life Sister Daily joined the church at Pleasant Hill Primitive Baptist and remained there for several years. She then joined another church and stayed there for a while.

She later moved to Michigan. When she came back on visits, she would visit our church and enjoyed herself very much. On the 29th of April, 1973 she reunited back with Pleasant Hill Church. She related that it was the church of her first love and how she did rejoice.

Sister Daily is sadly missed by her family, her church and her many friends.

Her body was taken back to Michigan and laid to rest by her husband.

We hope to meet again in the sweet by and by.

EARL W. BREWER

EARL W. BREWER, age 78, passed from this life November 30, 1972. He was a member of the Lenoir City Primitive Baptist Church and also a veteran

132

of World War I. Brother Earl leaves to mourn his passing, his wife, Stella Anderson Brewer. Two daughters, Mrs. Oneda Vincil and Mrs. Florence Clabough, both of Lenoir City. Three sons, Paul Brewer of Ringgold, Ga., Gordon and Marion (Wimpy) Brewer, both of Lenoir City. He also leaves 14 grandchildren and 19 great-grandchildren along with a great host of other relatives and friends. Funeral services were held Dec. 2, 1972 by Elder Charles Taylor and Rev. Raymond Phillips. His body was laid to rest in City Cemetery to await the final Resurrection.

DORA McNABB

DORA McNABB, age 82, passed from this life on Friday, August 3, 1973. She was a member of the Lenoir City Primitive Baptist Church. She is survived by one daughter, Iva Bryant of Lenoir City and one son, Vaughn Williams, also of Lenoir City. Stepchildren, Mrs. Arlie Galyon, Mrs. Helen White, and Edith Galyon, all of Loudon, Mrs. Melba Hyde of Lenoir City, Mose McNabb of Loudon. Brother, Kyle Anderson and sisters, Mrs. Stella Brewer, Mrs. Virgie Tinnell, and Ruth McNabb. She also leaves her grandchildren and other relatives and friends. Her kindness and smiles will be missed by all with whom she came into contact. Her funeral was held Sunday, August 5, 1973 with Elder Charles Taylor officiating. Her body was laid to rest in Lake View Cemetery to await the final call of her Lord in whom she trusted.

FRED R. WEAVER, SR.

FRED R. WEAVER, SR., age 74, passed from this life Sunday, February 25, 1973. He was a member of Lenoir City Primitive Baptist Church. He is survived by his companion Mrs. Mary Curtis Weaver; two daughters, Deloris Weaver of Lenoir City and Doris Jones of Washington, D. C. Three sons, Fred Jr. of Atlanta, Jim and Howard of Lenoir City. Besides these he leaves four grandchildren and one sisters. Also a vast host of friends. He was a faithful church member as long as health permitted. Graveside services were held at City Cemetery and his body was laid to rest to await that glad call from his Savior.

MISS GUSSIE HENSON

MISS GUSSIE HENSON, age 86, died Monday, April 16, 1973. She was a member of Lenoir City Primitive Baptist Church. She made her home with Mrs. Mary Lou Timmel by whom she is survived along with several nieces and nephews whom she loved as sons and daughters. Funeral services were held at Click Funeral Home with interment in Lenoir City Cemetery, Rev. J. E. Rush and Rev. Frankie Kagley officiating.

DAVID SPOON

DAVID SPOON, age 18, passed from this life September 20, 1972. He attended the Lenoir City Primitive Baptist Church which he loved very much. He had a wonderful talent for music and played the organ or piano for singing in the church. His friends were numbered by as many as he met in life. God saw fit to call him home but we all will miss him very much. His voice will be heard as long as we who remembered him live. He leaves to mourn his passing his father, Hubert Spoon; mother, Annie Spoon; two brothers, Jerry and Gary; three nieces and one nephews. Besides these are his grandmothers and a host of other relatives and friends. His funeral was held at the church he loved so well and his body was laid to rest in Lenoir City Cemetery to await the call of Jesus.

MATT PACKETT

MATT PACKETT, age 55, passed away Friday, September 8, 1972. He attended the Lenoir City Primitive Baptist Church. He loved and supported his church with all his means which God had given him. He will be sadly missed by his brothers and sisters in the church. He leaves to mourn hs passing, his wife, Della Spoons Packett; daughter, Ann Williams; two grandchildren, Michael and Lori Ann Williams. Also two sisters and two brothers. Brother Matt's loving disposition made him friends wherever he went. Funeral services were held at the church Sunday, September 10, 1972 with Elder Charles Taylor and Rev. Raymond Hudson officiating. His body was laid to rest in Lenoir City Cemetery to await the Resurrection morning.

HAZEL TINNEL SIMPSON

HAZEL TINNEL SIMPSON, age 56, passed from this life July 21, 1973. She was a faithful member of the Lenoir City Primitive Baptist Church. After a long and painful sickness God called her home to rest. Her talk with those who visited her was of the church and her Lord. We all will miss her encouragement to others. Her last request just before passing was for her pastor to pray with her and her loved ones standing by her bedside. She leaves to mourn her passing her husband, Paul Simpson; one daughter, Carrol Sims; one granddaughter, Nita; her mother, Mrs. R. E. Tinnel; one brother, Peter Tinnel. Also many other relatives and friends. Her funeral was conducted by Elder Charles Taylor. Her body was laid to rest in Lenoir City Cemetery to await the Masters Call.

FRANCIE ROSSON

MRS. FRANCIE ROSSON, 75, of New Tazewell, died Saturday October 21, 1972, at Claiborne County Hospital.

Survivors: sons, Billie, Lawrence, Elder Claude Rosson, New Tazewell, Carl Rosson, Halls, Tenn. Daughters, Mrs. Eula Gray Cupp, New Tazewell; 23 grandchildren; 15 great-grandchildren; sisters, Mrs. Eva Collins, Mrs. Allie Williams, Mrs. Lennie Keck, all of New Tazewell. Esco, Arlis, Dewey, Collins, all of New Tazewell. A host of relatives and friends.

Funeral services were held at 11 a.m. at Pleasant Point Baptist Church. Elder Walter Lyons officiating. Burial in Hopper Cemetery.

Pallbearers: grandsons, Glenn, Harold, Danty Lee, Marvin, Dale, Don Rosson. Coffey Mortuary Inc. in charge.

MRS. NORA TREECE

MRS. NORA TREECE was born June 15, 1887. She departed this life September 9, 1972, being 85 years, 3 months and 21 days of age. She was the daughter of Jeff and Manda Ludellia Treece.

She was married to Wiley Treece on May 27, 1906. To this union was born 11 children, 27 grandchildren and 41 great-grandchildren. A host of relatives and friends to mourn her loss.

Her husband and two sons preceded her in death.

She professed faith in Christ at an early age and joined the Primitive Baptist at Moyers Grove now known as Cedar Springs Church.

Later she and her husband came to Red Hill to help set up that church and after it was disbanded she went back to Cedar Springs and lived a faithful member until death. She was loved by all who knew her. Our loss is Heavens gain.

The Children.

SARAH ELLEN WILLIAMS

SARAH ELLEN WILLIAMS, age 77, passed away Sunday evening, January 14, 1973 in Norton, Virginia. She was a member of the Gibson Station Primitive Baptist Church. She leaves behind 9 children, 1 sister, 3 brothers and a host of grandchildren and great-grandchildren. Funeral services were conducted at the church January 17, 1973 with Elder Everett Berry and Elder Nelson Jones officiating. She was laid to rest in the Southern Cemetery til Jesus comes again. Sister Ell is missed very much by her church.

MRS. NOLA (White) SMITH

MRS. NOLA (White) SMITH, 72, of 156 Sharps Circle, La Follette, died at 12:08 a.m., Tuesday, April 3, at the LaFollette Community Hospital.

She is survived by her husband, Charlie Smith; three daughters, Mrs. A. J. Jones of Oak Ridge, Mrs. L. C. King, of Jacksboro and Mrs. Carthel Light, of Warren, Michigan; three sons, Duffey Smith of Oregon, Ohio; Wayne Smith of Knoxville; and Vitchue Smith of Jacksboro; four sisters, Mrs. Pearlie Weaver, of Knoxville; Mrs. Arletta Davis of Caryville; Mrs. Doshia Ivey of La-Follette and Mrs. Celia Ballew, of Detroit, Michigan; one brother, Alonzo White, of Fayetteville, Virginia; 14 grandchildren.

Funeral services were held (Thursday) April 5, at 2 p.m. at the Davis Chapel Primitive Baptist Church of which she was a member. Rev. Leonard White, and the Rev. Hugh Brummitt officiating. Burial was in Sunrise Cemetery.

Roach Mortuary, LaFollette, in charge of arrangements.

MRS. C. L. (Zona) GRAVES AULT

MRS. C. L. (Zona) GRAVES AULT, age 78, of 4106 Fulton Drive, Knoxville, Tenn., passed away 6:15 a.m. Tuesday, January 3, 1973, at St. Mary's Hospital. She was a member of Rocky Dale Baptist Church. Survivors: husband, Charles L. Ault, daughter, Mrs. T. R. Harrington, Jr., son, Leon Ault, all of Knoxville. Sisters, Mrs. George Rankin, of Port Charlotte, Florida, Mrs. Luther Hunter, of Panama City, Florida; brothers, Elmer, Fate and Dewey Graves, all of Corryton; grandsons, Tom R. Harrington III, Charles A. Harrington and Richard L. Harrington, of Knoxville, James A. Harrington, Atlanta; great-grandchildren, David, Susanne, and Amy Harrington. Services 4 p.m. Wednesday, January 4, at Gentrys Chapel, Dr. R. Frank Porter, Rev. William R. Wells officiating. Interment Lynnhurst Cemetery. Pallbearers: Ralph Kitts, Chester Ball, and grandsons, Tom R., Charles A., James A., and Richard L. Harrington. Gentrys in charge.

MRS. HENRY WALKER, (Rada)

MRS. HENRY WALKER, (Rada), passed away Sunday afternoon, March 11, at the home of her daughter, Mrs. Vaughn (Gladys) Browning, Maynardville. Survivors; daughter, grandchildren, Mrs. Clarence (Helen) Reasor, Mrs. Edsel (Wanda) Lett, Mrs. Don (Jewell) Flenniken, Ronald Browning, all of Knoxville, Buddy Browning, Kokomo, Ind.; sister, Mrs. Martha Harrison, Knoxville; brother, George Hundley, Florida; nine great-grandchildren. Funeral was held at 2 p.m. Wednesday at Oak Grove Baptist Church. Rev. Rob Williams, Rev. Lloyd England officiating. Burial in Stiner Cemetery. Ailors in charge.

JOHN RECTOR WILLIAMS

JOHN RECTOR WILLIAMS passed away December 19, 1972 at Claiborne Co. Nursing Home. He was 74 years old. Survivors: sister, Tina Williams Beeler, Greenback, Tenn. Several nieces and nephews. He was a member of Oak Grove Primitive Baptist Church. Funeral was held at Cook Funeral Home, Rev. Albert Davis officiating.

J. O. DANIELS (Roe)

J. O DANIELS (Roe), age 76, of Sharps Chapel, passed away Thursday morning at his home. Survivors: wife, Mrs. Ivey Daniels; daughters, Mrs. Bertha Cox, Mrs. Edder Peters, Mrs. Velma Adams, Sharps Chapel, Mrs. Eva Russell, Mrs. Ruth Woods, Halls; son, B. H. of Sharps Chapel; sisters, Mrs. Ena Whited, Maynardville, Mrs. Izora England, New Tazewell, Mrs. Grace Wilson, Elwood, Indiana; 23-grandchildren; nine great grandchildren. Funeral was held at 2 p.m. Saturday at Oak Grove Primitive Baptist Church, Elder W. M. Sparks, Elder J. C. Monday officiating. Interment church cemetery, Cooke Mortuary, in charge.

JAMES SHELBY

JAMES SHELBY, 80, of Rt. 4, New Tazewell, passed away Monday morning at Claiborne Hospital. Survivors, daughters, Mrs. Gracie Shoffner, Sharps Chapel, Mrs. Anna Mae Davis, New Tazewell; son, Willis Shelby, Bellevue, Ohio, 10 grandchildren; 11 great-grandchildren; brother, Herman Shelby, New Tazewell; sisters, Mrs. Pearly Moyers, New Tazewell, Mrs. Helen Brock, Marietta, Ga. Funeral was held at 2:30 p.m. Wednesday at Edwards Primitive Baptist Church. Interment, Stiner Cemetery. Coffey Funeral Home, in charge.

CHURCH	NAME OF DELEGATES	Restored	Recd. by Letter	Recd. by Baptism	Recd. by Relationship	Dismissed	Excluded	Deceased	Total Membership	Printing Minutes	Regular Meeting Time	Communion Time
BLACK FOX	Bros. Dale Capps, Bennie Capps, Calvin Capps, Roy Bailey and Arthur Terry. Sisters Ruth Capps, Sandra Capps, Flossie Capps, Roma Bailey, Naomi Cabbage, Mary Terry and Jessie Cabbage.	0	0	0	0	0	0	0	88	$15.00	Second and Third Sat. Night and Sunday	Sunday after the Second Sat. in June
BRADENS CHAPEL	Elder Noble Clawson, Elder J. C. Monday, Elder Wm. Sparks, Elder J. H. Branscomb. Sisters Helen Clawson, Winona Monday, Leecy Sparks, Lola Braden, Helen Branscomb, Rachel Lambert and Bro. Bill Lambert.	0	1	8	0	0	1	1	142	$10.00	First Sat. and Sunday in each Month	Sunday after the First Saturday in June
BRANTELY'S CHAPEL	Elder Clifford Brantley, Bro. Everett Brantley, Sister Mildred Brantley, Barsha Brantley and Linda Brantley.	0	0	0	0	0	2	0	86	$20.00	Second Sat.and Sun. ea. month	Sunday after the 2nd Sat. in July
CEDAR SPRINGS	Bros. Clifford Robertson, Bill Good and Sisters Eula Good, Ida Roberts and Veltie Munsey.	2						3	60	$10.00		
DAVIS CHAPEL	Elder Leonard White, Bro. Onie Parrott, Sister Mamie Parrott and Sister Mollie McCarty.	0	0	1	2	0	0	3	140	$20.00	3rd Sat. nite & Sun. & every Sun. nite	Sun. after Third Sat. in June
GIBSON STATION	Elder Joe Irving, Bros., Spurgeon Thompson, Harve Rhymer, Franklin Jones, Sisters Fannie Jones, Mellie Thompson, Mossie Cottrell, Edna Atkinson, and Evelyn Maples	0	0	0	1	0	0	1	91	$10.00		
KIRKWOOD	Elders R. H. Pettit, H. E. Brummitt, Walter Lyons, Bros. J. L. Sharp, S. B. Snodderly, Cambrose Sharp,										Every Sunday	Last Sunday

137

	Names									$	morning	in April
	Sisters Ruby Brummitt, Callie Lyons, Evelyn Sharp, Alta Snodderly, Frieda Sharp and Estelle Petree Sharp.	0	0	0	0	4	1	3	100	$25.00		
LENOIR CITY	Elders Charles Taylor, Alvin Graves, Bros. Henry Chamberlain, Hubert Spoon, Scott Collins, Sisters Estie Chamberlain, Annie Spoon, Agnes Taylor, Cora Hill, Edna Jo Collins and Ella Fields.	0	0	6	7	0	1	5	157	$30.00	Every Sunday and Sunday night	Sunday after the Third Sat. in May
MONROE, MICH.	Elder Lenvil Meyers, Bros. Herman Ayers, Dillard Sutton, Sisters Flossie Sutton, Marie Evans and Roxie Drummond.				2				14	$10.00	Third Sunday	Sunday after the Third Sat. in July
NOETON	Elder John Oliver, Bros. Charles Collins, Carroll Oliver and Sister Ruth Oliver.	0	0	3	0	0	0	2	32	$15.00	3rd Sat. & Sun. of each Month	3rd Sun. in May and September
OAK GROVE	Elder Toni Eastridge, Elder Johnny Atkins, Bros. Alfred Relford, and Aaron Cole, Sisters Tishie Creech, Francis Eastridge, Maggie Relford, Veda Cole, and Genice Brantley.	0	0	0	6	0	5	6	291	$20.00	First Sat. night and Sunday of each Month	Sunday after the First Saturday in May
PLEASANT	Elder Albert Davis, Bros. Glenn Davis, Millard Thompson, James Edwards, Verlin Edwards, Sisters Audry Davis, Lottie Berry, Faye Thompson and Aklin Edwards.	1	2	1	1	2	1		99	$20.00	Fourth Sat. and Sunday of each Month	Sunday after the Fourth Saturday in June
PLEASANT POINT	Elder Claude Rosson, Bra. George Williams, Sisters Allie Williams and Dorris Rosson.	0	0	0	0	0	0	1	118	$15.00	1st Sat. nite & 3rd Sun. morn.	Sun. after 1st Sat. in July
ROCKY DALE	Elders Everett Berry, Bill Berry, Joe Bush and Parnick Shelton, Bros. W. H. Taylor, Ralph Clapp, Elmer Graves, Sisters Trula Berry, Lola Berry, Wilma Shelton, Norma Jean Bush, Lou Emma Taylor, Fay Collett and Myrtle Bryant.	0	3	5	0	0	1	2	119	$25.00	Each Sunday and Sunday night	Sunday after the second Saturday in May

CHURCH	COUNTY	PASTOR	CLERK	ADDRESS
BLACK FOX	Grainger	Elder Alvin Graves	Bennie Capps Flossie Capps, Asst.	P. O. Box 91 Maynardville, Tenn.
BRADENS CHAPEL	Union	Elder Noble Lee Clawson Elder J. C. Monday, Asst.	Leecy Sparks	Speedwell, Tenn.
BRANTLEY'S CHAPEL	Blount	Elder J. C. Monday Elder Bill Berry, Asst.	Rina Johnson Daniel Brantley, Asst.	1217 Brown School Road, Maryville R. 10, Mint Rd. Maryville, Tenn.
CEDAR SPRINGS	Claiborne	Elder Claude Rosson Elder Johnny Ayers, Asst.	Eula Good Bonnie Miracle, Asst.	New Tazewell, Tenn.
DAVIS CHAPEL	Campbell	Elder Joe Bush Elder Leonard White, Asst.	Ruth Heatherly Lassie Ellison, Asst.	LaFollette, Tenn. Rt. 1
GIBSON STATION	Lee County, Va.	Elder Leonard White Elder Everett Berry, Asst.	Mossie Cottrell Lucille Fleemon, Asst.	Harrogate, Tenn. Ewing, Va.
KIRKWOOD	Knox	Elder Leonard White	Estelle Petree Sharp Alice T. Powers, Asst.	Rt. 27, Emory Rd., Knoxville 2923 Clearview Ave. N.E., Knoxville
LENOIR CITY	Loudon	Elder Charles Taylor	Scott Collins	707 W. 5th Ave. Lenoir City, Tenn.
MONROE, MICH.	Monroe	Elder Lenvil Mayers	Gertrude Zwack Roxie Drummonds, Asst.	1825 S. Paulding Rd. Monroe, Mich. 606 Ky. Ave., Monroe, Mich. 48161
NOETON	Grainger	Elder Gilbert Atkins	John Oliver Bessie Collins, Asst.	Bean Station, Tenn. Rt. 5, Morristown, Tenn.
OAK GROVE	Union	Elder J. C. Monday Elder Noble Lee Clawson, Asst.	Maggie Relford Ruth Shoffner, Asst.	Sharps Chapel, Tenn. Sharps Chapel, Tenn.
PLEASANT HILL	Claiborne	Elder Alvin Graves Elder Albert Davis, Asst.	William Branscomb Verlin Edwards, Asst.	Speedwell, Tenn. Speedwell, Tenn.
PLEASANT POINT	Claiborne	Elder Parnick Shelton Elder Claude Rosson, Asst.	Claude Rosson	Rt. 4, New Tazewell, Tenn. 37825 Tel. 626-3168
ROCKY DALE	Knox	Elder Hugh E. Brummitt	Edward Collett Avrell Graves, Asst.	Rt. 1, Luttrell, Tenn. Ph. 992-5710 Rt. 3, Corryton, Ph. 687-0206

1974 MINUTES

of the

POWELL VALLEY ASSOCIATION
OF PRIMITIVE BAPTIST

LENOIR CITY
PRIMITIVE BAPTIST CHURCH

ELDER CHARLES TAYLOR, PASTOR

Held with the Sister Church at Lenoir City
in Loudon County, Tennessee

AUGUST 16, 17, 18, 1974

THE ONE HUNDRED AND FIFTY-FIFTH
ANNUAL SESSION OF THE POWELL VALLEY ASSOCIATION
OF
PRIMITIVE BAPTIST

Held with the Sister Church at Lenoir City
in Claiborne County, Tennessee

AUGUST 16, 17, 18, 1974

Next Session will be held with the Sister Church at Kirkwood
in Knox County, Tennessee
to begin
On Friday before the Third Saturday in August, 1975
At 10:30 O'clock

Elder Albert Davis .... Moderator
Speedwell, Tenn. - Phone 869-3596

Elder Hugh Brummitt .... Assistant Moderator
1329 Brown Ave., Knoxville, Tenn. - Phone 546-7700

Bro. W. H. Taylor .... Clerk
Rt. 27, Knoxville, Tenn. - Phone 922-2143

Bro. Bennie Capps .... Assistant Clerk
Maynardville, Tenn.

141

FRIDAY, AUGUST 16, 1974

The one hundred and fifty fifth session of the Powell Valley Association of Primitive Baptist met with the Sister Church at Lenoir City in Loudon County, Tennessee, August 16, 1974, with Moderator Albert Davis presiding.

Song service began by singing Amazing Grace. After a good song service conducted by Elder Charles Taylor, prayer was offered by Elder Clifford Brantley of Brantleys Chapel Church.

After singing and prayer, Elder William Berry of Rocky Dale Church delivered a wonderful introductory sermon from the 20th chapter of Acts beginning at the 17th verse and holding to the theme of humbleness and faith and strength to resist the temptations of life.

After preaching, the congregation was dismissed in prayer by Elder Toni Eastridge, for a 15 minute intermission.

After intermission, the Association reconvened at the sound of singing and the moderator called for a moment of silent prayer in honor and respect to the memory of Brother O. R. Parrott and Brother Joshua Drummonds, two of our assistant clerks who have deceased.

Moderator then read from the 27th Psalm and called for prayer by Elder Parnick Shelton of Rocky Dale Church and then called for the business of the Association as follows:

1. The moderator called for the letters of the Sister Churches to be presented to the clerk for reading. Thirteen were received and read.
2. Call was given for members present but not delegated who wish to be seated as such to come forward. One came. Sister Susie Shoffner of Gibston Station Church.
3. Motion approved that we approve the letters and seat the delegates of the thirteen churches.
4. Moderator called for petitionary letters. Two were received from the corresponding Hiwassee Association. To wit: Headrick Chapel and Gethsemene, asking for admission and to become members of the Powell Valley Association.
5. Motion by Elder Everett Berry and second by Elder Charles Taylor was approved that we accept the churches of Gethsemane and Headricks Chapel of the Hiwassee Association and that we accept their petitions and seat their delegations.
6. Motion approved that the association re-elect Elder Albert Davis, Moderator, and Elder Hugh Brummitt, Assistant Moderator for the coming year.
7. The association voted to re-elect Brother W. H. Taylor, Clerk, and Brother Bennie C. Capps, Assistant Clerk in the place of Brother Parrott, who has since deceased.
8. Motion approved that the moderator be empowered to appoint all the committees for this business session.
9. Having been appointed to do so, the moderator made the following appointments:

COMMITTEE ON ARRANGEMENTS:
   Elder Alvin Graves
   Brother William B. Cook
   Brother Spurgeon Thompson

COMMITTEE ON PREACHING:
   Brother Henry Chamberlain
   Brother Franklin Jones
   Brother Cecil Godfrey

COMMITTEE ON CORRESPONDENCE:
   The only correspondence we had was with the Original Hiwassee Association and the two churches of that association petitioned and was admitted to the Powell Valley Association as full members, therefore, no committee on correspondence is necessary.

COMMITTEE ON REQUEST:
   Brother Scott Collins
   Brother James Heatherly
   Brother Tommy Carmichael

COMMITTEE ON FINANCE:
    Brother Glenn Abbott
    Elder Clifford Brantley
    Brother Clyde Abbott

10. The appointment of the committees having been completed, the association adjourned until 10:30 Saturday morning at which time they will reconvene for the remainder of the business session. Dismissed in prayer by Elder Walter Lyons.

SATURDAY, AUGUST 17, 1974

1. Saturday morning at 10:30, the association reconvened with a full house. After a wonderful song service by Elder Charles Taylor singing the good old songs of Zion, then Elder Hugh Brummitt, the Assistant Moderator, opened the service by reading the 111th Psalm. After a short talk he called for prayer by Elder Johnny Atkins of the Oak Grove Church.
2. The moderator called the association to order for the remainder of the business and asked for letters if any not received on Friday. One was received from the Sister Church of Noeton. The letter was accepted and the delegation seated.
3. Moderator called for the roll call of delegates which was completed and the absentees noted.
4. Moderator called for the report of the Committee on Arrangements, who gave the following report which was approved and the committee released.

   REPORT OF COMMITTEE ON ARRANGEMENTS:
   a. Call the roll of all delegates.
   b. Call for a report on the Committee on Preaching.
   c. Call for report of Committee on Request.
   d. Call for a report of Committee on Finance.
   e. Decide how many minutes we have printed and who shall supervise the printing and distribution of same, and how much he shall receive for his services, and where and when the next association shall be held who will deliver the introductory sermon and who will be the alternate.

   Respectfully submitted,
   Brother Spurgeon Thompson
   Brother William B. Cook
   Elder Alvin Graves

5. Call for the report of the Committee on Preaching which was given and approved as follows and the committee released.

REPORT OF COMMITTEE ON PREACHING:
    Friday Night: Elder Parnick Shelton, Elder Alvin Graves
    Saturday: Elder Johnny Atkins, Elder Glenn Abbott
    Saturday Night: Elder Joe Bush, Elder Clifford Brantley
    Sunday: Elder Hugh Brummitt, Elder Leonard White

   Respectfully submitted,
   Brother Henry Chamberlain
   Brother Franklin Jones
   Brother Cecil Godfrey

6. Moderator called for the report of the Committee on Request which was given as follows and was approved and the committee released.

REPORT OF COMMITTEE ON REQUEST:

We, the Committee on Request, recommend that we have printed 1,000 copies of the minutes and that we authorize the clerk to supervise the printing and distribution of same, and that he receive $50.00 for his service. We also ask that the next session of the association be held with the Sister Church at Kirkwood in Knoxville to begin on Friday before the third Saturday in August, 1975.

We further request that we re-initiate the practice of having a circular letter inserted in the minutes, and that the letter be written by an Elder appointed by the association, and that Elder Leonard White write the one for 1974 minutes and Elder Albert Davis write for 1975 minutes. These letters to be on any subject chosen by the writer.

Respectfully submitted:
Brother Scott Collins
Brother James Heatherly
Brother Tommy Carmichael

7. Moderator called for the report of the Committee on Finance which was received and the committee released.

REPORT OF COMMITTEE ON FINANCE:

Church	Amount
Black Fox	$15.00
Bradens Chapel	$10.00
Brantleys Chapel	$25.00
Cedar Springs	$10.00
Davis Chapel	$20.00
Gethsemane	$20.00
Gibson Station	$25.00
Headricks Chapel	$20.00
Kirkwood	$30.00
Lenoir City	$35.00
Monroe, Michigan	$10.00
Noeton	$20.00
Oak Grove	$25.00
Pleasant Hill	$30.00
Pleasant Point	$15.00
Rocky Dale	$30.00
Total	$340.00

Respectfully submitted:
Elder Glenn Abbott
Elder Clifford Brantley
Brother Clyde H. Abbott, Jr.

8. Motion approved that we honor the request of the committee and have 1,000 copies of the minutes printed and that we authorize the clerk to supervise the printing and distribution of same and that he be paid $50.00 for his services.

9. Motion approved that we hold the next session of the association with the Sister Church at Kirkwood in Knoxville, Tennessee, to begin on Friday before the third Saturday in August, 1975, at 10:30 A.M.

10. Motion approved that Elder Glenn Abbott deliver the introductive sermon and Elder Charles Taylor be the Alternate.

11. Motion that we extend to the Church at Lenoir City and to the good people of this community and everyone who had a part in showing us the friendliness, kindness, love and affection we have received while in your city, and as we leave you, we leave with a lingering prayer in our hearts for everyone of you and for your church. We also covet your prayers and may God bless you all.

The Churches of the Powell Valley Association of Primitive Baptist.
Dismissed in prayer by Elder Joe Bush.

Elder Albert Davis, Moderator
Elder Hugh Brummitt, Assistant Moderator
Brother W. H. Taylor, Clerk

144

SUNDAY, AUGUST 18, 1974

At the appointed hour of 10:30 A.M. a full house assembled at the sound of singing. After a spiritual song service, a short talk by Elder Charles Taylor and reading of the 133 Psalms, we were led in prayer by Elder Claude Rosson.

Elder Hugh Brummitt, Assistant Moderator of the association, then delivered the last sermon of the association reading from the 26th chapter of the Acts, delivered a wonderful, spiritual and touching sermon. Speaking on the life and travels of Paul and Gods power over man to do will at his good pleasure and time. Closing with much rejoicing and spiritual demonstrations. Dismissed in prayer by Elder Bill Berry.

ORDAINED MINISTERS

Elder Gilbert Atkins
Route # 3
Rutledge, Tenn.

Elder Johnny Atkins
Bean Station, Tenn.

Elder Johnny Ayers
New Tazewell, Tenn.

Elder Everett Berry
Route # 27
Knoxville, Tenn.
Phone 922-7004

Elder William Berry
Route # 27
Knoxville, Tenn.
Phone 922-2269

Elder J. H. Branscomb
Speedwell, Tenn.
Phone 869-3735

Elder Clifford Brantley
Brown School Road
Maryville, Tenn.
Phone 982-3735

Elder Hugh E. Brummitt
1329 Brown Avenue
Knoxville, Tenn.
Phone 546-7700

Elder Joe Bush
Corryton, Tenn.
Phone 687-7018

Elder Noble Clawson
Route # 4
Speedwell, Tenn.

Elder Albert Davis
Speedwell, Tenn.
Phone 869-3596

Elder Toni Eastridge
Louisville, Tenn.
Rt. # 3
Phone 983-1068

Elder Alvin Graves
Route # 3
Lenoir City, Tenn.

Elder Joe Irving
Gibson Station, Virginia

Elder Walter Lyons
1602 Garfield Street
Alcoa, Tenn.
Phone 984-3207

Elder Lenville Meyers
715 Scott Street
Monroe, Michigan

Elder J. C. Monday
Speedwell, Tenn.

Elder Shirdan Moore
Knoxville, Tenn.

Elder John Oliver
Bean Station, Tenn.

Elder R. H. Pettit
4907 Jacksboro Pike
Knoxville, Tenn.

Elder Claude Rosson
Route # 4
New Tazewell, Tenn.
Phone 626-3168

Elder Parnick Shelton
Corryton, Tenn.
Phone 687-6142

Elder W. M. Sparks
Speedwell, Tenn.
Phone 562-7997

Elder Charles Taylor
101 Rose Street
Lenoir City, Tenn.
Phone 986-8172

Elder Leonard White
LaFollette, Tenn.
Phone 562-5667

Elder Clay Widner
101 West Norris Street
Norris, Tenn.

Elder John E. Godfrey
Victorville, California

Elder Robert Walker
Knoxville, Tenn.

145

LICENTIATES

Brother Clyde H. Abbott
Knoxville, Tenn.

Brother Roscoe Branscomb
Speedwell, Tenn.

Brother Ray Walker
Knoxville, Tenn.

Brother Odell Carpenter
Maryville, Tennessee

Brother Spurgeon Thompson
Gibson Station, Virginia

RULES OF DECORUM

1. The churches composing the Powell's Valley Association shall not be confined to any set rules as to specific number of Messengers they shall have in the body, but shall have the right to name in their letters as many as they choose, and in addition all orderly members of and of the churches being present be entitled to seats in the body as Messengers of their respective churches, with all the rights and privileges of the same.

2. The Messengers thus assembled shall be denominated the Powell's Valley Primitive Baptist Association.

3. For the purpose of historical information and statistical edification, the Churches are required to state in letters, the number of members in fellowship, the number received by Baptism, by letter, by confession of Faith, the number dismissed, excluded and dead since last session; also the time of their meeting, their pastoral supply, and the amount of money contributed for ministers and other purposes together with any other information they deem appropriate for the edification of the saints and glory of God.

4. This Association shall have no power to answer queries, give advice, or dictate to the Churches in any case, or to lord it over God's heritage nor any power by which she can directly or indirectly fringe on the internal rights of the church or censure and try any church or member in reference to faith and practice and determine upon valigity of gospel ordinances. These things shall rest entirely with the churches; but henceforward our annual meetings shall be only for the purpose of hearing from each other, and for the worship of God and mutual comfort and edification of the Saints. To this end we reserve the privilege annually for the Third Friday in August and the two following days or at such other times as may be agreed upon with any church that may invite us having to protect our own standard, while in session, from heresay and disorder to recognize and invite any primitive Baptist minister or any lay brother to worship with us that may deem proper; to request the brethren of our body to visit other churches or bodies in our belief with whom we may desire to culture Christian fellowship; to publish in a minute of our proceedings.

5. Each session of the body shall have a Moderator and Clerk who shall hold office until re-elected.

6. Any order member of any church belonging to this body, when convened, being present shall be eligible to elect on as Moderator and Clerk or to sit on any committee appointed by the same.

7. In all election or questions that may be necessary to determine by vote, the vote shall be taken by churches, each church being entitled to three votes for any number less than one hundred, and one additional vote for every fifty or fraction thereof above the first hundred, but the Messengers of each church may divide their vote as they see proper.

8. All elections or questions coming to vote shall be determined by a majority vote cast, and it shall be the only duty of the minority to acquiesce in the decision thus reached.

9. If new churches desire to be admitted to this union they shall petition by letter and messengers and if voted for and recommended by one or more sister churches for her Presbytery constitutioning them, as orthodox and orderly they shall be received by the vote of the body and manifested by the Moderator giving the Messengers the right hand of fellowship.

10. Any motion or resolution clearly inconsistent with the above rules shall be promptly ruled out of order unless withdrawn by the mover.

11. Any Messenger being ruled out of order by the Moderator shall have the right to appeal to the body on the question of order, and if sustained shall be allowed to proceed, but if not take his seat.

12. Our meeting being held in the name of Christ and the worship of God; each Messenger is expected to observe due and proper therein.

13. It will not be considered good for any Messenger whose name has been enrolled as such to abruptly break off or absent himself from the Association without leave.

14. The Moderator shall be entitled to the same privilege of speech as other members provided the chair is filled.

15. The minutes of the Association shall be read and approved by the body and signed by the Moderator before adjourning.

16. The Association shall be opened and closed by prayer.

17. Amendments to these may be made at any time by a majority of the union voting by churches when they deem it necessary, provide such amendments do not compromise the sovereignty of the churches nor have tendency to give body undue power or jurisdiction over them.

ARTICLES OF FAITH

Article 1. We believe in only one true living God, as He is revealed to us in the Holy Scriptures - Father, Son, and Holy Ghost.

Article 2. We believe that the Scriptures of the old and new Testaments are the words of God and the only rule of all-saving knowledge and obedience.

Article 3. We believe in the doctrine of election according to the foreknowledge of God.

Article 4. We believe in the doctrine of original sin.

Article 5. We believe in man's impotency to rescue himself from the fallen state he is in, by his own will or ability.

Article 6. We believe that sinners are justified in the sight of God only by the imputed righteousness of Jesus Christ.

Article 7. We believe the elect, according to the foreknowledge of God will be called, converted, regenerated, and sanctified by the Holy Spirit.

Article 8. We believe the saints will persevere and never fall finally away.

Article 9. We believe that baptism and the Lord's Supper are ordinances of Jesus Christ, and that true believers are the only subject of these ordinances, and that the true mode of baptism is by immersion. We believe also that feet washing is an example of Jesus Christ and should be kept by his deciples until his second coming.

Article 10. We believe in the Resurrection of the dead and the General Judgement.

Article 11. We believe that the punishment of the wicked will be everlasting and that the joys of the righteous will be eternal.

Article 12. We believe that no minister has the right to administer the ordinances, except those who have been regularly baptized and called of God, and come under the imposition of hands of the presbytery.

148

Verda (Wilder) Brewer

Verda (Wilder) Brewer was united in marriage to Walter Brewer, while she was young and to this union was born several children. Sister Verda professed a hope and joined Pleasant Hill Primitive Baptist Church in June of 1921, and remained a member there until God called her home. She was the daughter of the late Elder & Mrs. Jim Matt Wilder. She is survived by her children, her grandchildren, her husband, one brother, Hollis Wilder, Berthat (Wilder) Harrison, Euretha Wilder, Claudia Wilder, Bennie Mae Wilder, and a host of relatives and friends.

Mrs. Lulu Estella Moneyham Toliver

Mrs. Lulu Estella Moneyham Toliver, 91, of Route 3, New Tazewell, Tennessee, passed away at Claiborne County Hospital at 1:15 P.M. Thursday, November 22, 1973. She was a member of Pleasant Point Baptist Church of New Tazewell. Survivors: Step sons, Milt Toliver of Sharps Chapel, Zan Toliver of Knoxville, Walter and Clarence Toliver of Mosheim, Jasper Toliver of Midway and Aaron Toliver of New Tazewell. Funeral services were held on November 25, 1973, at Coffeys Funeral Home with Elder Tony Eastridge and Elder Claude Rosson officiating. Interment in Pleasant Point Cemetery. Grandsons were used as pallbearers.

Dalis Ausmus Moyers

Dalis Ausmus Moyers, was born January 5, 1901, departed this life April 25, 1974, being 73 years old. She was married to Charles Moyers and to this union was born 3 children Wade, Gene and Kathryn. Her husband preceded her in death. Sister Dalis professed a Hope at an early age and joined Pleasant Hill Primitive Baptist Church May 1922, where she remained a member until God called her home. She is survived by her three children and some grandchildren; also one sister Edna (Ausmus) Davis, Curt, Floyd and Dr. Cas Ausmus, Sr. and a host of relatives and friends.

Edward Langston Sharpe

Edward Langston Sharpe, Age 32, died May 27, 1974. He attended Kirkwood Baptist Church until moving to Florida. He attended Bayshore Baptist Church after moving there. He was a veteran of the U. S. Air Force. Survivors: Two daughters, Sylinia and Maria Sharpe of Seminole, Florida, mother Zelma Sharpe of Clearwater, Fla., 2 brothers, R. H., Jr. of Atlanta, Georgia, Randolph of Knoxville; 1 sister Sherry Travis Old of Clearwater, Florida. Funeral services were held at Rose Chapel, Elder Hugh Brummitt officiating. Interment Lynnhurst Cemetery. Pallbearers, Donald Sharp, C. E. Goin, Tommy Langston, Robert Elwood, David Sharp, Ed Sharp, Wayne Gentry.

Mrs. Allie Collins Williams

Mrs. Allie Collins Williams was born January 29, 1904, passed away at her home Route #3 New Tazewell, June 8, 1974. She was united in marriage to George Williams April 21, 1928. To this union 2 children was born Annette and Roena which preceeded her in death. She leaves to mourn her passing, husband, George Williams, 2 sisters Eva Collins, Lennie Keck, 3 brothers Esco, Arlis and Dewey Collins all of New Tazewell, Tennessee. Several nieces and nephews, also a host of relatives and friends. She professed faith in Christ at an early age. She joined Pleasant Point Primitive Baptist Church in 1939 and was baptised by Elder Verlin Graves, and was a faithful member until her death. We loved her, but God loved her best. Written by her husband.

O. R. Parrott

It is with bowed heads and sad hearts that we announce the passing of our dearly beloved brother O. R. (Big Boy) Parrott. He was born, April 22, 1900 and died January 22, 1974.

He was married to Miss Mamie Lynch on July 9, 1920. To this union was born three children, Tilman, Carl, and June. Six grandchildren, one preceded him in death, three great grandchildren.

He professed faith in Christ in 1929 and in June of the same year at the waters edge he joined the church and was baptised and lived a faithful member until death.

On January 24, 1974, his body was carried to the church at Davis Chapel, his home church, at 2 P.M. The funeral orations were delivered by Elder Joe Bush and Elder Leonard White and under dark skies and downpour of rain his body was lain to rest in Sunrise Cemetery to await the dawn of a new day. He is still living in our hearts.

Lela Rachel (Bryant) Brittian Gibson

Our beloved Lela Gibson of Gibson Station Virginia, passed away November 7, 1973, at the age of 76 years old.

She professed faith in Christ at an early age and joined the Church at Gibson Station where she remained a faithful member until death.

She was the daughter of George and Amanda Bryant, and Granddaughter of George Southern, who donated the ground for our dear Primitive Baptist Church, more than one hundred years ago.

She was first married to Charlie Brittian at an early age, and to this union were born two children, Irene Dalton, and George Brittian. In later years she married John S. Gibson, and when death came, she left to mourn her loss, the two children, five grandchildren, and five great grandchildren. Funeral services were held at Gibson Station Primitive Baptist Church, with Elder Leonard White, and Elder Everett Berry, officiating. Interment in Southern Cemetery.

All who knew "Aunt Lee" loved her and she will be missed by children, her Church, and her friends.

"We loved you Aunt Lee, but God loved you best."

Edna Adkinson

Mrs. Hallie Russell

Mrs. Hallie Russell of Speedwell, Tenn. was born May 20, 1911, passed away December 28, 1973 at the Harlan Appalachian Hospital in Kentucky. She was a member of the Monroe, Michigan Primitive Baptist Church and also a deacon. She leaves to mourn her passing, her husband, Ditsy Russell, one son, Ralph Russell of Monroe, Michigan, two daughters Mrs. James H. Branscomb of Speedwell, Tenn., Mrs. Richard Brown of Monroe, Michigan, one daughter preceded her in death, eight grandchildren, one great grandson, two sisters, one brother.

Funeral services was held at the Pleasant Hill Baptist Church with the Elders, Albert Davis, Bill Sparks and J. C. Monday. Coffey's of Tazewell in charge. She was laid to rest in the family cemetery of Speedwell, Tenn. We loved you so much Mother. Home will never be the same but we have a hope to meet you some sweet day.

Joshua L. Drummonds

Joshua L. Drummonds was born April 19, 1888, and departed this life March 14, 1974 in the Memorial Hospital in Monroe, Michigan. Uncle Josh had been in ill health for three years, and in a serious condition for three weeks. He bore his illness with patience. Many times he would tell his family he was just waiting to go home.

He professed faith in Christ at an early age and joined the Primitive Baptist Church at Cedar Springs December, 1907. He and Aunt Delia were ordained deacon and deaconess November 23, 1913. He served as a faithful member and deacon until he was stricken with a heart attack in 1956. He moved to Monroe in 1956, but every year he was back home for the feet washing and communion until about four years ago. His mind was always back home with the church. He would talk and cry about how much he missed the old home church.

Uncle Josh married Delia Meyers May 26, 1912. She preceded him in death July 27, 1947. Three children were born to this union. Velma preceded him in death in March, 1939. He leaves two children to mourn his passing: Lloyd, Monroe, Mich. and Mrs. Robert (Alene) Campbell, Plymouth, Mich. There are 7 grandchildren: Jack and Glen Drummonds, Westland, Mich., Mrs. Jerry (Pansy) Smith, Pleasant Hill, Illinois, Melissa and Ralph Campbell, Plymouth, Mich.; Mrs. Ralph (Cornelia) Russell, Monroe, Mich.; and Richard Sowders, LaSalle, Mich.; ten great grandchildren, and a host of other relatives and friends.

Funeral services were held from the Coffey Morturary Chapel March 17, 1974 with Elders William Sparks and James Branscomb officiating. Music was rendered by a nephew, Wayne Poore; songs by nephews and nieces, the Bailey Family.

Pallbearers were: Isom Drummonds, Lonnie Meyers, Odra Drummonds, Durward Drummonds, Earl Poore, and William Poore.

Burial was in the Drummonds Cemetery.

John Morgan Collins

John Morgan Collins, age 68, departed this life Friday, March 8, 1974. He was a member of the Lenoir City Primitive Baptist Church. He is survived by his wife, Mrs. Annie Duggan Collins; Daughters, Mrs. Ralph Martin of Arizona, Mrs. Cecil Garner, Mrs. Joe Woodford, Mrs. Gene Vineyard, Mrs. Wayman Crawley. Sons, Marion, John M. Jr., George Arnold, Lloyd Lee, Gary, along with several grandchildren. Sisters; Mrs. Lee Parris, Mrs. Maude Parris, Mrs. Polly Kelly, and Mrs. Frances Lane. One brother; Scott Collins.

Funeral services were held Monday, March 11, 1974 with Elder Charles Taylor officiating. His body was laid to rest in the Lenoir City Memorial cemetery where it awaits the Resurrection Morning.

Jack C. Robinson

Jack C. Robinson, age 71, departed this life December 17, 1974. He was a member and Deacon of the Lenoir City Primitive Baptist Church. He is survived by his companion, sister Cora Robinson; one son, Eldon (Lum) Robinson; daughter-in-law, Fotchie Robinson; six grandchildren, Phoebe, Jack, Kristi, John, Mark, and Wade Robinson; three sisters, Mrs. Adelaide Tinnell, Mrs. Beulah Smith, and Marjorie Miller.

Funeral services were held at Click Funeral Home and his body was laid to rest in Lakeview Cemetery to await the call of his Savior. Brother Jack will be sadly missed by those he loved both in and out of the Church. Elder Charles Taylor and Rev. Charles Redmond officiated at the funeral.

Robert Paul Munsey

Robert Paul Munsey, age 59, passed away at his home on October 21, 1973, near Powder Springs. He professed faith in Christ at an early age and joined the Black Fox Primitive Baptist Church where he remained a member until death. He leaves to mourn his passing: Daughter, Mrs. Helen Graves, sons: Harold and Ronnie Munsey; Brothers: Bud, Luther, and Clarence Muncey; Sisters: Mrs. Hattie Bailey, Mrs. Rosie Bailey, Mrs. Flossie Frye, and Mrs. Cora Munsey; four grandchildren. Funeral services were conducted on October 24, 1973, at Black Fox Baptist Church with Elder Albert Davis officiating. Interment was in Cabbage Cemetery.

151

Tenn. Mrs. Ruby Keck, Morristown, Tenn., Mrs. Azalee Cook, Clinton, Tenn., and Mrs. Edith Houston, Knoxville, Tenn. Three sons, Clyde and Clifford of Sharps Chapel, Tenn. and Walter of Pulaski, Tenn. Twenty-one grandchildren and twenty-two great grandchildren. She joined Oak Grove Primitive Baptist Church in 1938. She loved her church dearly. Funeral services were held at Oak Grove Primitive Baptist Church Sept. 24, 1973. Elder Albert Davis officiated. The interment was in the Johnson Cemetery.

"We saw our dear Mother fading like a flower,
But she tried so hard to stay.
We nursed her with tender care
Until God called her away.
Although the world in which she lives
is free from care and pain,
Our world would be like heaven
if we had her back again.

It is only human we want her back,
But this we know is true, she can never
return to us but we can go to her.
We feel like our loss is Heaven's gain."

— Written by the children

Our dearest loved one passed away,
A precious one from us has gone.
A voice we loved is stilled.
A place is vacant in our home that never can be filled.
I do not need a special day to bring you to my mind.
The day I do not think of you are very hard to find.

Sadly missed by children,

Harold, Helen and Ronnie

Grace Boles Smith

Grace Boles Smith, born August 1, 1898, in Luttrell, Tennessee was married to the late Frank H. Smith, September 5, 1923. She passed away September 2, 1973 at 7:30 A.M. at St. Mary's Hospital. A member of Rocky Dale Primitive Baptist Church.

Survivors one son, Harold H. Smith; Odenton, Maryland; three daughters: Mrs. Bobbye Satterfield and Mrs. Maxine McKelvey of Corryton, Tennessee; Mrs. Nadine Powell of Marietta, Georgia. Eight grandchildren and two great grandchildren, several neices and nephews.

Funeral was Tuesday, September 4, at 1:30 P.M. at Stevens Chapel with Elder Hugh Brummitt, Elder Everett Berry and Elder Parnick Shelton officiating. Interment in Lynnhurst Cemetery.

She was so kind and loving, we all miss her so much.

Wanda Crumpley Clapp

Wanda Crumply Clapp, born March 5, 1910, passed away 2:45 A.M. October 27, 1973 at St. Mary's Hospital. She was a member of Rocky Dale Primitive Baptist Church. Survivors: husband, Ralph Clapp; daughters: Miss Bobbie Clapp, Mrs. Charles, Myrtle, Bryant; Mrs. Richard, Betty, Livingston; Mrs. Gordon, Sharon, Cantrell; all of Corryton; son, Roy Clapp of Chattanooga; Six grandchildren Brother, Archie Crumpley; sisters: Mrs. Gettys, Johnnie, Cannon and Mrs. Lon, Opal, Clapp. Services were held at Stevens Mortuary with Elder Hugh Brummitt and Elder Everett Berry officiating. Interment in Holston View Memory Gardens. Precious memories will remain forever.

Joseph Fate Dossett

Joseph Fate Dossett, age 71, 3606 East Marklin Avenue, Kokomo, Indiana born Sept. 15, 1902 in Sharps Chapel, Tenn. passed away at 9:30 a.m. Wednesday January 2, 1974 following an apparent heart attack. He was the son of John and Alice Graves Dossett. He professed faith in christ at an early age. He was married in 1925 to Rheba Kitts who survives. Surviving with the wife and father of Kokomo are three sisters, Mrs. Kenneth (Sarah) Brantlye of Sharps Chapel, Tenn., Mrs. Hobert (Goldia) White and Mrs. Eva Welling both of Kokomo. Three brothers, Cornelius and Vaughn of Kokomo and Matthew Dossett of Muncie, Indiana. A son, three brothers and one sister preceded him in death. Final resting place Albright Cemetery in Kokomo, Indiana.

Livia Johnson

Livia Johnson was born Aug. 13, 1895 and departed this life Sept. 22, 1973 at Claiborne County Hospital. She was married to Isaac Johnson Oct. 16, 1915 and to this union ten children were born. One preceded her in death, Ruble Johnson at the age of 18 years on Aug. 3, 1938. Her husband also preceded her in death on June 18, 1968. Survivors are six daughters, Mrs. Minnie Rogers, Mrs. Delta Hatmaker, Mrs. June Cook all of Sharps Chapel,

My Dear and Precious Brothers and Sisters in the Lord,

I have been chosen to write a circular letter for this association, which to many is something new but has been done by many in the past. When first used it was placed in the U.S. mail and circulated for a year hoping to find others of the same belief. So this letter is intended to circulate and reach all the churches of our association.

First, let's notice a few fundamental principles that God will not change and men cannot change.

God by his position is sovereign - this means He has a right to do as He will.

In Power HE is supreme.
In Knowledge HE is perfect.

He does not increase or diminish in knowledge or power as conditions change. "I do my will in Heaven and on earth and there is none who can stop me." He is telling us that we have no right to question him. Why?

Do you think God is confused and his plans frustrated and that after all man must take over or all will be lost?

Another fundamental: In Adam all died, then all are dead. Do you think the dead must take the first step in salvation? I pray, tell me, what can the dead do to live?

The Holy Spirit will find all the members of the Church of the first born. That Church will all be found and saved, even if the preacher is a little late. Jesus said, "All that the Father give me shall come to me and I will raise him up at the last day", all in number and all in substance.

I trust that all of our churches will love one another Churches, hold up the hands of your pastors because they so much need you.

In Christian ties, the very least of you all.

Elder Leonard White

STATISTICAL TABLE

CHURCHES	DELEGATES	COMMUNION TIME	REGULAR MEETING TIME	PRINTING MINUTES	TOTAL MEMBERSHIP	DECEASED	EXCLUDED	DISMISSED	RELATIONSHIP	BAPTISM	RECEIVED BY LETTER	RESTORED
Black Fox	Bros. Dale Capps, Bennie Capps; Sisters Mary Ruth Capps, Flossie Capps, Naomia Cabbage, Jessee Cabbage	Sunday after Second Sat. in June	Second and Third Sat. night and Sunday	15.00	88	1	0	0	0	1	0	0
Bradens Chapel	Letter Received - No Delegate present	First Sat. and Sunday in June	First Sat. and Sunday in each month	10.00	143	0	0	0	0	1	0	0
Brantley's Chapel	Elder Clifford Brantley, Brothers; Jeff Ellison, Everette Brantley, Daniel Brantley, Jerry McBee, Sisters: Barsha Brantley, Mildred Brantley, Linda Brantley, Sarah Brantley	Second Sunday in July	Each Sunday and Sunday night	25.00	86	0	1	5	5	1	0	0
Cedar Springs	Letter Received - No Delegate present	Fourth Sunday in May	Second and fourth Sat. night and Sunday	10.00	71	1	0	1	0	8	0	0
Davis Chapel	Brother James S. Heatherly; Sisters: Ruth Heatherly, Mamie Parrott, Ruby Hobbs, Debbie Hobbs, Mollie McCarty	Sunday after third Sat. in June	Third Sat. night and Sunday Every Sunday night	20.00	143	1	0	0	1	3	0	0
Gethsemane	Elder Glenn Abbott, Brothers: C. H. Godfrey, Tom Carmichael, Ray Godfrey; Sisters Billie Godfrey, June Carmichael, Mary Godfrey, Myrtle Cook	Fourth Sunday in May and Oct.		20.00	32							

155

Church								Members	Amount	Regular Meeting	Associational Meeting
Gibson Station — Elders: Joe Irwin Brothers: Spurgeon Thompson, Franklin Jones; Sisters: Jean Thompson, Mettie Thompson, Fannie Jones, Evelyn Maples, Edna Atkinson, Mossie Cottrell, Susie Shofener	0	0	3	1	0	1	1	93	25.00	First Sat. and Sat. night in each month	Second Sunday in June
Headrick Chapel — Elders: Shirdan Moore, Robert Walker; Brothers: Bill Cook, Clyde H. Abbott, Sr., Sister Grace Abbott		1	0	1	0	0	110	20.00	Sunday following first Saturday	First Sunday in May and Oct.
Kirkwood — Elders: H. E. Brummitt, Walter Lyons; Brothers: J. L. Sharp, C. A. Sharp; Sisters: Ruby Brummitt, Evelyn Sharp, Frieda Sharp, Estell Petree Sharp	0	0	0	0	0	0	100	30.00	Every Sunday morning	Last Sunday in April
Lenoir City — Elders: Charles Taylor, Alvin Graves; Brothers: Henry Chamberlain, Scott Collins, Hubert Spoons, Raymond Wilkerson, Millard Wilkerson, Clyde Abbott; Sisters: Estie Chamberlain, Ruby Williams, Annie Spoons, Ella Fields, Cora Hill, Jo Collins, Betty Abbott, Agnes Taylor	1	6	0	0	2	3	155	35.00	Every Sunday and Sunday night	Sunday after third Sat. in May
Monroe, Michigan — Letter Received - No Delegate present	0	0	0	2	0	1	12	10.00	Third Sunday	Sunday after the third Sat. in July
Noeton — Elder John Oliver; Brothers: Carroll Oliver, Charlie Collins; Sisters: Ruth Oliver, Mildred Oliver	0	3	0	0	0	0	35	20.00	Third Sat. and Sun. of each month	Third Sunday in May and Sept.
Oak Grove — Elder Toni Eastridge; Brother Leonard Eastridge; Sister Frances Eastridge	2	3	2	1	0	1	296	25.00	First Sat. night and Sunday of each month	First Sunday in May
Pleasant Hill — Elder Albert Davis, Brother Glenn Davis; Sister Audra Davis	0	8	0	0	0	2	105	30.00	Fourth Sat. and Sunday of each month	Sunday after fourth Sat. in June

Church	Officers									Value	Meeting time	Association
Pleasant Point	Brother: George Williams	0	0	2	0	0	0	2	117	15.00	First Sat. night and third Sunday morning	Sunday after first Sat. in July
Rocky Dale	Elders: Everette Berry, William Berry, Joe Bush, Parnick Shelton; Brothers: W. H. Taylor, Ralph Clapp, Dennis Branson, Sisters: Trula Berry, Norma Jean Bush, Myrtle Bryant, Fay Collett, Lou Emma Taylor	0	0	4	1	0	0	2	122	30.00	Each Sunday and Sunday night	Sunday after the second Sat. in May

CHURCH	COUNTY	PASTOR	CLERK	ADDRESS
Black Fox	Grainger	Elder Alvin Graves	Bennie Capps Flossie Capps, Asst.	Box 91, Maynardville, Tenn. 37807 Maynardville, Tenn. 37807
Bradens Chapel	Union	Elder Noble Clawson Elder J. C. Monday, Asst.	Leecy Sparks	Speedwell, Tenn,
Brantley's Chapel	Blount	Elder W.M. (Bill) Berry Elder Clifford Brantley, Asst.	Daniel Brantley D. C. Brantley, Asst.	Rt. 10, Mint Road, Maryville, Tn. 37801 2020 Bittle Road, Maryville, Tn. 37801
Cedar Springs	Claiborne	Elder Jimmy Branscomb	Eula Good Bonnie Miracle, Asst.	New Tazewell, Tenn,
Davis Chapel	Campbell	Elder Joe Bush Elder Leonard White, Asst.	Ruth Heatherly Lassie Ellison, Asst,	Rt. 1, LaFollette, Tn. 37766 Rt. 1, LaFollette, Tn. 37766
Gethsemane	Knox	Elder Walter Lyons	Tom Carmichael	729 Frank St, Knoxville, Tenn.
Gibson Station	Lee County, Va.	Elder Leonard White Elder Everette Berry, Asst.	Mossie Cottrell Lucille Fleemon, Asst.	Box 288, Harrogate, Tenn. Ewing, Va,
Headricks Chapel	Sevier	Elder Walter Lyons Elder Robert Walker, Asst,	Clyde Abbott	Rt. 7, Sevierville, Tenn.
Kirkwood	Knox	Elder Leonard White	Estelle Petree Sharp Alice T. Powers, Asst.	Rt. 27, Emory Rd., Knoxville, Tn. 2923 Clearview Ave., N.E. Knoxville, Tn.
Lenoir City	Loudon	Elder Charles Taylor	Scott Collins	705 W. 5th Ave. Lenoir City, Tenn. 37771

Church	County	Pastor	Clerk	Address
Monroe, Michigan	Monroe	Elder Lemvil Myers	Gertrude Zwack Roxie Drummonds, Asst.	1825 Spaulding Rd, Monroe, Mich. 606 Ky. Ave. Monroe, Mich. 48161
Noeton	Grainger	Elder Gilbert Atkins Elder John Oliver, Asst.	Elder John Oliver Bessie Collins, Asst.	Rt. 2, Bean Station, Tenn. Rt. 5, Morristown, Tenn.
Oak Grove	Union	Elder J. C. Monday Elder Noble Clawson, Asst.	Betty P. Sharp Mary Ann Walker, Asst.	Sharps Chapel, Tenn. Sharps Chapel, Tenn.
Pleasant Hill	Claiborne	Elder Alvin Graves Elder Albert Davis, Asst.	William Branscomb Verlin Edwards, Asst.	Speedwell, Tenn. Speedwell, Tenn.
Pleasant Point	Claiborne	Elder Parnick Shelton Elder Claude Rosson, Asst.	Elder Claude Rosson	Rt. 4, New Tazewell, Tenn. 37825
Rocky Dale	Knox	Elder Hugh E. Brummitt	Edward Collett Avrell Graves, Asst.	Rt. 1, Luttrell, Tenn. Rt. 3, Corryton, Tenn.

1975 MINUTES

of the

POWELL VALLEY ASSOCIATION
OF PRIMITIVE BAPTIST

KIRKWOOD PRIMITIVE BAPTIST CHURCH
ELDER EVERETT BERRY, PASTOR

Held with the Sister Church of Kirkwood in Knox County, Tennessee

AUGUST 15, 16, 17, 1975

THE ONE HUNDRED AND FIFTY SIXTH
ANNUAL SESSION OF THE POWELL VALLEY ASSOCIATION
OF
PRIMITIVE BAPTIST

HELD WITH THE SISTER CHURCH AT KIRKWOOD
IN KNOX COUNTY, TENNESSEE

AUGUST 15, 16, 17, 1975

NEXT SESSION WILL BE HELD WITH THE SISTER CHURCH
AT
GIBSON STATION
IN LEE COUNTY, VIRGINIA
TO BEGIN ON FRIDAY, BEFORE THE THIRD SATURDAY
IN AUGUST, 1976
AT 10:30 A.M.

OFFICERS

Elder Albert Davis. . . . . .Moderator
Speedwell, Tennessee Ph. 869-3596

Elder Hugh E. Brummitt. . . . . Assistant Moderator
1329 Brown Avenue, Knoxville, Tennessee Ph. 546-7700

Bro. W. H. Taylor . . . . Clerk
Route 27, Knoxville, Tennessee Ph. 922-2143

Bro. Bennie Capps. . . . . .Assistant Clerk
Maynardville, Tennessee Ph. 992-5571

Friday, August 15, 1975

The one hundred and fifty sixth session of the Powell Valley Association of Primitive Baptist met with the Sister Church at Kirkwood in Knox County, Tennessee, August 15, 16, and 17th, with Moderator Albert Davis presiding.

After singing, the Moderator called for opening prayer by Elder Walter Lyons of Kirkwood Church.

The moderator called on the entire congregation to stand for a moment of silent prayer in remembrance of the three Elders who have deceased since we last met. To wit: Elder Leonard White, Elder R. H. Pettit, Elder Gilbert Atkins.

Elder Glenn Abbott then delivered the introductory sermon, speaking from the 23rd Chapter of Numbers and delivered a wonderful lesson on the thought not to attempt in word or deed beyond what God has commanded.

After a song and testimony, we were dismissed in prayer by Elder Johnny Atkins of the Oak Grove Church for a 15 minute recess.

After recess the congregation reassembled at the sound of singing.

After the song service, the Moderator called the Association to order for the business and pleaded for harmony and peace to continue through out the association. He then read a lesson from the 13th Chapter of 1st Corinthians and called for prayer by Elder Alvin Graves of the Lenoir City Church, and then called for the business of the Association as follows:

1. Moderator called for the letters of the Sister Churches to be presented to the clerk for reading. Fourteen received.

2. Call for any member present but not named, who wished to be seated as delegate to come forward. Four came and were seated, to wit:

Elder Johnny Atkins of Oak Grove
Brother Clifford Robertson of Cedar Springs
Brother Donald Sharp of Rocky Dale, and
Sister Dorothy Johnson of Gibson Station

3. Motion approved that we receive the letters present and seat the delegates.

4. Called for petitionary letters, if any.

5. Motion approved that the Association re-elect Elder Albert Davis, Moderator and Elder Hugh Brummitt as Assistant Moderator.

6. Motion approved that the Association re-elect Brother W. H. Taylor as Clerk and Brother Bennie C. Capps, assistant clerk.

7. Motion that the Moderator be authorized to appoint all the committees.

8. The Moderator, having been appointed to do so, made the following committee appointments:

Committee on Arrangements	Elder Bill Berry Brother Bill Rhymer Brother Everett Brantley
Committee on Preaching	Brother Jeff Ellison Brother Charles Collins Brother J. L. Sharp
Committee on Request	Brother Donald Sharp Brother Orice McCarty Brother Tom Carmichael
Committee on Finance	Elder Charles Taylor Brother Clyde Abbott Brother Isom Drummonds

162

9. The committees all having been appointed, the Association was adjourned until Saturday Morning when we will re-convene at 10:30 a.m. Adjourned with prayer by Elder Clifford Brantley of Brantley's Chapel Church.

Saturday, August 16, 1975

1. Saturday morning at 10:30 at the sound of singing the crowd reassembled and Elder Albert Davis sang a short song, then Elder Hugh Brummitt the Assistant Moderator spoke for a short while and gave a wonderful talk on love and fellowship and read from the 12th chapter of Ecclesiastes and called for prayer by Elder Bill Sparks.

2. The Moderator then called the Association to order for the remainder of the business by calling for any letters of Sister Churches not received Friday. Two were received. One of Noeton Church and one of Oak Grove Church. The letters of the two churches were approved and their delegates seated.

3. Moderator called for a report of the Committee on Arrangements who gave the following report, which was approved and the committee released.

Report of Committee on Arrangements-
- a. Call for roll call of delegates.
       Call for report of Committee on Preaching
- c. Call for report of Committee on Request
- d. Call for report of Committee on Finance
- e. Decide how many minutes we have printed and who shall supervise the printing and distribution of same, and how much he shall receive for his services. Also, who shall preach the introductory sermon and who will be the alternate.

Respectfully submitted,
Elder Bill Berry
Brother Bill Rhymer
Brother Everett Brantley

4. Moderator called for roll call of delegates and absentees noted.

5. Call for the report of the Committee on Preaching which was accepted and committee released.

Report of Committee on Preaching:
Friday Night: Elder Walter Lyons, Elder Clifford Brantley
Saturday: Elder Pippins of South Carolina, Elder Johnny Atkins
Saturday Night: Elder Alvin Graves, Elder Toni Eastridge
Sunday: Elder Charles Taylor, Elder Everett Berry

Respectfully submitted,
Brother Jeff Ellison
Brother J. L. Sharp
Brother Charles Collins

6. Call for report of Committee on Request who gave the following report which was accepted and the committee released.

Report of Committee on Request:
We the committee on request make the following request, that we have printed 1,000 minutes and that the Clerk supervise the printing and distribution of same and receive $50.00 for his service; we also ask that

163

the next session be held with the Sister Church at Gibson Station in Lee County, Virginia, to begin on Friday before the third Saturday in August, 1976, at 10:30 a.m. We also request that a circular letter be written and placed in the minutes and that it be written by Elder Charles Taylor, and to be on a choosing of his own.

Respectfully submitted,
Brother Donald Sharp
Brother Orice McCarty
Brother Tom Carmichael

7. Call for the report of Committee on Finance who gave the following report which was accepted and the committee released.

Church	Amount	Amount
Black Fox		$15.00
Bradens Chapel		10.00
Brantley's Chapel		25.00
Cedar Springs		10.00
Davis Chapel		20.00
Gethsemane		20.00
Gibson Station		25.00
Headricks Chapel		20.00
Kirkwood		30.00
Lenoir City		30.00
Monroe, Michigan		10.00
Noeton		20.00
Oak Grove		25.00
Pleasant Hill		30.00
Pleasant Point		15.00
Rocky Dale		30.00
	Total	$340.00
	Balance in Bank	$311.50
		$651.50
	Expenses	335.00
	Balance	$316.50

Respectfully submitted,
Elder Charles Taylor
Brother Clyde Abbott
Brother Isom Drummonds

8. Motion approved that we have printed 1,000 copies of minutes and the clerk supervise the printing and distribution of same, and that we give him $100.00 instead of $50.00 for his services.

9. Motion approved that the next session of the Association be held with the Sister Church at Gibson Station, Virginia, to begin on Friday before the third Saturday in August, 1976, at 10:30 a.m. and continue the following two days and that Elder Charles Taylor, of Lenoir City Church, deliver the introductory sermon and Elder Everett Berry be the alternate.

10. Motion approved that Elder Charles Taylor be appointed to write a circular letter to be published in the next minutes.

11. Motion approved that the churches of this Association extend to the Sister Church of Kirkwood our thanks for the welcome, kindness, friendliness and wonderful food given us while at your church and as we leave you, we all request your prayers and may God bless you all.

Elder Albert Davis, Moderator
Elder Hugh Brummitt,
Assistant Moderator
Brother W. H. Taylor, Clerk
Brother Bennie C. Capps, Assistant Clerk

Sunday, August 17, 1975

Sunday at 10:30 a.m. the house filled to overflowing. After a good song service the Moderator opened the service by reading the first chapter of Psalmist David then called for prayer by Elder Bill Berry of Rocky Dale Church.

Elder Charles Taylor of Lenoir City Church read from the book of Revelations, chapter 22 and used as his text the 17th verse: "And the Spirit and the bride say come. And let him that heareth say come. And let him that is athirst come. And whosoever will, let him take the Water of Life freely," then preaching a wonderful sermon.

Elder Everett Berry then followed, using the 22 verse of Proverbs and using as his theme, "God's deliverance of his people" and delivering a wonderful discourse.

The service was closed by singing by the congregation and much rejoicing.

CIRCULAR LETTER

On August 17, 1974, the association while in session authorized me to write a circular letter, to be inserted in the 1975 minutes, of which I am an humble servant. I trust God will give me of his spirit as I undertake to prepare this letter. I will use as a starting point, I Corinthians 3rd Chapter, 11th verse, for other foundations can no man lay than that is laid which is Jesus Christ.

Now if any man build upon this foundation Gold, Silver, Precious stones, wood, hay, stubble, every man's work shall be made manifest for the day shall declare it.

This foundation has been tested by man all down through the ages to try to make this foundation to suit themselves and to meet their conditions.

The Psalmist David says in Psalms 11th Chapter, 3rd verse, if the foundations be destroyed, what can the righteous do? This foundation was laid even before the world began. For a proof text, Ephesians first chapter and 4th verse, the weak foundations that man trust in is like the foundations that Christ spoke of in St. Luke 6:49.

The sure foundation is found in I Peter 2nd Chapter, 6th verse, wherefore also is contained in the scriptures, Behold I lay in Zion the chief cornerstone, elect precious and he that believeth on him shall not be confounded.

I trust all who read this will read your Bible prayerfully and ask God to give you his spirit that you may stand upon this foundation that was laid by the God of this universe before the world began.

May God's servants feel the importance of preaching his true word without fear of favor, trusting God in everything in all our endeavors in bounds of Christian love.

Your Brother in hope of eternal life,
Elder Albert Davis

ORDAINED MINISTERS

Elder Glenn Abbott
1510 Paris St.
Knoxville, Tenn.

Elder Johnny Atkins
Bean Station, Tenn.

Elder Johnny Ayers
New Tazewell, Tenn.

Elder Everett Berry
Route 27
Knoxville, Tenn.
Ph. 922-7004

Elder William Berry
Route 27
Knoxville, Tenn.
Ph. 922-2269

Elder J. H. Branscomb
Speedwell, Tenn.
Ph. 869-3735

Elder Clifford Brantley
Brown School Road
Maryville, Tenn.
Ph. 982-3735

Elder Hugh Brummitt
1329 Brown Ave.
Knoxville, Tenn.
Ph. 546-7700

Elder Joe Bush
Corryton, Tenn.
Ph. 687-7018

Elder Noble Clawson
Route 4
Speedwell, Tenn.
Ph. 562-2004

Elder Albert Davis
Speedwell, Tenn.
Ph. 869-3596

Elder Toni Eastridge
Route 3
Louisville, Tenn.
Ph. 983-1068

Elder Alvin Graves
Route 3
Lenoir City, Tenn.

Elder Joe Irving
Gibson Station, Va.

Elder Walter Lyons
1602 Garfield St.
Alcoa, Tenn.
Ph. 984-3207

Elder Lenville Meyers
715 Scott Street
Monroe, Mich.

Elder J.C. Monday
Speedwell, Tenn.
Ph. 562-3068

Elder Shirdan Moore
Knoxville, Tenn.

Elder John Oliver
Bean Station, Tenn.

Elder Claude Rosson
Route 4
New Tazewell, Tenn.
Ph. 626-3168

Elder Parnick Shelton
Corryton, Tenn.
Ph. 687-6142

Elder W.M. Sparks
Speedwell, Tenn.
Ph. 562-7997

Elder Charles Taylor
101 Rose Street
Lenoir City, Tenn.
Ph. 986-8172

Elder Clay Widner
Route 1
Tazewell, Tenn.

Elder John E. Godfrey
Victorville, Calif.

Elder Robert Walker
Knoxville, Tenn.

LICENTIATES

Brother Clyde H. Abbott
Route 7
Sevierville, Tenn.

Brother Roscoe Branscomb
Speedwell, Tennessee

Brother Ray Walker
Route 1
Townsend, Tenn.

Brother Odell Carpenter
Maryville, Tennessee

Brother Spurgeon Thompson
Gibson Station, Va.

RULES OF DECORUM

1. The churches composing the Powell's Valley Association shall not be confined to any set rules as to specific number of Messengers they shall have in the body, but shall have the right to name in their letters as many as they choose, and in addition all orderly members of and of the churches being present be entitled to seats in the body as Messengers of their respective churches, with all the rights and privileges of the same.

2. The Messengers thus assembled shall be denominated the Powell's Valley Primitive Baptist Association.

3. For the purpose of historical information and statistical edification, the Churches are required to state in letters, the number of members in fellowship, the number received by Baptism, by letter, by confession of Faith, the number dismissed, excluded and dead since last session; also the time of their meeting, their pastoral supply, and the amount of money contributed for ministers and other purposes together with any other information they deem appropriate for the edification of the saints and glory of God.

4. This Association shall have no power to answer queries, give advice, or dictate to the Churches in any case, or to lord it over God's heritage nor any power by which she can directly or indirectly fringe on the internal rights of the church or censure and try any church or member in reference to faith and practice and determine upon valigity of gospel ordinances. These things shall rest entirely with the churches; but henceforward our annual meetings shall be only for the purpose of hearing from each other, and for the worship of God and mutual comfort and edification of the Saints. To this end we reserve the privilege annually for the Third Friday in August and the two following days or at such other times as may be agreed upon with any church that may invite us having to protect our own standard, while in session, from heresay and disorder to recognize and invite any primitive Baptist minister or any lay brother to worship with us that may deem proper; to request the brethren of our body to visit other churches or bodies in our belief with whom we may desire to culture Christian fellowship; to publish in a minute of our proceedings.

5. Each session of the body shall have a Moderator and Clerk who shall hold office until re-elected.

6. Any order member of any church belonging to this body, when convened, being present shall be eligible to elect on as Moderator and Clerk or to sit on any committee appointed by the same.

7. In all election or questions that may be necessary to determine by vote, the vote shall be taken by churches, each church being entitled to three votes for any number less than one hundred, and one additional vote for every fifty or fraction thereof above the first hundred, but the Messengers of each church may divide their vote as they see proper.

8. All elections or questions coming to vote shall be determined by a majority vote cast, and it shall be the only duty of the minority to acquiesce in the decision thus reached.

9. If new churches desire to be admitted to this union they shall petition by letter and messengers and if voted for and recommended by one or more sister churches for her Presbytery constitutioning them, as orthodox and orderly they shall be received by the vote of the body and manifested by the Moderator giving the Messengers the right hand of fellowship.

10. Any motion or resolution clearly inconsistent with the above rules shall be promptly ruled out of order unless withdrawn by the mover.

11. Any Messenger being ruled out of order by the Moderator shall have the right to appeal to the body on the question of order, and if sustained shall be allowed to proceed, but if not take his seat.

12. Our meeting being held in the name of Christ and the worship of God; each Messenger is expected to observe due and proper therein.

13. It will not be considered good for any Messenger whose name has been enrolled as such to abruptly break off or absent himself from the Association without leave.

14. The Moderator shall be entitled to the same privilege of speech as other members provided the chair is filled.

15. The minutes of the Association shall be read and approved by the body and signed by the Moderator before adjourning.

16. The Association shall be opened and closed by prayer.

17. Amendments to these may be made at any time by a majority of the union voting by churches when they deem it necessary, provide such amendments do not compromise the sovereignty of the churches nor have tendency to give body undue power or jurisdiction over them.

ARTICLES OF FAITH

Article 1. We believe in only one true living God, as He is revealed to us in the Holy Scriptures - Father, Son, and Holy Ghost.

Article 2. We believe that the Scriptures of the old and new Testaments are the words of God and the only rule of all-saving knowledge and obedience.

Article 3. We believe in the doctrine of election according to the foreknowledge of God.

Article 4. We believe in the doctrine of original sin.

Article 5. We believe in man's impotency to rescue himself from the fallen state he is in, by his own will or ability.

Article 6. We believe that sinners are justified in the sight of God only by the imputed righteousness of Jesus Christ.

Article 7. We believe the elect, according to the foreknowledge of God will be called, converted, regenerated, and sanctified by the Holy Spirit.

Article 8. We believe the saints will persevere and never fall finally away.

Article 9. We believe that baptism and the Lord's Supper are ordinances of Jesus Christ, and that true believers are the only subject of these ordinances, and that the true mode of baptism is by immersion. We believe also that feet washing is an example of Jesus Christ and should be kept by his deciples until his second coming.

Article 10. We believe in the Resurrection of the dead and the General Judgement.

Article 11. We believe that the punishment of the wicked will be everlasting and that the joys of the righteous will be eternal.

Article 12. We believe that no minister has the right to administer the ordinances, except those who have been regularly baptized and called of God, and come under the imposition of hands of the presbytery.

Elder Gilbert Atkins

Elder Gilbert Atkins, age 70, departed this life at Baptist Hospital, Knoxville, June 11, 1975. He is survived by wife Opal Atkins, three daughters, Mrs. Pearl Hipsher, Mrs. Georgia Coffey of Bean Station, Mrs. Mamie Moody of Rutledge; five sons, Monroe of Rutledge, Albert of Bean Station, Charlie, Matthew and Bill Ray of Morristown; 35 grandchildren. He joined Noeton Primitive Baptist Church in 1952 and was ordained to the full work of the Ministry in November, 1953. He was elected assistant pastor in 1953 and served until the death of Elder Matthew Oliver. He was elected Moderator in October, 1954. Funeral services were held Saturday, June 14, at Noeton Primitive Baptist Church with Elder John Oliver, Elder Olaf Atkins, officiating. Burial in Noe's Chapel Cemetery. Sleep on Dear Father til resurrection morn, we're sure he's gone to rest, we loved him, oh so dearly, but Jesus loved him best. We loved to walk the pathways, his dear feet have trod, because those paths will lead us all home. Written by wife and family.

Mrs. Doshia Mae Collins

Mrs. Doshia Mae Collins, age 57, passed away June 25, 1975, at Morristown Hamblen Hospital after a lingering illness. Survivors, husband, Charles A. Collins of Bean Station; daughter, Mrs. Herman (Brenda) Hurst of Rt. 7 Morristown; two grandchildren, Tammy and Anthony Hurst; parents, Mr. and Mrs. Pate Atkins of Bean Station; sisters, Mrs. Irene Singleton, Mrs. Sally Bowlin of Bean Station. Funeral services were conducted at 2 p.m. Saturday, June 28, at Noeton Primitive Baptist Church where she was a member for many years, with Elder John Oliver and Elder Olaf Atkins officiating. Burial in church cemetery. Stubbelfield Mortuary of Morristown, in charge.
I saw my Dear Mother fading like a flower
She tried so hard to stay cause she knowed
We would of wanted it that way.
Although we know she is
Free from pain and sorrow
We miss you so much
Cause she was such a
loyal wife and mother

Written by the daughter

Sister Pearlie (Mayes) Graves

Sister Pearlie (Mayes) Graves was born June 9, 1903 and passed away December 29, 1974. She was married to Elder George Mayes who passed away several years ago. In 1950, she was married to James Graves, and he too preceded her in death in 1971. Sister Pearlie professed a Hope in Christ at an early age and joined the church at Pleasant Point the fourth Saturday in March, 1951. She moved her membership to Pleasant Hill Primitive Baptist Church and remained there until death. She is survived by two sisters, one brother and several nephews and nieces and a host of relatives and friends.

Mrs. Wade Sharp McCroskey

Mrs. Wade Sharp McCroskey, 51, of Knoxville, passed away December 24, 1975. She was a devoted member of Kirkwood Primitive Baptist Church. She leaves to mourn her passing a son Richard L. McCroskey; one granddaughter,

170

Christie, a brother, Hilas Sharp, and many other relatives and friends. A beautiful memorial service was conducted at Kirkwood Church by Elder Leonard White.

Dave Wilson

Dave Wilson, age 69, of Route 3, Maynardville, formerly of Goin, passed away 12:20 Wednesday, December 24, 1974, at St. Mary's Hospital. Survivors: sisters, Mrs. Eulis Keck of Knoxville, Mrs. Agnes Tolliver, Mrs. Sara England, Mrs. Nancy Redmond of Maynardville; brother, Will Wilson of Maynardville; several nieces and nephews. He was a member of the Pleasant Point Baptist Church. Funeral services 2 p.m. Saturday at the Coffey Funeral Home Chapel. Interment at the Big Barren Cemetery in Union County. Family will receive friends at the Coffey Funeral Home in Tazewell, 7 to 9 p.m. Thursday and Friday evenings.

Curtis (CC) Keck

Curtis (CC) Keck, 69, of New Tazewell died Monday, November 25, 1974, at Claiborne County Hospital. He was a prominent farmer and life long citizen of Goin Community, member of Pleasant Point Baptist Church, member of Evening Star Lodge No. 180 F&AM, Tazewell Chapter No. 162 RAM. Survivors: wife, Mrs. Mae Surber Keck, New Tazewell; daughters, Mrs. David (Mary E.) Cline, Abingdon, Va., Mrs. Jack (Nancy K.) Rose, Tullahoma, Tn., one granddaughter, Tina Rose, Tullahoma; brothers, F. G. Keck, Russell Keck, New Tazewell; sisters, Mrs. Cecil Carey, Morristown, Mrs. Loalles Robinette, Kingston, Tn., Mrs. Lavetta Crawford, Powell, Mrs. Robert Carr, New Tazewell, Mrs. Rowena Barnes, New Tazewell. Funeral services were held at 2 p.m. Wednesday at Coffey Chapel with Rev. James Loy, officiating. Burial in Keck Family Cemetery. Pallbearers: Max Carey, M. F. Carey, Raymond Keck, Doug Barnes, Clay Cupp, John Curtis Crawford, Estill Robinette, Scottie Keck. Honorary pallbearers: Members of Masonic Lodge.

Mrs. Lora C. Goin

Mrs. Lora C. Goin, age 77, New Market, passed away Monday morning in Jefferson Memorial Hospital. Widow of the late Verlin T. Goin, a member of Pleasant Point Primitive Baptist Church, Claiborne County. Survivors: sons, Hoit of New Market, Kirby of Knoxville, Wade of Charlotte, N.C.; 13 grandchildren; 17 great grandchildren; several nieces and nephews. Funeral services Wednesday at 2 p.m. Fielden's Chapel. Rev. Lee Campbell, Rev. Joel Woods officiating. Interment Jefferson Memorial Garden. Family will receive friends Tuesday from 7-9 p.m. at the funeral home. Family is at the home of a son, Hoit Goin, Route 1, New Market.

Mrs. Nettie A. Cadle

Mrs. Nettie A. Cadle, age 80, of Route 1, died at UT Hospital at 2:30 p.m. Tuesday, October 15. She is survived by her husband, Charles R. Cadle; sons Herbert of Baltimore, Alvin of Pinconning, Mich., Harold of Bradenton, Fla., Wade of Knoxville; daughters, Mrs. Okle Barr of Indiana, Mrs. Thelma Bailey of Kentucky, Mrs. Lola Johnson of Georgia; sister, Flossie Miller, Maynardville; brother, Claude Weaver, Minn.; 45 grandchildren including Donnie and Danny Murr of Sevierville; 69 great grandchildren; and six great great grandchildren. Mrs. Cadle enjoyed quilting and sewing, and was a member of the Kirkwood Primitive Baptist Church. Funeral services were at 1 p.m. Friday at Rawling's Chapel. Interment was at Maynardville where Mrs. Cadle was originally from.

Edith Leona Clawson

Edith Leona Clawson, 61, of Speedwell, died January 25, at her home. She was a member of Bradens Chapel Church. She is survived by her daughter, Mrs. Bonnie Sue Bowman of Eaton, Ohio; grandchildren, Bart, Bret and Angela, also of Eaton; father, Donnie Clawson of Speedwell; sisters, Mell Berry and Lou Bullard of Speedwell, Nadine Owens of West Carrollton, Ohio; brothers, Noble Lee (Buster) of Speedwell, P. J. and Ray of Monroe, Mich., Johnny, Earl and Roy of Ohio, and a host of nieces, nephews and friends. Funeral services were held at 1 p.m. Tuesday at Braden Chapel by Elder J. C. Monday and Elder W. M. Sparks. Burial was in Braden Cemetery. Cross Funeral Home, LaFollette was in charge of the arrangements.

Mrs. Victoria Young

Mrs. Victoria Young, 89, wife of the late Steve Young, passed away Friday night, November 1, 1974, at her home in Middlesboro, Ky. She was a former resident of Gibson Station, Va., where she joined the Gibson Station Primitive Baptist Church in February, 1926. Survivors: six daughters, Mrs. Anna Brewer of Rose Hill, Va., Mrs. Herschel Jones of Ewing, Va., Mrs. Charles Johnson of Lousville, Ky., Mrs. Baye Seale of Baltimore, Md., Mrs. Richard Loop of Monroe, Mich., Miss Mable Young of Middlesboro, Ky; one son, John Young of Ewing, Va.; 26 grandchildren; two nieces; three nephews and a host of relatives and friends. Funeral services were held at Gibson Station Primitive Baptist Church with the Rev. W. B. Bingham and Rev. Floyd Davis officiating. She was laid to rest in the Southern Cemetery.

Mossie (Shoffner) Cottrell

Mossie (Shoffner) Cottrell, our beloved sister and sister-in-Christ, Mossie Cottrell, 74 years, 11 months, two days old, passed from this life at 2 a.m. Wednesday, April 2, 1975, in St. Mary's Hospital, Knoxville, Tenn. She was born April 23, 1900, daughter of the late Elder HIram and Sarah (Braden) Shoffner of Harrogate, Tenn. Mossie was a member of the Primitive Baptist Church at Gibson Station, Va., of which she had been a faithful member for 61 years. A member of Shawanee Order of Eastern Star, where she held office of Chaplin for several years and holds the Grand Cross of Cabor in the order of Rainbow for Girls. She was united in marriage on June 24, 1918, to the late Joe Cottrell. Survivors include one son, Wilburn Cottrell, two grand children; two sisters Edna Atkinson, Maggie Sanifer, one brother Rufus Shoffner, and two half sisters, Roxie Cadle and Blanch Ramsey. Funeral services were held at the dear old Primitive Baptist Church she so dearly loved with Elder Everett Berry and Elder Bill Berry in charge. Her body was laid to rest in the family Shoffner Cemetery where she is asleep in the arms of Jesus, sleep on dear sister, we loved you but God loved you best, She will sleep that no pain shall wake, night that no morn shall break till joy shall overtake their perfect peace. All who knew our dear beloved Sister loved and adored her and will be sadly missed by her son and family and sisters and brother and grandchildren, her place and presence will be missed by her church, she will live on in our hearts and by all who knew her.

——Written by Edna Atkinson

John L. Drummonds

John L. Drummonds of 2675 Blue Bush Road, Monroe, Michigan, formerly of New Tazewell, Tenn. passed away July 21, 1975, 4:48 a.m. in Memorial Hospital in Monroe, Mich. The son of Elijah Stephen and Margaret Wilson Drummonds, he was born August 10, 1911, in New Tazewell. He married Roxie A Lynch December 14, 1932, in New Tazewell. He professed faith in Christ and joined the Primitive Baptist Church at Meyers Grove and was baptised. He later moved his membership to 1234 Kentucky Avenue Church in Monroe, Michigan. Surviving are his wife Roxie A. Drummonds, one daughter Mrs. Roman S. (Elgie) Grabitz of Monroe, Mich. one son, William H. Drummonds of Phoenix, N.Y., one granddaughter, Mary Ann Grabitz, one grandson, Johnnie Ray Patterson of Monroe Michigan, two brothers Callie Drummonds of Morristown, Tenn., Isom Drummonds of Tazewell; four sisters, Mrs. Jake (Bertha) Drummonds, Mrs. Hurbert (Zora) McBee, Corryton, Tenn., Mrs. Arthur (Rutha) Henry, of Monroe, Mich., Mrs. Willis (Cretic) Atkins of Erie, Mich. Proceeding him in death, four brothers, William, Manie, Leonard, and Curtis Drummonds; two sisters, Mrs. Lee (Mae) Alston, Miss Mollie Gertrude Drummonds. Services were conducted in Earle Little Funeral Home by Elder Linvil Meyers in Monroe, Mich., and Elder James Branscomb and Elder Alvin Graves at Meyers Grove Primitive Baptist Church. Coffey's Funeral Home in charge. Pallbearers: Wallace and Larry Lynch, Fay Neely, Dillace McGeorge, Johnnie Ray Patterson, Charles Harrell and Bob Drummonds. His body was laid to rest in the Drummonds Cemetery, New Tazewell, Tenn. We love you so very much darling, Home will never be the same, but through the mercies of God we all hope to meet you in the Glory Lane. Sadly missed by wife, children, grandchildren, and all who knew him. You will never be forgotten.

James J. Johnson

James J. Johnson, age 84, passed away at his home Sharp's Chapel, Tenn. 5:30 p.m. Wednesday, December 11, 1974. He was a member of Oak Grove Baptist Church since 1918. Survivors: wife, Mrs. Thelma B. Johnson, Sharp's Chapel; daughters, Mrs. Edna Cadle, Maryville, Mildred Johnson, Sharp's Chapel; sons, Rina Johnson, Maryville, Winfred Johnson, Landon, Ky.; sister, Mrs. Beatrice Linde, Knoxville; brothers, W. T. Johnson, Tazewell, Clay Johnson, Sharp's Chapel; five grand children; four great grandchildren. Funeral services at 2 p.m. at Oak Grove Baptist Church with Elder Albert Davis officiating, interment Johnson Cemetery. We miss you Dad, in the morning when day has just begun, we miss you in the evening with the setting of the sun. Our home it was so happy before you went away. The sky was so sunny, so suddenly turned to gray. But Heaven we know is brighter Dad, with your kind eyes of Blue and some day when this life is over again we'll be with you. Wife, Thelma Johnson and children.

Eva Mae McMahan

Eva Mae McMahan, age 48, 222 Boardman Avenue, Maryville, Tenn., born August 15, 1926, in Sharps Chapel, Tenn., passed away at 11:00 a.m. Sunday, June 8, 1975, at Blount Memorial Hospital. She was the daughter of Hughie A. Cox and the late Sally Ousley Cox; stepmother, Albie Cox. Survivors: husband, Glenn McMahan Sr.; daughter Lois Albright; three sons, Glenn (Sonny) McMahan Jr., Roger Dale and Kenneth Andrew McMahan; sister, Ada McBee; one deceased sister, Ruby Cox Welch; three grandchildren, and many friends.

Funeral Services were held at Smith's Mortuary Chapel, Tuesday, June 10, 1975. Interment Brantley's Chapel Cemetery, Maryville, Tenn. Elder Clifford Brantley and Elder William Berry, officiating.

It broke our hearts to lose you, But you did not go alone.
For part of us went with you The day God called you home.
The world may change from year to year, And friends from day to day,
But never will the one we love, From memory pass away.
The love we shared together Are the memories we hold dear.
And the happiness you gave us, Keeps forever near.

> ——At Rest But Not Forgotten
> Glenn (Sonny) McMahan Jr.
> Ada McBee

Edith Magnolia Boruff

Miss Edith Boruff, of Ridgeview Road, Rt. 1, Corryton, Tenn., was born June 26, 1916, and passed away unexpectedly Friday evening, February 14, 1975, at her home. She professed faith in Christ, August 12, 1937, and joined Rocky Dale Primitive Baptist Church on May 3, 1942. She was baptised by Elder Leonard White, June 28, 1942.

She was the oldest daughter of the late Marion and Lucy Boruff. She leaves to mourn her passing one brother, James Boruff, Knoxville; six sisters, Mrs. Clay (Ruth) Russell, Knoxville, Mrs. Josh (Ima Lee) Stapleton, Powell, Mrs. Glen (Beatrice) Johnson, Corryton, Mrs. Edward (Fay) Collett, Luttrell, Mrs. Charles (Christine) Earl, Strawberry Plains, Mrs. Moses (Opal) Norton, Corryton; six nieces; eleven nephews and thirteen great nieces and nephews.

Services were at 2:30 p.m. on Monday at Rocky Dale Primitive Baptist Church with Elder Hugh Brummitt and Elder Everett Berry officiating. Her body was lain to rest, beside her mother and father, in Clapp's Chapel Cemetery, as the beautiful warm sun shined down from above, to await the second coming of our blessed Savior.

When Jesus called you quickly went, without a pain or tear;
It breaks our heart each time we think, not one of us were near.
But when He called for you to go, He knew you were alone;
The King, so gently, took your hand, and led you to His home.

Sarah (Sallie) Davis

Sarah (Sallie) Davis was born November 2, 1882, and passed away November 7, 1974, being 92 years old. She was married to Samuel Davis in 1900 and to this union was born 11 children. She professed faith in Christ at an early age and joined the Primitive Baptist Church at Black Fox where she remained a member. She leaves to mourn her passing two daughters: Mrs. Goldie Gose, Knoxville, and Mrs. Lorene Dyer, Luttrell; six sons, Odra, Maynardville, Clayton of Corryton, Fred, Washburn, Murphy and Austin, Knoxville, and Verlin of Luttrell; twenty three grandchildren, 23 great grand children, and four great great grandchildren. She was preceded in death by two sons and a daughter.

Elder R. H. Pettit

Elder R. H. Pettit died on January 27, 1975, at Fort Sanders Hospital at the age of 89. He was survived by one son, Cliff; five grandchildren; nine great grandchildren; two great great grandchildren; one brother, Oscar Pettit of Vonore, Tenn., one sister, Mrs. Lemma Howard of Marietta, Georgia. Elder Pettit was one of seven children born to B. M. and Cashie Pettit of Jasper, Georgia. He came to Tennessee as a young man and met and married Mollie Wiggins of Lenoir City who died on December 27, 1966. Elder and Mrs. Pettit also raised a granddaughter, Betty. Elder Pettit helped to start Kirkwood Primitive Baptist Church of which he was a member at his death. Elder Pettit was ordained as a Primitive Baptist Minister on January 9, 1943.

Mattie Sharp Cunningham

Mattie Sharp Cunningham was born in Union County at Sharp's Chapel August 8, 1895. She passed away at Madison Hospital in Madison, Tenn. after an operation, April 21, 1975. She was 79 years, eight months and 13 days old. She was converted at an early age and joined the Oak Grove Primitive Baptist Church of which she was a member until the Kirkwood Church was organized, she then moved her membership to that church where she was an active and faithful member until she became ill with age. She was a widow of Buell Cunningham. She professed faith in Christ at every opportunity. We know she is at rest. She leaves four step children and nieces and nephews. Funeral services were conducted at Naves Funeral Home in Lebanon, Tenn. Rev. Donald Owens officiated. Interment Watertown Cemetery, Watertown, Tenn.

Coy Lee Gossage

Coy Lee Gossage was born January 30, 1912, and died May 31, 1975. Making his stay here 63 years. He professed faith in Christ at an early age and joined the Lenoir City Primitive Baptist Church. His life was of a wonderful Christian nature and a loving companion and father. He developed a heart condition which forced him into early retirement and recently required open heart surgery. His testimony was one of resignation to God's will being done in his life. Brother Coy's life work was involved with young people; helping them in any way possible to become better citizens. His life was filled with benevolent deeds for others. We will miss him very much. He leaves to mourn his passing his wife, Imogene; daughter, Mrs. Amos (Gail) Manzer; sons, James G. and Lee Gossage; seven grandchildren; one brother; one sister; two half brothers; one half sister; and a host of relatives and friends. Funeral services were conducted June 2, 1975, with Elder Charles Taylor officiating. Burial was in Loudon County Memorial Gardens.

Mrs. Ruby (Lynch) Hobbs

Mrs. Ruby Louisa (Lynch) Hobbs, age 58, of Route 4, LaFollette, passed away Saturday evening, August 31, 1974, at the LaFollette Community Hospital. She was a faithful member of the Davis Chapel Primitive Baptist Church, since her profession of faith in November 1928. She was the daughter of the late James F. and Cordelia V. Spangler Lynch and wife of the late Lonnie Tyler Hobbs. She is survived by two daughters, Mrs. Doris Fields of Kingsport and Mrs. Debra McNeeley of LaFollette; one son, Warren Gene Hobbs, of LaFollette; two sisters, Mrs. Mamie Parrott and Mrs. Mildred Ellison both of LaFollette; four brothers, Mr. Joe Lynch of Wyandotte, Mich., Mrs. Walter Lynch, of Riverview, Mich., Mr. Clyde Lynch of Taylor, Mich., and Mr. Robert (Bob) Lynch of LaFollette; one grandson, Stephen Tyler Fields of Kingsport.

Funeral services were Tuesday, September 3, 1974, at 2 p.m. at the Davis Chapel Primitive Baptist Church. Elder Leonard White and Joe Bush officiated. Her body was lain to rest in Sunrise Cemetery at Davis Chapel.

Our many fond memories shall live on for our beloved mother.

Gene, Doris and Debbie

Kenneth Brantley

Kenneth Brantley was born Oct. 7, 1904. Died June 9, 1975. He was a member of Oak Grove Primitive Baptist Church. He is survived by his wife Sarah Brantley and four children. Wayne of Maryville, Tenn., Delona of Sharps Chapel, Tenn., Gniece Brantley of Sharps Chapel, Tenn., and Mrs. Barbara Lamb of Rockvale, Tenn.; one brother, Lonnie Brantley of Knoxville, Tenn.; one sister Mrs. Beatrice Weaver also of Knoxville; two grandsons and seven granddaughters; one great granddaughter; several nieces and nephews. Funeral was held at Oak Grove Church June 12, 1975, at 2 p.m. with Elder W.M. Sparks, Elder Noble Lee Clawson and Elder J.C. Monday officiating. Burial in Church Cemetery.

WE LOVED HIM SO VERY MUCH BUT WE FEEL OUR LOSS IS HIS ETERNAL GAIN.

Rhoda Berry

Rhoda Berry, age 72, of Sharps Chapel passed away suddenly Nov. 8, 1974. Survivors, one sister, Mrs. Tishie Creech of Sharps Chapel; several nieces and nephews and a host of friends. She was a member of Cave Springs Primitive Baptist Church until it disbanded and later joined Oak Grove Primitive Baptist Church. Funeral services were held on Sunday, Nov. 10, 1974, at 2 p.m. at Oak Grove Church with Elders W.M. Sparks, J.C. Monday and Noble Lee Clawson officiating. Burial was in Church Cemetery.

GREATLY MISSED BY SISTER AND RELATIVES AND FRIENDS.

Mrs. Frances Yadon Liford

Mrs. Frances Yadon Liford was born in 1886 and passed away June 10, 1975, being 88 years, nine months and three days old. She was married to James G. Lofird. She professed faith in Christ at an early age and joined the Primitive Baptist Church at Black Fox where she remained a member. Survivors were one daughter, Mrs. Myrtle Farmer, seven grand children and 15 great grand children and a host of friends, nieces and nephews.

Laura Hines Wright

Laura Hines Wright was born October 8, 1885, and died August 25, 1974. She was almost 89 years of age. She was a faithful member of the Lenoir City Primitive Baptist Church from very early in life until God called her to rest. Her last years were spent not being able to attend her church on accounty of poor health, yet her desire was for the peace and welfare of her brothers and sisters in Christ.

She is survived by one daughter, Mrs. Nannie Mae Rosson; many nieces and nephews; and a host of friends and relatives. Funeral services were conducted by Elder Charles Taylor and she was lain to rest beneath a blanket of beautiful flowers to await the Resurrection morning. Her place is vacant but her works live on in our memories.

Elder Leonard White

It was on the cold, dark, and dreary day of January 24, 1975, that we followed the casket to its last resting place at Sunset Cemetery near Davis Chapel Church, Campbell County, Tennessee. The gathering of family, friends, and loved ones stood in hushed silence and with bowed heads as the committal was pronounced by Elder Hugh Brummitt and the remains of our beloved Elder Leonard White was lowered into the mother earth to await the Resurrection morning.

Elder Leonard White was born in Union County, Tennessee, April 8, 1883, and passed from this life January 21, 1975. He attended school from 1888-1905 which included the years 1900-1905 which were spent at Hills Academy. Following this he taught school in the counties of Union, Claiborne, and Campbell during the years 1904-1932.

He professed faith in Christ January 2, 1903 and united with Mossy Springs Church in Union County. He was licensed to preach either in the year of 1905 or 1906. On April 13, 1907, he was ordained to the full work of the ministry as an Elder of the Primitive Baptist Churches. For nearly 68 years brother White was faithful in this work which God had called him to and the church of long ago had sent him out to do. Always preaching the unsearchable riches of Jesus Christ. He went as one who possessed nothing of his own — yet being given all things through God who had called him into this glorious work.

On April 28, 1907, Elder White was united in marriage to his childhood sweetheart, Miss Mossie C. McBee with the late Elder S.M. Petree performing the marriage ceremony. To this union was born four children: Emerson and Con White, both of LaFollette; two daughters, Mrs. Geneva Irwin of LaFollette, and Miss Oral White of Oak Ridge, Tennessee.

During his ministry, Elder White served the following churches as pastor: Cave Springs, Pleasant Hill, Mossy Spring, Red Hill, Gibson Station (Va.), Pleasant Point, Oak Grove, Rocky Dale, Davis Chapel, Lenoir City, Hensley's Chapel, Poplar Spring, Macedonia, and Kirkwood. Of these 14 churches he was instrumental in bringing three of them into the Powell Valley Association. Namely: Red Hill, Davis Chapel, and Kirkwood.

Elder White was blessed with a wonderful memory. This was used well in being able to recall Scriptures when he so ably expounded on the Word of God in preaching. Also it was a wonderful asset in almost instant recall of names, faces and events. His spontaneous love and able admonition caused the younger ministers to consider him in the same capacity of the Apostle Paul to the young man Timothy. It can never be said that he unduly criticized but rather stood ready to advise and help.

It is with sorrow in our hearts that we give him up to God. Yet the time of his departure is at hand. He has "fought a good fight," he has "kept the faith," henceforth there is laid up for him a "crown of righteousness." May this sorrow only serve to quicken us who are left behind to attain to the life which Elder White projected. Funeral services were conducted at the Davis Chapel Church with Elder Charles Taylor, Elder Everett Berry, Elder Joe Bush, and Elder Hugh Brummitt officiating. It seemed only fitting to use a favorite poem that Elder White so often used:

"Crossing The Bar"

Sunset and evening star, and one clear call for me,
And may there be no moaning of the bar, when I put out to sea.
But such a tide as moving seems asleep, too full for sound and foam,
When that which drew from out the boundless deep, turns again home.
Twilight and evening bell, and after that the dark!
And may there be no sadness of farewell, when I embark;
For tho' from out our bourne of time and place,
the flood may bear me far,
I hope to see my pilot face to face, when I have crossed the bar.

——Alfred Tennyson

Bertha Nevada Turner

Mrs. Bertha Nevada Turner, daughter of the late Henry C. and Rosa Hoskins, was born on June 4, 1902, and departed this life on February 4, 1975. She professed faith in Christ at an early age and joined Gibson Station Primitive Baptist Church where she remained a faithful member. Her husbands preceded her in death. She leaves to mourn her loss: one son, Ray Brooks, and one daughter, Mrs. Pearl Martell of Toledo, Ohio; two brothers, Paschal Hoskins of Harrogate, Tenn. and Syllus Hoskins of Toledo, Ohio; two sisters, Bessie West, Morristown, Tenn. and Lucille Ball of Dundee, Mich.; eight grandchildren. Funeral services were held at Gibson Station Primitive Baptist Church with Elders Everett Berry and Joe Irvin officiating. She was lain to rest in Shoffner's Cemetery. Our loss is Heaven's gain.

Oscar Verlin Edwards

Oscar Verlin Edwards was born November 7, 1895, and departed this life on April 10, 1975, at St. Mary's Hospital in Knoxville, Tenn. He was married to Cecil Graves on April 8, 1922. To this union 12 children were born, three of whom preceded him in death.

Survivors are his wife, eight sons, Coy, Kenneth, Condis, Boyd and Carl of Speedwell, Tenn.;two brothers, James and Alonzo of Speedwell; four sisters, Edna Robbins and Minnie Collingworth of Madisonville, Tenn., Lou Lambert of Speedwell and Mae Pace of Eva, Tenn.; 18 grandchildren, five step-grandchildren; four great grandchildren; and eight step great grandchildren.

He joined Pleasant Hill Primitive Baptist Church in 1917 and was a faithful member until death. He was assistant clerk for 47 years.

Funeral services were held by Elders Alvin Graves, James Henry Branscomb, Albert Davis and Tony Eastridge. Burial in the Hunter Cemetery.

STATISTICAL TABLE

CHURCHES	DELEGATES	Printing Minutes	Total Membership	Deceased	Excluded	Dismissed by Letter	Relationship	Baptism	Received by Letter	Restored	REGULAR MEETING TIME;	COMMUNION TIME
BLACK FOX	Bros. Dale Capps, Arthur Terry, Bennie Capps; Sisters Mary Ruth Capps, Pamela Capps, Mary Terry	$15	88	2	0	0	0	2	0	0	Second Sat. night & Sunday. Third Sat. night & Sunday.	Second Sunday in June
BRADEN'S CHAPEL	Elders W.M. Sparks, J.C. Monday; Sisters Helen Clawson, Leecy Sparks, Winona Monday	$10	138	1	1	10	2	4	0	0	First Saturday & Sunday of each month	First Sunday in July
BRANTLEY'S CHAPEL	Elder Clifford Brantley, Bros. Everett Brantley, Daniel Brantley, Jeff Ellison, Jerry McBee, Sisters Barsha Brantley, Mildred Brantley, Linda Brantley, Lela Ellison	$25	84	0	1	1	0	1	0	0	Second Saturday night, Every Sunday	Second Sunday in July
CEDAR SPRINGS	Bros. Isom Drummonds, Clay Widner, Clifford Robertson, Sisters Velt Muncey, Wanda Widner	$10	74	0	0	0	0	0	0	3	Second Saturday night and Sunday, Fourth Sat. night and Sunday	Fourth Sunday in May
DAVIS CHAPEL	Bros. James S. Heatherly, Orice McCarty, Seth Welch, Robert Lynch, Sisters Ruth Heatherly, Mollie McCarty, Ollie Welch	$20	141	2	0	0	0	0	0	0	Third Saturday night, Every Sunday and Sunday night	Third Sunday in June
GETHSEMANE	Elders Glenn Abbott, Brothers, Tom Carmichael, Jimmy Estes, C.H. Godfrey, Sisters June Carmichael, Rhoda Estes, Myrtle Cook, Billie Godfrey.	$20	32	0	0	0	0	0	0	0		Fourth Sunday May and October

Church	Delegates									$		
GIBSON STATION	Elder Joe Irwin, Bros. Spurgeon Thompson, Bill Rhymer, Franklin Jones, Sisters Fannie Jones, Karen Rhymer, Evelyn Maples, Dorothy Johnson	0	0	0	2	0	0	3	78	$25	First Sat. and Sunday, Every Sunday and Sunday night	First Sunday in June
HEADRICK CHAPEL	Bros. Clyde Abbott, Bill Cook, Sister Grace Abbott	0	0	0	0	0	0	0	110	$20	Sunday Following First Saturday	First Sunday in May and October
KIRKWOOD	Elders H.E. Brummitt, Walter Lyons, Bros. J.L. Sharp, C.A. Sharp, Jack Cook, Sisters Ruby Brummitt, Evelyn Sharp, Frieda Sharp, Dottie Cook	0	13	0	0	1	0	4	108	$30	Every Sunday	Last Sunday in April
LENOIR CITY	Elders Alvin Graves, Charles Taylor, Bros. Henry Chamberlain, Hubert Spoons, Clyde Abbott, Raymond Wilkerson, Scott Collins, Jerry Spoons, Sisters Estie Chamberlain, Annie Spoons, Betty Abbott, Ella Fields, Ruby Williams, Cora Hill, Agnes Taylor, Janice Spoons	0	0	0	0	2	0	3	150	$35	Every Sunday and Sunday night	Sunday after third Sat. in May
MONROE, MICHIGAN	Letter Received — No Delegates Present	0	2	0	0	0	0	1	13	$10	Third Sunday	Sunday after the third Sat. in July
NOETON	Elder John Oliver, Bros. Carroll Oliver, Charlie Collins	1	2	0	0	0	0	2	36	$20	Third Saturday and Sunday of each month	Third Sunday May and September
OAK GROVE	Elders Toni Eastridge, Johnny Atkins, Bros. Jim Sharp, Sisters Francis Eastridge, Laura Lou Walker, Betty Sharp, Sandra Gail Walker	0	13	10	0	0	0	4	313	$25	First Sat. night and Sunday of each month	First Sunday in May
PLEASANT HILL	Elders Albert Davis, James Henry Branscomb, Sisters Audra Davis Helen Ruth Branscomb	8	4	0	0	1	0	3	113	$30	Fourth Saturday of each month	Fourth Sunday in June

181

PLEASANT POINT	Elders Claude Rosson, Bros. Lawrence Rosson, Mitchell Johnson, Sister Glossie Rosson	0	0	1	0	0	0	3	115	$15	First Sat. night and Sunday Third Sunday	First Sunday in July
ROCKY DALE	Elders Everrett Berry, Parnick Shelton, Joe Bush, Bill Berry, Bros. Donald Sharp, Bill Taylor Ralph Clapp, Elmer Graves, Sisters Trula Berry, Lola Berry, Lou Emma Taylor, Grace Graves, Fay Collett	0	0	0	2	0	1	2	121	$30	Every Sunday and Sunday night	Second Sunday in May

CHURCH	COUNTY	PASTOR	CLERK	ADDRESS
Black Fox	Grainger	Elder Alvin Graves	Bennie Capps Flossie Capps, asst.	Box 92, Maynardville, Tn. Maynardville, Tn.
Bradens Chapel	Union	Elder Noble Clawson Elder J.C. Monday, asst.	Jimmie Edwards Phyllis Wilson, asst.	Speedwell, Tn. Speedwell, Tn.
Brantley's Chapel	Blount	Elder J. C. Monday	D. C. Brantley Mildred Brantley, asst.	2020 Bittle Read, Maryville, Tn. 804 Brown School Road, Maryville, Tn. 37801
Cedar Springs (Meyers Grove)	Claiborne	Elder Clay Widner Elder Jimmy Branscomb, assistant	Eula Good Bonnie Miracle, assistant	New Tazewell, Tn. New Tazewell, Tn.
Davis Chapel	Campbell	Elder Joe Bush	Ruth Heatherly Lassie Ellison, asst.	Rt. 1, Lafollette, Tn. Rt. 1, Lafollette, Tn.

Church	County	Pastor	Clerk	Address
Gethsemane	Knox	Elder Walter Lyons Elder Glenn Abbott, asst.	Tom Carmichael	729 Frank Street Knoxville, Tn.
Gibson Station	Lee Virginia	Elder Everette Berry	Dorothy Johnson Floyd Cobb, asst.	Rt. 2, Ewing, Va. Rt. 2, Ewing, Va.
Headrecks Chapel	Sevier	Elder Walter Lyons	Clyde Abbott	Rt. 7, Sevierville, Tn.
Kirkwood	Knox	Elder Everette Berry	Estelle Petree Sharp Alice Tindell Powers	Rt. 27, Emory Rd., Knoxville, Tn. 2923 Clearview Ave., Knoxville
Lenoir City	Loudon	Elder Charles Taylor	Scott Collins	705 W. 5th Avenue, Lenoir City, Tn.
Monroe Mich.	Monroe	Elder Lenvil Myers	Gertrude Zwack	1825 Spaulding Road, Monroe, Mich.
Noeton	Grainger	Elder John Oliver	Elder John Oliver Bessie Collins, asst.	Rt. 2, Bean Station, Tn. Rt. 7, Morristown, Tn.
Oak Grove	Union	Elder J. C. Monday Elder Noble Clawson, asst.	Betty P. Sharp Mary Ann Walker, asst.	Sharps Chapel, Tn. Sharps Chapel, Tn.
Pleasant Hill	Claiborne	Elder Alvin Graves Elder Albert Davis, asst.	William Beanscomb Larry Anderson, asst.	Speedwell, Tn. Speedwell, Tn.
Pleasant Point	Claiborne	Elder Parnick Shelton Elder Claude Rosson, asst.	Elder Claude Rosson	Rt. 4, New Tazewell, Tn.
Rocky Dale	Knox	Elder Hugh E. Brummitt	Edward Collett Dennis Branson, asst.	Rt. 1, Luttrell, Tn. Rt. 13, Knoxville, Tn.

1976 MINUTES

of the
POWELL VALLEY ASSOCIATION
OF PRIMITIVE BAPTIST

GIBSON STATION BAPTIST CHURCH
ELDER EVERETT BERRY, PASTOR

Held with the Sister Church
at
Gibson Station in Lee County, Va.
—— AUGUST 20, 21, 22, 1976 ——

THE ONE HUNDRED AND FIFTY SEVENTH ANNUAL SESSION

OF THE

POWELL VALLEY ASSOCIATION

OF

PRIMITIVE BAPTIST

HELD WITH THE SISTER CHURCH OF GIBSON STATION IN LEE COUNTY, VIRGINIA AUGUST 20, 21, 22, 1976

NEXT SESSION WILL BE HELD WITH THE SISTER CHURCH OF BRANTLEY'S CHAPEL IN BLOUNT COUNTY, TENNESSEE TO BEGIN ON FRIDAY, BEFORE THE THIRD SATURDAY IN AUGUST, 1977 AT 10:30 A.M.
ELDER JOHNNY ATKINS WILL DELIVER THE INTRODUCTORY SERMON AND ELDER GLENN ABBOTT WILL BE THE ALTERNATE.

OFFICERS

Elder Albert Davis ....Moderator
Speedwell, Tennessee Ph. 869-3596

Elder Hugh E. Brummitt..............Assistant Moderator
1329 Brown Ave., Knoxville, Tennessee Ph. 546-7700

Bro. W. H. Taylor ....Clerk
Rt. 27 Emory Rd., Knoxville, Tennessee Ph. 922-2143

Bro. Bennie Capps ....Assistant Clerk
Maynardville, Tennessee Ph. 922-2143

Friday, August 20, 1976

The Powell Valley Association of Primitive Baptist met with the Sister Church at Gibson Station in Lee County Virginia on August 20, 1976, at 10:30 A.M. for the one hundred and fifty seventh annual session, with Elder Albert Davis presiding. After a good spiritual song service directed by Elder William Berry of Rocky Dale Church, the congregation was led in prayer by Elder Berry.

The Moderator then read the 19th Psalm and gave a welcome to Sister Churches then gave way to Elder Charles Taylor of the Lenoir City Church for the introductory sermon.

Elder Taylor read from the 6th Chapter of 2nd Kings and using the 2nd verse as his text. He preached a wonderful sermon which was attentive and graciously received by the congregation.

After the introductory sermon, the Association was recessed for 15 minutes.

After recess, the Association was reassembled at the sound of singing.

After singing, the Moderator Elder Albert Davis called for the opening prayer by Elder Parnick Shelton of Rocky Dale Church.

The Moderator then called the Association to order for the business of the Association.

1. The Moderator called for the letters of the Sister Churches to be presented to the clerk for reading. Fifteen were received.

2. Moderator called for anyone from the Sister Churches present and not named as delegate who wish to be seated to come forward and give the clerk their name. Four came forward, namely: Elwood Evans and Velma Evans of Kirkwood Church, Elder Johnny Atkins of Oak Grove Church and Edward Collett of Rocky Dale Church.

3. Motion approved that we accept the letters and seat the delegates of said churches.

4. The Moderator then called for petitionary letters if any. One was received from Faith Primitive Baptist

Church of Spartanburg, South Carolina. After being recommended by Elder Charles Taylor, Elder Brantley, Elder Anderson and Abbott, motion approved that we accept and welcome this addition to the Powell Valley Association.

5. Motion by Elder Walter Lyons and seconded by Elder Godfrey was approved that we re-write the 4th article of the Rules of Decorum.

6. Motion that we re-elect Elder Albert Davis as Moderator and Elder Hugh E. Brummitt as Assistant Moderator was approved.

7. Motion approved that the Association re-elect Brother W. H. Taylor as Clerk and Brother Bennie C. Capps, Assistant Clerk.

8. Motion approved that the Moderator be authorized to appoint all the committees.

9. The Moderator being authorized to do so, made the following committee appointments:

Committee on Arrangements:

Elder Glenn Abbott
Brother Clyde Abbott
Brother Daniel Brantley

Committee on Preaching:

Brother Elwood Evans
Brother Tommy Carmichael
Brother Franklin Jones

Committee on Request:

Brother Cecil Godfrey
Brother Spurgeon Thompson
Elder Bill Berry

Committee on Finance:

Elder Larry Anderson
Elder Parnick Shelton
Brother Isom Drummonds

10. Motion to pay W. H. Taylor for extra 100 minutes.

11. Motion approved that the Association be adjourned until Saturday morning when it will be re-convened at 10:30. Dismissed in prayer by Elder John Oliver of the Noeton Church.

SATURDAY, August 21, 1976

1. Saturday morning at the appointed hour of 10:30, the Association re-convened and after singing, the Assistant Moderator Elder Hugh E. Brummitt made a short and interesting talk and read the 5th Chapter of Psalms and called for prayer by Brother Burkhalter of Alabama.

2. The Moderator then called the Association to order and called for the letter from the Sister Church of Braden's Chapel not received Friday. The letter was received, accepted and the delegation seated.

3. Moderator called for anyone who was not named and wished to be seated as delegate to come forward, one came, Sister Susie Shoffner of Gibson Station Church.

4. Moderator called for report of Committee on Arrangements which was received and the committee released.

Report of Committee on Arrangements:

    a. Call for roll call of Delegates.
    b. Call for report of Committee on Preaching.
    c. Call for report of Committee on Request.
    d. Call for report of Committee on Finance.
    e. Decide how many minutes we have printed, who shall supervise the printing and distribution of same, and how much he shall receive for his services. Also, where will the next session of the Association be held and who shall preach the introductory Sermon and who shall be the alternate.

                Respectfully submitted,
                Elder Glenn Abbott
                Brother Clyde Abbott, Jr.
                Brother Daniel Brantley

5. The Moderator then called for the roll call of

delegates and absentees to be noted.

6. Call for the report of the Committee on Preaching, which was accepted as follows and the committee released.

Report of Committee on Preaching:
Friday Night: Elder Alvin Graves and Elder Scott
Saturday: Elder Clifford Brantley and Brother Don Burkhalter
Saturday Night: Elder John Godfrey, Elder Howard Pippin
Sunday: Elder Johnny Atkins and Elder Albert Davis

Respectfully submitted,
Brother Elwood Evans
Brother Tommy Carmichael
Brother Franklin Jones

7. Called for report of committee on Request who gave the following report and was released:

Report of Committee on Request:

We request that the Association have printed 1,150 copies of the minutes and that the clerk supervise the printing and distribution of same and that he receive $100.00 for this service. We also request that the next session of this Association be held with the Sister Church of Brantley's Chapel in Blount County Tennessee to begin on the third Friday in August 1977, at 10:30 A.M. We also request that a circular letter be written for placement in the minutes and that it be written by Elder Johnny Atkins.

Respectfully submitted:
Brother Spurgeon Thompson
Brother C. H. Godfrey
Elder Bill Berry

8. Called for report on Committee on Finance which was accepted as follows and the committee released:

Committee on Finance:

Church	Amount
Black Fox	$ 20.00
Braden's Chapel	15.00
Brantley's Chapel	25.00
Davis Chapel	20.00
Faith Primitive Baptist	20.00
Gethsemane	25.00
Gibson Station	25.00
Headrick Chapel	25.00
Kirkwood	30.00
Lenoir City	35.00
Monroe, Michigan	10.00
Meyers Grove	20.00
Noeton	20.00
Oak Grove	25.00
Pleasant Hill	30.00
Pleasant Point	15.00
Rocky Dale	30.00
Total	$390.00

Respectfully submitted,
Elder Larry Anderson
Elder Parnick Shelton
Brother Isom Drummonds

9. Motion approved as requested that we print 1,150 minutes and that the clerk supervise the printing and distribution of same and that he receive $100.00 for his services.

10. Motion approved that the next session of this Association be held with the Sister Church of Brantley's Chapel in Blount County, Tennessee to begin on Friday before the Third Saturday in August, 1977, at 10:30 A.M

11. Motion approved that Elder Johnny Atkins preach the introductory sermon and Elder Glenn Abbott be the alternate.

12. Motion that Elder Johnny Atkins write the circular letter for the minute.

13. Motion approved that we appoint Elder Clifford Brantley, Elder Glenn Abbott, Brother Cecil Godfrey and Brother Clyde Abbott, Jr. to represent the Powell Valley Association of Primitive Baptist in love and

fellowship at the Elk River Association in Alabama, and in love, appreciation of their fellowship here with us in our Association.

14. The Association by a standing vote wishes to extend to the Church of Gibson Station and the entire community our heart felt thanks and our love and our prayers for the kindness, love, and fellowship we have enjoyed while here with you. As we leave you, may Gods richest blessings rest upon all of you. We desire your prayers. With these words, the Moderator declared the Association closed with prayer by Elder W. M. Sparks

Elder Albert Davis, Moderator
Elder Hugh E. Brummitt, Assistant Moderator
W. H. Taylor, Clerk
Bennie C. Capps, Assistant Clerk

Sunday, August 22, 1976

Sunday at the appointed hour of 10:30, the congregation at the sound of singing filled the house to overflowing. After singing, Elder Joe Irving, Assistant Pastor of the host church, gave the welcome to the Sister Churches of the Association, then called on Elder Bill Berry of the Rocky Dale Church for prayer. After prayer, Elder Johnny Atkins of the Oak Grove Church introduced the service by reading from the 2nd Chapter of the book of Daniel and using the 44th verse for a test. After preaching a good sermon for 35 minutes, he was followed by Elder Albert Davis who delivered a good sermon for 25 minutes. He was followed by song, hand shake, rejoicing and testimonies. Then the congregation was dismissed in prayer by Elder Howard Pippin of Spartanburg, South Carolina.

CIRCULAR LETTER 1976 *Elder Charles Taylor*

Very Dear Brethren,

I feel that I am not worthy to carry out the appointment which this Association placed upon me while in session one year ago. However, I will endeavor to carry out their determination with all love and humility by submitting in print a message preached by your humble servant over Radio Station W.G.A.P., Alcoa, Tenn. July 1965. This was one year before you began publishing me on your minutes as an elder in the Powell Valley Association. Through prayerful examination of my belief, I find it to be the same now as it was then. I pray that you will examine this letter and if it be found orthodox, spread it on our minutes this year.

In examining the type of preaching and practice among many churches, it is our earnest belief that we have, to say the least, forsaken our basic principles of doctrine. To say the most, a great number of our people do not believe these great doctrines of truth. Through this condition, we have become weakened. The borders of our land have become encrouched upon by intruders who, if allowed to stay here, will destroy our inheritance and lead our people into the same bondage that some of our worldly church friends are servants of. We have opened our churches and pulpits to these intruders and they have used us to the advantage of satan. I realize that this is a serious charge and I do not make it without first making prayer and supplication to God. Not just for an hour or a day, but for a long period of time. I shall endeavor to show my reasons as I go along. Please let us reason together whether these things be true.

ARTICLE OF FAITH #3. "We believe in the doctrine of election according to the foreknowledge of God." I Peter 1:2; "Elect according to the foreknowledge of God the Father, through sanctification of the Spirit, unto obedience and sprinkling of the blood of Jesus Christ: grace unto you, and peace be multiplied." Ephesians 1:4; "According as He hath chosen us in Him before the foundation of the world, that we should be holy and without blame before Him in love."

We want to retain in our minds the word "foreknowledge". The mind is finite. It cannot fathom the knowledge of God who stood before the creation and determined the destiny of the world and of His people. This same God chose us in Him (Christ) before the foundation of the world. Ephesians 1:4; I Peter 1:2; II Thessalonians 2:13; I Thessalonians 1:4; Colossians 3:12. These, along with all the Word of God, are consistent in declaring the omnipotent Sovereignty of a loving God toward His Elect. This should draw our hearts closer to this loving God who saw us as individuals and chose us to Salvation, having predestinated us to the adoption of children through Jesus Christ our Saviour, redeeming us by His blood, justifying us by His faith, and making us accepted in the Beloved. He finished our faith by raising Christ from the dead and promised us a like resurrection.

The great church groups (institutions) around us have put pressure on us to the extent that we must turn to these Bible truths or become extinct. This Gospel of Christ originating from the Holy Spirit as it moved upon men of old causing them to speak and write as the Spirit gave utterance does not conform to the carnal desires of men. When we use the word "carnal", we include all the institutions for the conversion of the world. In this category fall all the machinery of missionism such as: educational facilities for the ministers and field workers that they in turn might go out and educate the heathen, children, and every person who would stop to listen into christianity. This, along with other strange sounds, has excluded the work of the Holy Spirit and left it to the carnal knowledge of man, causing their churches to be filled with unregererated persons who lead others to licentuousness. If man is not controlled by the Holy Spirit of God, he must be controlled by the Law. The office of ministry of the Gospel must then be turned into an office of law givers and law enforcers. The Church ceases to be a place to receive food for the soul and becomes a Levitical priesthood with an altar where sacrifices must be made. If these were not performed under the Levitical priesthood then the people could find no justification. I fear the same thing binds our people today that bound those under the Law. Instead of liberty of the Spirit of Christ Jesus there is the yoke of bondage which Paul said that neither we nor our fathers were able to bear. Instead of justification by the blood of Christ through the supreme sacrifice on the Cross, there is justification by works. At least this is what people are led to believe. The only conclusion we can arrive at, if this be the case, is that if it is our works, it is no more of Grace. So those that are on that side have, in deeds and actions, denied the blood of Christ and put Him to an open shame. "With their lips they do honor me, but their hearts are far from me."

How far then can we go on the subject of Election? I believe we can go to the bounds of eternity. While we cannot conceive the bounds of eternity, in that it is unmeasurable, neither is the mind of man able to conceive the full boundry of election. I do know that hungering, thirsting, poor, destitute sinners can be assured by the very description given by our Lord, that a loving, merciful God had them in mind when He determined this plan of Salvation. For Jesus said in Matthew, chapter 5: "Blessed are the poor in spirit: for theirs is the kingdom of heaven. Blessed are they that mourn for they shall be comforted. Blessed are they which do hunger and thirst after righteousness: for they shall be filled."We do not fail to include into these assurances the meek. He said, "blessed are the meek: for they shall inherit the earth." I believe this inheritance meant the true Church made up of true believers. It is hard to see much meekness in these that have been proselyted into the churches today through these means.

Some would tell us that we don't give any encouragement to poor sinners by this doctrine; that it will offend some so that they will never accept Christ and will die and go to hell. I believe this is on the contrary! The only Gospel which does give any encouragement to the poor sinner, because the simple statement that he is poor means that he has spent all of his gifts and offerings, sacrifices, and prayers, yea, every resource at his disposal. Yet he has not obtained that for which his soul longs after. In this state of extreme poverty, ready to perish and die, the Covenant God of Abraham and all Israel gives him the riches of Grace and the knowledge of Jesus his Saviour! Then can he realize the fulfillment of the longing Church represented in the Songs of Solomon chapter 3: "By night on my bed I sought Him whom my soul loveth; I sought Him but I found Him not. I will rise now, and go about the city in the streets, and in the broad ways I will seek Him whom my soul loveth: I sought Him but I found Him not. The watchmen (Preachers) that go about the city found me: to whom I said, saw ye Him whom my soul loveth? It was but a little that I passed from them, but I found Him whom my soul loveth: I held Him and would not let Him go, until I had brought Him into my mother's house, and into the chamber of her that conceived me." Beyond the preacher; beyond the physical church; just a little beyond their reach; the poor hungry, thirsty, longing child can find the Lord of Salvation. They which are born, not of blood, nor of the will of the flesh, nor of the will of man, but of God; finds this and brings it into the physical church. There he enjoys all the blessings and benefits of the Bride of Christ.

Armenian teaching tells the sinner that we have no love for him; that we have no desire to see him saved; and that in general we don't care whether he goes to hell or not. The believers in election refute this even though the statements themselves are not worthy of notice. If we did not have compassion we could join with them and tell the sinner that it is his decision to make. That he can choose to either reject or to receive Christ as Saviour. That his eternal destiny (Heaven or hell) depends on "what he is willing to let God do for him". If this be our gospel then God's work has been done in vain. The doctrine of the Holy Bible testifies there are multitudes of God's elect in Babylonian institutions. They are not feeding on the green pastures nor drinking from the still clear pools of the waters of Salvation. We pray for every one of them that God might see fit to lead them out and let them find a home with their brethren in Canaan land.

Today we stand at the altar to witness and choose between the god baal, or the Lord God Jehovah of Elijah. Baal is not a god of salvation. Yet much "free-will" and "armenianism", with all their priests who stand and smite their bodies, saying they are willing to die for the profit of seeing numbers added to their church, have almost persuaded our people and many preachers that this is the right way. As for me, I want to stand with Elijah and tell them to cry louder because I know the baal of self-will and of self-service has no ears to hear nor a voice to answer. Neither has he the power to consume the sacrifice. While the God of Salvation is strong to the pulling down of mighty strong-holds. Able to consume the offering and bless His people.

Let us re-affirm our position on these issues! Let us cast out these intruders who with their false doctrines and practices are sowing wild seed in the borders of our land! And let us stand where all of those who possessed the land before us stood. Also, most of all, let us not fear! Be Strong! Quit like men! God will fight our battles for us. AMEN.

ELDER CHARLES TAYLOR

ORDAINED MINISTERS

Elder Glenn Abbott
1801 Cherrybrook Drive
Knoxville, Tennessee
Phone 949-6875

Elder Larry Anderson
Speedwell, Tennessee

Elder Johnny Atkins
Bean Station, Tenn.
Phone 767-2397

Elder Johnny Ayers
New Tazewell, Tenn.

Elder Everette Berry
Route #27
Knoxville, Tennessee
Phone 922-7004

Elder William Berry
Route #27
Knoxville, Tennessee
Phone 922-2269

Elder J.H. Branscomb
Speedwell, Tennessee
Phone 562-6361

Elder Clifford Brantley
Brown School Road
Maryville, Tennessee
Phone 982-3735

Elder Hugh E. Brummitt
1329 Brown Avenue
Knoxville, Tenn.
Phone 546-7700

Elder Toni Eastridge
Route #3
Louisville, Tennessee
Phone 983-1068

Elder Alvin Graves
122 Oak Wood
Lenoir City, Tenn.
Phone 986-9725

Elder Joe Irving
Rt. #2
Ewing, Virginia

Elder Walter Lyons
1602 Garfield Street
Alcoa, Tennessee
Phone 984-3207

Elder J.C. Monday
Speedwell, Tennessee
Phone 562-3068

Elder Sheridan Moore
Knoxville, Tennessee

Elder John Oliver
Bean Station, Tenn.

Elder Howard M Pippin
7435 Loan Oak Blvd.
Spartanburg, S.C.
Phone (803) 578-7220

Elder Claude Rosson
Route #4
New Tazewell, Tenn.
Phone 626-3168

Elder Joe Bush
Corryton, Tenn.
Phone 687-7108

Elder Parnick Shelton
Corryton, Tennessee
Phone 687-6142

Elder Noble Clawson
Route #4
Speedwell, Tenn.
Phone 562-2004

Elder William M Spark
Speedwell, Tenn.
Phone 562-7997

Elder Charles Taylor
101 Rose Street
Lenoir City, Tenn.
Phone 986-8172

Elder Albert Davis
Speedwell, Tenn.
Phone 869-3596

Elder Clay Widner
Route #1
Tazewell, Tenn.
Phone 523-2746

Elder John Godfrey
15443 Valleoga
Victorville, California
Phone (714) 243-4661

Elder Robert Walker
Knoxville, Tennessee

LICENTIATES

Brother Clyde H. Abbott
Route #7
Sevierville, Tennessee

Brother Bill Rhymer
Route #2
Harrogate, Tennessee

Brother Roscoe Branscomb
Speedwell, Tennessee

Brother Roy Walker
Route #1
Townsend, Tennessee

Brother Odell Carpenter
Maryville, Tennessee

Brother Spurgeon Thompson
Box 36
Shawanee, Tennessee

RULES OF DECORUM

1. The churches composing the Powell's Valley Association shall not be confined to any set rules as to specific number of Messengers they shall have in the body, but shall have the right to name in their letters as many as they choose, and in addition all orderly members of and of the churches being present be entitled to seats in the body as Messengers of their respective churches, with all the rights and privileges of the same.

2. The Messengers thus assembled shall be denominated the Powell's Valley Primitive Baptist Association.

3. For the purpose of historical information and statistical edification, the Churches are required to state in letters, the number of members in fellowship, the number received by Baptism, by letter, by confession of Faith, the number dismissed, excluded and dead since last session; also the time of their meeting, their pastoral supply, and the amount of money contributed for ministers and other purposes together with any other information they deem appropriate for the edification of the saints and glory of God.

4. This Association shall have no power to dictate to the churches in any case, or to lord it over God's heritage, nor any power by which she can directly or indirectly infringe on the internal rights of any church. However, in order to protect the standards of the churches composing this body, this Association shall reserve the right to answer queries, give advice, and if the need arises, shall reserve the right to "table" the letter of a church deemed to be in disorder until such time that said church shall set her house in order. Our annual meetings shall be for the purpose of hearing from each other, and for the worship of God and mutual comfort and edification of the Saints. To this end we reserve the privilege annually for the Third Friday in August and the two following days or at such other times as may be agreed upon with any church that may invite us, having due regard to priority of claims and the good of the cause; to protect our own stand while in session, from heresy and disorder; to recognize and invite any visiting Primitive Baptist

minister or lay brother to worship with us, that we may deem proper; to request the brethren of our own body to visit other churches or bodies in our behalf, with whom we may desire to cultivate church fellowship; to publish a minute of our proceedings.

5. Each session of the body shall have a Moderator and Clerk who shall hold office until re-elected.

6. Any other member of any church belonging to this body, when convened, being present shall be eligible to elect on as Moderator and Clerk or to sit on any committee appointed by the same.

7. In all election or questions that may be necessary to determine by vote, the vote shall be taken by churches, each church being entitled to three votes for any number less than one hundred, and one additional vote for every fifty or fraction thereof above the first hundred, but the Messengers of each church may divide their vote as they see proper.

8. All elections or questions coming to vote shall be determined by a majority vote cast, and it shall be the only duty of the minority to acquiesce in the decision thus reached.

9. If new churches desire to be admitted to this union they shall petition by letter and messengers and if voted for and recommended by one or more sister churches for her Presbytery constitutioning them, as orthodox and orderly they shall be received by the vote of the body and manifested by the Moderator giving the Messengers the right hand of fellowship.

10. Any motion or resolution clearly inconsistent with the above rules shall be promptly ruled out or order unless withdrawn by the mover.

11. Any Messenger being ruled out of order by the Moderator shall have the right to appeal to the body on the question of order, and if sustained shall be allowed to proceed, but if not take his seat.

12. Our meeting being held in the name of Christ and the worship of God; each Messenger is expected to observe due and proper therein.

13. It will not be considered good for any Messenger whose name has been enrolled as such to abruptly break off or absent himself from the Association without leave.

14. The Moderator shall be entitled to the same privilege of speech as other members provided the chair is filled.

15. The minutes of the Association shall be read and approved by the body and signed by the Moderator before adjourning.

16. The Association shall be opened and closed by prayer.

17. Amendments to these may be made at any time by a majority of the union voting by churches when they deem it necessary, provide such amendments do not compromise the sovereignty of the churches nor have tendency to give the body undue power or jurisdiction over them.

ARTICLES OF FAITH

Article 1. We believe in only one true living God, as He is revealed to us in the Holy Scriptures - Father, Son, and Holy Ghost.

Article 2. We believe that the Scriptures of the old and new Testaments are the words of God and the only rule of all-saving knowledge and obedience.

Article 3. We believe in the doctrine of election according to the foreknowledge of God.

Article 4. We believe in the doctrine of original sin.

Article 5. We believe in man's impotency to rescue himself from the fallen state he is in, by his own will or ability.

Article 6. We believe that sinners are justified in the sight of God only by the imputed righteousness of Jesus Christ.

Article 7. We believe the elect, according to the foreknowledge of God will be called, converted, regenerated, and sanctified by the Holy Spirit.

Article 8. We believe the saints will persevere and never fall finally away.

Article 9. We believe that baptism and the Lord's Supper are ordinances of Jesus Christ, and that true believers are the only subject of these ordinances, and that the true mode of baptism is by immersion. We believe also that feet washing is an example of Jesus Christ and should be kept by his disciples until his second coming.

Article 10. We believe in the Resurrection of the dead and the General Judgement.

Article 11. We believe that the punishment of the wicked will be everlasting and that the joys of the righteous will be eternal.

Article 12. We believe that no minister has the right to administer the ordinances, except those who have been regularly baptized and called of God, and come under the imposition of hands of the presbytery.

Cassie Verniece Braden

Cassie Verniece Braden, 54, was born May 13, 1921 and passed away September 9, 1975. Survivors: husband, Willie Braden of Speedwell, Tennessee; two daughters, Mrs. Charles Breeding of Adrian, Michigan and Mrs. Raymond Duncan, Jr. of Middlesboro, Kentucky; two sons, Bill Braden of LaFollette, Tennessee and Tom Braden of Speedwell, Tennessee; two grandchildren, Kenneth Breeding and Jennifer Duncan; sisters, Mrs. Brice Braden, Mrs. Milton Braden, and Mrs. Verlin Maddox; brothers, Alba and Walter Lambert; mother Mrs. Lou Lambert of Speedwell, Tennessee. She professed faith in Christ at an early age and joined the Pleasant Hill Primitive Baptist Church. Some years later she moved her letter to Braden's Chapel Primitive Baptist Church where she attended regularly as long as she was able. Funeral services were held at 2:00 P.M. Friday, September 12, 1975, at the Braden's Chapel Church with Elder Bill Sparks, Elder J.C. Monday, and Elder Noble Lee Clawson officiating. Interment was in the Braden's Cemetery. "Our loss is heaven's gain."

Roy F. Clawson

Roy F. Clawson, age 42 years, born May 30, 1933, passed away at his home Tuesday, May 25, 1976. He was survived by his wife, Maxine Clawson; 3 sons, Jack, Danny, Terry all of Ohio, and one who preceded him in death; 2 grandchildren, Debbie and Angie of Ohio; his father, Donnie Clawson of Speedwell, Tennessee; 2 sisters Nadine Owens of West Carrollton, Ohio, Lou Bullard of Speedwell, Tennessee; 5 brothers, Johnny and Earl of Ohio, Ray and P.J. of Michigan, and Noble Lee of Speedwell, Tennessee. His mother, Lizzie Clawson, one brother, and 2 sisters preceded him earlier in death. He professed a hope in Christ at an early age and was a member of Braden's Chapel Church.

Harley Otto Berry, Sr.

Harley Otto Berry, Sr. age 80 of Clapps Chapel Road, Route 1 Corryton, passed away at St. Mary's Medical Center 3 p.m. Saturday, August 21, 1976. He was a member of Rocky Dale Primitive Baptist Church. Survivors: wife, Mrs. Ida Belle Berry; daughters, Mrs. C.M. (Ethel) Robison, Mrs. Hairl (Bertha) Kear, Mrs. Ralph (Jean) Kear all of Knoxville, Mrs. J.D. (Margie) Lively of Corryton; sons, Luther Berry, Charlotte, N.C., Clyde, Elmer, Ross, Harley, Jr., Charles, Edward, Rev. Billy Joe, Rev. Ronnie, all of Corryton, and Elder Everette Berry of Knoxville; 39 grandchildren; 41 great-grandchildren; 2 great-great-grandchildren; brother, Alberty Berry of S.C. Services 2 p.m. Tuesday Mynatt's Chapel, Rev. Roger Barnes, Rev. Kenneth Perkins, and Elder Hugh Brummitt officiating. Interment Clapps Chapel Cemetery. Grandsons will be pallbearers. Family will receive friends from 7 to 9 p.m. Monday at Mynatt's.

Fred Brantley

Fred Brantley, age 82, of Rt. 1 Speedwell, passed away at Claiborne County Hospital Friday afternoon. Survivors: wife, Mrs. Gilley Brantley, Speedwell; Daughters, Mrs. Gladys Denton, Miss Mildred Brantley, both of Knoxville, Mrs. Anette Romines, Speedwell; Sons, W. C. Brantley, Maryville; 6 grandchildren; 8 great grandchildren; sister, Mrs. Edna Rogers, Jacksboro; brothers, Clyde Brantley, Jacksboro, Roy Brantley Sr., Nashville, Otto Brantley, Elizabethton, Michigan. Funeral service 2 p.m. Monday at Carrs Chapel Baptist Church, Rev. Ellis Hoskins officiating. He was a member of Pleasant Hill Baptist Church.

William C. Capps

William C. Capps was born May 9, 1896, and departed this life April 7, 1976, being 79 years, 10 months and 28 days old. He professed faith in Christ at an early age and joined Black Fox Primitive Baptist Church where he remained a faithful member. He was a Veteran of World War I. Survivors to mourn his passing: wife, Flossie; daughter, Maxine; sons, Bennie, all of Maynardville, Tennessee, Cecil and Dale of Knoxville, Tennessee. Nine grandchildren and one great grandchild. Sisters: Mrs. Kate Lay, Mrs. Iva Davis, and Mrs. Dollie Helton, all of Washburn, Tennessee, Mrs. Gertrude Greene of Corryton, Tennessee, and Mrs. Lula Campbell of Morristown, Tennessee. Funeral services were conducted April 10, 1976, at Black Fox Church with Elder Alvin Graves, Elder Parnick Shelton and Rev. Walter Smith officiating. Interment in Cabbage Cemetery. Pallbearers were nephews: Otis and Basel Cabbage, Ralph and Earl Helton, Bobby and Billy Lay. Ailor's of Maynardville in charge.

Billy Charles Cobb

Billy Charles Cobb age 28 of Cumberland Gap, Tennessee, passed away at Bowling Green, Ohio, on August 14, 1976. Son of the late Hershell and Roxie (Ball) Cobb. He was a member of the Primitive Baptist Church of Gibson Station. Survivors: wife, Mary; son, Lee of Cumberland Gap. Three brothers, James Cobb of Copperas Cove, Texas, Danny Cobb of Archibold, Ohio, Floyd Cobb of Napeleon, Ohio. Several nieces and nephews. Host of relatives and friends.

Oscar Verlin Edwards

Oscar Verlin Edwards was born November 7, 1895, and departed this life on April 10, 1975, at St. Mary's Hospital in Knoxville, Tennessee. He was married to Cecil Graves on April 8, 1922. To this union 12 children were born, three of whom preceded him in death. Survivors are his wife; eight sons, Coy, Kenneth, Condis, Boyd and Carl of Speedwell, Tennessee; Loyd, Austion, and Terry of Dayton, Ohio; one daughter, Mrs. William Branscomb of Speedwell, Tennessee; two brothers, James and Alonzo of Speedwell; four sisters, Edna Robbins and Minnie Collingworth of Madisonville, Tennessee, Lou Lambert of Speedwell, Tennessee, and Mae Pace of Eva, Tennessee; 18 grandchildren, five step-grandchildren; four great grandchildren; and eight step great grandchildren. He joined Pleasant Hill Primitive Baptist Church in 1917 and was a faithful member until death. He was assistant clerk for 47 years. Funeral services were held by Elders Alvin Graves, James Henry Branscomb, Albert Davis and Tony Eastridge. Burial in the Hunter Cemetery.

Flossie Odella (Yadon) Keck
Mrs. Flossie Odella Yadon Keck, age 83, of 1916 McCroskey Avenue, passed away at 4 a.m. Thursday at the home. She was the widow of Otis Keck who died in 1954. She was a member of the Kirkwood Primitive Baptist Church. She was born in Grainger County, the daughter of Mr. and Mrs. Jasper David (Jay) Yadon. She is survived by one daughter, Mrs. Eddie Strader, of Knoxville; sons, William B. Keck, of Gastonia, N.C., Roy Otis Keck, Jr., and James Frank Keck, both of Knoxville. One sister, Mrs. Lucie Yadon McDonald, Knoxville, and 7 grandchildren and 7 great grandchildren. Funeral services at 2 p.m. Friday at Stevens Chapel, Elder E.M. Berry officiating. Interment Lynnhurst Cemetery. Pallbearers: Grandsons. Honorary pallbearers, Deacons of Kirkwood Primitive Baptist Church.

Mrs. Roxie Ellen Beason Keck
Mrs. Roxie Ellen Beason Keck was born October 16, 1885, died May 5, 1976 at the age of 91 years. She was married to J.L. Keck and to this union was born three children. She was preceded in death by her

husband a n d one s o n. She is s u r v i v e d by two daughters: Mrs. Bertha Heath and Mrs.Edith Moyers, both of New Tazewell. One brother: Hubert Beason, Knoxville, Tennessee. Five grandchildren, eight great grandchildren. She professed Faith in Christ at an early age and joined Pleasant Point Primative Baptist Church where she remained a member until death. She was an inspiration to the ones who loved and cared fo r her a n d bore her illness wit h so much patience. May She Rest In Peace With God.

Mary Ann McFarland

Mary Ann McFarland age 78 years, passed away June 1, 1976. She leaves to mourn her loss: one brother, Emmet McFarland of Corryton, Tennessee; one sister, Arletta Shoffner of Knoxville, Tennessee; several nieces and nephews. She professed hope in Christ at an early age and joined Davis Chapel Primitive Baptist Church where she remained a member until her death. Funeral services were held at Rose Funeral Home Chapel on June 3, 1976, Elder H. E. Brummitt and Elder Everett Berry officiating. She was laid to rest in Lynnhurst Cemetery.

Elder Linvel I. Meyers

Elder Linvel I. Meyers was born February 1, 1897 and departed this life April 18, 1976. Making his stay here 79 years, 2 months, and 17 days. He joined the Monroe, Michigan Primitive Baptist Church July 8, 1950 and faithfully pastored this church till God called him home.

Elder Meyers was united in marriage to Ida Mae Lynch on April 29, 1917. To this union was born 7 children. 3 sons: Leon of Maynardville, Tenn.; Lynn, of Sarasota, Florida; and Calvin of Monroe, Michigan. Daughter: Mrs. Charles (Ruby) Simmons of Sarasota, Florida; Mrs. Wayne (Lorene) Pope of Monroe, Michigan; Mrs. Victor (Wanda) Peles of Pennsylvania; and one daughter who preceded him in death. His wife, Ida Mae, also preceded him in death, October 1, 1962.

He is survived by his present wife, Virginia Poore Meyers, whom he married December 7, 1963. Other survivors are: 1 brother, C.A. Meyers; 1 sister, Mrs. Chester (Dorsie) Minton; 17 grandchildren, and 17 great-grandchildren.

Elder Meyers was an able minister whom God had blessed to have great insight into the Holy Word. He spent many hours in study and meditation on the Bible. He will be greatly missed by those whom he knew and loved. But "...we know that if our earthly house of this tabernacle were dissolved, we have a building of God, an house not made with hands, eternal in the heavens."

Funeral services were conducted by Elder Charles Taylor at Monroe, Michigan on April 21, 1976, and his body was laid to rest in the cemetery nearby to await the resurrection morning.

Haley Paradine Owens

Haley Paradine Owens of Route 3 Speedwell, Tennessee was born January 14, 1896, to the late James and Cumy Edwards. Departed this life December 9,

1975, at the age of 79 years. She was married to Ossero Owens April 25, 1914. She leaves to morn her husband, Ossero Owens of Speedwell; five sons, Albert, James, Marshall, and Claude Owens, all Dayton, Ohio. Dave Owens of Knoxville, Tennessee. Five daughters, Mrs. Bonnie Hagewood, Mrs. Dale (Marie) Evans both of Monroe, Michigan; Mrs. Harold (Alida) Drummonds of Phoenix, New York; Mrs. Ditsy (Cleo) Russell, Miss Nila Owens both of Speedwell, Tennessee. Her oldest daughter (Myrtle) preceded her in death December 25, 1954. 21 grandchildren, 15 great grandchildren. She also leaves one brother, Dock Henry Edwards of Middlesboro, Kentucky. She professed hope in Christ at an early age and joined the Pleasant Hill, Primitive Baptist Church, where she remained a true member. Funeral services were held at the Pleasant Hill, Primitive Baptist Church on December 12 with Elder Alvin Graves and Elder Tony Eastridge officiating. Her body was laid to rest in the Ausmus Cemetery at Speedwell.

Mother, you're no longer with us on this earth anymore
But by the Grace of God, we'll meet again on that beautiful shore
Where there'll be no parting, no tears to dim the eyes
We'll live up there forever in the sweet bye and bye.
(Written by daughter, Mrs. Harold Drummonds)

Mrs. Meldia Paul

Mrs. Meldia Paul, age 62 of Speedwell, passed away Saturday, August 16, 1975, at the Caliborne County Hospital. She was survived by her daughters; Mrs. Virie Wright, Speedwell, Mrs. Geneva Irvin, Cumberland Gap, Mrs. Jerldeen Pritchard, Speedwell, Mrs. Annie Sutton, Somerville, Ohio, Mrs. Linda Douglas, LaFollette, Miss Gracie Paul, Speedwell; sons, Alonzo Paul, Hamilton, Ohio, Curtis Paul, Cumberland Gap, Lonas Paul, Tazewell, James Paul, Piqua, Ohio, Willis Paul, Billy Paul, Johnny Paul of Speedwell. Brothers: Rufus Miracle, Lexington, Ky., Andy Miracle, T.J.

Miracle, Billy G. Miracle, of New Tazewell, Sisters: Mrs. Katie Cupp, Tazewell, Mrs. Rose Annie Tuttle, Crossville, and a host of other relatives and friends to mourn her passing. The funeral services were held Tuesday 2 p.m. at Meyers Grove Baptist Church with Rev. George Douglas and Rev. Don Douglas officiating. Interment Drummonds Cemetery. Reeces in charge.

Mary (Miracle) Roberts

Mary (Miracle) Roberts was born March 3, 1900, departed this life November 11, 1975. She was married to George Roberts and to this union were born 8 children: Lloyd, Irving, Robert, Lena Henderson, Betty Petree, Ruth Hawkins, Bertha Hawkins, Aggie Schmidt, and Lee Roberts who prededed her in death. Sister Mary professed a hope in Christ and later joined the Primitive Baptist at Pleasant Hill Church and lived a faithful member until God called her home. She is sadly missed by her husband, her children, 30 grandchildren and 6 great-grandchildren. Pleasant Hill has lost a wonderful member.

Mrs. Loalles Keck Robinette

Mrs. Loalles Keck Robinette, age 62, of Route 2 Buttermilk Road, Kingston, passed away Sunday morning. She was a member of Pleasant Point Primitive Baptist Church. Survivors: husband, Fanoy Robinette; daughter, Mrs. Howard (Jo Ann) Silvis of Kingston; son, Estal Robinette, Kingston; 1 grandchild, Annette Burchfield; sister, Mrs. Dan (Cecil) Carey of Morristown, Mrs. John (Lovetta) Crawford of Powell, Mrs. Major (Roberta) Carr and Mrs. Hughes (Rowena) Barnes of Tazewell; 2 brothers, Fay and Russell Keck of Tazewell; several nieces and nephews; many friends. Funeral 2 p.m. Tuesday at Bradbury United Methodist Church, Rev. Bob Cantrell, Rev. Virtrue Sharp officiating. Burial in church cemetery. The body will be at the family home after 2 p.m. Monday Click Funeral Home, Lenoir City in charge.

Harvie Rhymer

Harvie Rhymer passed away Friday, April 16, 1976 at the Claiborne County Hospital at the age of 86. He was a Member and a Deacon of Gibson Station Primitive Baptist Church which he had loved and attended faithfully till death. He leaves to mourn his passing: Wife, Hazel Rhymer, Ewing, Va.; Sons, George of Wauseon, Ohio, Paul of Hamilton, Ohio, Leroy of Bluefield, West Virginia, Esco of LaFollette, Tenn., Clyde in the U.S. Army, Germany, and Bill of Harrogate, Tenn.; Daughters: Mae Carson of La-Follette, Tenn., Anna Bateman, Ruth Warf, June Ball, and Margaret Rhymer, all of Ewing, Va. He also had 35 grandchildren, 37 great-grandchildren, and a host of relatives and friends. Funeral services were held at Gibson Station Primitive Baptist Church with Elders Everett Berry, Larry Anderson, and Spurgeon Thompson officiating. Pallbearers: Doyle Bolton, Rev. Hubert Munsey, Grant Carmack, Elder Bill Berry, Elder Charles Taylor, Wayne Bolton, and Claude Sandifer. He was laid to rest in the Southern Cemetery with Reece Funeral Home in charge.

John L. Sharp

John L. Sharp, of Halls Cross Roads, was born January 9, 1905 at Maynardville, Tennessee and passed away July 5, 1976 at 5 A.M. He was married to Evelyn Petree, June 9, 1929. He was a member of Kirkwood Primitive Baptist Church. Funeral Service was conducted at Mynatt Mortuary by Elder Everette Berry and Elder Bill Berry. The body was interred at Lynnhurst Cemetery. He will be dearly missed by family and friends.

Charlie Payne Shoffner

Charlie Payne Shoffner age 56, passed away 5:00 p.m. Tuesday, October 7, 1975 at Sharps Chapel, Tennessee. He was a Deacon and a Faithful member of Oak Grove Primitive Baptish Church. Survivors: Wife, Edna Shoffner, Daughters: Mrs. Wanda Sheckels,

Mrs. Ann Weaver and Mrs. Donna Flatford all of Sharps Chapel. Mrs. Glenda Hunley of Corryton and Mrs. Kathy Keck of New Tazewell. Sons: J.D. of Heiskell, Tennessee, Jack, Tom, and Steve of Sharps Chapel. 12 grandchildren. Brother: Mannie Shoffner of Sharps Chapel. Sisters: Mrs. Nelle Sherritze of New Tazewell, Mrs. Belle Moore of Kokomo, Ind. and Mrs. Francis Eastridge of Louisville, Tenn. Funeral services were held on Friday October 10, 1976 at 11:00 a.m. at Oak Grove Primitive Baptist Church with Rev. Lloyd England and Elder J.C. Monday officiating. Interment was in the Rush Strong Cemetery, Pallbearers: Malcolm Walker, Aaron Cole, Alfred Relford, Woodrow Cole, Monte Cole, Jim Sharp and Doc England. "Wake to sleep no more, Dad; We love you but God loved you more." The Family

Lydia (Granny) Spoons

Mrs. Lydia (Granny) Spoons was born August 6, 1875, and passed from this life October 21, 1975. Making her stay on earth 100 years, 2 months, and 15 days. She had been a member of the Lenoir City Primitive Baptist Church for many years. She was faithful in her devotion to the church during all these years and spoke of her desire to be able to attend services even when she was no longer able to get to her church meetings. Her faithfulness is evidenced by the large number of her offspring who are now members following in the footsteps of her and her beloved husband. Surely her "works do follow after her". She will be greatly missed by her children, their children, and all who knew and loved her. She is survived by her daughters, Mrs. Myra McLaughlin, Mrs. Cora Arden, Mrs. Lucy Graves, and Mrs. Della Packett, all of Lenoir City, and Mrs. Maggie Petty of Nashville; son, Roy Spoons of Lenoir City; one sister, Mrs. Maggie Wilson of Ringold, Georgia; 32 grandchildren, 59 great-grandchildren, and 31 great-great-grandchildren. Funeral services were conducted by Elder Charles Taylor and Rev. Roy Arwood, October 24 at Click Funeral Home. Her body was laid to reat in Lenoir City Cemetery to await the call of her blessed Redeemer at the resurrection morning.

STATISTICAL TABLE

CHURCHES	DELEGATES	Restored	Received by Letter	Baptism	Relationship	Dismissed by Letter	Excluded	Deceased	Total Membership	Printing Minutes	REGULAR MEETING TIME	COMMUNION TIME
BLACK FOX	Bros. Dale Capps, Bennie Capps, Sisters: Flossie Capps, Mary Ruth Capps, Pamela Capps	0	0	0	0	0	0	1	87	$20	Second Sat. night and Sunday. Third Sat. night and Sunday.	Second Sunday in June
BRADEN'S CHAPEL	Elders W.M. Sparks, Noble Clawson, Bros. Timmie Edwards, Matthew Edwards, Sisters: Helen Clawson, Leecy Sparks, Racheal Lambert	0	0	3	7	1	0	2	140	$15	First Saturday & Sunday of each month	First Sunday in July
BRANTLEY'S CHAPEL	Elder Clifford Brantley, Bros. Everett Brantley, Daniel Brantley, Sisters: Barsha Brantley, Mildred Brantley, Linda Brantley	0	0	0	1	1	1	0	83	$25	Second Sat. night Every Sunday and Sunday night	Second Sunday in July
DAVIS CHAPEL	Bros. James Heatherly, Orice McCarty, Seth Welch, Sisters: Ruth Heatherly, Mamie Parrott, Mollie McCarty, Ollie Welch, Lassie Ellison	0	0	0	0	0	0	1	140	$20	Third Sat. night Every Sunday & Sunday night	Third Sunday in June
FAITH	Elder Howard M. Pippin, Sister Phylis J. Pippin	0	0	0	0	0	0	0	5	$20	Every Sunday & Sunday night	Fourth Sunday in Sept.
GETHSEMANE	Elders Glenn Abbott, John Godfrey, Bros. C.H. Godfrey, Tommy Carmichael, Sisters: Myrtle Cook, Mary Godfrey, Billie Godfrey, June Carmichael	0	0	0	0	0	1	0	31	$25		Fourth Sunday in May and October

Church	Officers and Members									Fee	Meeting Time	Association Time
GIBSON STATION	Elder Joe Irving, Bros. Franklin Jones, Bill Rhymer, Spurgeon Thompson, Sisters: Fannie Jones, Sally Brittain, Evelyn Maples, Karen Rhymer, Mellie Thompson, Virginia Bolton, Dorothy Johnson, Susas Shoffner	0	0	0	0	0	0	1	80	$25	First Sat. & Sat. night of each month and Sunday & Sunday night	First Sunday in June
HEADRICK CHAPEL	Elder Robert Walker, Bros. William B. Cook, Clyde Abbott, Sr., Sister: Grace Abbott	1	0	0	0	0	0	0	108	$25	Sunday following first Sat. following third Saturday	First Sun in May and October
KIRKWOOD	Elders H.E. Brummitt, Walter Lyons, Bros. C.A. Sharp, Elwood Evans, Sisters: Ruby Brummitt, Freida Sharp, Velma Evans	0	2	0	0	0	0	2	108	$30	Every Sunday morning	Last Sunday in April
LENOIR CITY	Elders Alvin Graves, Charles Taylor, Bros. Hubert Spoons Clyde Abbott, Raymond Wilkerson, Sisters: Anne Spoons, Betty Abbott, Shirley Graves	0	0	4	2	0	1	1	154	$35	Every Sunday and Sunday night	Third Sunday in May
MONROE, MICHIGAN	Letter received no delegates presented	0	0	1	0	0	0	1	13	$10	Third Sunday of each month	Sunday after third Saturday in July
MYERS GROVE	Elder Clay Widner, Bros. Clifford Robertson, Isom Drummonds, Sisters Ioa Robertson, Wanda Widner, Velt Muncey	0	0	0	0	0	0	1	70	$20	Second Sat. night & Sunday Fourth Sat. night & Sunday	Fourth Sunday in May
NOETON	Elder John Oliver, Bros. Carroll Oliver, Charlie Collins, Sisters Ruth Oliver, Dora Collins	0	0	4	0	0	0	0	40	$20	First Sunday Third Sat. night and Sunday	Third Sunday in May and September
OAK GROVE	Elders Johnny Atkins, Toni Eastridge, Bros. Aaron Cole, Malcolm Walker, Jim Sharp, Sisters: Veda Cole, Francis Eastridge,	0	0	9	9	0	0	4	327	$25	First Sat. and Sunday	First Sunday in May

PLEASANT HILL	Elders Albert Davis, Larry Anderson, James H. Branscomb, Bros. Jerry Lynn Hensley, Sisters Audry Davis, Myra Anderson, Helen Ruth Branscomb	0	1	2	0	2	0	3	111	$30	Fourth Sat. & Sunday	Fourth Sunday in June
PLEASANT POINT	Elder Claude Rosson, Bros. Lawerence Rosson, Sister Doris Rosson	0	0	1	0	0	0	2	117	$15	First Sat. night and Sunday / Third Sunday	First Sunday in July
ROCKY DALE	Elders Everett Berry, Parnick Shelton, Joe Bush, William Berry, Bros. W.H. Taylor, Donald Sharp, Sisters Trula Berry, Lola Berry, Lou Emma Taylor, Dorothy Sharp, Fay Collett	0	0	9	0	2	0	0	127	$30	Every Sunday & Sunday night	Second Sunday in May

CHURCH	COUNTY	PASTOR	CLERK	ADDRESS
Black Fox	Grainger	Elder Alvin Graves	Bennie Capps / Flossie Capps	P. O. Box 91, Maynardville, Tn. 37807 / Maynardville, Tn. 37807
Braden's Chapel	Union	Elder Noble Clawson / Elder J. C. Monday, Asst.	Jimmie B. Edwards / Phyllis Wilson, Asst.	Speedwell, Tn. / Speedwell, Tn.
Brantley's Chapel	Blount	Elder Clifford Brantley	D. C. Brantley / Daniel Brantley, Asst.	2020 Biddle Rd., Maryville, Tn. / Rt. 10, Mint Road, Maryville, Tn.
Davis Chapel	Campbell	Elder William Berry	Ruth Heatherly / Lassie Ellison, Asst.	Rt. 1, Davis Chapel Rd., LaFollette, Tn. / 918 Carwynn Rd., LaFollette, Tn.

Church	County	Minister	Clerk	Address
Faith		Elder Howard M. Pippin	Inez M. Pippin	c/o Elder Howard M. Pippin 7435 Lone Oak Blvd. Spartanburg, South Carolina 29303
Gethsemane	Knox	Elder Walter Lyons	Tom Carmichael	729 Frank St., Knoxville, Tn.
Gibson Station	Lee Virginia	Elder Joe Irving, Asst. Elder Everette Berry	Dorothy Johnson Shirley Sandifer	Rt. 2, Ewing, Va. Rt. 2, Harrogate, Tn.
Headrick Chapel	Knox	Elder Glenn Abbott	Clyde Abbott, Sr.	Rt. 7, Sevierville, Tn.
Kirkwood	Knox	Elder Everette Berry	Estelle Petree Sharp Alice Tinell Powers	Rt. 27, Emory Road, Knoxville, Tn. 2923 Clearview Ave., Knoxville, Tn.
Lenoir City	Loudon	Elder Charles Taylor	Scott Collins	705 W. 5th Ave., Lenoir City, Tn.
Monroe, Michigan	Monroe		Gertrude Zwack Roxie Drummonds, Asst.	1825 Spaulding Rd., Monroe, Michigan 2675 Blue Bush Rd., Monroe, Michigan
Myers Grove	Claiborne	Elder Clay Widner Elder Jimmy Branscomb, Asst.	Bonnie Miracle Harold Cupp, Asst.	Rt. 2, Box 194, New Tazewell, Tn. Rt. 2, New Tazewell, Tn.
Noeton	Grainger	Elder John Oliver	Carroll Oliver Bessie Collins, Asst.	Rt. 2, Box 512, Bean Station, Tn. Rt. 5, Morristown, Tn.
Oak Grove	Union	Elder J. C. Monday	Betty P. Sharp Betty Shoffner, Asst.	Sharp Chapel, Tn. Sharp Chapel, Tn.

Church	County			
Pleasant Hill	Claiborne	Elder Alvin Graves	William Branscomb	Speedwell, Tn.
		Elder Albert Davis, Asst.	Larry Anderson	Speedwell, Tn.
Pleasant Point	Claiborne	Elder Parnick Shelton	Elder Claude Rosson	Rt. 4, New Tazewell, Tn.
Rocky Dale	Knox	Elder Hugh Brummitt	Edward Collett	Rt. 1, Luttrell, Tn.
			Dennis Branson	Rt. 13, Knoxville, Tn.

1977 MINUTES

of the
POWELL VALLEY ASSOCIATION
OF PRIMITIVE BAPTIST

BRANTLEY'S CHAPEL CHURCH

Held with the Sister Church
at
BRANTLEY'S CHAPEL CHURCH
IN BLOUNT COUNTY, TENN.
AUGUST 19, 20, 21, 1977

THE ONE HUNDRED FIFTY-SEVENTH
ANNUAL SESSION
OF THE
POWELL VALLEY ASSOCIATION
OF
PRIMITIVE BAPTIST

WAS HELD WITH THE SISTER CHURCH AT
BRANTLEY'S CHAPEL IN BLOUNT COUNTY
TENNESSEE AUGUST 19, 1977

NEXT SESSION WILL BE HELD WITH THE
SISTER CHURCH AT ROCKY DALE IN KNOX
COUNTY, TENNESSEE TO BEGIN ON FRIDAY
BEFORE THE THIRD SATURDAY IN AUGUST
1978 TO BEGIN AT 10:30 A.M. AND CONTINUE
FOR THREE DAYS, WITH ELDER WILLIAM
BERRY DELIVERING THE INTRODUCTORY
SERMON AND ELDER WALTER LYONS AS
THE ALTERNATE.

OFFICERS

Elder Albert Davis .... Moderator
Speedwell, Tennessee Ph. 869-3596

Elder Hugh E. Brummitt...Assistant Moderator
1329 Brown Ave., Knoxville Ph. 546-7700

Bro. W. H. Taylor .... Clerk
Rt. 27 - Knoxville, Tennessee Ph. 922-2143

Bro. Bennie Capps .... Assistant Clerk
Maynardville, Tennessee Ph. 992-5571

Friday, August 19, 1977

The one hundred fifty-eighth annual session of the Powell Valley Association of Primitive Baptist met with the sister church at Brantley's Chapel in Blount County, August 19, 20, and 21, 1977 at 10:30 a.m.

After the song service, the Moderator introduced the service by quoting some scripture from memory then calling for a song.

After singing, Elder Johnny Atkins of Oak Grove Church preached the introductory sermon, using the 3rd Chapter of Acts, verses 22 through 26, staying with the theme of God's Sovereignty and God's Grace and Righteousness and preaching a wonderful sermon. After this and a song, the Association was dismissed in prayer by Elder Pippin of Lenoir City for a 15 minute recess.

After recess and at the sound of singing, the Association was again convened and the Moderator read from the 4th Chapter of 1st Timothy, then called for the opening prayer by Elder Walter Lyons. Then went into the business session.

1. The Moderator called for the letters of the Sister Churches to be presented to the Clerk for reading. Sixteen were received.

Called for any one from the Sister Chur-
hes present and not delegated who
wish to come and give the Clerk your
name and the church you are from. None
came.

3. A motion was approved that we accept
the letters of the 16 churches and seat
the delegates of these churches.

4. The Moderator called for petitionary
letters, if any from churches of the
same faith. None was received.
Motion approved that the Association
re-elect Elder Albert Davis as Moderator, and Elder Hugh E. Brummitt as
Assistant Moderator.

6. Motion approved that we re-elect Brother Bennie Capps as Assistant Clerk.

7. Motion approved that the Moderator appoint all the committees for this session.

8. The Moderator, after being authorized,
made the appointments as follows:
Committee on Arrangements
Brother Robert P. Bridges
Brother Clyde Abbott, Jr.
Elder Toni Eastridge
Committee on Preaching
Brother Jeff Ellison
Brother C. H. Godfrey
Brother Carroll Oliver

Committee on Request
Brother Clyde Abbott, Sr.
Elder Larry Anderson
Elder Spurgeon Thompson
Committee on Finance
Brother Vaughn Beason
Elder Bill Berry
Elder Alvin Graves

9. Motion approved that the Association be recessed until Saturday morning at 10:30 when it will re-convene at the sound of singing. After a song, we were dismissed in prayer by Elder John Oliver of Noeton Church.

Saturday, August 20, 1977

1. Saturday morning the Association re-convened at 10:30 A.M. at the sound of singing. After a good song service, the Assistant Moderator, Elder Hugh E. Brummitt introduced the service by making a good and humble talk and reading from the 3rd Chapter of Proverbs, then Called for prayer by Elder William Sparks of Braden's Chapel Church.

2. Moderator, Elder Albert Davis, then continued the business of the Association by calling for any letters not pre-

sented on Friday. One was received from the Sister Church at Braden's Chapel. The letter was accepted and the delegates seated.

3. The Moderator called for any one not delegated, who wish to be seated as such to come forward. None came.

4. Call was made for the report of the Committee on Arrangements who made the following report, which was accepted and the committee released.

Report of Committee on Arrangements

a. Call for the roll call of delegates.

b. Call for the report of Committee on Preaching.

c. call for the report of Committe on Request.

d. call for the report of the Committee on Finance.

e. Decide how many minutes to have printed, who shall supervise the printing and distribution of same, how much he shall receive for this service. Also, where will the next session of the Association be held and who shall preach the introductory sermon and who shall be the alternate.

Respectfully submitted,

Elder Toni Eastridge
Brother Clyde Abbott, Jr.
Brother R. P. Bridges

5. The Moderator called for the roll call of delegates and the absentees noted. Called for the report of the Committee on Preaching, who gave the following report which was accepted and the committee released.

Report of Committee on Preaching

We, the Committee on Preaching, beg to submit the following report for the preaching services.

Friday Night Elder Walter Lyons
               Elder Parnick Shelton

Saturday   Elder John Oliver
               Elder Hugh Brummitt

Saturday Night
               Elder Larry Anderson
               Elder Spurgeon Thompson

Sunday   Elder Bill Sparks
               Elder Bill Berry

Respectfully submitted,

Brother Carroll Oliver
Brother Jeff Ellison
Brother C. H. Godfrey

7. Called for the report of the Committee on Request, who made the following request which was accepted and the committee released.

We the Committee on Request, wish to request that we have 1,150 copies of the Minutes printed and that the clerk supervise the printing and distribution of the same and that he be paid $100.00 for this service. We also request that the next session of this Association be held with the Sister Church of Rocky Dale in Knox County, Tennessee to begin on Friday, before the third Saturday in August, 1978, at 10:30 A.M. We also request that a Circular letter be printed in the minutes and that it be written by Elder Joe Irving of Gibson Station.

Respectfully submitted,

Elder Larry Anderson
Elder Spurgeon Thompson
Brother Clyde Abbott, Sr.

8. Call for the report of the Committe on report.
Report of the finance as follows, was accepted and the committee released.

Report of Finance Committee

Church	Amount
Black Fox	$20.00
Braden's Chapel	15.00
Brantley's Chapel	25.00
Davis Chapel	20.00
Faith Primitive Baptist	15.00
Gethsemane	25.00
Gibson Station	25.00
Headrick Chapel	25.00
Kirkwood	30.00
Lenoir City	35.00
Monroe, Michigan	10.00
Meyers Grove	20.00
Noeton	20.00
Oak Grove	25.00
Pleasant Hill	30.00
Pleasant Point	15.00
Rocky Dale	30.00
	$385.00

Respectfully submitted

Elder Bill Berry

Elder Alvin Graves

Brother Vaughn Beason

9. Motion approved that we grant the request of the Committee and have 1,150 minutes printed and that the Clerk supervise the printing and distribution of

10. Motion approved that, as requested, the next session be held with the Sister Church of Rocky Dale in Knox County, Tennessee, to begin on Friday before the third Saturday in August, 1978, at 10:30 A.M.

11. Motion approved that Elder Bill Berry shall preach the introductory sermon, and that Elder Walter Lyons be the alternate.

12. Motion approved that Elder Joe Irving shall prepare the Circular letter to be printed in minutes for 1978.

13. Motion approved that we drop the paragraph inserted in article four of the Rules of Decorum, and insert in the minutes the article four as it read in the previous minutes through 1975

14. Motion approved that we do not letter and delegate to the Elk River Association since they did not with our Association.

15. Motion approved that we extend to the Church and the entire Community and people at Brantley's Chapel our heart felt thanks for the love and kindness and good food while in your church. And as we leave you, we leave with love and prayers that God's richest

blessing rest with you till we meet
again. The Association then was
closed with a song and much rejoicing
and testifying, then dismissed in prayer
by Elder Parnick Shelton.

Elder Albert Davis, Moderator
Elder Hugh E. Brummitt, Asst. Moderator
Brother W. H. Taylor, Clerk
Brother Bennie Capps, Asst. Clerk

Sunday, August 21, 1977

Sunday at the appointed hour of 10:30 A.M.
and at the sound of singing, the house was
filled to capacity. After singing the good songs
of Zion, Elder Clifford Brantley of Brantley's
Chapel, the host church, gave a talk and welcomed the congregation and called on Elder
Bill Rhymer of Gibson Station Church for prayer.

Following prayer and a song, Elder William
Sparks of Braden's Chapel Church came forward
and preached a wonderful sermon, reading from
the 2nd Chapter of 1st Corinthians. He followed the theme of God's Love for his people
and Faith in God.

After a wonderful lesson by Elder Sparks,
Elder Bill Berry of Rocky Dale Church followed and used as his starting point, the 68th, and

69th verses of the 1st Chapter of St. Luke. Elder Berry gave a very spiritual and touching sermon which was followed by much rejoicing and testimony after which the service was closed in prayer by Elder Claude Rosson.

Circular Letter

Dear Brothers and Sisters in Christ, I was appointed by the Association to write a circular letter to be carried in the minutes for the session of 1977.

The purpose of this letter among all the churches of the same faith ahd belief. So let us look at a few of the things we believe. We believe that God is Sovereign and never changes and that He will do His will and none can hinder or stay his hand. We believe that Salvation is by the Grace of God and that every one that is saved this way will be found, because Jesus said, all that the Father give Me shall come to Me and I will raise them up at the last day. We believe that He is God in Heaven and God on earth beneath and if He had the power to create this earth and set the Sun, Moon and Stars in place, why is He not able to save and do His Will despite the efforts of feeble men.

Knowing this, I pray God that you will hold to God's unchanging hand and uphold and pray for your pastors and love your Brothers and Sisters with that love that only God can give and remember your unworthy servant when you pray.

Elder Johnny Atkins

MINISTERS DIRECTORY

Elder Glenn Abbott
1801 Cherrybrook Drive
Knoxville, Tennessee
Phone 957-6895

Elder Larry Anderson
Speedwell, Tennessee

Elder Johnny Atkins
Bean Station, Tennessee
Phone 767-2397

Elder Johnny Ayers
New Tazewell, Tennessee

Elder Everette Berry
Route #24
Knoxville, Tennessee
Phone 922-7004

Elder William Berry
Route #24
Knoxville, Tennessee
Phone 922-2269

Elder J. H. Branscomb
Speedwell, Tennessee
Phone 562-6361

Elder Clifford Brantley
Brown School Road
Maryville, Tennessee
Phone 982-3735

Elder Hugh E. Brummitt
1329 Brown Ave.
Knoxville, Tennessee
Phone 546-7700

Elder J. C. Monday
Speedwell, Tennessee
Phone 562-3068

Elder Sheridan Moore
Route #1
Townsend, Tennessee

Elder John Oliver
Bean Station, Tennessee

Elder Howard Pippin
101 Rose Street
Lenoir City, Tennessee

Elder Claude Rosson
Route #4
New Tazewell, Tennessee
Phone 626-3168

Elder Joe Bush
Corryton, Tennessee
Phone 687-2108

Elder Noble Clawson
Rt. #4
Speedwell, Tennessee
Phone 562-2004

Elder Albert Davis
Speedwell, Tennessee
Phone 869-3596

Elder Clay Widner
Route #1
Tazewell, Tennessee
Phone 523-2746

(Ministers Directory cont'd)

Elder Toni Eastridge
Route #3
Louisville, Tennessee
Phone 983-1068

Elder Alvin Graves
122 Oak Wood Drive
Lenoir City, Tennessee
Phone 986-9725

Elder Joe Irving
Route #2
Ewing, Virginia

Elder Walter Lyons
1602 Garfield Street
Alcoa, Tennessee
Phone 984-3207

Elder John Godfrey
15443 Valleoga
Victoryvill, California
Phone (714)243-4661

Elder Robert Walker
Sevierville, Tennessee

Elder Parnick Shelton
Corryton, Tennessee
Phone 687-6142

Elder William Sparks
Speedwell, Tennessee
Phone 562-7997

Elder William Rhymer
Route #2
Harrogate, Tennessee

Elder Spurgeon Thompson
Box #36
Shawanee, Tennessee

Licentiates

Brother Clyde Abbott
Route #7
Sevierville, Tennessee

Brother Roscoe Branscomb
Speedwell, Tennessee

Brother Odell Carpenter
Maryville, Tennessee

Brother Ray Walker
Route #1
Townsend, Tennessee

RULES OF DECORUM

1. The churches composing the Powell's Valley Association shall not be confined to any set rules as to specific number of Messengers they shall have in the body, but shall have the right to name in their letters as many as they choose, and in addition all orderly members of and of the churches being present be entitled to seats in the body as Messengers of their respective churches, with all the rights and privileges of the same.

2. The Messengers thus assembled shall be denominated the Powell's Valley Primitive Baptist Association.

3. For the purpose of historical information and statistical edification, the Churches are required to state in letters, the number of members in fellowship, the number received by Baptism, by letter, by confession of Faith, the number dismissed, excluded and dead since last session; also the time of their meeting, their pastoral supply, and the amount of money contributed for ministers and other purposes together with any other information they deem appropriate for the edification of the saints and glory of God.

4. This Association shall have no power to answer queries, give advice, or dictate to the Churches in any case, or to lord it over God's heritage nor any power by which she can directly or indirectly fringe on the internal rights of the church or censure and try any church or member in reference to faith and practice and determine upon valigity of gospel ordinances. These things shall rest entirely with the churches; but henceforward our annual meetings shall be only for the purpose of hearing from each other, and for the worship of God and mutual comfort and edification of the Saints. To this end we reserve the privilege annually for the Third Friday in August and the two following days or at such other times as may be agreed upon with any church that may invite us having to protect our own standard, while in session, from heresay and disorder to recognize and invite any primitive Baptist minister or any lay brother to worship with us that may deem proper; to request the brethren of our body to visit other churches or bodies in our belief with whom we may desire to culture Christian fellowship; to publish in a minute of our proceedings.

5. Each session of the body shall have a Moderator and Clerk who shall hold office until re-elected.

6. Any order member of any church belonging to this body, when convened, being present shall be eligible to elect on as Moderator and Clerk or to sit on any committee appointed by the same.

7. In all election or questions that may be necessary to determine by vote, the vote shall be taken by churches, each church being entitled to three votes for any number less than one hundred, and one additional vote for every fifty or fraction thereof above the first hundred, but the Messengers of each church may divide their vote as they see proper.

8. All elections or questions coming to vote shall be determined by a majority vote cast, and it shall be the only duty of the minority to acquiesce in the decision thus reached.

9. If new churches desire to be admitted to this union they shall petition by letter and messengers and if voted for and recommended by one or more sister churches for her Presbytery constitutioning them, as orthodox and orderly they shall be received by the vote of the body and manifested by the Moderator giving the Messengers the right hand of fellowship.

10. Any motion or resolution clearly inconsistent with the above rules shall be promptly ruled out of order unless withdrawn by the mover.

11. Any Messenger being ruled out of order by the Moderator shall have the right to appeal to the body on the question of order, and if sustained shall be allowed to proceed, but if not take his seat.

12. Our meeting being held in the name of Christ and the worship of God; each Messenger is expected to observe due and proper therein.

13. It will not be considered good for any Messenger whose name has been enrolled as such to abruptly break off or absent himself from the Association without leave.

14. The Moderator shall be entitled to the same privilege of speech as other members provided the chair is filled.

15. The minutes of the Association shall be read and approved by the body and signed by the Moderator before adjourning.

16. The Association shall be opened and closed by prayer.

17. Amendments to these may be made at any time by a majority of the union voting by churches when they deem it necessary, provide such amendments do not compromise the sovereignty of the churches nor have tendency to give the body undue power or juris-diction over them.

ARTICLES OF FAITH

Article 1. We believe in only one true living God, as He is revealed to us in the Holy Scriptures - Father, Son, and Holy Ghost.

Article 2. We believe that the Scriptures of the old and new Testaments are the words of God and the only rule of all-saving knowledge and obedience.

Article 3. We believe in the doctrine of election according to the foreknowledge of God.

Article 4. We believe in the doctrine of original sin.

Article 5. We believe in man's impotency to rescue himself from the fallen state he is in, by his own will or ability.

Article 6. We believe that sinners are justified in the sight of God only by the imputed righteousness of Jesus Christ.

Article 7. We believe the elect, according to the foreknowledge of God will be called, con-verted, regenerated, and sanctified by the Holy Spirit.

Article 8. We believe the saints will persevere and never fall finally away.

Article 9. We believe that baptism and the Lord's Supper are ordinances of Jesus Christ, and that true believers are the only subject of these ordinances, and that the true mode of baptism is by immersion. We believe also that feet washing is an example of Jesus Christ and should be kept by his deciples until his second coming.

Article 10. We believe in the Resurrection of the dead and the General Judgement.

Article 11. We believe that the punishment of the wicked will be everlasting and that the joys of the righteous will be eternal.

Article 12. We believe that no minister has the right to administer the ordinances, except those who have been regularly baptized and called of God, and come under the imposition of hands of the presbytery.

Mossie Williamston Braden was born May 1, 1902. She married John Dave Braden and to this union were born 6 children, 3 sons and 3 daughters. He preceded her in death. She professed a hope in Christ at an early age. In May of 1949, she joined the church at Pleasant Hill Baptist and lived a loyal member until she was called home to be with Jesus, June 6, 1977. Our church has suffered a great loss, but God knows best. She is survived by her 6 children, 3 step-children, 3 step-daughters, 3 brothers, 5 sisters, 22 grandchildren, 2 great-grandchildren and a great host of friends.

Lonnie Ellison, born May 30, 1898, passed away at the age of 78 years, 11 months and 24 days. He was a member of the Oak Grove Primitive Baptist Church. He is survived by his wife, Maudie Ellison, and one daughter, Mrs. Ima Bridges. Two children, Anna Belle Ford and Lee Ellison preceded him in death. Other survivors: a sister, Ebbie Beeler and a foster daughter, Mrs. Lona Ray: six grandchildren, four great-grandchildren, a host of an nieces, nephews and friends. Funeral was held at the Oak Grove Primitive Baptist Church on

May 26, 1977, at 2:00 P.M. with Elders J.C. Monday and W. M Sparks officiating. Burial in Church Cemetery.

> Our dear loved one passed away
> A precious one from us is gone
> A voice is vacant in our home that
> never can be filled. I do not need
> a special day to bring you to my mind.
> The days I do not think of you are very
> hard to find.

Written by wife and children

Mrs. Laura Goin Helton, age 44, of Washburn, passed away at Claiborne County Hospital, 4:30 A.M. Wednesday, November 24, 1976. Survivors: husband: Ralph Helton. Sons: Gary and Jerry Helton of Washburn. Mother: Mrs. Mossie Perry. Sisters: Miss Ethel Goin, Mrs. Bonnie Nicely, of Washburn, Tennessee. Half-sister: Mrs. Juanita Russell, Corryton, Tennessee. Funeral 2:00 P.M. Friday at Beeler's Chapel Methodist Church. Interment in Liberty Hill Cemetery. Elder Parnick Shelton and Red Clyde Helton officiating. Ailor's Funeral Home Maynardville, in charge.

> A place is vacant in our home
> A voice we loved is still
> There's an empty place within our hearts
> That no one else can fill
> Sadly missed by husband, sons, mother and sisters.

Allice Hopper, age 87, passed away June 18, 1977. Survivors: daughter, Mrs. Ophelia Wilson of Knoxville; son, Levi Hopper of Maynardville; brothers, Jake Lemarr of Tuscon, Arizona and David Lemarr of LaFollette; six grandchildren, ten great-grandchildren. She was a member of the Oak Grove Primitive Baptist Church where services were held on June 21, 1977, at 2:30 P.M. with Elder Clifford Brantley officiating. Burial was in the Church cemetery

Louvenia Edwards Lambert was born March 25, 1893, passed away July 24, 1977, being 84 years, 3 months and 29 days of age. She married Pryor Carr Lambert, September 20, 1914, who preceded her in death. And to this union 7 children were born, Hettie Lambert Morgan and Cassie Lambert Braden, daughters, both of whom preceded her in death; Lola Lambert Braden and Marie Lambert Maddox, both of Speedwell, Tennessee; Wilma Lambert Braden of Monroe, Michigan. Sons; Alba C. Lambert of Speedwell, Tennessee, and Walter E. Lambert of Radcliff, Kentucky. Two sisters; and three brothers preceded her in death. Living sisters: Minnie Collingsworth and Edna Robbins of Madisonville, Tennessee: Mae Pace of Eva, Tennessee. Brothers: Jim and Alonzo

Edwards of Speedwell, Tennessee. 17 living grandchildren, 1 deceased grandson, 15 great-grandchildren and a host of friends and relatives. She professed faith in Christ at an early age and joined Pleasant Hill Baptist Church in 1910 where she remained a member until death. Our loss is Heaven's gain.

Mamie Abbott Lee of Route 3, Sevierville, was born March 13, 1894, to the late Elder D. J. and Mary Ellen Abbott. She departed this walk of life on March 1, 1977, at the age of 82 years, 11 months, and 15 days old. She professed faith in Christ at the age of 12 years and joined Headrick's Chapel Primitive Baptist Church. She remained a faithful member until her death. Survivors are as follows. Husband: Charles A. Lee. Daughters: Mrs. Robert (Mary) Walker and Mrs. Ralph (Emmalene) Dobson. Son: Harold A. Lee. 11 grandchildren, 14 great-grandchildren. Sisters: Mrs. Myrtle Cook, Mrs. Minnie Godfrey. Brothers: Louie

Clyde, and Walter Abbott. 9 nieces and 18 nephews. Funeral services were held March 3, 1977, at Atchley's Chapel, Sevierville. Elder Walter Lyons officiating. Pallbearers were grandsons. Interment, Headrick's Chapel Cemetery.

Haley Paradine Owens, Route 3, Speedwell, Tennessee, was born January 14, 1896, to the late James and Cumy Edwards. Departed this life December 9, 1975, at the age of 79 years. She was married to Ossero Owens April 25, 1914. She leaves to mourn: husband: Ossero Owens of Speedwell. Five sons: Albert, James Marshall, and Claude Owens, all of Dayton, Ohio; Dave Owens of Knoxville, Tennessee. Five daughters: Mrs. Bonnie Hagewood, Mrs. Dale (Marie) Evans, both of Monroe, Michigan; Mrs. Harold (Alida) Drummonds of Phoenix, New York; Mrs. Ditsy (Cleo) Russell; Miss Nila Owens, both of Speedwell, Tennessee. Her eldest daughter (Myrtle) preceded her in death December 25, 1954. 21 grandchildren. 15 great-grandchildren. She also leaves one brother, Dock Henry Edwards of Middlesboro, Kentucky. She professed hope in Christ at an early age and joined the Pleasant Hill Primitive Baptist Church, where she remained a true member. Funeral services were held at the Pleasant

Hill Primitive Baptist Church on December 12, with Elder Alvin Graves and Elder Tony Eastridge. Her body was laid to rest in the Ausmus Cemetery at Speedwell.

> Mother, you're no longer with us on the earth anymore
> But by the Grace of God, we'll meet again on that
> beautiful shore
> Where there'll be no more parting, no tears to dim
> the eyes
> We'll live up there forever in the sweet by and bye.

Written by daughter, Mrs. Harold Drummons

Mrs. Tilda Simmons, age 87, wife of the late Ewin Simmons of New Tazewell, passed away June 4, 1977, at the home of her grand-daughter, Susie Skipper of Knoxville. She professed faith in Christ at an early age and was a member of Meyers Grove Primitive Baptist Church. Survivors are as follows. Daughters: Mrs. Myrtle Mathews and Mrs. Bonnie Meyers of Knoxville. Sons: Parlin Simmons of Knoxville, Verlin Simmons of New Tazewell. 38 grandchildren. 67 great-grandchildren. 7 great-great-grandchildren. Sister: Mrs. Lollas Russel of New Tazewell. Brothers: Alvis, Fred and Selby Treece of New Tazewell; Louis Treece of Knoxville. A host of nieces and nephews, relatives and friends. She was preceded in death by one son, Rev. Virgil Simmons and two daughters, Mrs. Hattie Dunsmore and and Mrs. Beatrice Dunsmore. Funeral services were held Monday, June 6, at 2:00 p.m. at the Coffey Funeral Home Chapel, with Rev. W. M. Sparks, Rev. Lynn Simmons officiating. Pallbearers: Lenis, Coy Von, Jerry Simmons, Clay, Mathews, Loy and Billy Dunsmore. Song by Liberty Quartet.

Virgil Anderson Tinnel, age 69, passed away at St. Mary's Hospital at 2:30 p.m. Oct. 9, 1976. She was the widow of W. H. Tinnel. She was a member of Kirkwood Primitive Baptist Church. She is survived by the following. Son: James H. Tinnel. Two daughters: Mrs. W. E. (Joyce) Johnson and Mrs. Marvin (Alice) Powers. 9 grandchildren and 1 great--granddaughter. 2 sisters: Mrs. Ruth McNabb and Mrs. Stella Brewer. Brother: Kyle Anderson. Funeral services were held at Rose Mortuary, October 11, at 3:30 p.m. Elder Hugh Brummitt and Elder Everett Berry officiating. Burial in Lenoir City Cemetery.

Lewis White, age 93 of Route 2 LaFollette,, Tennessee, died on December 26, 1976, at LaFollette Community Hospital. He was a retired farmer. He was survived by the following: wife: Lou Beeler White. Daughters: Mrs. Ike

Miller and Mrs. Mack Heatherly. Sons: Verlin Leonard, Maney, William, Howard, and Jack White all of LaFollette. 26 grandchildren, 43 great-grandchildren. 5 great-great-grandchildren. Services were held on Wednesday, December 29th at Davis Chapel Primitive Baptist Church of which he was a member. The services were conducted by Rev. Theodore Carroll and Elder William Sparks. Interment was in Sunrise Cemetery at Davis Chapel.

Pearlie Larmer, age 81, passed away 1:30 Sunday, October 31, 1976, at St. Mary's Medical Center. Survivors: a host of nieces and nephews. Funeral at Black Fox Primitive Baptist Church of which she was a member, with Rev. Andy Vance and Rev. Clyde Helton officiating. Interment in Cabbage Cemetery.

Millard Welch of Maryville, Tennessee, born November 27, 1902 and departed this life February 21, 1977. His stay 74 years, 2 months and 24 days. He married Luda Brantley May 21, 1921. She survives him. To their union 6 children were born. Daughter: Jessie Coppinger of Maryville: sons: Oras, Leon, Hillured and Arnold all of Maryville. Alvin was killed in World War II. Sisters: Helen Berry, Maryville,, Lester Singleton, Bonnie Brantley, of Sharp's Chapel, Gladys Baker of Arizona, Ola Loop of Michigan, Edith Helton of Knoxville. Brothers Chester of Strawberry Plains, Amon, Alex, and Sillis, all of Michigan. Twenty grandchildren, ten great-grandchildren. He professed faith in Christ at an early age and joined the Cave Springs Primitive Baptist Church, Union County. The Norris Dam caused him to leave, and the church disbanded. In 1936 he moved to Maryville, he and his wife and six children. In 1948 Brantley Chapel Primitive Baptist Church was organized and he became one of the leaders of the church and remained faithful until death. Funeral services were conducted at Smith's Funeral Home Chapel by Elder J. C. Monday, Elder Carl McCarty, Elder Clifford Brantley. He was laid to rest in Sherwood Memorial Gardens. He is missed by the family, and the church.

The Family

STATISTICAL TABLE

CHURCHES	DELEGATES	Restored	Rec'd by Letter	Baptism	Relationship	Dism'd by Letter	Excluded	Deceased	Total Membership	Printing Minutes	REGULAR MEETING TIME	COMMUNION TIME
BLACK FOX	Bros.: Dale Capps, Bennie Capps, Arthur Terry Sisters: Flossie Capps, Mary Ruth Capps, Pamela Capps, Mary Terry	0	0	2	1	1	1	1	87	$20.	Second Saturday Night and Sunday Third Saturday Night and Sunday	Second Sunday in June
BRADEN'S CHAPEL	Elder W. M. Sparks Sisters: Leecy Sparks, Winona Monday	0	0	2	0	2	0	0	140	$15.	First Saturday and Sunday of each month	First Sunday in July
BRANTLEY'S CHAPEL	Elder Clifford Brantley Bros.: Everett Brantley, Glenn Beason, Jeff Ellison, Vaughn Beason and Rina Johnson Sisters: Barsha Brantley, Mildred Brantley, Hazel Johnson, Linda Brantley Polly Ward, Lela Ellison	0	0	1	0	1	4	1	80	$25.	Second Saturday Night Every Sunday and Sunday Night	Second Sunday in July
DAVIS CHAPEL	Bros.: James Heatherly, Orice McCarty, Seth Welch Sisters: Ruth Heatherly, Mamie Parrott, Mollie McCarty, Ollie Welch, Lina Lynch	0	0	0	0	0	0	2	138	$20.	Third Saturday and Sunday Every Sunday and Sunday Night	Third Sunday In June
FAITH	Elder Howard M. Pippin Sister: Phylis J. Pippin	0	0	0	0	0	0	0	5	$15.	Every Sunday and Sunday night Fourth	Fourth Sunday in September

Church	Officers									Members	Amount	Meeting Times	Association Meeting
GETHSEMANE	Elders: Glenn Abbott Bros.: Tom Carmichael, C. H. Godfrey, William Glenn Abbott Sisters: Mary Godfrey, Myrtle Cook, Billie Godfrey, June Carmichael, Flora Wilson, Rhoda Estes	0	0	0	1	0	0	0	0	32	$25.	Fourth Sunday of each Month	Fourth Sunday in May and October
GIBSON STATION	Elders: Joe Irving, Spurgeon Thompson, Bros.: Franklin Jones Sisters: Fannie Jones, Karen Rhymer, Evelyn Maples, Sally Brittain, Mellie Thompson, Susie Shoffner	0	0	0	0	0	0	1		79	$25.	First Saturday and Saturday Night of each Month Every Sunday and Sunday Night	First Sunday in June
HEADRICK CHAPEL	Elders: Robert Walker Bros.: Clyde Abbott, Sr. Bill Cook Sisters: Gady Sutton	1	0	0	0	0	0	1		110	$25.	Sunday Following First and Thir Daturday	Sunday following First Saturday in May and October
KIRKWOOD	Elders: Hugh E. Brummitt and Walter Lyons; Bros.: C. A. Sharp, R. P. Bridges, M.E. Evans, E.P. Cook; Sisters: Ruby Brummitt, Callie Lyons, Freida Sharp, Ora Bridges, Velma Evans, Dottie Cook	0	7	0	0	0	0	1		114	$30.	Every Sunday Morning	Last Sunday in April
LENOIR CITY	Elders: Howard Pippin and Alvin Graves; Bros.: Henry Chamberlain, Hubert Spoons, Clyde Abbott, Jr., Raymond Wilkerson; Sisters: Esta Chamberlain, Annie Spoons, Betty Abbott, Ruby Williams, Cora Hill	1	0	1	0	4	0	0		152	$35.	Every Sunday and Sunday Night	Third Sunday in May
MONROE MICHIGAN	Letter Received- No delegate presented	0	0	1	0	0	0	0		14	$10.	Third Sunday of each Month	Sunday after Third Saturday in July
AYERS GROVE	Elders: Johnny Ayers; Bros.: Clifford Robertson, Isom Drummonds; Sisters, Ida Robertson, Gipsy Ayers, Lisa Ayers, Velta Muncey	0	1	0	0	0	1			67	$20.	Fourth Saturday Night and Sunday	Sunday following Third Saturday in May and September
JOETON	Elder John Oliver,; Bros.: Carroll Oliver, Charlie Collins Sisters: Ruth Oliver, Dora Collins	0	2	0	0	0	0	0		42	$20.	First Sunday Third Saturday Night and Sunday	

OAK GROVE	Elders: Johnny Atkins, Toni Eastridge; Bros.: Malcolm Walker; Sisters: Laura Lou Walker, Veda Cole, Nelle Sherritze, Edna Faye Sexton, Francis Eastridge	0	0	1	7	0	0	0	2	334	$25.	First Saturday Night and Sunday Thirs Dunday	First Sunday in May
PLEASANT HILL	Elders: Albert Davis, Larry Anderson, James Branscomb, Sisters: Audra Davis, Myra Anderson, Helen Ruth Branscomb	0	0	1	0	0	0	0	2	110	$30.	Fourth Saturday and Sunday	Fourth Sunday in June
PLEASANT POINT	Letter Received- No delegate Presented	0	0	1	0	0	0	0	1	115	$15.	First Saturday Night and Sunday Third Sunday	First Sunday in July
ROCKY DALE	Elders: Everett Berry, Parnick Shelton, Joe Bush, William Berry; Bros.: W. H. Taylor, Dennis Branson; Sisters: Lou Emma Taylor, Trula Berry, Norma Jean Bush	0	0	3	0	0	0	1	1	128	$30.	Every Sunday and Sunday Night	Second Sunday in May

CHURCH	COUNTY	PASTOR	CLERK	ADDRESS
Black Fox	Grainger	Elder Alvin Graves	Bennie Capps Flossie Capps	P. O. Box 91, Maynardville, Tn. 37807 Maynardville, Tn. 37807
Braden's Chapel	Union	Elder Noble Clawson Elder J. C. Monday, Asst.	Jimmie B. Edwards Phyllis Wilson, Asst.	Speedwell, Tn. Speedwell, Tn.
Brantley's Chapel	Blount	Elder Clifford Brantley	D. C. Brantley Daniel Brantley, Asst.	2020 Biddle Rd., Maryville, Tn. Rt. 10, Mint Road, Maryville, Tn.
Davis Chapel	Campbell	Elder William Berry	Ruth Heatherly Lassie Ellison, Asst.	Rt. 1, Davis Chapel Rd. LaFollette, Tn. 918 Carwynn Rd., LaFollette, Tn.

Church	County	Pastor	Clerk	Address
Faith		Elder Howard M. Pippin	Inez M. Pippin	c/o Elder Howard M. Pippin, 101 Rose St., Lenoir City, Tn. 37771
Gethsemane	Knox	Elder Walter Lyons	Tom Carmichael	729 Frank St., Knoxville, Tn.
Gibson Station	Lee Virginia	Elder Joe Irving, Asst. / Elder Everette Berry	Dorothy Johnson / Shirley Sandifer	Rt. 2, Ewing, Va. / Rt. 2, Harrogate, Tn.
Headrick Chapel	Knox	Elder Walter Lyons	Clyde Abbott, Sr.	Rt. 7, Sevierville, Tn.
Kirkwood	Knox	Elder Everette Berry	Estelle Petree Sharp / Alice Tinell Powers	Rt. 27, Emory Road, Knoxville, Tn. / 2923 Clearview Ave., Knoxville, Tn.
Lenoir City	Loudon	Elder Howard M. Pippin	Scott Collins	705 W. 5th Ave., Lenoir City, Tn.
Monroe, Michigan	Monroe, Michigan		Gertrude Zwack / Roxie Drummonds, Asst.	1825 Spaulding Rd., Monroe, Michigan / 2675 Blue Bush Rd., Monroe, Michigan
Myers Grove	Claiborne	Elder Johnny Avers / Elder Clay Widner, Asst.	Bonnie Miracle / Harold Cupp, Asst.	Rt. 2, Box 194, New Tazewell, Tn. / Rt. 2, New Tazewell, Tn.
Noeton	Grainger	Elder John Oliver	Carroll Oliver / Bessie Collins, Asst.	Rt. 2, Box 512, Bean Station, Tn. / Rt. 5, Morristown, Tn.
Oak Grove	Union	Elder J. C. Monday / Elder Noble Clawson, Asst.	Betty P. Sharp / Betty Shoffner, Asst.	Sharp Chapel, Tn. / Sharp Chapel, Tn.

Pleasant Hill	Claiborne	Elder Larry Anderson	William Branscomb	Speedwell, Tn.
		Elder Albert Davis, Asst.		Speedwell, Tn.
Pleasant Point	Claiborne	Elder Jimmy Branscomb	Elder Claude Rosson	Rt. 4, New Tazewell, Tn.
		Elder Larry Anderson, Asst.		
Rocky Dale	Knox	Elder Hugh Brummitt	Edward Collett	Rt. 1, Luttrell, Tn.
			Dennis Branson	Rt. 13, Knoxville, Tn.

247

1978 MINUTES
of the
ONE HUNDRED FIFTH-EIGHTH SESSION
of the
POWELL VALLEY ASSOCIATION
OF PRIMITIVE BAPTIST

ROCKY DALE PRIMITIVE BAPTIST CHURCH

**POWELL VALLEY ASSOCIATION
OF PRIMITIVE BAPTISTS**

**held with the Sister Church at
ROCKY DALE
in KNOX COUNTY, TENNESSEE
AUGUST 18, 19, 20, 1978**

Next Session to be held with the Sister Church at Oak Grove in Union County, Tennessee to begin on Friday before the Third Saturday in August 1979 at 10:30 A.M. Elder Howard Pippin will preach the Introductory Sermon and Elder Spurgeon Thompson the Alternate.

THE ONE HUNDRED FIFTY-EIGHTH SESSION
OF THE POWELL VALLEY ASSOCIATION
OF
PRIMITIVE BAPTIST

HELD WITH THE SISTER CHURCH AT ROCKY DALE
IN KNOX COUNTY, TENNESSEE
AUGUST 18, 19, 20, 1978
NEXT SESSION WILL BE HELD WITH THE SISTER CHURCH
AT
OAK GROVE
IN UNION COUNTY, TENNESSEE
TO BEGIN ON FRIDAY BEFORE THE THIRD SATURDAY
IN AUGUST, 1979
AT 10:30 A.M.
ELDER HOWARD PIPPIN WILL DELIVER THE INTRODUCTORY
SERMON AND ELDER SPURGEON WILL BE THE ALTERNATE

OFFICERS

Elder Albert Davis .... Moderator
Speedwell, Tenn. - Phone 869-3596

Elder Hugh Brummitt .... Assistant Moderator
1329 Brown Ave., Knoxville, Tenn. - Phone 546-7700

Bro. W. H. Taylor .... Clerk
Rt. 27, Knoxville, Tenn. - Phone 922-2143

Bro. Bennie Capps .... Assistant Clerk
Maynardville, Tenn.

FRIDAY'S PROCEEDINGS

1. According to previous arrangements, the one hundred and fifth-eighth session of the Powell Valley Association met pursuant to adjournment.

2. After singing praise and prayer by Elder Toni Eastridge of Oak Grove Church, Moderator Davis read from the psalmist David.

3. Elder Wm. Berry then delivered a very wonderful introductory sermon from the 85th Psalm, Verse 10, ((mercy and truth are met together. *Righteousness and peace have kissed each other.)*

4. After a song, and prayer by Elder Johnny Atkins, the Association was recessed for 15 minutes.

5. After intermission, and at the sound of singing, the Association re-assembled and was led in prayer by Elder Walter Lyons of Kirkwood Church.

6. After prayer, the Moderator called the Association to order of business.

7. The Moderator called for letters of the Sister Churches be delivered to the Clerk for reading. (All churches of the Association except one were represented by letter.)

8. All letters presented were accepted and the delegates seated.

9. An opportunity was given for any member of these Sister churches present but not delegated and wishing to be seated as such to come forward. The following members came: Millie Thompson of Gibson Station Church, John Godfrey of Gethsemane Church and Geraldine Abbott of Headricks Chapel Church.

10. Called for petitionary letters if any—there were none.

11. Motion approved to re-elect Elder Albert Davis Moderator and also Elder Hugh E. Brummitt Assistant Moderator.

11. Motion carried that the Association re-elect Bro. W. H. Taylor as Clerk and Bro. Bennie Capps as Assistant Clerk.

13. Motion approved that the Moderator appoint the following committees:

A. **COMMITTEE ON ARRANGEMENTS**
Bro. Elwood Evans
Bro Isom Drummons
Elder Glenn Abbott

B. **COMMITTEE ON PREACHING**
Bro. E. D. Graves
Bro. Henry Chamberlain
Bro. Malcolm Walker

C **COMMITTEE ON REQUESTS**
Elder Larry Anderson
Elder William Rhymer
Bro. Orice McCarty

D. **COMMITTEE ON FINANCE**
Elder Howard Pippin
Elder John Godfrey
Bro. Daniel Brantley

14. After the committees were all appointed, the Association voted to adjourn until Saturday at 10:30 A.M. and was dismissed in prayer by Elder Clifford Brantley of Brantley's Chapel Church.

SATURDAY'S PROCEEDINGS

1. Saturday morning at the appointed hour of 10:30 and at the sound of singing, a crowd assembled that overflowed into the Sunday School addition.

2. After singing praises, Assistant Moderator Hugh E. Brummitt gave a welcome and a very good spiritual talk and reading the 13th chapter of 1st Corinthians then called for prayer by Elder Noble Clawson of Bradens Chapel.

3. Moderator Elder Davis then called for any letters of Sister Churches not received on Friday. One was received from the sister church at Bradens Chapel.

4. Motion approved that we accept the letter and seat the delegates of Bradens Chapel Church.

5. Moderator called for anyone not named in the letter and wishing to be seated as delegate to come forward and give their name and church. None came.

6. Moderator called for the report of the Committee on Arrangements who gave the following report, which was accepted and the committee released.

REPORT OF COMMITTEE ON ARRANGEMENTS

A. Call for roll call of delegates
B. Call for report of Committee on Preaching.
C. Call for report of Committee on Request.
D. Call for report of Committee on Finance.
E. Suggest how many minutes we shall have printed and who shall supervise the printing and distribution of same and how much he shall receive for his services. Where will the next Association be held and who shall preach the introductory sermon and who shall be the alternate.

> **Respectfully submitted,**
> **Elder Glenn Abbott**
> **Bro. Elwood Evans**
> **Bro. Isom Drummons**

7. Call for the roll call of delegates and note to be made of all absent.

8. Call for the report of the Committee on Preaching. The following report

was accepted and the committee released after substituting for Elder Walter Lyons and Elder Clawson as both reported they could not be present at the time delegated to them.

REPORT OF COMMITTEE ON PREACHING

Friday Night	Elder Everett Berry
	Elder Glenn Abbott
Saturday	Elder Spurgeon Thompson
	Elder Noble Clawson
Saturday Night	Elder Toni Eastridge
	Elder Howard Pippin
Sunday	Elder Larry Anderson
	Elder Clifford Brantley

Respectfully submitted,

Bro. Malcolm Walker
Bro. Henry Chamberlain
Bro. E. D. Graves

9. Call for report of the Committee on Request who submitted the following report which was accepted and the committee released.

REPORT OF COMMITTEE ON REQUEST

We the Committee on Request suggest that we have 1,150 copies printed of the minutes and that the Clerk supervise the printing and distribution of same and that he receive $100.00 for his services.

Respectfully submitted,

Elder Larry Anderson
Elder William Rhymer
Bro. Orice McCarty

10. Call for report of Committee on Finance and the following report of the Finance Committee was accepted and released.

Black Fox	$20.00
Bradens Chapel	$20.00
Brantleys Chapel	$30.00
Davis Chapel	$20.00
Gethsemane	$25.00
Gibson Station	$25.00
Headricks Chapel	$25.00
Kirkwood	$30.00
Lenoir City	$35.00
Monroe, Mich.	$10.00

Meyers Grove	$20.00
Norton	$20.00
Oak Grove	$25.00
Pleasant Hill	$35.00
Pleasant Point	$15.00
Rocky Dale	$40.00
	$395.00
Balance in Bank	$419.00
Grand Total	$814.00
Expenses 1978	-385.00
Balance in Bank	$429.00

Respectfully submitted,

Elder Howard Pippin
Elder John Godfrey
Bro. Daniel Brantley

1. Motion approved that we accept the request of the committee and have 1,150 copies of the minutes printed and that the Clerk supervise the printing and distribution of the same and that he receive $100.00 for his services. *Black Fax*

2. Motion approved that the next session of the Association be held with the Sister Church of Oak Grove in Union County, Tennessee to begin on Friday at 10:30 A.M. before the 3rd Saturday in August 1979.

13. Motion approved that Elder Howard Pippin deliver the introductory sermon and that Elder Spurgeon Thompson be the alternate.

14. Motion approved that Elder William Sparks write a circular letter to be published in the next minutes.

15. Motion that the entire Association of Sister Churches thank the host church of Rocky Dale for the welcome, warmth, fellowship and love we felt while in your church and community and the wonderful food you gave us all. May God's richest blessings rest on each and every one of you is our prayer.

SUNDAY SERVICES

Sunday at the appointed hour of 10:30 the church was filled to capacity. After singing the old songs of Zion, the service was continued by Elder Larry Anderson of Pleasant Hill Church reading from different books and chapters and delivering a very good and interesting sermon. Following Elder Anderson was Elder Clifford Brantley of Brantleys Chapel Church who spoke from the book of Genesis also from Zechariah and delivered a good spiritual sermon. After singing praise and much rejoicing this wonderful Association was closed out by the Assistant Moderator, Elder Hugh E. Brummitt.

Elder Albert Davis, Moderator   Bro. W. H. Taylor, Clerk
Edler Hugh E. Brummitt, Asst. Moderator   Bro. Bennie Capps, Asst. Clerk

SUPPLEMENT BY THE CLERK

Allow us to say that the preaching of this Association was wonderful from the beginning.

Elder Willism Berry delivered a wonderful introductory sermon on Friday. Followed by Elder Noble Clawson and Elder Spurgeon Thompson on Saturday. Then on Saturday Night Elder Toni Eastridge and Elder Howard Pippin did some very good preaching. Then they were followed by Elder Larry Anderson and Elder Clifford Brantley on Sunday.

We just thank the Lord for the many good ministers in our Association.

W. H. Taylor, Clerk

W. H. Taylor, Clerk

CIRCULAR LETTER

Dear Brethren and Sisters in Christ composing the Powell Valley Association of Churches:

I was appointed by the Association to write this letter for the 1978 session. Greetings. I pray God we will always live in peace and love and fellowship and not let any confusion arise in our churches. (2nd Timothy-Chapter 3-*This know also, that in the last days perilous times shall come. For men shall be lovers of their own selves, covetous, boasters, proud, blasphemers, disobedient to parents, unthankful, unholy, without natural affection, truce breakers, false accusers, incontinent, fierce, despisers of those that are good.*) (1st Timothy-Chapter 2—*I exhort therefore, that first of all, supplication, prayers, intercessions, and giving of thanks be made for all men.*) 2 verse, *For this is good and acceptable in the sight of God our Savior*).

Remember me in your prayers.

Elder Joe S. Irving

MINISTERS DIRECTORY

Elder Glenn Abbott, 1801 Cherrybrook Drive, Knoxville, Tn., Ph. 947-6875

Elder Larry Anderson, Speedwell, Tennessee, Ph. 869-4635

Elder Johnny Atkins, Bean Station, Tennessee, Ph. 767-2397

Elder Johnny Ayres, New Tazewell, Tennessee

Elder Everette Berry, Rt. #24, Knoxville, Tn., Ph. 922-7004

Elder William Berry, Rt. #13, Knoxville, Tn., Ph. 922-9189

Elder J. H. Branscomb, Speedwell, Tn., Ph. 562-6361

Elder Clifford Brantley, Brown School Rd., Maryville, Tn., Ph. 982-3735

Elder Hugh E. Brummitt, 1329 Brown Ave., Knoxville, Tn., Ph. 546-7700

Elder J. C. Monday, Speedwell, Tn., Ph. 562-3068

Elder Sheridan Moore, Route #1, Townsend, Tn., Ph. 581-5039

Elder Howard Pippin, 101 Rose Street, Lenoir City, Tennessee

Elder Claude Rosson, Rt. #4, New Tazewell, Tn., Ph. 626-3168

Elder Joe Bush, Corryton, Tennessee, Ph. 687-2108

Elder Noble Clawson, Rt. #4, Speedwell, Tn., Ph. 562-2004

Elder Albert Davis, Speedwell, Tn., Ph. 869-3596

Elder Clay Widner, Rt. #1, Tazewell, Tn., Ph. 626-3893

Elder Toni Eastridge, Rt. #3, Louisville, Tn., Ph. 983-1068

Elder Alvin Graves, 122 Oak Wood Dr., Lenoir City, Tn., Ph. 986-9725

Elder Joe Irving, 111 Eighth St., Middlesboro, Ky.

Elder Walter Lyons, 1602 Garfield St., Alcoa, Tn., Ph. 984-3207

Elder John Godfrey, 15443 Valleoga, Victoryvill, Calif., Ph. (714) 243-4661

Elder Robert Walker, Sevierville, Tn., Ph. 453-2753

Elder Parnick Shelton, Corryton, Tn., Ph. 687-6142

Elder William Sparks, Speedwell, Tn., Ph. 562-7997

Elder William Thymer, Rt. #2, Harrogate, Tn. Ph. 869-3082

Elder Spurgeon Thompson, Box #36, Shawanee, Tn., Ph. 869-8175

Elder John Oliver, Bean Station, Tn., Ph. 581-5039

LICENTIATES

Bro. Clyde Abbott, Route #7, Sevierville, Tn., Ph. 453-2329

Bro. Roscoe Branscomb, Speedwell, Tennessee

Bro. Jim Campbell, Louisville, Tennessee

Brother Odell Carpenter, Maryville, Tennessee

Brother Ray Walker, Route #1, Townsend, Tennessee

RULES OF DECORUM

1. The churches composing the Powell's Valley Association shall not be confined to any set rules as to specific number of Messengers they shall have in the body, but shall have the right to name in their letters as many as they choose, and in addition all orderly members of and of the churches being present be entitled to seats in the body as Messengers of their respective churches, with all the rights and privileges of the same.

2. The Messengers thus assembled shall be denominated the Powell's Valley Primitive Baptist Association.

3. For the purpose of historical information and statistical edification, the Churches are required to state in letters, the number of members in fellowship, the number received by Baptism, by letter, by confession of Faith, the number dismissed, excluded and dead since last session; also the time of their meeting, their pastoral supply, and the amount of money contributed for ministers and other purposes together with any other information they deem appropriate for the edification of the saints and glory of God.

4. This Association shall have no power to answer queries, give advice, or dictate to the Churches in any case, or to lord it over God's heritage nor any power by which she can directly or indirectly fringe on the internal rights of the church or censure and try any church or member in reference to faith and practice and determine upon valigity of gospel ordinances. These things shall rest entirely with the churches; but henceforward our annual meetings shall be only for the purpose of hearing from each other, and for the worship of God and mutual comfort and edification of the Saints. To this end we reserve the privilege annually for the Third Friday in August and the two following days or at such other times as may be agreed upon with any church that may invite us having to protect our own standard, while in session, from heresay and disorder to recognize and invite any primitive Baptist minister or any lay brother to worship with us that may deem proper; to request the brethren of our body to visit other churches or bodies in our belief with whom we may desire to culture Christian fellowship; to publish in a minute of our proceedings.

5. Each session of the body shall have a Moderator and Clerk who shall hold office until re-elected.

6. Any order member of any church belonging to this body, when convened, being present shall be eligible to elect on as Moderator and Clerk or to sit on any committee appointed by the same.

7. In all election or questions that may be necessary to determine by vote, the vote shall be taken by churches, each church being entitled to three votes for any number less than one hundred, and one additional vote for every fifty or fraction thereof above the first hundred, but the Messengers of each church may divide their vote as they see proper.

8. All elections or questions coming to vote shall be determined by a majority vote cast, and it shall be the only duty of the minority to acquiesce in the decision thus reached.

9. If new churches desire to be admitted to this union they shall petition by letter and messengers and if voted for and recommended by one or more sister churches for her Presbytery constitutioning them, as orthodox and orderly they shall be received by the vote of the body and manifested by the Moderator giving the Messengers the right hand of fellowship.

10. Any motion or resolution clearly inconsistent with the above rules shall be promptly ruled out of order unless withdrawn by the mover.

11. Any Messenger being ruled out of order by the Moderator shall have the right to appeal to the body on the question of order, and if sustained shall be allowed to proceed, but if not take his seat.

12. Our meeting being held in the name of Christ and the worship of God; each Messenger is expected to observe due and proper therein.

13. It will not be considered good for any Messenger whose name has been enrolled as such to abruptly break off or absent himself from the Association without leave.

14. The Moderator shall be entitled to the same privilege of speech as other members provided the chair is filled.

15. The minutes of the Association shall be read and approved by the body and signed by the Moderator before adjourning.

16. The Association shall be opened and closed by prayer.

17. Amendments to these may be made at any time by a majority of the union voting by churches when they deem it necessary, provide such amendments do not compromise the sovereignty of the churches nor have tendency to give body undue power or jurisdiction over them.

ARTICLES OF FAITH

Article 1. We believe in only one true living God, as He is revealed to us in the Holy Scriptures - Father, Son, and Holy Ghost.

Article 2. We believe that the Scriptures of the old and new Testaments are the words of God and the only rule of all-saving knowledge and obedience.

Article 3. We believe in the doctrine of election according to the foreknowledge of God.

Article 4. We believe in the doctrine of original sin.

Article 5. We believe in man's impotency to rescue himself from the fallen state he is in, by his own will or ability.

Article 6. We believe that sinners are justified in the sight of God only by the imputed righteousness of Jesus Christ.

Article 7. We believe the elect, according to the foreknowledge of God will be called, converted, regenerated, and sanctified by the Holy Spirit.

Article 8. We believe the saints will persevere and never fall finally away.

Article 9. We believe that baptism and the Lord's Supper are ordinances of Jesus Christ, and that true believers are the only subject of these ordinances, and that the true mode of baptism is by immersion. We believe also that feet washing is an example of Jesus Christ and should be kept by his deciples until his second coming.

Article 10. We believe in the Resurrection of the dead and the General Judgement.

Article 11. We believe that the punishment of the wicked will be everlasting and that the joys of the righteous will be eternal.

Article 12. We believe that no minister has the right to administer the ordinances, except those who have been regularly baptized and called of God, and come under the imposition of hands of the presbytery.

257

Mattie Haskew "Ma" Mason

Mattie Haskew "Ma" Mason, age 75, passed away August 14, 1978. Survivors: Daughters; Mrs. Tyson (Maureen) Shoffner, Mrs. Charles (Juanita) Shoffner, and Mrs. Robert (Aliene((Thomas, all of Tazewell, Tn. Brother, Carl Haskew, Harrogate, Tn. Grandchildren, Eddie Shoffner, Tazewell, Tn., Carolyn Ledford, Cinn., Ohio, Janie Turnblazer, Maynardville, Tn., Celia Hall, Speedwell, Tn. and Bobby Thomas, Harrogate, Tn. Great-grandchildren; Autumne, Jill and Wendy Shoffner, Julie and Renee Ledford, Jennifer hall, Jason Turnblazer, and Steve Thomas.

She attended the church at Gibson Station, Va. where she was loved by all. Her sweet smile and beautiful testimonies will always be remembered.

Funeral services were held at Harrogate United Methodist Church, where she was a member, with Rev. Robert Boy and Elder Everett Berry officiating.

She was laid to rest in Harrogate Cemetery.
ASLEEP IN JESUS

Pryor Lee Berry

Pryor Lee Berry passed away September 14, 1977, at the age of 90.

He is survived by his wife, Nellie Berry, Knoxville, 2 sons, Marshall Berry, Louisville, Ky., and Grover Berry, Speedwell. 4 daughters, Ruth A. Berry, Knoxville, Malinda Williamson, Speedwell, Vina Eisenberg, Knoxville, Hedy Dalton, Knoxville, 20 grandchildren, 1 sister, Della Berry, Maynardville, and a host of other relatives and friends to mourn his passing.

He joined the Pleasant Hill Primitive Baptist Church in 1958 and was a faithful member until death.

By his wife and children

Seth E. Welch

Seth E. Welch, age 79, departed this life January 13, 1978. He was a faithful member of Davis Chapel Primitive Baptist Church.

Survivors: wife, Ollie White Welch, 5 daughters, 1 stepdaughter, 6 sons, 1 step son, two sisters, 23 grandchildren, 4 step-grandchildren, 12 great-grandchildren and 2 step great-grandchildren.

Funeral services were held at 2 p.m., January 16, 1978, at the Davis Chapel Church, by Elder William Sparks and Elder Billy Berry. Interment in Fincastle Cemetery.

Robert Walter Ray

Robert Walter Ray, age 85, of LaFollette, died Wednesday, January 4, 1978, in Park West General Hospital, Knoxville. Member of Davis Chapel Primitive Baptist Church.

Survivors: daughters, Mrs. Lowell (Thelma) Bowers, LaFollette, Mrs. Georgia Testo of Dayton, Ohio, Mrs. Lois Adlich of Detroit, Michigan. Sons, James Ray of LaFollette, Albert Ray of Dayton, Ohio. 7 grandchildren, 8 great-grandchildren.

Services 2:00 p.m., Saturday, Davis Chapel Primitive Baptist Church. Elder Paul Heatherly officiated. Interment, Sunrise Cemetery.

Martha Anderson Leeper

Martha Anderson Leeper of Knoxville, Tennessee was born June 7, 1921, passed away January 31, 1978. She was united in marriage January 27, 1940 to her surviving husband, Henry F. Leeper. Her church membership was with Kirkwood Primitive Baptist Church in Knoxville, Tennessee. Other survivors are the two daughters; Miss Pamela Leeper and Mrs. Joe Moultz (Emily), both of Washington, D.C., one grandson, John Addison Moultz and one brother, Ben F. Anderson, Clarksville, Tennessee.

Funeral services were conducted at Weaver's by her cousin Elder Richard Martin. Interment was in Highland Memorial Cemetery.

Russell Odell McCarty

Russell Odell McCarty, age 44, of 258 South 31st Street, Richmond, Indiana, passed away at his home on May 31, 1978. He served in the U. S. Army as a paratrooper and was an engineer by profession.

He was the son of Orice and Mollie McCarty of LaFollette. He was married to Helen Taylor in 1956. To this union was born one daughter, Brenda Kaye.

He professed faith in Christ at an early age and joined the Primitive Baptist Church at Davis Chapel. His interment was in Memorial Park in Dayton, Ohio.

Mrs. Minnis Hill Boruff

Mrs. Minnis (Hill) Boruff, 84, of 510 East Beech Street, LaFollette, died on July 17, 1978, at Jellico Community Hospital. She was the wife of the late Amon Boruff and a member of Davis Chapel Primitive Baptist Church.

Mrs. Boruff is survived by three daughters: Mrs. Sylvia Wilson of West Alexander, Ohio, Mrs. Cleo Miracle and Mrs. Arletta Parton, both of LaFollette; two sons; Virgil Boruff of New Lexington, Ohio, and Buster Boruff of LaFollette; one sister, Mrs. Linda Turner of LaFollette. 22 grandchildren, 55 great-grandchildren, and 2 great-great-grandchildren.

Funeral services were held at the Independent Baptist Church in LaFollette. Burial was in Sunrise Cemetery.

Herbert E. Davis

Herbert E. Davis, age 82, Route 2, Washburn, passed away April 17, 1978, at 12:00 at his home. He was a member of Black Fox Church. Survivors: Wife, Edith, son, Herbert, Jr. of Washburn; daughters, Mrs. Marie Lay of Corryton, Mrs. Jean Keck of Michigan, 11 grand children. Brother Loarn (Lo) Davis of Knoxville. Funeral was conducted at Ailor's Chapel with Elder Parnick Shelton officiating. Burial was in Thomas Cemetery.

Washie Coffey

Washie Coffey passed away January 1, 1978 at Morristown-Hamblen Hospital. He was a member of Norton Primitive Baptist Church. Survivors: sons, Gene and Daniel, Morristown; daughters, Mary France, Jefferson City; Martha Carpenter of Morristown; 14 grandchildren; brothers, Walt, Tommy, and Henry all of Bean Station; sisters, Vara Wallace, Bean Station; Dexter Hedrick, Whitesburg, Ofie Coffey of Ohio, Irene Mallicoat, Knoxville. Funeral services were held at Norton Baptist Church with Elder Johnny Atkins officiating. Burial in Atkins Cemetery. West Side Chapel in charge.

Lemie L. Spires

Lemie L. Spires, 64, Route 2, Bean Station, died October 7, 1977 at Morristown-Hamblen Hospital. He was a member of Norton Primitive Baptist Church. Survivors: sisters, Mrs. Avery Coffey, Rutledge and Mrs. Mae Sinard, Greeneville; brother, Harding Spires, Rutledge; half-brother, Sam Blair, Franklin, Ohio.

Funeral services were held at Norton Primitive Baptist Church with Elder John Oliver and Rev. Olof Atkins officiating. Burial in church cemetery. Stubblefield of Morristown in charge.

Rhoda Bridges Dunn

Rhoda Bridges Dunn, daughter of Elvin and Elizabeth Weaver, was born January 6, 1883 at Sharp's Chapel. She passed away May 20, 1978, at the home of her son, Maldon T. Bridges, in Knoxville, Tennessee at the age of 95 years, 4 months and 14 days.

She joined the Mossy Springs Primitive Baptist Church at an early age. She later joined the Oak Grove Church when Norris Lake covered the Mossy Spring Church.

Rhoda married Elvin L. Bridges on December 25, 1904. To this union was born 3 sons, Maldon T. Bridges, Knoxville, Robert Palmer Bridges, Maryville, Tennessee, and Duke Bridges of Redlands, California. After the death of her husband, Elvin, she married Maston C. Dunn of Corryton, Tennessee. She then joined the Rocky Dale Primitive Baptist Church where whe remained a member until her death.

In addition to her 3 sons, she is survived by 4 grandchildren, 2 great-grand-children, stepson, Elmer Dunn of Johnson City, Tennessee, step-daughters, Virgie Collins, Fern Whited and Emma Dunn all of Corryton. 6 step-grandchildren, 7 step great-grandchildren, a sister, Mrs. F. A. Petree of Clifton, Illinois and a host of nieces and nephews.

Funeral services were held at Rodky Dale Baptist Church May 22, 1978 by Elders Hugh Brummitt and Everett Berry. Burial was in Blue Springs Cemetery, Sharps Chapel, Tennessee.

Sadie Proffitt Keck Rouse

Sadie Proffitt Keck Rouse was born July 7, 1899, died January 14, 1977 at 11:45 P.M. at Claiborne County Hospital. Perofessed Christ at an early age. She was a member of Pleasant Point Church since 1915.

Survivors: daughter, Mrs. Hershel Bowen of New Tazewell; son, Arie Rouse of New Tazewell; 10 grandchildren; 2 great-grandchildren. Step sons, Harlie Rouse of New Tazewell and Willis Rouse of Spring City. 11 step-grandchildren, 12 great-great grandchildren. Sister Lou Mae Keck of New Tazewell. Brother Theodore Proffitt of Youngstown, Ohio. Several nieces and nephews, and a host of relatives and friends to mourn her passing.

She loved everybody.

Elcaney Key

Elcaney Key, age 95, of 615 Bon Street, Lenoir City, Tennessee, passed away Wednesday afternoon, July 5, 1978, at Loudon County Memorial Hospital. He had been a member of Lenoir City Primitive Baptist Church for many years, during which he faithfully served his God and Church. He is survived by his wife, Mrs. Annie Parks Key; Sister, Mrs. Mallie Smithey, Maryville, Tennessee; Sister-in-Law, Mrs. Cora Hill, Lenoir City, Tennessee; several nieces and nephews. Funeral services were conducted by Elder Howard Pippin, Elder Harold Hunt, and Rev. A. A. Carlton, at Click Funeral Home, Friday, July 7. He was laid to rest in Lenoir City Cemetery, there to await the resurrection morning and the call of his blessed Redeemer.

William E. Plemons

William E. Plemons, age 77, of 808 Bon Street, Lenoir City, Tennessee, passed away Monday Morning, October 17, 1977 after a long illness. He is a member of Lenoir City Primitive Baptist Church. He is survived by his wife, Mrs. Sarah E. Webster Plemons; daughters, Mrs. Aline Watkins, Mrs. Martha Hill, Mrs. Alice Mills and Mrs. Dorothy Lowe, all of Lenoir City. Sons, Walter, William E., Jr., and Dexter of Lenoir City. Calvin of Missouri and Virgil of Virginia. 13 grandchildren. Brother Tom, Lenoir City. The funeral was conducted at Hawkins Funeral Chapel October 19 by Rev. Raymond Phillips. Interment at Lakeview Cemetery.

Virgie Ethel Weaver Welch

Virgie Ethel Weaver Welch, of Strawberry Plains, Tennessee, born August 31, 1907, passed away Easter Sunday morning, March 26, 1978, at St. Mary's Medical Center. On January 9, 1927, she married Chester Welch, who survives. Other survivors; Son, Robert Welch, Louisville, Tenn. Daughters, Wanda Pigusch, Arkansas, and Annale Welch, Strawberry Plains. Granddaughter Karen Bobo of Florida. Sister, Addie Belle Petree, Illinois.

Preceded in death by 3 grandchildren, 3 brothers, and 1 sister. Funeral services were held Tuesday, March 28, at Brantley's Chapel Primitive Baptist Church, of which she was a member. Rev. Clifford Brantley, Rev. Everett Berry, and Rev. J. W. Lusk, officiating. Interment: Church Cemetery.

WE STILL MISS YOU
THE FAMILY

Charles A. Lee

Charles A. Lee of Route 3, Sevierville, was born August 26, 1893, to the late Omer H. and Nola Lee. he departed this walk of life August 19, 1978 at the age of 84 years, II months and 23 days. Preceded in death by his wife Mamie Abbot Lee. He was a faithful member of Gethsemane Primitive Baptist Church until his death. Survivors are as follows: daughters, Mrs. Robert (Mary) Walker and Mrs. Ralph (Emmalene) Bobson; son, Harold A. Lee. 11 grandchildren, 15 great-grandchildren. Sisters: Hessie Teffeteller and Nula Gentry. Brothers, Henry and Earl Lee, and a host of nieces and nephews. Funeral services were held August 21, 1978, at Atchley's Chapel, Sevierville. Elder Walter Lyons officiating. Pallbearers were grandsons. Interment, Headrick Chapel Cemetery.

262

Abraham Maples

Mr. Abraham Maples of Harrogate, Tennessee, passed away January 20, 1978 at the Claiborne County Nursing Home. He was born September 24, 1890 in Claiborne County, Tennessee.

He was a long time resident of Middlesboro and was a veteran of World War I. He was a member of the Red Man Oniska Tribe, No. 149 and a member of the Gibson Station Primitive Baptist Church.

He is survived by his wife Evelyn Maples, Harrogate. Two sons, Clyde of Middlesboro, Ky. and Abraham Maples, Jr., Green Cove Springs, Florida.

Three Grandsons: Hobart Dale Sowders, David Maples of Middlesboro and Gordon Maples, San Diego, California, and a host of relatives and friends.

Funeral services were conducted at the Gibson Station Primitive Baptist Church with the Elder Everette Berry and Reverend Nelson Jones officiating.

Pall Bearers were Rev. Randy Duncan, Rev. Bill Parker, Bryant Duncan, Danny Jones, Wilburn Cottrell, and Joe Shumate.

Interment followed in the Shoffner Cemetery with Reece Funeral Home of New Tazewell in charge.

Mary Magnolia Harrison

Mary Magnolia Harrison, age 85, passed away at the Claiborne County Nursing Home on March 17, 1978 after a lengthy illness.

She was married to John Harrison about 52 years ago. Nolia professed a hope at an early age and joined the Pleasant Hill Primitive Baptist Church in March of 1912 and lived a faithful member until God called her home to live with him. She was also a member of the Cumberland Mountain Eastern Star Chapter No. 137.

She is survived by: 3 sons, Joe of Pontiac Michigan, Clyde of Maumee, Ohio, and Oakie of Speedwell, Tennessee. 8 grandchildren, at least 10 great-grandchildren, 3 sisters: Annette Ellison of Dundee, Michigan; Malinda Owens of Ashland, Kentucky; and Harriet Brewer of Speedwell, Tennessee. 2 brothers, John F. Russell of Monroe, Michigan; and Clarence Russell of Speedwell, Tennessee, and a host of relatives and friends.

Our loss is her eternal gain.

Olive Marie Lambert Maddox

Olive Marie Lambert Maddox, who was born February 5, 1927, passed away May 19, 1978, being 51 years, 3 months, and 14 days of age. She was united in marriage to Verlin Maddox in 1949 and to this union was born 3 children.

Survivors:
Husband, Verlin Maddox, Speedwell, Tennessee. Daughters, Mrs. Charlene Jones, Nicholasville, Ky. and Mrs. Donna Meadors, Speedwell, Tennessee. Two grand-daughters and two grandsons. Sisters: Mrs. Lola Braden of Speedwell, Tennessee, and Mrs. Wilma Braden, Monroe, Michigan. Brothers: Alba Lambert, Speedwell, Tennessee and Walter Lambert, Radcliff, Kentucky.

She was preceded in death by her parents and two sisters.

She professed faith in Christ at an early age and joined Pleasant Hill Baptist Church where she remained a faithful member until death.

OUR LOSS IS HEAVEN'S GAIN.

STATISTICAL TABLE

CHURCHES	DELEGATES	Restored	Received by Letter	Baptism	Relationship	Dismissed by Letter	Excluded	Deceased	Total Membership	Printing Minutes	REGULAR MEETING TIME;	COMMUNION TIME
BLACK FOX	Bros. Dale Capps, Bennie Capps. Sisters Flossie Capps, Mary Ruth Capps, Pamela Capps	0	0	0	0	0	0	1	86	$20.00	Second Saturday Night and Sunday. Fourth Saturday Night and Sunday	Second Sunday in June
BRADEN'S CHAPEL	Elders: Noble N. Clawson and W. M. Sparks. Sisters: Helen Clawson, Leely Sparks, Winona Monday	0	0	5	0	1	0	1	143	$20.00	First Saturday Night and Sunday of each month	First Sunday in July
BRANTLEY'S CHAPEL	Elder Clifford Brantley. Bros. Everett Brantley, Daniel Brantley, Robert Welch. Sisters: Mildred Brantley, Linda Brantley, Barsha Brantley, Blanch Welch	0	0	2	2	0	3	2	80	$30.00	Second Saturday Night, Every Sunday and Sunday Night	Second Sunday in July
DAVIS CHAPEL	Bros. James S. Heatherly, Orice McCarty, Bob Lynch. Sisters Ruth Heatherly, Mollie McCarty, Ollie Welch, Lassie Ellison	0	0	0	0	0	10	7	114	$20.00	Third Saturday Night and Sunday. Every Sunday and Sunday Night	Third Sunday in June
GETHSEMANE	Elder Glen Abbott. Bros. Jim Campbell, June Carmichael, Mary Godfrey, Myrtle Cook	0	2	0	3	0	0	0	37	$25.00	Fourth Sunday of each Month	Fourth Sunday in May and October
GIBSON STATION	Elders William Rhymer, Spurgeon Thompson, Joe Irving. Sisters Karen Rhymer, Jean Thompson, Evelyn Irving, Sally Brittain, Susie Shofiner, Dorothy Johnson, Millie Thompson	0	0	0	0	0	2	1	76	$25.00	Each Sunday and Sunday Night	First Sunday in June
HEADRICK CHAPEL	Bros. Bill Cook, Clyde Abbott, Sr. Sisters Grace Abbott, Geraldine Abbott	0	0	0	0	0	0	0	110	$25.00	First Sunday of each month	First Sunday in May and October
KIRKWOOD	Elders H. E. Brummitt, Walter Lyons. Bros. C. A. Sharp, R. P. Bridges, M. E. Evans. Sisters Ruby Brummitt, Fredia Sharp, Ora Bridges, Velma Evans	0	0	2	0	0	0	1	115	$30.00	Every Sunday Night	Last Sunday in April

									Business Meeting	Association
LENOIR CITY	Elder Howard Pippin. Bros. Henry Chamberlain, Hubert Spoon, Raymond Wilkerson. Sisters Estie Chamberlain, Anna Spoon, Ruby Williams, Phyllis Pippin	0	2	0	0	4	2	146	$35.00	Every Sunday and Sunday Night	Third Sunday in May
MONROE, MICH.	Roxie Drummonds	0	0	1	0	0	1	13	$10.00	Third Sunday of each month	Third Sunday in July
MYERS GROVE	Elders Johnny Ayers, Clay Widner. Bros. Harold Cupp. Isom Drummonds.	0	0	4	0	0	1	70	$20.00	Second Saturday Night and Sunday Fourth Saturday night and Sunday	Fourth Sunday in May
NOETON	Elder John Oliver. Bros. Carroll Oliver, Charlie Collins. Sisters Ruth Oliver and Dora Collins.	0	0	0	0	0	2	40	$20.00	First Sunday Third Saturday night and Sunday	Third Saturday and Sunday in May and September
OAK GROVE	Elders Johnny Atkins, Tonie Eastridge. Bro. Malcolm Walker. Sisters Frances Eastridge, Laura Lou Walker.	0	0	2	0	1	0	335	$25.00	First Saturday and Sunday Third Sunday	First Sunday in May
PLEASANT HILL	Elders: Larry Anderson, Albert Davis Sisters: Myra Anderson, Audra Davis	0	0	0	0	0	3	107	$35.00	Fourth Saturday night and Sunday	Fourth Sunday in June
PLEASANT POINT	Letter Received. No Delegate Present.	0	0	0	0	0	2	113	$15.00	First Saturday Night and Sunday Third Sunday	First Sunday in July
ROCKY DALE DALE	Elders Everett Berry, William Berry, Joe Bush, Parnick Shelton. Bros. W. H. Taylor, Ralph Clapp, E. D. Graves, Dewey Graves, Dennis Branson. Sisters Trula Berry, Lou Emma Taylor, Norma Jean Bush, Helen Branson, Grace Graves.	0	0	2	1	0	1	129	$40.00	Every Sunday and Sunday Night	Second Sunday in May

CHURCH	COUNTY	PASTOR	CLERK	ADDRESS
Black Fox	Grainger	Elder Parnick Shelton	Bennie Capps Flossie Capps	P. O. Box 91, Maynardville, Tn. 37807 Maynardville, Tn. 37807
Braden's Chapel	Union	Elder Noble Clawson Elder J. C. Monday, Asst.	Jimmie B. Edwards Phyllis Wilson, Asst.	Speedwell, Tn. Speedwell, Tn.
Brantley's Chapel	Blount	Elder Clifford Brantley	Daniel Brantley D. C. Brantley, Asst.	Rt. 10, Mint Road, Maryville, Tn 2020 Biddle Road, Maryville, Tn.
Davis Chapel	Campbell	Elder William Berry	Ruth Heatherly Lassie Ellison, Asst.	Rt. 1, Davis Chapel Rd. LaFollette, Tn. 918 Carwynn Rd., LaFollette, Tn.
Gethsemane	Knox	Elder Walter Lyons	Tom Carmichael	729 Frank St., Knoxville, Tn.
Gibson Station	Lee Virginia	Elder William Rhymer Elder Everette Berry	Dorothy Johnson Shirley Sandifer, Asst.	Rt. 2, Ewing, Va. Rt. 2, Harrogate, Tn.
Headrick Chapel	Knox	Elder Walter Lyons	Clyde Abbott, Sr.	Rt. 7, Sevierville, Tn.
Kirkwood	Knox	Elder Everette Berry	Estelle Petree Sharp Alice Tinell Powers	Rt. 24, Emory Road, Knoxville, Tn. 7525 Temple Acre Dr., Knoxville, Tn.

Church	County	Minister	Clerk	Address
Lenoir City	Loudon	Elder Howard M. Pippin	Scott Collins	705 W. 5th Ave., Lenoir City, Tn.
Monroe, Michigan	Monroe		Gertrude Zwack	1825 Spaulding Rd., Monroe, Michigan
			Roxie Drummonds, Asst.	2675 Blue Bush Rd., Monroe, Michigan
Myers Grove	Claiborne	Elder Noble Clawson	Bonnie Miracle	Rt. 2, Box 194, New Tazewell, Tn.
		Elder Clay Widner, Asst.	Harold Cupp, Asst.	Rt. 2, New Tazewell, Tn.
Noeton	Grainger	Elder John Oliver	Carroll Oliver	Rt. 2, Box 512, Bean Station, Tn.
			Bessie Collins, Asst.	Rt. 5, Morristown, Tn.
Oak Grove	Union	Elder J. C. Monday	Betty P. Sharp	Sharp Chapel, Tn.
		Elder Noble Clawson, Asst.	Betty Shoffner, Asst.	Sharp Chapel, Tn.
Pleasant Hill	Claiborne	Elder Larry Anderson	William Branscomb	Speedwell, Tn.
		Elder Albert Davis, Asst.		
Pleasant Point	Claiborne	Elder Claude Rosson	Beatrice Williams	New Tazewell, Tn.
		Elder Larry Anderson, Asst.		
Rocky Dale	Knox	Elder Hugh Brummitt	Edward Collett	Rt. 1, Box 17, Luttrell, Tn
			Dennis Branson	4633 Marshall Drive, Knoxville, Tn.

1979 MINUTES

of the

ONE HUNDRED FIFTY-NINTH SESSION

of the

POWELL VALLEY ASSOCIATION

OF PRIMITIVE BAPTIST

OAK GROVE PRIMITIVE BAPTIST CHURCH

held with the Sister Church at
OAK GROVE
in UNION COUNTY, TENNESSEE
AUGUST 17, 18, 19, 1979

The next Session will be held with the Sister Church at Black Fox in Grainger County, Tenn., to begin on Friday before the Third Saturday in August 1980 at 10:30 A.M.

THE ONE HUNDRED FIFTY-NINTH SESSION
OF THE POWELL VALLEY ASSOCIATION
OF
PRIMITIVE BAPTIST

**HELD WITH THE SISTER CHURCH AT OAK GROVE
IN UNION COUNTY, TENNESSEE
AUGUST 17, 18, 19, 1979
NEXT SESSION WILL BE HELD WITH THE SISTER CHURCH
AT
BLACK FOX
IN GRAINGER COUNTY, TENNESSEE
TO BEGIN ON FRIDAY BEFORE THE THIRD SATURDAY
IN AUGUST, 1980
AT 10:30 A.M.
ELDER HUGH BRUMMITT WILL DELIVER THE INTRODUCTORY
SERMON, AND ELDER WALTER LYONS WILL BE THE ALTERNATE**

OFFICERS

Elder Albert Davis   Moderator
Speedwell, Tenn. - Phone 869-3596

Elder Hugh Brummitt   Assistant Moderator
1329 Brown Ave., Knoxville, Tenn. - Phone 546-7700

W. H. Taylor   Clerk
Rt. 27, Knoxville, Tenn. 37918 - Phone 922-2143

Bennie Capps   Assistant Clerk
Maynardville, Tenn. - Phone 992-5571

FRIDAY, AUGUST 17, 1979

According to previous arrangements, the one hundred and fifty ninth session of the Powell Valley Association of Primitive Baptist met with the sister church at Oak Grove in Union County, Tennessee, August 17, 18 and 19.

After singing, prayer was offered by Elder Jim Campbell after which the good old song of "Hold to God's Unchanging Hand" was sung by the congregation.

The introductory sermon was delivered by Elder Howard Pippin who used the first seven verses of the Book of Isaiah and preaching a very good sermon.

After the introductory sermon the congregation sang a song and was recessed for fifteen minutes by prayer by Elder Everett Berry.

After intermission and at the sound of singing, the Association reassembled and gave a moment of silent prayer in memory of our beloved departed minister, Elder Tonie Eastridge. Then followed with prayer by Elder Walter Lyons.

After prayer Moderator Davis called the Association to order for the business session of the Association not finished before recess.

The Moderator called for the letters of sister churches to be presented to the Clerk for reading.

Letters from all the sister churches with the exception of Bradens Chapel Church were read and approved, and the delegates were seated.

The Moderator called for anyone from the sister churches not delegated and wishing to be seated as such to come forward and give your name and the church you are from. None came.

The Moderator called for any petitionary letter if there should be one. There was no response.

Motion approved that the Association re-elect Elder Albert Davis as Moderator and Elder Hugh E. Brummitt as Assistant Moderator for the coming year.

Motion approved to re-elect Bro. W. H. Taylor as Clerk and Bro. Bennie Capps as Assistant Clerk.

The Association appointed Elder Davis the Moderator to appoint all the committees.

The Moderator, after being delegated to do so, appointed the committees as follows:

A.   **COMMITTEE ON ARRANGEMENTS**
Bro. Robert Bridges
Bro. Isom Drummons
Bro. Charlie Collins

B.   **COMMITTEE ON PREACHING**
Bro. Elwood Evans
Bro. Aaron Cole
Bro. Daniel Brantley

C.   **COMMITTEE ON REQUEST**
Bro. Orice McCarty
Elder Joe Bush
Elder Jim Campbell

D.   **COMMITTEE ON FINANCE**
Bro. Rina Johnson
Elder William Rhymer
Elder James Branscomb

The committees all being appointed, the Association adjourned until 10:30 A.M. Saturday. After a song the Association was dismissed in prayer by Elder Brantley of Brantleys Chapel Church.

SATURDAY, AUGUST 18, 1979

Saturday at the appointed hour of 10:30 A.M., at the sound of singing, the Association reassembled with a full house.

After singing praise, the Assistant Moderator, Elder Hugh Brummitt, gave the welcome and read the 23rd Psalm and gave a very stirring and spiritual talk and called for prayer by Elder John Oliver of the Noeton Church.

The Moderator called for any church letter not received on Friday. One was presented from the sister church at Bradens Chapel.

A motion was approved to receive their letter and seat their delegates.

A call was given for anyone from the sister churches not sent as a delegate and wishing to be seated as such to come forward. None came.

The Moderator called for the report of the Committee on Arrangements, who gave the following report which was accepted and the committee was released.

REPORT ON ARRANGEMENTS

Call for roll call of all delegates.
Call for report of Committee on Preaching.
Call for report of Committee on Request.
Call for report of Committee on Finance.
To suggest how many minutes we shall have printed and who shall supervise the printing and distriution of same, and how much he shall receive for his services. Where the next Association shall be held and who shall preach the introductory sermon and who shall be his alternate.

Respectfully submitted,

Bro. Robert Bridges
Bro. Isom Drummons
Bro. Charlie Collins

Call for the roll call of delegates of all the sister churches and the absentees to be noted.

Call for the report of the Committee on Preaching which was givin, and after making substitutions for some who could not be present at the appointed time, the report was given as follows and the committee was released.

REPORT ON PREACHING

Friday Night	Elder William Berry
	Elder Joe Bush
Saturday	Elder Jim Campbell
	Elder Clifford Brantley
Saturday Night	Elder Claude Rosson
	Elder Noble Clawson
Sunday	Elder William Rhymer
	Elder Everett Berry

273

Respectfully submitted,

Bro. Elwood Evans
Bro. Aaron Cole
Bro. Daniel Brantley

Called for the report of the Committee on Request which was received and after one amendment was approved and accepted and the committee released.

REPORT ON REQUEST

We the committee request that we have 1,150 copies of the minutes printed and that the Clerk supervise the printing and distribution of the same and receive $100.00 (as amended $125.00) for his services. We also request that Elder Hugh Brummitt of Rocky Dale Church write a circular letter to be placed in the minutes. Also that the next Association be held with the sister church at Black Fox in Grainger County and may peace and love of our Lord be with us through the remainder of the session.

Submitted with love,

Elder Jim Campbell
Bro. Orice McCarty

274

Call for the report of the Committee on Finance who gave the following report which was accepted and the committee released.

REPORT ON FINANCE

Black Fox	$20.00
Bradens Chapel	$20.00
Brantleys Chapel	$25.00
Davis Chapel	$25.00
Gethsemane	$25.00
Gibson Station	$30.00
Headricks Chapel	$20.00
Kirkwood	$30.00
Lenoir City	$35.00
Monroe, Mich.	$10.00
Meyers Grove	$20.00
Noeton	$20.00
Oak Grove	$25.00
Pleasant Hill	$35.00
Pleasant Point	$15.00
Rocky Dale	$40.00
TOTAL	$395.00
TOTAL COLLECTION	$395.00
BALANCE IN BANK	$429.00
TOTAL	$824.00
EXPENSES FOR 1979	$413.00
BALANCE TO DATE	$411.00

Respectfully submitted,

Elder James H. Branscomb
Elder William Rhymer
Bro. Rina Johnson

Motion approved that we accept the request of the committee and have printed 1,150 copies of the minutes and that the Clerk supervise the printing and distribution of same and that he receive $125.00 for his services.

Motion approved that the next Association shall be held with the sister church at Black Fox in Grainger County, Tennessee to begin on Friday before the third Saturday in August 1980 at 10:30 A.M.

Motion approved that Elder John Oliver of Noeton Church shall preach the introductory sermon and Elder Walter Lyons of Kirk-

Call for the report of the Committee on Finance who gave the following report which was accepted and the committee released.

REPORT ON FINANCE

Black Fox	$20.00
Bradens Chapel	$20.00
Brantleys Chapel	$25.00
Davis Chapel	$25.00
Gethsemane	$25.00
Gibson Station	$30.00
Headricks Chapel	$20.00
Kirkwood	$30.00
Lenoir City	$35.00
Monroe, Mich.	$10.00
Meyers Grove	$20.00
Noeton	$20.00
Oak Grove	$25.00
Pleasant Hill	$35.00
Pleasant Point	$15.00
Rocky Dale	$40.00
TOTAL	$395.00
TOTAL COLLECTION	$395.00
BALANCE IN BANK	$429.00
TOTAL	$824.00
EXPENSES FOR 1979	$413.00
BALANCE TO DATE	$411.00

Respectfully submitted,

Elder James H. Branscomb
Elder William Rhymer
Bro. Rina Johnson

Motion approved that we accept the request of the committee and have printed 1,150 copies of the minutes and that the Clerk supervise the printing and distribution of same and that he receive $125.00 for his services.

Motion approved that the next Association shall be held with the sister church at Black Fox in Grainger County, Tennessee to begin on Friday before the third Saturday in August 1980 at 10:30 A.M.

Motion approved that Elder John Oliver of Noeton Church shall preach the introductory sermon and Elder Walter Lyons of Kirkwood Church be the alternate.

Motion approved that Elder Hugh Brummitt prepare a circular letter to be placed in the minutes.

‣ We the sister churches that compose this Association wish to express our heart-felt thanks for the love, fellowship and warm welcome and the wonderful food you have given us. May the good Lord bless each one of you is our prayer as we leave you. Dismissed in prayer by Elder Walter Lyons.

SUNDAY, AUGUST 19, 1979

Sunday at the appointed hour of 10:30 the Association assembled at the sound of singing. Elder Davis introduced the service and read from the 13th Chapter of Corintians and called for prayer by Elder Parnick Shalton of Rocky Dale Church. After prayer Elder William Rhymer taking for his sermon the first few verses of St. John. (In the beginning was the word and the Word was God) was his starting words. Elder Rhymer was blessed with a good spirit and preached a wonderful, wonderful sermon.

Following this was Elder Everett Berry preaching from the 3rd Chapter of 1st Timothy. Elder Berry came to the pulpit filled with the spirit and delivered another soul stirring sermon which was followed by much rejoicing and praising God.

This being the last service of this Association we have to say that we have been wonderfully blessed with the best of preaching.

We now leave you with our humble prayer that God will bless each and every one of you as you go back to your churches.

Dismissed in prayer by Elder Hugh Brummitt.

> Elder Albert Davis, Moderator
> Elder Hugh Brummitt, Asst. Moderator
> W. H. Taylor, Clerk
> Bennie Capps, Asst. Clerk

This Association is blessed with a fine group of ministers, as was illustrated during this session. Time would not permit but a small number of them to have the opportunity to preach.

On Friday, Elder Howard Pippin of the Lenoir City Church did a wonderful introductor sermon. Then on Friday night Elder Jim Campbell of the Gethsemane Church delivered a good sermon speaking from the 8th Chapter of Romans the 23rd Verse.

277

Elder Campbell was followed by Elder Bill Berry from Rocky Dale Church speaking from the 105th Psalm, Verses 1 thru 11, and delivering a wonderful lesson.

Then on Saturday, Elder Jim Campbell introduced the preaching service speaking from the 1st Chapter of Genesis followed by Elder Clifford Brantley of Brantleys Chapel Church speaking from the 25th Chapter of Isaiah on the power and the covenants of God which was a wonderful sermon.

Then on Saturday night, Elder Rossen of Pleasant Point Church delivered a good sermon from the 15th Chapter of St. John, using for his text "The True Vine". This was followed by Elder Noble Clawson of Bradens Chapel Church using as his subjects "The Three Hebrew Children and the Firey Furnace" and "The Worship of Idol Gods" and gave a wonderful lesson.

Then on Sunday, Elder William Rhymer of Gibson Station Church did a wonderful sermon with lots of spirit using the text "The Word was with God and the Word was God". Elder Rhymer being followed by Elder Everett Berry from Rocky Dale who did a very spiritual sermon from the book of 1st Tomothy followed by much praise and rejoicing.

MINISTERS DIRECTORY

Elder Glenn Abbott, 1801 Cherrybrook Drive, Knoxville, Tn., Ph. 947-6875

Elder Larry Anderson, Speedwell, Tennessee, Ph. 869-4635

Elder Johnny Atkins, Bean Station, Tennessee, Ph. 767-2397

Elder Johnny Ayres, Rt. 3 Box 159, Bean Station, Tn., Ph. 586-5401

Elder Everette Berry, Rt. #24, Knoxville, Tn., Ph. 922-7004

Elder William Berry, Rt. #13, Knoxville, Tn., Ph. 922-9189

Elder J. H. Branscomb, Speedwell, Tn., Ph. 562-6361

Elder Clifford Brantley, Brown School Rd., Maryville, Tn., Ph. 982-3735

Elder Hugh E. Brummitt, 1329 Brown Ave., Knoxville, Tn., Ph. 546-7700

Elder J. C. Monday, Speedwell, Tn., Ph. 562-3068

Elder Sheridan Moore, Route #1, Townsend, Tn., Ph. 581-5039

Elder Howard Pippin, 101 Rose Street, Lenoir City, Tennessee

Elder Claude Rosson, Rt. #4, New Tazewell, Tn., Ph. 626-3168

Elder Joe Bush, Corryton, Tennessee, Ph. 687-2108

Elder Noble Clawson, Rt. #4, Speedwell, Tn., Ph. 562-2004

Elder Albert Davis, Speedwell, Tn., Ph. 869-3596

Elder Clay Widner, Rt. #1, Tazewell, Tn., Ph. 626-3893

Elder Alvin Graves, 122 Oak Wood Dr.. Lenoir City, Tn., Ph. 986-9725

Elder Joe Irving, 111 Eighth St., Middlesboro, Ky.

Elder Walter Lyons, 1602 Garfield St., Alcoa, Tn., Ph. 984-3207

Elder John Godfrey, 15443 Valleoga, Victoryvill, Calif., Ph. (714) 243-4661

Elder Robert Walker, Sevierville, Tn., Ph. 453-2753

Elder Parnick Shelton, Corryton, Tn., Ph. 687-6142

Elder William Sparks, Speedwell, Tn., Ph. 562-7997

Elder William Rhymer, Rt. #2, Harrogate, Tn. Ph. 869-3082

Elder Spurgeon Thompson, Box #36, Shawanee, Tn., Ph. 869-8175

Elder John Oliver, Bean Station, Tn., Ph. 581-5039

Elder Jim Campbell, Louisville, Tn., Ph. 983-1654

Elder Clyde Abbott, Jr., Rt. 8, Holton Rd., Maryville, Tn., 37801

LICENTIATES

Brother Roscoe Branscomb, Speedwell, Tennessee

Brother Odell Carpenter, Maryville, Tennessee

Brother Ray Walker, Route #1, Townsend, Tennessee

Elder Clyde Abbott, Sr., Rt. 7, Sevierville, Tn., Ph. 453-2329

RULES OF DECORUM

1. The churches composing the Powell's Valley Association shall not be confined to any set rules as to specific number of Messengers they shall have in the body, but shall have the right to name in their letters as many as they choose, and in addition all orderly members of and of the churches being present be entitled to seats in the body as Messengers of their respective churches, with all the rights and privileges of the same.

2. The Messengers thus assembled shall be denominated the Powell's Valley Primitive Baptist Association.

3. For the purpose of historical information and statistical edification, the Churches are required to state in letters, the number of members in fellowship, the number received by Baptism, by letter, by confession of Faith, the number dismissed, excluded and dead since last session; also the time of their meeting, their pastoral supply, and the amount of money contributed for ministers and other purposes together with any other information they deem appropriate for the edification of the saints and glory of God.

4. This Association shall have no power to answer queries, give advice, or dictate to the Churches in any case, or to lord it over God's heritage nor any power by which she can directly or indirectly fringe on the internal rights of the church or censure and try any church or member in reference to faith and practice and determine upon validity of gospel ordinances. These things shall rest entirely with the churches; but henceforward our annual meetings shall be only for the purpose of hearing from each other, and for the worship of God and mutual comfort and edification of the Saints. To this end we reserve the privilege annually for the Third Friday in August and the two following days or at such other times as may be agreed upon with any church that may invite us having to protect our own standard, while in session, from heresay and disorder to recognize and invite any primitive Baptist minister or any lay brother to worship with us that may deem proper; to request the brethren of our body to visit other churches or bodies in our belief with whom we may desire to culture Christian fellowship; to publish in a minute of our proceedings.

5. Each session of the body shall have a Moderator and Clerk who shall hold office until re-elected.

6. Any order member of any church belonging to this body, when convened, being present shall be eligible to elect on as Moderator and Clerk or to sit on any committee appointed by the same.

7. In all election or questions that may be necessary to determine by vote, the vote shall be taken by churches, each church being entitled to three votes for any number less than one hundred, and one additional vote for every fifty or fraction thereof above the first hundred, but the Messengers of each church may divide their vote as they see proper.

8. All elections or questions coming to vote shall be determined by a majority vote cast, and it shall be the only duty of the minority to acquiesce in the decision thus reached.

9. If new churches desire to be admitted to this union they shall petition by letter and messengers and if voted for and recommended by one or more sister churches for her Presbytery constitutioning them, as orthodox and orderly they shall be received by the vote of the body and manifested by the Moderator giving the Messengers the right hand of fellowship.

10. Any motion or resolution clearly inconsistent with the above rules shall be promptly ruled out of order unless withdrawn by the mover.

11. Any Messenger being ruled out of order by the Moderator shall have the right to appeal to the body on the question of order, and if sustained shall be allowed to proceed, but if not take his seat.

12. Our meeting being held in the name of Christ and the worship of God; each Messenger is expected to observe due and proper therein.

13. It will not be considered good for any Messenger whose name has been enrolled as such to abruptly break off or absent himself from the Association without leave.

14. The Moderator shall be entitled to the same privilege of speech as other members provided the chair is filled.

15. The minutes of the Association shall be read and approved by the body and signed by the Moderator before adjourning.

16. The Association shall be opened and closed by prayer.

17. Amendments to these may be made at any time by a majority of the union voting by churches when they deem it necessary, provide such amendments do not compromise the sovereignty of the churches nor have tendency to give body undue power or jurisdiction over them.

ARTICLES OF FAITH

Article 1. We believe in only one true living God, as He is revealed to us in the Holy Scriptures - Father, Son, and Holy Ghost.

Article 2. We believe that the Scriptures of the old and new Testaments are the words of God and the only rule of all-saving knowledge and obedience.

Article 3. We believe in the doctrine of election according to the foreknowledge of God.

Article 4. We believe in the doctrine of original sin.

Article 5. We believe in man's impotency to rescue himself from the fallen state he is in, by his own will or ability.

Article 6. We believe that sinners are justified in the sight of God only by the imputed righteousness of Jesus Christ.

Article 7. We believe the elect, according to the foreknowledge of God will be called, converted, regenerated, and sanctified by the Holy Spirit.

Article 8. We believe the saints will persevere and never fall finally away.

Article 9. We believe that baptism and the Lord's Supper are ordinances of Jesus Christ, and that true believers are the only subject of these ordinances, and that the true mode of baptism is by immersion. We believe also that feet washing is an example of Jesus Christ and should be kept by his disciples until his second coming.

Article 10. We believe in the Resurrection of the dead and the General Judgement.

Article 11. We believe that the punishment of the wicked will be everlasting and that the joys of the righteous will be eternal.

Article 12. We believe that no minister has the right to administer the ordinances, except those who have been regularly baptized and called of God, and come under the imposition of hands of the presbytery.

Hattie Bailey

Mrs. Hattie Bailey, age 73, Route 2 Washburn passed away Jan. 20, 1979. She was a member of Black Fox Primitive Baptist Church. Survivors: husband, Ora Bailey; Sisters Mrs. Rosie Bailey, Mrs. Cora Munsey, Mrs. Flossie Fry, brothers Luther and James Munsey. Funeral services were conducted at Black Fox Primitive Baptist Church with Rev. Ralph Munsey and Rev. Andy Vance officiating. Interment in Cabbage Cemetery.

John H. Bailey

John H. Bailey age 35 of Maynardville passed away November 1, 1978, at Baptist Hospital. He was a member of Black Fox Primitive Baptist Church. Survivors: wife, Delores Bailey, daughter, Sherry; sons Freddy and Gregg Bailey; sisters Mrs. Reba Nicely, Mrs. Rachel Ingle and Mrs. Polly Beeler, brothers; Junior and Judson. Parents Mr. & Mrs. Roy Bailey. Funeral services were conducted at Black Fox Church with interment in Cabbage Cemetery.

Roma Liford Bailey

Mrs. Roma Liford Bailey, age 69 of Washburn passed away January 8, 1979, at her home. She was a member of Black Fox Primitive Baptist Church. Survivors: Husband, Roy, daughters, Mrs. Reba Nicely, Mrs. Rachel Ingle, Mrs. Polly Beeler, sons; Judson and Junior. Sisters: Mrs. Alma Munsey, Mrs. Cleva Carver, brothers; Fred and Claude Liford, 12 grandchildren, 2 greatgrandchildren. She was preceded in death by a son John Bailey. Funeral services were conducted at Black Fox Church with Elder Parnick Shelton and Elder Albert Davis officiating. Interment in Cabbage Cemetery.

Vaughn W. Beason

Vaughn W. Beason, 61, of 619 Brown School Road, Maryville, passed away at his home June 15, 1979.

He was a Charter Member of Brantley's Chapel Primitive Baptist Church. He was also a member of New Providence Masonic Lodge.

Survivors; wife Jeanette Beason, Sons, David, Glenn and Bill Beason all of Maryville. Daughters, Barbara Johnson of Talbot, Carolyn Stapleton of Maryville, Peggy Pack of Fayetteville, Ga. Mother, Zanie Beason of Union Co. Twelve grandchildren. Brother, Voyd Beason of Knoxville, Lee Beason of Union Co. Sisters, Ruth Shoffner of Union Co., Mona Rogers of Corryton, Dona Keck of Knoxville.

Funeral services were held at Brantley's Chapel Church, with Elders Clifford Brantley and J. C. Monday. Burial in Church Cemetery.

Sadly missed by wife and family.

Malissa Hurst Cadle

Malissa Hurst Cadle 84, Rt. 8 Brown School Rd., Maryville, passed away March 21, 1979 at Blount Memorial Hospital. She was a member of Brantley's Chapel Primitive Baptist Church. Daughter, Mrs. Hazel Johnson of Maryville, Sons, Riley Cadle of Maryville, John Cadle of New Market.

Malissa Hurst Cadle, 84, Rt. 8 Brown Schoo Rd. Maryville, passed away March 21, 1979 at Blount Memorial Hospital. She was a member of Brantley's Chapel Primitive Baptist Church. Daughter, Mrs. Hazel Johnson of Maryville, Sons, Riley Cadle of Maryville, John Cadle of New Market.

Six grandchildren, eight great-grandchildren. Funeral was held at Brantley's Chapel Church, with Elder Clifford Brantley and Elder William Berry officiating. Interment in Church Cemetery.

It broke our heart to lose you
But you did not go alone,
For part of us went with you
The day God called you home,
From your bed to heavenly rest
God took you home to be his
  guest.
The love we shared together
Are the memories we hold dear,
And the happiness you gave us,
Keeps forever near.
Peaceful be thy rest dear
  Mother;
It is sweet to breathe thy name,
In life we loved you dearly
And in Death we do the same.

Forever Missed;
Daughter & Sons

Oma N. Capps

Mrs. Oma N. Capps, age 85 of Knoxville passed away December 23, 1978. She was a member of Black Fox Primitive Baptist Church. Survivors: Daughters Mrs. Irene Clevenger and Mrs. Reva Braden. Sons: Woodrow, Claude, John, Carl and Loren; step-son Herman Capps, step-daughter Caltha Street. Services were conducted at Mynatt's Chapel with Elder John Foster and Rev. Lewis Fortner officiating. Interment in Borruff Cemetery.

Tonie Ira Eastridge

Elder Tonie Ira Eastridge, born February 16, 1912 departed this life Jan. 26, 1979 at Blount Memorial Hospital after a short illness. Age 66 years, 11 months, & 10 days. He was the son of Garett and Ella Cardwell Eastridge. He was married to Francie Shaffner Eastridge Dec. 25, 1932. To this union one daughter was born, Eula Gray Eastridge, who preceeded him in death. One son, Leonard Eastridge. One brother, Robert Eastridge; 5 sisters. One sister and 3 brothers preceeded him in death. His mother and father preceeded him in death. He joined the church when he was 12 years old and was ordained Oct. 7, 1950 at Oak Grove Primitive Baptist Church of which he was a member. He pastored churches until he was disabled. He loved all the churches and ministers and was strong in his belief. He loved to visit all the churches in their Communions and feet washing. He was a Free Mason for many years and a 32 Scottish Rite.

Our home is so lonesome. We loved him so much, but God had a place for him where there is no more pain.

The funeral was conducted at Oak Grove Church Jan. 29, 1979. Laid to rest in Rush Strong Cemetery to await the morning of the Resurrection. Funeral conducted by Elder W. M. Sparks, Elder J. C. Monday, Elder Clifford Brantley. Pallbearers: nephews, and honorary pallbearers were a host of dear Elders who were present. We are thankful for every one of them. Our home is so sad and will never be the same, but we hope to meet him again in the "Sweet By and By".

His Wife and Family

Lucinda Moyers

Lucinda Moyers, daughter of Elder and Mrs. Phillip Moyers. She was united in matrimoney to Elder W. A. (Bill) Moyers April 1914. To this union were born 12 children. Eight have preceded her in death. Also preceded in death by her husband in 1960. Survivors; one daughter Nadine; three sons, Robert Lee, Earl Ray and Kenneth Bruce.

She professed faith in Christ at an early age and joined the church at Pleasant Hill. She really loved her church but due to her afflictions she was unable to attend in her last years. Our loss is her eternal gain.

Annie Parks Key

Mrs. Annie Parks Key, 88, of 615 Bon Street, Lenoir City. Wife of the late Elcaney Key, died Monday, Nov. 13 at Loudon County Memorial Hospital. She was a member of Bon Street Primitive Baptist Church and a retired knitter with the Charles H. Bacon Company. Survivors are: sister, Cora Hill of Lenoir City, several nieces and nephews. Annie joined the church at an early age and remained a loyal and faithful member as long as her health permitted. She loved her church and was a mother to the ministers and visitors who came and made their home a welcome place for them. She will be sadly missed by relatives, church and all who knew her and loved her.

Funeral services were held at 2:30 p.m., Wednesday, Nov. 15 at Click Funeral Home chapel, with Elder Howard Pippin, Elder Harold Hunt and Rev. A. A. Carlton officiating. Burial in Lenoir City Cemetery.

284

Anna Hurst Overbay

Anna Hurst Overbay, age 87, passed away July 8, 1979. Survivors: two daughters; Minnie Overbay and Mrs. Melba Stubblefield of Bean Station. One sister, Mrs. Polly Long of Spring City, Tenn., two brothers, Floyd Hurst of Knoxville, Ernest Hurst of Spring City. Three grandchildren, three great-grandchildren.

She was a member of Noeton Primitive Baptist Church where services were held on July 11, 1979 at 2:30 p.m. with Elder John Oliver, Rev. Olof Atkin and Rev. Billy Carroll officiating. Burial in Noeton Cemetery.

Betty Sayers

Mrs. Betty Sayers, age 67, died Jan. 22, 1979 at Doctor's Hospital at Morristown. She was a member of Noeton Primitive Baptist Church. She is survived by sisters; Edith Bunch of Morristown, Susie Oliver of Bean Station; Brother, Oscar Hurst of Morristown. Several nieces and nephews.

Funeral services at Noeton Primitive Baptist Church with Elder John Oliver, Rev. Olof Atkins officiating. Burial in Acuff Cemetery in Washburn. Stubblefield Funeral Home of Morristown in charge.

Alta J. (Sharp) Snodderly

Alta J. (Sharp) Snodderly, age 68, passed from this life on April 1, 1979. She was preceded in death by her husband, the late Silas B. Snodderly. Survivors: daughter, Mrs. James K. (Reba) Whitson; granddaughter, Maresa Kelly Whitson; brother, R. E. Sharp, Knoxville; sister, Mrs. R. O. (Myrtle) Taylor, Knoxville; nieces and nephews. Services were held on April 3, 1979, at Mynatt's Chapel. Elder Everett Berry, Elder Bill Berry and Rev. Chad Wayland officiating. Interment at Sherwood Memorial Gardens.

Silas B. Snodderly

Silas B. Snodderly, age, 74, passed from this life on September 18, 1978. Survivors: wife, Alta J. Snodderly; daughter, Mrs. James K. (Reba) Whitson; granddaughter, Maresa Kelly Whitson; brother, Lee Snodderly, Maryville; several nieces and nephews. Services were held Wednesday, September 20, 1978, at Mynatt's Chapel. Elder Everett Berry, Elder Bill Berry and Rev. Chad Wayland officiating. Interment at Sherwood Memorial Gardens.

Della Stigall

Mrs. Della Stigall 86, of Ewing, Va., passed away Thursday, Feb. 15, 1979, at the Middlesboro Community Hospital. She is survived by two daughters: Pearl Mae Barnes, Ewing and Topsie Harve Brooks of Monroe, Michigan. A son: Floyd Stigall and foster son Kestrell Stigall of Ewing, Va., and one sister: Eva Collins of Ben Hur, Va., and many relatives and friends.

Funeral services were conducted at 1:00 p.m., Monday, Feb. 19 at the Gibson Station Primitive Baptist Church of which she was a member, with the Elder Everette Berry and Elder William Rhymer officiating. She was laid to rest in Gibson Cemetery.

Nora Treece

Mrs. Nora Treece age 80, of New Tazewell, passed away February 10, 1978 at Claiborne County Hospital.

She was a member of Pleasant Point Baptist Church.

Survivors: son, Earl Treece, Monroe, Mich., daughters, Mrs. Jean Billingsley, New Tazewell, Mrs. Opal Cardwell, Tazewell, five grandchildren, five great grandchildren, one sister, Mrs. Harriet Simmons, New Tazewell, one brother, Walter Wilcox, New Tazewell. Her husband Herbert Treece and one son preceded her in death.

Funeral services were held 11 a.m. Sunday at Coffey Chapel with burial in Fairview Cemetery. Rev. William Sparks officiating.

Pallbearers: Kenneth Simmons, Clayton Jones, Jack Treece, Bob Russell, Archie Russell, and Hoy Treece.

Songs were by Verlin Simmons Singers.

Coffey Funeral Home in charge.

Luda Brantley Welch

Luda Brantley Welch of Maryville, born Jan. 11, 1904, deceased Oct. 3, 1978, age 74 years 8 months and 23 days. Married to Millard Welch in May 1921. She was preceded in death by her husband in Feb. 1977. To this union were born six children. Sons, Hillard, Leon and Arnold, all of Maryville. Son Alvin was killed in World War II. Daughter Jessie Coppinger of Maryville. Sisters, Elizabeth and Bessie Loy of Clinton. Martha, who preceded her in death in Jan. 1978. Twenty grandchildren and twelve great-grandchildren. One great-granddaughter deceased.

Luda professed faith in Christ at an early age, and joined the Cave Springs Primitive Baptist Church in Union County in 1948. She moved from the Norris Basin to Blount County and became a charter member of the newly organized church of Brantleys Chapel where she remained a loyal and faithful member until death. Services conducted at Smiths Funeral Home chapel by Elder Clifford Brantley and Elder J. C. Monday. Laid to rest in Sherwood Memorial Garden.

Sadly missed by family and church.

STATISTICAL TABLE

CHURCHES	DELEGATES	Restored	Rec'd by Letter	Baptism	Relationship	Dismiss by Letter	Excluded	Deceased	Total Membership	Printing Minutes	REGULAR MEETING TIME	COMMUNION TIME
BLACK FOX	Bros. Dale Capps, Arthur Terry, Bennie Capps. Sisters: Flossie Capps, Mary Ruth Capps, Pamela Capps, Mary Terry, Naomi Cabbage	0	0	0	0	0	0	5	81	$20.00	Second Saturday Night and Sunday Fourth Saturday Night and Sunday	Second Sunday in June
BRADEN'S CHAPEL	Elders: W. M. Sparks, Noble Clawson. Bros: Coy Edwards. Sisters: Leecy Sparks, Helen Clawson.	0	1	0	0	4	0	0	140	$20.00	First Saturday Night and Sunday of each month	Saturday and First Sunday in July
BRANTLEY'S CHAPEL	Elder Clifford Brantley. Bros. Brian Brantley, Daniel Brantley, Everett Brantley, Rina Johnson. Sisters: Angela Brantley, Barsha Brantley, Linda Brantley, Mildred Brantley	0	0	10	3	0	0	3	85	$25.00	Second Saturday Night. Every Sunday and Sunday Night	Saturday and Second Sunday in July
DAVIS CHAPEL	Bros. Orice McCarty, Bob Lynch, Clyde Lynch. Sisters: Mamie Parrot, Mollie McCarty, Ollie Welch, Pearl Lynch	0	0	0	1	0	5	0	110	$25.00	Third Saturday Night. Every Sunday and Sunday Night	Third Sunday in June
GETHSEMANE	Elders: Glenn Abbott, Jim Campbell. Sisters: Myrtle Cook, Carolyn Campbell, Flo Wilson	0	0	1	0	0	1	0	38	$25.00	Every Sunday except the First Sunday of each month	Saturday and Fourth Sunday in May and October
GIBSON STATION	Elders: William Rhymer, Joe Irving, Spurgeon Thompson. Bros. Curtis Ball, Franklin Jones. Sisters: Fannie Jones, Lucille Ball, Karen Rhymer, Evelyn Irving, Dorothy Johnson, Shirley Sandifur	0	0	0	0	0	0	1	75	$30.00	First Saturday and Saturday Night of each month. Every Sunday and Sunday Night	Saturday and First Sunday in June
HEADRICK CHAPEL	Sister: Grace Abbott, Geraldine Abbott	0	0	0	0	0	0	0	110	$20.00	First and Third Sunday	First Sunday in May and October

Church	Delegates / Officers							No.	Amount	Communion	Annual Meeting
KIRKWOOD	Elders: H. E. Brummitt, Walter Lyons. Bros: Palmer Bridges, Ambrose Shard, Elwood Evans. Sisters: Ruby Brummitt, Ora Bridges, Freida Sharp, Velma Evans, Dola Webb.	0	2	0	0	0	2	115	$30.00	Every Sunday Morning	
LENOIR CITY	Elder Howard Pippin. Bros: Henry Chamberlain, Raymond Wilkerson, Hubert Spoon. Sisters: Estie Chamberlain, Anna Spoon, Phylis Pippin	0	0	0	1	0	4	147	$35.00	Every Sunday and Sunday Night	Third Sunday in May
MONROE, MICHIGAN	Letter Received - No Delegate Present	0	0	0	0	0	0	15	$10.00	Third Sunday of each month	Third Sunday in July
MYERS GROVE	Bros: Isom Drummonds, Clifford Robinson. Sisters: Ida Robinson, Florence Drummonds, Velt Muncey	0	3	0	0	0	0	73	$20.00	Second Saturday Night and Sunday. Fourth Saturday Night and Sunday	Saturday and Fourth Sunday in May
NOETON	Elder: John Oliver, Bros: Carroll Oliver, Charlie Collins. Sisters: Dora Collins	0	2	0	0	0	0	40	$20.00	First Sunday of each month Third Saturday Night and Sunday of each month	Third Saturday and Sunday in May and September
OAK GROVE	Elders: Johnny Atkins. Bros: Malcolm Walker, Aaron Cole. Sisters: Veda Cole, Ruth Shoffner, Frances Eastridge	0	3	2	2	1	4	333	$25.00	First Saturday and Sunday Third Sunday	Saturday First Sunday in May
PLEASANT HILL	Elders: Albert Davis, Larry Anderson, James Branscomb. Sisters: Audra Davis, Myra Anderson, Helen Ruth Branscomb	0	0	0	1	0	1	105	$35.00	Fourth Saturday Night and Sunday	First Sunday in June
PLEASANT POINT	Elder: Claude Rosson. Sisters: Doris Rosson	0	0	0	0	0	0	113	$15.00	First Saturday Night and Sunday Third Sunday	First Sunday in July
ROCKY DALE	Elders: William Berry, Everett Berry, Joe Bush, Parnick Shelton. Bros: W. H. Taylor, Herbert Graves, Curtis Johnson, Sisters: Trula Berry, Norma Jean Bush, Lou Emma Taylor	0	1	0	0	0	0	130	$40.00	Every Sunday and Sunday Night	Saturday and Second Sunday in May

288

CHURCH	COUNTY	PASTOR	CLERK	ADDRESS
Black Fox	Grainger	Elder Parnick Shelton	Bennie Capps Flossie Capps	P.O. Box 91, Maynardville, Tn. 37807 Maynardville, Tn. 37807
Braden's Chapel	Union	Elder Noble Clawson Elder J. C. Monday, Asst.	Jimmie B. Edwards Phyllis Wilson, Asst.	Speedwell, Tn. 37870 Speedwell, Tn. 37870
Brantley's Chapel	Blount	Elder Clifford Brantley	Jennifer Johnson Rina F. Johnson	1217 Brown School Rd., Maryville, Tn. 37801 1217 Brown School Rd., Maryville, Tn. 37801
Davis Chapel	Campbell	Elder William Berry	Ruth Heatherly Lassie Ellison, Asst.	Rt. 1, Davis Chapel Rd. LaFollette, Tn. 37766 918 Carwynn Rd., LaFollette, Tn. 37766
Gethsemane	Knox	Elder Walter Lyons	Tom Carmichael	729 Frank St., Knoxville, Tn. 37919
Gibson Station	Lee Virginia	Elder William Rhymer, Asst. Elder Everette Berry	Dorothy Johnson	Rt. 2, Ewing, Va. 24248
Headrick Chapel	Knox	Elder Walter Lyons	Clyde Abbott, Sr.	Rt. 7, Sevierville, Tn. 37862
Kirkwood	Knox	Elder Everette Berry	Estelle Petree Sharp Alice Tinell Powers	Rt. 24, Emory Road, Knoxville, Tn. 37918 7525 Temple Acre Dr., Knoxville, Tn. 37918
Lenoir City	Loudon	Elder Howard M. Pippin	Scott Collins	705 W. 5th Ave., Lenoir City, Tn. 37771

Monroe, Michigan	Monroe		Gertrude Zwack Roxie Drummonds, Asst.	1825 Spaulding Rd., Monroe, Michigan 48161 2675 Blue Bush Rd., Monroe, Michigan
Myers Grove	Claiborne	Elder Noble Clawson	Bonnie Miracle Harold Cupp, Asst.	Rt. 2, Box 194, New Tazewell, Tn. 37825 Rt. 2, Box 166, New Tazewell, Tn. 37825
Noeton	Grainger	Elder John Oliver	Carroll Oliver Bessie Collins, Asst.	Rt. 2, Box 512, Bean Station, Tn. 37708 Rt. 5, Morristown, Tn.
Oak Grove	Union	Elder J. C. Monday Elder Noble Clawson, Asst.	Betty P. Sharp Betty Shoffner, Asst.	Sharp Chapel, Tn. 37866 Sharp Chapel, Tn. 37866
Pleasant Hill	Claiborne	Elder Larry Anderson Elder Albert Davis, Asst.	William Branscomb	Speedwell, Tn. 37870
Pleasant Point	Claiborne	Elder Claude Rosson Elder Larry Anderson, Asst.	Beatrice Williams	Rt. 2, Box 156, Rogersville, Tn. 37857
Rock Dale	Knox	Elder Hugh Brummitt	Edward Collett Dennis Branson	Rt. 1, Box 17, Luttrell, Tn. 37779 4633 Marshall Drive, Knoxville, Tn. 37918

1980 MINUTES

OF THE

ONE HUNDRED SIXTIETH SESSION

OF THE

POWELL VALLEY ASSOCIATION
OF PRIMITIVE BAPTIST

Held with the Sister Church at
BLACK FOX
in
GRAINGER COUNTY TENNESSEE
AUGUST 15, 16, 17, 1980

THE ONE HUNDRED SIXTIETH SESSION
OF THE POWELL VALLEY ASSOCIATION
OF
PRIMITIVE BAPTIST
HELD WITH THE SISTER CHURCH AT BLACK FOX
IN GRAINGER COUNTY, TENNESSEE
AUGUST 15, 16,17, 1980
NEXT SESSION WILL BE HELD WITH THE SISTER CHURCH
AT PLEASANT HILL
IN CLAIBORNE COUNTY TENNESSEE
TO BEGIN ON FRIDAY BEFORE THE THIRD SATURDAY
IN AUGUST 1981
AT 10:30 A.M.
ELDER WALTER LYONS WILL DELIVER THE INTRODUCTORY
SERMON, AND ELDER WILLIAM RHYMER WILL BE THE ALTERNATE.

OFFICERS

Elder Albert Davis   Moderator
Speedwell, Tenn. - Phone 869-3596

Elder Hugh Brummitt   Assistant Moderator
1329 Brown Ave., Knoxville, Tenn. - Phone 546-7700

W. H. Taylor   Clerk
Rt. 27, Knoxville, Tenn. 37918 - Phone 922-2143

Bennie Capps   Assistant Clerk
Maynardville, Tenn. - Phone 992-5571

FRIDAY, AUGUST 15, 1980

The one hundred and sixtieth session of the Powell Valley Association of Primitive Baptist met with the Sister Church at Black For in Grainger, Tennessee, on August 15, 16 and 17, 1980.

After singing the Moderator, Elder Albert Davis welcomed the congregation and pleading for peace and love to abide through the entire association, and called for prayer by Elder J.H. Branscomb of Pleasant Hill Church.

Following prayer, Elder John Oliver of the Noeton Church delivered the introductory sermon and gave a very good lesson from the 3rd Chapter of St. John beginning at the Fourth verse.

After the introductory sermon they sang a song and was dismissed in prayer by Elder Parnick Shelton, pastor of the host church. The Association was to reconvene after a 15 minute recess.

After recess the crowd reassembled in the church at the sound of singing. Following a song the moderator asked the association to be in silent prayer in honor and memory of a dear departed Elder Everett Berry, deceased since we last met.

The moderator then read a lesson from the 3rd Chapter of 2nd Timothy and called for prayer by Elder Clifford Brantley of brantley's Chapel Church.

The moderator then asked for the order of business, and called for the letters of the Sister Churches to be presented to the clerk for reading, 13 were received.

The letters presented were read and approved and the delegates were seated.

The moderator called for anyone present from any of the Sister Churches not named as a delegate and desired to be seated as such to come forward and give the clerk your name and the name of your church. None came.

Call for petitionary letter if there should be one. There was none.

Motion approved that the association re-elect Elder Albert Davis as Moderator, Elder Hugh Brummitt as Assistant Moderator, W.H. Taylor as Clerk, and Benny Capps as Assistant Clerk for the coming year.

Motion was approved that we elect Elder Davis to appoint all the committees to serve this session.

The moderator, having been appointed to do so, named the committees as follows:

COMMITTEE ON ARRANGEMENTS

Bro. Cecil Godfrey
Bro. Curtis Ball
Bro. Donald Sharp

COMMITTEE ON PREACHING
Bro. Elwade Evans
Bro. Arthur Terry
Bro. Coy Edwards

COMMITTEE ON REQUEST
Bro. Orice McCarty
Bro. Robert Bridges
Elder Parnick Shelton

COMMITTEE ON FINANCE
Elder Larry Anderson
Elder Spurgeon Thompson
Bro. Rina Johnson

The Committees all having been appointed and accepted, the association moved to adjourn until 10:30 Saturday morning. They sang a song and was dismissed in prayer by Elder Spurgeon Thompson of the Sister Church of Gibson Station, Virginia.

SUNDAY, AUGUST 17, 1980

Sunday morning at the appointed hour of 10:30, after singing, Elder Parnick Shelton, Pastor of the host church, opened the service and called for prayer by Elder Clifford Brantley.

After prayer Elder Albert Davis occupied the pulpit and read the 10th Chapter of Revelations, following the theme "The Little Book" which is the Gospel and preached a wonderful sermon.

Elder Davis was followed by Elder Hugh E. Brummitt, Pastor of Rocky Dale Church. Elder Brummitt read the second verse of the fourth Chapter of Second Timothy, "Preach the word, be instant in season, out of season, reprove, rebuke, exhort with all longsuffering and doctrine," preaching a wonderful spiritual sermon, thus closing out the service with singing and rejoicing in the altar. Service dismissed in prayer by Elder Parnick Shelton.

SATURDAY AUGUST 16, 1980

Saturday at the appointed hour of 10:30, at the sound of singing the association reasembled to a full house.

After singing, the Assistant Moderator Elder Hugh E. Brummitt, gave a very spiritual and uplifting talk and then read the one hundred and eleventh Psalm. Then called for prayer by Elder Claude Rosson of Pleasant Point Church.

After prayer the moderator called the association to order for the remainder of the business.

The moderator called for any letters from Sister Churches not received on Friday. Letters were received from the Sister Churches of Meyers Grove and Lenior City.

Motion was approved to accept the letters and seat the named delegates.

The moderator called for anyone from either of the churches who were present and desired to be seated as delegates to come forward. None came.

Moderator then called for the report of the Committee on Arrangements who submitted the following arrangement which was accepted and the committee was released.

REPORT ON ARRANGEMENTS

Call for roll call of delegates.
Call for report of Committee on Preaching.
Call for report of Committee on Request.
Call for report of Committee on Finance.
To suggest how many minutes to have printed and who shall supervise the printing and distribution of same; how much he shall receive for his service. Where shall the next session be held and who shall preach the introductory sermon and who shall be the alternate.

Respectfully submitted,
Bro. Cecil Godfrey
Bro. Curtis Bell
Bro. Donald Sharp

Call for the roll call of delegates of all the Sister Churches and check the absentees.

Call for the report of the Committee on Preaching, which was given as follows and was accepted and the committee released.

REPORT OF COMMITTEE ON PREACHING

Friday Night   Elder Clifford Brantley
                    Elder Bill Rhymer

Saturday   Elder Larry Anderson
              Elder Spurgeon Thompson

Saturday Night   Elder Bill Berry
              Elder J. H. Branscomb

Sunday   Elder Albert Davis
                    Elder Hugh Brummitt

Respectfully submitted,
Bro. Coy Edwards
Bro. Arthur Terry
Bro. Elwood Evans

Call for the report of the Committee on request, which was accepted and the committee released.

REPORT OF COMMITTEE ON REQUEST

We, the Committee on Request, request that we have 1150 minutes printed and that the clerk supervise the printing and distribution of same and that he receive $125.00 for his service.

We also request that Elder J. H. Branscomb write a circular letter to be printed in the minutes, also that the next session of the association be held with the Sister Church of Pleasant Hill in Claiborne County, Tennessee, to begin on Friday before the 3rd Saturday in August 1981, and may the love and peace that is here continue through the remainder of this association.

Respectfully submitted,
Bro. Orice McCarty
Bro. Robert Bridges
Elder Parnick Shelton

We the Committee on Finance submit the following which was accepted and the committee released.

REPORT OF FINANCE COMMITTEE

Black Fox	$25.00
Bradens Chapel	$20.00
Brantleys Chapel	$35.00
Davis Chapel	$35.00
Gethsemane	$25.00
Gibson Station	$30.00
Headricks Chapel	$20.00
Kirkwood	$30.00
Lenoir City	$35.00
Meyers Grove	$25.00
Noeton	$20.00
Oak Grove	$25.00
Pleasant Hill	$35.00
Pleasant Point	$15.00
Rocky Dale	$40.00
TOTAL	$415
BALANCE IN BANK	$411.00
GRAND TOTAL	$826.00

Respectfully submitted,
Bro. Rina Johnson
Elder Larry Anderson
Elder Spurgeon Thompson

Motion approved that we grant the request of the committee and have 1150 copies of the minutes printed and that the clerk supervise the printing and distribution of the same and that he receive $125.00 for his service.

Motion approved that the next association be held with the Sister Church of Pleasant Hill in Claiborne County, Tennessee, to begin on Friday before the Saturday in August at 10:30 A.M.

Motion approved that Elder Walter Lyons deliver the introductory sermon and Elder Bill Rhymer be the alternate.

Motion approved that Elder J.H. Branscomb of Pleasant Hill Church write a circular letter for the 1981 minutes.

Motion approved that we request each ordained minister in the Powell Valley Association to prepare a circular letter as early as possible and file it some place or with the family where it will be available at any time. Then when their time arrives to prepare the letter they can use it, or if they prefer they can prepare another one. Then if anything should happen to the minister his letter can still be used.

Motion that the churches of this Powell Valley Association extend to this church and the people of Black Fox our heart felt thanks and our prayers for the love, fellowship and kindness and good food while here with you. May the Good Lord Bless and Keep You is our prayer.

Motion to adjourn, trusting the Lord to permit us to meet again with the Sister Church at Pleasant Hill in Claiborne County, Tennessee, on Friday before the third Saturday in August 1981.

Dismissed in prayer by Elder Bill Berry.

Elder Albert Davis Moderator
Elder Hugh E. Brummitt, Asst. Moderator
W.H. Taylor, Clerk
Bennie Caps, Asst. Clerk

MINISTERS DIRECTORY

Elder Glenn Abbott, 1801 Cherrybrook Drive, Knoxville, TN., Ph. 947-6875.
Elder Larry Anderson, Speedwell, Tennessee, Ph. 869-4635.
Elder Johnny Atkins, Bean Station, Tennessee, PH. 767-2397.
Elder Johnny Ayres, Rt. 3 Box 159, Bean Station, TN., Ph. 586-5401.
Elder William Berry, Rt. #13, Knoxville, TN., Ph. 922-9189.
Elder J. H. Branscomb, Speedwell, TN., Ph. 562-6361.
Elder Clifford Brantley, Brown School Rd. Maryville, TN., Ph. 982-3875.
Elder Hugh E. Brummitt, 1329 Brown Ave., Knoxville, TN., Ph. 546-7700
Elder J.C. Monday, Speedwell, TN., Ph. 562-3068.
Elder Sheridan Moore, Route #1 Townsend, TN., Ph. 581-5039.
Elder Howard Pippin, 101 Rose Street, Lenior City, Tennessee 986-2791.
Elder Claude Rosson, Rt. #4, New Tazewell, TN., Ph. 626-3168.
Elder Joe Bush, Corryton, Tennessee, Ph. 687-2108.
Elder Noble Clawson, Rt. #4, Speedwell, TN., Ph. 562-2004.
Elder Albert Davis, Speedwell, TN., Ph. 869-3596.
Elder Clay Widner, Rt. #1, Tazewell, TN., Ph. 626-3893.
Elder Alvin Graves, 122 Oak Wood Dr., Lenior City, TN., Ph. 986-9725.
Elder Joe Irving, 111 Eighth St., Middlesboro KY.
Elder Walter Lyons, 1602 Garfield St., Alcoa TN., Ph. 984-3207.
Elder John Godfrey, 15443 Valleoga, Victoryvill, Calif., Ph. (714) 243-4661.
Elder Robert Walker, Sevierville, TN., PH. 453-2753.
Elder Parnick Shelton, Rt. 4 Corryton, TN.
Elder William Sparks, Speedwell, TN., Ph. 562-7997.
Elder William Rhymer, Rt. #3, Harrogate, TN., Ph. 861-3092.
Elder Spurgeon Thompson, Box #36, Shawanee, TN., Ph. 869-8175.
Elder John Oliver, Rt. 2 Box 513 Bean Station, TN., Ph. 581-5039.
Elder Jim Campbell, Louisville, TN., Ph. 983-1654.
Elder Clyde Abbott, Jr., Rt. 8, Holton Rd., Maryville, TN., 379801.

LICENTIATES

Brother Roscoe Branscomb, Speedwell, Tennessee
Brother Odell Carpenter, Maryville, Tennessee.
Brother Ray Walker, Route #1, Townsend, Tennessee
Bro. Clyde Abbott, Sr., Rt. 7, Sevierville, TN., Ph. 453-2329
Bro. Danny E. Turner, 101 Rose St. Lenior City, Tennessee, Ph. 986-2791.

CIRCULAR LETTER

Dear Brothers and Sisters in Christ:

I was appointed by the Association to write a circular letter to be placed in our Minutes. This is very hard to do because I don't feel worthy.

Let us use as our thought the statement that is found in Jude. Verse Three (3)--and exhort you that he should earnestly contend for the faith which was once delivered unto the Saints. This is very important to us today. For us to have the same faith as they had, we must contend for this same faith and our churches should demand this, for this is the only thing that will comfort in the time of trouble.

Our Association was founded upon this faith. Our churches also are set upon this faith. I have studied the Articles of our Faith and have found them to be true according to what I can understand. I said when I was ordained that I would uphold these Articles of Faith; and, churches it is your duty to demand that this Faith be preached in your church. I know that it is not popular but, as the poet once said "give me the old time religion, it will do when I am dying," it teaches a great God and very little man.

I love the Powell Valley Association and what it stands for. I want to live with you and I want to die with you, and most of all, I want to meet you all on the other side of life where God will be all and all and we will sing the song of Victory in Jesus. May God bless you all is my prayer   Please remember me in your prayers.

Your Unworthy Servant,
Elder Hugh E. Brummitt

We are blessed with a fine group of ministers as was illustrated by those who had the opportunity to preach. We regret that time will not permit more of them to preach.

On Friday Elder John Oliver delivered the introductory sermon reading from the 3rd Chapter of St. John and delivering a very interesting sermon "Verily I say unto you no man can come to me except he be born of Spirit and water."

Then on Friday night Elder Parnick Shelton opened the service and called for prayer by Elder William Berry then Elder Clifford Brantley of Brantleys Chapel Church preached a wonderful sermon from the 1st Chapter of Luke, "Things to fall in place." Elder Brantley was followed by Elder William Rhymer of Gibson Station who preached a good sermon on the power of God, the Garden of Eden and the forbidden fruit.

Then on Saturday Elder Larry Anderson of Pleasant Hill Church gave a wonderful lesson in Thessalonians which was well delivered.

Following this was Elder Spurgeon Thompson of Gibson Station Church who gave a wonderful sermon, speaking from the 25th Chapter of Acts and the 26th Verse, also using some passages from the 26th Chapter.

Then on Saturday night, after prayer by Elder Spurgeon Thompson of Gibson Station, Elder James Branscomb preached a good sermon on the 10th Chapter of Romans, using the passage "man's going is of the Lord."

Following this was Elder William Berry of Rocky Dale Church who preached a real good sermon using as his line of thought taken from the 9th Chapter of Second Samuel, "The Covenant between God and his Son."

RULES OF DECORUM

1. The churches composing the Powell's Valley Association shall not be confined to any set rules as to specific number of Messengers they shall have in the body, but shall have the right to name in their letters as many as they choose, and in addition all orderly members of any of the churches being present be entitled to seats in the body as Messengers of their respective churches, with all the rights and privileges of the same.

2. The Messengers thus assembled shall be denominated the Powell's Valley Primitive Baptist Association.

3. For the purpose of historical information and statistical edification, the Churches are required to state in letters, the number of members in fellowship, the number received by Baptism, by letter, by confession of Faith, the number dismissed, excluded and dead since last session; also the time of their meeting, their pastoral supply, and the amount of money contributed for ministers and other purposes together with any other information they deem appropriate for the edification of the saints and glory of God.

4. This Association shall have no power to answer queries, give advice, or dictate to the Churches in any case, or to lord it over God's heritage nor any power by which she can directly or indirectly fringe on the internal rights of the church or censure and try any church or member in reference to faith and practice and determine upon validity of gospel ordinances. These things shall rest entirely with the churches; but henceforward our annual meetings shall be only for the purpose of hearing from each other, and for the worship of God and mutual comfort and edification of the Saints. To this end we reserve the privilege annually for the Third Friday in August and the two following days or at such other times as may be agreed upon with any church that may invite us having to protect our own standard, while in session, from heresay and disorder to recognize and invite any primitive Baptist minister or any lay brother to worship with us that may deem proper; to request the brethren of our body to visit other churches or bodies in our belief with whom we may desire to culture Christian fellowship; to publish in a minute of our proceedings.

5. Each session of the body shall have a Moderator and Clerk who shall hold office until re-elected.

6. Any order member of any church belonging to this body, when convened, being present shall be eligible to elect on as Moderator and Clerk or to sit on any committee appointed by the same.

7. In all election or questions that may be necessary to determine by vote, the vote shall be taken by churches, each church being entitled to three votes for any number less than one hundred, and one additional vote for every fifty or fraction thereof above the first hundred, but the Messengers of each church may divide their vote as they see proper.

8. All elections or questions coming to vote shall be determined by a majority vote cast, and it shall be the only duty of the minority to acquiesce in the decision thus reached.

9. If new churches desire to be admitted to this union they shall petition by letter and messengers and if voted for and recommended by one or more sister churches for her Presbytery constitutioning them, as orthodox and orderly they shall be received by the vote of the body and manifested by the Moderator giving the Messengers the right hand of fellowship.

10. Any motion or resolution clearly inconsistent with the above rules shall be promptly ruled out of order unless withdrawn by the mover.

11. Any Messenger being ruled out of order by the Moderator shall have the right to appeal to the body on the question of order, and if sustained shall be allowed to proceed, but if not take his seat.

12. Our meeting being held in the name of Christ and the worship of God; each Messenger

is expected to observe due and proper therein.

13. It will not be considered good for any Messenger whose name has been enrolled as such to abruptly break off or absent himself from the Association without leave.

14. The Moderator shall be entitled to the same privilege of speech as other members provided the chair is filled.

15. The minutes of the Association shall be read and approved by the body and signed by the Moderator before adjourning.

16. The Association shall be opened and closed by prayer.

17. Amendments to these may be made at any time by a majority of the union voting by churches when they deem it necessary, provide such amendments do not compromise the sovereignty of the churches nor have tendency to give body undue power or jurisdiction over them.

Obituaries

Elder Everett M. Berry

Elder Everett M. Berry was born September 18, 1918 and departed this life on February 11, 1980 at age 61 years, 4 months and 24 days.

He professed faith in Christ and joined the church at Rocky Dale on February 20, 1932, where he remained a faithful member until God called him home.

He was ordained as a deacon of the church on December 18, 1955. He was licensed to preach the gospel on October 14, 1956 and was ordained to the full work of the ministry on November 24, 1957.

In January, 1958, he was elected assistant pastor of the church at Gibson Station and served until 1975, at which time he was elected pastor and moderator and served until his death.

He also was pastor and/or assistant pastor of Brantley's Chapel Church of Maryville from 1963 to 1970. He helped as supply pastor at Lenoir City and Pleasant Point churches in the absence of their pastors. In 1975, he was called to Kirkwood Church to complete the term of Elder Leonard White and remained as pastor until his death.

Everett was the son of Ida Bell Berry and the late Harley Berry. On April 22, 1939, he was united in marriage to Trula Wolfenbarger. To this union were born two children, Elder William Berry and Mrs. Dennis (Helen) Branson. He also had five grandchildren whom he loved dearly, Steve and John Berry, Robin, Scott and Todd Branson.

Survivors also include: mother, brothers, Clyde, Elmer, Ross, Charles, Harley Jr, Ronnie, Edward, Billy, all of Corryton, TN, Luther of Charlotte, N.C.; sisters, Ethel Robinson, Bertha and Jean Kear of Knoxville, and Margie Lively of Corryton, Tn.

Funeral services were conducted at Mynatt's Chapel on February 13, 1980, with Elders William Berry, H.E. Brummitt, Clifford Brantley and William Rhymer officiating. He was laid to rest in Clapp's Chapel Cemetery to await the resurrection morning.

Everett loved all the churches and ministers of the Powell's Valley Association. We would like to thank each one for the prayers, kind words, flowers and cards. Also, the ministers who acted as pallbearers. Everyone's kindness meant so much and was greatly appreciated. Words can never express our gratitude. May God bless you all.

The Berry Family

ON THE OTHER SIDE OF DEATH

Death is a gateway we all must pass through
To reach that fair land where the soul's born anew.
For man's born to die and his sojourn on earth,
Is a short span of years beginning with birth.
And like pilgrims we wander until death takes our hand,
And we start on our journey to God's promised land.
A place where we'll find no suffering nor tears,
Where time is not counted by days, months, or years.
And in this fair city that God has prepared,
Are unending joys to be happily shared.
With all of our loved ones who patiently wait,
On death's other side to open "The Gate."

Helen Steiner Rice

Ruth Berry

Ruth Berry ws born June 20, 1917. She was the daughter of the late Pryor Lee Berry and Nellie Berry. She departed this life August 24, 1979 being 62 years old at the time of death.

Sister Ruth professed a hope in Christ at an early age and joined Pleasant Hill Primitive Baptist Church in March of 1942 and lived a devoted member until God called her home to be with him.

303

She was a bright light in our church, in her home and neighborhood.

She leaves to mourn her loss her mother, Nellie Berry; brothers, Grover Lee Berry, Milton Berry; sisters, Mrs. Malinda Williamson, Mrs. Vina Eisenberg and Mrs. Ethel Dalton; several nieces and nephews and a host of relatives and friends.

Our church has lost a precious jewel. We feel our loss is her eternal gain.

Verlin Berry

Verlin Berry, born December 23, 1906, departed this life April 2, 1980 at the age of 73. He joined Pleasant Hill Primitive Baptist Church and was a faithful member until death. He was the son of the late Lafate and Tilda Berry. He was married to Lottie Lambert Berry December 25, 1925. He was a Mason for 49 years. He leaves to mourn his passing wife, 2 daughters, Imogene Owens and Azilee Davis, 2 sons Don and Marson Berry, 7 grandchildren and 3 great grandchildren, 5 sisters, 5 brothers and a host of relatives and friends.

It broke our hearts to lose you, but you did not go alone for part of us went with you the day God called you home.

Sadly missed by,
Wife and Family

William Frank (Buck) West

William Frank (Buck) West was born September 14, 1914 to Jack and Dora Agee West and passed away January 4, 1980 near Morristown, Tennessee where he lived with his wife Bessie Hoskins West.

He professed faith in Christ at an early age, and joined the Primitive Baptist Church near Arthur, Tenn. where he remained a member. But in later years he attended the Primitive Baptist Church at Gibson Station, Virginia with his wife and helped to support our church and was loved by our church.

He leaves to mourn his passing: one daughter, Audrey Elsner of Courtland, New York; two sons, J. C. West, Cleveland, Tenn. and Mike West, Monroe, Michigan; four grandsons and two grand-daughters; one sister, Juanita Welch, Speedwell, Tenn.; four brothers, Roy of Harrogate, Luther of Arthur, Edd and Leamon of Detroit, Michigan; and a host of other relatives and friends.

Services were held on January 7, 1980 at 10:30 a.m. at Coffey Funeral Home in Tazewell, Tennessee by Elder Everette Berry and Rev. Clarence Powell, and laid to rest in the Shoffner Cemetery.

Tip Carpenter

Tip Carpenter was born on March 30, 1891 in Claiborne

County, Tennessee, to the late Charlie and Tishie Carpenter. Departed this life suddenly on December 31, 1958. He was 67 years 9 months and 1 day old. He was united in marriage to Belle Thomas on February 4, 1925. To this union was born 10 children. 6 daughters: Mrs. Ethridge (Annis) Keys, Mrs. Carl (Pauline) Sands, Mrs. Earnest (Stella) Lowery, all of Corryton, Tennessee. Loula Belle, Virgie, and Ruth, remaining at home. 3 sons: J. C., Vaughn, Odell and Fred all of Corryton, Tennessee. Other survivors are: 1 step brother, George Barnard of Sharps Chapel; and 10 grandchildren. He professed faith in Christ, joined and was baptised into White Hollow, Primitive Baptist Church, by Elder Virlin Graves. He later moved his membership to Oak Grove, then to Rocky Dale Primitive Baptist Church. Later in life he joined; Bethel, Missionary Baptist Church, where he remained a member until death.

Funeral services were conducted by Rev. Earnest Rush, Rev. Fred Atkins and Rev. Jack Day at Bethel, Baptist Church on January 4, 1959 at 2 p.m. His body was laid to rest in Little Flat Creek Cemetery to await the coming of the Lord. Sadly missed by wife and children.

Wanda Godfrey Casker

Wanda Godfrey Casker died March 11, 1980. She was born September 12, 1932. She joined the Headricks Chapel Church in Sevier County, Tennessee at an early age and remained a member until her death. She is survived by her husband William Casker, daughters Sandra, Patricia and Tammy; mother Mary Godfrey, brothers Arthur, Cecil, John; sisters Mrs. June Carmichael and Mrs. Pauline Brown.

She was a dear little sister of whom we all miss her sweet smile and wonderful personality. When her eyes closed in this life we have the hope by her testimony here that we will see her over on the Golden Shores of Heaven where we all shall ever be with the Lord. She is sadly missed by her family.

Hala Dossett

Hala Dossett, 1636 W. 8th Street died early Saturday in Ball Hospital following a one month illness. She was born in Union County, Tennessee and moved to Muncie, Indiana twelve years ago from Galion, Ohio. She was a member of Oak Grove Baptist Church in Sharps Chapel, Tennessee. She is survived by her husband William Dossett, one son William C. Dossett of Banner Springs, Tenn. Five daughters, Mrs. Willie (Edna) Atkins, Mrs. Clayton (Pauline) Bicknell, Mrs. Delbert (Maxine) York, Mrs. Paul (Ruth) Burks and Mrs. Thomas (Ruby) Beaty all of Muncie. A brother, Roy Ellison of Sharps Chapel, Tenn. 17 grandchildren, 10 great-grandchildren and several nieces and nephews. Services were held at 10 a.m.

Monday at Parson Mortuary with Rev. Marshall L. Calloway officiating. Burial was in the Elm Ridge Cemetery.

John H. Dossett

John H. Dossett, age 101 of 4111 E. Boulevard, Kokomo, Ind. passed away at Howard Community Hospital at 6:35 p.m. Thursday, July 10, 1980 following an illness of three months. He was born in Union County, Tenn. July 28, 1878, the son of Matthew and Sarah (Berry) Dossett. He was married to Alice M. Graves who died in 1947. He was a retired farmer and a member of the Junior Odd Fellows and a former member of Caves Springs Primitive Baptist Church both of Union County. Survivors are three sons: Scott of Muncie, Ind., Cornelius and Vaughn both of Kokomo, Ind. Three daughters: Sarah Brantley of Union County, Goldie White and Eva Turner both of Kokomo, Ind. A sister, Minta Ellison of Union County, 23 grandchildren, several great grandchildren and several great, great grandchildren. A sister, a daughter and four sons preceded him in death. Services were held at 12:30 p.m. on Saturday at Ellers Mortuary with the Rev. Logan Sparling officiating. Burial was in the Allbright Cemetery. We Loved Him Very Much.

Written by Children

Tonie Ira Eastridge

Elder Tonie Ira Eastridge, born February 16, 1912, departed this life Jan. 26, 1979 at Blount Memorial Hospital after a short illness. Age 66 years, 11 months and 10 days. He was the son of Garett and Ella Cardwell Eastridge. He was married to Francie Shaffner Eastridge Dec. 25, 1932. To this union one daughter was born, Eula Gray Eastridge, who preceeded him in death. One son, Leonard Eastridge. One brother, Robert Eastridge; 5 sisters. One sister and 3 brothers preceeded him in death. His mother and father preceeded him in death. He joined the church when he was 12 years old and was ordained Oct. 7, 1950 at Oak Grove Primitive Baptist Church of which he was a member. He pastored churches until he was disabled. He loved all the churches and ministers and was strong in his belief. He loved to visit all the churches in their Communions and feet washing. He was a Free Mason for many years and a 32 Scottish Rite.

Our home is so lonesome. We loved his so much, but God had a place for him where there is no more pain.

306

The funeral was conducted at Oak Grove Church Jan. 29, 1979. Laid to rest in Rush Strong Cemetery to await the morning of the Resurrection. Funeral conducted by Elder W. M. Sparks, Elder J. C. MOnday, Elder Clifford Brantley Pallbearers: nephews, and honorary pailbearers were a host of dear Elders who were present. We are thankful for every one of them. Our home is so sad and will never be the same, but we hope to meet him again in the "Sweet By and By."

His Wife and Family

Ray E. Godfrey

Ray E. Godfrey died January 4, 1980. He was born January 14, 1928 living just 10 days short of 52 years.

He joined the Headricks Chapel Church in Sevier County at an early age and was a faithful member and later joined the Gethsemane Church in Knoxville, Tenn. where he remained a member until death.

He is survived by his wife, Geneva Godfrey; son, Timothy; daughters, Mrs. Mary Joyce Ledford, Mrs. Tina Ellison, Mrs. Teresa Helton; mother, Mary Godfrey; brothers, Arthur, Cecil, John; sisters, Mrs. June Carmichael, Mrs. Pauline Brown and Mrs. Wanda Casker (since deceased.)

He was a bright light in the little church and everytime he was able to come to church the Lord would bless him and he would rejoice in The Spirit and it would be an uplifting to all present.

He is sadly missed by all who knew him.

Herman Hayworth

Brother Herman Hayworth, age 66, died on Monday, November 26, 1979. Brother Herman united with the Lenoir City Primitive Baptist Church in May of 1948. He is survived by his wife, Sister Geneva Hayworth; Son, Glenn Hayworth of Tucson, As; daughter, Mrs. Helen Smallen of Lenoir City; grandchildren, Greg and Maxine Hayworth of Tucson, Az. and Robin Wade, DeAnn and Stacey Smallen, all of Lenoir City, and 5 Sisters. The funeral services were held on November 28, 1979 at the Hawkins Mortuary Chapel with Elder Howard Pippin and Rev. Joe Wampler officiating, burial was in the City Cemetery. May our heavenly Father ease the loss and loneliness with His blessed love and peace.

Alice L. Sharp Keck

Mrs. Alice L. Sharp Keck, of Goin Community, New Tazewell, died of cancer Tuesday morning, July 1, 1980, at her home.

Survivors: husband F. G. (Fay) Keck; daughter, Mrs. Evelyn Moyers; son-in-law, John C. Moyers, Oak Ridge, daughter, Mrs. Alice F. Dixon; son-in-law Leon Dixon. Columbia, Tn.; grandchildren Jan and Clif

Moyers, Oak Ridge, and Lenise and Gina Dixon of Columbia; sister, Mrs. Ida Sharp Lowe, Knoxville; brother, Ambrose (C.A.) Sharp, Knoxville.

She was the daugher of the late Isaac Calvin and Elvira P. Sharp, Sharps Chapel. She was a member of Oak Grove Primitive Baptist Church, Sharps Chapel.

Funeral services were conducted at 10:30 Thursday morning, July 3, 1980, at Coffey Funeral Home Chapel with the Rev. Hugh Brummitt and Rev. J. C. Monday officiating. The music was rendered by Mrs. Enna Faye and Mark Sexton. Burial was in Lynnhurst Cemetery, Knoxville.

Pallbearers: Joe Lewis, Herman Cupp, Harold Cupp, George Lynn (Glenn) Cupp, Brian Cole, Kennie Keck, Kenneth Bailey and Kenny Delynn Widner. Honorary pallbearers were nephews.

Coffey Funeral Home in charge.

Arlis Joshua Keck

Arlis Joshua Keck, age 84, of Route 3 New Tazewell, Tn., passed away May 15, 1980 at the Claiborne County Hospital.

He attended Pleasant Point Baptist Church.

Survivors: one son, Arnold J. Keck, Jefferson City, Tn,; two daughters, Mrs. John (Daisy) Lynch, New Tazewll; Mrs. Albert (Mattie) Simmons, Copper Cove, Texas; brother, Lee Keck, New Tazewell; 13 grandchildren and 11 great grandchildren.

He was preceded in death by his wife and two sons, James Ralph and Forster Keck.

Funeral services were held at 11 a.m. Saturday May 17 at Pleasant Point Baptist Church with Rev. Claude Rosson and Rev. Rupert Hopper officiating. Burial was in the Keck Cemetery.

Songs rendered by the Leather Wood Quartet.

Pallbearers were Clive Keck, Wade Keck, Marvin Rosson, Clebert Keck, Doug Keck, Von Widner, Dana Lee Rosson and Bobby Maddox.

Coffey Funeral Home in charge.

Scotty A. Keck

Scotty A. Keck, age 30, of Route 4, New Tazewell, passed away Sunday, May 11, 1980 at the Claiborne County Hospital.

He was a member of Pleasant Point Primitive Baptist Church.

Survivors include: his wife, Mrs. Charlene Love Keck of New Tazewell, one son, Jamie Keck, New Tazewell; parents, Mr. and Mrs. Robert Keck, New Tazewell; sister, Mrs. Connie Gent, New Tazewell; three nephews, one niece; several aunts and uncles and a host of friends.

Funeral services were held Wednesday, May 14 at 11 a.m. at the Coffey Funeral Home Chapel with Rev. Claude Rosson, Rev. George Walker officiating. Burial in Cole Cemetery.

Pallbearers: Beagle Hopper, Ronald Keck, Rex Keck, Don Johnson, Johnny Johnson, Tommy Johnson and Ronnie Tolliver.

Songs rendered by the Verlin Simmons Singers.

Coffey Funeral Home in charge.

VIRGIL MADDOX

Virgil Maddox, age 68 of New Tazewell passed away May 17, 1980 at the Baptist Hospital in Knoxville.

He was a member of Leatherwood Baptist Church.

Survivors: wife, Mrs. Ruby Maddox, New Tazewell; daughter, Mrs. Betty Lou Carrico, Blissfield, Michigan; sons: Wade Maddox, Monroe, Michigan, Swan Joe Maddox, New Tazewell 12 grandchildren. 7 great-grandchildren. A host of step grandchildren; stepson, Emory and Bruce Keck, Kokomo, Indiana, Swan Drummonds, Maynardville; step daughters, Mrs. Bessie Coker, Mrs. Arlee Maples, Monroe, Michigan, Mrs. Rosa Miracle, New tazewell; sisters, Mrs. Pearl Keck, La Salle, Michigan, Mrs. Sarah McDaniel, Monroe, Michigan, Mrs. Nancy Housley, Lenoir City, Tenn., Mrs. Mary Williams, New Market, Mrs. Mattie Simms, Knoxville, Mrs. Georgia Thomas, Knoxville; brothers, Clarence Maddox, New Tazewell, Tilmon Maddox, Lenoir City and John Maddox, Corryton.

Funeral services were held Monday, May 19 at 2 p.m. at Coffey Funeral Home Chapel with Rev. Lloyd England, Rev. Don Fannon and Rev. John Robinson officiating. Burial in Keck Cemetery.

Pallbearers: Anderson Cockrum, Kenny Coker, Glenn Miracle, David Drummonds, Doug Maples, Lonnie Maddox and Syllus Miracle.

Songs rendered by the Turner family singers. Coffey Funeral Home in charge.

Iva Jane Shelby McFarland

Iva Jane Shelby McFarland was born on July 25, 1910 and departed this life March 28, 1980.

She was the daughter of the late Milo and Katie Shelby. She was married to Emit McFarland on July 3, 1926. To this union were born two sons, Roy and Edgar McFarland.

She joined Rocky Dale Primitive Baptist Church at an early age, being one of the early members of the church. Although she did not get to attend the church, she remained a member until her death.

Survivors are: husband, Emit; sons, Roy and Edgar; two grandchildren; three sisters and one brother.

Funeral services were conductedd at Gentry's Chapel with interment in Greenwood Cemetery.

Calvin C. Meyers

Calvin C. Meyers born July 3, 1923 in Middlesboro, Ky. died March 30, 1980 at 6:30 in Veterans Hospital Ann Arbor, Mich. He was the son of Linvel I. and Ida M. (Lynch) Meyers and was married to Ruby Burchett of Jonesville, Va. on July 3, 1942. He married and went to Monroe, Mich. in 1936 and was employed at Consolidated Pakaging as a Machinist and Foreman and Time Container Corp. as Foreman.

He was a member of Monroe Primitive Baptist Church, Floral City Chapter of disabled veterans and Monroe Post 1138 Veterans of Foreign Wars. He is survived by wife Ruby, daughter Mrs. David (Linda) Diroff of Plymouth, Mick, sisters Ruby Simmons and Mrs. Wayne (Lorene) Pope of Monroe and Mrs. (Wanda) Victor Peles of Bernville, Pa. and one grandson Bryan Calvin Diroff. Brothers Leon of Tazewell, Tenn. and Linvel Jr. of Sarasota, Fla. Services were held Wednesday, 3 p.m. at the Earle Little Funeral Home with Rev. Timothy Mavery and Rev. James Krider officiating.

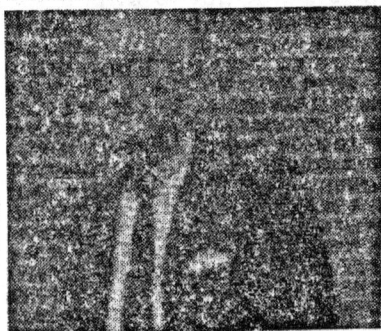

R. E. Sharp

R. E. (Edd) Sharp, 92, passed away July 5, 1980. He professed faith in Christ at an early age and joined the Primitive Baptist Church. In later years he moved to Knoxville and joined the Kirkwood Primitive Baptist Church as long as his health permitted. Survivors are one sister, Mrs. R.O. (Myrtle) Taylor. Granddaughter, Carol Lopez. Grandsons, Pat Norris, John and Hu-Ed Sharp. A host of friends and relatives.

He began his professional life as a school teacher in Union County. In later years he moved to Knoxville where he operated a successful grocery business until his retirement. Graveside services were conducted by Elder Hugh E. Brummit at Lynnhurst Cemetery with Rose Funeral Home in charge.

Mrs. Versey R. Powers

Mrs. Versey R. Powers, age 82, passed away at 4 a.m., May 9, 1980 at East Tennessee Baptist Hospital. She was a faithful member of Kirkwood Primitive Baptist Church. She is survived by two sons, Frank Carpenter and Marvin Powers, 6 grandchildren and three great-grandchildren Funeral conducted by Elder Bill Berry at Berry Funeral Home on Sunday, May 11, and burial was at Mt. Olive Cemetery. Grandsons served as pallbearers.

Estelle Petree Sharp

Estelle Petree Sharp, of Knoxville, was born November 12, 1907 in Union County, Tennessee and passed away April 28, 1980 approximately 1:30 p.m. at her home.

She was united in marriage to L. Oden Sharp September 7, 1928 who preceded her in death October 17, 1972. To this union no children were born.

She was a charter member and Church Clerk of Kirkwood

310

Primitive Baptist Church.

Funeral service was conducted at Gentry-Griffey Mortuary by Elder Billy Berry. The body was interred at Lynnhurst Cemetery.

She will be greatly missed by her church, family and many friends.

Roxie Ann Shoffner Cadle

Roxie Anna Shoffner Cadle born April 4, 1888 died October 8, 1979, at the age of 91 years, 6 months & 4 days.

She professed a hope at an early age and was a life long member of the Gibson Station Primitive Baptist Church.

She was the daughter of Elder Hiram A. Shoffner and Martha "Kink" Seals Shoffner.

She was married to Oscar Cadle until his death in 1948.

To this union were born seven children - five boys & two girls.

The five boys - Othnal, Thornton, Dee, Ancil and Raymond - preceeded her in death. The daughters are Treecy Cadle Cardwell of Middlesboro, KY, and Janet Cadle Cowgill of Fairbanks, Alaska.

Services were held at Binghamtown Baptist Church with Reverent W.B. Bingham and Elder Everette Berry officiating.

Charlie Smith

Charlie Smith, age 85, passed away July 12, 1980. He was a member and deacon of Davis Chapel Primitive Baptist Church. He was preceded in death by his wife, Nola White Smith, and son, Wayne Smith.

Survivors: three daughters; Dorothy Jones, Oak Ridge; Margie King, LaFollette; Myrtle Light, Arkansas. Two sons; Duffa Smith, Ohio; Vitchue Smith, LaFollette; thirteen grandchildren, seven great-grandchildren.

Funeral services were held at 2 p.m. Tuesday, July 15, 1980 at Davis Chapel Primitive Baptist Church with the Elders William Berry and Hugh Brummitt officiating. Interment in Sunrise Cemetery, LaFollette.

Mrs. Martha Thomas

Mrs. Martha Thomas, age 81 of Washburn, Tenn. passed away 10:30 a.m. Tuesday. She was a member of Black Fox Primitive Baptist Church for many years. She was preceded in death by a son, James Thomas. Survivors: Husband, Will Thomas, Washburn; daughter, Mrs. Neal Haynes, Maynardville; sons, Fred Thomas, California, Rev. Charles Thomas, Maynardville, Frank Thomas, Chattanooga, Junior Thomas, North Carolina, Mack and Robert Thomas, Knoxville, Rev. Ford Thomas, Corryton, and John Thomas, Washburn. 42 grandchildren; several great-grandchildren and great-great grandchildren. Funeral services were conducted at Ailor's Chapel with Elder Parnick Shelton officiating. Interment Thomas Cemetery. Grandsons were pallbearers.

Chester Dewey Welch

Chester Dewey Welch of Strawberry Plains, Tennessee, born September 25, 1905, passed away Saturday morning, December 1, 1979. Preceded in death by wife Virgie Ethel Weaver Welch. Survived by : Son, Robert Welch, Louisville, Tennessee; Daughters Wanda Pigusch, Arkansas, and Annale Welch, Strawberry Plains. Granddaughter Karen Bobo of Florida. Sisters: Mrs. Luster Singleton, Mrs. Bonnie Brantley, Mrs. Helen Berry, Mrs. Edythe Helton of Tennessee, Mrs. Ola Loop of Michigan, and Mrs. Gladys Baker of Arizona. Brothers: Alex, Amon and Silas Welch all of Monroe, Michigan. Several nieces and nephews. Preceded in death by 3 grandchildren and 1 brother. Funeral services were held Monday, December 3, 1979 at Brantley's Chapel Primitive Baptist Church of which he was a member. Rev. Clifford Brantley and Rev. J. C. Monday, officiating, interment at the church cemetery.

We still miss you too, Dad. The Family.

312

STATISTICAL TABLE

CHURCHES	DELEGATES	Restored	Received By Letter	Baptism	Relationship	Dismissed By Letter	Excluded	Deceased	Total Membership	Printing Minutes	REGULAR MEETING TIME	COMMUNION TIME
BLACK FOX	Bros. Bennie Capps, Dale Capps, Arthur Terry. Sisters: Mary Terry, Mary Ruth Capps, Namoi Cabbage, Sarah Hopson, Flossie Capps, Mossie Perry, Ethel Helton, Rachel Ingle, Sue Atkins, Pamela Capps.	0	0	0	0	0	0	1	80	$25.00	Second Saturday Night and Sunday Fourth Saturday Night and Sunday	Sunday following Second Saturday in June
BRADEN'S CHAPEL	Bros. Coy Edwards	0	0	0	7	5	0	1	142	$20.00	First Saturday Night and Sunday of each month	Sunday following first Saturday in July
BRANTLEY'S CHAPEL	Elder: Clifford Brantley, Bros. Everett Brantley, Daniel Brantley, Rina Johnson, Corum Berry. Sisters: Hazel Johnson, Mildred Brantley.	0	1	2	4	1	1	2	88	$35.00	Second Saturday Night Every Sunday and Sunday Night	Sunday following Second Saturday in July
DAVIS CHAPEL	Bros. Orice McCarty, Clyde Lynch. Sisters: Mollie McCarty, Ollie Welch.	1	0	0	0	0	1	0	108	$35.00	Third Saturday Night Every Sunday and Sunday Night	Third Sunday in June
GETHSEMANE	Bros. C. H. Godfrey Sister Myrtle Cook	0	0	1	0	2	0	1	36	$25.00	Every Sunday except the First Sunday of each month	Sunday following fourth Sunday in May and October
GIBSON STATION	Elders: William Rhymer, Spurgeon Thompson, Joe Irving. Bros. Franklin Jones, Curtis Ball, Claude Sandifer. Sisters: Fannie Jones, Lucille Ball, Karen Rhymer, Jean Thompson, Shirley Sandifer, Elvin Irving	0	0	1	0	0	0	1	75	$30.00	First Saturday and Saturday Night of each month Every Sunday and Sunday Night	Sunday following first Saturday in June
HEADRICK CHAPEL	Bros. Adam Abbott, Sisters: Geraldine Abbott, Grace Abbott, Angela Abbott, Margo Abbott	0	0	3	0	0	0	0	113	$20.00	First and Third Sunday	Sunday following first Saturday in May & Oct.
KIRKWOOD	Elders: H. E. Brummitt, Bros. C.A. Sharp, R. P. Bridges, M. E. Evans, E. P. Cook, Sisters: Ruby Brummitt, Frieda Sharp, Ora Bridges, Velma Evans, Dola Webb.	0	0	1	3	1	2	2	112	$30.00	Every Sunday Morning	Last Sunday in April
LENOIR CITY	Bros. Henry Chamberlain, Hubert Spoon Sisters: Anna Spoon, Estie Chamberlain, Cora Hill.	0	1	5	0	2	1	1	142	$35.00	Every Sunday and Sunday Night Every Wednesday Night	Wednesday night before Easter Sunday
MONROE, MICHIGAN	No Letter Received - No Delegates	0	2	0	0	0	0	1	15	$10.00	Third Sunday of each month	Third Sunday in July
MYERS GROVE	Bros. Isom Drummonds.	0	0	0	1	0	0	1	78	$25.00	Second Saturday Night and Sunday Fourth Saturday Night and Sunday	Sunday following fourth Saturday in May
NOETON	Elder: John Oliver; Bros. Charlie Collins, Carroll Oliver, Sister: Dora Collins.	0	0	2	0	0	0	0	42	$20.00	Third Saturday and Sunday First Sunday of each month	Sunday following third Saturday in May & Sept.
OAK GROVE	Sister: Frances Eastridge	0	0	1	0	0	0	3	331	$25.00	First Saturday Night and Sunday Third Sunday	Sunday following first Saturday in May
PLEASANT HILL	Elders: Albert Davis, Larry Anderson, James Branscomb. Sisters: Audra Davis, Myra Anderson	0	0	0	0	0	0	2	103	$35.00	Fourth Saturday Night and Sunday	Sunday following fourth Sat. in June
PLEASANT POINT	Elder: Claude Rosson Sister: Doris Rosson	0	0	0	0	0	0	2	110	$15.00	First Saturday Night Third Sunday	Sunday following first Sat. in July
ROCKY DALE	Elders: William Berry, Parnick Shelton, Bros. W. H. Taylor, Herbert Graves, Curtis Johnson, Harry Graves, Donald Sharp, Sisters: Lola Berry, Trula Berry, Evelyn Graves, Fay Anderson, Dorothy Sharp.	0	0	0	1	1	0	2	130	$40.00	Every Sunday and Sunday Night	Sunday following second Saturday in May

CHURCH	COUNTY	PASTOR	CLERK	ADDRESS
Black Fox	Grainger	Elder Parnick Shelton	Bennie Cappa Flossie Cappe	P. O. Box 91, Maynardville, Tn. 37807 Maynardville, Tn. 37807
Braden's Chapel	Union	Elder Noble Clawson Elder J. C. Monday, Asst.	Jimmie B. Edwards Phyllis Wilson, Asst.	Speedwell, Tn. 37870 Speedwell, Tn. 37870
Brantley's Chapel	Blount	Elder Clifford Brantley	Jennifer Johnson Rina F. Johnson	1217 Brown School Rd., Maryville, Tn. 37801 1217 Brown School Rd., Maryville, Tn. 37801
Davis Chapel	Campbell	Elder William Berry	Ruth Heatherly	Rt. 1, Davis Chapel Rd. LaFollette, Tn. 37766
Gethsemane	Knox	Elder Walter Lyons	Tom Carmichael	729 Frank St., Knoxville, Tn. 37919
Gibson Station	Lee Virginia	Elder William Rhymer Elder Spurgeon Thompson, Asst.	Dorothy Johnson	Rt. 2, Ewing, Va. 24248
Headrick Chapel Kirkwood	Knox	Elder Walter Lyons	Clyde Abbott, Sr.	Rt. 7, Sevierville, Tn. 37862
Kirkwood	Knox	Elder William Berry Elder Parnick Shelton, Asst.	Alice Tinell Powers	7525 Temple Acre Dr., Knoxville, Tn. 37918
Lenoir City	Loudon	Elder Howard M. Pippin	Scott Collins	705 W. 5th Ave., Lenoir City, Tn. 37771
Monroe, Michigan	Monroe		Gertrude Zwack Roxie Drummonds, Asst.	1825 Spaulding Rd., Monroe, Michigan 48161 2675 Blue Bush Rd., Monroe, Michigan
Myers Grove	Claiborne	Elder Noble Clawson	Bonnie Miracle Harold Cupp, Asst.	Rt. 2, Box 194, New Tazewell, Tn. 37825 Rt. 2, Box 166, New Tazewell, Tn. 37825
Noeton	Grainger	Elder John Oliver	Carroll Oliver Bessie Collins, Asst.	Rt. 2, Box 512, Bean Station, Tn. 37708 Rt. 5, Morristown, Tn.
Oak Grove	Union	Elder J. C. Monday Elder Noble Clawson, Asst.	Betty P. Sharp Betty Shoffner, Asst.	Sharp Chapel, Tn. 37866 Sharp Chapel, Tn. 37866
Pleasant Hill	Claiborne	Elder William Rhymer	William Branscomb	Speedwell, Tn. 37870
Pleasant Point	Claiborne	Elder Albert Davis, Asst. Elder James Branscomb, Asst.	Claude Rosson	Rt. 4, New Tazewell, Tn. 37825
Rock Dale	Knox	Elder Larry Anderson Elder Hugh Brummitt	Edward Collett Dennis Branson	Rt. 1, Box 17, Luttrell, Tn. 37779 4633 Marshall Drive, Knoxville, Tn. 37918

ARTICLES OF FAITH

Article 1. We believe in only one true living God, as He is revealed to us in the Holy Scriptures - Father, Son, and Holy Ghost.

Article 2. We believe that the Scriptures of the old and new Testaments are the words of God and the only rule of all-saving knowledge and obedience.

Article 3. We believe in the doctrine of election according to the foreknowledge of God.

Article 4. We believe in the doctrine of original sin.

Article 5. We believe in man's impotency to rescue himself from the fallen state he is in, by his own will or ability.

Article 6. We believe that sinners are justified in the sight of God only by the imputed righteousness of Jesus Christ.

Article 7. We believe the elect, according to the foreknowledge of God will be called, converted, regenerated, and sanctified by the Holy Spirit.

Article 8. We believe the saints will persevere and never fall finally away.

Article 9. We believe that baptism and the Lord's Supper are ordinances of Jesus Christ, and that true believers are the only subject of these ordinances, and that the true mode of baptism is by immersion. We believe also that feet washing is an example of Jesus Christ and should be kept by his disciples until his second coming.

Article 10. We believe in the Resurrection of the dead and the General Judgement.

Article 11. We believe that the punishment of the wicked will be everlasting and that the joys of the righteous will be eternal.

Article 12. We believe that no minister has the right to administer the ordinances, except those who have been regularly baptized and called of God, and come under the imposition of hands of the presbytery.

1981 MINUTES

OF THE

ONE HUNDRED SIXTY—FIRST SESSION

OF THE

POWELL VALLEY ASSOCIATION
OF PRIMITIVE BAPTIST

**HELD WITH THE SISTER CHURCH AT
PLEASANT HILL
CLAIBORNE COUNTY TENNESSEE
AUGUST 14, 15, 16, 1981**

THE ONE HUNDRED SIXTY-FIRST SESSION
OF THE POWELL VALLEY ASSOCIATION
OF
PRIMITIVE BAPTIST
HELD WITH THE SISTER CHURCH AT PLEASANT HILL
IN CLAIBORNE COUNTY, TENNESSEE
AUGUST 14,15,16,1981

NEXT SESSION WILL BE HELD WITH THE SISTER CHURCH
AT
LENOIR CITY
IN LOUDON COUNTY TENNESSEE
TO BEGIN ON FRIDAY BEFORE THE THIRD SATURDAY
IN AUGUST 1982
AT 10:30 A.M.

ELDER WALTER LYONS WILL DELIVER THE INTRODUCTORY
SERMON, AND ELDER JERRY MCBEE
WILL BE THE ALTERNATE

OFFICERS

ELDER HUGH BRUMMITT   MODERATOR
1329 BROWN AVENUE, KNOXVILLE, TENN., PHONE 546-7700
ELDER CLIFFORD BRANTLEY   ASSISTANT MODERATOR
809 BROWN SCHOOL RD. MARYVILLE, TENN., PHONE 982-3875
BENNIE CAPPS   CLERK
P.O. BOX 91, MAYNARDVILLE, TENN., PHONE 992-5571
RINA JOHNSON   ASSISTANT CLERK
1217 BROWN SCHOOL ROAD, MARYVILLE, TENN., PHONE 983-2774

FRIDAY, AUGUST 14, 1981

The one hundred and sixty-first session of the Powell Valley Association of Primitive Baptist met with the Sister Church at Pleasant Hill in Claiborne County, Tennessee, on August 14, 15, and 16, 1981.

After singing the Moderator, Elder Albert Davis, welcomed the congregation and pleaded for peace and love to abide through the entire Association and called for prayer by Elder Nelson Jones of Gibson Station.

Following prayer, Elder William Rhymer of the Gibson Station church delivered the introductory sermon and gave a very good sermon using as his text "BEING IN THE KINGDOM" in the absence of Elder Walter Lyons.

After the introductory sermon, they sang a song and was dismissed in prayer by Elder Noble Clawson of Braden's Chapel. The Association was to reconvene after a 15 minute recess.

After recess, the crowd reassembled in the church. After singing, the Moderator Elder Albert Davis quoted the first chapter of Psalms and called for prayer by Elder Howard Pippin of Lenoir City Church.

The Moderator then asked for the order of business for the following transactions:

1st. Motion approved that we release the church at Monroe, Michigan as a member of the Powell Valley Association to take up membership in the Sanlick Association of Michigan.

2nd.: Called for the letters of the sister churches to be presented to the clerk for reading, 13 were received.

3rd.: The letters presented were read and motion approved that the delegates be seated.

4th The moderator called for anyone present from any of the sister Churches not named as a delegate and desire to be seated as such to come forward and give the clerk their name and the name of their church. None came.

5th.: Called for petitionary letter if there should be one. There was none.

6th.:　　Move and second, that Elder Albert Davis be re-elected as Moderator and Elder Hugh Brummitt be re-elected as Assistant Moderator. The move and second was withdrawn.

7th.:　　Motion approved that the Association elect Elder Hugh Brummitt as Moderator and Elder Clifford Brantley as Assistant Moderator for the ensuing year.

The Association then gave Elder Albert Davis a standing ovation in appreciation of all the years of loyal and devoted services to the Association.

8th.:　　Move and second, Brother W. H. Taylor be re-elected Clerk and Brother Bennie Capps be re-elected Assistant Clerk for the ensuing year. This motion and second was withdrawn.

9th.:　　Motion approved athat Brother Bennie Capps be elected Clerk and Brother Rina Johnson be elected Assistant Clerk for the ensuing year.

10th.:　　Motion was approved that we elect Elder Brummitt to appoint all the committees to serve this session.

11th.:　　The Moderator, having been appointed to do so, named the committees as follows:

COMMITTEE ON ARRANGEMENTS
Brother Orice McCarty
Brother Raymond Wilkerson
Brother Arthur Terry

COMMITTEE ON PREACHING
Brother Hubert Spoon
Brother Elwood Evans
Brother Coy Edwards

COMMITTEE ON REQUEST
Brother Robert Bridges
Elder :arry Anderson
Brother W. H. Taylor

COMMITTEE OF FINANCE
Brother Everett Brantley
Elder Spurgeon Thompson
Elder Noble Clawson

12th.:　　Called for the finances to be turned in to the Finance committee.

13th.:　　The committees all having been appointed and accepted, the

Association moved to adjourn until 10:30 Saturday morning. They sang a song and was dismissed in prayer by Elder Claude Rosson of the Sister Church at Pleasant Point.

SATURDAY, AUGUST 15, 1981

Saturday at the appointed hour of 10:30, at the sound of singing, the Association reassembled to a full house.

After singing, the Assistant Moderator, Elder Clifford Brantley, gave a very spiritual and uplifting talk and then read part of the 8th. Chapter of Romans. Then called for prayer by Elder Johnnie Atkins of Oak Grove Church.

After prayer, the Moderator called the Association to order for the remainder of the business.

1st.:   The Moderator called for any letters from Sister Churches not received on Friday. Letters were redeived from the Sister Churches of Meyer's Grove and Headrick Chapel.

2nd.:   Motion was approved to accept the letters and seat the named delegates.

3rd.:   The Moderator called for anyone from either of the churches who were present and desired to be seated as delegates to come forward. Sister Ida Robertson from Meyer's Grove came forward.

4th.:   The Moderator then called for the report of the Committee on on Arrangements who submitted the following arrangements which was accepted and the committee was released:

REPORT ON ARRANGEMENTS:
Call for roll call of delegates.
Call for report of Committee on Preaching.
Call for report of Committee on Request
Call for Report of Committee on Finance.
Decide how many minutes to have printed, who shall supervise the printing and distribution of same, and how much he shall receive for his services. Who shall preach the introductory sermon and who will be the alternate.

Respectfully submitted,
Brother Arthur Terry
Brother Orice McCarty

5th.:   Call the roll call of delegates of all the Sister Churches and check the absentees.

6th.:   Called for the report of the committee on Preaching, which was given as follows and was accepted and the committee was released;

REPORT OF COMMITTEE ON PREACHING

Friday Night:	Elder Bill Berry
	Elder Larry Anderson
Saturday:	Elder Johnnie Atkins
	Elder Spirgeon Thompson
Saturday Night:	Elder John Oliver
	Elder Claude Rosson
Sunday:	Elder Clifford Brantley
	Elder James Branscomb

Respectfully submitted,
Brother Elwood Evans
Brother Hubert Spoon
Brother Coy Edwards

7th.:   Call for the report of the Committee on Request which was accepted and the committee was released.

REPORT OF COMMITTEE ON REQUEST:

We, the Committee on Request, request that we have 1,150 minutes printed and that the clerk supervise the printing and distribution of the same and that he receive $125.00 for his services. We also request that Elder Noble L.Clawson write a circular letter to be printed in the minutes, also that the next session of the Association be held with the Sister Church of Lenoir City in :Loudon County, Tennessee, to begin on Friday before the 3rd. Saturday in August, 1982, and may the love and peace that is here continue through the remainder of this Association.

Respectfully submitted,
Brother Robert Bridges
Brother W.H. Taylor
Elder Larry Anderson

8th.;   Call for the Committee on Finance which was accepted and the committee was released.

REPORT OF FINANCE COMMITTEE:

Black Fox	$25.00
Braden's Chapel	20.00

Brantley's Chapel	35.00
Davis Chapel	35.00
Gethsemane	30.00
Gibson Station	40.00
Headricks Chapel	20.00
Kirkwood	30.00
Lenoir City	35.00
Meyers Grove	25.00
Noeton	20.00
Oak Grove	25.00
Pleasant Hill	35.00
Pleasant Point	20.00
Rocky Dale	40.00
	$435.00
Contribution (Monroe Michigan)	10.00
Donation	20.00
	$465.00
Balance in Bank	376.00
	$841.00
Expenses for 1981	564.00
Balance in Bank	$277.00

Respectfully submitted,
Elder Spurgeon Thompson
Brother Everett Brantley
Elder Noble Clawson

9th.: Motion approved that we grant the request of the committee and have 1,150 copies of the minutes printed and that the clerk supervise the printing and distribution olf the same and that he receive $125.00 for his services.

10th.: Motion approved that the next session of the Association be held with the Sister Church of Lenoir City in Loudon County, Tennessee, to begin on Friday before the thirdSaturday in August, 1982, at 10:30 A.M.

11th.: Motion approved that Elder Walter Lyons deliver the introductory sermon and Elder Jerry McBee be the alternate.

12th.: Motion approved that Elder Nobel L. Clawson of Braden's Chapel write a circular letter for the 1982 minutes.

13th.: Motion approved that the churches of the Powell Valley Association extend to the church and the people of Pleasant Hill our heart felt thanks and our prayers for the love, fellowship and kindness and good food, while we were here with you. May the Good Lord Bless and keep you is our prayers.

14th.:   Motion to adjourn, trusting the Lord to permit us to meet again with the Sister Church at Lenoir City in Loudon County, Tennessee, on Friday before the third Saturday in August, 1982, at 10:30 A.M.

Dismissed in Prayer by Elder Albert Davis.

Elder Hugh Brummitt, Moderator
Elder Clifford Brantley, Assistant Moderator
Brother Bennie Capps, Clerk
Brother Rina Johnson, Assistant Clerk

SUNDAY, AUGUST 16, 1981

Sunday services were conducted by Elder Clifford Brantley who preached from the 42nd Chapter of Isaiah. He was then followed by Elder James Branscomb who preached from the 28th. Chapter of Isaiah.

SUMMARY

We are blessed with a fine group of minister as was illustrated by those who had the opportunity to preach. We regret that time will not permit more of them to preach.

On Friday, Elder William Rhymer delivered the introductory sermon.

Then on Friday night, after singing, prayer was by Brother Orice McCarty. Elder Larry Anderson preached from the 1st. Chapter of Hebrews. IT was a wonderful spiritual meeting with God richly blessing his children.

Then on Saturday morning, after prayer by Elder Joe Irving, Elder Spurgeon Thompson read part of the 4th. Chapter of Second Timothy, using as his text "I instruct you therefore to preach the Word". He was then followed by Elder Johnnie Atkins who preached a wonderful sermon on "As the Eagle spread the feather then gather them up, as Christ gathers up His children.

Saturday night services were opened in prayer by Brother Brice Braden; then Elder Claude Rosson read the 17th. Chapter of Second Samuel using as his text "Is there not a cause." Then Elder William Rhymer read 1st. Chapter of Acts with his text "Promise of the Holy Ghost", he was then followed by Elder William Berry. The meeting was very spiritual and God's children rejoiced greatly in the love of Jesus Christ. Dismissed by Elder Larry Anderson.

Sunday services was conducted by Elder Clifford Brantley who preached from the 42nd. Chapter of Isaiah. He was then followed by Elder James Branscomb who preached from the 28th. Chapter of Isaiah.

RULES OF DECORUM

1. The churches composing the Powell's Valley Association shall not be confined to any set rules as to specific number of Messengers they shall have in the body, but shall have the right to name in their letters as many as they choose, and in addition all orderly members of any of the churches being present be entitled to seats in the body as Messengers of their respective churches, with all the rights and privileges of the same.

2. The Messengers thus assembled shall be denominated the Powell's Valley Primitive Baptist Association.

3. For the purpose of historical information and statistical edification, the Churches are required to state in letters, the number of members in fellowship, the number received by Baptism, by letter, by confession of Faith, the number dismissed, excluded and dead since last session; also the time of their meeting, their pastoral supply, and the amount of money contributed for ministers and other purposes together with any other information they deem appropriate for the edification of the saints and glory of God.

4. This Association shall have no power to answer queries, give advice, or dictate to the Churches in any case, or to lord it over God's heritage nor any power by which she can directly or indirectly fringe on the internal rights of the church or censure and try any church or member in reference to faith and practice and determine upon validity of gospel ordinances. These things shall rest entirely with the churches; but henceforward our annual meetings shall be only for the purpose of hearing from each other, and for the worship of God and mutual comfort and edification of the Saints. To this end we reserve the privilege annually for the Third Friday in August and the two following days or at such other times as may be agreed upon with any church that may invite us having to protect our own standard, while in session, from heresay and disorder to recognize and invite any primitive Baptist minister or any lay brother to worship with us that may deem proper; to request the brethren of our body to visit other churches or bodies in our belief with whom we may desire to culture Christian fellowship; to publish in a minute of our proceedings.

5. Each session of the body shall have a Moderator and Clerk who shall hold office until re-elected.

6. Any order member of any church belonging to this body, when convened, being present shall be eligible to elect on as Moderator and Clerk or to sit on any committee appointed by the same.

7. In all election or questions that may be necessary to determine by vote, the vote shall be taken by churches, each church being entitled to three votes for any number less than one hundred, and one additional vote for every fifty or fraction thereof above the first hundred, but the Messengers of each church may divide their vote as they see proper.

8. All elections or questions coming to vote shall be determined by a majority vote cast,

and it shall be the only duty of the minority to acquiesce in the decision thus reached.

9. If new churches desire to be admitted to this union they shall petition by letter and messengers and if voted for and recommended by one or more sister churches for her Presbytery constitutioning them, as orthodox and orderly they shall be received by the vote of the body and manifested by the Moderator giving the Messengers the right hand of fellowship.

10. Any motion or resolution clearly inconsistent with the above rules shall be promptly ruled out of order unless withdrawn by the mover.

11. Any Messenger being ruled out of order by the Moderator shall have the right to appeal to the body on the question of order, and if sustained shall be allowed to proceed, but if not take his seat.

12. Our meeting being held in the name of Christ and the worship of God; each Messenger is expected to observe due and proper therein.

13. It will not be considered good for any Messenger whose name has been enrolled as such to abruptly break off or absent himself from the Association without leave.

14. The Moderator shall be entitled to the same privilege of speech as other members provided the chair is filled.

15. The minutes of the Association shall be read and approved by the body and signed by the Moderator before adjourning.

16. The Association shall be opened and closed by prayer.

17. Amendments to these may be made at any time by a majority of the union voting by churches when they deem it necessary, provide such amendments do not compromise the sovereignty of the churches nor have tendency to give body undue power or jurisdiction over them.

CIRCULAR LETTER

Dear Brothers and Sisters in Christ who compose the Powell Valley Association of the Primitive Baptist. I was appointed by the Association to write this letter to be printed in the minutes of the 1981 session. Greetings with love to everyone.

I count it a great joy to speak of the Association and the love and fellowship we have together. As time goes by I can see a greater need of attending the Association and to help in any way that I can. I hope others can see that too. Hebrews 12:1, "Let us lay aside every weight, and the sin which doth so easily beset us, and let us run with patience the race that is set before us. May God Bless every one is my prayers. Remember me when you pray.

Elder James H. Branscomb

Elder Jerry McBee, 2433 Pennsylvania Ave., Maryville, TN., 37801
Elder Glenn Abbott, 1801 Cherrybrook Drive, Knoxville, TN., Ph. 947-6875.
Elder Larry Anderson, Speedwell, Tennessee, Ph. 869-4635.
Elder Johnny Atkins, Bean Station, Tennessee, PH. 767-2397.
Elder Johnny Ayres, Rt. 3 Box 159, Bean Station, TN., Ph. 586-5401.
Elder William Berry, Rt. #13, Knoxville, TN., Ph. 922-9189.
Elder J. H. Branscomb, Speedwell, TN., Ph. 562-6361.
Elder Clifford Brantley, Brown School Rd. Maryville, TN., Ph. 982-3875.
Elder Hugh E. Brummitt, 1329 Brown Ave., Knoxville, TN., Ph. 546-7700
Elder J.C. Monday, Speedwell, TN., Ph. 562-3068.
Elder Sheridan Moore, Route #1 Townsend, TN., Ph. 581-5039.
Elder Howard Pippin, 101 Rose Street, Lenior City, Tennessee 986-2791.
Elder Claude Rosson, Rt. #4, New Tazewell, TN., Ph. 626-3168.
Elder Joe Bush, Corryton, Tennessee, Ph. 687-7018
Elder Noble Clawson, Rt. #4, Speedwell, TN., Ph. 562-2004.
Elder Albert Davis, Speedwell, TN., Ph. 869-3596.
Elder Clay Widner, Rt. #1, Tazewell, TN., Ph. 626-3893.
Elder Alvin Graves, 122 Oak Wood Dr., Lenior City, TN., Ph. 986-9725.
Elder Joe Irving, 111 Eighth St., Middlesboro KY. Ph. 248-8349
Elder Walter Lyons, 1602 Garfield St., Alcoa TN., Ph. 984-3207.
Elder John Godfrey, 15443 Valleoga, Victoryvill, Calif., Ph. (714) 243-4661.
Elder Robert Walker, Sevierville, TN., PH. 453-2753.
Elder Parnick Shelton, Rt. 4 Corryton, TN. Ph. 687-6142
Elder William Sparks, Speedwell, TN., Ph. 562-7997.
Elder William Rhymer, Rt. #3, Harrogate, TN., Ph. 861-3092.
Elder Spurgeon Thompson, Box #36, Shawanee, TN., Ph. 869-8175.
Elder John Oliver, Rt. 2 Box 513 Bean Station, TN., Ph. 581-5039.
Elder Jim Campbell, Louisville, TN., Ph. 983-1654.
Elder Nelson Jones, Rt. 1, Harrogate, TN., Ph. 869-3703

LICENTIATES

Brother Roscoe Branscomb, Speedwell, Tennessee
Brother Odell Carpenter, Maryville, Tennessee.

Bro. Clyde Abbott, Sr., Rt. 7, Sevierville, TN., Ph. 453-2329
Bro. Danny E. Turner, 101 Rose St. Lenior City, Tennessee, Ph. 986-2791.

Obituaries

JAMES T. ATKINS

James t. Atkins, departed this life October 4, 1980, at the age of 53 years. He joined Noeton Primitive Baptist Church and was a faithful member until death. He made his home with his cousins, Mr. & Mrs. Nelson ATkins of Bean Station, Tennessee. Other survivors, 3 half-brothers and 4 half-sisters. Several neices and nephews. Funeral was held at 1:00P.M. on Monday, October 6, with Elder John Oliver and Elder Johnny Atkins officiating. Burial in Noeton Church Cemetery. Smith Funeral Home of Rutledge in charge.

LORA BUSSELL BRADEN

Braden, Mrs. H. F. (Lora Bussell)- age 87, of Corryton, Route 2, Idumea Road died 3 P.,M. Wednesday October 1, 1980 at Knoxville Health Care Center. She was a member of Rocky Dale Primitive Baptist Church since November 1940.Survivors: daughters, Mrs Henry (Mildred) Sing of Knoxville, tennessee, Mrs. James (Wilma) Phillips, Dalton, Ga., Mrs. Robert (Minnie) Faulkner of Corryton, Tennessee and Mrs.Keith (Florence) Baker, Hazel Park, Mich.; Sons, Johnny Braden of Mascot, Tennessee, Amos Fred Braden of Corryton, Tennessee and Troy Braden of Warsaw, Ind.; Sisters, Mrs Mae Braden, Middlesboro, Ky., Miss Minnie Bussell, Knoxville, Tennessee; Brother, Everett Bussell of Middleboro, Ky.; 24 grandchildren, 39 great-grandchildren; 2 great-great-grandchildren; several nieces and nephews. Funeral services 10 A.M. Saturday at McCarty Chapel, Elder H.E. Brummett and Rev. Lloyd Henry officiating. Interment , Taylors Grove Cemetery in Union County. Grandsons were pallbearers. The family received friends 7-9 P.M. onFriday at McCarty Mortuary.

STELLA ANDERSON BREWER

Stella Anderson Brewer age 80, Lenoir City passed away February 5, 1981 at her home. She was a member of Primitive Baptist Church. Survivors: 2 daughters; Mrs. Oneda Vincil and Mrs. Florence Clabough of Lenoir City. 3 sons; Gordon and Marion of Lenoir City and Paul Brewer of Dalton, Georgia. 12 grandchildren, 32 great-grandchildren and 1 great-great-grandchild. Sister; Kyle Anderson of Lenoir City. Several nieces and nephews.

Funeral services were held 2:30 Sunday, February 8. at the Click Funeral Home Chapel. Elder Howard Pippin and Rev. Clarence Gresham, officiating. Burial was in the City Cemetery.

FLOSSIE CAPPS

Mrs. Flossie Capps, born April 19, 1907, passed away at St. Mary's Medical Center on June 13, 1981, being 74 years old. She professed faith in Christ at an early age and joined Black Fox Church in September, 1938 where she remained a faithful member as long as the Lord let her stay here. She was preceded in death by husband, William C. Capps. Survivors to mourn her passing, 4 children, Maxine NS Bennie of Manardville. Cecil and Dale of Knoxville, 1 brother, Robert Snyder, 1 sister, Mrs. Lucy hite, and 1 niece Brenda Hite all of Morristown.,9 grand children 2 great-grandchildren. Funeral services were conducted at Black Fox on June 15, 1981, with Elder Hugh Brummitt, Elder Parnick Shelton,and Rev. Walter Smith officiating. Pallbearers were:Gregory and Randy Capps, Donnie Smith, Ott Cabbage, Bill Lay, and Arthur Terry. She was laid to rest in the Cabbage Cemetery to await the coming of Christ. She will be greatly missed by all who knew her.

EVA M. COLLINS

Eva M. Collins was born November 27, 1899. Passed away May 27, 1981 at the age of 81 years and 6 months. She professed faith in Christ at an early age. She is survived by two brothers, Arlis and Dewey Collins, one sister, Linnie Keck all of New Tazewell. Fourteen nieces and nephews, a host of other relatives and friends. She was preceded in death by three sisters, and one brother. "Our loss is Heavens Gain". She was a member of Pleasant Point Baptist Church.

MARGARET SHARP COUNTISS

Margaret Sharp Countiss, Greenville, South Carolina, formerly a resident of Knoxville, passed away March 14, 1981. She was a member of Kirkwood Baptist Church and formerly with Hall-Tate Clothing. Survivors: Daugher, Helen Tomason, Greenville; Son, Wendell C. Countiss, Norris; Sister, Lucy S. Martin, Chattanooga; 4 grandchildren; 6 great-grandchildren; 1 great-great-grandchild. Funeral Service 2 P.M. Wednesday at Rose Chapel, Rev William Berry officiating. Interment in Greenwood Cemetery. Pallbearers; Michael McCall, Bill Martin, Scott Sharp, Dr. Buddy Gipson, joe lombardo, Mike Countiss, Eddie Allison.

ANNA JANE (DYKES) GRAVES

MRS. Anna Jane (Dykes) Graves, age 77, passed away May 12, 1981 at her home in Maynardville, Tennessee after a lingering illness. She was a member of Oak Grove Primitive Baptist Church.

Survivors: Husband, Leslie Graves, Daughters, Jessie M. Graves, Mrs. V.H. (Pearl) Kitts, Mrs Robert (Bertie) Campbell, Mrs. Leonard (Loretta) Padgett and Mrs. Jean Richardson. Sons: Charles, Bill, Roy and Coy all of Maynardville, Tennessee. Twenty Grandchildren, seventeen great-grandchildren. Sister, Mrs Aaron (Rova) Rouse of Monroe, Mich. Several nieces and nephews and a very special friend: Mrs. Fausteen Marsee. Funeral was held 2:30 P.M. May 14th. at Ailor's Chapel with Rev. Leonard Padgett and Roscoe Harless officiating. Interment in Monroe Cemetery. Pallbearers: Grandsons.

Honorary Pallbearer: Jerry Muncey

Flower Girls: Granddaughters.

Singers: Hubbs Grove Quartet.

STELLA B. GRAVES

Stella B.(White) Graves, age 84 of LaFollette, died on October 8, 1980. She was a member of Davis Chapel Primitive Baptist Church. She was the daughter of the late Elza and Polly White of Union County and Widow of the late Elder Verlin H. Graves.

Survivors are three daughters, Mrs. James D. (Edna) Gluff of Bradenton, Florida, Mrs J.S. (Annarene) Welch of Atlantic Beach,Florida, Mrs. George R. (Maxine) Asbury of LaFollette, one son, Joseph H. Graves of Dearborn Heights, Michigan, 13 grandchildren and 10 great-grandchildren Funeral services were 11:00 A.M. Friday at Walters Chapel with the Rev. Bob Cross officiating. Burial was in Lynnhurst Cemetery, Knoxville. Walters Funeral Home, LaFollette, was in charge of the arrangements.

JOHN PETER HEMBREE

John Peter Hembree, age 80 of Maryville, passed away Saturday, Nov. 29, 1980. Survivors: Wife of 60 years, Ellen; four sons, Clarence and hubert of Maryville, David of Oak Ridge, and Chester of Rockford. Five daughters Mrs. Mildred Peacock of Alabama, MISS Freda Hembree of Knoxville, Mrs Frances Davis of Maryville, Mrs Edith walker of Rockford, Mrs Gaye Lee of Townsend; 28 grandchildren; 20 great-grandchildren; 2 brothers, 4 sisters. Funeral services were conducted at Miller's Funeral Home by Elder Clifford Brantley. Interment at Tuclaleechee Primitive Baptist Church. He was a member of Brnatley's Chapel Church.''He is missed dearly and the memories of him are not forgotten''.

OSCAR W. HURST

Oscar W. Hurst, Departed this life May 2, 1981, at the age of 74. He was a faithful menber of Noeton Primitive Baptist Church. He is survived by wife: Pauline Hurst of Rutledge. Daughters: Mrs. Jackie Hurst and Mrs. Ray Harrell both of Morristown. Sons: Fred Davis Hurst of Morristown, Carl Edward Hurst, Talbott. Sisters: Edith Bunch, Morristown, Susie Oliver, Bean Station, 12 grandchildren. Funeral services 2 p.M. Tuesday, May 5, at Noeton Primitive Baptist Church with Elder John Oliver, amd Rev. Olaf Atkins officiating. Burial in Acuff Cemetery at Washburn. Stubbelfield Funeral Home of Morristown in charge.

LUNDA COX KECK

Mrs. Lunda Cox Keck-age 90, passed away at 7:25 A.M. Saturday at ST. Mary's Medical Center. She was a member of Pleasant Point Baptist and widow of J.D. Keck. Survivors: daughter Mrs. Lydia Owen; sons, Carl Keck, Maynardville, Pat Keck, Knoxville. Graveside service 2 P.M. Monday, Lynnhurst Cemetery, Rev. Charles Plumlee officiating. Rose Mortuary in charge.

ESTHER ELLISON MCBEE

Ester Ellison McBee-Born April 23, 1916, departed this life, November 18, 1980 at Blount Memorial Hospital, Maryville. Her home was in Kokomo Ind. She was a mamber of Brantley's Chapel Church, Maryville.

Survivors: Husband Leonard McBee, Kokoma, one daughter Geneva Maddock, Kokoma; three grandchildren, Julie, Cindy, & Gregory. Sisters; Ottie McBee and Sara Brantley of Maryville, Dinia Barnard & Bessis McCarty of Sharp's Chapel, and Irene Bridges of Nashville. Three brothers Jeff Ellison, Maryville, Swan Ellison of Sharp's Chapel & Ulysess Ellison, Walton, Ind.; several nieces and nephews.

Funeral services were at Smith Mortuary, Maryville, with the Elder Clifford Brantley and Jerry McBee officiating. The body was sent to Ellers Funeral home, Kokomo, Indiana for burial.

Sadly missed by relatives and friends...Gone but not forgotten.

Written by niece, Arretus McBee

ANDERSON MUNSEY

Anderson Munsey age 91 of New Tazewell, passed away at the Claiborne County Hospital in Tazewell, Sept. 8, 1980. He was preceded in death by his wife Barbara Earl Munsey and two grand sons Ronnie and Kenneth Munsey. He was a member of Union Chapel Baptist. He is survived by his wife, Velta Drummonds Munsey. Three sons, Lawrence, Jack and Whitt and one daughter Lourene, all of New Tazewell.several grandchildren and a host of relatives and friends to mourn his passing. Funeral services were conducted at the Coffey Funeral Home Chapel by Elder Bill Sparks and Rev.Claude Brooks, he was laid to rest in the Shoemaker Cemetery. We miss you so much darling. Written by his wife.

LINNIE PEARL AUSMUS PIERCE

Linnie Pearl Ausmus Pierce was born April 3, 1898 and passed this life on January 20, 1981, being 82 years, 9 months and 17 days of age. She joined Pleasant Hill Church and remained a member until her death. She was married to Howard Pierce in 1918; he preceded her in death. Left to mourn her passing is: One daughter, Mrs. Adrian (Oklen) Edwards of Speedwell, Tenn.,2 sons: Carl Pierce of LaFollette, Tenn. and Cole Pierce of Wyandotte, Mich., 9 grandchildren; 8 great-grand children and a host of relative and friends. Services were held Friday January 23, 1981, 2 P.M. at Pleasant Hill Church. The services were conducted by Elder Albert Davis and Elder Bill Rhymer. Interment was in the Ausmus Cemetery. The grandsons were pallbearers. She is sadly missed by her family.

MAGGIE LONEAL ROBERTSON

Maggie Loneal Robertson was born to Tannie and Jane Drummonds on March 22, 1898. She passed away April 20, 1981, making her 83 years and 1 month old. She professed faith at an early age and joined Myers Grove Primitive Baptist Church. She married Charlie Robertson at age 16 and from this marriage there were 10 children born. Two sons and husband preceded her in death. She is survived by four sons: Clifford and Otis Robertson of New Tazewell, Tn., HOY Robertson, Belleville, Mich, and Lawrence Robertson of Detroit, Michigan. Four Daughters: Mrs. Mattie Holt and Eula Gray Good both of New Tazewell, Tn., Mrs Irene Elliott of Woodfine, KY., and Mrs. Easter Good of Pomutus, Mich. One Sister Mrs Velt Munsey of New Tazewell. 24 Grandchildren, 36 Great Grand-children and 4 great-great-grandchildren and a host of friends and relatives She was loved by everyone who ever met her. She was a Mother that will never be forgotten. Funeral services were held at Meyers Grove Church at 11:00 A.M. on the 23 of April and she was laid to rest at the Drummons Cemetery. Coffey Mortuary was in charge. Her pallbearers were her grandsons: Roger Mickle, Ronnie Good, Richard Elliott, Hollis Robertson, Beazer Watson and Clay Widner. The singers were Elder Johnny Ayers and his singers, and Elder Claude Rosson and his wife Doris. The services were held by ElderNoble Clawson and Elder Claude Rosson. May she always rest in peace with Christ is our prayer.

J. VICTOR SHARP

J. Victor Sharp born December 30, 1933 died June 18, 1981 in Johnson City Medical Center.

He professed faith in Christ at an early age and joined the Primitive Baptist Church at Kirkwood in Knoxville. He owned and operated an old fashioned butcher shop in Kingsport.

Survived by wife, Kizzy Sharp of Elizabethton, son Calvin, daughters Donna Ruth and Shirley Ann Sharp, parents Ambrose and Freda Sharp, brother Don Sharp, sisters Joyce ann McFalls and Shirley Bowden all of Knoxville. Funeral services 2 P.M. Saturday June 20 at Weaver Funeral Home. Elder Hugh Brummitt and Elder Earl Chapman officiating.

He was laid to rest in LynnHurst Cemetery, the most beautiful cemetery in the southland, to await the glorious resurrection of the dead. By Mother.

MILLARD (SHORTY) THOMPSON

Millard (shorty) Thompson, age 76, a life-long Bell County resident, passed away Thursday, October 16. 1980, at the Veterans Hospital in Lexington, Ky., after a long illness. Mr. Thompson was born January 7, 1904, in Bell County, the son of the late Weaver and Nevada Hoskins Thompson. He was a vetern of World War Two, a retired Bell County school teacher and a member of Pleasant Hill Primitive Baptist Church. He loved the church and enjoyed going when he was able. He is survived by his wife, Faye Greene Thompson and one daughter Joy Saylor and one grand-daughter Leigh Ann Saylor all of Calvin, Ky. Five brother and three sisters and many other friends. His parents and two brothers preceded him in death. Funeral services were held Sunday October 19, 1980, at 2 P.M.

at the Arnett Funeral Home Chapel with Elder Albert Davis and Elder Bill Rymer officiating. Burial was in Roselawn Memorial Gardens in Middlesboro, Ky. The pallbearers were his nephews. "The love we shared together are the memories I hold dear. It broke my heart to lose you after 35 years" Sadly missed by wife Faye and all.

TRULA WALKER

Trula Walker age 81, passed away October 1, 1980. She was a member of Oak Grove Primitive Baptist Church. Survivors: Daughters, Mrs Betty Hylemon, Knoxville, Mrs. Dean Russ, Gladwin, Michigan and Mrs. Lilias Clawson of Monroe, Michigan. Sons, Tyson of Knoxville, Leonard of California, Theodore of Nashville and Willie of Toledo, Ohio. 22 grand-children; 26 great-grandchildren; and two great-great-grandchildren. Sister , Mrs Clatie Dykes of Sharps Chapel. Brothers, Kyle and Earl Welch both of Knoxville, She was preceeded in death by a daughter, Mrs. Mildred Lee, and husband, Elmer.

Funeral Services were held at 1:00 P.M. on Saturday at the Oak Grove Primitive Baptist Church with Elder William Sparks and Elder J.C. Monday officiating. Interment was in Church Cemetery.

PEARL (LYNCH) WELCH

Pearl (Lynch) Welch-Born January 27, 1904, died November 3, 1980. She was preceded in death by her husband, Francis and one daughter, Nola Faye.

Survivors: Daughters, Etta Mae Monroe, Sharps Chapel, Anna Myrle Burnett, Kokomo, Ind. and Trula Fern Cox, Wasbash, Ind. Son, James Welch, Sharps Chapel. Sisters, Mrs. Etha Maples, Mrs.Roy Roe both of Sharps Chapel and Mrs. W.C. Robertson, Knoxville.

Funeral Services were held at Oak Grove, where she was a member. Elder J.C. Monday officiating. Interment was in Church Cemetery.

GEORGE W. WILLIAMS

George Washington Williams, age 74, New Tazewell, died October 10, 1980 at Claiborne County Hospital.

He was a member of Pleasant Point Primitive Baptist Church. He was preceded in death by his wife, Mrs. allie Williams, in 1974, and two-daughters.

He is survived by sisters, Mrs. Vernie Irick, New Tazewell, Mrs Lora Goforth, Mrs Ada Rouse, Mrs Florence Patton, Knoxville, and Mrs. Bertha Maddox, Lenoir City; brothers Rev. Robert and John of New Tazewell and Jim , Maynardville; several nieces and nephews.

Funeral services were held at 10 A.M. Monday, October 13, at Pleasant Point Church with Elder Walter Lyons and Elder Parnick Shelton officiating. Burial was in the Pleasant Point Cemetery.

Pallbearers wer nephews: Ralph Maddox, Steve, Bruce, and Wade Williams, Wade Keck and J.D. McBee. Coffey Mortuary in charge.

EDGAR WILLS

Wills, Edgar-age 64. of Route 1, Dandridge, Tennessee passed away at 1:30 P.M. Sunday, June 7, 1981 at V.A. Hospital, Mountain Home, after a lingering illness. He was a member of Rocky Dale Primitive Baptist Church since January 6, 1963. Former employee of Baneberry Country Club. Vereran of WW2 and a member of the V.F.W. Post of Maynardville, Tennessee. Survivors: wife, Mrs. Opal Weaver Wills, Dandridge; son Edgar Wills, Jr., Bloomington, Ill.;daughter, Mrs Robert   (Geraldine) Boltz, Vancover, Washington; Stepson, Robert Beecher, Madison, Wis. 9 grandchildren; 1 great-grandchild; 2 sisters, Mrs Hazel Bushman, Mrs Lois Jones, both of Mahomit, Ill.; several nieces and nephews. Funeral services were 8 P.M. Tuesday at Farrar's Chapel. Elder Hugh Brummitt officiating. Interment 10 A.M. Wednesday in Dandridge

Memorial Gardens. The family received friends 7-8 P.M. Tuesday at Farrar's Chapel.

STATISTICAL TABLE

CHURCHES	DELEGATES	Restored	Rec'd. by Letter	Baptism	Relationship	Dismiss by Letter	Excluded	Deceased	Total Membership	Printing Minutes	REGULAR MEETING TIME	COMMUNION TIME
BLACK FOX	Bros: Arthur Terry, Dale Capps, Bennie Capps; Sisters: Mary Terry, Mary Ruth Capps, Pamela Capps	0	0	0	0	0	0	1	79	$25.00	Second Saturday Night and Sunday Fourth Sunday	Sunday following Second Saturday in June
BRADEN'S CHAPEL	Elders: Noble Clawson; Bros: Coy Edwards, James Pierce; Sisters: Helen Clawson, Sue Pierce	0	0	4	3	6	0	2	144	$20.00	First Saturday Night and Sunday of each month	Sunday following First Saturday in July
BRANTLEY'S CHAPEL	Elders: Clifford Brantley, Jerry McBee; Bros: Daniel Brantley, Rina Johnson, Cyrus McBee, Chester Hembree, Everett Brantley; Sisters: Hazel Johnson, Mildred Brantley, Barsha Brantley	0	3	12	8	0	1	2	110	$35.00	Second Saturday Night Every Sunday and Sunday Night	Sunday following Second Saturday in July
DAVIS CHAPEL	Bros: Clyde Lynch, James S. Heatherly, Orice McCarty, Bob Lynch; Sisters: Ruth Heatherly, Mollie McCarty, Ollie Welch, Pearl Lynch	0	0	2	1	0	0	1	110	$35.00	Third Saturday Night. Every Sunday and Sunday Night	Third Sunday in June
GETHSEMANE	Sisters: Myrtle Cook	0	0	2	0	1	0	0	37	$30.00	Every Sunday except First Sunday of each month.	Sunday following Fourth Saturday in May & Oct.
GIBSON STATION	Elders: William Rhymer, Spurgeon Thompson, Joe Irving, Nelson Jones; Bros: Franklin Jones; Sisters: Karen Rhymer, Jean Thompson, Fannie Jones, Evelyn Irving, Dorothy Johnson, Polly Jones	0	0	2	2	0	0	0	79	$40.00	First Saturday and Saturday Night. Every Sunday and Sunday Night of each month.	Sunday following Second Saturday in June
HEADRICK CHAPEL	Bros: Clyde Abbott, Sr., Bill Cook; Sisters: Geraldine Abbott, Margo Abbott, Angela Abbott	0	0	1	0	0	0	0	114	$20.00	First and Third Sunday	Sunday following First Saturday in May & Oct.

Church	Leadership							Members	Salary	Services	Homecoming
KIRKWOOD	Elders: H. E. Brummitt; Bros: C. A. Sharp, R. P. Bridges, M. E. Evans, E. P. Cook; Sisters: Ruby Brummitt, Frieda Sharp, Ora Bridges, Velma Evans, Dottie Cook, Dola Webb	0	0	0	0	0	2	106	$30.00	Every Sunday Morning	Last Sunday in April
LENOIR CITY	Elder: Howard Pippin; Bros: Raymond Wilkerson, Henry Chamberlain, Hubert Spoon; Sisters: Estie Chamberlain, Annie Spoon	0	0	0	0	3	1	131	$35.00	Every Sunday and Sunday Night	Wednesday night before Easter Sunday. Third Sunday in October
MYERS GROVE	Sisters: Vett Munsey	0	6	0	0	0	2	77	$25.00	Second Saturday Night and Sunday. Fourth Saturday Night and Sunday	Sunday following Fourth Saturday in May
NOETON	Elder: John Oliver; Bros: Carroll Oliver, Charlie Collins; Sisters: Ruth Oliver, Mildred Oliver, Dora Collins	0	1	0	0	0	2	40	$20.00	First Sunday of each month. Third Saturday and Sunday of each month	Sunday following Third Saturday in May and Sept.
OAK GROVE	Elders: Johnnie Atkins; Sisters: Frances Eastridge	0	5	1	0	3	3	334	$25.00	First Saturday Night and Sunday. Third Sunday	Sunday following First Saturday in May
PLEASANT HILL	Elders: Albert Davis, Larry Anderson, James H. Branscomb; Sisters: Audry Davis, Helen Ruth Branscomb, Myra Anderson	0	2	0	0	0	2	103	$35.00	Fourth Saturday Morning and Saturday night. Fourth Sunday Every Sunday night.	Sunday following Fourth Saturday in June
PLEASANT POINT	Elders: Claude Rosson	0	0	0	0	0	3	107	$20.00	First Saturday night and Sunday. Third Sunday	Sunday following First Saturday in July
ROCKY DALE	Elders: Parnick Shelton, William Berry, Herbert Graves, Curt Johnson, Donald Sharp; Sisters: Wilma Shelton, Trula Berry, Dorothy Sharp	0	0	0	0	4	2	124	$40.00	Every Sunday and Sunday Night	Sunday following Second Saturday in May

CHURCH	COUNTY	PASTOR	CLERK	ADDRESS
Black Fox	Grainger	Elder Larry Anderson	Bennie Capps	P.O. Box 91, Maynardville, TN 37807
Braden's Chapel	Union	Elder Noble Clawson Elder J. C. Monday, Asst.	Jimmie B. Edwards Phyllis Wilson, Asst.	Speedwell, TN 37870 Speedwell, TN 37870
Brantley's Chapel	Blount	Elder Clifford Brantley Elder Jerry McBee, Asst.	Jennifer Johnson Vickie Irwin, Asst.	1217 Brown School Rd.-Maryville, TN 37801 Rt. 14, Box 61, Maryville, TN 37801
Davis Chapel	Campbell	Elder William Berry	Ruth Heatherly Katheryn Angel, Asst.	Rt. 1 - Box 528, LaFollette, TN 37766 Rt. 4 - Box 80, LaFollette, TN 37766
Gethsemane	Knox	Elder Walter Lyons	Tom Carmichael	729 Frank St., Knoxville, TN 37919
Gibson Station	Lee, Va.	Elder William Rhymer Elder Spureon Thompson, Asst.	Dorothy Johnson Shirley Sandifur, Asst.	Rt. 2, Box 114, Ewing, Va. 24248 Rt. 2 - Harrogate, TN
Headrick Chapel	Sevier	Elder Sheridan Moore, Asst.	Clyde Abbott, Sr.	Rt. 7, Box 288 - Sevierville, TN 37862
Kirkwood	Knox	Elder William Berry Elder Parnick Shelton, Asst.	Mrs. Alice Powers Miss Truly Berry, Asst.	7525 Temple Acres Drive Knoxville, TN 37918 Rt. 8 - Brown School Road Maryville, TN 37801
Lenoir City	Loudon	Elder Howard Pippin	Thelma Brown	319 Bussell Ferry Rd., Lenoir City, TN 37771
Meyer's Grove	Claiborne	Elder Noble Clawson	Bonnie Miracle Harold Cupp, Asst.	Rt. 2, Box 91, New Tazewell, TN 37825 Rt. 2, Box 166, New Tazewell, TN 37825
Noeton	Grainger	Elder John Oliver	Carroll Oliver Bessie Collins	Rt. 2, Box 513, Bean Station, TN 37708 Rt. 5, Morristown, TN 37814
Oak Grove	Union	Elder J. C. Monday Elder Jerry McBee, Asst.	Betty P. Sharp Betty Shoffner	Sharps Chapel, TN 37866 Sharps Chapel, TN 37866
Pleasant Hill	Claiborne	Elder William Rhymer Elder Albert Davis, Asst.	William Branscomb Dennis Edwards, Asst.	Speedwell, TN 37870 Speedwell, TN 37870
Pleasant Point	Claiborne	Elder Larry Anderson	Elder Claude Rosson	Rt. 4, New Tazewell, TN 37825
Rocky Dale	Knox	Elder Hugh Brummitt	Edward Collett Dennis Branson	Rt. 1, Box 17, Luttrell, TN 37779 Rt. 13, 4633 Marshall Dr. Knoxville, TN 37918

337

ARTICLES OF FAITH

Article 1. We believe in only one true living God, as He is revealed to us in the Holy Scriptures - Father, Son, and Holy Ghost.

Article 2. We believe that the Scriptures of the old and new Testaments are the words of God and the only rule of all-saving knowledge and obedience.

Article 3. We believe in the doctrine of election according to the foreknowledge of God.

Article 4. We believe in the doctrine of original sin.

Article 5. We believe in man's impotency to rescue himself from the fallen state he is in, by his own will or ability.

Article 6. We believe that sinners are justified in the sight of God only by the imputed righteousness of Jesus Christ.

Article 7. We believe the elect, according to the foreknowledge of God will be called, converted, regenerated, and sanctified by the Holy Spirit.

Article 8. We believe the saints will persevere and never fall finally away.

Article 9. We believe that baptism and the Lord's Supper are ordinances of Jesus Christ, and that true believers are the only subject of these ordinances, and that the true mode of baptism is by immersion. We believe also that feet washing is an example of Jesus Christ and should be kept by his disciples until his second coming.

Article 10. We believe in the Resurrection of the dead and the General Judgement.

Article 11. We believe that the punishment of the wicked will be everlasting and that the joys of the righteous will be eternal.

Article 12. We believe that no minister has the right to administer the ordinances, except those who have been regularly baptized and called of God, and come under the imposition of hands of the presbytery.

1982 Minutes

OF THE

ONE HUNDRED SIXTY-SECOND SESSION

OF THE

POWELL VALLEY ASSOCIATION OF PRIMITIVE BAPTIST

HELD WITH THE SISTER CHURCH AT
LENOIR CITY
LOUDON COUNTY, TENNESSEE
AUGUST 20, 21, 22, 1982

THE ONE HUNDRED SIXTY-SECOND SESSION
OF THE POWELL VALLEY ASSOCIATION
OF
PRIMITIVE BAPTIST
HELD WITH THE SISTER CHURCH AT LENOIR CITY
IN LOUDON COUNTY, TENNESSEE
AUGUST 20, 21, 22, 1982

NEXT SESSION WILL BE HELD WITH THE SISTER CHURCH
AT
GIBSON STATION
IN LEE COUNTY, VIRGINA
TO BEGIN ON FRIDAY BEFORE THE THIRD SATURDAY
IN AUGUST 1983
AT 10:30 A.M.

ELDER CLIFFORD BRANTLEY WILL DELIVER THE
INTRODUCTORY SERMON, AND ELDER WILLIAM
RHYMER WILL BE THE ALTERNATE

OFFICERS

ELDER HUGH BRUMMITT   MODERATOR
1329 BROWN AVENUE, KNOXVILLE, TENN., PHONE 546-7700
ELDER CLIFFORD BRANTLEY   ASSISTANT MODERATOR
809 BROWN SCHOOL RD. MARYVILLE, TENN., PHONE 982-3875
BENNIE CAPPS   CLERK
P.O. BOX 91, MAYNARDVILLE, TENN., PHONE 992-5571
RINA JOHNSON   ASSISTANT CLERK
1217 BROWN SCHOOL ROAD, MARYVILLE, TENN., PHONE 983-2774

ARTICLES OF FAITH

Article 1. We believe in only one true living God, as He is revealed to us in the Holy Scriptures - Father, Son, and Holy Ghost.

Article 2. We believe that the Scriptures of the old and new Testaments are the words of God and the only rule of all-saving knowledge and obedience.

Article 3. We believe in the doctrine of election according to the foreknowledge of God.

Article 4. We believe in the doctrine of original sin.

Article 5. We believe in man's impotency to rescue himself from the fallen state he is in, by his own will or ability.

Article 6. We believe that sinners are justified in the sight of God only by the imputed righteousness of Jesus Christ.

Article 7. We believe the elect, according to the foreknowledge of God will be called, converted, regenerated, and sanctified by the Holy Spirit.

Article 8. We believe the saints will persevere and never fall finally away.

Article 9. We believe that baptism and the Lord's Supper are ordinances of Jesus Christ, and that true believers are the only subject of these ordinances, and that the true mode of baptism is by immersion. We believe also that feet washing is an example of Jesus Christ and should be kept by his disciples until his second coming.

Article 10. We believe in the Resurrection of the dead and the General Judgement.

Article 11. We believe that the punishment of the wicked will be everlasting and that the joys of the righteous will be eternal.

Article 12. We believe that no minister has the right to administer the ordinances, except those who have been regularly baptized and called of God, and come under the imposition of hands of the presbytery.

Friday, August 20, 1982

The one hundred and sixty-second session of the Powell Valley Association of Primitive Baptist met with the sister church at Lenoir City in Loudon County, Tennessee on August 20, 21, and 22, 1982.

After Elder William Berry led the congregation in singing Amazing Grace" and "How Firm A Foundation", the Moderator, Elder Hugh Brummitt welcomed the congregation and pleaded for peace and love to abide through the entire Association and called for prayer by Elder Albert Davis of Pleasant Hill Church.

Following prayer, Elder Jerry McBee, Brantley's Chapel delivered the introductory sermon and gave a very good sermon from 1st Kings and the 8th Chapter using as his text "Stranger that came into the Land" in the absence of Elder Walter Lyons.

After the introductory sermon, they sang a song and was dismissed in prayer by Elder Spurgeon Thompson of Gibson Station. The Association was to reconvene after a 15 minute recess.

After recess, the crowd reassembled in the church; Elder Albert Davis led the congregation in "Pass Me Not", the Moderator, Elder Hugh Brummitt, read the entire 13th Chapter of First Corinthians speaking on love, faith, hope and charity, then called for prayer by Elder Howard Pippin of Lenoir City Church.

The Moderator then asked for the order of business for the following transactions.:

1st   Called for letters of the Sister Churches to be presented to the clerk for reading. Fourteen (14) were received.

2nd   The letters presented were read and motion approved that the delegates be seated.

3rd   The moderator called for anyone present from any of the sister churches not named as a delegate and desired to be seated as such to come forward and give the clerk their name and the name of the church. Two came: Sister Letha Heath of Pleasant Point and Sister Polly Ward of Brantley's Chapel.

4th   Called for petitionary letter if there should be one. There was none.

5th   Motion approved that the Association re-elect Elder Hugh Brummitt as Moderator and Elder Clifford Brantley as Assistant Moderator for the ensuing year.

6th Motion approved that Brother Bennie Capps be re-elected Clerk and Brother Rina Johnson be re-elected Assistant Clerk for the ensuing year.

7th Motion was approved that we empower Elder Brummitt to appoint all the committees to serve this session.

8th The Moderator, having been empowered to do so, named the committee as follows:

> Committee on Arrangements:
> > Brother Orice McCarty
> > Brother Donald Sharp
> > Brother Everett Brantley
>
> Committee on Preaching:
> > Brother Raymond Wilkerson
> > Brother Arthur Terry
> > Elder Elwood Evans
>
> Committee on Request:
> > Elder John Oliver
> > Elder William Berry
> > Elder Larry Anderson
>
> Committee on Finance:
> > Elder Howard Pippin
> > Brother Henry Chamberlain
> > Elder Parnick Shelton

9th Called for the finances to be turned into the Finance Committee.

10th The committees all having been appointed and accepted, the Association moved to adjourn until 10:30 Saturday morning. They sang a song and was dismissed in prayer by Elder William Rhymer of the Sister Church at Gibson Station.

Saturday, August 21, 1982

Saturday, at the appointed hour of 10:30, and at the sound of singing, the Association reassembled to a full house.

After singing, the Assistant Moderator, Elder Clifford Brantley, gave a very spiritual and uplifting talk and then read part of the 22nd Chapter of Psalms, then called for prayer by Elder William Berry of Rocky dale Church.

After prayer, the Moderator called the Association to order for the remainder of the business.

1st The Moderator called for any letters from Sister Churches not received on Friday. Letter was received from the Sister Church at Davis Chapel.

2nd Motion was approved to accept the letter and seat the named delegates.

3rd The Moderator called for anyone from any of the churches who were present and desired to be seated as delegate to come forward. None came.

4th The Moderator then called for the report of the Committee on Arrangements who submitted the following arrangements which was accepted and the committee released.

Report on Arrangements:

Call for roll call of delegates
Call for report of Committee on Preaching
Call for report of Committee on Request
Call for report of Committee on Finance

Decide how many minutes to have printed, who shall supervise the printing and distribution of same, and how much he shall receive for services.

Who shall preach the introductory sermon and who will be the alternate.

Respectfully submitted,
Brother Everett Brantley
Brother Donald Sharp
Brother Orice McCarty

5th Called the roll call of delegates of all the Sister Churches and check the absentees.

6th Called for the report of the Committee on Preaching, which was given as follows and was accepted and the committee was released.

Report of Committee on Preaching:

Friday Night,	Elder William Berry
Friday Night,	Elder Howard Pippin
Friday Night,	Elder Parnick Shelton
Friday Night	Elder James H. Branscomb
Saturday Night,	Elder James H. Branscomb
Saturday Night,	Elder William Rhymer
Saturday Night,	Elder Hugh Brummitt
Sunday,	Elder Hugh Brummitt
Sunday,	Elder Clifford Brantley

Respectfully submitted,
Brother Raymond Wilkerson
Brother Arthur Terry
Brother Elwood Evans

7th Called for the report of the Committee on Request which was accepted and the committee was released.

Report of Committee on Request:

We, the Committee on Request, request that we have 1,150 minutes printed and that the clerk supervise the printing and distribution of same and that he receive $125.00 for his services. We also request that Elder J. C. Monday write a circular letter to be printed in the minutes, also that the next session of the Association be held with the Sister Church of Gibson Station in Lee County, Virginia, to begin on Friday before the third Saturday in August, 1983, and may the love and peace that is here continue through the remainder of this Association.

Respectfully submitted,
Elder William Berry
Elder John Oliver
Elder Lary Anderson

8th Called for the Committee on Finance which was accepted and the committee was released.

Report of Finance Committee:

Black Fox	$25.00
Braden's Chapel	25.00
Brantley's Chapel	35.00
Davis' Chapel	35.00
Gethesemane	25.00
Gibson Station	40.00
Headricks Chapel	25.00
Kirkwood	40.00
Lenoir City	35.00
Meyers Grove	25.00
Noeton	20.00
Oak Grove	25.00
Pleasant Hill	35.00
Rocky Dale	40.00
Total	$450.00
Balance in Bank	277.00
	727.00
Expenses for 1982	550.00
Balance in Bank	$177.00

Respectfully Submitted:
Elder Howard Pippin
Brother Henry Chamberlain
Elder Parnick Shelton

9th Motion approved that we grant the request of the committee and have 1,250 copies of the minutes printed and that the clerk supervise the printing

10th Motion approved that the next session of the Association be held with the Sister Church of Gibson Station in Lee County Virginia, to begin on Friday before the third Saturday in August, 1983, at 10:30 A.M.

11th Motion that Elder Walter Lyons deliver the introductory sermon and Elder William Berry be the alternate. This motion was withdrawn.

12th Motion approved that Elder Clifford Brantley deliver the introductory sermon and Elder William Rhymer be the alternate.

13th Motion approved that Elder J. C. Monday of Braden's Chapel write a circular letter for the 1983 minutes.

14th Motion approved that the churches of the Powell Valley Association extend to the church and the people of Lenoir City our heart felt thanks and our prayers for the love, fellowship and kindness and food while we were here with you. May the Good Lord Bless and keep you is our prayers.

15th Motion to adjourn, trusting the Lord to permit us to meet again with the Sister Church at Gibson Station in Lee County, Virginia, on Friday before the third Saturday in August, 1983, at 10:30 A.M.

Dismissed in prayer by Elder Robert Walker.

> Elder Hugh Brummitt, Moderator
> Elder Clifford Brantley, Assistant Moderator
> Brother Bennie Capps, Clerk
> Brother Rina Johnson, Assistant Clerk

Sunday, August 22, 1982

After Singing by Elder William Berry, Elder Howard Pippin gave a very interesting talk, then called on Elder Joe Bush for prayer, after which Elder Clifford Brantley read 26 chapters of Acts, starting with the 6th Verse and preached concerning Paul's journey in Egypt and the blood was applied to the door post and upon the mantle. Then Elder Hugh Brummitt read the 5th Verse of 1st Chapter of Joshua and preached a very spiritual sermon concerning Moses being sent to Egypt to bring out his people. Dismissed by Brother Rina Johnson of Brantley's Chapel.

The following four (4) churches requested the Association for 1983: Black Fox, Brantley's Chapel, Gibson Station and Lenoir City.

SUMMARY

We are blessed with a fine group of ministers as was illustrated by those who had the opportunity to preach. We regret that time will not permit more of them to preach when we meet with the Association

On Friday, Elder Jerry McBee delivered the introductory sermon.

Friday night sermons were delivered by Elder William Berry and Elder Howard Pippin.

Then on Saturday morning, Elder Parnick Shelton preached a wonderful sermon from the 3rd Chapter of First Corinthians and the 10th Verse. using as his theme According to the Grace of God, and Man buildeth upon the Rock. He was then followed by Elder Spurgeon Thompson who read the 1st Chapter of Ephesians and used "Chosen in Him before the Foundation of the world." Dismissed by Brother Orice McCarty.

Saturday night sermons were delivered by Elder James H. Branscomb and Elder William Rhymer.

Sunday services were conducted by Elder Clifford Brantley who preached concerning Moses being sent to Egypt to bring our His people.

RULES OF DECORUM

1. The churches composing the Powell's Valley Association shall not be confined to any set rules as to specific number of Messengers they shall have in the body, but shall have the right to name in their letters as many as they choose, and in addition all orderly members of any of the churches being present be entitled to seats in the body as Messengers of their respective churches, with all the rights and privileges of the same.

2. The Messengers thus assembled shall be denominated the Powell's Valley Primitive Baptist Association.

3. For the purpose of historical information and statistical edification, the Churches are required to state in letters, the number of members in fellowship, the number received by Baptism, by letter, by confession of Faith, the number dismissed, excluded and dead since last session; also the time of their meeting, their pastoral supply, and the amount of money contributed for ministers and other purposes together with any other information they deem appropriate for the edification of the saints and glory of God.

4. This Association shall have no power to answer queries, give advice, or dictate to the Churches in any case, or to lord it over God's heritage nor any power by which she can directly or indirectly fringe on the internal rights of the church or censure and try any church or member in reference to faith and practice and determine upon validity of gospel ordinances. These things shall rest entirely with the churches; but henceforward our annual meetings shall be only for the purpose of hearing from each other, and for the worship of God and mutual comfort and edification of the Saints. To this end we reserve the privilege annually for the Third Friday in August and the two following days or at such other times as may be agreed upon with any church that may invite us having to protect our own standard, while in session, from heresay and disorder to recognize and invite any primitive Baptist minister or any lay brother to worship with us that may deem proper; to request the brethren of our body to visit other churches or bodies in our belief with whom we may desire to cul-

347

ture Christian fellowship; to publish in a minute of our proceedings.

5. Each session of the body shall have a Moderator and Clerk who shall hold office until re-elected.

6. Any order member of any church belonging to this body, when convened, being present shall be eligible to elect on as Moderator and Clerk or to sit on any committee appointed by the same.

7. In all election or questions that may be necessary to determine by vote, the vote shall be taken by churches, each church being entitled to three votes for any number less than one hundred, and one additional vote for every fifty or fraction thereof above the first hundred, but the Messengers of each church may divide their vote as they see proper.

8. All elections or questions coming to vote shall be determined by a majority vote cast, and it shall be the only duty of the minority to acquiesce in the decision thus reached.

9. If new churches desire to be admitted to this union they shall petition by letter and messengers and if voted for and recommended by one or more sister churches for her Presbytery constitutioning them, as orthodox and orderly they shall be received by the vote of the body and manifested by the Moderator giving the Messengers the right hand of fellowship.

10. Any motion or resolution clearly inconsistent with the above rules shall be promptly ruled out of order unless withdrawn by the mover.

11. Any Messenger being ruled out of order by the Moderator shall have the right to appeal to the body on the question of order, and if sustained shall be allowed to proceed, but if not take his seat.

12. Our meeting being held in the name of Christ and the worship of God; each Messenger is expected to observe due and proper therein.

13. It will not be considered good for any Messenger whose name has been enrolled as such to abruptly break off or absent himself from the Association without leave.

14. The Moderator shall be entitled to the same privilege of speech as other members provided the chair is filled.

15. The minutes of the Association shall be read and approved by the body and signed by the Moderator before adjourning.

16. The Association shall be opened and closed by prayer.

17. Amendments to these may be made at any time by a majority of the union voting by churches when they deem it necessary, provide such amendments do not compromise the sovereignty of the churches nor have tendency to give body undue power or jurisdiction over them.

CIRCULAR LETTER

Dear Brothers and Sisters in Christ,

I was appointed by the Association to write a circular letter to be placed in our Minutes of the 1982 session.

Let us use the Scriptures: St. John 3:16-17, "For God so loved the world, that He gave His only begotten Son, that whosoever believeth in Him should not perish, but have everlasting life." "For God sent not His Son into the world to condemn the world; but that the world through Him might be saved." 1 John 4:8-12, (8) "He that loveth not knoweth not God; for God is love." (9) "In this was manifested the love of God toward us, because that God sent his Son to be the propitiation for our sins." (11) "Beloved, if God so loved us, we ought also to love one another. (12) No man hath seen God at any time. If we love one another, God dwelleth in us, and his love is perfected in us.''

Let us seek peace and love in our Association. Remember God's word and abide by it. May God bless you is my prayer.

Elder Noble L. Clawson

MINISTERS DIRECTORY

Elder Jerry McBee, 2433 Pennsylvania Ave., Maryville, TN 37801
Elder Larry Anderson, Speedwell, TN 869-4635
Elder Johnny Atkins, Bean Station, TN Ph. 767-2397
Elder Johnny Ayres, Rt. 3-Box 159, Bean Station, TN Ph. 586-5401
Elder William Berry, Rt. #13, Knoxville, TN Ph. 922-9189
Elder J. H. Branscomb, Speedwell, TN, Ph. 562-6361
Elder Clifford Brantley, Brown School Rd., Maryville, TN, Ph. 982-3735
Elder Hugh H. Brummitt, 1329 Brown Ave., Knoxville, TN Ph. 546-7700
Elder J. C. Monday, Speedwell, TN, Ph. 562-3068
Elder Sheridan Moore, Route #1 Townsend, TN, Ph. 448-6430
Elder Howard Pippin, 101 Rose Street, Lenoir City, TN, Ph. 986-2791
Elder Claude Rosson, Rt. #4, New Tazewell, TN, Ph. 626-3168
Elder Joe Bush, Corryton, TN, Ph. 687-7018
Elder Noble Clawson, Rt. #4, Speedwell, TN, Ph. 562-2004
Elder Albert Davis, Speedwell, TN, Ph. 869-3596
Elder Clay Widner, Rt. #1, Tazewell, TN, Ph. 626-3893
Elder Alvin Graves, 122 Oak Wood Dr., Lenoir City, TN, Ph 986-9725
Elder Joe Irving, Rt. 3, Box B101, Middlesboro, KY, Ph. 248-8349
Elder Walter Lyons, 1602 Garfield St., Alcoa, TN, Ph. 984-3207
Elder John Godfrey, 15443 Valleoga, Victoryvill, Calif., Ph. (714)243-4661
Elder Robert Walker, Sevierville, TN, Ph. 428-1527
Elder Parnick Shelton, Rt. 4, Corryton, TN., Ph. 687-6142
Elder William Sparks, Speedwell, TN, Ph. 562-7997
Elder William Rhymer, Rt. #3, Harrogate, TN, Ph. 861-3092
Elder Spurgeon Thompson, Box 36, Shawanee, TN, Ph. 869-8175
Elder John Oliver, Rt. 2, Box 513, Bean Station, TN, Ph. 581-5039
Elder Jim Campbell, Louisville, TN, Ph. 983-1654
Elder Nelson Jones, Rt. 1, Harrogate, TN, Ph. 869-3703

LICENTIATES

Brother Roscoe Branscomb, Speedwell, TN
Brother Odell Carpenter, Maryville, TN
Brother Clyde Abbott, Sr., Rt. 7, Sevierville, TN, Ph. 453-2329
Brother Danny E. Turner, 101 Rose St., Lenoir City, TN, Ph. 986-2791

Obituaries

In memory of Glenn E. Abbott, who was born in Alcoa, Tennessee, April 2, 1939 and departed this life April 23, 1982, making his stay here 43 years and 21 days.

Brother Glenn married Audrey Ann Mays Aug. 6, 1960 by Elder Sherdian Moore; to this union was born 3 children — 2 boys and 1 girl. Brother Glenn was preceded in death by his mother, Louisa Evelyn (Eva) Abbott. He leaves to mourn his departure his wife, Audrey; sons, William Glenn (Billy) Abbott, Ricky Lynn Abbott; daughter, Deborah Ann Abbott; granddaughter, Rachel Diane Abbott, all of Knoxville, Tennessee. His father, Louia H. Abbott; step-mother, Goldie R. Abbott of Riverside, California; five brothers, William Jackson Abbott, Fred Daniel Abbott of Knoxville, John Raymond Abbott, Harold Wayne Abbott and Clarence Wiley Abbott of California; one sister, Wilma Jean Green of California; also a host of aunts and uncles, nieces, nephews, and friends.

Brother Glenn professed a hope in Christ and joined the Oliver's Chapel Primitive Baptist Church, and was baptised in Riverside California in 1961. He began to speak in the church and said he felt that the Lord had called him to preach, and the Lord blessed him wonderfully and he began to speak with the understanding. In 1970 brother Glenn moved to Knoxville where he united with the Gethsemane Church, and onMarch 24, 1974 he was presented to a Presbytery of qualified elders and sister churches; He was questioned and examined thoroughly by the presbytery with the church standing by and was found sound in the Doctrine of the Bible. The charge was read and given and the laying on of hands with prayer (as the Bible instructed). Then the Presbytery turned Brother Glenn back over to the church as an ordained Minister of the Gospel.

Brother Glenn was called to assist the pastor at Gethsemane where he preached and carried out the ordinances of the church in the absences of the pastor. He visited various churches and preached, and was well liked by all who knew him.

So now, let us as wife, children, father, brothers, sister, and kindred, and friends, take up the Cross and press on until we too shall be called to that great homecoming where we will ever be with the redeemed of God.

ACUFF, BETSY WILLIAMS — age 78, of 6913 Wilson Drive, Knoxville, died 9:06 p.m. Wednesday in Fort Sanders Hospital. She was a native of Washburn in Grainger County and a member of Black Fox Primitive Baptist Church. Survivors: son, Conda of Knoxville; daughters, Mrs.

Dorothy Nicely, Mrs. Mary McMahan, Mrs. Betty Faye Dowing all of Knoxville, Mrs. Bertha Standifer, Louisville, Ky., Mrs. Eloise Purvis, Austell, Ga.; brothers, Jim of Knoxville, Elvin of Luttrell & Rector Williams, Maynardville; sisters, Mrs. Lilly Munsey, Knoxville, Mrs. Edna Shelton, Washburn; 12 grandchildren; 2 great-grandchildren. Funeral service 2:00 p.m. Saturday, Oak Grove Baptist Church, Washburn, Rev. Andy Vance, Rev. Gary Beeler officiating. Burial in Fox Cemetery. Pallbearers: Grandsons. Smith Funeral Home in charge.

LEE ALSTON -age 81, Rt. 2, New Tazewell, Tenn., passed away at 6:15 p.m. Wednesday, October 17 at the Claiborne County Hospital. Alston was a member of Myers Grove Primitive Baptist Church.

He is survived by a daughter, Mrs. Reva J. Golden of Tazewell, Tenn. three sons, Jesse A. Alston of Seymour, Tenn., Andrew Alston of Newport, Mich., and David Alston of Carlton, Mich.; and 23 grandchildren, 19 great-grandchildren, and two great-great-grandchildren.

Funeral services were held at 2 p.m. Saturday, October 20 at the First Baptist Church in New Tazewell. Dr. James Loy officiated. Burial was in the Drummonds Cemetery. Coffey Funeral Home was in charge of all arrangements.

CURT AUSMUS — was born October 3, 1905 at Speedwell, Tennessee and was a life time resident there. He joined Pleasant Hill Primitive Baptist Church and was baptised in August of 1974, where he lived a faithful member. He loved his church very much. He departed this life in March, 1982. He is survived by his wife and 3 children.

MRS. BERTHA SUSAN BORUFF — age 92 of Knoxville, Passed away Friday morning, January 22, 1982 at East Tennessee Baptist Hospital. She was a member of Rocky Dale Baptist Church since September 26, 1926. Survivors: sons, Luna L. Boruff, V.T. Boruff, Knoxville; grandsons, Bob and James Boruff; grandaughters, Mrs. Shirley Weaver, Knoxville, Miss Patricia Mayo, Livonia, Michigan; 5 great-grandchildren; Graveside services, were held Monday, 11:00 a.m. at Lynnhurst Cemetery, Dr. Calvin S. Metcalf officiating. Pallbearers: Lee Graves, Willie Houston, Gawain Houston, Charles Weaver, Dee S. Jones and Bart Monroe. The family received friends 7-9 p.m. Sunday at Mynatt's.

DONNIE CLAWSON — age 87, of Speedwell, passed away July 20 at his home. Survivors, sons, Elder Noble Lee Clawson, Speedwell, Ray Clawson, P.J. Clawson, Monroe, Michigan; daughters, Lou Bullard, Speedwell, Nadine Owens, Dayton, Ohio; 43 grandchildren, 59 great-grandchildren, 3 great-great-grandchildren; brothers, Sebern Clawson, Speedwell,

Hubert Clawson, LaFollette; sisters, Sarah Vennie Braden, Speedwell, Arletta Leach, Dayton, Ohio, and a host of relatives and friends.

He was preceded in death by his wife Elizabeth Foust Clawson, Sons, Howard, Hillard, Roy and Earl Clawson, Daughters, Edith Clawson, Mell Berry.

Funeral Services were held Friday at 2 p.m. at Bradens chapel Baptist Church with Elders J.C. Monday, LeRoy Braden officiating, songs by the church singers, with interment in the Braden Cemetery.

Pallbearers: James Monday, Mack Clawson, Bill Clawson, Randy Clawson, Gary Clawson, Boss Berry, Jr.

Reece Funeral Home was in charge.

CLAYTON HENRY DAVIS — age 76 of Corryton, passed away 8:30 p.m. Friday April 16, 1982 in St. Mary's Medical Center. Member of Black Fox Primitive Baptist Church. Survivors: wife, Reba K. Davis, Corryton; daughter, Mrs. Jay (Erma Lee) Wyrick, Talbott; sons, Edward and Ralph Davis, both of Corryton, Larry Davis, Concord; 6 grandchildren; sisters, Mrs. Bill (Goldie) Gose, Knoxville, Mrs. Conley (Lorene) Dyer, Luttrell; brothers, Rev. Odra and Fred Davis, both of Maynardville, Verlin Davis, Luttrell, Murphy and Austin Davis, both of Knoxville. Funeral service 3:30 p.m. Monday, Ailor's Chapel, Rev. Parnick Shelton, Rev. Herman Lakin & Rev. Gary Beeler officiating. Interment in Dyer Cemetery. Pallbearers: nephews. Ailors, Maynardville, in charge.

MRS. JULIA EARL, - age 58, of Red Hill of Speedwell, was born May 10, 1924, passed away at Doctors Hospital, Morristown, Tenn., July 22, 1982. She was a member of Meyers Grove Primitive Baptist Church. She is survived by her husband, Bill of Red Hill, sons, George W. of Bean Station, Billy of Red Hill, Ada Rowlette of Mississippi, Eva Jones of Middlesboro, Ky., brother Ray Treece of Red Hill, Junior, Ottie, Clifford Treece of Monroe, Michigan. She was preceded in death by her parents, Wiley and Nora Treece, and 2 brothers, Herzal and Lloyd. Funeral services were at 11:00 a.m. Saturday, July 24, 1982, at Red Hill Baptist Church with Red Hoskins and Rev. Hollis Simmons officiating. Burial was in Red Hill Cemetery. Pallbearers were Kenny Treece, Terry Evans, Gordon Bright, Franklin Wright, Joe and Roger Evans. Coffey Mortuary, Inc. in charge.

MRS. MAUDIE E. ELLISON — age 71, of Sharps Chapel, passed away December 19, 1981 in the Claiborne County Hospital. Her Husband, Lonnie Ellison preceded her in death. She was a member of Oak Grove Primitive Baptist Church. Survivors: daughter, Mrs. Ima Bridges, Sharps Chapel; 7 grandchildren; 6 great-grandchildren; sisters, Emma Brantley, LaFollette, Celia Marcum, Speedwell, Carrie Braden, Typhenia McKart, both of Monroe, Michigan; several nieces and nephews. Funeral services were at 2 p.m. Monday at Oak Grove Baptist Church, Rev. Johnny Robison and Elder J.C. Monday officiating. Interment in Church Cemetery.

Mrs. Mossie (Jones) Graves was born March 19, 1904, departed this life October 30, 1981. She was united in marriage to the late McKinley Graves in the year of 1920, who preceded her October 12, 1966. Also, she gave up one son, Loyd Milton Graves in World War II in the year 1945. She professed a hope in Christ and united with the church at Pleasant Hill March, 1942 and lived a loyal, faithful member until death. She leaves to mourn her loss four other children, 17 grandchildren, and 10 great-grandchildren; two sisters, and three half sisters, and a host of relatives and friends. She was laid to rest in the Ausmus Cemetery in Speedwell, Tennessee to await the glorious resurrection.

FRANKIE HAYES, — age 76, of Route 16, Tarwater, Knoxville, Tenn., died July 31, 1981 at Brakebill Nursing Home in Knoxville. She was a member of Myers Grove Baptist Church. She is survived by sisters, Mrs. Gertrude Zwack and Mrs. Dora Lundy, both of Monroe, Michigan; brothers, Willie Drummonds, New Tazewell, Carlie Drummonds, Monroe, Michigan, and Virgil Drummonds, Knoxville. Funeral Services were held at 11 a.m. Sunday, August 2, at Coffey Mortuary Chapel with Rev. Buster Clawson officiating. Singers were Goins Chapel Quartet. Burial was in Robin Cemetery. Pallbearers were Lloyd Drummonds, Bobby Drummonds, Toye Drummonds, Ronnie Drummonds, Lester Jones, and Dale Bolin.

MARY THELMA JOHNSON — age 82, passed away at her home at 5 a.m. Saturday April 24, 1982. She was preceded in death by her husband, the late James J. Johnson. Survivors: daughters, Miss Mildred Johnson, Sharps Chapel, Mrs. Riley (Ina) Cadle, Maryville; sons, Rina Johnson, Maryville, Winfred Johnson, London, Kentucky; sisters, Mrs. Rona Cook, Maynardville, Miss Ina Brewer, Knoxville; five grandchildren, four great-grandchildren: several nieces and nephews. Services were held at Oak Grove Primitive Baptist Church, where she was a member. Elder Clifford Brantley and Elder Albert Davis officiating. Interment, Johnson Cemetery.

> Mother, because you were so dear to us,
> Your memory will live on,
> Just as a flower's fragrance
> Lingers after it is gone.
> Mother, your kind endearing ways
> In thought are with us still,
> For in the hearts that love you,
> You live on, and always will.
> Oh! how we miss you.

> Mildred, Edna, Rina and Winfred

MRS. HELEN HARRELL JOHNSON — age 54, of Brown Gap Road, Knoxville, passed away 3:40 a.m. Sunday, January 17, 1982 at St Mary's Medical Center in Knoxville. She was a member of Rocky Dale Primitive Baptist Church. Survivors; husband, Estle Johnson; son and daughter-in-law, Ricky and Glenda Johnson; son, Ted Johnson of Halls; grand-daughter, April Johnson; sisters, Mrs. Thomas (Rose) Johnson of Mich., Mrs. Don (Peggy) Noe, Mrs. Martha Cottrill, both of California; brothers, Harvey Harrell of Corryton, William Thomas Harrell of Georgia, Frank, George and Bobby Harrell, all of Texas; father-in-law, Curtis Johnson of Halls. Funeral was at 2:00 p.m. on Tuesday at Ailor's Chapel, Elder Hugh Brummitt officiating. Interment in Monroe Cemetery. The family received friends 7-9 p.m. on Monday at Ailor's Mortuary in Maynardville.

MRS. NANNIE HEATHERLY KITTS — age 86, died on September 6, 1981. She was the oldest member of Davis Chapel Primitive Baptist Church. She was preceded in death by her husband, James Merton Kitts, and a son, Jesse L. Kitts. Survivors: daughters, Mrs. Evelyn McCoin, Cleveland, Tennessee, Mrs. Margie Bentley of Centerville, Ohio; son, George Kitts of Dayton, Ohio; sister, Elsie Sutton of Dayton, Ohio; brothers, James S. Heatherly of LaFollette, Tennessee and Homer Heatherly of Dayton, Ohio. Eight grandchildren and 4 great-grandchildren. Funeral services were held at Davis Chapel Church with Rev. Paul Heatherly officiating. Burial was in Sunrise Cemetery.

RUBLE MAPLES — age 62, Route 11, Thomas Weaver Road, Knoxville, passed away Monday evening March 29, 1982, at U.T. Hospital in Knoxville. He was a member and trustee of Rocky Dale Primitive Baptist Church, and a veteran of world War II. Survivors: wife, Clydia Maples; sons, Phillip Maples, Nashville, Gilbert Maples, Ocean Side, California; daughter, Carolyn Maples Lassiter, Knoxville; 6 grandchildren; mother, Mrs. Etha Maples, Sharps Chapel; sisters, Mrs. Ova Bridges, Maynardville, Mrs. Jean Cook, Sharps Chapel, Mrs. Ollie Oaks, Knoxville. Services 8:00 p.m. on Thursday at Mynatt's Chapel, Elder H.E. Brummitt, Elder Joe Bush officiating. Interment 11:00 a.m. Friday, in Greenwood Cemetery. Pallbearers: Steve Maples, David Roach, Mike Smith, Leon Ellison, Lewis Bridges and Walter Cook. The family received friends from 6:30-8:00 p.m. on Thursday at Mynatt's.

RUTH McNABB — Route 1, Philadelphia, Tennessee departed this life June 24, 1982. She was a member of Lenoir City Primitive Baptist Church. Survivors: daughter, Hazel Riddle, 3 sons, Curtis of Loudon. George of College Park, Ga., Carl of Newport News, Va.; brother Kyle Anderson; 12 grandchildren, 8 great-grandchildren. Funeral services June 27, 1982, at Clicks Chapel with Elder Howard Pippin, Rev. Ogle Wattenbarger, and Rev. Thomas Lynn officiating. Burial at Lakeview Cemetery.

FLOSSIE WEAVER MILLER — age 82, was born October 31, 1899, passed away suddenly at her home on Tuesday, May 18, 1982. She was a member of Oak Grove Primitive Baptist Church of Sharp's Chapel, Tennessee. She was the daughter of the late C.B. and Louisa Brantley Weaver. She was preceded in death by her husband Andrew Curtis Miller and a daughter, Velma Hankins. Survivors: daughters, Dorothy Beason, with whom she made her home and Evelyn Holloway of Maynardville; sons, Rev. Lee Miller of Knoxville, Chalmer and Delone Miller of Maynardville; 19 grandchildren and 28 great-grandchildren; brother, Claude Weaver of Minnesota; Pallbearers: Grandson, Bill Holloway, Ronnie, Donnie and Wayne Miller, Billy Hankins and Jeffrey Lee. Funeral Services were held Thursday, May 20, 1982 at Milan Baptist Church with Rev. Ralph Cox officiating. Interment in Union Church Cemetery near Maynardville.

We feel Our loss is her Eternal gain.

                                                    Written by Children.

NORA S. OLIVER — age 68, of 2126 Newcut Road, died Saturday morning in Morristown-Hamblen Hospital following a lingering illness. She was a member of Noeton Primitive Baptist Church.   Survivors include her husband, Ted J. Oliver of Morristown, sons, Ted J. Oliver, Jr. of Kingsport and Don C. of Rogersville; daughters, Mrs. Hal (Dot) Sams of Morristown and Mrs. Darrell (Doris) Patterson of Ivenhoe, Virginia; brothers, Mack Shepherd of Georgia; 17 grandchildren and three great-grandchildren. Services at 2:00 p.m. Monday in Noeton Primitive Baptist Church with Elder John Oliver officiating. Burial in Church Cemetery.

MISS DELTA A. OUSLEY — age 88, of Warner-Robbins, Georgia, passed away April 18, 1982 at the home of her niece and husband, Mr. and Mrs. William Mitchell. She was a member of Oak Grove Baptist Church in Union County. Survivors: sisters, Mrs. K. D. Lively of Seymour, Texas, Mrs. Victor Edwards of Kokomo, Indiana, Mrs. H. E. Anderson of Knoxville, Mrs. E. B. Edgemon of Ten Mile; brothers, O. C. Ousley of Maynardville, Deward Ousley of Briceville, W. T. Ousley of Kokomo, Indiana; many nieces and nephews. Funeral services 2 p.m. Wednesday, Gentry-Griffey Chapel, Rev. Ray F. Brown officiating. Interment in Bethel Cemetery, Emory Road.

WILLIAM (LEE) PARRIS — age 78, of Oak Street, Lenoir City, and Care Inn Nursing Home departed from this life on Thursday, January 7, 1982 at Loudon County Memorial Hospital. He united whith the Lenoir City Primitive Baptist Church in September of 1938, and was an active member as long as his health permitted; serving the church for several years as custodian. He was survived by his wife Mrs. Mary Colling Parris; sisters, Mrs. Stella Stewart of Cleveland, Tennessee and Mrs. Melba Diggs of Calumet City, Illinois; brother, Cecil Parris of Oliver Springs, Tennessee; several nieces and nephews. Funeral services were held at 2:30 January 10, 1982 at Click Funeral Home Chapel with Elder Howard Pippin officiating. Brother Parris was laid to rest in the Lenoir City Cemetery.

DORIS KECK ROSSON, born August 8, 1920, passed away July 23, 1982, at the age of 61 years, 11 months and 15 days. She was a member of the Pleasant Point Primitive Baptist Church. Survivors: husband, Elder Claude Rosson; sons, Danty and Marvin Rosson; grandchildren, Ronnie, Amy, Misty, and Chad Rosson; daughter-in-laws, Tiny and Pat Rosson, all of New Tazewell, Tennessee; sisters, Mrs. Nell Dooley, Mrs. Blache Meyers, Mrs. Hettie Cupp; brothers, Lewis, Lloyd, Walter, Jackie and Chester Keck, all of New Tazewell, Tennessee; several nieces, nephews and a host of relatives and friends. Funeral services were held at 11:00 a.m. Sunday, July 25, 1982, at Coffey Mortuary Chapel with Elder Larry Anderson, Elder J. C. Monday officiating. Burial in Keck Cemetery. Singers were the Shoffner Family. Pallbearers: R. M. and Milton Dooley, Roy, Hoy, Terry, Michael, Mitchell and Dennis Keck and Randall Meyers.

STEVEN C. SANDLIN — age 22, Blue Spring Hollow Road, Speedwell, died suddenly Sunday, May 30, 1982, in a swimming accident in Norris Lake. Survivors: mother and step-father, Mr. & Mrs. Eugene Braden of Speedwell; father and step-mother, Mr. & Mrs. Herbert Sandlin of Covington, Kentucky; sister, Mrs. Sharon Thomason of Niota, Tennessee. Services 2:00 p.m. Wednesday at Braden's Chapel Baptist Church, Elder J. C. Monday, Elder Buster Clawson and Rev. Bill Braden officiating. Interment in Braden Cemetery. Family will receive friends 7-9 p.m. Tuesday June 1, at Roach Mortuary, LaFollette. Services June 2, 1982 at Braden's Chapel.

DELLA RALEY WEAVER — age 91, Dandridge Tennessee, passed away 6:10 p.m. Wednesday June 16, 1982 at Jefferson County Nursing Home, Dandridge Tennessee after a lingering illness. Widow of the late Marcus Austin Weaver. She was born December 13, 1890 in Union County, Tennessee. A daughter of LaFayette and Sarah Oakes Raley. She married Marcus A. Weaver, February 14, 1907. He died in 1957. Member of Rocky Dale Primitive Baptist Church of Corryton, Tennessee; preceded in death by infant daughter, Inis Weaver; son Raymond; a grandson, three brothers and two sisters. Survivors: daughters, Opal Wills, Dandridge, Tennessee, Felcie Stroh, Sibley, Illinois, Jessie Finn, Mesa, Arizona; 7 grandchildren; 11 great-grandchildren; 3 great-great-grandchildren; brother, Raymond Raley, Maynardville, Tennessee; several nieces and nephews. Funeral 8:00 p.m. Thursday at Farrars Chapel in Dandridge, Elder Hugh Brummitt officiating. Graveside service, Friday , 4 p.m. in Drummer Township Cemetery at Gibson City, Illinois, Rev. Donald Swenson officiating. In lieu of flowers, memorials may be made to Rocky Dale Baptist Church.

STATISTICAL TABLE

CHURCHES	DELEGATES	Restored	Rec'd. by Letter	Baptism	Relationship	Dismiss by Letter	Excluded	Deceased	Total Membership	Printing Minutes	REGULAR MEETING TIME	COMMUNION TIME
BLACK FOX	Bros. Arthur Terry, Bennie Capps Sisters: Mary Terry, Mary Ruth Capps	0	0	0	0	0	1	3	75	$25.00	Second Saturday and Sunday Fourth Sunday Night	Sunday following Second Saturday in June
BRADEN'S CHAPEL	Letter Received No Delegates Present	0	0	2	4	0	3	1	146	$25.00	First Saturday Night and Sunday	Sunday following First Saturday in July
BRANTLEY'S CHAPEL	Elders Clifford Brantley, Jerry McBee Bros: Rina Johnson, Eskle Boruff, Chester Hembree, Everett Brantley, Cyrus McBee, Jeff Ellison, Thurman Razor, William Irwin Sisters: Barsha Brantley, Hazel Johnson, Edith Hembree, Mildred Brantley, Lela Ellison, Vicki Irwin, Vannessa Irwin, Suzzette Irwin, Josie Razor, Burnice McBee	0	0	3	2	0	4	0	110	$35.00	Second Saturday Night Every Sunday and Sunday Night	Sunday following Second Saturday in July
DAVIS CHAPEL	Bros: Orice McCarty, Clyde Lynch Sisters: Mollie McCarty, Pearl Lynch Ollie Welch	0	0	1	1	0	0	2	113	$35.00	Third Saturday Night Every Sunday and Sunday Night	Third Sunday in June
GETHSEMANE	Bros: Tom Carmichael Sisters: June Carmichael, Myrtle Cook	0	0	2	2	0	0	1	38	$25.00	Every Sunday except the First Sunday	Sunday following Fourth Saturday in May & Oct.
GIBSON STATION	Elders: William Rhymer, Spurgeon Thompson, Joe Irwin Bros: Curtis Ball Sisters: Karen Rhymer, Evelyn Irving, Lucille Ball, Dorothy Johnson	0	0	0	0	0	1	0	78	$40.00	First Saturday and Saturday Night Every Sunday and Sunday Night	Sunday following Second Saturday in June
HEADRICK CHAPEL	Elders: Robert Walker Bros: Clyde Abbott, Bill Cook Sisters: Grace Abbott, Geraldine Abbott, Angie Abbott	0	0	0	0	0	0	0	113	$25.00	First Sunday of each Month	Sunday following First Saturday in May & Oct.

357

Church	Officers / Delegates								Members	Dues	Services	Conference
KIRKWOOD	Elders: H.E. Brummitt Bros.: M. E. Evans Sisters: Ruby Brummitt, Frieda Sharp, Velma Evans, Dottie Cook, Dola Webb, Alice Powers	0	1	0	0	0	2	0	105	$40.00	Every Sunday Morning	Last Sunday in April
LENOIR CITY	Elder: Howard Pippin Bros: Raymond Wilkerson, Henry Chamberlain, Hubert Spoon Sisters: Estie Chamberlain, Annie Spoon	0	0	0	0	1	2	2	126	$35.00	Every Sunday and Sunday Night	Wednesday night before Easter Sunday. Third Sunday in October
MYERS GROVE	Letter Received No Delegate Present	0	0	1	0	0	0	2	77	$25.00	Second Saturday Night and Sunday. Fourth Saturday Night and Sunday	Sunday following Fourth Saturday in May
NOETON	Elder: John Oliver Bros: Charlie Collins, Carroll Oliver, Tim Oliver Sisters: Dora Collins	0	0	1	0	0	0	1	40	$20.00	First Sunday of each month. Third Saturday and Sunday of each month	Sunday following Third Saturday in May and Sept.
OAK GROVE	Elder: Johnnie Atkins Sister: Frances Eastridge	0	0	6	1	2	1	6	332	$25.00	First Saturday Night and Sunday. Third Sunday	Sunday following First Saturday in May
PLEASANT HILL	Elders: Albert Davis Larry Anderson, James H. Branscomb Sister: Audra Davis	0	1	0	0	0	2	2	100	$35.00	Fourth Saturday Morning and Saturday night. Fourth Sunday. Every Sunday night.	Sunday following Fourth Saturday in June
PLEASANT POINT	Letter Received No Delegate Present	0	0	0	0	0	0	1	106	$20.00	First Saturday night and Sunday. Third Sunday	Sunday following First Saturday in July
ROCKY DALE	Elders: Parnick Shelton, William Berry Bros: Curt Johnson, Herbert Graves, Donald Sharp Sisters: Wilma Shelton, Trula Berry, Dottie Sharp	0	0	1	3	0	0	4	118	$40.00	Every Sunday and Sunday Night	Sunday following Second Saturday in May

CHURCH	COUNTY	PASTOR	CLERK	ADDRESS
Black Fox	Grainger	Elder Larry Anderson	Bennie Capps	P.O. Box 91, Maynardville, TN 37807
Braden's Chapel	Union	Elder Noble Clawson Elder J. C. Monday, Asst.	Jimmie B. Edwards Phyllis Wilson, Asst.	Speedwell, TN 37870 Speedwell, TN 37870
Brantley's Chapel	Blount	Elder Clifford Brantley Elder Jerry McBee, Asst.	D. C. Brantley n Jennifer Johnson, Asst.	2020 Bittle Heights, Maryville, TN 37801 1217 Brown Schook Road, Maryville, TN 37801
Davis Chapel	Campbell	Elder William Berry Elder Parnick Shelton, Asst.	Katheryn Angel Sondra Wright, Asst.	Rt. 4, Box 80, LaFollette, TN 37766 1256 Middlesboro Hwy., LaFollette, TN 37766
Gethsemane	Knox	Elder Walter Lyons	Tom Carmichael	729 Frank St., Knoxville, TN 37919
Gibson Station	Lee, Va.	Elder William Rhymer Elder Spureon Thompson, Asst.	Dorothy Johnson Shirley Sandifur, Asst.	Rt. 2, Box 114, Ewing, Va. 24248 Rt. 2 - Harrogate, TN
Headrick Chapel	Sevier	Elder Walter Lyons	Clyde Abbott, Sr.	Rt. 7, Box 288 - Sevierville, TN 37862
Kirkwood	Knox	Elder William Berry Elder Parnick Shelton, Asst.	Mrs. Alice Powers Mrs. Sarah Jean Harmon, Asst.	7525 Temple Acres Drive Knoxville, TN 37918 7120 Chermont Circle, Knoxville, TN 37918
Lenoir City	Loudon	Elder Howard Pippin	Thelma Brown	319 Bussell Ferry Rd., Lenoir City, TN 37771
Meyer's Grove	Claiborne	Elder Noble Clawson	Bonnie Miracle Harold Cupp, Asst.	Rt. 2, Box 91, New Tazewell, TN 37825 Rt. 2, Box 166, New Tazewell, TN 37825
Naeton	Grainger	Elder John Oliver	Carroll Oliver Bessie Collins	Rt. 2, Box 512 , Bean Station, TN 37708 Rt. 5, Morristown, TN 37814
Oak Grove	Union	Elder J. C. Monday Elder J~ry McBee, Asst.	Betty P. Sharp Betty Shoffner	Sharps Chapel, TN 37866 Sharps Chapel, TN 37866
Pleasant Hill	Claiborne	Elder William Rhymer Elder Albert Davis, Asst.	William Branscomb Dennis Edwards	Speedwell, TN 37870 Speedwell, TN 37870
Pleasant Point	Claiborne	Elder Larry Anderson	Elder Claude Rosson Beatrice Williams	Rt. 4, New Tazewell, TN 37825 Rt. 2, Box 156, Rogersville, TN 37857
Rocky Dale	Knox	Elder Hugh Brummitt	Edward Collett Dennis Branson, Asst.	Rt. 1, Box 17, Luttrell, TN 37779 Rt. 13, 4633 Marshall Dr. Knoxville, TN 37918

Minutes 1983

OF THE
ONE HUNDRED SIXTY-THIRD SESSION
OF THE

POWELL VALLEY ASSOCIATION
OF PRIMITIVE BAPTIST

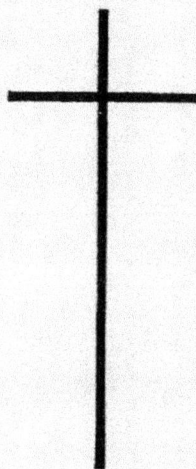

HELD WITH THE SISTER CHURCH AT
GIBSON STATION
LEE COUNTY, VIRGINIA
AUGUST 19, 20, and 21, 1983

THE ONE HUNDRED SIXTY-THIRD SESSION
OF THE POWELL VALLEY ASSOCIATION
OF
PRIMITIVE BAPTIST
HELD WITH THE SISTER CHURCH AT GIBSON STATION
LEE COUNTY, VIRGINIA
AUGUST 19, 20, 21, 1983

NEXT SESSION WILL BE HELD WITH THE SISTER CHURCH
AT
BRANTLEY'S CHAPEL
BLOUNT COUNTY, TENNESSEE
TO BEGIN ON FRIDAY BEFORE THE THIRD SATURDAY
IN AUGUST 1984
AT 10:30 A.M.

ELDER WILLIAM RHYMER WILL DELIVER THE
INTRODUCTORY SERMON, AND ELDER LARRY ANDERSON
WILL BE THE ALTERNATE

OFFICERS

ELDER HUGH BRUMMITT   MODERATOR
1329 BROWN AVENUE, KNOXVILLE, TENN., PHONE 546-7700
ELDER CLIFFORD BRANTLEY   ASSISTANT MODERATOR
809 BROWN SCHOOL RD. MARYVILLE, TENN., PHONE 982-3875
BENNIE CAPPS   CLERK
P.O. BOX 91, MAYNARDVILLE, TENN., PHONE 992-5571
RINA JOHNSON   ASSISTANT CLERK
1217 BROWN SCHOOL ROAD, MARYVILLE, TENN., PHONE 983-2774

ARTICLES OF FAITH

Article 1. We believe in only one true living God, as He is revealed to us in the Holy Scriptures - Father, Son, and Holy Ghost.

Article 2. We believe that the Scriptures of the old and new Testaments are the words of God and the only rule of all-saving knowledge and obedience.

Article 3. We believe in the doctrine of election according to the foreknowledge of God.

Article 4. We believe in the doctrine of original sin.

Article 5. We believe in man's impotency to rescue himself from the fallen state he is in, by his own will or ability.

Article 6. We believe that sinners are justified in the sight of God only by the imputed righteousness of Jesus Christ.

Article 7. We believe the elect, according to the foreknowledge of God will be called, converted, regenerated, and sanctified by the Holy Spirit.

Article 8. We believe the saints will persevere and never fall finally away.

Article 9. We believe that baptism and the Lord's Supper are ordinances of Jesus Christ, and that true believers are the only subject of these ordinances, and that the true mode of baptism is by immersion. We believe also that feet washing is an example of Jesus Christ and should be kept by his disciples until his second coming.

Article 10. We believe in the Resurrection of the dead and the General Judgement.

Article 11. We believe that the punishment of the wicked will be everlasting and that the joys of the righteous will be eternal.

Article 12. We believe that no minister has the right to administer the ordinances, except those who have been regularly baptized and called of God, and come under the imposition of hands of the presbytery.

Friday, August 19, 1983

The one hundred and sixty-third session of the Powell Valley Association of Primitive Baptists met with the sister church at Gibson Station in Lee County, Virginia on August 19, 20, and 21, 1983.

After Bro. Donald Sharp led the congregation in singing, "Hold to God's Unchanging Hands", "How Firm a Foundation" and "Amazing Grace", the Moderator, Elder Hugh Brummitt welcomed the congregation and pleaded for peace and love to abide through the entire Association and called for prayer by Elder Spurgeon Thompson of Gibson Station Church.

Following prayer, Elder Clifford Brantley of Brantley's Chapel delivered the introductory sermon and gave a very good sermon from the 9th chapter of Acts, second verse, using as his text "Of This Way".

After the introductory sermon, they sang a song and were dismissed in prayer by Elder Howard Pippin of Lenoir City Church. The Association was to reconvene after a 15 minute recess.

After recess, the crowd reassembled in the church; Elder Bill Berry led the congregation in "I'll Fly Away"; Moderator Elder Hugh Brummitt read the entire 23rd chapter of Psalms, then called for prayer by Elder Parnick Shelton of Rocky Dale Church.

The Moderator then asked for the order of business for the following transactions:

1st: Called for letters of the Sister Churches to be presented to the clerk for reading. Fourteen (14) were received.

2nd: The letters were presented and read and motion approved that the delegates be seated.

3rd: The Moderator called for anyone present from any of the Sister Churches not named as a delegate and desired to be seated as such to come forward and give the clerk their name and the name of their church. Seven came. Bro. Bill Good from Myers' Grove; Bro. Cecil Godfrey, Michael Beal and Scott Campbell from Gethsemane: Sister Lottie Berry from Pleasant Hill; Sister Dola Webb from Halls and Sister Alvada Dykes from Oak Grove.

4th: Called for petitionary letter if there should be one. There was none.

5th: Motion approved that the Association re-elect Elder Hugh Brummitt as Moderator and Elder Clifford Brantley as Assistant Moderator for the ensuing year.

6th: Motion approved that Brother Bennie Capps be re-elected Clerk

363

and Brother Rina Johnson be re-elected Assistant Clerk for the ensuing year.

7th Motion was approved that we empower Elder Brummitt to appoint all the committees to serve this session.

8th The Moderator, having been empowered to do so, named the committee as follows:

Committee on Arrangements: Bro. Orice McCarty, Bro. Bill Good, Bro. Arthur Terry

Committe on Preaching: Bro. Elwood Evans, Bro. Coy Edwards, Bro. Curtis Ball

Committee on Request: Bro. Cecil Godfrey, Bro. Donald Sharp, Elder Jimmy Campbell

Committee on Finance: Bro. Hubert Spoon, Elder Howard Pippin, Elder Spurgeon Thompson

9th: Called for the finances to be turned in to the Finance Committee.

10th: The committees all having been appointed and accepted, the Association moved to adjourn until 10:30 Saturday morning. They sang a song and was dismissed in prayer by Elder Joe Irving of Gibson Station.

Saturday, August 20, 1983

At the appointed hour of 10:30 Saturday, and at the sound of singing, the Association reassembled to a full house.

After singing, the Assistant Moderator, Elder Clifford Brantley gave a very spiritual and uplifting talk and then read verses 4-13 of the 15th chapter of Romans, then called for prayer by Elder John Oliver of Noeton Church.

After prayer, the Moderator called the Association to order for the remainder of the business:

1st: The Moderator called for any letters from Sister Church at Noeton.

2nd. Motion was approved to accept the letter and seat the named delegates.

3rd: The Moderator called for anyone from any of the churches who were present and desired to be seated as delegate to come forward. None came.

4th: The Moderator then called for the report of the Committee on Arrangements who submitted the following Arrangements which were accepted and the committee released.

Report on Arrangements:

Call for roll call of delegates
Call for report of Committee on Preaching
Call for report of Committee on Request
Call for report of Committee on Finance

Decide how many minutes to have printed, who shall supervise the printing and distribution of same, and how much he shall receive for services.

Who shall preach the introductory sermon and who shall be the alternate.

Respectfully submitted,
Bro. Orice McCarty, Bro. Bill Good, Bro. Arthur Terry

5th Called the roll call of delegates of all the Sister Churches and check the absentees.

6th: Called for the report of the Committee on Preaching:

Friday night:	Elder Bill Berry
	Elder Jimmy Branscomb
Saturday morning:	Elder Bill Rhymer
	Elder Hugh Brummitt
Saturday night:	Elder Larry Anderson
	Elder Nelson Jones
Sunday morning:	Elder Parnick Shelton
	Elder Spurgeon Thompson

Respectfully submitted,
Bro. Curtis Ball
Bro. Coy Edwards
Bro. Elwood Evans

7th: Called for the report of the Committee on Request which was accepted and the committee was released.

Report of Committee on Request:

We the Committee on Request, request that we have 1,100 minutes printed and that the clerk supervise the printing and distribution of same and that he receive $135.00 for his services. We also request that Elder Walter Lyons write a circular letter to be printed in the minutes; also, that the next session of the Association be held with the Sister Church of Brantley's Chapel in Maryville, Tennessee to begin on Friday before the third Saturday in August, 1984, and may the love and peace that is here continue throughout the remainder of this Association.

Respectfully submitted,
Bro. Cecil Godfrey, Elder Jimmy Campbell, Bro. Donald Sharp

8th: Called for the Committee on Finance which was accepted and the committee was released.

Report of Finance Committee:

Black Fox	$25.00
Braden's Chapel	35.00
Brantley's Chapel	35.00
Davis Chapel	45.00
Gethsemane	35.00
Gibson Station	40.00
Headricks Chapel	25.00
Halls	40.00
Lenoir City	35.00
Meyer's Grove	25.00
Noeton	20.00
Oak Grove	25.00
Pleasant Hill	35.00
Pleasant Point	20.00
Rocky Dale	40.00
	$480.00
Donations	20.00
	$500.00
Balance in bank	177.00
	677.00
Expense for 1983	560.00
Balance in bank	$117.00

9th: Motion approved that we grant the request of the committee and 1,100 minutes printed and the clerk to receive $135.00 for his services.

10th: Motion approved that the next session of the Association be held with the Sister Church at Brantley's Chapel in Blount County, Tennessee to begin on Friday before the third Saturday in August, 1984, at 10:30 a.m.

11th: Motion approved that Elder Walter Lyons write the circular letter for the 1984 minutes.

12th: Motion approved that Elder Bill Rhymer deliver the introductory sermon and Elder Larry Anderson be the alternate.

13th: Motion approved that the churches of the Powell Valley Association extend to the church and the people of Gibson Station our heartfelt thanks and our prayers for the love, fellowship, kindness and food while we were here with you. May the Good Lord bless and keep you is our prayers.

14th: Motion to adjourn, trusting the Lord to permit us to meet again with the Sister Church at Brantley's Chapel in Blount County, Tennessee on Friday before the third Saturday in August, 1984, at 10:30 a.m.

Dismissed in prayer by Elder Albert Davis.

Elder Hugh Brummitt, Moderator
Elder Clifford Brantley, Asst.Moderator
Brother Bennie Capps, Clerk
Brother Rina Johnson, Asst. Clerk

Sunday, August 21, 1983

After singing, and prayer, Elder Parnick Shelton preached a wonderful sermon from the 18th Chapter of Matthew, using as his text "Kingdom of God, Kingdom of Heaven and Works". Then Elder Spurgeon Thompson preached a very spiritual message from the 9th Chapter of Hebrew, verses 24th, 25th, and 26th. The congregation was dismissed in prayer by Brother Orice McCarty.

SUMMARY

We are blessed with a fine group of ministers as was illustrated by those who had the opportunity to preach. We regret that time will not permit more of them to preach when we meet with the Association.

On Friday, Elder Clifford Brantley delivered the introductory sermon, and gave a very good sermon from the 9th chapter of Acts, second verse using as his text "Of This Way".

Friday night sermons were delivered by Elder William Berry who preached from the 3rd chapter of Second Peter, verse 9. He was then followed by Elder James Branscomb who used as his text, "Spirit."

Then on Saturday morning, Elder William Rhymer preached from the 24th and 29th chapter of Genesis which was a very spiritual and uplifting sermon. He was then followed by Elder Hugh Brummitt who delivered a wonderful message from the second chapter of Eph., Verse 1.

Saturday night message was by Elder Larry Anderson and Elder Nelson Jones.

Sunday morning, Elder Parnick Shelton preached a wonderful message from the 18th chapter of Matthew. He was then followed by Elder Spurgeon Thompson who used verses 24, 25, and 26 from the 9th chapter of Hebrews. Both sermons were very uplifting.

Special Announcements:

Halls Primitive Baptist Church was formerly known as Kirkwood Primitive Baptist Church. The church was relocated and renamed since the last meeting of the Association. All church officers remain the same.

Brantley's Chapel has their Sunday night services every Sunday night at 7 p.m. in the summer months and at 6 p.m. in the winter months.

Rocky Dale has changed their Communion Services to the Sunday after the third Saturday in May.

The following four churches asked for the Association for 1984. Black Fox, Brantley's Chapel, Lenoir City, and Oak Grove.

367

CIRCULAR LETTER

I can not put on paper what is in my heart to say. When I was called to preach I became a servant unto all, as Jesus taught.

We are persuaded that those things which we have learned have brought to our souls the assurance that this is the way and we are most happy to walk in it. We further consider of whom we have learned these truths which we hold dear. Those that come before us and know the Lord by patient continuance in well doing, seeking glory, honor, immortality, and eternal life. Many of those have passed on to their reward, having received the end of their faith even the salvation of their soul. They believed the promise of God, were persuaded by them and confession that they were strangers and pilgrims on this earth. By their faith, declared plainly that they looked for a heavenly country wherefore God is not ashamed to be called their god.

We too are searching for the same country.

May God bless
Elder J. C. Monday

Obituaries

Dora Wilson Brantley - age 87, Route 7, Shady Lane, Knoxville, TN went home to be with Jesus on Tuesday, 9:15 p.m., October 12, 1982.

She was a member of Kirkwood Primitive Baptist Church. She was preceded in death by her husbank: Jahue Brantley; two daughters: Roena Brantley Hall and Evoline Brantley Ezell.

Survivors: one son; Rev. Trumer Brantley, Greenville, Tn.: four daughters: Mrs. Elwood (Velma) Evans, Mrs. Vance (Irene) Harmon, Mrs. Charles (Vandella) Weaver, all of Knoxville and Mrs. Steve (Wanda) Booth of Pensacola, Fla.; one brother, Clondis Wilson of Knoxville; 20 grandchildren, 26 great-grandchildren, 4 great-great-grandchildren; several nieces and nephews.

Sadly missed by family and friends

Miss Edith Brantley, of Route 1, Speedwell, was born May 8, 1926 and departed this life March 20, 1983 at the age of 56 years at Claiborne County Hospital.

She professed faith in Christ and was a member of Pleasant Hill Baptist Church.

She was a retired school teacher and a member of Powell Valley OES 484. She was preceded in death by her father, James Brantley.

Survivors: mother, Mrs. Ada Brantley, Speedwell; brothers, and sisters-in-law, Odus and Dorothy Brantley, of Speedwell, Ottis and Frances Brantley of Harrogate; one nephew, James Edward Brantley, Speedwell, and a host of relatives .nd friends.

Funeral services were held at 2 p.m. Wednesday, March 23, 1983 at the Red Hill Baptist Church with Rev. Hollis Simmons and Elder Clifford Brantley officiating. Singers were the Red Hill Church Choir. Burial in the Red Hill Cemetery.

Charity Ellen "Hopper" Carr, age 98, of New Tazewell, passed away September 5, 1981 at the home of her daughter in New Tazewell. She was born September 14, 1883, and was the daughter of Daniel Milton and Elizabeth "Dunn" Hopper.

She was preceded in death by her husband, James M. Carr and one son, Gillis Carr. She was a member of Cave Springs Primitive Baptist Church.

Survivors: daughter, Mrs. Arlis (Rubie) Collins, New Tazewell, son, Elbert Carr of Middlesboro, Kentucky; three granchildren, James, Tazewell, Mrs.Thelma Carr, Middlesboro, Ky.; 7 great-grandchildren; 1 great-great-grandchild.

Funeral services were held 10 a.m. Tuesday, September 8 at Coffey Funeral Home with Rev. Rupert Hopper and Elder Albert Davis Officiating. Burial in Carr Cemetery in POwell Valley.

Sister Nora Lela Chilcote, age 80, died on February 6, 1983. She was a faithful member of Davis Chapel Primitive Baptist Church in LaFollette, Tennessee. Funeral Services and burial were in Terre Haute, Indiana.

Sister Hettie Dossett Cox, age 70, of Davis Chapel, LaFollette, Tenn., died July 8, 1983 at the LaFollette Nursing Home. She was the widow of Richard Cox and a member of Davis Chapel Primitive Baptist Church with

Elders Bill Berry and Parnick Shelton officiating. Burial was in Sunrise Cemetery.

Survivors include one sister, Mrs. Asilee White of LaFollette; brothers, John and C. E. Dossett, both of LaFollette; step-mother, Ellie Dossett of LaFollette; step-daughter, Mrs. Dora Hatmaker of Lake City, one step-son, Emmit Cox of Jacksboro.

Tishie Cox, age 84, Sharps Chapel, passed away May 21, 1983 at St. Mary's Medical Center. She was a member of Oak Grove Primitive Baptist Church.

Survivors: daughters, Mrs. Clayton (Edna) Sharp and Mrs. Theodore (Georgia) Ellison, both of Sharps Chapel, Mrs. Fred (Opal) Blevins of New Tazewell,, Mrs. Bill (Maggie) Lawson of Alcoa, Mrs. Charles (Mae) Duncan, of California, Mrs. Ruth McMillan of Louisville, Tenn.; sons, Robert of Murfreesboro, John H. and Daniel, both of Monroe Michigan; sisters, Mrs. Sarah Tinnell, Mrs. Lillian Maddox and Mrs. Louetta Birchfield, all of Knoxville; brothers, John H., Huey, and Ruble, all of Monroe, Michigan, Charles and Devine of Knoxville, and Theodore of New Tazewell; 36 grandchildren, 58 great-grandchildren and 4 great-great-grandchildren.

Funeral services were held at 2:00 p.m. Tuesday, May 24, at the Oak Grove Primitive Baptist Church with Elder J. C. Monday and Elder Jerry McBee officiating.. Interment was in the Cox Cemetery.

Jefferson Monroe Ellison, born Oct. 25, 1907 at Sharps Chapel, Union County, Tennessee, departed this life June 20, 1983. He professed faith in Jesus Christ at an early age and later joined Oak Grove Primitive Baptist Church and was baptized. After moving to Blount County from Union County he was instrumental in organizing Brantley Chapel Primitive Baptist Church of which he was a Charter Member and Trustee.

Feb. 3, 1929 he married Lela Mae Sharp of Sharps Chapel, Tenn. and to this union were born four children: three daughters, Helen, Rebecca, and Brenda; one son, J. M.; daughter Rebecca preceded him in death in 1944.

Surviving, other than his wife and children are: grandchildren, Kim and Shane Ellison, Stephanie, Alison and Michael Adams; daughter-in-law, Linda Ellison; sons-in-law, Odell Carpenter and Lawrence Adams; sisters, Sarah Brantley and Ottie McBee of Maryville, Bessie McCarty and Dinah Barnard of Sharps Chapel, Irene bridges of Nashville; brothers, U.J. Ellison of Walton, Ind., and Swan Ellison of Sharps Chapel.

Elbert L. (Ebb) Moore, age 72, of 174 North 400 East, Kokomo, Ind., formerly of Sharps Chapel, passed away 1 a.m. on a Monday. He professed faith in Christ at an early age. Preceded in death by parents, Mr.and Mrs. LaFayette Moore.

Survivors: wife, Belle Moore; daughter, Mrs. Beecher (Georgia) Cole; granddaughter, Mrs. David (Mary Lee) Edwards; great-grandson, Joel, all of Kokomo, Ind.; sisters, Mrs. Carsie Holt of New Tazewell, Mrs. Reaford Parker of Maybee, Michigan, Mrs. Edith Houston of Knoxville; brothers, Fred Moore of Maynardville, Earl Moore of Powell, Tennessee;

several nieces and nephews; Funeral 11 a.m. a Thursday, Oak Grove Baptist Church, Elder Clifford Brantley, Elder J. C. Monday, Rev. Robert Williams officiating. Interment in Shoffner Cemetery.

Thomas Herman Munsey, age 85 was born December 3, 1897 in Grainger County, Tennessee and passed away February 3, 1983 at his home or Branville Road, Knoxville, Tennessee, after a lingering illness. Mr. Munsey was a member of Kirkwood Primitive Baptist Church.

Funeral Services were held at McCarty Mortuary on February 7, 1983, Elder William Berry and Parnick Shelton officiating. Burial was in Cabbage Cemetery, Grainger County, Tennessee.

Nora S. Oliver, age 68, of 2126 Newcut Road, Morristown, died Saturday morning in Morristown Hamblen Hospital following a lingering illness. She was a member of Noeton Primitive Baptist Church.

Survivors: husband, Ted J. Oliver of Morristown; sons, Ted, J. Jr. of Kingsport, and Don C. of Rogersville; daughters, Mrs. Hal (Dot) Sams, Mrs. James (Donna) Hodge, Mrs. Jerrie D. Southerland of Morristown, and Mrs. Darrell (Dorris) Patterson of Ivenhoe, Virginia; brother, Mack Shepherd of Georgia; 17 grandchildren, 3 great-grandchildren.

Services were at 2 p.m. on a Monday in Noeton Primitive Baptist Church with Elder John Oliver Officiating. Burial in Church Cemetery.

Susie H. Oliver, Bean Station, Tennessee, Rt. 1, was born Feb. 18, 1904, departed this life March 7, 1983. She was married to the late James OLiver, May 17, 1930.

She leaves to mourn her departure: daughter and son-in-law, Mary and Nelson Atkins of Bean Station; sister, Edith Bunch, Morristown; nieces, nephews, and friends.

She professed a hope in Christ at an early age and joined Noeton Primitive Baptist Church.

Funeral services at Noeton Church with Elder Johnny Atkins and Elder John Oliver officiating. Burial in Church Cemetery.

Mother you are no longer with us on this earth anymore;
Mother, you did not go alone, for part of us went with you the day God called you home, where there is no pain, all happiness.
The love we shared together are the memories we hold dear.
By the grace of God we will meet you on that beautiful shore,
Where there will be no tears to dim the eyes. We will live there forever in the sweet by and by.
Peaceful be thy rest, Dear Mother.

Forever missed by daughter
Mrs. Mary Atkins

Harley Fred Parris, age 78, Lenoir City, Tennessee, passed away April 20, 1983 at U.T. Hospital. He united with the Lenoir City Primitive Baptist Church in May 1948 and remained a member until his death.

He was preceded in death by a brother, Joe. Survivors: wife, Mabel Graves Parris; daughters, Marion Anderson of Chicago, Ill. and Frankie

Brown of Lenoir City; son, Fred Parris, Jr. of W. Chicago, Ill; five grand-children; sister Thelma Hattley of Lenoir City; brothers, Ben of Galion, Ohio, and Edd of Lenoir City.

Funeral services were held April 23 at Lenoir City Primitive Baptist Church, Elder Howard Pippin Officiating. Interment was at Loudon County Memorial Gardens.

Cyrus Ambrose Sharp, born April 5, 1907, departed this life May 26, 1983 at Ft. Sanders Presbyterian Hospital in Knoxville after a lingering illness.

He professed faith in Christ at an early age. He joined Kirkwood Church shortly after it was organ- ized, remaining a faithful loving member until in- terrupted by failing health.

He was preceded in death by J. Victor Sharp, a son.

Survived by: wife, Freda (Weaver) Sharp; son, Donald; daughters, Mrs. Joyce McFalls, and Mrs. Shirley Bowden, both of Knoxville.

Funeral services were conducted by Elder Hugh Brummitt and Elder Bill Berry at Weaver Mortuary Chapel.

He was laid to rest to await the coming of our Lord Jesus in the Lynn-hurst Cemetery. He will be sadley missed by all who knew him.

Wife

Elder William Sparks, age 76, born September 7, 1906 and passed away suddenly January 23, 1983 at the LaFollette Medical Center.

He was a member and former pastor of Braden's Chapel Church. He was also former pastor of other churches. He was preceeded in death by his mother, father, one sister and one brother.

Survivors: wife, Leecy Bean Sparks, son, T.J. Sparks of Speedwell; daughter, Winona Monday of Speedwell; brothers, Harrison, Brad and Clarence of Middlesboro, Kentucky and H. M. Sparks of Virginia. sisters, Ruby Sutton and Pearl Ledford, both of Middlesboro; three grandchildren and two great-grandchildren.

Funeral services were held at 2 p.m. a Tuesday at Bradens Chapel Church, Elder Noble Lee Clawson, Rev. Bill Braden, and Elder Lee Roy Braden officiating. Burial in Bradens Cemetery.

Our home is so sad and we miss him bad, but I know he's at rest. We hope to meet him again in the "Sweet by and by."

The Family

Ray Wiley Treece, age 61, of Speedwell passed away at Veterans Hospital, Johnson City on May 30, 1983.

He was a member of Red Hill Baptist Church and a veteran of World War II. He was preceded in death by his parents, Wiley and Nora Treece; brothers, Hershel and Lloyd and sister, Julie Earls.

Survivors: wife, Mrs. Betty Treece, Speedwell; son, Kenny Treece, Harrogate; daughter, Kay Robertson, Speedwell; grandchildren, David

Robertson, Speedwell, Jody and Shannon Johns, of Harrogate; brothers, Clifford Treece, Junior Treece, and Ottie Treece of Monroe; sisters, Eva Jones, Middlesboro, Viola Treece, Maggie Wright, Speedwell and Ada Rowlette, Ocean Springs, Miss.; several nieces and nephews.

Funeral services were held at 2 p.m. Wednesday, June 1, at Red Hill Baptist Church with Rev. Hollis Simmons officiating. Singer was Junior Cinningham. Burial in the Red Hill Cemetery.

Ida Ann Stinnitt Walker, was born October 24, 1882. She departed this life May 10, 1983, making her stay with us 100 years, 6 months and 15 days. She outlived her brothers and sisters, husband, 5 children, and in-laws. She married James Thomas Walker November 22, 1902 and has 8 living children from this union. Her parents were Tipton and Sarah Roberts Stinnitt. She professed faith in Christ at the age of 22 and joined Headrick's Chapel Church on the fourth Sunday in August, 1904, and was baptized the same day with 28 others who had joined the church with her. She was a member for 79 years and loved the church until her death.

Left to mourn her are: sons, Louis, Luther, Tom, Bill, Robert, Richard, and Harold; daughter, Mamie Blalock; grandchildren, great-grandchildren and great-great-grandchildren, and a host of friends.

Funeral service was at Headrick's Chapel Church with Elder Walter Lyons and Elder Sheridan Moore officiating. She was laid to rest in the church cemetery to await the coming of the Lord.

Mother, we miss your sweet voice and smile.

We know God knew best. He had a place prepared for you beyond the veil of tears — where all of God's children will never say goodby.

Sadly missed by all who knew her

Mary M. Lee Walker passed away at 8:30 p.m. Friday, June 10, 1983 at Baptist Hospital after a brief illness. She was born December 17, 1921 to Charles and Mamie Abbott Lee, making her stay on earth 61 years, 5 months and 24 days. She married Robert A. Walker September 17, 1938 and has six children living. She joined Headrick's Chapel Church July 2, 1939 and was baptized July 3, and remained a faithful member until her death. She leaves her husband, Robert; sons, Robert, R., Charles Ray, Donald Oton; daughters, Gada Lea Sutton, Shirley Carol Dixon, and Gladys Inez Trentham; 12 grandchildren, 2 great-grandchildren; brother, Harold A. Lee; sister, Emmalene Dobson; several nieces and nephews, aunts, uncles, cousins and a host of friends.

Funeral services were held at 2 p.m. Monday, June 13 at Atchley's Chapel, Elder Sheridan Moore and Elder Wayne Gehman officiating. Interment in Headrick's Chapel Cemetery.

St John 11:25: Jesus said unto her, I am the resurrection, and the life; he that believeth in me, though he were dead, yet shall he live.

††✝

RULES OF DECORUM

1. The churches composing the Powell's Valley Association shall not be confined to any set rules as to specific number of Messengers they shall have in the body, but shall have the right to name in their letters as many as they choose, and in addition all orderly members of any of the churches being present be entitled to seats in the body as Messengers fo their respective churches, with all the rights and privileges of the same.

2. The Messengers thus assembled shall be denominated the Powell's Valley Primitive Baptist Church.

3. For the purpose of historical information and statistical edification, the Churches are required to state in letters, the number of members in fellowship, the number received by Baptism, by letter, by confession of Faith, the number dismissed, excluded and dead since last session; also the time of their meeting, their pastoral supply, and the amount of money contributed for ministers and other purposed together with any other information they deem appropriate for the edification of the saints and glory of God.

4. This Association shall have no power to answer queries, give advice, or dictate to the Churches in any case, or to lord it over God's heritage nor any power by which she can directly or indirectly fringe on the internal rights of the church or censure and try any church or member in reference to faith and practice and determine upon validity of gospel ordinances. These things shall rest entirely with the churches; but henceforward our annual meetings shall be only for the purpose of hearing from each other, and for the worship of God and mutual comfort and edification of the Saints. To this end we reserve the privilege annually for Friday before the Third Saturday in August and the two following days or at such other times as may be agreed upon with any church that may invite us having to protect our own standard, while in session, from heresay and disorder to recognize and invite any primitive Baptist minister or any lay brother to worship with us that may deem proper; to request the brethren of our body to visit other churches or bodies in our belief with whom we may desire to culture Christian fellowship; to publish in a minute of our proceedings.

5. Each session of the body shall have a Moderator and Clerk who shall hold office until re-elected.

6. Any order member of any church belonging to this body, when convened, being present shall be eligible to elect on as Moderator and Clerk or to sit on any committee appointed by the same.

7. In all election or questions that may be necessary to determine by vote, the vote shall be taken by churches, each church being entitled to three votes for any number less than one hundred, and one additional vote for every fifty or fraction thereof above the first hundred, but the Messengers of each church may divide their vote as they see proper.

8. All elections or questions coming to vote shall be determined by a majority vote cast, and it shall be the only duty of the minority to acquiesce in the decision thus reached.

9. If new churches desire to be admitted to this union they shall petition by letter and messengers and if voted for and recommended by one or more sister churches for her Presbytery constitutioning them, as orthodox and orderly they shall be received by the vote of the body and manifested by the Moderator giving the Messengers the right hand of fellowship.

10. Any motion or resolution clearly inconsistent with the above rules shall be promptly ruled out of order unless withdrawn by the mover.

11. Any messenger being ruled out of order by the Moderator shall have the right to appeal to the body on the question of order, and if sustained shall be allowed to proceed, but if not take his seat.

12. Our meeting being held in the name of Christ and the worship of God; each Messenger is expected to observe due and proper therein.

13. It will not be considered good for any Messenger whose name has been enrolled as

such to abruptley break off or absent himself from the Association without leave.

14. The Moderator shall be entitled to the same privilege of speech as other members provided the chair is filled.

15. The minutes of the Association shall be read and approved by the body and signed by the Moderator before adjourning.

16. The Association shall be opened and closed by prayer.

17. Amendments to these may be made at any time by a majority of the union voting by churches when they deem it necessary, provide such amendments do not compromise the sovereignty of the churches nor have tendency to give body undue power or jurisdiction over them.

MINISTERS DIRECTORY

Elder Larry Anderson, Speedwell, TN 869-4635

Elder Johnny Atkins, Bean Station, TN Ph. 767-2397

Elder Johnny Ayres, Rt. 3 - Box 159, Bean Station, TN Ph. 586-5401

Elder William Berry, Rt. #13, Knoxville, TN Ph. 922-9189

Elder LeRoy Braden, 2305 Middlesboro Hwy.LaFollette, TN 562-9353

Elder J. H. Branscomb, Speedwell, TN, Ph. 562-6361

Elder Clifford Brantley, Brown School Rd., Maryville, TN Ph. 982-3735

Elder Hugh H. Brummitt, 1329 Brown Ave., Knoxville, TN Ph. 546-7700

Elder Joe Bush, Corryton, TN, Ph. 687-7018

Elder Jim Campbell, Louisville, TN Ph. 983-1654

Elder Noble Clawson, Rt. 4, Speedwell, TN Ph. 562-2004

Elder Albert Davis, Speedwell, TN Ph. 869-3596

Elder Joe Irving, RT. #, Box B101, Middlesboro, KY Ph. 248-8349

Elder Nelson Jones, Rt. 1, Harrogate, TN Ph. 869-3703

Elder Gohn Godfrey, 15443 Valleoga, Victoryvill, CA Ph. 714-243-4661

Elder Alvin Graves, 122 Oak Wood Dr., Lenoir City, TN Ph. 986-9725

Elder Walter Lyons, 1602 Garfield St., Alcoa, TN Ph. 984-3207

Elder Jerry McBee, 2433 Pennsylvania Ave., Maryville, TN 37801 ~~984-1643~~

Elder Sheridan Moore, Route 1, Townsend, TN Ph. 448-6430   982-6915

Elder J. C. Monday, Speedwell, TN Ph. 562-3068

Elder John Oliver, Rt. 2, Box 513, Bean Station, TN Ph. 581-5039

Elder Howard Pippin, 101 Rose Street, Lenoir City, TN Ph. 986-2791

Elder William Rhymer, Rt. 3, Harrogate, TN Ph. 861-3092

Elder Parnick Shelton, Rt. 4, Corryton, TN Ph. 687-6142

Elder Spurgeon Thompson, Box 36, Shawanee, TN Ph. 869-8175

Elder Claude Rosson, Rt. 4, New Tazewell, TN Ph. 626-3168

Elder Robert Walker, Sevierville, TN Ph. 428-1527

Elder Clay Widner, Rt. 1, Tazewell, TN Ph. 626-3893

LICENTIATES

Brother Clyde Abbott, Sr., Rt. 7, Sevierville, TN Ph. 453-2329

Brother Roscoe Branscomb, Speedwell, TN

Brother Odell Carpenter, Maryville, TN

14

CHURCH	COUNTY	PASTOR	CLERK	ADDRESS
Black Fox	Grainger	Elder Larry Anderson	Bennie Capps	P.O.: Box 91, Maynardville, TN 37807
Braden's Chapel	Union	Elder Noble Clawson Elder LeRoy Braden, Asst.	Jimmie Edwards Phyllis Wilson, Asst.	Speedwell, TN 37870 Speedwell, TN 37870
Brantley's Chapel	Blount	Elder Clifford Brantley Elder Jerry McBee, Asst.	Gaye Lee EllenCoppinger, Asst.	Rt. 1, Box 128, Townsend, TN 37822 Rt. 8, Box 29, Brown School Road Maryville, TN 37801
Davis Chapel	Campbell	Elder William Berry Elder Parnick Shelton, Asst.	Katheryn Angel Sondra Wright, Asst.	Rt. 4, Box 80, LaFollette, TN 37766 1256 Middlesboro Hwy. LaFollette, TN 37766
Gethsemane	Knox	Elder Walter Lyons	Tom Carmichael	729 Frank St., Knoxville, TN 37919
Gibson Station	Lee, Va	Elder William Rhymer Eld. Spurgeon Thompson, Asst.	Dorothy Johnson Shirley Sandifur, Asst.	Rt. 2, Box 320, Ewing VA 24248 Rt. 2, Harrogate, VA 37752
Halls	Knox	Elder William Berry Elder Parnick Shelton, Asst.	Alice Powers Sarah Jean Harmon, Asst.	7525 Temple Acre Dr., Knoxville TN 37938 7120 Chermont Circle Knoxville, TN 37938
Headrick's Chapel	Sevier	Elder Walter Lyons Eld. Sheridan Moore, Asst.	Clyde H. Abbott, Sr. Geraldine Abbott, Asst.	Rt. 7, Sevierville, TN 37862 Rt. 6, Box 204A, Sevierville, TN 37862
Lenoir City	Loudon	Elder Howard Pippin	Thelma Brown	319 Bussell Ferry Rd. Lenoir City, TN 37771
Meyers' Grove	Claiborne	Elder LeRoy Braden	Bonnie Miracle Harold Cupp, Asst.	Rt.2, Box 91, New Tazewell, TN 37825 Rt. 2, Box 166, New Tazewell, TN 37825
Noeton	Grainger	Elder John Oliver	Caroll Oliver Bessie Collins, Asst.	Rt. 2, Box 512, Bean Station, TN 37708 Route 5, Morristown, TN
Oak Grove	Union	Elder J. C. Monday Elder Jerry McBee, Asst.	Betty P. Sharp Betty Shoffner, Asst.	Sharps Chapel, TN 37866 Sharps Chapel, TN 37866
Pleasant Hill	Claiborne	Elder William Rhymer Elder Albert Davis, Asst.	William Branscomb Dennis Edwards, Asst.	Speedwell, TN 37870 Speedwell, TN 37870
Pleasant Point	Claiborne	Elder Larry Anderson	Elder Claude Rosson Beatrice Williams, Asst.	Rt. 4, New Tazewell, TN 37825 Rt. 2, Box 156, Rogersville, TN 37857
Rocky Dale	Knox	Elder Hugh Brummitt	Edward Collett Dennis Branson, Asst.	Rt. 1, Box 17, Luttrell, TN 37779 Rt. 13, 4633 Marshall Drive Knoxville, TN 37918

STATISTICAL TABLE

CHURCHES	DELEGATES	Restored	Rec'd. by Letter	Baptism	Relationship	Dismiss by Letter	Excluded	Deceased	Total Membership	Printing Minutes	REGULAR MEETING TIME	COMMUNION TIME
Black Fox	Bros.: Dale Capps, Arthur Terry, Bennie Capps; Sisters: Mary Ruth Capps, Pamela Capps, Mary Terry, Debbie Sexton, Sarah Hopson	0	0	0	0	0	0	0	75	$25.00	Second Saturday Night and Sunday Sunday after Fourth Saturday	Sunday Following Second Saturday in June
Braden's Chapel	Bro. Coy Edwards	0	0	1	3	0	0	1	149	$35.00	First Saturday Night and Sunday	Sunday following First Saturday In April
Brantley's Chapel	Elder: Clifford Brantley; Bros.; Rina Johnson, Everett Brantley, Robert Welch, Eskie Boruff; Sisters: Barsha Brantley, Hazel Johnson, Mildred Brantley, Blanch Welch	0	0	0	2	2	1	1	106	*35.00	Second Saturday Night Every Sunday and Sunday Night	Sunday following Second Saturday In July at 10:30 a.m.
Davis Chapel	Bros.: Bob Lynch, Clyde Lynch, O.D. McCarty; Sisters: Pearl Lynch, Molly McCarty, Ollie Welch	0	0	0	2	0	2	2	111	$45.00	Third Saturday Night Every Sunday and Sunday Night	Sunday following Third In June.
Gethsemane	Eld.: Jim Campbell; Sisters: Myrtle Cook, Carolyn Campbell, Beth Campbell	0	0	0	2	0	0	0	40	$35.00	Every Sunday except the First Sunday	Sunday following Fourth Saturday In May & October.
Gibson Station	Elders: William Rhymer, Spurgeon Thompson, Joe Irving, Nelson Jones; Bros.: Curtis Ball, Claude Sandifur; Sisters: Karen Rhymer, Jean Thompson, Evelyn Irving, Polly Jones, Shirley Sandifur, Lucille Ball, Dorothy Johnson	0	0	1	0	0	0	0	79	$40.00	First Saturday and Saturday Night Every Sunday and Sunday Night	Sunday following First In June.
Halls	Elder: Hugh Brummitt Bro.: Elwood Evans Sisters: Ruby Brummitt, Velna Evans, Trula Berry	0	5	2	2	0	3	3	110	$40.00	Every Sunday Morning	Last Sunday in April

Church	Officers										Meeting	
Headrick's Chapel	Bros.: Clyde Abbott, Sr., Bill Cook Sisters: Geraldine Abbott, Grace Abbott, Angela Abbott, Margo Abbott	0	0	0	0	0	0	2	111	$25.00	First And Third Sunday of each Month	First Sunday in May & October
Lenoir City	Elder: Howard Pippin Bros: Hubert Spoon, Scott Collins Sister: Annie Spoon	0	0	1	0	0	6	1	120	$35.00	Every Sunday and Sunday Night	Wednesday Night before Easter Sunday; Third Sunday in October
Myers Grove	Bros: Isom Drummonds Sister: Velt Muncey	0	0	0	0	0	0	0	77	$25.00	Second Saturday Night and Sunday; Fourth Saturday Night and Sunday	Sunday following Fourth Saturday in May
Noeton	Elder: John Oliver Bros.: Charlie Collins, Ted Oliver Sisters: Ruth Oliver, Dora Collins, Vernia Brantley	0	0	0	0	0	0	1	39	$20.00	First Sunday of each Month Third Saturday and Sunday of each Month	Sunday following Third Saturday in May & September
Oak Grove	Elder: Johnnie Atkins Sister: Francis Eastridge	0	0	13	2	0	5	2	340	$25.00	First Saturday Night and Sunday Third Sunday	Sunday following First Saturday in May
Pleasant Hill	Elders: James Henry Branscomb, Larry Anderson, Albert Davis Sisters: Helen Ruth Branscomb, Myra Anderson, Audra Davis	0	0	0	0	0	1	1	98	$35.00	Fourth Saturday Morning and Saturday Night Fourth Sunday Every Sunday Night	Sunday following Fourth Sunday in June
Pleasant Point	Letter Received No delegates present	0	0	0	0	0	0	0	106	$20.00	First and Third Sunday	Sunday following First Saturday in July at 11:00 a.m.
Rocky Dale	Elders: Parnick Shelton, Bill Berry Bros.: Donald Sharp Sisters: Dottie Sharp	0	0	0	3	0	0	0	115	$40.00	Every Sunday and Sunday Night	Sunday following Third Saturday in May

1984 Minutes

OF THE
ONE HUNDRED SIXTY-FOURTH SESSION
OF THE

POWELL VALLEY ASSOCIATION
OF PRIMITIVE BAPTIST

HELD WITH THE SISTER CHURCH AT
BRANTLEY'S CHAPEL
BLOUNT COUNTY, TENNESSEE
AUGUST 17, 18, and 19, 1984

THE ONE HUNDRED SIXTY–FOURTH SESSION
OF THE POWELL VALLEY ASSOCIATION
OF
PRIMITIVE BAPTIST
HELD WITH THE SISTER CHURCH AT BRANTLEY'S CHAPEL
BLOUNT COUNTY TENNESSEE
AUGUST 17, 18, and 19, 1984

NEXT SESSION WILL BE HELD WITH THE SISTER CHURCH
AT
BLACK FOX
GRAINGER COUNTY, TENNESSEE
TO BEGIN ON FRIDAY BEFORE THE THIRD SATURDAY
IN AUGUST, 1985
AT 10:30 A.M.

ELDER LARRY ANDERSON WILL DELIVER THE
INTRODUCTORY SERMON
ELDER SPURGEON THOMPSON WILL BE THE ALTERNATE

OFFICERS

ELDER HUGH BRUMMITT   MODERATOR
1329 BROWN AVENUE, KNOXVILLE, TENN., PHONE 546-7700
ELDER CLIFFORD BRANTLEY   ASSISTANT MODERATOR
809 BROWN SCHOOL RD. MARYVILLE, TENN., PHONE 982-3875
BENNIE CAPPS   CLERK
P.O. BOX 91, MAYNARDVILLE, TENN., PHONE 992-5571
RINA JOHNSON   ASSISTANT CLERK
1217 BROWN SCHOOL ROAD, MARYVILLE, TENN., PHONE 983-2774

Friday, August 17, 1984

The one hundred and sixty-fourth session of the powell Valley Association of Primitive Baptists met with the sister church at Brantley's Chapel in Blount County, Tennessee, on August 17, 18, and 19, 1984.

After Bro. Glenn Walker led the congregation in singing "A Beautiful Life", "Near the Cross", and Amazing Grace" the Moderator, Elder Hugh Brummitt welcomed the congregation and pleaded for peace and love to abide through the entire Association and called for prayer by Bro. Clarence Hicks of the Lenoir City Church.

Following prayer, Elder William Rhymer of Gibson Station delivered the introductory sermon—a very good sermon— from the 17th chapter of St. John, using as his text "Covenant of Grace".

After the introductory sermon, they sang a song and were dismissed in prayer by Elder Walter Lyons of Halls Church. The Association was to reconvene after a 15 minute recess.

After recess, the crowd reassembled in the church; Elder Jerry McBee led the congregation in "Hand in Hand with Jesus". Moderatory Elder Hugh Brummitt read from the 3rd chapter of Proverbs, then called for prayer by Elder Johnnie Atkins of Oak Grove Church.

The Moderator then asked for the order of business for the following transactions;

1st: Called for letters of the Sister Churches to be presented to the clerk for reading. Fifteen (15) were received.

2nd: The letters were presented and read and motion approved that the delegates be seated.

3rd: The Moderator called for anyone present from any of the Sister Churches not named as a delegate who desired to be seated as such to come forward and give the clerk their name and the name of their church. Two came. Sister Alvada Dykes from Oak Grove and Sister Irene Harmon from Halls.

4th: Called for petitionary letter if there should be one. There was none.

5th: Motion approved that the Association re-elect Elder Hugh Brummitt as Moderator and Elder Clifford Brantley as Assistant Moderator for the ensuing year.

6th: Motion approved that Brother Bennie Capps be re-elected Clerk and Brother Rina Johnson be re-elected Assistant Clerk for the ensuing year.

7th: Motion was approved that we empower Elder Brummitt to appoint all the committees to serve this session.

8th: The Moderator, having been empowered to do so, named the committees as follows:

Committee on Arrangements:	Bro. Carroll Oliver
	Bro. Tom Carmichael
	Bro. Bill Taylor
Committee on Preaching:	Bro. Everett Brantley
	Bro. Elwood Evans
	Bro. Hubert Spoons
Committee on Request:	Elder William Berry
	Bro. Robert Welch
	Bro. Orice McCarty
Committee on Finance:	Elder Jerry McBee
	Elder Howard Pippin
	Bro. Joe Culvahouse

9th: Called for the finances to be turned in to the Finance Committee.

10th: The committees all having been appointed and accepted, the Association moved to adjourn until 10:30 Saturday morning. They sang a song and were dismissed in prayer by Elder Albert Davis, from Pleasant Hill Church.

Saturday, August 18, 1984

At the appointed hour of 10:30 Saturday morning, and at the sound of singing, the Association reassembled to a full house.

After singing, the Assistant Moderator, Elder Clifford Brantley gave a very spiritual and uplifting talk and read from the third chapter of Galatians, then called for prayer by Elder Arnold Thompson from Ohio.

After prayer, the Moderator called the Association to order for the remainder of the business:

1st: The moderator called for any letters from Sister Churches not received on Friday. There was none.

2nd: The Moderator called for anyone from any of the churches who were present and desired to be seated as delegate to come forward. Four came: Sisters Vicki Irwin, Suzette Irwin, Vanessa Irwin and Brother William Irwin, all from Brantley's Chapel.

3rd: The Moderator then called for the report of the Committee on Arrangements who submitted the following report:

Report on Arrangements:
Call for roll call of delegates
Call for report of Committee on Preaching
Call for report of Committee on Request
Call for report of Committee on Finance
Decide how many minutes to have printed, who shall supervise the printing and distribution of same, an how much he shall receive for services. Who shall preach the introductory sermon and who shall be the alternate.
the alternate.

Respectfully submitted,
Bro. Bill Taylor
Bro. Tom Carmichael
Bro. Carroll L. Oliver

4th: Motion approved to receive the above report and release the committee.

5th: Called the roll call of delegates of all the Sister Churches and check the absentees.

6th: Called for the report of the Committee on Preaching:

Friday Night:	Elder Bill Berry
	Elder Clifford Brantley
Saturday Morning:	Elder Larry Anderson
	Elder Spurgeon Thompson
Saturday Night:	Elder Hugh Brummitt
	Elder Jimmy Branscomb
Sunday Morning:	Elder Albert Davis
	Elder Parnick Shelton

Respectfully Submitted,   Bro. Everett Brantley
Bro. Hubert Spoon
Bro. Elwood Evans

7th: Motion approved to receive the above report and release the committee.

8th: Called for the report of the Committee on Request.

Report on Committee on Request:

We, the Committee on Request, request that we have 1,100 minutes printed and the clerk supervise the printing and distribution of same and that he receive $135.00 for his services. We request that Elder Parnick Shelton write a circular letter to be printed in the minutes, that the next session of the Association be held with the Sister Church of Black Fox in Grainger County, Tennessee, to begin on Friday before the third Saturday in August, 1985, and may the love and peace that is here continue throughout the remainder of this Association.

Respectfully submitted,

Bro. O. D. McCarty
Bro. Robert Welch
Eld. Bill Berry

9th: Motion approved to receive the above report and release the committee.

10th: Called for the report of the Committee on Finance, which submitted the following report:

(CONTINUED PAGE 5)

Report of Finance Committee:

Black Fox	$25.00
Braden's Chapel	$35.00
Brantley's Chapel	$40.00
Davis Chapel	$45.00
Gethsemane	$35.00
Gibson Station	$50.00
Headricks Chapel	$25.00
Hall's	50.00
Lenoir City	45.00
Meyers Grove	25.00
Noeton	25.00
Oak Grove	30.00
Pleasant Hill	35.00
Pleasant Point	25.00
Rocky Dale	40.00

	$530.00
Donation	20.00
	40.00
	$590.00
Balance in Bank	117.00
	$707.00
Expense for 1984	560.00
Balance in Bank	$147.00

Respectfully Submitted,
Elder Jerry McBee
Elder Howard Pippin
Bro. Joe Culvahouse

11th: Motion approved to receive the above report and release the committee.

12th: Motion approved that we grant the request of the committee and have 1,100 minutes printed and the clerk to receive $135.00 for his services.

13: Motion approved that the next session of the Association be held with the Sister Church at Black Fox in Grainger County, Tennessee, to begin on Friday before the third Saturday in August, 1985, at 10:30 a.m.

14th: Motion approved that Elder Parnick Shelton write

the circular letter for the 1985 minutes.

15th: Motion approved that Elder Larry Anderson deliver the introductory sermon and Elder Spurgeon Thompson be the alternate.

16th: Motion approved that the churches of the Powell Valley Association extend the church and the people of Brantley's Chapel our heart felt thanks and our prayers for the love, fellowship, kindness and food while we were here with you. May the good Lord bless and keep you is our prayers.

17th: Motion to adjourn, trusting the lord to permit us to meet again with the Sister Church at Black Fox in Grainger County, Tennessee, on Friday before the third Saturday in August, 1985, at 10:30 a.m.

Dismissed in prayer by Elder Joe Irving.

Elder Hugh Brummitt, Moderator
Elder Clifford Brantley, Assistant Moderator
Brother Bennie Capps, Clerk
Brother Rina Johnson, Assistant Clerk

Sunday, August 19, 1984

After singing and prayer, Elder Clifford Brantley read from the 22nd chapter of Genesis; then Elder Albert Davis read from the 1st chapter of Haggai and preached a wonderful sermon using as his text "Let Us Consider Our Ways". Next, Elder Parnick Shelton preached a very uplifting sermon from the 4th chapter of Hebrews, using as his text "There remaineth therefore a rest to the people of God". The congregation was dismissed in prayer by Brother Orice McCarty.

SUMMARY

We are blessed with a fine group of ministers as was illustrated by those who had the opportunity to preach. We regret that time will not permit more of them to preach when we meet with the Association.

On Friday, Elder William Rhymer of Gibson Station delivered the introductory sermon and gave a very good sermn from the 17th chaper of St. John, using as his text "Covetous of Grace".

On Friday night, Elder Hugh Brummitt spoke of love, and yet the love of many has waxed cold and have left their first love. Then Elder Clifford Brantley read from Genesis 28, verse 15, concerning Bethel, or the House of God, and I will bring you once again to this good land. He was followed by Elder Bill Berry who read from 1st John, 3rd chapter, 2nd verse, and preached fro we shall see Him as He is and shall be conformed to His image in that day.

Then on Saturday morning, Elder Larry Anderson preached from the 53rd chapter of Isaiah, and used "Redeem thur Jesus" as his text. Then Elder Spurgeon Thompson spoke a few minutes on the blood and then turned his time over to Elder Arnold Thompson, of Ohio, who preached a wonderful and spiritual sermon on the "Goodness of God"

On Saturday night, Elder James Branscomb read from Romans, 5th chapter:4th verse and preached on He that believeth and shall be baptised shall be saved. Elder Hugh Brummitt then read from 2nd chapter of Ephesians, "It is by Grace and that not of yourself lest any man should boast"

Sunday sermons were by Elder Albert Davis and Elder Parnick Shelton.

SPECIAL ANNOUNCEMENTS

Brantley's Chapel has their Sunday night services every Sunday night at 7 p.m. in the summer months and at 6 p.m. in the winter months.

The following four churches asked for the Association for 1985. They were: Black Fox, Brantley's Chapel, Gibson Station, and Lenoir City.

Please make your contribution payable to: Powell Valley Association.

CIRCULAR LETTER TO THE POWELL VALLEY ASSOCIATION OF PRIMITIVE BAPTIST

Being called upon to write this letter, I hope by God's grace to strengthen those who read it.

My subject being—Saved by Grace. (Eph. 2:8-9).

Grace we know is unmerited favor bestowed upon undeserving creatures. If grace is unmerited, then we do not work for it. If we are undeserving, then we are, by nature, unworthy of it. So if we are saved by grace, as the scriptures teach, then it is a free gift of God.

Man, by nature, hates this doctrine because it takes all the glory from man and gives it to God. Man, by nature, wants credit for everything good that happens, but this is one thing that excludes man's works. Poor mortal man is on the receiving end of the greatest gift that has ever been given, the Son of God, that man may stand justified in the presence of a Just, Holy and Merciful God. Men great and small have been trying for centuries to explain away this doctrine. It is here to stay and will stand when the world is on fire!

Jesus said in John 10:27-29, ''My sheep hear my voice, and I know them, and they follow me: and I give unto them eternal life; and they shall never perish, neither shall any man pluck them out of my hand. My Father, which gave them me, is greater than all; and no man is able to pluck them out of my Father's hand.''

You brother in Christ. May God bless you is my prayer.

Elder Walter G. Lyons

389

CHURCHES AND THEIR DELEGATES

BLACK FOX: Brothers: Dale Capps, Bennie Capps
Sisters: Mary Ruth Capps and Pamela Capps
BRADEN'S CHAPEL: Letter received, no delegate present
BRANTLEY'S CHAPEL: Elders: Clifford Brantley, Jerry McBee
Brothers: Rina Johnson, Everett Brantley, Glen
Walker, Robert Welch, Daniel Brantley, David Beason,
Richard Walker, Leonard Eastridge, Eskie Boruff
Sisters: Hazel Johnson, Mildred Brantley, Edith Walker,
Blanch Welch, Linda Brantley, Sherry Beason, Barsha
Brantley, Vanessa McBee and Linda Eastridge
DAVIS CHAPEL: Brothers: Clyde Lynch, O. D. McCarty
Sisters; Pearl Lynch, Molly McCarty, Ollie Welch
GETHSEMANE: Brother: Tom Carmichael
Sisters: Myrtle Cook, June Carmichael
GIBSON STATION: Elders: William Rhymer, Spurgeon
Thompson, Joe Irving
Brothers: Curtis Ball, Franklin Ball
Sisters: Karen Rhymer, Evelyn Irving, Lucile Ball,
Dorothy Johnson, Shirley Sandifur, Fannie Jones
HALLS: Elders: Hugh Brummitt, Walter Lyons
Brothers: Elwood Evans, Joe Culvahouse, Bill Taylor
Sisters: Ruby Brummitt, Velna Evans, Betty Culvahouse,
Wilma Shelton, Trula Berry, Dola Webb, Frieda Sharp
HEADRICK CHAPEL: Elders: Robert Walker
Brothers: Clyde Abbott, Sr., Bill Cook
Sisters: Grace Abbott, Geraldine Abbott, Margo Abbott
LENOIR CITY: Elders: Howard Pippin
Brothers: Clarence Hicks, Hubert Spoon, Scott Collins
Sisters: Annie Spoon
MYERS GROVE: Letter received. No delegates listed
NOETON: Elders; John Oliver
Brothers: Charlie Collins, Carroll Oliver
Sisters: Mildred Oliver
OAK GROVE: Elders: Johnnie Atkins
Sisters: Francis Eastridge
PLEASANT HILL: Elders: James Henry Branscomb
Larry Anderson, Albert Davis
Sisters: Myra Anderson, Audra Davis
PLEASANT POINT: Letter received. No delegates present
ROCKY DALE: Elders: Parnick Shelton, Bill Berry
Brothers: Donald Sharp, Josh Stapleton
Sisters: Dottie Sharp, Ima Lee Stapleton

STATISTICAL TABLE

	Restored	Rec'd by Letter	Baptism	Excluded	Dismiss by Letter	Relationship	Deceased	Total Membership	Printing Minutes	REGULAR MEETING TIME	COMMUNION TIME
Black Fox	0	0	0	1	0	0	3	73	$25.00	Second Saturday Night and Sunday after Fourth Saturday	Sunday Following Second Saturday in June
Braden's Chapel	0	0	9	0	2	0	0	156	35.00	First Saturday Night and Sunday	Sunday Following First Saturday in April
Brantley's Chapel	0	1	1	2	0	2	2	108	40.00	Second Saturday Night– Every Sunday and Sunday Night	Sunday following Second Saturday in July at 10:30 a.m.
Davis Chapel	0	0	0	0	0	2	3	106	45.00	Third Saturday Night-Every Sunday and Sunday Night	Sunday following Third Saturday in June
Gethsemane	0	0	0	0	1	0	0	39	35.00	Every Sunday except the First Sunday	Fourth Sunday in May and and October
Gibson Station	0	0	0	0	0	2	1	78	50.00	First Saturday and Saturday Night- Every Sunday and Sunday Night	Sunday following First Sunday in June
Halls	0	4	0	0	1	0	1	110	50.00	Every Sunday and Sunday Night	Last Sunday in April
Headrick's Chapel	0	0	0	0	0	0	0	111	25.00	First and Third Sunday of each Month	First Sunday in May and October
Lenoir City	0	1	10	0	1	0	1	129	45.00	Every Sunday and Sunday Night	Wednesday Night before Easter Sunday –Third Sunday in October
Myers Grove	0	0	3	1	2	0	0	77	25.00	2nd Saturday Night & Sunday 4th Saturday Night & Sunday	Sunday following Fourth Saturday in May
Noaton	0	0	0	0	0	0	1	38	25.00	First Sunday–Third Saturday and Sunday of each Month	Sunday following Third Saturday in May & September
Oak Grove	0	0	3	1	0	1	5	338	30.00	First Saturday Night and Sunday– Third Sunday	Sunday following the First Saturday in May
Pleasant Hill	0	0	1	0	0	2	3	94	35.00	4th Sat. Morning & Sat. Night 4th Sun.–Every Sun. Night	Sunday following Fourth Sunday in June at 11 a.m.
Pleasant Point	0	0	0	0	0	0	3	103	25.00	Sunday Following Fourth Saturday	Sunday following first Saturday in July
Rocky Dale	0	0	0	0	2	0	5	108	40.00	Every Sunday Morning	Sunday following Third Saturday in May

CHURCH	COUNTY	PASTOR	CLERK	ADDRESS
Black Fox	Grainger	Elder Larry Anderson	Bennie Capps	P.O. Box 91, Maynardville, TN 37807
Braden's Chapel	Union	Elder Noble Clawson Elder LeRoy Braden, Asst.	Jimmie Edwards Phyllis Wilson, Asst.	Speedwell, TN 37870 Speedwell, TN 37870
Brantley's Chapel	Blount	Elder Clifford Brantley Elder Jerry McBee, Asst.	Gaye Lee Ellen Coppinger, Asst.	Rt. 1, Box 128, Townsend, TN 37822 Rt. 8, Box 210, Maryville, TN 37801
Davis Chapel	Campbell	Elder William Berry Elder Parnick Shelton, Asst.	Katheryn Angel Sondra Wright, Asst.	Rt. 4, Box 80, LaFollette, TN 37766 1256 Middlesboro Hwy.- LaFollette, TN37766
Gethsemane	Knox	Elder Walter Lyons	Tom Carmichael	729 Frank St., Knoxville, TN 37919
Gibson Station	Lee Va.	Elder William Rhymer Eld. Spurgeon Thompson,Asst.	Dorothy Johnson Shirley Sandifur, Asst.	Rt. 2, Box 320, Ewing, VA 24248 Rt. 2, Harrogate, TN 37752
Halls	Knox	Elder William Berry Elder Parnick Shelton, Asst.	Alice Powers Sarah Jean Harmon,Asst.	7525 Temple Acre Dr.,Knoxville,TN37938 7120 Chermont Cir.,Knoxville,TN 37938
Headrick's Chapel	Sevier	Elder Walter Lyons	Clyde H. Abbot, Sr.	Rt. 7, Sevierville, TN 37862
Lenoir City	Loudon	Elder Howard Pippin	Thelma Brown	319 Bussell Ferry Road Lenoir City, TN 37771
Meyers' Grove	Claiborne	Elder LeRoy Braden Elder Clay Widner,Asst.	Bonnie Miracle Harold Cupp, Asst	Rt.,Box 91,New Tazewell,TN 37825 Rt. 2,,Box 166,New Tazewell,TN 37825
Noeton	Grainger	Elder John Oliver	Carroll Oliver Bessie Collins, Aisst.	Rt. 2,Box 512,Bean Station,TN37708 Rt. 5, Morristown, TN 37814
Oak Grove	Union	Elder J. C. Monday Elder Jerry McBee, Asst.	Betty P. Sharp Betty Shoffner, Asst.	Rt. 1, Box 250, Sharps Chapel, TN 37866 Sharps Chapel, TN 37866
Pleasant Hill	Claiborne	Elder William Rhymer Elder A'bert Davis, Asst.	William Branscomb Dennis Edwards, Asst.	Speedwell, TN 37870 Speedwell, TN 37870
Pleasant Point	Claiborne	Elder Larry Anderson	Elder Claude Rosson Beatrice Williams, Asst.	Rt. 4, New Tazewell, TN 37825 Rt. 2, Box 156 Rogersville,TN 37857
Rocky Dale	Knox	Elder Hugh Brummitt	Edward Collett Saundra Boruff	Rt. 1, Box 17, Luttrell, TN 37779 6916 Weaver Rd.,Knoxville,TN

RULES OF DECORUM

1. The churches composing the Powell's Valley Association shall not be confined to any set rules as to specific number of Messengers they shall have in the body, but shall have the right to name in their letters as many as they choose, and in addition all orderly members of any of the churches being present be entitled to seats in the body as Messengers fo their respective churches, with all the rights and privileges of the same.

2. The Messengers thus assembled shall be denominated the Powell's Valley Primitive Baptist Church.

3. For the purpose of historical information and statistical edification, the Churches are required to state in letters, the number of members in fellowship, the number received by Baptism, by letter, by confession of Faith, the number dismissed, excluded and dead since last session; also the time of their meeting, their pastoral supply, and the amount of money contributed for ministers and other purposed together with any other information they deem appropriate for the edification of the saints and glory of God.

4. This Association shall have no power to answer queries, give advice, or dictate to the Churches in any case, or to lord it over God's heritage nor any power by which she can directly or indirectly fringe on the internal rights of the church or censure and try any church or member in reference to faith and practice and determine upon validity of gospel ordinances. These things shall rest entirely with the churches; but henceforward our annual meetings shall be only for the purpose of hearing from each other, and for the worship of God and mutual comfort and edification of the Saints. To this end we reserve the privilege annually for Friday before the Third Saturday in August and the two following days or at such other times as may be agreed upon with any church that may invite us having to protect our own standard, while in session, from heresay and disorder to recognize and invite any primitive Baptist minister or any lay brother to worship with us that may deem proper; to request the brethren of our body to visit other churches or bodies in our belief with whom we may desire to culture Christian fellowship; to publish in a minute of our proceedings.

5. Each session of the body shall have a Moderator and Clerk who shall hold office until re-elected.

6. Any order member of any church belonging to this body, when convened, being present shall be eligible to elect on as Moderator and Clerk or to sit on any committee appointed by the same.

7. In all election or questions that may be necessary to determine by vote, the vote shall be taken by churches, each church being entitled to three votes for any number less than one hundred, and one additional vote for every fifty or fraction thereof above the first hundred, but the Messengers of each church may divide their vote as they see proper.

8. All elections or questions coming to vote shall be determined by a majority vote cast, and it shall be the only duty of the minority to acquiesce in the decision thus reached.

9. If new churches desire to be admitted to this union they shall petition by letter and messengers and if voted for and recommended by one or more sister churches for her Presbytery constitutioning them, as orthodox and orderly they shall be received by the vote of the body and manifested by the Moderator giving the Messengers the right hand of fellowship.

10. Any motion or resolution clearly inconsistent with the above rules shall be promptly ruled out of order unless withdrawn by the mover.

11. Any messenger being ruled out of order by the Moderator shall have the right to appeal to the body on the question of order, and if sustained shall be allowed to proceed, but if not take his seat.

12. Our meeting being held in the name of Christ and the worship of God; each Messenger is expected to observe due and proper therein.

13. It will not be considered good for any Messenger whose name has been enrolled as

such to abruptley break off or absent himself from the Association without leave.

14. The Moderator shall be entitled to the same privilege of speech as other members provided the chair is filled.

15. The minutes of the Association shall be read and approved by the body and signed by the Moderator before adjourning.

16. The Association shall be opened and closed by prayer.

17. Amendments to these may be made at any time by a majority of the union voting by churches when they deem it necessary, provide such amendments do not compromise the sovereignty of the churches nor have tendency to give body undue power or jurisdiction over them.

MINISTERS DIRECTORY

Elder Doyle Ausmus, Rt. 2, Speedwell, TN 566-0433

Elder Larry Anderson, Speedwell, TN 869-4635

Elder Johnny Atkins, Bean Station, TN 767-2397

Elder Johnny Ayres, Rt. e - Box 159, Bean Station, TN 586-5401

Elder William Berry, Rt. 13, Knoxville, TN 922-9189

Elder LeRoy Braden, 2305 Middlesboro Hwy., LaFollette, TN 562-9353

Elder J. H. Branscomb, Speedwell, TN 562-6361

Elder Clifford Brantley, Brown School Rd., Maryville, TN 982-3735

Elder Hugh H. Brummitt, 1329 Brown Ave., Knoxville, TN 546-7700

Elder Joe Bush, Rt. 3, Corryton, TN 687-7018

Elder Jim Campbell, 601 Frank St., Knoxville, TN 525-2019

Elder Noble Clawson, Rt. 4, Speedwell, TN 562-2004

Elder Albert Davis, Speedwell, TN 869-3596

Elder Joe Irving, Rt. 3, Box B101, Middlesboro, KY 248-8349

Elder Nelson Jones, Rt. 1, Harrogate, TN 869-3703

Elder John Godfrey, 15443 Valleoga, Victoryville, CA 714-243-4661

Elder Alvin Graves, 122 Oak Wood Dr., Lenoir City, TN 986-9725

Elder Walter Lyons, 1602 Garfield St., Alcoa, TN 984-3207

Elder Jerry McBee, 2433 Pennsysvania Ave.,Maryville,TN 37801-982-6915

Elder Sheridan Moore, Route 1, Townsend, TN 448-6430

Elder J. C. Monday, Speedwell, TN 562-3068

Elder John Oliver, Rt. 2, Box 513, Bean Station, TN 581-5039

Elder Howard Pippin, 101 Rose Street, Lenoir City 986-2791

Elder William Rhymer, Rt. 3, Box 266, Harrogate, TN 861-3092

Elder Parnick Shelton, Rt. 4, Corryton, TB 687-6142

Elder Spurgeon Thompson, Box 36, Shawanee, TN 869-8175

Elder Claude Rosson, Rt. 4, New Tazewell, TN 626-3168

Elder Robert Walker, Sevierville, TN 428-1527

Elder Clay Widner, Rt. 1, Tazewell, TN 626-3893

LICENTIATES

Brother Clyde Abbott, Sr., Rt. 7, Sevierville, TN 453-2329

Brother Roscoe Branscomb, Speedwell, TN

Brother Odell Carpenter, Maryville, TN

Brother Clarence Hicks, Lenoir City, TN

OBITUARIES

KATHERINE ATKINS, Rt. 3, Bean station, died January 11, 1984. She was a member of Noeton Primitive Baptist Church. Survivors: daughters: Sally Bowlin, Irene Singleton of Bean Station; Bonnie West, Morristown; 10 grandchildren, 14 great-grandchildren; sister, Sarah Campbell of Bean Station. Services were held at Noeton Primitive Baptist Church with Elder John Oliver and Rev. Olaf Atkins officiating. Burial was in church cemetery. Westside Chapel Funeral Home, Morristown in charge.

SEAGLE E. BEELER, age 91, of Sallings Road, Luttrell, Tennessee passed away at 1:18 p.m. Friday, May 25, 1984 at Ridgeview Nursing Home. He was a member of Rocky Dale Primitive Baptist Church. Survivors: wife, Mrs. Ibbie (Ellison) Beeler; daughter, Thelma Taylor; 7 grandchildren; sister, Zelphia Stern, Knoxville. Graveside service was at 2:30 p.m. on Sunday at Stiner Cemetery, Rev. Gary Beeler officiating. Cooke Mortuary, Maynardville, in charge.

WILLIE ANDREW BRADEN, son of John Dave Braden, 86 years of age, departed this life Nov. 12, 1983. Bro. Willie professed a hope in Christ at an early age and joined pleasant Hill Primitive Baptist Church several years ago. He lived a loyal and faithful life in the church and is sadly missed by the church. He is survived by 1 daughter, Becky Rouse; 3 sons, Emerson, Carl and Ricky Braden; 2 sisters, 1 brother, 3 half-sisters, and 4 half brothers; also 8 grandchildren and 5 great-grandchildren. We feel our loss is his eternal gain.

RALPH E. CLAPP, age 85 of 6912 Boruff Road, Corryton, Tennessee, passed away June 26, 1984 at his home. He was a very devoted and faithful member of Rocky Dale Primitive Baptist Church. Survivors: daughters, Bobby Clapp, Mrs. Charles (Myrtle) Bryant, Betty Livingston, Mrs. Gordon (Sharon) Cantrell, all of Corryton; son, Roy Clapp of Chattanooga; 7 grandchildren, 2 great-grandchildren; brothers, Henry Clapp, Knoxville, Ross Clapp, Knoxville. Funeral service 8 p.m. June 28, 1984, Mynatt's Chapel, Elder H.E. Brummitt officiating. Interment in Highland Memorial Cemetery, East.

> Family and friends were gathered in the chapel that night
> The organ played so softly and everything seemed so quiet
> When it seemed a voice was speaking coming down from God's throne
> "Rejoice, dear ones, be happy your loved one has just reached home"
> The minister spoke so softly of the beautiful home beyond
> Where our dear precious loved one had so much longed to go
> To meet with friends and loved ones across the mystic foam
> To hear the angels singing "Another Child Has Just Reached Home"

SARAH MALINDA ELLISON BRANTLEY, 1717 Brown Scholl Road, Maryville, Tenn., was born in Sharps Chapel December 3, 1894 and died May 4, 1984 after a brief illness. She was 89 years, 5 month, and 1 day of age. While living in Sharps Chapel, Union County, Tenn., she attended Big Sinks School. She professed faith in Christ in 1910 at the age of 15 while attending a revival at Cave Springs Church. The late Elder Leonard White conducted this revival. Sarah often told how she met the Lord and recalled that Elder White spoke from the 15th Chapter of Luke during this revival on a Saturday. She joined the church at Cave Springs and was baptized. She later moved her membership to Oak Grove.

On May 5, 1912, Sarah married Daniel Milton Brantley who preceded her in death. To this union were born five children: Clifford, Everett and Doyle Brantley, all of Maryville, Tenn.; Mrs. Norma Jean Bush, Corryton, and Mrs. Juanita Brantley of Kokomo, Ind., Sarah had 13 grandchildren and 20 great-grandchildren. Surviving brothers and sisters were, U. J. Ellison of Walton, Ind., Swan Ellison of Sharps Chapel, Mrs. Bessie McCarty, LaFollette, Mrs. Dinah Barnard, Mrs. Ottie McBee, Maryville, and Irene Bridges, Nashville. After moving to Maryville in 1948, she joined Brantley Chapel Church where she remained a faithful member until death. Funeral services were held at Brantley Chapel on Monday, May 7, 1984 at 11:00 a.m. Elder Clifford Brantley and Elder Joe Bush conducted the service. Burial was in the church cemetery. Pallbearers were grandsons.

Written by Family

OLLIE MYRTLE COX, age 86, of Sharps Chapel, passed away 10:30 a.m. December 16, 1983 at Claiborne County Hospital. She was preceded in death by son, J.W. Cox. Survivors: son and daughter-in-law, Bobby and Wade Cox, Corryton; grandchildren, Melissa Cox, Corryton, Jimmy Cox, Florida, Jerry, Terry and Jamie Cox, Knoxville; great-granddaughter, Allisha Cox; step-children, Dewey Cox, Tazewell, Hetty Shoffner, Maryville, Nancy Brewer, Powell. Funeral 2 p.m. Monday, Oak Grove Primitive Baptist Church, of which she was a member, Elder J.C. Monday, Elder Albert Davis officiating. Interment in Church cemetery.

HUGHIE A. (COTTON) COX, 841 Cherry St., Alcoa, TN, 84 years of age and formerly of Union County. Born May 24, 1899, passed away Monday, October 31, 1983, at Colonial Hills Nursing Center, Maryville. He joined Oak Gr ove Primitive Baptist Church at an early age. Survivors, wife, Mrs. Albia White Cox; daughter, Mrs. Ada McBee, Maryville;

sisters, Nancy Brewer, Powell, Hettie Shoffner, Rockwood; brother, Dewey Cox, Tazewell; half-brother, Bob Cox, Knoxville; 5 grandchildren, 4 great-grandchildren. Funeral 2 p.m. on Thursday, Brantley's Chapel Church with Elder Clifford Brantley and Elder Jerry McBee officiating. Interment, church cemetery. - Sadly missed by family and friends and our loss is Heaven's gain.

ETHEL IRENE DALTON, died August 16, 1983, in St. Mary's Medical Center, Knoxville. Survivors, husband, LeRoy Dalton, Morristown; sons, Doyle and Jerry Dalton, Morristown, Donnie, Austin, Texas and Freddie of Mt. Juliet; daughter, Mrs. Dorothy Beckham, Knoxville; brothers, Estel Bunch, Winstead, Conn., Glenn Bunch, Indianapolis, Ind., R. S., James, Carl and Horace Bunch, Morristown; sisters, Mrs. Gladys McKinney, Mrs. Sarah Majors, Mrs. Eula Hatcher and Mrs. Cleta Holloway, all of Morristown. 7 grandchildren, and 1 great-grandson. Services were conducted by Elder John Oliver and Rev. Eugene Winstead with burial in Hamblin Memory Gardens.

McKINLEY A ELLISON was born December 3,, 1895, at Sharps Chapel in Union County, Tennessee. He passed away April 14, 1984, at the LaFollette Medical Center. He was a member and trustee of Davis Chapel Primitive Baptist Church in LaFollette, Tennessee.

On January 12, 1913, JcKinley and Bedie Wyrick were married. To this union were born four children; three boys and one daughter. Sons, woodrow and Robert preceeded their father in death. Their mother, Bedie died April 1, 1946.

On January 17, 1948, McKinley and Lassie Cannon were married. Survivors, wife, Lassie; son, Carl, Lake City; daughter, Naomi Longmire, LaFollette, and a devoted daughter-in-law, Mrs. Robert (Ethel) Ellison of Ridgely, Maryland; sister, Vestie Dyke, Sharps Chapel, and brother, Charlie Ellison, Sharps Chapel; 14 grandchildren, 20 great-grandchildren, and 2 great-great-grandchildren. He was laid to rest in the Sunrise Cemetary at Davis Chapel.

MRS. EVELYN L. GRAVES, age 55, of 8313 Emory Road, Corryton, died 12:55 p.m. Wednesday, May 9, 1984 at East Tennessee Baptist Hospital. She was a member of Rockydale Primitive Baptist Church, a charter member of Adiel Temple No 147 Daughters of the Nile, Corryton Chapter No 337 O.E.S. and former employee of Corryton Post Office. Survivors: husband, Harry Graves; daughters and sons-in-law, Mrs. Pat and Deve Wright, Mrs. Gwen and Larry Buckner, Myra Roberts, all of Corryton; son and daughter-in-law, Bob and Judy Roberts, Corryton, son and daughter-in-law, Bob and Judy Conners, Elgin, Ill; grandchildren, Bill Wright, Angela Roberts, Tessie and Timmy Drew, Carla, Ronnie and Erin Conners; father, S.T. Davis, Corryton; sisters, Mrs. Estelle Kirkland, Mrs. Nancy Weaver, Martha Davis, all of Knoxville; brothers, Joe Davis,

Tazewell, Frank Davis, Sharps Chapel, Ralph Davis, Corryton; several nieces and nephews. O.E.S. Memorial Service 8 p.m. Thursday, Stevens Chapel, by the Corryton Chapter No. 337, followed by the Adiel Temple Service which will be followed by funeral service, Elder Hugh Brummitt, Rev. Vince Jones officiating. Graveside service & interment 11 a.m. Friday in Rocky Dale Cemetery.

MRS. RUTH BEATRICE ELLISON HEATHERLY, 79, of Route 1, LaFollette, died May 15, 1984, at LaFollette Medical Center. She was a faithful member and former church clerk of Davis Chapel Primitive Baptist Church. Survivors include her husband, James S. Heatherly of LaFollette; two sons, Roy L. Heatherly, Knoxville and Arnold Heatherly of Detroit, Mich.; daughter, Mrs. Trulene H. Nash of Washington, D.C.; sisters Mrs. H. D. Gross, Nora Ellison, Mrs. D. W. Lambin and Mrs. Charles Roberson, all of LaFollette; brother, Everett Ellison, LaFollette; three grandchildren. Funeral services were held at Davis Chapel Primitive Baptist Church, Elder William Berry and Parnick Shelton officiating. Burial was in Sunrise Cemetery.

CURTIS JOHNSON, age 87, Knoxville, passed away 8 a.m. Friday, Dec. 23, 1983 at Hillcrest Nursing Home. He was a faithful member of Rocky Dale Primitive Baptist Church. Survivors: son, Estle Johnson; grandsons, Rick and Ted Johnson; great-granddaughter, April Johnson, all of Knoxville; sister, Mrs.Lottie Shelly, Sharps Chapel; several nieces and nephews. Funeral 2 p.m. Monday at Ailor's chapel, Elder Hugh Brummitt officiating. Interment, Monroe Cemetery.

CLARVEL DEVINE (GOB) KECK, age 90, was born April 7, 1893 and passed away August 21, 1983 at 10 p.m. at his home in Goin, Tennessee. He joined the Pleasant Point Primitive Baptist Church in 1927 and was ordained as a deacon on May 1, 1938. He remained a faithful member and deacon until his death and spoke of his church often. He was a retired farmer and livestock dealer; was the son of the late Thomas C. Keck and Katie Jane Hopper. He was preceded in death by his wife, Mrs. Mertie Mays Keck, two sons, Kermit and Kirby Keck, four brothers and three sisters. Survivors: wife, Mrs. Marjorie Lynch Keck, New Tazewell; daughter and son-in-law, Reba and Vaughn Widner, New Tazewell; grandchildren, Patricia Ann White, Lenoir City, Coy D. Keck, Cleveland, Tn. Sandra Gail Keck, Knoxville, and Kenny De-Lynn Widner and Denise Keck, both of New Tazewell; sister, Mrs. Bessie Collins, New Tazewell; several nieces and nephews, relatives and friends. He bore his illness with never a word of complaint and with such courage that it was amazing to his family and loved ones who cared for him so tenderly. At the last moment of life when he could no longer speak he smiled at the ones who were so patiently watching by his bed side.

Funeral services were held 11 a.m. Wednesday, August 24 at Pleasant

Point Primitive Baptist Church with Rev. Dallas Harrell, Rev. Andy Vance, and Elder Parnick Shelton Officiating. Interment in the Keck Cemetery. Songs were by the Oak Wood Quartet; Pallbearers were, Verlin Simmons, Odra Drummonds, Forrest Keck, R. M. Dooley, Tom Elmore, White Collins, Marvin Keck, and Ted Keck. Evans was in Charge.

MRS. LAURA J. KECK, age 91, Kokomo, Indiana, was born March 18, 1891 and passed away at Howard Community Hospital in Kokomo, September 6, 1982. She was a member of Pleasant Point Baptist Church and was married to Wendfield Keck in 1921. Her residence has been in Kokomo for the past 20 years. Her previous residence was Goin where she was postmaster for 20 years and a teacher 10 years. Survivors: sons, Homer Keck, Alexandria, Virginia, Corum Keck, Kokomo; brothers Milton Gray, Santa Ana and Burlie A. Gray, Knoxville; 6 grandchildren, 5 great-grandchildren. She was preceded in death by her husband, Wendfield Keck, February 7, 1949; two sons, three sisters and four brothers. Funeral services were held at 11 a.m. Thursday, September 9, at Coffey Funeral Home with Rev. George Walker officiating. Burial in the Pleasant Point Cemetery. Singers were David and Eddie Cole, Roger and Gary Walker and pianist was Janet Walker. Pallbearers were Jerry, Mike, Jeff and Rick Keck, Mike Bliss and Jay Walker.

LOUIS J. LAMB, 78, of Kanakee, Illinois, died March 10, 1984 at the Americana Healthcare Center in Kankakee. He was born November 13, 1905 in DeKalb, Alabama. He was a retired employee of Carson, Pirie Scott and Company, and was also employed at the A.O. Smith Corporation. He was an active member of the Salvation Army and a member of the League of Mercy for Shut-Ins and the Northside Senior Citizens. He was a member of Mossey Springs Primitive Baptist Church until it was dis-

banded to the T.V.A. He was preceded in death by two grandchildren, a brother and sister, and parents. Survivors include: wife, the former Cora Weaver; three sons, Ray of Aroma Park, Illinois; Earl of Bourbonnais, Illinois and Orsro, St. Anne, Illinois; a daughter, Carrie Lue Popstein of Bourbonnais, Illinois; three sisters, Molly McCarty, LaFollette, Sarah, St. Louis, Mo. and Esther of Newport, Kentucky; two brothers, Archie, Florida and Frank, Georgia; 15 grandchildren and 12 great-grandchildren. funeral services were at the Salvation Army in Kankakee with Captain Herbert Dahl officiating. Burial was in Aroma Park Cemetery.

PLUMMER McBEE, age 82, of Rt. 2, Middle-settlements Rd., Maryville, was born July 3, 1901 and passed away Sunday evening October 9, 1983 at Colonial Hills Nursing Center, Maryville. He was a Charter member and deacon of Brantley's Chapel Church. Survivors: wife, Mrs. Ottie Ellison McBee; sons, Cyrus and Junior McBee, both of Maryville; daughter, Ms. Arretus McBee, Maryville; brothers, Lora McBee, Knoxville, Lawrence McBee, Loyston amd Leonard McBee of Indiana; sisters, Mrs. Zettia Bruce and Mrs. Mae Arwood, both of Indiana; 4 grandchildren, Bill McBee, Vickie McBee Irwin, Phyllis McBee Goins and Jerry McBee all of Maryville; 8 great-grandchildren. Funeral services 2 p.m. Wednesday at Brantley's Chapel Church, Elder Clifford Brantley, Elder J. C. Monday officiating. Interment in the church cemetery. The family received friends 7-9 p.m. Tuesday at Smith Mortuary, Maryville.

Sadly missed by family and friends, but not forgotten.

MOSES NORTON, age 50, of Ridgeview Road, passed away 2:10 a.m. Wednesday, April 25, 1984 at St. Mary's Medical Center. He was a member of Rocky Dale Primitive Baptist Church. Survivors: wife, Mrs. Opal Norton; daughter, Judy Norton; daughter and son-in-law, Debbie and Roy Sharp; grandchildren, Laura, Jason and Adam Sharp; brothers, Mitchell, Ronnie and Clifford Norton; sisters, Gracie Smith, Alvada Wilkerson, Virgie Daniels, Mamie Ward, Opal Cooper, Edith Collins, and Pauline Williams; several nieces and nephews. Services at 2 p.m. Friday, at Mynatt's chapel, Elder Joe Bush and Elder Bill Berry officiating. Interment Clapp's Chapel Cemetery. Pallbearers, Buddy Daniels, David Wilkerson, LE. Smith, Larry Johnson, Ronnie Boruff and Tim Wheeler; Honorary Pallbearers, Employees of Robertshaw Control Co.

GRACIE ELDORA BREWER RUSSELL, age 82, of Sharps Chapel, passed away Tuesday, December 20, 1983 at 2:20 a.m at Baptist Hospital. She was a member of Oak Grove Primitive Baptist Church. Survivors: husband, Allen Willoughby Russell; daughters, Mrs. Ed (Alvada) Dyke, Zella Dyke, Mrs. Troy (Gladys) Lambdin, Mrs. Elbert(Margie) Hunley,all of Knoxville. Mrs. Wonnie (Meda Jean) Perry, Bradford, Ill, Mrs. Billy (Doris) Cole, New Tazewell; sons, James Russell, Sharps Chapel and Allen R. Russell of Monroe Michigan; 31 grandchildren, 37 great-grandchildren, several nieces and nephews. Funeral services were held on Thursday, Dec. 22, 1983 at 2:30 p.m. at Cooke Mortuary chapel with Elder J. C. Monday, Rev. John Robinson and Rev. Greg Sharp officiating. Singers were Trula Berry, Estelle Smith and Helen Brabson.Interment, Cris Keck Cemetery.

ALLEN WILLOUGHBY RUSSELL, age 87, of Sharps Chapel, passed away Monday, January 2, 1984 at 11:25 a.m. at Baptist Hospital. He was a member of Pleasant Hill Primitive Baptist Church, Speedwell, Tennessee. He was preceded in death 13 days by his wife Gracie Eldora Russell. Survivors: daughters, Mrs. Ed (Alvada) Dyke, Zella Dyke, Mrs. Troy (Gladys) Lambdin, Mrs. Elbert (Margie) Hunley, all of Knoxville. Mrs. Wonnie (Meda Jean) Perry, Bradford, Ill. and Mrs. Billy (Doris) Cole of New Tazewell; sons, James Russell of Sharps Chapel and Allen R. Russell, Monroe, Michigan. 31 grandchildren, 37 great-grandchildren; sisters, Clema Raley, Maynardville, Clara Rutledge, Morton, Mississippi, Francie Monroe of Ontario, Oregon. Brothers, Charlie and Denzil Russell, Sharps Chapel, Otis of Maynardville, and Ditsy, Milburn and Loyd, all of Speedwell, Tennessee; several nieces and nephews. Funeral services were held on Thursday, January 5, 1984, 2:30 p.m. at Cooke Mortuary chapel with Elder J. C. Monday, Rev. John Robison and Rev. Greg Sharp officiating. Singers were Mannie Shoffner Family and Dannie Peters. Interment in Chris Keck Cemetery.

DITSY STIRL RUSSELL, age 76, of Route 3, Speedwell was born February 16, 1908, passed away at Ft. Sanders Hospital on July 16, 1984. He was a member and deacon of Pleasant Hill Primitive Baptist Church. He was also a veteran of World War II. He was preceded in death by his first wife, Hallie Pierce Russell and one daughter, Barbara Ann. Survivors: wife, Mrs. Cleo Owens, Berry Russell, Speedwell: daughters, Mrs. James (Helen) Branscomb, and Mrs. Richard (Wilma) Brown both of Speedwell; son Ralph Russell, Monroe, Michigan, brothers, Milburn Russell, Lloyd Russell, Charlie Russell, Sharps Chapel, Denzil Russell, Sharps Chapel, Otis Russell, Maynardville; sisters, Clema Raley, Maynardville, Clara Rutledge, Morton, Mississippi, Francis Monroe, Ontario, Oregon; step-daughters, Mrs. Bennie Berry Grace, Middlesboro, Ky., Mrs. N. Lou Berry Ferris, Monroe, Mich.; 4 grandsons, one step-grandson, three granddaughters; nine great-grandchildren; several nieces and nephews. Funeral services were held at 2 p.m. Thursday, July 19 at Pleasant Hill Baptist Church with Elder Bill Thymer, Elder Larry Anderson officiating. Songs by church choir. Interment in the Cawood Cemetery. Pallbearers were Billy Wayne Russell, David Russell, Don Russell, Billy Lee Raley, Verlin Maddox and Vic Graves.

CON E. WHITE, age 70, of Davis Chapel Community, died on April 1, 1984. He was a son of the late Elder Leonard and Mossie White. He was a member of LaFollette Masonic Lodge No. 623 F&AM. He was a retired painter. Survivors: wife, Naomie White; son and daughter-in-law, Bobby Lynn and Sue Gartrell White; 3 grandchildren; brother, Emerson White; sisters, Mrs. Wheeler (Geneva) Irwin, and Oral White. Funeral services were held on April 4 at Davis Chapel Primitive Baptist Church with Elders

401

William Berry, Parnick Shelton and Hugh Brummitt officiating. Interment was in Sunrise Cemetery with Masons in charge.

CLETIS A. SIMMONS, 76, of 3111 S. Grove St., Grand Beach, died at 3 a.m. in Flower Hospital, Sylvania, Ohio. He had been hospitalized since Feb. 22. Friends were received after 6 p.m. Saturday in the Earle Little Funeral Home, where services were held at 11 a.m. Monday. The Rev. Damon Patterson of Monroe Missionary Baptist Church officiated and interment was in Roselawn Memorial Park, LaSalle, Mich. He was born May 20, 1907, in Union County, Tenn., he was the son of Marshall C. and Nancy (O'Dell) Simmons. He married Hattie Stiner Feb. 27, 1927, in Union County. They moved to Monroe in 1941 from Tennessee.

He had been employed by Consolidated Packaging Corp., northside plant, as a beater operator for more than 29 years, retiring in 1972.

He was a member of the Oak Grove Primitive Baptist Church, Sharps Chapel, Tenn.

Surviving are his wife; his step-parents, Mr. and Mrs. Joseph Zwack of Monroe; three daughters, Mrs. Russel (Mildred) Billings and Mrs. George (Barbara) Taylor, both of Chicago, Ill., and Mrs. Jack (Bonnie) Sharp of Monroe; a brother, Marshall Orlander Simmons of Indiana; two sisters, Mrs. Lela Drummonds of Monroe and Mrs. Robert (Norma) Taber of Indiana; six grandchildren, and two great-grandchildren.

He was preceded in death by two brothers.

SUSIE M. KECK SHOFFNER, age 87, of Harrogate, widow of Isaac M. Shoffner, passed away Monday, January 16, at UT Hospital. Member of Gibson Station Baptist Church and Eastern Star Lodge NO. 436, Shawanee. Preceded in death by step-children, Roy, Goldie and Ott Shoffner. Survivors: daughter, Hazel Felix of South Hollywood, Ca.; sons, Tyson and Charles Shoffner of Harrogate; 7 grandchildren; 19 great-grandchildren; 2 step-grandchildren; 7 step-great-grandchildren; brother, Londy Keck of Tuscon, Ariz.; sisters, Hassie Cole of New Market, Coba Stanley of Harrogate. Funeral service 2 p.m. Thursday, January 19, Reece Funeral Home, Elder Bill Berry, Elder William Rhymer officiating. Interment Shoffner Cemetery.

MRS. LOU WHITE, 96, died on Oct. 15, 1983, at LaFollette Community Hospital Nursing Home. She was the oldest member of Davis Chapel Primitive Baptist Church. She was preceded in death by her husband, Lewis White. Survivors include daughters, Oma Miller and Ruby Heatherly of LaFollette; sons, Leonard, Verlin, Maney, Wid, Howard and Jack White all of LaFollette; brothers, Harrison and Joe Beeler of LaFollete; 23 grandchildren; 47 great-grandchildren and 12 great-great-grandchildren. Funeral services were held at Davis Chapel Church with Elders William Berry and Parnick Shelton Officiating. Burial was in Sunrise Cemetery.

1985 Minutes

OF THE
ONE HUNDRED SIXTY-FIFTH SESSION
OF THE

POWELL VALLEY ASSOCIATION
OF PRIMITIVE BAPTIST

**HELD WITH THE SISTER CHURCH AT
BLACK FOX
GRAINGER COUNTY, TENNESSEE
AUGUST 16, 17, and 18, 1985**

THE ONE HUNDRED SIXTY-FIFTH SESSION
OF THE POWELL VALLEY ASSOCIATION
OF
PRIMITIVE BAPTIST
HELD WITH THE SISTER CHURCH AT BLACK FOX
GRAINGER COUNTY, TENNESSEE
AUGUST 16, 17, and 18, 1985

NEXT SESSION WILL BE HELD WITH THE SISTER CHURCH
AT
HALLS
KNOX COUNTY, TENNESSEE
TO BEGIN ON FRIDAY BEFORE THE THIRD SATURDAY
IN AUGUST, 1986
AT 10:30 A.M.

ELDER SPURGEON THOMPSON WILL DELIVER THE
INTRODUCTORY SERMON
ELDER CHARLES TAYLOR WILL BE THE ALTERNATE

OFFICERS

ELDER HUGH BRUMMITT   MODERATOR
1329 BROWN AVENUE, KNOXVILLE, TENN., PHONE 546-7700
ELDER CLIFFORD BRANTLEY   ASSISTANT MODERATOR
809 BROWN SCHOOL RD. MARYVILLE, TENN., PHONE 982-3875
BENNIE CAPPS   CLERK
P.O. BOX 91, MAYNARDVILLE, TENN., PHONE 992-5571
RINA JOHNSON   ASSISTANT CLERK
1217 BROWN SCHOOL ROAD, MARYVILLE, TENN., PHONE 983-2774

ARTICLES OF FAITH

Article 1. We believe in only one true living God, as He is revealed to us in the Holy Scriptures - Father, Son, and Holy Ghost.

Article 2. We believe that the Scriptures of the old and new Testaments are the words of God and the only rule of all-saving knowledge and obedience.

Article 3. We believe in the doctrine of election according to the foreknowledge of God.

Article 4. We believe in the doctrine of original sin.

Article 5. We believe in man's impotency to rescue himself from the fallen state he is in, by his own will or ability.

Article 6. We believe that sinners are justified in the sight of God only by the imputed righteousness of Jesus Christ.

Article 7. We believe the elect, according to the foreknowledge of God will be called, converted, regenerated, and sanctified by the Holy Spirit.

Article 8. We believe the saints will persevere and never fall finally away.

Article 9. We believe that baptism and the Lord's Supper are ordinances of Jesus Christ, and that true believers are the only subject of these ordinances, and that the true mode of baptism is by immersion. We believe also that feet washing is an example of Jesus Christ and should be kept by his disciples until his second coming.

Article 10. We believe in the Resurrection of the dead and the General Judgement.

Article 11. We believe that the punishment of the wicked will be everlasting and that the joys of the righteous will be eternal.

Article 12. We believe that no minister has the right to administer the ordinances, except those who have been regularly baptized and called of God, and come under the imposition of hands of the presbytery.

1985 MINUTES OF THE ONE HUNDRED SIXTY-FIFTH SESSION

Friday, August 16, 1985

The one hundred and sixty-fifth session of the Powell Valley Association of Primitive Baptists met with the Sister Church at Black Fox, in Grainger County, Tennessee on August 16, 17, and 18, 1985.

After Elder Albert Davis led the congregation in "Amazing Grace" and Elder Charles Taylor led "How Firm A Foundation", the Moderator, Elder Hugh Brummitt welcomed the congregation and pleaded for peace and love to abide through the entire Association and called for prayer by Elder John Oliver of Noeton Church.

Following prayer, Elder Larry Anderson of Pleasant Hill Church delivered the introductory sermon, from 52nd Chapter of Isaiah, using as his text "Awaken Out of the Darkness" and preached a very uplifting sermon.

After the introductory sermon, they sang a song and were dismissed in prayer byElder Walter Lyons of Halls Church. The Association was to reconvene after a 15 minute recess.

After recess, the crowd reassembled in the church. Elder Albert davis led the congregation in "Children of the Heavenly King". Moderator elder Hugh Brummitt read from the 2nd chapter of Revelation, Verses 1-5, then called for prayer by Elder Charles Taylor fró Lenoir City Church.

The Moderator then asked for the order of business for the following transactions:

1st: Called for letters of the Sister Churches to be presented to the clerk for reading. Fifteen (15) were received.

2nd: The letters were presented and read and motion approved that the delegates be seated.

3rd:The moderator called for anyone present from any of the Sister Churches not named as delegate who desired to bι be seated as such to come forward and give the clerk their name and the name of their church. Three came: Sisters, Hazel Lambert and Ada Jones from Pleasant Hill. Sister Alvada Dykes from Oak Grove.

4th: Called for petitionary letter if there should be one. None Came.

5th: Motion approved to take up correspondence with the Red Bird Association. Messengers appointed were: Elder James H. Branscomb, Elder Spurgeon Thompson, Bro.Clyde Abbott,Sr., and Brother Elwood Evans.

6th: Motion approved that the clerk be empowered to write the letter of correspondence and send to the Association.

7th: Motion approved that the Association re-elect Elder Hugh Brummitt as Moderator and Elder Clifford Brantley as Assistant Moderator for the ensuing year.

8th: Motion approved that Brother Bennie Capps be re-elected Clerk and Brother Rina Johnson be re-elected Assistant Clerk for the ensuing year.

9th: Motion was approved that we empower Elder Brummitt to appoint all the committees to serve this session.

10th: The Moderator, having been empowered to do so, named the committees as follows:

Committee on Arrangements:	Bro. Robert Welch
	Bro. Bill Taylor
	Bro. Arthur Terry
Committee on Preaching:	Bro. Elwood Evans
	Bro. Ross Wilkerson
	Bro. Glen Walker
Committee on Request:	Bro. Orice McCarty
	Elder John Oliver
	Bro. Bill Cook
Committee on Finance:	Bro. Joe Culvahouse
	Bro. Clarence Hicks
	Bro. Mannie Shoffner

11th: Called for the finances to be turned in to the Finance Committee.

12th: The committees all having been appointed and accepted, the Association moved to adjourn until 10:30 Saturday morning. They sang a song and were dismissed in prayer by Bro. Clyde Abbott, Sr. of Headrick's Chapel Church.

Saturday, August 17, 1985

At the appointed hour of 10:30 Saturday morning, and at the sound of singing, the Association reassembled to a full house.

After singing, the Assistant Moderator, Elder Clifford Brantley gave a very spiritual and uplifting talk and read from the 32nd chapter of Deuteronomy, beginning with verse 7, then called for prayer by Bro. Steve Taylor of Lenoir City Church.

After prayer, the Moderator called the Association to order for the remainder of the business:

1st: The Moderator called for any letters from Sister Churches not received on F riday. There was none.

2nd: The Moderator called for anyone from any of the churches who were present and desired to be seated as delegate to come forward. There was none.

3rd: The moderator then called for the report of the Committee on Arrangements who submitted the following report:

Report on Arrangements:
  Call for the roll call of delegates.
  Call for report of Committee on Preaching
  Call for report of Committee on Request.
  Call for report of Committee on Finance.
  Decide how many minutes we have printed, who shall
  supervise the printing and delivery of same, which
  sister church shall host the next association and who will
  preach the introductory sermon and who will be the
  alternate. Who will prepare Circular Letter.

  Respectfully Submitted,
  Bro. Bill Taylor
  Bro. Arthur Terry,
  Bro. Robert Welch

4th: Motion approved to receive the above report and release the Committee.
5th: Called the roll call of delegates of all the Sister Churches and check the absentees.
6th: Called for the report of the Committee on Preaching:

Friday Night:	Elder Spurgeon Thompson
	Elder Bill Berry
Saturday Morning:	Elder William Rhymer
	Elder Clifford Brantley
Saturday Night:	Elder Albert Davis
	Elder Parnick Shelton
Sunday Morning:	Elder Hugh Brummitt
	Elder Charles Taylor

  Respectfully Submitted,
  Bro. Glen Walker
  Bro. Raymond Wilkerson
  Bro. Elwood Evans

7th: Motion approved to receive the above report and release the committee.
8th: Called for the report of the Committee on Request.
  Report on Committee on Request:
8th: We, the Committee on Request, request that we have 1,100 minutes printed and the clerk supervise the printing and distribution of same and that he receive $135.00 for his services. We request that Elder Clifford Brantley write a circular letter to be printed in the minutes, that the next session of the Association be held with the Sister Church of Halls in Knox County,

Tennessee, to begin on Friday before the third Saturday in August, 1986, and may the love of peace that is here continue throughout the remainder of this Association.

Respectfully Submitted,
Bro. O. D. McCarty
Eld. John Oliver
Bro. William Cook

9th: Motion approved to receive the above report and release the committee.

10th: Called for the report of the Committee on Finance, which submitted the following report:

Report of Finance Committee:

Black Fox	$ 25.00
Braden's Chapel	35.00
Brantley's Chapel	40.00
Davis Chapel	45.00
Gethsemane	35.00
Gibson Station	50.00
Halls	100.00
Headrick's Chapel	25.00
Lenoir City	45.00
Meyer's Grove	35.00
Noeton	25.00
Oak Grove	35.00
Pleasant Hill	45.00
Pleasant Point	25.00
Rocky Dale	40.00
Total collection	$605.00
Donation	40.00
Collection	200.00
Balance in Bank	147.00
	$992.00
Expenses for 1985	560.00
Balance in Bank	432.00

Respectfully submitted,
Bro. Joe Culverhouse
Bro. Mannie Shoffner
Bro. Clarence Hicks

410

11th: Motion approved to receive the above report and release the committee.

12th: Motion approved that we grant the request of the committee and have 1,100 minutes printed and the clerk to receive $135.00 for his services.

13th: Motion approved that the next session of the Association be held on Friday before the third Saturday in August, 1986, at 10:30a.m.

14th: Motion approved that Elder Clifford Brantley write the circular letter for the 1986 minutes.

15th: Motion approved that Elder Spurgeon Thompson deliver the introductory sermon and Elder Charles Taylor be the alternate.

16th: Motion approved that the churches of the Powell Valley Association extend to the church and the people of Black Fox our heart felt thanks and our prayers for the love, fellowship, kindness and food while we were here with you. May the good Lord bless and keep you is our prayers.

17th: Motion to adjourn, trusting the Lord to permit us to meet again with the sister church at Hall in Knox County, Tennessee, on Friday before the third Saturday in August, 1986, at 10:30 A.M.

Dismissed in prayer by Bro. Clarence Hicks
Elder Hugh Brummitt, Moderator
Elder Clifford Brantley, Assistant Moderator
Brother Bennie Capps, Clerk
Brother Elna Johnson, Assistant Clerk

LETTER OF CORRESPONDENCE

We, the Powell Valley association of Primitive Baptist, now in session with the Black Fox Church, convening August 16, 17, and 18, 1985, send greetings to the Red Bird Association.

Our very dear Brothers and Sisters we desire to establish correspondence with you. We have chosen as messengers to bear the epistle of love to you, Elder James H. Branscomb, Elder Spurgeon Thompson, Brother Clyde Abbott, Sr., and Brother Elwood Evans.

We look forward to having your delegate with us next year when we convene with the church at Halls in Knox, Tennessee, to commence on Friday before the third Saturday in August, 1986.

- Special Announcements -

Brantley's Chapel has their Sunday night services every Sunday night at 7 p.m. in the summer months and at 6 p.m. in the winter months.

The following churches asked for the Association for 1986: Black Fox, Brantley's Chapel, Gibson Station, Halls, Lenoir City, and Pleasant Hill.

Please make your contribution payable to: Powell Valley Association.

SUMMARY

We are blessed with a fine group of ministers as was illustrated by those who had the opportunity to preach. We regret that time will not permit more of them to preach when we meet with the Association.

On Friday night, Elder Bill Berry preached from the 2nd chapter of Daniel, 44th verse, using as his text "The Kingdom of Heaven" and preached a very spiritual and uplifting sermon. He was followed by Elder Spurgeon Thompson who spoke from the 2nd chapter of First Corinthians, verse 8, and preached a very good sermon.

Then on Saturday morning, Elder Clifford Brantley spoke from the 1st chapter of 2nd Timothy, 9th verse, using as his text "What Jesus Christ Came to Do", and preached a very spiritual sermon. He was then followed by Elder Charles Taylor, who spoke from the 17th chapter of John, using as his text "Unity" and preached a sermon that was enjoyed by all.

On Saturday Night, Elder James Branscomb brought a wonderful sermon concerning the birth of Christ and the purpose of His birth. He was then followed by Elder Parnick Shelton who read from the 17th chapter of John and using as his text "Love" and brought a very uplifting sermon.

On Sunday morning, Elder William Rhymer preached a very spiritual and uplifting sermon concerning the "Kingdom of God". He was then followed by Elder Hugh Brummitt who also brought a very spiritual and uplifting sermon using "Hope" as his text.

RULES OF DECORUM

1. The churches composing the Powell's Valley Association shall not be confined to any set rules as to specific number of Messengers they shall have in the body, but shall have the right to name in their letters as many as they choose, and in addition all orderly members of any of the churches being present be entitled to seats in the body as Messengers fo their respective churches, with all the rights and privileges of the same.

2. The Messengers thus assembled shall be denominated the Powell's Valley Primitive Baptist Church.

3. For the purpose of historical information and statistical edification, the Churches are required to state in letters, the number of members in fellowship, the number received by Baptism, by letter, by confession of Faith, the number dismissed, excluded and dead since last session; also the time of their meeting, their pastoral supply, and the amount of money contributed for ministers and other purposed together with any other information they deem appropriate for the edification of the saints and glory of God.

4. This Association shall have no power to answer queries, give advice, or dictate to the Churches in any case, or to lord it over God's heritage nor any power by which she can directly or indirectly fringe on the internal rights of the church or censure and try any church or member in reference to faith and practice and determine upon validity of gospel ordinances. These things shall rest entirely with the churches; but henceforward our annual meetings shall be only for the purpose of hearing from each other, and for the worship of God and mutual comfort and edification of the Saints. To this end we reserve the privilege annually for Friday before the Third Saturday in August and the two following days or at such other times as may be agreed upon with any church that may invite us having to protect our own standard, while in session, from heresay and disorder to recognize and invite any primitive Baptist minister or any lay brother to worship with us that may deem proper; to request the brethren of our body to visit other churches or bodies in our belief with whom we may desire to culture Christian fellowship; to publish in a minute of our proceedings.

5. Each session of the body shall have a Moderator and Clerk who shall hold office until re-elected.

6. Any order member of any church belonging to this body, when convened, being present shall be eligible to elect on as Moderator and Clerk or to sit on any committee appointed by the same.

7. In all election or questions that may be necessary to determine by vote, the vote shall be taken by churches, each church being entitled to three votes for any number less than one hundred, and one additional vote for every fifty or fraction thereof above the first hundred, but the Messengers of each church may divide their vote as they see proper.

8. All elections or questions coming to vote shall be determined by a majority vote cast, and it shall be the only duty of the minority to acquiesce in the decision thus reached.

9. If new churches desire to be admitted to this union they shall petition by letter and messengers and if voted for and recommended by one or more sister churches for her Presbytery constitutioning them, as orthodox and orderly they shall be received by the vote of the body and manifested by the Moderator giving the Messengers the right hand of fellowship.

10. Any motion or resolution clearly inconsistent with the above rules shall be promptly ruled out of order unless withdrawn by the mover.

11. Any messenger being ruled out of order by the Moderator shall have the right to appeal to the body on the question of order, and if sustained shall be allowed to proceed, but if not take his seat.

12. Our meeting being held in the name of Christ and the worship of God; each Messenger is expected to observe due and proper therein.

13. It will not be considered good for any Messenger whose name has been enrolled as

such to abruptley break off or absent himself from the Association without leave.

14. The Moderator shall be entitled to the same privilege of speech as other members provided the chair is filled.

15. The minutes of the Association shall be read and approved by the body and signed by the Moderator before adjourning.

16. The Association shall be opened and closed by prayer.

17. Amendments to these may be made at any time by a majority of the union voting by churches when they deem it necessary, provide such amendments do not compromise the sovereignty of the churches nor have tendency to give body undue power or jurisdiction over them.

MINISTERS DIRECTORY

Elder Larry Anderson, Speedwell, TN 869-4635
Elder Johnny Atkins, Bean Station, TN Ph. 767-2397
Elder Johnny Ayres, Rt. 3 - Box 159, Bean Station, TN Ph. 586-5401
Elder William Berry, Rt. #13, Knoxville, TN Ph. 922-9189
Elder LeRoy Braden, 2305 Middlesboro Hwy.LaFollette, TN 562-9353
Elder J. H. Branscomb, Speedwell, TN, Ph. 562-6361
Elder Clifford Brantley, Brown School Rd., Maryville, TN Ph. 982-3735
Elder Hugh H. Brummitt, 1329 Brown Ave., Knoxville, TN Ph. 546-7700
Elder Joe Bush, Corryton, TN, Ph. 687-7018
Elder Jim Campbell, Louisville, TN Ph. 983-1654
Elder Noble Clawson, Rt. 4, Speedwell, TN Ph. 562-2004
Elder Albert Davis, Speedwell, TN Ph. 869-3596
Elder Joe Irving, RT. 3, Box B101, Middlesboro, KY Ph. 248-8349
Elder Nelson Jones, Rt. 1, Harrogate, TN Ph. 869-3703
Elder Gohn Godftey, 15443 Valleoga, Victoryvill, CA Ph. 714-243-4661
Elder Alvin Graves, 122 Oak Wood Dr., Lenoir City, TN Ph. 986-9725
Elder Walter Lyons, 1602 Garfield St., Alcoa, TN Ph. 984-3207
Elder Jerry McBee, 2433 Pennsylvania Ave., Maryville, TN 37801 984-1643
Elder Sheridan Moore, Route 1, Townsend, TN Ph. 448-6430
Elder J. C. Monday, Speedwell, TN Ph. 562-3068
Elder John Oliver, Rt. 2, Box 513, Bean Station, TN Ph. 581-5039
Elder Howard Pippin, 101 Rose Street, Lenoir City, TN Ph. 986-2791
Elder William Rhymer, Rt. 3, Harrogate, TN Ph. 867-3092 762
Elder Parrick Shelton, 6001 McGinnis Rd., Corryton, TN 687-6142
Elder Spurgeon Thompson, Box 36, Shawanee, TN Ph. 869-8175
Elder Claude Rosson, Rt. 4, New Tazewell, TN Ph. 626-3168
Elder Robert Walker, Sevierville, TN Ph. 428-1527
Elder Clay Widner, Rt. 1, Tazewell, TN Ph. 626-3893

LICENTIATES

Brother Clyde Abbott, Sr., Rt. 7, Sevierville, TN Ph. 453-2329
Brother Roscoe Branscomb, Speedwell, TN
Brother Odell Carpenter, Maryville, TN
Brother Clarence Hicks, Maryville, TN 984-8881
Brother Steve Taylor, Lenoir City, TN

CHURCHES AND THEIR DELEGATES

BLACK FOX: Brothers, Dale Capps, Arthur Terry, and Bennie Capps; **Sisters:** Mary Ruth Capps, Pamella Capps, Naomi Cabbage, Mary Terry, Sarah Hopson, Debbie Sexton, Rachael Ingle and Sue Atkins

BRADEN'S CHAPEL: No delegate listed

BRANTLEY'S CHAPEL: Elder Clifford Brantley; **Brothers:** Glen Walker, Dan Walker, Robert Welch, Rina Johnson, Eskie Boruff, David Beason, Chester Hembree, and Everett Brantley; **Sisters,** Edith Walker, Barcie Brantley, Hazel Johnson, Blanche Welch, Sherry Beason,Mildred Brantley

DAVIS CHAPEL: Bros., Clyde Lynch, O. D. McCarty; **Sisters,** Ruby Boruff, Pearl Lynch, Molly McCarty and Ollie Welch

GETHSEMANE: Elders, William Rhymer, Spurgeon Thompson, Joe Irving and Nelson Jones; **Bros.,** Franklin Jones, Curtis Ball and Claude Sandifur; **Sisters,** Karen Rhymer, Evelyn Irving, Polly Jones, Fannie Jones, Lucille Ball, Shirley Sandifur and Dorothy Johnson

HALLS: Elders, Parnick Shelton, Hugh Brummitt and Walter Lyons; **Bros.,** Elwood Evans, Joe Culvahouse, Vance Harmon, Vance Harmon, Jr, and Bill Taylor; **Sisters:** Wilma Shelton, Ruby Brummitt, Velna Evans, Betty Culvahouse, Irene Harmon, Cookie Harmon and Trula Berry

HEADRICK'S CHAPEL: Elder: Robert Walker; **Bros.:** Clyde Abbott, and Bill Cooke

LENOIR CITY: Elder, Charles Taylor; **Bros.,** Clarence Hicks, Raymond Wilkerson and Hubert Spoon; **Sisters,** Annie Spoon and Ruby Williams

MYERS GROVE: Bro. Bill Good

NOETON: Elder John Oliver; **Bro.** Charlie Collins, Carroll Oliver and Tim Oliver; **Sister,** Dora Collins

OAK GROVE: Elder, Johnnie Atkins; **Bro.,** Mannie Shoffner; **Sisters,** Frances Eastridge and Ruth Shoffner

PLEASANT HILL: Elders, James Henry Branscomb, Larry Anderson and Albert Davis; **Sisters:** Helen Ruth Branscomb, Myra Anderson and Audra Davis

ROCKY DALE: Elders, Joe Bush and Bill Berry; **Bros.,** Josh Stapleton; **Sisters;** Norma Jean Bush and Ima Lee Stapelton

CIRCULAR LETTER

by Elder Parnick Shelton

Very Dear Brethren,

May God help me to express my love to all of our Churches in the Powell Valley Association of Primitive Baptist. We should count it a blessing to meet for three days once a year.

I wish more people would attend, as we are brothers and sisters in Christ Jesus. I always look forward to the Association. I love to see the people of God, to be with them, and to hear the Gospel of our Lord preached, and to see the people rejoice in our Saviour's love and the Salvation that we have, given freely by God.

I love to see God's Spirit manifest among his people. There are pleanty of blessings for us if we obey the spirit. God gives us of his spirit to manifest. It is by God's love, mercy, and grace, that we are children of of God. All our praise, honor, and glory we owe to him. As the Apostle Paul has written, "By the grace of god I am what I am." So are we, by his unmerited favor and grace. I love what our churches are founded upon, which is Jesus Christ. The Truths of God's Word. It should be believed by our people and be preached by our preachers. So if it is the truth, let us contend for the truth and rejoice in truth. We must worship in spirit and truth.

Study the Articles of Faith that you will find in our Minutes, which our churches are founded upon. We believe them to be solid and will stand, a firm foundation, because his word will back it up. God is a wonderful and great God; a sovereign God, unbounded by space. We can not measure God. In Romans Chapter 9--Verse 20 and 21 it states "He is the potter and we are the clay". Who are we to question God?

I love Salvation by Grace which is free. I love Election, the foreknowledge of God. In II Thessalonians, Chapter II, Verse 12, the Bible says, "That they all might be damned who believe not the truth, but had pleasure in unrighteousness. We are to believe the Truth to please Him. May God bless you all is my prayer.

CHURCH	COUNTY	PASTOR	CLERK	ADDRESS
Black Fox	Grainger	Elder Larry Anderson	Bennie Capps	P.O. Box 91, Maynardville, TN 37807
Braden's Chapel	Union	Elder Noble Clawson Elder LeRoy Braden, Asst.	Jimmie Edwards Linda Bean, Asst.	Speedwell, TN 37870 Speedwell, TN 37870
Brantley's Chapel	Blount	Elder Clifford Brantley	Gaye Lee Mildred Lee, Asst.	Rt. 1, Box 128, Townsend, TN 37822 Rt. 1, Box 128, Townsend, TN 37822
Davis Chapel	Campbell	Eld. LeRoy Braden	Katheryn Angel Sondra Wright, Asst.	Rt. 5, Box 170, LaFollette, TN 37766 1766 1256 Middlesboro Hwy. LaFollette, TN37766
Gethsemane	Knox	Elder Walter Lyons	Tom Carmichael	729 Frank St., Knoxville, TN 37919
Gibson Station	Lee Va.	Elder William Rhymer Eld. Spurgeon Thompson, Asst.	Dorothy Johnson Shirley Sandifur, Asst.	Rt. 2, Box 320, Ewing, VA 24248 Rt. 2, Harrogate, TN 37752
Halls	Knox	Elder William Berry Elder Parnick Shelton, Asst.	Alice Powers Sarah Jean Harmon, Asst.	7525 Temple Acre Dr., Knoxville, TN37938 7120 Chermont Cir., Knoxville, TN 37938
Headrick's Chapel	Sevier	Elder Walter Lyons	Clyde H. Abbot, Sr.	Rt. 7, Sevierville, TN 37862
Lenoir City	Loudon	Eld. Charles Taylor	Libby Hicks	Rt. 13, Box 67-13, Maryville, TN 37801
Meyers' Grove	Claiborne	Elder LeRoy Braden Elder Clay Widner, Asst.	Bonnie Miracle Kathy Keck, Asst.	Rt., Box 91, New Tazewell, TN 37825 Rt. 2, Box 52, New Tazewell, TN 37825
Noeton	Grainger	Elder John Oliver	Carroll Oliver Bessie Collins, Asst.	Rt. 2, Box 512, Bean Station, TN37708 Rt. 5, Morristown, TN 37814
Oak Grove	Union	Elder J. C. Monday Elder Jerry McBee, Asst.	Betty P. Sharp Betty Shoffner, Asst.	Rt. 1, Box 250, Sharps Chapel, TN 37866 Sharps Chapel, TN 37866
Pleasant Hill	Claiborne	Elder William Rhymer Elder Albert Davis, Asst.	William Branscomb Jerry Hensley, Asst.	Speedwell, TN 37870 Speedwell, TN 37870
Pleasant Point	Claiborne	Elder Larry Anderson	Elder Claude Rosson Beatrice Williams, Asst.	Rt. 4, New Tazewell, TN 37825 Rt. 2, Box 156 Rogersville, TN 37857
Rocky Dale	Knox	Elder Hugh Brummitt	Edward Collett Saundra Boruff	Rt. 1, Box 17, Luttrell, TN 37779 6916 Weaver Rd., Knoxville, TN

11

STATISTICAL TABLE

Church	Printing Minutes	Total Membership	Deceased	Relationship	Dismiss by Letter	Excluded	Baptism	Rec'd by Letter	Restored	REGULAR MEETING TIME	COMMUNION TIME
Black Fox	$25.00	71	2	0	0	0	0	0	0	Second Saturday Night and Sunday after Fourth Saturday	Sunday Following Second Saturday in June
Braden's Chapel	35.00	155	0	1	3	2	3	0	0	First Saturday Night and Sunday	Sunday Following First Saturday in April
Brantley's Chapel	40.00	107	0	0	4	0	2	0	0	Second Saturday Night- Every Sunday and Sunday Night	Sunday following Second Saturday in July at 10:30 a.m.
Davis Chapel	45.00	106	0	1	0	1	0	0	0	Every Sunday and Sunday Night	Sunday following Third Saturday in June
Gethsemane	35.00	31	1	0	7	0	0	0	0	Every Sunday except the First Sunday	Fourth Sunday in May and October
Gibson Station	50.00	76	2	0	0	0	0	0	0	First Saturday and Saturday Night- Every Sunday and Sunday Night	Sunday following First Sunday in June
Halls	100.00	110	0	1	0	1	0	1	0	Every Sunday and Sunday Night	Last Sunday in April
Headrick's Chapel	25.00	110	0	0	0	1	1	0	0	First and Third Sunday of each Month	First Sunday in May and October 11 A.M.
Lenoir City	45.00	129	2	0	0	1	1	2	0	Every Sunday and Sunday Night	Wednesday Night before Easter Sunday -Third Sunday in October
Myers Grove	35.00	74	1	0	1	1	0	0	0	Every Sunday Morning 4th Saturday Night & Sunday	Sunday following Fourth Saturday in May
Noston	25.00	38	0	0	0	0	0	0	0	First Sunday-Third Saturday and Sunday of each Month	Sunday following Third Saturday in May & September
Oak Grove	35.00	339	5	2	0	4	8	0	0	First Saturday Night and Sunday- Third Sunday	Sunday following the First Saturday in May
Pleasant Hill	45.00	90	2	0	0	3	0	0	0	4th Sat. Morning & Sat. Night 4th Sun.-Every Sun. Night	Sunday following Fourth Sunday in June at 10:30 a.m.
Pleasant Point	25.00	103	0	0	0	0	0	0	0	Sunday Following Fourth Saturday	Sunday following first Saturday in July
Rocky Dale	40.00	104	3	1	2	0	0	0	0	Every Sunday Morning	Sunday following Third Saturday in May

ANDERSON, EASTER FAYE, age 79, of Emory Road,, Corryton, Tennessee passed away Wednesday evening, February 20, 1985, at the home of her son, Bill Anderson. She was the Widow of Ernest Anderson and a member of Rocky Dale Baptist Church. Survivors: Daughter, Mrs. Sam (Gail) Shields, Lebanon, Tn; sons; William (Bill) Anderson, and Keith Anderson, both of Corryton, TN; 8 grandchildren; 1 great-granddaughter; sister, Mrs. Stella Clapp, Corryton, TN; brother, Clun Hill, Knoxville, TN and very devoted friends, Mack and Brenda Dyer and family. Funeral service was held at 2 p.m. on Saturday at Gentry-Griffey Chapel, Elder Hugh Brummitt, Elder Parnick Shelton and Elder Joe Bush officiated. Interment was in Greenwood Cemetery. Pallbearers were: Gary Hill, Floyd Loy, Bill Wright, James Thompson, Mack Dyer, and Mackie Dyer. The family received friends from 6:30 -9 p.m. on Friday at Gentry-Griffey Chapel. She is sadly missed by family, church and neigbors.

So many times I've heard her say
If Jesus would only come today
And take His children to that sweet home
Where no more heartaches ever come.
How sweet 'twill be to reach Heaven's shore
And live with Jesus forever more.
I'll trust His gentle hand to guide
Me safely to the other side -
To see friends and loved ones gone before.
They're waiting me near Heaven's door.

Trula M. Berry

BERRY, IDA BELLE, 82, Clapps Chapel Road, Corryton, TN, was born July 24, 1902, and passed away November 5, 1984 She was married to Harley Berry on August 10, 1917. She was preceded in death by her husband and one son, Elder Everett Berry. One son, Clyde, passed away on November 23, 1984. Survivors are: daughters, Mrs. Bertha Kear, Mrs. Jean Kear, and Mrs. Ethel Robinson of Knoxville, TN, and Mrs Margie Lively of Corryton, TB; sons, Elmer, Ross, Edward, Harley, Jr., Rev. Ronnie and Rev. Billy Berry of Corryton, TN, Charles Berry of Knoxville, TN, AND Luther Berry of Charlotte, N.C. There were 38 grandchildren. She was survived by one sister, Mamie Murphy, St. Louis, MO, and one brother, Edward Shelby, Corryton, TN.

She was a devoted and faithful member of Rocky Dale Primitive Baptist Church. Funeral services were held at Mynatt's Mortuary at 1 p.m. on November 7, 1984, with Elder H.E. Brummitt, Rev.Roger Barnes, and Rev. John Dawsey officiating. Burial was in Clapps Chapel Cemetery.

DYKE, MRS. CLATIS (WELCH) — age 92, of Sharps Chapel, passed away

4:20 p.m. Wednesday, January 23, 1985, at the home of her daughter, Mrs. Mary Ellison. Member of Oak Grove Primitive Baptist Church. She was the widow of the late James Dyke. Survivors: daughters, Mary Ellison, Sharps Chapel, Maggie Dale, Maynardville, Fern Ellison, Walton, Indiana; sons, Robert Dyke, Knoxville, Lonnie Dyke, Sharps Chapel, Carl Dyke, Maynardville, Jay Dyke, Chattanooga; 26 grandchildren; 43 great-grandchildren; 4 great-great grandchildren; 6 step-grandchildren; Half-brothers, Kyle and Earl Welch, both of Knoxville; several nieces and nephews. Funeral service at 2:30 p.m. Saturday at Oak Grove Primitive Baptist Church. Elder J. C. Monday, Rev. Johnny Robison and Rev. Larry Dyke Officiated. Interment was in Church Cemetery.. Pallbearers: grandson. The family received friends 7-9 p.m. Friday at Cooke's Mortuary in Maynardville.

Mama, we miss you so much but we know you are resting in the arms of Jesus.

EDWARDS, MRS. HASSIE, age 89, died at the Laurel Manor Nursing Home September 17, 1984.

She is survived by her sons, Harold Edwards, Virgil Edwards, and Roy Edwards, all of Speedwell, TN; brother, Everett Harmon, Speedwell, TN; sisters, Harriett Moyers, LaFollette, TN, Hattie Brust, Cleveland, Ohio; 14 grandchildren and 14 great-grandchildren.

Services were held at 4:30 p.m. Wednesday at the Pleasant Hill Primitive Baptist Church with burial in Hunter Cemetery in Speedwell, TN. Evans Funeral Home was in charge of arrangements.

HILL, CORA PARKS, age 84, of 615 Bon Street, Lenoir City, TN, passed away November 30, 1985 at ParkWest Hospital. Member of Halls Primitive Baptist Church of Knoxville, TN. He was a retired knitter of Charles Bacon Company. Survivors: nephews: Willard and Carson Parks, Both of Texas, Jack Parks of Loudon, TN, Hubert Parks of Lenoir City, TN; nieces: Iva Kagley and Neva Jean Robbins, Both of Lenoir Ciry, Rosa Bridges of California, Sarah Ford of Greenback, TN, Georgia Quillen and Irene Davis, both of Florida; a very devoted and loving friend, Mollie Rogers.

Funeral service was at 2 p.m. December 2, 1985 at Click Funeral Home Chapel, Lenoir City, TN. Elder Harold Hunt and Bill Berry officiated. Interment in City Cemetery. The family received friends 7-9 Saturday at Click's Funeral Home. Pallbearers: William Taylor, Jack Cook, Sam Hardeman, David Sharp, Tommy Scarbrough and Vance Harmon.

IRVIN, MRS. ZULA, was born in Tennessee on January 14, 1909 and departed this life in Claiborne County Hospital on June 14, 1985 at the age of 76 after a long illness. She was preceded in death by her husband, John Irvin. She was a member of Gibson Station Primitive Baptist Church Her survivors include: a nephew, Frank Willis of Ewing VA; a niece, Sue Hicks of Morristown, TN and many, many friends.

Funeral services were held at Sturgill Funeral Home in Rose Hill, VA, with Elder William Rhymer and Elder Spurgeon Thompson officiating. She was laid to rest in Southern Cemetery at Gibson Station, VA.

LAMB, CORA LILLIS WEAVER, 77 , of Kankakee, Illinois, died June 20, 1985 at her home, following a short illness. She was born February 16, 1908 in Lost Creek to Elder and Mrs. Manna Weaver. She was married to Louis Lamb on January 27, 1927 in Union County. He died February 4, 1984. They both were members of mossey Springs Primitive Baptist Church unti it was disbanded to the Tenessee Valley Authority.

Mrs. Lamb had been employed by Bear Band Hosiery Company and was a 35 year member of the Salvation Army. She also was a member of the League of Mercy Shut-Ins and the Home League. Survivors include: three sons, Ray, Earl, and Osro; a daughter, Carrie Lue Popstein; 15 grandchildren: 13 great-grandchildren; two sisters, Freida Sharp of Knoxville (Halls) and Ruby Boruff of LaFollette, (Davis Chapel); two brothers and three sisters are deceased. Funeral services and burial were in Illinois.

MIRACLE, EVERT, age 53, New Tazewell, passed away at Claiborne County Hospital July 20, 1985. He professed faith in Christ and was a member and deacon of Myers Grove Primitive Baptist Church. Survivors: wife, Mrs. Rosa Drummonds Miracle, New Tazewell; daughters: Ms. Bonnie Miracle, Knoxville; Mrs. Johnny (Carolyn) Day, Knoxville; Mrs. John (Kathern) Mike, Harrogate; Ms. Wanda Miracle, Ms. Patsy Miracle, Ms. Abigail Miracle, Ms. Lillie Mae, all of Tazewell; sons: Glen, Syllus, Bradley and Troy Miracle, all of New Tazewell; grandchildren: Jason Lynn and Crystal Dawn Day, both of Knoxville; parents, Andy and Flora Miracle, New Tazewell; brothers: Matthew Miracle, Blaine, Carson Miracle, Winchester, Ky; Dane Miracle, New Tazewell; Sisters: Esther Drummonds, and Oma West, Monroe, Mich.; several nieces and nephews. He was preceded in death by one son, Steve Miracle and one half-brother, Dewey Keller. Funeral services were held at 2 p.m. Tuesday, July 23 at Coffey Funeral Home Chapel, New Tazewell with Rev. J.C. Monday and Rev. Buster Clawson officiating. Burial in the Drummonds Cemetery. Coffey Funeral Home in Charge.

NEELY, MRS. DOROTHY DRUMMONDS, age 77, of New Tazewell,

(SEE PICTURE PAGE 18)

421

was born May 6, 1911, departed this life September 28, 1984 at Claiborne County Hospital. She professed faith in Christ at an early age. Survivors: husband, H. C. (Clayton) Neely of New Tazewell;brother, Ray Drummonds of New Tazewell; sister, Miss Hazel Drummonds, Tazewell; three nieces and three nephews, several great-nieces and nephews and other relatives. She was preceded in death by three sons. Funeral services were held at 2 p.m. Monday, Oct. 1 at Coffey Funeral Home Chapel with Rev. Hugh Vancel, Rev. Danny Drummonds officiating. Songs byVerlin Simmons Singers. Interment in the Drummond Cemetery. Pallbearers were Gerald and Richard Hansard, Jeff Walker, Dennis Drummonds, Doyle Hansard, Edsel Leabow, Richard Neely and Dale Neely. Coffey Mortuary, Inc., in charge.

MOYERS, ROBERT LEE, son of William A. and Lucinda Moyers, passed away December 1, 1984, at the Veterans Administration Hospital in Murfreesboro, TN after a long illness. He was born Oct. 14, 1921. He was married to Juanita Sweet February 6, 1946. To this union was born two children: Billy Ray Moyers of Powell, TN and Mrs. James (Mildred) Wise of Dandridge,TN and 4 grandchildren: 1 grandchild, Janet Gail Wise preceded him in death. Surviving grandchildren are: James and Barbie Wise of Dandridge, TN, and Billy Wayne Moyers of New Tazewell, TN; two brothers, Earl Ray Moyers of Monroe Mich., and Rev. Kenneth B. Moyers of Washburn, TN; sister, Mrs. Nadine Ray, Maynardville, TN and several nieces and nephews and many friends. He joined Pleasant Hill Primitive Baptist Church at Speedwell, TN several years ago but has been sick for a long time and unable to attend.
Our loss is Heaven's gain.

ROE, CLYDE R., age 77, of Route 4, Oak St., Maynardville, passed away 2:15 a.m. Friday, May 24, 1985 at St. Mary's Medical Center. Member of Oak Grove Primitive Baptist Church, retired employee of Union Carbide, Kokomo, Ind., former Sheriff of Union County. Preceded in death by parents, Paris and Maggie (King) Roe; brother, Audrey Row. Survivors: wife, Mrs. Frances (Walker) Roe; daughters, Helen Bailey, Kokomo, Ind., Joann Mulkey, Greentown, Ind., Marcella Chesney, Seymour; sons, Larry and Gary Roe, both of Maynardville, Darrell Roe, of Gatlinburg; 14 grandchildren; 6 great-grandchildren; 1 great-great-grandchild; sister, Pearl Turntaugh, Russiaville, Ind., brothers, Vibert Roe, Kokomo, Ind., Clatis Roe, Speedwell, Roy Roe, Sharps Chapel; several nieces and nephews. Funeral service at 2 p.m. Sundat, Cooke Mortuary Chapel, Eld. Hugh Brummitt and Rev. Gary Beeler officiating. Interment Pleasant View Cemetery, Maynardville. Pallbearers: Wayne Walker, David Hunley, Troy Holloway, Harold Daniels, Lon Cooke, Bob Dykes. The family received friends 7-9 p.m. Saturday at Cooke Mortuary, Maynardville.

SHOFFNER, MRS. AUDREY MAE (BAILEY) —age 42, of Rt. 1, Heiskell, passed away suddenly 11 a.m. Tuesday October 23, 1984 at Talmadge Memorial Hospital, Augusta, GA. She was a dedicated member of Oak Grove Baptist Church. Employee of St. Mary's Medical Center. Survivors: husband, J.D. Shoffner, Heiskell; daughter, Teresa Satterfield, Maryville; sons, Tim and Troy Lee Shoffner, both of Heiskell; mother, Mamie Bailey, Heiskell; sisters, Irene Nicks, Geraldine Hunley, Charlotte Capshaw, Aretta Day, Evely Mynatt; brothers, L.E. and Esco Bailey, Clarence Flatford; several nieces and nephews. Funeral services were held 11 a.m. Friday at Oak Grove Baptist Church, Elder J.C. Monday, Elder Jerry McBee officiating. Interment in Stiner Cemetery. The family received friends 7-9 p.m. Thursday at Cooke Mortuary, Maynardville.

She was loved by all who knew her.

SHOFFNER, LILLIE M. (AUNT LILLIE) — age 95, of 3094 S. 800 W., Russiaville, Ind., passed away 4:08 p.m. Sunday, Dec. 23, 1984 at St. Joseph's Memorial Hospital, Kokomo, Ind. Preceded in death by son, daughter, brother, and four sisters. Survivors: daughters, Ruth Edwards, New Tazewell, Leath Simmons, Kokomo, Ind., Floy Cole and Veda Cole, both of Sharps Chapel, June Irwin, Russiaville, Ind., sons, Taylor Shoffner, Rutledge, Tilus Shoffner, Kokomo, Ind., Gene Shoffner, Bunker Hill, Ind.; 24 grandchildren; 10 great-grandchildren. Funeral services were held 11 a.m. Thursday at Oak Grove Primitive Baptist Church, Elder J.C. Monday officiating. Interment Shoffner Cemetery. The family received friends 7-9 p.m. Wednesday at Ailor's, Maynardville.

Sadly missed by family and friends.

THOMAS, WILL — age 93, passed away Sunday afternoon at Knoxville Health Care Center. He was a member and deacon at Black Fox Church for many years. Survivors: daughter, Mrs. Neal(Agatha) Haynes of Maynardville; sons: Fred Thomas, California, Rev. Charles Thomas, Maynardville, Frank Thomas, Chattanooga, Mac and Robert (Bob) Thomas, Knoxville, Rev. Ford Thomas, Corryton, John Thomas, Washburn; 42 grandchildren, many great-grandchildren and great-great grandchildren. Funeral was at 2 p.m. Tuesday at Ailor's Mortuary, burial in Thomas Cemetery. Elder Parnick Shelton and Rev. Andy Vance officiated. Pallbearers were sons.

WILLIS, ANNA GIBSON, — age 75, of Gibson Station, VA, died Sunday, May 5, 1985, at Morristown Humana Hospital in Morristown, TN. She was a member of Gibson Station Primitive Baptist Church. She was preceded in death by husband and daughter. Survivors: son, Frank Willis of Ewing, VA, daughter, Sue Hicks of Morristown, TN; 5 grandchildren and 2 stepchildren. Elder William Rhymer and Elder Spurgeon Thompson conducted the funeral serviced at Coffey Funeral Home on Tuesdy May 7. Burial was in the Willis Cemetery.

WARD, ELDRIDGE OKLEY — Son of Samuel H. and Almedia Kelley Ward, was born April 3, 1910 and departed this life December 3, 1984, age, 74 years and 8 months. He was preceded in death by his father, mother, and brother, Dr. H.H. Ward. In his early youth, he professed faith in Christ Jesus, and was baptized into the Primitive Baptist Church, in which he lived a consistent and devoted member until Jesus called him home. Truly, it can be said, "The fruits of the spirit were evident in his daily life." His church membership was with the Marion Robinette Memorial Primitive Baptist Church in Hawkins Co., TN. After making his home in Mayville, he regularly attended and enjoyed the fellowship of Brantley's Chapel Church. He was married to Polly Robinett on July 21, 1931. God blessed this union with 53 years and the birth of one son, Dennis Okley. Survivors include: wife, son and daughter-in-law: Gary and Tina Ward, Jeffrey and Diane Ward, and Brian Ward; great-grandson, samuel Todd Ward, all of Maryville; two nephews of Miami, Florida. A funeral service was held at 8 p.m. at Smith Mortuary in Maryville, and another service was held the following day at the Robinette Memorial Church in Hawkins County, Rogersville, TN. The officiating ministers were Elders Clifford Brantley, John Arnett and Jerry McBee. His body was laid to rest in the church cemetery to await that Glorious Ressurection.

DOROTHY (DRUMMONDS) NEELY
(See P. 15-16)

1986 Minutes

OF THE
ONE HUNDRED SIXTY-SIXTH SESSION
OF THE

POWELL VALLEY ASSOCIATION
OF PRIMITIVE BAPTIST

HELD WITH THE SISTER CHURCH AT
HALLS
KNOX COUNTY, TENNESSEE
AUGUST 15, 16, AND 17, 1986

THE ONE HUNDRED SIXTY-SIXTH SESSION
OF THE POWELL VALLEY ASSOCIATION
OF
PRIMITIVE BAPTIST
HELD WITH THE SISTER CHURCH AT HALLS
KNOX COUNTY, TENNESSEE
AUGUST 15, 16, AND 17, 1986
NEXT SESSION WILL BE HELD WITH THE SISTER CHURCH
AT
LENOIR CITY
LOUDON COUNTY, TENNESSEE
TO BEGIN ON FRIDAY BEFORE THE THIRD SATURDAY
IN AUGUST, 1987
AT 10:30 A.M.

ELDER CHARLES TAYLOR WILL DELIVER THE
INTRODUCTORY SERMON
ELDER WILLIAM BERRY WILL BE THE ALTERNATE

OFFICERS

ELDER HUGH BRUMMITT   MODERATOR
1329 BROWN AVENUE, KNOXVILLE, TENN., PHONE 546-7700
ELDER LARRY ANDERSON   ASSISTANT MODERATOR
RT. #, BOX 314-A, SPEEDWELL, TENN. PHONE 869-4635
BENNIE CAPPS   CLERK
P. O. BOX 91, MAYNARDVILLE, TENN., PHONE 992-5571
RINA JOHNSON   ASSISTANT CLERK
1217 BROWN SCHOOL RD., MARYVILLE, TN, PHONE 983-2774

Friday, August 15, 1986

The one hundred sixty-sixth session of the Powell Valley Association of Primitive Baptists met with the Sister Church at Halls in Knox County, Tennessee, on August 15, 16, and 17, 1986.

After Elder Bill Berry led the congregation in singing "Amazing Grace" and "Did You Think To Pray", Moderator Elder Hugh Brummitt welcomed the congregation and pleaded for peace and love to abide throughout the entire Association and called for prayer by Elder Lee Price of Georgia.

Following prayer, Elder Spurgeon Thompson of Gibson Station Church delivered the introductory sermon from the 6th chapter of Jeremiah, 16th verse, and preached a very uplifting and spiritual sermon, using as his text "Search out the old pathway". Then, Elder Charles Taylor spoke for a few minutes from the 53rd chapter of Isaiah, verse 11.

After the introductory sermon, they sang a song and were dismissed in prayer by Elder Joe Irving of Gibson Station Church. The Association was to reconvene after a 15 minute recess.

After recess, the crowd reassembled in the church. Elder William Berry led the congregation in singing, and then Moderator Elder Hugh Brummitt read from the 111 Chapter of Psalms, verse 1-9, then called for prayer by Elder Albert Davis from Pleasant Hill Church.

The Moderator then asked for the order of business for the following transactions:

1st: Called for letters of the Sister Churches to be presented to the clerk for reading. Fifteen (15) were received.

2nd: The letters were presented and read and motion approved that the delegates be seated.

3rd: The Moderator called for anyone present from any of the Sister Churches not named as delegate who desired to be seated as such to come forward and give the clerk their name and the name of their church. Two came: Brother Edmond Graves and Sister Grace Graves from Rocky Dale.

4th:Called for petitionary letter if there should be one. None came.

5th: Called for correspondence letter from the Red Bird Association, but the letter was not received.

6th: Motion approved that the clerk be empowered to write the letter of correspondence and send to the Association. Delegates: Elder Spurgeon Thompson; Brothers: Clyde Abbott, Sr., Eldwood Evans and Dale Capps; Sisters: Mary Ruth Capps and Pamela Capps.

7th: Motion approved that the Association re-elect Elder Hugh Brummitt as Moderator and Elder Larry Anderson as Assistant Moderator for the ensuing year.

427

8th: Motion approved that Brother Bennie Capps be re-elected clerk and Brother Rina Johnson be re-elected Assistant Clerk for the ensuing year.

9th: Motion was approved that we empower Elder Brummitt to appoint all the committees to serve this session.

10th: The Moderator, having been empowered to do so, named the committees as follows:

Committee on Arrangements:	Brother Robert V. Welch
	Brother O. D. McCarty
	Brother Charlie Collins
Committee on Preaching:	Brother Raymond Wilkerson
	Brother Junior McBee
	Brother Elwood Evans
Committee on Request	Brother Coy Edwards
	Brother Clyde Lynch
	Brother Bill Taylor
Committee on Finance:	Brother Joe Culvahouse
	Brother Bill Berry
	Elder John Oliver

11th: Called for the finances to be turned in to the Finance Committee.

12th: Motion approved that Elder Clifford Brantley be made Honorary Assistant Moderator.

13th: The Committees all having been appointed and accepted the Association moved to adjourn until 10:30 Saturday morning. They sang a song and were dismissed in prayer by Elder Walter Lyons, of Halls Church.

Saturday, August 16, 1986.

At the appointed hour of 10:30 Saturday morning and at the sound of singing the Association reassembled to a full house.

After singing, the Assistant Moderator, Elder Larry Anderson gave a very spiritual and uplifting talk and read from the 2nd chapter of John, and called for prayer by Brother Clarence Hicks of Lenoir City Church.

After prayer, the Moderator called the Association to order for the remainder of the business:

1st: The Moderator called for any letters from Sister Churches not received on Friday. There was none.

2nd: The Moderator called for anyone from any of the churches who were present and desired to be seated as delegate to come forward and give the clerk their name and church. Ten came: Brothers, Jim Sharp, Mannie Shoffner; Sisters, Betty Sharp and Ruth Shoffner from Oak Grove; Brother Chester Lee Hembree from Brantley's Chapel; Sisters, Ruby Hill and Linnie White and Brother Ulyss White from Davis Chapel; Sisters, Amy Sandifur and Angie Sandifur from Gibson Station Church.

3rd: The Moderator then called for the repor ~f the Committee on Arrangement who submitted the following report:
Report on Arrangements:

Call for the roll call of delegates.

Call for report of Committee on Preaching.

Call for report of Committee on Request.

Call for report of Committee on Finance.

Decide how many minutes we have printed, who shall supervise the printing and delivery of same, which sister church shall host the next association and who will preach the introductory sermon and who will be the alternate.

Who will prepare the Circular Letter.

> Respectfully Submitted,
> Brother Robert V. Welch
> Brother O. D. McCarty
> Brother Charlie Collins

4th: Motion approved to receive the above report and release the committee.

5th: Called the roll call of delegates of all the Sister Churches and check the absentees.

Who will prepare the Circular Letter.

> Respectfully Submitted,
> Brother Robert V. Welch
> Brother O. D. McCarty
> Brother Charlie Collins.

4th: Motion approved to receive the above report and release the committee.

5th: Called the roll call of delegates of all the Sister Churches and check the absentees.

6th: Called for the report of the Committee on Preachingz;

Friday Night:	Elder Larry Anderson
	Elder Bill Berry
Saturday Morning:	Elder Nelson Jones
	Elder John Oliver
Saturday Night:	Elder Parnick Shelton
	Elder Charles Taylor
Sunday Morning:	Elder William Rhymer
	Elder Hugh Brummitt

Respectfully Submitted,
Brother Raymond Wilkerson
Brother Junior McBee
Brother Elwood Evans

7th: Motion approved to receive the above report and release the committee.

8th: Called for the report of the Committee on Request, which was given:

We, the Committee on Request, request that we have 1,100 minutes printed and the clerk, Bennie Capps, supervise the printing and distribution of same, and that he receive $135.00 for his services. We therefore request Elder John Oliver write a circular letter to be printed in the minutes. We further request that the next session of the Powell Valley Association be held with the Sister Church at Lenoir City, Tennessee, in Loudon County to begin at 10:30 A.M. on Friday morning before the third Saturday in August, 1987, and to continue three days. We also request that Elder Charles Taylor preach the introductory sermon and Elder William Berry be the alternate.

Respectfully submitted,
Brother Coy Edwards,
Brother Clyde Lynch
Brother Bill Taylor

9th: Motion approved to receive the above report and release the committee.

10th: Called for the report of the Committee on Finance, which submitted the following report:

Black Fox	$25.00
Braden's Chapel	35.00
Brnatley's Chapel	40.00
Davis Chapel	45.00
Gethsemane	35.00
Gibson Station	50.00
Halls	100.00
Headrick's Chapel	25.00
Lenoir City	45.00
Meyers' Grove	25.00
Noeton	30.00
OakGrove	35.00
Pleasant Hill	45.00
Pleasant Point	25.00
Rocky Dale	40.00

Total Collection	$600.00
Donation	100.00
Balance in Bank	432.00
	1,082.00
Expenses for 1986	560.00
Balance in Bank	522.00

Respectfully Submitted:
Brother Joe Culvahouse
Elder Bill BERRY
Elder John Oliver

11th: Motion approved to receive the above report and release the committee.

12: Motion approved that we grant the request of the committee and have 1100 minutes printed and the clerk to receive $135.00 for his services.

13: Motion approved that the next session of the Association be held at the Sister Church of Lenoir City to commence on Friday before the third Saturday in August, 1987, at 10:30 A.M.

14: Motion approved that Elder John Oliver write the circular letter for the 1987 minutes.

15th: Motion approved that Elder Charles Taylor deliver the introductory sermon and Elder Bill Berry be the alternate.

16th: Motion approved that the churches of the Powell Valley Association extend to the church and the people of Halls our heart felt thanks and our prayers for the love, fellowship, kindness and food while we were with you. May the good Lord bless and keep you is our prayers.

17th: Motion approved to adjourn, trusting the Lord to permit us to meet again with the sister church at Lenoir City in Loudon County, Tennessee, on Friday before the third Saturday in August, 1987, 10:30A.M.

Dismissed in prayer by Elder William Berry.

Elder Hugh Brummitt, Moderator

Elder Hugh Brummitt, Moderator
Elder Larry Anderson, Assistant Moderator
Brother Bennie Capps, Clerk
Brother Rina Johnson, Assistant Clerk

SPECIAL ANNOUNCEMENTS

Brantley's Chapel has their second Saturday night service at 7P.M.;

every Sunday morning at 10:30 a.m.; Sunday night at 7 p.m. in the summer months and 6 p.m. in the winter months.

The following churches for the Association for 1987: Black Fox, Brantley's Chapel, Gibson Station, Lenoir City, and Pleasant Hill.

Date of ordination of the following Elders:

Elder Larry Anderson, October, 1975
Elder James Branscomb, June, 1956
Elder Nelson Jones, July 17, 1981
Elder Charles Taylor, April 1959

Please make your contribution payable to: Powell Valley Association.

SUMMARY

We are blessed with a fine group of ministers as was illustrated by those who had the opportunity to preach. We regret that time will not permit more of them to preach when we meet with the Association.

On Friday night, Elder Bill Berry read from the 8th chapter of Romans, verses 28, 29 and 30, preached a very uplifting and spiritual sermon on, "All things work together for good to them that love God". He was followed by Elder Lee Price of Georgia who preached a uplifting sermon, using as his text "All Things." He was then followed by Elder Larry Anderson who spoke on Faith and Love from 1st John, the 5th chapter and brought a sermon enjoyed by all.

Then on Saturday morning, Elder Nelson Jones read the 1st chapter of John, verses 1-12 and preached a good sermon on the beginning of them and the creation of man.;;He was followed by Elder John Oliver who brought a good sermon using as his text "Prayer".

On Saturday night, Elder James Branscomb opened up the service and read from the 32nd chapter of Deuteronomy, verse 7 and spoke on the "True and Living God". He was then followed by Elder Parnick Shelton who preached a wonderful sermon from the 17th chapter of John, using as his text "The World that God so loved". He was followed by Elder Charles Taylor who brought a very uplifting and spiritual sermon concerning "The Will of Man" from the 10th chapter of Isaiah, verse 5.

On Sunday morning, Elder Bill Berry opened up the service and read from the 13th chapter of First Corinthians and spoke a few minutes on "Love". He was then followed by Elder William Ryhmer who preached a spiritual sermon from the 1st chapter of Matthew, verse 21 concerning "The Works and Will of God. Elder Hugh Brummitt then preached from the 4th chapter of First Thessalonians, and brought a very uplifting and spiritual sermon concerning "Comforting you therefore one another with the Word".

MINISTERS DIRECTORY

Elder Larry Anderson, Rt. 3, Box 314-A,Speedwell, TN 869-4635
Elder JohnnyAtkins, Bean Station, TN Ph. 767-2397
Elder Buford Doyle Ausmus, Rt. 2, Speedwell, TN Ph. 566-0433
Elder Johnny Ayres, Rt. 3-Box 159, Bean Station, TN Ph. 586-5401
Elder William Berry, Rt. 13, Knoxville, TN Ph. 922-9189
Elder LeRoy Braden, 2305 Middlesboro, Hwy., LaFollette, TN 562-9353
Elder J. H. Branscomb, Speedwell, TN, Ph. 562-6361
Elder Hugh H. Brummitt, 1329 Brown Ave., Knoxville, TN Ph. 546-7700
Elder Joe Bush, Rt. 3, Corryton, TN, Ph. 687-7018
Elder Jim Campbell, Louisville, TN Ph. 983-1654
Elder Noble Clawson, Rt. 4, Speedwell, TN Ph. 562-2004
Elder Albert Davis, Speedwell, TN Ph. 869-3596
Elder Joe Irving, Rt. 3, Box B101, Middlesboro, KY Ph. 248-8349
Elder Nelson Jones, Rt. 1 - Box 343, Harrogate, TN Ph. 869-3703
Elder John Godfrey, 15443 Valleoga, Victoryvill, CA Ph. 714-243-4661
Elder Alvin Graves, 122 Oak Wood Dr., Lenoir City, TN Ph. 986-9725
Elder Walter Lyons, 1602 Garfield St., Alcoa, TN Ph. 984-3207
Elder Jerry McBee, 2433 Pennsylvania Ave., Maryville, TN 37801 984-1643
Elder Sheridan Moore, Rt. 1, Townsend, TN Ph. 448-6430
Elder J. C. Monday, Speedwell, TN Ph. 562-3068
Elder John Oliver, Rt. 2, Box 513, Bean Station, TN Ph. 581-5039
Elder Howard Pippin, 101 Rose Street, Lenoir City, TN Ph. 986-2791
Elder William Rhymer, P.O. Box 12, Shawanee, TN Ph. 869-3092
Elder Parnick Shelton, 6601 McGinnis Rd., Corryton, TN 687-6142
Elder Charles Taylor, 101 Rose St., Lenoir City, TN 37771
Elder Spurgeon Thompson, Box 36, Shawnee, TN Ph. 869-8175
Elder Claude Rosson, Rt. 4, New Tazewell, TN Ph. 626-3168
Elder Robert Walker, Sevierville, TN Ph. 428-1527
Elder Clay Widner, Rt. 1, Tazewell, TN Ph. 626-3893

LICENTIATES

Brother Clyde Abbott, Sr., Rt. 7, Sevierville, TN Ph. 453-2329
Brother Roscoe Branscomb, Speedwell, TN
Brother Odell Carpenter, Maryville, TN
Brother Chester Hembree, Maryville, TN
Brother Clarence Hicks, Maryville, TN 984-8881
Brother Mark Taylor, Lenoir City, TN
Brother Steve Taylor, Lenor City, TN
Brother Richard Walker, Maryville, TN

LETTER OF CORRESPONDENCE

We, the Powell Valley Association of Primitive Baptist now in session with Halls Primitive Baptist Church, convening August 15, 16, and 17, 1986, send greetings to the Red Bird Association.

Our very dear Brothers and Sisters, we desire to establish correspondence with you. We have chosen as messengers to bear the epistle of love to you, Elder Spurgeon Thompson, Brother Clyde Abbott, Sr., Brother Elwood Evans, Brother Dale Capps; Sister Mary Ruth Capps and Sister Pamela Capps.

We look forward to having your delegate with us next year when we convene with the church at Lenoir City Primitive Baptist Church in Loudon County, Tennessee, to commence on Friday before the third Saturday in August, 1987.

Elder Hugh Brummitt, Moderator
Elder Larry Anderson, Assistant Moderator
Brother Bennie Capps, Clerk
Brother Rina Johnson, Assistant Clerk

CHURCHES AND THEIR DELEGATES

Black Fox: **Brothers,** Dale Capps and Bennie Capps; **Sisters:** Mary Ruth Capps, Pamela Capps and Naomi Cabbage

BRADEN'S CHAPEL: Brother Coy Edwards

BRANTLEY'S CHAPEL: Brothers, Everett Brantley, Rina Johnson, Glenn Walker, Chester Hembree, Junior McBee, Eskie Boruff, Richard Walker, and Robert Welch; **Sisters,** Mildred Brantley, Hazel Johnson, Edith Walker, Edith Hembree and Blanch Welch

DAVIS CHAPEL: **Brothers,** Bob Lynch, Clyde Lynch and O. D. McCarty; **Sisters,** Pearl Lynch, Mollie McCarty and Ollie Welch

GETHSEMANE: **Brother,** Tom Carmichael; **Sister,** June Carmichael

GIBSON STATION: Elders: William Rhymer, Spurgeon Thompson, Joe Irving and Nelson Jones; **Brothers,** Franklin Jones, Curtis Ball and Claude Sandifur; **Sisters,** Karen Rhymer, Polly Jones, Fannie Jones, Evelyn Irving, Lucille Ball, Shirley Sandifur and Dorothy Johnson

HALLS: Elders, Bill Berry, Parnick Shelton, Hugh Brummitt and Walter Lyons; **Brothers,** Joe Culvahouse, Vance Harmon, Vance Harmon, Jr., Edward Sharp and Elwood Evans; **Sisters,** Wilma Shelton, Ruby Brummitt, Betty Culvahouse, Irene Harmon, Cookie Harmon, Kaye Sharp, Trula Berry, Frieda Sharp and Dola Webb

HEADRICK'S CHAPEL: **Elder,** Robert Walker, **Brother,** Clyde Abbott, Sr., **Sisters,** Gearldine Abbott, Margo Abbott, and Rachael Abbott

LENOIR CITY: **Elder,** Charles Taylor; **Brothers,** Hubert Spoon, Raymond Wilkerson, Clarence Hicks and Gary Hicks; **Sisters,** Ruby Williams, Libby Hicks, Annie Spoon and Debbie Hicks

MYERS' Grove: Sister, Velt Munsey

NOETON: Elder, John Oliver; **Brothers,** Charlie Collins and Carroll Oliver; **Sisters,** Dora Collins and Mary Atkins

OAK GROVE: **Sisters,** Alvada Dykes and Frances Eastridge

PLEASANT HILL: Elders, James Henry Branscomb, Larry Anderson and Albert Davis; **Sisters,** Helen Ruth Branscomb, Myra Anderson and Audra Davis

PLEASANT POINT: No delegates present

ROCKY DALE: **Brothers,** Joe Palmer and Edward Collett; **Sisters,** Leola Palmer and Fay Collett

STATISTICAL TABLE

Church	Restored	Rec'd by Letter	Baptism	Excluded	Dismiss by Letter	Relationship	Deceased	Total Membership	Printing Minutes	REGULAR MEETING TIME	COMMUNION TIME
Black Fox	0	0	0	1	0	0	2	68	$25.00	Second Sat. Night and Sun. Sunday after Fourth Saturday	Sunday Following Second Saturday in June
Braden's Chapel	0	0	1	0	5	0	0	152	35.00	First Saturday Night and Sunday	Sunday Following First Saturday in April
Brantley's Chapel	1	0	0	1	1	1	1	106	40.00	Second. Saturday Night— Every Sunday and Sunday Night	Sunday Following Second Saturday in July at 10:30 a.m. 1:30 a.m.
Davis Chapel	0	0	0	0	1	0	5	93	45.00	Every Sunday and Sunday Night	Sunday following Third Saturday in June
Gethsemane	0	0	0	0	0	0	1	30	35.00	Every Sunday except the First Sunday	Fourth Sunday in May and and October
Gibson Station	0	0	0	0	0	0	1	75	50.00	First Saturday and Saturday Night— Every Sunday and Sunday Night	Sunday following First Sunday in June
Halls	0	2	0	0	0	1	1	112	100.00	Every Sunday and Sunday Night	Last Sunday in April
Hedrick's Chapel	0	0	0	0	0	0	1	109	25.00	First and Third Sunday of each Month	First Sunday in May and October 11 A.M.
Lenoir City	0	3	5	2	3	0	5	137	45.00	Every Sunday and Sunday Night	Wednesday Night before Easter Sunday
Myers Grove	0	0	0	0	0	0	0	74	25.00	4th Saturday Night & Sunday	Sunday following Fourth Saturday in May
Noeton	0	0	1	0	0	0	0	39	30.00	First Sunday—Third Saturday and Sunday of each Month	Sunday following Third Saturday in May & September
Oak Grove	1	0	8	4	2	0	2	336	35.00	First Saturday Night and Sunday— Third Sunday	Sunday following the First Saturday in May
Pleasant Hill	0	1	1	1	0	1	3	90	45.00	4th Sat. Morning & Sat. Night 4th Sun.—Every Sun. Night	Sunday following Fourth Sunday in June at 10:30 a.m.
Pleasant Point	0	0	0	0	0	1	1	102	25.00	First Sunday	Sunday following first Saturday in July
Rocky Dale	0	1	1	0	2	1	0	102	40.00	Every Sunday Morning	Sunday following Third Saturday in May

CHURCH	COUNTY	PASTOR	CLERK	ADDRESS
Black Fox	Grainger	Elder Larry Anderson	Bennie Capps	P.O. Box 91,Maynardville,TN 37807
Braden's Chapel	Union	Elder LeRoy Braden Elder Noble Clawson	Jimmie Edwards Linda Bean, Asst.	Speedwell, TN 37870 Speedwell, TN 37870
Brantley's Chapel	Blount		Gaye Lee Mildred Davis, Asst.	Rt. 1,Box 128,Townsend, TN 37882 Rt. 1,Box 344,Townsend, TN 37882
Davis Chapel	Campbell	Elder LeRoy Braden	Katheryn Angel Sondra Wright, Asst.	Rt. 5,Box 170,LaFollette,TN 37766 1256 Middlesboro Hwy., LaFollette,TN 37766
Gethsemane	Knox	Elder Walter Lyons Elder Robert Walker, Asst.	Tom Carmichael	729 Frank St., Knoxville, TN 37919
Gibson Station	Lee, Va.	Elder William Rhymer Eld. Spurgeon Thompson,Asst.	Dorothy Johnson Shirley Sandifur,Asst.	Rt.2,Box 320,Ewing,VA 24258 Rt.2,Box 416,Harrogate,TN 37752
Halls	Knox	Elder William Berry Elder Parnick Shelton,Asst.	Alice Powers Sara Jean Harmon,Asst.	7525TempleAcreDr.,Knoxville 37919 7120ChermontCir.,Knoxville, 37938
Headrick's Chapel	Sevier	Elder Walter Lyons Eld. Sheridan Moore,Asst.	Clyde H. Abbott,Sr. Geraldine Abbott,Asst.	Rt. 7,Box288,Sevierville,TN 37862 Rt.6,Box 204A,Sevierville,TN 37862
Lenoir City	Loudon	Elder Charles Taylor	Libby Hicks	Rt. 13,Box 67BMaryville,TN 37801
Meyers' Grove	Claiborne	Elder J. C. Monday	Bonnie Miracle Kathy Downes, Asst.	Rt., Box91,NewTazewell,TN 37825 New Tazewell, TN 37825
Noeton	Grainger	Elder John Oliver	Carroll Oliver Bessie Collins,Asst.	Rt.2,Box512,BeanStation,TN 37708 Rt. 5, Morristown, TN 37814
Oak Grove	Union	Elder J. C. Monday Elder Jerry McBee,Asst.	Betty P. Sharp Betty Shoffner,Asst.	Rt.1,Box250,SharpsChapel,TN 37866 Sharps Chapel, TN 37866
Pleasant Hill	Claiborne	Elder William Rhymer Elder Albert Davis, Asst.	William Branscomb Jerry Hensley, Asst.	Speedwell, TN 37870 Speedwell, TN 37870
Pleasant Point	Claiborne	Elder Larry Anderson	Elder Claude Rosson Beatrice Williams,Asst.	Rt.4, New Tazewell, TN 37825 Rt.Box 156,Rogersville,TN 37857
Rocky Dale	Knox	Elder Hugh Brummitt	Edward Collett Saundra Boruff,Asst.	Rt.1, Box 17,Luttrell,TN 37779 6916 Weaver Rd.,Knoxville, TN

RULES OF DECORUM

1. The churches composing the Powell's Valley Association shall not be confined to any set rules as to specific number of Messengers they shall have in the body, but shall have the right to name in their letters as many as they choose, and in addition all orderly members of any of the churches being present be entitled to seats in the body as Messengers fo their respective churches, with all the rights and privileges of the same.

2. The Messengers thus assembled shall be denominated the Powell's Valley Primitive Baptist Church.

3. For the purpose of historical information and statistical edification, the Churches are required to state in letters, the number of members in fellowship, the number received by Baptism, by letter, by confession of Faith, the number dismissed, excluded and dead since last session; also the time of their meeting, their pastoral supply, and the amount of money contributed for ministers and other purposed together with any other information they deem appropriate for the edification of the saints and glory of God.

4. This Association shall have no power to answer queries, give advice, or dictate to the Churches in any case, or to lord it over God's heritage nor any power by which she can directly or indirectly fringe on the internal rights of the church or censure and try any church or member in reference to faith and practice and determine upon validity of gospel ordinances. These things shall rest entirely with the churches; but henceforward our annual meetings shall be only for the purpose of hearing from each other, and for the worship of God and mutual comfort and edification of the Saints. To this end we reserve the privilege annually for Friday before the Third Saturday in August and the two following days or at such other times as may be agreed upon with any church that may invite us having to protect our own standard, while in session, from heresay and disorder to recognize and invite any primitive Baptist minister or any lay brother to worship with us that may deem proper; to request the brethren of our body to visit other churches or bodies in our belief with whom we may desire to culture Christian fellowship; to publish in a minute of our proceedings.

5. Each session of the body shall have a Moderator and Clerk who shall hold office until re-elected.

6. Any order member of any church belonging to this body, when convened, being present shall be eligible to elect on as Moderator and Clerk or to sit on any committee appointed by the same.

7. In all election or questions that may be necessary to determine by vote, the vote shall be taken by churches, each church being entitled to three votes for any number less than one hundred, and one additional vote for every fifty or fraction thereof above the first hundred, but the Messengers of each church may divide their vote as they see proper.

8. All elections or questions coming to vote shall be determined by a majority vote cast, and it shall be the only duty of the minority to acquiesce in the decision thus reached.

9. If new churches desire to be admitted to this union they shall petition by letter and messengers and if voted for and recommended by one or more sister churches for her Presbytery constitutioning them, as orthodox and orderly they shall be received by the vote of the body and manifested by the Moderator giving the Messengers the right hand of fellowship.

10. Any motion or resolution clearly inconsistent with the above rules shall be promptly ruled out of order unless withdrawn by the mover.

11. Any messenger being ruled out of order by the Moderator shall have the right to appeal to the body on the question of order, and if sustained shall be allowed to proceed, but if not take his seat.

12. Our meeting being held in the name of Christ and the worship of God; each Messenger is expected to observe due and proper therein.

13. It will not be considered good for any Messenger whose name has been enrolled as

such to abruptley break off or absent himself from the Association without leave.

14. The Moderator shall be entitled to the same privilege of speech as other members provided the chair is filled.

15. The minutes of the Association shall be read and approved by the body and signed by the Moderator before adjourning.

16. The Association shall be opened and closed by prayer.

17. Amendments to these may be made at any time by a majority of the union voting by churches when they deem it necessary, provide such amendments do not compromise the sovereignty of the churches nor have tendency to give body undue power or jurisdiction over them.

ARTICLES OF FAITH

Article 1. We believe in only one true living God, as He is revealed to us in the Holy Scriptures - Father, Son, and Holy Ghost.

Article 2. We believe that the Scriptures of the old and new Testaments are the words of God and the only rule of all-saving knowledge and obedience.

Article 3. We believe in the doctrine of election according to the foreknowledge of God.

Article 4. We believe in the doctrine of original sin.

Article 5. We believe in man's impotency to rescue himself from the fallen state he is in, by his own will or ability.

Article 6. We believe that sinners are justified in the sight of God only by the imputed righteousness of Jesus Christ.

Article 7. We believe the elect, according to the foreknowledge of God will be called, converted, regenerated, and sanctified by the Holy Spirit.

Article 8. We believe the saints will persevere and never fall finally away.

Article 9. We believe that baptism and the Lord's Supper are ordinances of Jesus Christ, and that true believers are the only subject of these ordinances, and that the true mode of baptism is by immersion. We believe also that feet washing is an example of Jesus Christ and should be kept by his disciples until his second coming.

Article 10. We believe in the Resurrection of the dead and the General Judgement.

Article 11. We believe that the punishment of the wicked will be everlasting and that the joys of the righteous will be eternal.

Article 12. We believe that no minister has the right to administer the ordinances, except those who have been regularly baptized and called of God, and come under the imposition of hands of the presbytery.

439

Abbott, Gracie Mae Hurst - age 61, of 312 Cox St., Knoxville, Tennessee, passed away July 26, 1985 at Sevier County Hospital of Heart failure. She was a long time and faithful member of Headrick's Chapel Primitive Baptist Church in Sevier County. Her survivors are: son, Elder Clyde Abbott, Jr., Knoxville; daughter, Alice G. (Geri) Abbott of Sevierville; grandchildren, Adam S. Abbott, Margo Abbott, Rachael Abbott, and Lori Abbott; brother, Ralph (Bid) Hurst of Sevierville; several nieces and nephews; special friends, Harold and Ina Lee, of Knoxville.

Funeral services were held at Atchley's Funeral Home Chapel at 7 P.M. Monday, July 29, 1985, with Elder Charles Taylor officiating. Burial in the Black Oak (Hurst) Cemetery at 10a.m. July 30, 1985.

Atkins, Nelson - 62, of Bean Station, passed away August 25, 1985 at Morristown -Hamblen Hospital. He was a retired farmer and attended Noeton Primitive Baptist Church. Survivors include wife, Mary Atkins of Bean Station; sisters, Mrs. Bertha Hurst of Morristown, Mrs. Dora Cameron of Rutledge, Mrs. Lizzie Hollifield of Morristown; brother, Archie Atkins of Rutledge.

Services were held August 28 at Noeton Primitive Baptist Church with Elders: Johnny Atkins, John Oliver and Rev. Olaf Atkins officiating. Burial in church cemetery. Smith Funeral Home of Rutledge in charge.

My dearest husband, it's been so lonesome since you passed away.
Our home will never be the same;
But I know you are happy in your new home, where there's no more heartaches or sickness. So sleep on and someday we'll be together again, and never to part any more.

Submitted by Wi e
Mary Atkins

Brantley, Elder Clifford K - Pastor and Moderator of Brantley's Chapel Primitive Baptist Church He was born April 14, 1913, departed this life August 17, 1986 at 10:15 a.m. at UT Hospital, Knoxville, Tennessee, passed away at the age of 73 years, 4 months and 3 days. He professed faith in Christ at an early age; joined Oak Grove Primitive Baptist Church in Union County, Tennessee, February 7, 1943; baptized May 2, 1943. He came to Blount County Tennessee, in 1937: helped organize the Church at Brantley's

Chapel in 1948, and was a Charter Member of the Church. Elder Brantley was licensed to preach February 14, 1959; ordained to full ministry of the Gospel April 12, 1959; elected Pastor and Moderator of Brantley's Chapel Primitive Baptist Church on August 8, 1959, and was either Moderator or Assistant moderator until his death. Elder Brantley was the son of the late D. Milton and Sarah M. Brantley. He was assistant moderator of the Powell Valley Primitive Baptist Association; retired employee of Alcoa and a member of the 25 Year Club.

Survivors: wife, Mrs. Barsha Ogle Brantley; sons and daughters-in-law: Daniel and Linda Brantley, Truman and Deedie Brantley, all of Maryville, Tennessee, Dennis and Brenda Brantley, Lithis Springs, Georgia; grand-children: Angela, Brian, Mike, Tina, Gina, and Ginger Brantley; brothers: Everett and Doyle Brantley, both of Maryville; sisters: Mrs. Norma Jean Bush of Corryton, Mrs. Juanita Brantley of Indiana.

Funeral Services were conducted at 2 p.m. Wednesday, August 20, 1986 at Brantley's Chapel Primitive Baptist Church. Elder William Berry and Elder William Rhymer officiating. Interment Church Cemetery. Honorary Pallbearers: Elders of Powell Valley Primitive Baptist Association. The family received friends 7-9 p.m. Tuesday, August 19, 1986 at Smith Mortuary, Maryville, Tennessee.

> Though absent you are always near;
> Still loved, still miss, still very dear.
> Time takes away the edge of grief,
> But memory turns back every leaf.
> Your memory is a keepsake
> With which we will never part.
> Though God has you in His keeping,
> We still have you in our hearts.

The Family

Brewer, Paul, age 61, died March 3, 1986. He was a member of the Lenoir City Primitive Baptist Church for many years. He is survived by his wife, Hazel Brewer; three sons, Dan, Carl, and Clyde Brewer; one daughter, Kathy; he also leaves 7 grandchildren. He had made his home in Georgia for several years before his death.

His funeral was held at Funeral Chapel, and his body was laid to rest in the City Cemetery February 28, 1986 to await the resurrection. Jesus said, "I am the resurrection, and the life; he that believeth in me, though he were dead, yet shall he live; and whosoever liveth and believeth in me shall never die.

Chamberlain, Estie Williams - passed from this life July 31, 1986. She was 77 years of age. Sister Estie suffered several years and bore it patiently. God has call her home where there is no more suffering, disappointment, or tears.

She leaves to mourn her passing her husband, J. Henry Chamberlain;

sister, Cinda Williams, both of Lenoir City. She also leaves several nieces and nephews and cousins.

Sister Estie was a faithful member of the Lenoir City Primitive Baptist Church. When she was able there was no time when she was not at her place in Church. We will miss her very much.

Funeral services were conducted on August 3, at Click Funeral Chapel with Elder Charles Taylor conducting the services. Burial was in Lakeview Cemetery wher her body awaits the resurrection and the call of her Savior.

Clawson, P.J. - 58 of Monroe Michigan, formerly of Speedwell, born May 30, 1928, died July 24, at St. Vincent Medical Center in Toledo, Ohio. He was retired from Ford Motor Co., and a Veteran of World War II.
Survivors include his wife, Alda Edwards Clawson; sons, Roger G.Clawson, Larry D., Randy H., P.J. Lee, Jeffrey S. Clawson, all of Monroe Michigan and Phillip Clawson of Temperance Michigan; daughters, Brenda L. Goins, Peggy Tyniu, Joann Paul, all of Monroe, Michigan; Sandra Chumley of Speedwell, Tennessee; brothers, Noble Lee Clawson, Speedwell; Ray Clawson, Monroe; sisters, Lou Bullard, Speedwell, Nadine Owens of West Carrollton, Ohio; 11 grandchildren.

We loved him so much, but we feel our loss is Heaven's gain.

Noble Lee Clawson

Edwards, Lonzo - 85, Speedwell, died Monday, May 12, 1986 at his home. He joined Pleasant Hill Primitive Baptist Church May, 1921 and remained a member until death. He was preceded in death by his first wife, Pearlie Mae Bean Edwards and 3 infant children; also one infant son, Earl Glen, from his second marriage. He leaves to mourn their loss, his wife Dalis M. Edwards and their daughter, Kasonda; 5 other children from his first marriage: Sybol, Vandola, Wonda, Kelburn, and Allen; three sisters, Mal Pace of Texas, Edna Robins and Minnie Collingworth, both of Madisonville.

Edwards, Jim - age 83, of Speedwell, was born March 25, 1902, passed away at his home 1:15 A.M. Friday, January 17, 1986. He was a member of the Pleasant Hill Primitive Baptist Church and the , alley Star Masonic Lodge # 577. He was preceded in death by his wife, Mrs. Hattie Owen Edwards; son, Clavin Doyle Edwards; daughter, Mrs. Ella Kay Braden, and step-son, John Delmar Brantley.

Survivors; wife, Mrs. Emma Mae Braden Edwards, Speedwell; daughters, Mrs. Barbara Sue Whaley, Petersburgh, Michigan, Mrs. Velma Berniece Shephard, of LaSalle, Michigan, Mrs. Alda Clawson, Dayton, Ohio, Mrs. Jane Whaley, Mrs. Ruby Jean Bratcher, Mrs. Helen Clawson, all of Speedwell, Mrs. Alberta Leach, LaFollette; sons, Matthew Edwards and Glen Edwards, both of Speedwell; step-son, Ivo Brantley, Speedwell; 55 grandchildren, 59 great-grandchildren; sisters, Mrs. Mae

Pace, Texas, Mrs. Edna Robbins and Mrs. Minnie Collingsworth, both of Tennessee; brother, Mr. Lonzo Edwards, of Tennessee.

Funeral services were held at Pleasant Hill Primitive Baptist Church by Elder James H. Branscomb and Elder Johnny Monday. Burial was in the Ausmus Cemetery, Speedwell.

Evans, Velna Esta, - Daughter of Jahue and Dora Wilson Brantley was born on July 24, 1916 and departed this life on May 18, 1986 at the home on Crippen Road, Knoxville, Tennessee. She was preceded in death by her parents and two sisters, Mrs. Roena Hall and Mrs. Evolena Ezell.

Survivors; husband, Elwood Evans, daughter, Iretis Watson, Euless, Texas; son, Paul Evans, Knoxville; sisters, Irene Harmon and Vandella Duncan, both of Knoxville, Wanda Booth, Pensacola, Florida; brother, Trumer Brantley, Greenville; three grandsons, Charles Hickman, Euless, Texas, Travis Evans and Jason Evans, both of Knoxville; several nieces and nephews.

She was a devoted and faithful member of Halls Primitive Baptist Church and a member of Fountain City Charter No. 160 O.E.S. Funeral services were held on Wednesday at 2:00 P.M. May 21, 1986, with Elder Bill Berry and Elder Parnick Shelton officiating. Pallbearers were Charles Hickman, Travis Evans, Vance Harmon, Jr., Jimmy Harmon, Mark Foust, and David Weaver. Burial was in Lynnhurst Cemetery.

She is sadly missed by family, friends, and neighbors.

Our loss is heaven's gain.

Gossage, Wafey - died March 3, 1986. She joined the Lenoir City Primitive Baptist Church many years prior to her death. She had lived away for most of the following years.

Funeral services were conducte at Click Funeral Chapel with burial in City Cemetery. Jesus said, "And this is the Father's will which hath sent me, that of all which he hath given me I should lose nothing, but should raise up again at the last day."

Graves, Dewey - age 85, of Knoxville, Tennessee, passed away Tuesday, March 4, 1986 in Decatur, Alabama. He was a member of Rocky Dale Primitive Baptist Church and was a retired employee of Robert Shaw Controls. He was preceded in death by wife, Clara Sharp Graves, and and daughter, Mrs. James (Mildred) Foster. Survivors: daughters, Mrs. Hubert (Lucile) Woods, Mrs. george (Catherine) Clevenger, both of Knoxville, Mrs. Bill (Joanne) Boruff, Madison, Alabama; son, Leroy Graves, Knoxville; 14 grandchildren; 11 great-grandchildren; sisters, Mrs. Mada Gwatney, Panama City, Florida; brothers, Elmer and Fate Graves, both of Corryton.

Funeral services were held at 8 P.M. on Friday, at Mynatt's Chapel, Elder Hugh Brummitt officiating. Family and friends met at Greenwood Cemetery for graveside service and interment at 10 A.M. on Saturday. The family received friends 7-8 P.M. Thursday at Mynatt's.

He was a very faithful member as long as his health permitted, and is sadly missed by the church at Rocky Dale.

Hill, James Hugh - Age 63, died on October 31, 1985. He was a member and deacon of Davis Chapel Primitive Baptist Church where he taught Sunday School for many years. He was a veteran of World War II, a farmer, and had served on the A.S.C.S. Committee for several years. He was preceded in death by his mother, Ada, and half-brother, Junior. Survivors are: wife, Ruby Turner Hill; son and daughter-in-law, Sanford and Debbie Hill; daughter, son-in-law, and grandson, Katheryn, Eddie, and Johnny Angel; father and step-mother, Bob and Rosie Hill; sisters and step-sister, Georgia Lumpkins, Bonnie Cooper, Mae Hood, Jean Hill, Emma West, and Aileen Queener; brother, Dewey.

Funeral Service was at Davis Chapel Primitive Baptist Church with Elders, LeRoy Braden, William Berry, and Parnick Shelton officiating. Burial was in Sunrise Cemetery.

IRWIN, JERRY, died July 10, 1986. He was the grandson of the late Elder Leonard White. He was a member of Davis Chapel Primitive Baptist Church in LaFollette.

Survivors are: wife, Linda; son, Todd; mother, Geneva; sister, Gail Roy. Funeral services were at Cross Chapel with Brother Don Whited officiating. Burial was in Sunrise Cemetery.

King, Margie Smith, died June 18, 1986. She was a member of Davis Chapel Primitive Baptist Church in LaFollette. She was the daughter of the late Charlie and Lola Smith.

Survivors are: husband, L. C. Smith; son, Gary; daughter, Brenda; brothers, Vitchue and Duffie Smith; sisters, Myrtle Light and Dorothy Jones.

Funeral services were at Martin Funeral Home with Brother Leonard Dabney officiating. Burial was in Campbell Memorial Gardens.

Miller, Issac Ike - age 80, died July 23, 1986. He was a member of Davis Chapel Primitive Baptist Church in LaFollette.

Survivors are: wife, Neoma; sons, John L. Austin and Bobby Miller; sisters, Martha Ford and Ada Riggs; brother, Marion; six grandchildren and two great-grandchildren.

Funeral services was at Little Coolidge Ridge Missionary Baptist Church with Brothers Frank Shown and Millard T. Cox officiating. Interment was in Bakers Forge Cemetery.

Ousley, Ott - age 89, of Route 3, Maynardville, passed away 10:19 P.M. Saturday, February 15, 1986 at Claiborne County Hospital. He was a member of Oak Grove Primitive Baptist Church. He served as superintendent of the Union County Highway Dept. for several years and as sheriff of Union County from 1936-1938. He was preceded in death by wife, Lizzie (Lig) Ousely.

Survivors: daughters, Mrs. Willard (Aldilva) Carr, Maynardville, Mrs. Edmond (Anna Lou) Campbell, Powell, Mrs. Paul (Billie) Talley, Atlanta, Georgia; six grandchildren; four great-grandchildren; sisters, Mrs. K.D. (Cecil) Lively, Seymour, Texas, Mrs. H.E. (Belvia) Anderson, Knoxville, Mrs. Victor (Alma) Edwards, Kokomo, Indiana, Mrs. Ed (Helen) Edgemon Ten Mile; brothers, Deward Ousley, Riceville, Tennessee, Bill Ousley, Kokomo; step-daughters, Mrs. Walter (Blanche) Sexton, Maynardville, Mrs. Keith (Ruth) Cole, Toledo, Ohio; step-sons, Jim Edmondson,Temperance, Michigan, Johnny and Lee Edmondson, Maynardville; several step-grandchildren, nieces and nephews.

Funeral service was held at 2 P.M. Tuesday February 18, at Cooke Mortuary Chapel, Rev. Walter Smith and Elder J.C. Monday officiating. Interment in Big Barren Cemetery.

Pallbearers: grandsons; Jimmy and Ronald Carr, Doug and Bob Sexton, Ronnie and Johnnie Edmondson.

Parris, Maude Collins, - age 73 years, passed from this life June 7, 1986 after an illness of several weeks. She has left the suffering of life to be at rest with God. Sister Maude was a faithful member of the Lenoir City Primitive Baptist Church. She was always read to help with things which God laid at her hands to do, and will be greatly missed by all those who knew her.

She leaves to mourn her passing her husband, Ed Parris; daughters, Mrs. Jery (Janice) Spoons, Mrs. Lena Donnept, Miss Jane Parris, all of Lenoir City, Jeweline Heard of California; sons, John and Ron Parris, Lenoir City, Harold Parris, Houston, Texas; 12 grandchildren; 13 great-grandchildren; sisters, Sallie Anderson, Lenoir City, Mary Parris, Care Inn, Loudon; brother, Scott Collins, Sr., Lenoir City.

Funeral services were held at Click's Funeral Home and her body was laid to rest in the City Cemetery, with Elder Charles Taylor Conducting the services. She awaits the glorious resurrection of the last day.

Sharp, Nellie S., age 89, died Friday, May 2, 1986. She was a faithful member of Lenoir City Primitive Baptist Church and attended to it lovingly for as long as she was able. She spent the last several years of her life suffering with several illnesses. Her hands were always busy making things which she mostly gave to her friends and loved ones. She will always remain in the hearts of all who knew her. Her love reached far and near. She spoke often of the hope which lay deep within her heart.

She leaves as survivors: sons, L.E. Sharp Knoxville, R.A. Sharp of Winchester Virginia, G.K. Sharp of Detroit, Michigan; daughter, Mrs Margurite Miller of Ooltewah; nine grandchildren; 11 great-grandchildren.

Funeral services were held Monday, May 5, 1986 at Weaver Chapel and conducted by Elder Charles Taylor. She was laid to rest in New Gray Cemetery to await the time when Jesus comes to claim her for His own in the Resurrection. She rests from her labor and her works do follow her.

Sharp, Clayton G. (Jerry) - age 76, of Sharps Chapel, passed away 1:20 a.m. Sunday, February 9, 1986 at his home after a lingering illness. He was of the Baptist faith and attended Oak Grove Primitive Baptist Church. His parents, Charlie Alice Sharp and one brother, Rector (Tobe) Sharp preceded him in death.

Survivors: wife, Edna (Polly) Sharp; son, Jerry (Jim) Sharp; daughters, Mrs. Malcolm (Laura Lou) Walker and Mrs. Lee (Bobbie) Beason, all of Sharps Chapel and Mrs. Bert (Mary Ann) Savage of Fortville, Indiana; six grandchildren; three great-grandchildren; brother, Luna Sharp of Sharps Chapel; several nieces and nephews. Funeral services were held on Tuesday, February 11, 1986 at Oak Grove Primitive Baptist Church with Elder J.C. Monday and Elder Jerry McBee officiating. Interment was in the Cox Cemetery. Pallbearers were grandsons and nephews: Jerry Lynn Walker, Keith and Arnold Beason and C.B., Ralph and Larry Sharp. Ailor's, Maynardville, in charge.

GONE BUT NOT FORGOTTEN

Shoffner, Tyson Walter - Entered into Eternal Rest March 22, at the Mountain Home VA Hospital in Johnson City, Tennessee.

He believed in the Primitive Baptist Faith. He was a former road superintendent in Claiborne County. He was a World War II Veteran, a charter member of New Tazewell VFW Post #8779, and a member of the Masonic Lodge #546.

Survivors are wife, Maureen Mason Shoffner of Harrogate, Tennessee; two daughters, Carolyn Ledford of Cincinnati, and Celia Hall of Speedwell, Tennessee; one brother, Charles Shoffner of Harrogate; one sister, Hazel Felix of Studio City, California; six grandchildren; Julie, Renee and Richard Ledford, Jennifer and David Hall.

Services were conducted at the Reece Funeral Home and Valley Chapel, with Elder Bill Berry and Elder Bill Rhymer speaking. Full military Honors were condcted by the Claiborne County Honor Guard.

Brother Tyson was laid to rest in the Shoffner Cemetery until the Glorious and Resurrection Dawn!

Thompson, Mellie Lee - Age 77 years and 24 days, entered into eternal rest August 26, 1985 at the Laurel Manor Health Care.

She professed faith in Christ and joined the Gibson Station Primitive Church in 1923, and was baptized by Elder Leonard White. She was the daughter of Elder and Mrs. Charlie and Sallie Redmond. She is survived by one son, Elder Spurgeon O. Thompson, Shawanee, Tennessee; one daughter, Virginia Bolton, Lakeland, Florida; one foster daughter, Donna

Fern Rizzo, Oak Lawn, Illinois; daughter-in-law, Jean Thompson and son-in-law, Doyle Bolton; 4 grandchildren, 1 great-grandchild, 1 grand-daughter-in-law.

Funeral services were conducted at the church with Elder Bill Berry and Elder Bill Rhymer, whom she loved very much! She was laid to rest until Jesus comes, in the Southern Cemetery. She was taken care of by her dear and faithful friends at the Reece Funeral Home, especially Davis Reece who she loved very much!

Mommy loved her church, preachers, and all her brothers and sisters in Christ. The last 2½ years whe would ask me about them, when I had seen them, how they were doing and she would always say I love them so. Mommy would sit in her chair, and with her fragil voice, she would sing the old hymns! Her favorite was, "I'll Be Satisfied". Before she became so ill, I heard her sing "Amazing Grace, How Sweet The Sound, That Saved A Wretch Like Me; I Once Was Lost But Now I'm Found, Was Blind But Now I See"!

Mommy is SATISFIED

White, Hasten O., age 70, died August 8, 1986. He was a member of Davis Chapel Primitive Baptist Church in LaFollette.

Survivors are: sisters, Rushie Hill, Beddie White, Mossie Bailey, Dovie Stanford, June Wilhoit, and Trula McFarland; brothers, Dewey, Conley, and Claude White.

Funeral services were at Martin Funeral Home with Brothers Clyde Ellison and O.D. Hill, Nephew, officiating. Burial was in Sunrise Cemetery.

Terry, Mary D. - age 72, of Route 2, Washburn, passed away 4:25 a.m. Tuesday, February 25, 1986, at her home. She was a member of Black Fox Primitive Baptist Church.

Survivors: husband, Arthur Terry, Washburn; daughters, Mary Ruth Capps, Edna Patterson, both of Knoxville, Sue Atkins, Washburn, Debbie Sexton, Maynardville; sons, Carl Thomas, Blaine, Stanely, Maynardville and Steve Terry, Knoxville; grandchildren, Rick and Ronnie Thomas, Sandy, Randy and Pam Capps, Chuck, Robbie and David Patterson, Mark, Chris and Beth Atkins, Crystal and April Terry, Jason

Sexton; great-grandchild, Josh; sisters, Jessie Cabbage, Maynardville, Sarah Hopson and Naomi Cabbage, both of Washburn, Bessie Lay, Knoxville; several nieces and nephews; a host of friends.

Funeral service was at 2 p.m. Thursday, at Black Fox Primitive Baptist Church, Elder Larry Anderson, Elder Bill Rhymer and Elder Parnick Shelton officiating. Interment Thomas Cemetery. Grandsons will serve as pallbearers. The family will receive friends 7-9 on Wednesday at Ailor's Maynardville.

Just when her days seemed brightest,
Just when her hopes seemed best,
God called her from amongst us,
to her eternal rest.
What we would give to see your smile,
to sit and talk with you awhile.
We often sit and think of you,
And the things you used to say and do;
And looking back with tenderness
Along the path you trod,
We bless the years we had with you,
And leave the rest to God.

We miss you Mommy — The Family

1987 Minutes

POWELL VALLEY ASSOCIATION
OF PRIMITIVE BAPTIST

**THE ONE HUNDRED SIXTY-SEVENTH SESSION
OF THE POWELL VALLEY ASSOCIATION
OF PRIMITIVE BAPTIST
HELD WITH THE SISTER CHURCH AT LENOIR CITY
LOUDON COUNTY, TENNESSEE
AUGUST 14, 15 AND 16, 1987
NEXT SESSION WILL BE HELD WITH THE SISTER
CHURCH
AT ROCKY DALE, KNOX COUNTY, TENNESSEE
TO BEGIN ON FRIDAY BEFORE THE THIRD
SATURDAY IN AUGUST, 1988 AT 10:30 A.M.
ELDER WILLIAM RHYMER WILL DELIVER
THE INTRODUCTORY SERMON
ELDER JOHN OLIVER WILL BE THE ALTERNATE**

OFFICERS

ELDER HUGH BRUMMITT   MODERATOR
1329 BROWN AVENUE, KNOXVILLE, TENN., PHONE 546-7700
ELDER LARRY ANDERSON   ASSISTANT MODERATOR
RT. 3, BOX 314-A, SPEEDWELL, TENN., PHONE 869-4635
BENNIE CAPPS   CLERK
P.O. BOX 91, MAYNARDVILLE, TENN., PHONE 992-5571
RINA JOHNSON   ASSISTANT CLERK
1217 BROWN SCHOOL RD., MARYVILLE, TN., PHONE 983-2774

Statistical Table	Communion Time	Regular Meeting Time	Printing Minutes	Total Membership	Deceased	Relationship	Dismiss by Letter	Excluded	Baptism	Rec. by Letter	Restored
Black Fox *25.00*	Sunday following Second Saturday in June	Second Sat. Night and Sun. Sunday after Fourth Saturday	$25.00	69	1	0	0	0	0	0	0
Braden's Chapel	Sunday following First Saturday in July	First Saturday Night and Sunday	35.00	155	1	0	0	0	4	0	0
Brantley's Chapel *100.00*	Sunday Following Second Saturday in July at 10:30 a.m.	Second Saturday Night - Every Sunday and Sunday Night	100.00	114	2	0	0	1	8	0	3
Davis Chapel *45.00*	Sunday following Third Saturday in June	Every Sunday and Sunday Night	45.00	76	5	1	0	0	1	0	1
Gethsemane *35.00*	Fourth Sunday in May and October	Every Sunday except the First Sunday	-	-	-	-	-	-	-	-	-
Gibson Station *50.00*	Sunday following First Sunday in June	First Saturday and Saturday Night - Every Sunday and Sunday Night	50.00	73	0	0	0	4	2	0	0
Halls *100.00*	Last Sunday in April	Every Sunday and Sunday Night	100.00	109	4	0	0	0	1	0	0
Hedrick's Chapel	First Sunday in May and October 11 a.m.	First and Third Sunday of each Month	25.00	108	1	1	0	1	0	0	0
Lenoir City *45.00*	Wednesday Night before Easter Sunday	Every Sunday and Sunday Night	45.00	131	5	0	10	0	7	2	0
Myers Grove *25.00*	Sunday following Fourth Saturday in May	4th Saturday Night & Every Sunday	25.00	79	0	0	0	0	4	0	0
Nocton *30.00*	Sunday following Third Saturday in May & September	First Sunday - Third Saturday and Sunday of each month	30.00	38	0	1	0	0	1	0	0
Oak Grove *35.00*	Sunday following the First Saturday in May	First Saturday Night and Sunday Third Sunday	35.00	329	5	0	2	4	4	0	0
Pleasant Hill	Sunday following the Fourth Sunday in June at 10:30 a.m.	4th Sat. Morning & Sat. Night 4th Sun. - Every Sun. Nght	45.00	89	1	0	2	1	1	0	0
Pleasant Point	Sunday following first Saturday in July	First Sunday	25.00	99	3	0	0	0	0	0	0
Rocky Dale *50.00*	Sunday following Third Saturday in May	Every Sunday Morning	50.00	99	2	0	1	0	0	0	0

MINUTES OF THE ONE HUNDRED SIXTY-SEVENTH SESSION

Friday, August 14, 1987

The one hundred sixty-seventh session of the Powell Valley Association of Primitive Baptists met with the Sister Church at Lenoir City in Loudon County, Tennessee, on August 14, 15 and 16, 1987.

After Brother Glenn Walker led the congregation in singing "Amazing Grace" and "There is a Fountain", moderator Elder Hugh Brummitt welcomed the congregation and pleaded for peace and love to abide throughout the entire Association, and called for prayer by Elder William Berry of Halls.

Following prayer, Elder William Berry of Halls Church delivered the introductory sermon from the 1st. chapter of Peter, 2nd. verse and preached a very uplifting and spiritual sermon, using as his text, Election and Foreknowledge of God. Elder Charles Taylor was scheduled for the introductory sermon but was not present.

After the introductory sermon, they sang a song and were dismissed in prayer by Elder Spurgeon Thompson, of Gibson Station. The Association was to reconvene after a 15 minute recess.

After recess, the crowd reassembled in the church. Brother Glenn Walker led the congregation in singing, and then Moderator Elder Hugh Brummitt read from the 7th. chapter od Second Chronicles, verse 12, then called for prayer by Orice McCarty, from Davis Chapel Church.

The Moderator then asked for the order of business for the following transactions:

1st: Called for letters of the Sister Churches to be presented to the clerk for reading. Fourteen (14) were received.

2nd. The letters were presented and read and motion approved that the delegates be seated.

3rd: The Moderator called for anyone present from any of the Sister Churches not named as delegate who desired to be seated as such to come forward and give the clerk their name and the name of their church. Three came. Brother William Beason, Brantley's Chapel; Sister Maggie Welch, Oak Grove; Sister Ruby Williams of Lenoir City Church.

4th: Called for petitionary letter if there should be one. None came.

5th: Called for correspondence letter from the Red Bird Association, but the letter was not received.

6th: Motion approved that we drop our correspondence with the Red Bird Association.

7th: Motion approved that the Association re-elect Elder Hugh Brummitt as Moderator and re-elect Elder Larry Anderson as Assistant Moderator for the ensuing year.

8th: Motion approved that Brother Bennie Capps be re-elected clerk and Brother Rina Johnson be re-elected Assistant Clerk for the ensuing year.

9th: Motion was approved that we empower Elder Brummitt to appoint all the committees to serve this session.

10th: The Moderator, having been empowered to do so, appointed the committees as follows:

Committee on Arrangements: Brother Clyde Lynch
Brother Everett Brantley
Brother Hubert Spoon

Committee on Preaching: Brother Robert V. Welch
Brother John Franklin
Brother Elwood Evans

Committee on Request: Brother Bill Taylor
Brother O.D. McCarty
Brother Joe Culvahouse

Committee on Finance: Brother Raymond Wilkerson
Elder William Rhymer
Brother Vance Harmon, Jr.

11th: Called for the finances to be turned in to the Finance Committee.

12th: The Committee all having been appointed and accepted, the Association moved to adjourn until 10:30 Saturday morning. They sang a song and were dismissed in prayer by Elder Parnick Shelton, of Halls.

Saturday, August 15, 1987

At the appointed hour of 10:30 Saturday morning and at the sound of singing, the Association reassembled.

After Elder William Berry led the congregation in singing "Amazing Grace" and "Tarry with Me," the Assistant Moderator, Elder Larry Anderson gave a very spiritual and uplifting talk and read from the 3rd Chapter of Exodus and called for prayer by Elder Joe Bush of Rocky Dale Church.

After prayer, the Moderator called the Association to order for the remainder of the business:

1st: Called for any letters from Sister Churches not received on Friday. There was none.

2nd: Called for anyone from any of the churches who were present and desired to be seated as delegate to come forward and give the clerk their name and their church. Five came, Sister Edna Atkinson, Gibson Station, Sister Bernice McBee, Brantley's Chapel, and Brother Cyrus McBee of Brantley's Chapel.

3rd: Called for the report of the Committee on Arrangements who submitted the following report:

Report on Arrangements:

Call for roll call of delegates.

Call for report of Committee on Preaching.

452

Call for report of Committee on Request
Call for report of Committee on Finance.

Decide how many minutes we have printed, who shall supervise the printing and delivery of the same, which sister church shall host the next association and who will preach the introductory sermon and who will be the alternate.

Who will prepare the Circular Letter.

Respectfully Submitted,
Brother Clyde Lynch
Brother Everett Brantley
Brother Hubert Spoon

4th: Motion approved to receive the above report and release the committee.

5th: Called the roll call of delegates of all the Sister Churches and check the absentees.

6th: Called for the report of the Committee on Preaching:
Committee on Preaching:

Friday Night:	Elder Spurgeon Thompson
	Elder Jimmy Branscomb
Saturday Morning:	Elder Jerry McBee
	Elder Parnick Shelton
Saturday Night:	Elder Hugh Brummitt
	Elder Bob Bullion
Sunday Morning:	Elder Bill Rhymer
	Elder Larry Anderson

John Oliver
Larry Anderson

Respectfully Submitted,
Brother Robert V. Welch
Brother John Franklin
Brother Elwood Evans

7th: Motion approved to receive the above report and release the committee.

8th: Called for the report of the Committee on Request, which was given:

We, the Committee on Request, wish to request as follows, that we have 1,100 minutes printed and the clerk supervise the printing and distribution of same and that he receive $135.00 for his services. We also request that the next session of the Powell Valley Association be held with the Sister Church at Rocky Dale in Knox County to begin on Friday before the third Saturday in August, 1988, at 10:30 A.M. and continue three days. We also request that Elder William Rhymer preach the introductory sermon and Elder John Oliver be the alternate. We request that Elder William Berry write a circular letter for the minutes for 1988.

Respectfully Submitted,
Brother Bill Taylor
Brother O.D. McCarty

9th: Motion approved to receive the above report and release the committee.

10th: Called for the report of the Committee on Finance, which submitted the following report:

Black Fox	$25.00
Braden's Chapel	35.00
Brantley's Chapel	100.00
Davis Chapel	45.00
Gethsemane	
Gibson Station	50.00
Halls	100.00
Headrick's Chapel	25.00
Lenoir City	45.00
Meyer's Grove	25.00
Noeton	30.00
Oak Grove -	35.00
Pleasant Hill	45.00
Pleasant Point	25.00
Rocky Dale	50.00
Total Collection	635.00
Donation	10.00
Balance in Bank	522.00
	1,167.00
Expenses for 1987	550.00
Balance in Bank	$617.00

Respectfully Submitted
Brother Raymond Wilkerson
Elder William Rhymer
Brother Vance Harmon, Jr.

11th: Motion approved to receive the above report and release the committee.

12th: Motion approved that we grant the request of the committee and have 1,100 minutes printed and the clerk to receive $135.00 for his services.

13th: Motion approved that the next session of the Association be held with the Sister Church at Rocky Dale to commence on Friday before the third Saturday in August, 1988, at 10:30 A.M.

14th: Motion approved that Elder William Berry write the circular letter for the 1988 minutes.

15th: Motion approved that Elder William Rhymer deliver the introductory sermon and Elder John Oliver be the alternate.

16th: Motion approved that the churches of the Powell Valley Association extend to the church and the people of Lenoir City our heart felt thanks and our prayers for the love, fellowship, kindness and food while we were with you. May the good Lord bless and keep you is our prayer.

17th: Motion approved to adjourn, trusting the Lord to permit us to meet again with the Sister Church at Rocky Dale in Knox County, Tennessee, on Friday before the third Saturday in August, 1988, at 10:30 A.M.

Dismissed in prayer by Elder Robert Walker.

Elder Hugh Brummitt, Moderator
Elder Larry Anderson, Assistant Moderator
Brother Bennie Capps, Clerk
Brother Rina Johnson, Assistant Clerk

SPECIAL ANNOUNCEMENTS

Brantley's Chapel has their second Saturday night services at 7 P.M., every Sunday morning at 10:30 A.M.; Sunday night at 7 P.M. in the summer months and at 6:00 P.M. in the winter months.

The following churches requested the Association for 1988: Black Fox, Brantley's Chapel, Gibson Station, Pleasant Hill and Rocky Dale.

Please make your contributions payable to: Powell Valley Association.

Dates of ordination of the following Elders:
     Elder Joe Irving, October 1, 1949
     Elder Hugh Brummitt, December 12, 1954
     Elder James Branscomb, June 23, 1956
     Elder Charles Taylor, April, 1959
     Elder Parnick Shelton, December 11, 1960
     Elder Claude Rosson, July 4, 1964
     Elder Joe Bush, April 27, 1969
     Elder Johnny Ayres, June 28, 1969
     Elder Bill Berry, August 27, 1972
     Elder Larry Anderson, October 24, 1975
     Elder Spurgeon Thompson, December 17, 1976
     Elder Bill Rhymer, December 17, 1976
     Elder Jerry McBee, April 26, 1981
     Elder Nelson Jones, July 17, 1981
     Elder Steve Taylor, September 26, 1986
     Elder Clearance Hicks, September 26, 1986

SUMMARY

We are blessed with a fine group of ministers as was illustrated by those who had the opportunity to preach. We regret that time will not permit more of them to preach when we meet with the Association.

Friday night services were conducted by Elder Spurgeon Thompson and Elder James H. Branscomb. On Saturday morning, Elder Parnick Shelton of Halls Church preached from the 3rd chapter of First Corinthians, and the 10th verse, preached a very uplifting and spiritual sermon on "The Foundation that Christ has laid." He was followed by Elder Jerry McBee who read from the 4th chapter of Nehemiah, 19 verse, preached a wonderful sermon on "Standing on the Solid Rock." Saturday night services were conducted by Elder Hugh Brummitt and Elder Bob Bullion. On Sunday morning Elder Bob Bullion opened up the service and read from the 15th chapter of Acts concerning "The Man which came down from Judaea." He was then followed by Elder Larry Anderson, who read from the 16th chapter of Ezekiel, concerning "The Fallen State of Man." He was then followed by Elder Rhymer who spoke on "The Promise of God." Both preached a very uplifting and spiritual sermons.

CHURCHES AND THEIR DELEGATES

BLACK FOX: Brothers, Dale Capps and Bennie Capps; **Sisters,** Mary Ruth Capps and Pamela Capps

BRADEN'S CHAPEL: Brother Coy Edwards

BRANDLEY'S CHAPEL: Elder Jerry McBee; **Bothers,** Daniel Brantley, Richard Walker, Rina Johnson, Robert Welch, Evertt Brantley, and Glenn Walker; **Sisters,** Hazel Johnson, Blanch Welch, Mildred Brantley, and Barsha Brantley

DAVIS CHAPEL: Brothers, Clyde Lynch, O.D. McCarty; **Sisters,** Pearl Lynch, Mollie McCarty, and Ollie White

GETHSEMANE: No letter received

GIBSON STATION: Elders, William Rhymer, Spurgeon Thompson; **Sisters,** Karen Rhymer and Evelyn Irving

HALLS: Elders, Bill Berry, Parnick Shelton, Hugh Brummitt; **Brothers,** Elwood Evans, Edward Sharp, Bill Taylor, Vance Harmon, Vance Harmon, Jr., Joe Culvahouse; **Sisters,** Wilma Shelton, Ruby Brummitt, Lou Emma Taylor, Irene Harmon, Cookie Harmon, Betty Culvahouse, Trula Berry and Frieda Sharp.

HEADRICK'S CHAPEL: Elder Robert Walker; **Brothers**, Clyde Abbott, Sr., and Bill Cook; **Sister** Gearldine Abbott

LENOIR CITY: Elder Robert Bullion; **Brothers**, Hubert Spoon, Tommy Scarbrough, John Franklin, and Raymond Wilkerson; **Sister** Annie Spoon

MEYER'S GROVE: Letter received, no delegate present.

NOETON: Letter received, no delegate present.

OAK GROVE: Sister Frances Eastridge

PLEASANT HILL: Elders, James H. Branscomb, Larry Anderson and Albert Davis; **Sister** Myra Anderson

PLEASANT POINT: Letter received, no delegate present.
ROCKY DALE: Elder Joe Bush; **Sister** Norma Jean Bush

MINISTERS DIRECTORY

Elder Larry Anderson, Rt. 3, Box 314-A, Speedwell, TN 869-4635
Elder Johnny Atkins, Bean Station, TN Ph. 767-2397
Elder Buford Doyle Ausmus, Rt. 2, Speedwell, TN ph. 566-0433
Elder Johnny Ayres, Rt. 3-Box 159, Bean Station, TN 588-5401
Elder William Berry, Rt. 13, Knoxville, TN Ph. 922-9189
Elder LeRoy Braden, 2305 Middlesboro , LaFollette, TN 562-9353
Elder J.H. Branscomb, Speedwell, TN, Ph. 562-6361
Elder Hugh H. Brummitt, 1329 Brown , Knoxville, TN 546-7700
Elder Joe Bush, Rt. 3, Corryton, TN, Ph. 687-7018
Elder Jim Campbell, Louisville, TN, Ph. 983-1654
Elder Noble Clawson, Rt. 4, Speedwell, TN, Ph. 562-2004
Elder Albert Davis, Speedwell, TN, Ph. 869-3596
Elder Joe Irving, Rt.3, Box B101, Middlesboro, KY, Ph. 248-8349
Elder Clarence Hicks, Maryville, TN
Elder Nelson Jones, Rt. 1 - Box 343, Harrogate, TN, Ph. 869-3703
Elder John Godfrey,15443Valleoga,Victoryville,CA,714-243-4661
Elder Alvin Graves, 122 Oak Wood Dr., Lenoir City, TN 986-9725
Elder Jerry McBee, 901 Chaparral , Seymour, TN 37865, 577-2669
Elder Sheridan Moore, Rt. 1, Townsend, TN, Ph. 448-6430
Elder J.C. Monday, Speedwell, TN, Ph. 562-3068
Elder John Oliver, Rt. 2, Box 513, Bean Station, TN, Ph. 581-5039
Elder Howard Pippin, 101 Rose Street, Lenoir City, TN, 986-2791
Elder William Rhymer, P.O. Box 12, Shawnee, TN, Ph. 869-3092
Elder Parnick Shelton, 6001 McGinnis , Corryton, TN 687-6142
Elder Charles Taylor, 101 Rose St., Lenoir City, TN 37771
Elder Steve Taylor, Lenoir City, TN
Elder Spurgeon Thompson, P.O. Box 36, Shawnee, TN, 869-8175
Elder Claude Rosson, Rt. 4, New Tazewell, TN Ph. 626-3168
Elder Robert Walker, Sevierville, TN, Ph. 428-1527
Elder Clay Widner, Rt. 1, Tazewell, TN, Ph. 626-3893

LICENTIATES

Brother Clyde Abbott, Sr., Rt. 7, Sevierville, TN, Ph. 453-2329
Brother Roscoe Branscomb, Speedwell, TN
Brother Odell Carpenter, Maryville, TN
Brother Chester Hembree, Maryville, TN
Brother Mark Taylor, Lenoir City, TN
Brother Richard Walker, Maryville, TN

CIRCULAR LETTER TO
POWELL VALLEY ASSOCIATION

I pray that the Lord will help me while I try to express a few words of Love.

I have met many wonderful ministers and people as I visited our churches.

(Job 19:23-24) Job said, "Oh that my words were now written! Oh that they were printed in a book! That they were graven with an iron pen and lead in the rock forever." Without Christ as our rock all our hopes would be in vain. Christ is the anchor to our soul. When God sent Adam and Eve from the garden, He already had a plan that he would redeem man back through his Son Jesus Christ. His plan was finished there on the Cross. Jesus said: "Father it is finished." (John 15:13) Greater love hath no man than this, that a man lay down his life for his friends. God loved us so that he gave his only Son, through him that we might have Eternal Life. (Matt. 24: 11-12-13) And in the last days many false prophets shall rise and shall deceive many. And because iniquity shall abound, the love of many shall Wax Cold. But he that shall endure unto the end, the same shall be saved.

So friends, love is what its all about. We must worship God in spirit and truth. May the Love of Christ Jesus rest and abide on all. May God bless everyone.

Elder John Oliver

RULES OF DECORUM

1. The churches composing the Powell's Valley Association shall not be confined to any set rules as to specific number of Messengers they shall have in the body, but shall have the right to name in their letters as many as they choose, and in addition all orderly members of any of the churches being present be entitled to seats in the body as Messengers fo their respective churches, with all the rights and privileges of the same.

2. The Messengers thus assembled shall be denominated the Powell's Valley Primitive Baptist Church.

3. For the purpose of historical information and statistical edification, the Churches are required to state in letters, the number of members in fellowship, the number received by Baptism, by letter, by confession of Faith, the number dismissed, excluded and dead since last session; also the time of their meeting, their pastoral supply, and the amount of money contributed for ministers and other purposed together with any other information they deem appropriate for the edification of the saints and glory of God.

4. This Association shall have no power to answer queries, give advice, or dictate to the Churches in any case, or to lord it over God's heritage nor any power by which she can directly or indirectly fringe on the internal rights of the church or censure and try any church or member in reference to faith and practice and determine upon validity of gospel ordinances. These things shall rest entirely with the churches; but henceforward our annual meetings shall be only for the purpose of hearing from each other, and for the worship of God and mutual comfort and edification of the Saints. To this end we reserve the privilege annually for Friday before the Third Saturday in August and the two following days or at such other times as may be agreed upon with any church that may invite us having to protect our own standard, while in session, from heresay and disorder to recognize and invite any primitive Baptist minister or any lay brother to worship with us that may deem proper; to request the brethren of our body to visit other churches or bodies in our belief with whom we may desire to culture Christian fellowship; to publish in a minute of our proceedings.

5. Each session of the body shall have a Moderator and Clerk who shall hold office until re-elected.

6. Any order member of any church belonging to this body, when convened, being present shall be eligible to elect on as Moderator and Clerk or to sit on any committee appointed by the same.

7. In all election or questions that may be necessary to determine by vote, the vote shall be taken by churches, each church being entitled to three votes for any number less than one hundred, and one additional vote for every fifty or fraction thereof above the first hundred, but the Messengers of each church may divide their vote as they see proper.

8. All elections or questions coming to vote shall be determined by a majority vote cast, and it shall be the only duty of the minority to acquiesce in the decision thus reached.

9. If new churches desire to be admitted to this union they shall petition by letter and messengers and if voted for and recommended by one or more sister churches for her Presbytery constitutioning them, as orthodox and orderly they shall be received by the vote of the body and manifested by the Moderator giving the Messengers the right hand of fellowship.

10. Any motion or resolution clearly inconsistent with the above rules shall be prompt- ly ruled out of order unless withdrawn by the mover.

11. Any messenger being ruled out of order by the Moderator shall have the right to appeal to the body on the question of order, and if sustained shall be allowed to proceed, but if not take his seat.

12. Our meeting being held in the name of Christ and the worship of God; each Messenger is expected to observe due and proper therein.

13. It will not be considered good for any Messenger whose name has been enrolled as

such to abruptley break off or absent himself from the Association without leave.

14. The Moderator shall be entitled to the same privilege of speech as other members provided the chair is filled.

15. The minutes of the Association shall be read and approved by the body and signed by the Moderator before adjourning.

16. The Association shall be opened and closed by prayer.

17. Amendments to these may be made at any time by a majority of the union voting by churches when they deem it necessary, provide such amendments do not compromise the sovereignty of the churches nor have tendency to give body undue power or jurisdiction over them.

ARTICLES OF FAITH

Article 1. We believe in only one true living God, as He is revealed to us in the Holy Scriptures - Father, Son, and Holy Ghost.

Article 2. We believe that the Scriptures of the old and new Testaments are the words of God and the only rule of all-saving knowledge and obedience.

Article 3. We believe in the doctrine of election according to the foreknowledge of God.

Article 4. We believe in the doctrine of original sin.

Article 5. We believe in man's impotency to rescue himself from the fallen state he is in, by his own will or ability.

Article 6. We believe that sinners are justified in the sight of God only by the imputed righteousness of Jesus Christ.

Article 7. We believe the elect, according to the foreknowledge of God will be called, converted, regenerated, and sanctified by the Holy Spirit.

Article 8. We believe the saints will persevere and never fall finally away.

Article 9. We believe that baptism and the Lord's Supper are ordinances of Jesus Christ, and that true believers are the only subject of these ordinances, and that the true mode of baptism is by immersion. We believe also that feet washing is an example of Jesus Christ and should be kept by his disciples until his second coming.

Article 10. We believe in the Resurrection of the dead and the General Judgement.

Article 11. We believe that the punishment of the wicked will be everlasting and that the joys of the righteous will be eternal.

Article 12. We believe that no minister has the right to administer the ordinances, except those who have been regularly baptized and called of God, and come under the imposition of hands of the presbytery.

460

Obituaries

Boruff, Ruby Weaver – Age 80, of LaFollette, died on August 17, 1986. She was a member of Davis Chapel Primitive Baptist Church. She was preceded in death by her husband, Dewey Boruff. She is survived by her sister, Frieda Sharp and several nieces and nephews. Funeral services were at Walter's Funeral Home with Elder Billy Berry and Rev. Don Reynolds, officiating.

Collins, Scott – **Age** 71, died October 28, 1986, after a lingering illness. He joined the Lenoir City Primitive Baptist Church June 18, 1961, where he was a faithfull member until his health failed him.

He leaves to mourn his passing his wife, Jo Collins; 2 sons, Scott, Jr., and Doug; 3 daughters, Charlotte, Betty, and Judy; several grandchildren, nieces and nephews.

Funeral services were held October 30, 1986, at Click Funeral Home and the body was laid to rest at Lakeview Cemetery to waint for the final ressurection day. Elder Charles Taylor officiated at the services. "And this is the Fathers will which should raise it up at the last day."

Ellison, Lassie Cannon – Age 84, of the Davis Community in LaFollette died on February 11, 1987. She was a retired school teacher and a faithful member of Davis Chapel Primitive Baptist Church. She was preceded in death by her husband, McKinley Ellison. Survivors include, stepson, Carl Ellison; step-daughter, Naomi Longmire, brother, Paris Parrott; and sisters, Helen Childress and Lela Busseni. Funeral services were held at Cross Funeral Home with Elder Billy Berry officiating. Interment was in Fincastle Cemetery.

Graves, Elmer H. – Age 95, of Corryton, died 3:40 a.m. Sunday, April 12, 1987, at St. Mary's Medical Center. Charter member of Rocky Dale Primitive Baptist Church and a retired farmer. Preceded in Death by wife, Mrs. Bessie Cardwell Graves. Survivors: daughters, Mrs. Ruth Clapp, Mrs. Lorene Hubbs and Mrs. Alma Clapp, all of Corryton, Mrs. Fern Perrin, Knoxville, Betty Graves, Miami, Florida; daughter in law, Mrs. Geneva Graves, Corryton; sons, Harry Graves, Avrell Graves; son-in-law, Dan Clapp, all of Corryton; 14 grandchildren; 27 great-grandchildren; six great-great-grandchildren; sisters, Mrs. Mada Gwatney, Panama City, Florida, Mrs. Cleo Rankin, Knoxville; brother, Fate Graves, Corryton; several nieces and nephews. Funeral services were at 8 p.m. on Tuesday at Stevens Chapel,

Elders Parnick Shelton, Joe Bush and Hugh Brummitt officiating. Family and friends met at 9:45 a.m. on Wednesday at Rocky Dale Cemetery, Corryton, for 10 a.m. gravesite service and interment. Pallbearers were grandsons and great-grandsons. The family received friends 6-8 p.m. on Tuesday at Stevens Mortuary.

Graves, Herbert D. – Age 83, of Knoxville, passed away at 11:25 p.m. October 2, 1986, at Fort Sanders Hospital, after a lengthy illness. He was a member of Rocky Dale Primitive Baptist Church, 50 year member of Blazing Star Lodge No. 455, and veteran of WWII. Survivors: son and daughter-in-law, Ronnie and Sharon Graves, Knoxville; daughter, Betty Carolyn Stubs of Switzerland; granddaughter, Tammie Renee; grandson, Ronnie E. Graves Jr., Knoxville. The family received friends 6-8 p.m. on Sunday at Ailor's Chapel. Masonic services were held by Blazing Star Lodge No. 455 at 8 p.m. in Ailor's Chapel. Funeral service followed at 8:30 p.m. with Rev. Dewey Cooper officiating. Interment 1 p.m. Monday, in Union Cemetery, Maynardville. Ailor's Mortuary, in charge.

Hopper, Horace Virley – In memory of Horace Virley Hopper born January 26, 1885, passed away April 10, 1963. Wife Alice Lemarr Hopper born August 30, 1889, passed away June 18, 1977. They were married July 7, 1918. They were members and deacons of Oak Grove Primitive Baptist Church. She was baptized July 8, 1908, being a member for 69 years. Sadly missed by children, grandchildren, and great grandchildren. Our loss is Heaven's gain.

Johnson, Dustie L. (Smith) – was born January 22, 1905, passed away November 19, 1986, at St. Mary's Medical Center in Knoxville. She joined Pleasant Point Primitive Baptist Church and was baptized the first Sunday in May, 1930. She was married to Robert Ellsworth Johnson, January 28, 1926. He preceded her in death January 28, 1958. Her parents and 12 sisters and brothers also preceded her in death. Survivors family, Frances Smith, Ruby Earl, and Dossie Watson all of Knoxville, Ruth Collins, New Tazewell, Cora Sherrod, Kokomo, Indiana, Conley Smith and Buddy Watson both of Knoxville, several nieces and nephews. Step-daughter Marie England, New Tazewell; step-sons, Mitchell Johnson, New Tazewell, and Henry B. Johnson of Knoxville, several step-grandchildren. Funeral services were held at 11:00 a.m. Friday November 21, 1986, at Coffey Funeral Home Chapel, Elder Larry Anderson, Rev. Lloyd England and Rev. Yadon Howard officiating. Burial in Shoemaker Cemetery. Written by a sister.

Keck, Lennie Collins – Mrs. Lennie Collins Keck, age 73, formerly of Claiborne County was born March 7, 1913 and passed away at the home of her daughter and son-in-law on October 31, 1986.

She professed faith in Christ and joined Pleasant Point Primitive Baptist Church. She was preceded in death by her husband, Spencer Keck.

Survivors: daughter, Inez K. Lakin; son-in-law, Joe E. Lakin; grandson and wife, David and Sharon Lakin; grandson, Dennis Lakin, all of Knoxville; brothers, Arlis and Dewey Collins both of New Tazewell; several nieces and nephews.

Funeral service was held at 11 a.m. Monday, November 3, 1986, at Pleasant Point Primitive Baptist Church with Elders Claude Rosson and Larry Anderson officiating. Songs by Willis Byrd. Interment in the Keck Family Cemetery.

Pallbearers: Mike Ramsey, Steve Nicely, Lawrence Rosson, DeLoy Collins, Billy Rosson and Isaac Collins.

Coffee Mortuary, Inc., Tazewell, was in charge.

Larmer, Carrie N. – was born February 14, 1906, departed this life September 28, 1986, at St. Mary's Medical Center at 11:22. She was a member of Black Fox Primitive Baptist Church. She is survived by daughter, Bernice Larmer of the home. Foster children, Susan, Jimmy, and Sonja Munsey, foster grandchildren Tonya, Aaron, January; Sister Lidia Mincey of Ridgeview Terrace Nursing Home, Rutledge, Tennessee, Orleane Collins, Washburn, Tennessee. Several nieces and nephews. Funeral services 2:30 p.m. Wednesday, Black Fox Primitive Baptist Church, Rev. Andy Vance and Rev. Richard Nicely officiating. Interment Cabbage Cemetery. Pallbearers sons of the late Conley Collins. Honorary pallbearers, Terry Dalton, Harold Seals, and Jerry Savage. Singers Beach Grove Quartet. Sadly missed by daughter and foster children, friends and relatives. Gone but not forgotten.

Lyons, James A. – Age 94, died August 19, 1987. Member of Halls Primitive Baptist Church. Preceded in death by sons, Elder Walter G. Lyons, Harley and Dayton Lyons. Survivors: Daughter, Mrs. Jack (Dottie) Cook of Knoxville, 6 grandchildren, 14 great grandchildren, 6 great-great-grandchildren. Burial was in Lynnhurst Cemetery. L.G. Hutchens, officiating minister.

Elder Walter G. Lyons

Age 73 of Alcoa, died June 30, 1987

Elder Lyons was Paster of Gethsemane, and Headrick's Chapel Primitive Baptist Churches. Member of Halls Primitive Baptist Church. Vetern of WWII. Retired employee of H.H. Lyons Food Markets.

He was preceded in death by his mothers Martha Lyons Brown and bothers Harley H and Dayton Lyons.

Survivors: Wife of 53 years, Callie Ausmus Lyons; daughters Georgia Ruth Hamilton of Abilene, Texas, Rhoda Johnson, Walland Glenda Murrell of Alcoa. Seven grandchildren. Three great grandchildren. Father, James A. Lyons of Maryville, Sister Mrs. Jack Cook, Knoxville, Aunt, Bernice Bean, Knoxville. Several Nieces and nephews.

Funeral services were held at 2:00 p.m. Friday July 3, 1987 at Brantley's Chapel Primitive Baptist Church. Elder Bill Berry, Elder Parnick Shelton officiating.

He was laid to rest in Church Cemetery. Honorary pallbearers: Elders of Powell Valley Primitive Baptist Association.

Maples, Etha Lynch – Age 92, of Sharps Chapel, passed away June 7, 1987 at Laurel Manor Nursing Home. Member of the Oak Grove Primitive Baptist Church. Widow of the Late James Maples. Survivors: daughters, Ova Bridges, Maynardville, Ollie Oaks, Knoxville, Olta Jean Cook, Sharps Chapel; 11 grandchildren, 13 great grandchildren, two great-great grandchildren; sisters, Seguina Robertson, Powell, Louise (Eliza) Roe, Kokomo, Indiana; several nieces, nephews and a host of friends. Funeral service 2 p.m. Tuesday, Oak Grove Baptist Church, Rev. Johnny Robinson Officiating. Interment Oak Grove Cemetery. Pallbearers were nephews. The family received friends from 7:00 to 9:00 p.m. Monday at Cooke Mortuary in Maynardville.

Maples, James H. (Buster) – Age 36, of Rt. 3, Old Valley Road, Maynardville, passed away suddenly 9 p.m. Saturday, January 17, 1987 at his home. Member of Oak Grove Primitive Baptist Church, member and Past Master of Blazing Star 455 F & AM. He was a 5th Degree Isshinryu Karate Black Belt; Staff Manager for Home Beneficial Life Insurance Company. Survivors: wife, Deborah F. Maples; Son, James Stacy maples; daughter, Karen Michelle Maples all of Maynardville. Parents, Herman and Doris (Johnson) Maples; sister, Kathy Woods; nephew, Tim Woods·

grandmother, Nancy Maples all of Sharps Chapel. Funeral services were held at 2:00 p.m. on Tuesday at Cooke Mortuary Chapel with Elder J.C. Monday officiating. Interment was in Oak Grove Church Cemetery. Honorary Pallbearers were Harold Long and Pete Mills. Active Pallbearers: Stewart Asher, Jerry Smith, Pete Harness, Rick Brooks, Kim Cox and L.A. Woods. The family received friends from 7:00 to 9:00 p.m. on Monday at Cooke Mortuary in Maynardville.

Ottie E. Ellison McBee

Born February 19, 1903, departed this life, July 20, 1987 at her home on Middlesettlements Road, Maryville, Tennessee. She was a charter member of Brantley's Chapel Church . Preceded in death by her husband, Plumer McBee, Sr.

Survivors include: daughter, Arretus McBee; sons and daughters-in-law, Cyrus and Bernice McBee, Plumer Jr. and Ada McBee, all of Maryville; grandchildren Vicki Irwin, Phyllis Goins, both of Maryville, Bill J. McBee of Georgia, Elder Jerry McBee, Seymour; 10 great-grandchildren; Sisters, Bessie McCarty, LaFollette, Dinah Barnard, Sharp's Chapel Irene Bridges, Nashville; brother Swan Ellison Sharp's Chapel; several nieces and nephews.

Funeral services were at 2 p.m. Thursday, July 23, 1987 at Brantley's Chapel Church with Elders J.C. Monday and Jerry McBee officiating. Interment was at the church cemetery. Smith Mortuary was in charge of the arrangements.

Sadly missed by relatives and friends, but our love for her will remain in our hearts forever.

McKinney, Margaret – Age 82, of Davis Chapel Community in LaFollette, died on October 28, 1986. She was a member of Davis Chapel Primitive Baptist Church. She was preceded in death by her husband, James Curtis McKinney. Survivors include: daughter, Nellie Myers; sisters, Mary McFarland and Cynthia Heatherly, and two grandsons. Funeral services were held at Walter's Funeral Home. Interment was in Fincastle Cemetery.

Newman, Floyd – Age 89, died October 14, 1986, at the Baptist Health Care Center where he had been a resident for several months. he united with the Lenoir City Primitive Baptist Church in May 1948. He loved to attend the services at the church, until his health kept him from attending. He will be sadly missed by his Brothers and Sisters at the Church.

He leaves as his survivors his son, Jack, and daughter, Carol; several grandchildren and great grandchildren; and a host of nieces, nephews and cousins.

Brother Floyd was laid to rest and now awaits the final resurrection day. Elder Charles Taylor officiated at the services. "I go to prepare a place for you — that where I am, there ye may be also."

Parrott, Tilman C. - Age 66 of LaFollette, died Friday, June 26, 1987, at Veterans Administration Medical Center in Nashville. He was of the Baptist faith and was a Veteran of World War II. Funeral services were Monday, June 29, 1987, at Walter's Funeral Home Chapel with Elder LeRoy Barden and Rev. J.L. Thacker officiating. Interment was in Sunrise Cemetery with military honors presented by D.A.V. 105. Preceded in death by his father, O.R. Parrott. Survivors include his wife, Ruby Myers Parrott of LaFollette; a son, Martin Parrott of Oak Ridge; mother Mamie Parrott of Monroe, Michigan; brother Carl Parrott of Knoxville; a host of relatives and friends. Our loss is Heaven's gain.

Patrick, Zella Oliver Long - passed away August 11, 1987, at her home in Morristown. She was a member of Noeton Primitive Baptist Church. She was the widow of Joe W. Long and Clarence G. Patrick. Survivors are, son, Raymond W. Long of White Pine; daughter, Mrs. Fuller (Fayrene) Reed, Mrs. Ernest (Opal Jean) Woods, both of Morristown; sisters, Mrs. Raymond (Aileen) Childers of Bean Station, Vina Haun of Morristown, Hettie Keitts and Mary McDaniel of Columbia, S.C., brothers, Elder John Oliver, and Jack Oliver of Bean Station, Ted Oliver of Morristown; 10 grand children, 10 great-grandchildren; 4 great-great-grandchildren. Services 11 a.m. Friday, August 14, 1987, at Mayes Mortuary in Morristown with the Rev. Hubert Bunch officiating. Burial in Hamblen Memory Gardens.

Petree, James C., Jr. - Age 71, of Knoxville, died at Brakebill Nursing Home. Member of Halls Primitive Baptist Church. Survivors: sons, Richard A. Petree, Des Moines, Iowa, James L. Petree, Atlanta, Georgia; daughters, Susan P. Burnett, Knoxville, Sara P. Simpson, Charlotte, North Carolina; eight grandchildren; one great grandchild; sisters, Mrs. Sam (Jessie May) Hardman, Mrs. John L. (Evelyn) Sharp; several nieces and nephews. Graveside services were at Old Gray Cemetary, Elder Bill Berry Officiated. Memorials made be made to Halls Primitive Baptist Church or the American Lung Association. Friends may call 7–9 p.m. Monday at Mann's Heritage Chapel.

Edna Lavada Edwards Robbins

Age 75, of 211 Monroe St., Madisonville, passed away 12:30 a.m. Saturday, October 11, 1986, at Sweetwater Hospital. Member of Pleasant Hill Primitive Baptist Church, Speedwell.

Survivors: husband, Richard Robbins; daughters and sons-in-law, Patsy Whited, Sweetwater, Mildred and Phil Newton, Savannah, Georgia, Ina and Larry R. Morgan, Corryton, Shirley and Tom Toomey, Madisonville, Joan and R.L. Hicks, Athens; sons and daughters-in-law, Paul and Carrie Mae Robbins, Richard M. and Patsy Hodge Robbins, Roger and Faye Robbins, all of Madisonville; 28 grandchildren; 10 great-grandchildren; sisters, Mae Pace of Texas, Minnie Collingsworth, Madisonville; several nieces and nephews. Preceded in death by son, Kenneth Eugene Robbins; two grandsons, Timothy Vaughn Morgan and James Ray Morgan and James Ray Robbins. Funeral 2 p.m. Monday, Biereley-Hale Chapel, Elder Kenneth Robbins, Elder Harold Hunt officiating. Interment in Sunset Cemetery. Arrangements by Biereley-Hale Funeral Home, Madisonville.

Russell, Walter Lee, Sr. – Walter Lee Russell, Sr., 74, of Route 3, Speedwell, Tennessee, died Tuesday, August 4, at his home.

He was born in Claiborne County on June 22, 1913, son of the late William J. Russell and Mary Jane Owens Cawood. He was a member of Braden's Chapel Church.

He was preceded in death by his parents William J. Russell and Mary Jane Owens Russell Cawood.

Survivors include his wife, Gladys McCreary Russell, Speedwell; five sons, James, Harrison, Eddie, Walter, Jr., and Milton Russell, all of Speedwell; five daughters, Bobbie Myers, Mary Ann Russell, Katherine Harrison, and Nancy Jesse, all of Speedwell and Betty Russell, Maynardville, Tennessee; 17 grandchildren and 15 great grandchildren; two brothers: Jim Cawood, Middlesboro, and Harrison Cawood, Jr., Columbus, Indiana; three sisters, Nellie Cawood and Mattie Frye, both of Middlesboro, and Betty Price, Speedwell.

Services were held at Reece Valley Chapel with J.C. Monday and Noble Clawson presiding. Burial is in Ausmus Cemetery. Music by the Braden's Chapel singers.

Pallbearers were Marvin Bean, Lee Roy Braden, Roger Russell, Russ Wilson, Kelburn Edwards, Clarence Breeding, Bill Graves, and Don Pierce.

Reece Funeral Home & Valley Chapel of Harrogate, Tennessee was in charge of arrangements.

Sharp, Alma Sowder – Age 68, of Sharps Chapel, passed away Thursday, August 21, at UT Hospital. Member of Oak Grove Primitive Baptist Church. Survivors: husband, Pascal Sharp; daughters, Mrs. Lorene Collins, both of Sharps Chapel, Mrs. Hilda Braden, Mrs. Joyce Lee, both of New Tazewell, Mrs. Bessie Johnson, Davisburg, Michigan, Mrs. Dottie Williams, Monroe, Michigan; sons, Bob Sharp, James C. Sharp, Luna Sharp, all of Sharps Chapel, Ralph Sharp, New Tazewell, Monterey Sharp, Ft. Lauderdale, Florida; twin sister, Mrs. Alta Miller (who followed her in death four months later); 15 grandchildren, 7 great grandchildren. Funeral service was at Oak Grove Primitive Baptist Church, Elder John C. Monday and Rev. Lloyd England officiated. Music was by the Charlie Shoffner Family. Interment at Brogan Family Cemetery.

Shoffner, Flora M. – Age 78, of Kokomo, Indiana, passed away at the Howard Community Hospital. She was born July 24, 1909, in Sharp's Chapel, Tennessee, the daughter of Troy and Zinie Weaver Kivett. in 1930 she married Lucas Earl Shoffner. He preceded her death on October 19, 1973. Member of the Oak Grove Primitive Baptist Church. Survivors: sons, Winfred (Luke) Shoffner, New Tazewell, Joe N. Shoffner, Kokomo, Indiana, Doyle A. Shoffner, Greentown, Indiana, Donald I. Shoffner, Fountain City, Tennessee; daughters, Mrs. Esther Lou Webb, Middlesboro, Kentucky, Mrs. Jack (Lassie) Z. Kidwell, Kokomo, Mrs John (Ruth) Cornell, Galveston, Indiana; brothers, Carlos R. Kivett, Knoxville, Richard Kivett, Sharp's Chapel; aunt, Willie Kivett Dillman; 20 grandchildren, five great-grandchildren; several nieces and nephews. Funeral sevices were at Ellers Mortuary, Elder James Mitchell Smith and Elder Kenneth Morgan officiated. Entombment at Sunset Memory Gardens, Kokomo.

Smithey, Mallie – Age 99, died in October 1986. Sister Mallie joined the Lenoir City Primitive Baptist Church in 1915. She had a great zeal and love for the Church and although she had not been able to attend for several years, due to sickness, she was constantly in prayer for those she loved. She leaves several loved ones to mourn her passing.

Her body is now at peace where she sleeps in Jesus until the last trump shall sound and all the dead in Christ shall rise to be with Him in glory forever.

Taylor, Myrtle E. – age 92, of 5311 Jacksboro Pike, passed away Friday, October 3, 1986 at St. Mary's Medical Center. Member of Halls Primitive Baptist Church. Before coming to Knoxville she joined the Oak Grove Primitive Baptist Church in Union County.

She later became a charter member when the Kirkwood Primitive Baptist Church of Knoxville was organized. She then came with the church when it moved to Halls. she was a retired school teacher and owner and operator of Fountain City Kindergarten for 19 years. Survivors: husband, Raymond O. Taylor; daughter, Joyce Huffstetler; grandchildren, Mrs. Eugene (Gwendolyn) McClure, James Taylor Huffstetler; three great grandchildren. Funeral services were conducted at Rose's Chapel, Broadway Elder Bill Berry officiated. Service at the Cemetery with Rev. Eugene McClure. Pallbearers: William H. Taylor, Herman Webb, Elwood Evans, Marvin Powers, Hilas Sharp, and David Sharp.

Tinnel, R.R. (Pete), – 71, died on September 8, 1986, after a lingering illness. He was a member of the Lenoir City Primitive Baptist Church for many years. He has left the suffering of this life to be at rest with his Lord.

Brother Pete leaves to mourn his passing, his beloved children, 2 sons, Lanny (Sonny) and Sid; 2 daughters Wanda and Sylvia; 10 grandchildren, and several great-grandchildren.

Funeral services were held at Click Funeral Home Chapel on September 10, 1986 and the body now rests at Memorial Gardens in Lenoir City, to await the coming of our Lord and Saviour. Elder Charles Taylor and Rev. Charles Sullivan conducted the services.

Toliver, Arthur Milton – Arthur Milton (Milt) Toliver, age 80, of Sharps Chapel, passed away October 9, 1986, at his home. He was a member of Pleasant Point Church.

He was preceded in death by his parents, Lilburn and Marget Toliver, five brothers and two sisters.

Survivors: wife, Margaret I. Turner Toliver of Sharps Chapel; daughter Zella Toliver Gervais of Sharps Chapel; granddaughter Angela Dawn Gervais of Marrero, LA; several stepchildren; brothers: Aaron Toliver of New Tazewell and Jasper Toliver of Greene County, TN; several nieces and nephews.

Funeral Services were held October 12, 1986 at Coffee Funeral Home Chapel with Rev. John Robinson officiating. Singers were the Better Way Quartet. Burial in the Fairview Cemetery.

Pallbearers: Johnny Omary, Glen Yadon, Larry Anderson, Bob Dockins, Tippy Dockins, and Kenneth Toliver.

Coffee Funeral Home, Tazewell, in charge.

White, Emerson – Age 75, of the Davis Chapel Community in LaFollette, died on July 19, 1987. He was a retired farmer. He was member and trustee of Davis Chapel Primitive Baptist Church. He was preceded in death by parents, Elder Leonard and Mossie White; wife, Edna Smith White; and son, Estel White. Survivors include: son, Earl E. White; sisters, Oral White and Geneva Irwin; three grand children; and two great grand children. Funeral services were at Davis Chapel Primitive Baptist Church with Elder Billy Berry officiating. Interment was in Sunrise Cemetery.

White, James Maney – Age 70, of the Davis Chapel Community in LaFollette, died on September 11, 1986. He was a retired electrician and member of Davis Chapel Primitive Baptist Church. He is survived by: wife, Christine White; daughters, Fleda Kolp and Freda Moses; sons, Jerry and Gary White; sisters, Oma Miller and Ruby Heatherly; brothers, Leonard Verlin, Wid Howard, and Jack White; fourteen grandchildren, and eleven great grand children. Funeral services were held at Roach's Mortuary. Interment was in Baker's Forge Cemetery.

Dewey Drefus Wilson age 87 Was born in Knoxville, Tennessee April 14, 1900. Passed away June 5, 1987 at Baptist Hospital.

He was a member of Halls Primitive Baptist Church and a World War One Navy Veteran. He was preceded in death by his sister Lucille McCoy Eades. Survived by Nieces and Nephews.

Funeral services 8 p.m. June 7 at Mynatt Funeral Home Chapel. Elder Bill Berry and Elder Parnick Shelton officiating. Graveside services 11 a.m. June 8 at Lynhurst Cemetery. A certificate of recognition in his memory was awarded him for devoted service to the United States signed by Ronald Reagan, President.

CHURCH	COUNTY	PASTOR	CLERK	ADDRESS
Black Fox	Grainger	Elder Larry Anderson	Bennie Capps	P.O. Box 91, Maynardville, TN 37807
Braden's Chapel	Union	Elder LeRoy Braden Elder Noble Clawson	Linda Bean Phyllis Wilson, Asst.	Speedwell, TN 37870 Speedwell, TN 37870
Brantley's Chapel	Blount	Elder Jerry McBee	Gaye Lee Mildred Davis, Asst.	Rt. 1, Box 128, Townsend, TN 37882 Rt. 1, Box 344, Townsend, TN 37882
Davis Chapel	Campbell	Elder LeRoy Braden	Katheryn Angel Sondra Wright, Asst.	Rt. 5, Box 170, LaFollette, TN 37766 1256 Middlesboro Hwy., LaFollette, TN 37766
Gethsemane	Knox		Tom Carmichael	729 Frank St., Knoxville, TN 37919
Gibson Station	Lee, Va.	Elder William Rhymer Eld. Spurgeon Thompson, Asst.	Dorothy Johnson Shirley Sandifur, Asst.	Rt. 2, Box 320, Ewing, VA 24248 Rt. 1, Box 416, Harrogate, TN 37752
Halls	Knox	Elder William Berry Elder Parnick Shelton, Asst.	Alice Powers Sara Jean Harmon, Asst.	7425 Tample Acre Dr., Knoxville 37938 7120 Chermont Cir., Knoxville 37938
Headrick's Chapel	Sevier	Elder Sharidan Moore	Geraldine Abbott Clyde H. Abbott, Sr. Asst.	Rt. 6, Box 204A, Sevierville, TN 37938 Rt. 7, Box 288, Sevierville, TN 37862
Lenoir City	Loudon	Elder Robert Bullion	Janice Spoon	1001 Bell Ave. Lenoir City, TN 37771
Meyers' Grove	Claiborne	Elder J.C. Monday Elder Doyle Ausmus, Asst.	Bonnie Miracle Kathy Downes, Asst.	Rt. 2, Box 91, New Tazewell, TN 37825 New Tazewell, TN 37825
Nocton	Grainger	Elder John Oliver	Carroll Oliver Bessie Collins, Asst.	Rt. 2 Box 512, Bean Station, TN 37708 Rt. 5, Morristown, TN 37814
Oak Grove	Union	Elder J.C. Monday Elder Jerry McBee, Astt.	Betty P. Sharp Betty Shoffner, Asst.	Rt. 1, Box 250, Sharps Chapel, TN 37866 Sharps Chapel, TN 37866
Pleasant Hill	Claiborne	Elder William Rhymer Elder Albert Davis, Asst.	William Branscomb Jerry Hensley, Asst.	Speedwell, TN 37870 Speedwell, TN 37870
Pleasant Point	Claiborne	Elder Larry Anderson	Elder Claude Rosson Beatrice Williams, Asst.	Rt. 4, New Tazewell, TN 37825 Rt. Box 156, Rogersville, TN 37857
Rocky Dale	Knox	Elder Hugh Brummitt	Edward Collett Saundra Boruff, Asst.	Rt. 1, Box 17, Luttrell, TN 37779 6916 Weaver Rd., Knoxville, TN

471

1988 Minutes

POWELL VALLEY ASSOCIATION
OF PRIMITIVE BAPTIST

THE ONE HUNDRED SIXTY-EIGHTH SESSION
OF THE POWELL VALLEY ASSOCIATION
OF PRIMITIVE BAPTIST
HELD WITH THE SISTER CHURCH AT ROCKY DALE
KNOX COUNTY, TENNESSEE
AUGUST 19, 20, 21, 1988
NEXT SESSION WILL BE HELD WITH THE SISTER CHURCH
AT OAK GROVE, UNION COUNTY, TENNESSEE
TO BEGIN ON FRIDAY BEFORE THE THIRD
SATURDAY IN AUGUST, 1989 AT 10:30 A.M.
ELDER JOHN OLIVER, WILL DELIVER
THE INTRODUCTORY SERMON
ELDER WILLIAM BERRY WILL BE THE ALTERNATE

OFFICERS

ELDER HUGH BRUMMITT   MODERATOR
1329 BROWN AVENUE, KNOXVILLE, TENN., PHONE 546-7700
ELDER LARRY ANDERSON   ASSISTANT MODERATOR
RT. 3, BOX 314-A, SPEEDWELL, TENN., PHONE 869-4635
BENNIE CAPPS   CLERK
P.O. BOX 91, MAYNARDVILLE, TENN., PHONE 992-5571
RINA JOHNSON   ASSISTANT CLERK
1217 BROWN SCHOOL RD., MARYVILLE, TN., PHONE 983-2774

Statistical Table	Restored	Rec. by Letter	Baptism	Excluded	Dismiss by Letter	Relationship	Deceased	Total Membership	Printing Minutes	Regular Meeting Time	Communion Time
Black Fox	0	0	0	0	0	0	2	65	$25.00	Second Sat. Night and Sun. Sunday after Fourth Saturday	Sunday following Second Saturday in June
Braden's Chapel	0	0	2	0	2	0	3	152	40.00	First Saturday Night and Sunday	Sunday following First Saturday in July
Brantley's Chapel	0	1	4	1	0	0	2	115	100.00	Second Saturday Night - Every Sunday and Sunday Night	Sunday Following Second Saturday in July at 10:30 a.m.
Davis Chapel	0	0	1	0	0	0	1	76	45.00	Every Sunday and Sunday Night	Sunday following Third Saturday in June
Gethsemane	0	0	0	0	1	0	2	27	35.00	Second and Fourth Sunday	Fourth Sunday in May and October
Gibson Station	0	0	1	0	0	0	2	72	50.00	First Saturday Night - Every Sunday and Sunday Night	Sunday following First Saturday in June
Halls	0	1	1	0	0	0	0	112	100.00	Every Sunday and Sunday Night	Last Sunday in April
Hedrick's Chapel	0	1	0	0	0	0	0	109	25.00	First and Third Sunday of each Month	First Sunday in May and October 11 a.m.
Lenoir City	0	1	11	1	5	3	3	143	45.00	Every Sunday and Sunday Night	Wednesday Night before Easter Sunday
Myers Grove	0	1	0	0	0	0	0	78	25.00	4th Saturday Night & Every Sunday	Sunday following Fourth Saturday in May
Noeton	0	1	1	0	0	0	0	39	30.00	First Sunday - Third Saturday and Sunday of each month	Sunday following Third Saturday in May & September
Oak Grove	0	0	5	0	1	0	3	332	35.00	First Saturday Night and Sunday - Third Sunday	Sunday following the First Saturday in May
Pleasant Hill	0	0	0	0	1	0	1	87	50.00	4th Sat. Morning & Sat. Night Every Sun. and Sun. Night	Sunday following the Fourth Sunday in June at 10:30 a.m.
Rocky Dale	0	0	0	3	0	0	1	95	50.00	Every Sunday Morning	Sunday following Third Saturday in May

MINUTES OF THE ONE HUNDRED SIXTY-EIGHTH SESSION

Friday, August 19, 1988

The one hundred sixty-eighth session of the Powell Valley Associationof Primitive Baptists met with the Sister Church at Rocky Dale in Knox County, Tennessee, on August 19, 20, and 21, 1988.

After Brother Don Sharp led the congregation in singing, "Amazing Grace", "I Will Sing the Wondrous Story", "Victory in Jesus", and "Near the Cross", the Moderator Elder Hugh Brummitt welcomed the congregation and pleaded for peace and love to abide throughout the entire Association and called for prayer by Elder Albert Davis of Pleasant Hill Church.

Following prayer, Elder William Rhymer of Gibson Station Church delivered the introductory sermon from the 8th chapter of Romans, and the 28th verse and preached a very uplifting and spiritual sermon, of Paul writing to the church at Rome.

After the introductory sermon, they sang a song and were dismissed in prayer by Orice McCarty, of Davis Chapel Church. The Association was to reconvene after a 15 minute recess.

After recess, the crowd reassembled in the church. Brother Don Sharp led the congregation in singing, and then Moderator Elder Hugh Brummitt read from the 1st John, verses 1-13, the called for prayer by Elder Bob Bullion of Lenoir City Church.

The Moderator then asked for the order of business for the following transactions:

1st: Called for letters of the Sister Churches to be presented to the clerk for reading. Twelve (12) were received.

2nd: The letters were presented and read and motion approved that the delegates be seated.

3rd: The Moderator called for anyone present from any of the Sister Churches not named as delegate who desired to be seated as such to come forward and give the clerk their name and the name of their church. Three came. Francis Eastridge, Alvada Dykes and Mona Rogers all from Oak Grove Church.

4th: Called for petitionary letter if there should be one. None came.

5th: Motion approved that the Association re-elect Elder Hugh Brummitt as Moderator and re-elect Elder Larry Anderson as Assistant Moderator for the ensuing year.

6th: Motion approved that Brother Bennie Capps be re-elected Clerk and Brother Rina Johnson be re-elected Assistant Clerk for the ensuing year.

7th: Motion was appoved that we empower Moderator Elder Brummitt to appoint all the committees to serve this session.

8th: The Moderator, having been empowered to do so, appointed the committees as follows:

Committee on Arrangements:	Brother Carroll L. Oliver 5 Many
	P Brother Clyde Lynch
	Brother Franklin Jones
Committee on Preaching:	Brother Junior McBee
	Brother Hubert Spoon
	Brother Elwood Evans
Committee on Request:	Brother O.D. McCarty
	Elder Robert Bullion
	Brother Josh Stapleton
Committee on Finance:	¢ Elder Parnick Shelton
	Brother Joe Culvahouse
	Brother Vance E. Harmon, Jr.

9th: Called for the finances to be turned in to the Finance Committee.

10th: The committees all having been appointed and accepted, the Association moved to adjourn until 10:30 Saturday morning. They sang a song and were dismissed in prayer by Elder Spurgeon Thompson of Gibson Station Church.

Saturday, August 20, 1988

At the appointed hour of 10:30 Saturday morning and at the sound of singing, the Association reassembled.

After Brother Edward Collett led the congregation in singing "Some Glad Day", "Redeemed" and "Holy Manna", the Assistant Moderator Elder Larry Anderson gave a very spiritual and uplifting talk and read from the 1st chapter of Second Peter, verses 1-10 and called for prayer by Elder William Berry of Halls Church.

After prayer, the Moderator called the Association to order for the remainder of the business:

1st: Called for any letters from Sister Churches not received on Friday. There was one.

2nd: The letter was presented and read and motion approved that the delegates be seated.

3rd: Called for anyone from any of the churches who were present and desired to be seated as delegate to come forward and give the clerk their name and their church. Two came. Sister Ruby Hill of Davis Chapel and Sister Ruth Shoffner of Oak Grove.

4th: Called for the report of the Committee on Arrangements who submitted the following report:

Report on Arrangements:

Call for roll call of delegates.

Call for report of Committee on Preaching.

Call for report of Committee on Request.

Call for report of Committee on Finance.

Decide how many minutes we have printed, who shall supervise the printing and delivery of the same, which sister church shall host the next association and who will preach the introductory sermon and who will be the alternate. Who will prepare the Circular Letter.

Respectfully Submitted,
Brother Carroll L. Oliver
Brother Clyde Lynch
Brother Franklin Jones

5th: Motion approved to receive the above report and release the committee.

6th: Called the roll call of delegates of all Sister Churches and check the absentees.

7th: Called for the report of the Committee on Preaching:

Committee on Preaching:

Friday night:	Elder Robert Bullion
	Elder Joe Bush
Saturday morning:	Elder Robert Walker
	Elder Spurgeon Thompson
Saturday night:	Elder Jerry McBee
	Elder Parnick Shelton
Sunday morning:	Elder John Oliver
	Elder Larry Anderson

Respectfully submitted,
Brother Junior McBee
Brother Hubert Spoon
Brother Elwood Evans

8th: Motion approved to receive the above report and release the committee.

9th: Called for the report of the Committee on Request, which was given:

We, the Committee on Request, wish to request as follows, that we have 1,100 minutes printed and the clerk supervise the printing and distribution of same and that he recieve $135.00 for his services. We also request that the next session of the Powell Valley Association be held with the Sister Church at Oak Grove in Union County, to begin on Friday before the third Saturday in August, 1989, at 10:30 A.M. and continue three days. We also request that Elder John Oliver preach the introductory sermon and Elder William Berry be the alternate. We also request that Elder Claude Rosson write a circular letter for the minutes for 1989.

Respectfully submitted,
Brother O.D. McCarty
Elder Robert Bullion
Brother Josh Stapleton

10th: Motion approved to receive the above report and release the committee.

11th: Called for the report of the Committee on Finance, which submitted the following report:

Black Fox	$25.00
Braden's Chapel	40.00
Brantley's Chapel	100.00
Davis Chapel	45.00
Gethsemane	35.00
Gibson Station	50.00
Halls	100.00
Headrick's Chapel	25.00
Lenoir City	45.00
Meyer's Grove	25.00
Noeton	30.00
Oak Grove	35.00
Pleasant Hill	50.00
Rocky Dale	50.00
Total Collection	655.00
Donations	50.00
	705.00
Balance in bank	617.00
	1,322.00
Expenses for 1988	585.00
Balance in bank	737.00

Respectfully Submitted,
Elder Parnick Shelton
Brother Joe Culvahouse
Brother Vance E. Harmon, Jr.

12th: Motion approved to receive the above report and release the committee.

13th: Motion approved that we grant the request of the committee and have 1,100 minutes printed and the clerk to receive $135.00 for his services.

14th: Motion approved that the next session of the Association be held with the Sister Church at Oak Grove to commence on Friday before the third Saturday in August, 1989, at 10:30 A.M.

15th: Motion approved that Elder Claude Rosson write the circular letter for the 1989 minutes.

16th: Motion approved that Elder John Oliver deliver the introductory sermon and Elder William Berry be the alternate.

17th: Motion approved that the churches of the Powell Valley Association extend to the church and the people of Rocky Dale our heart felt thanks and our prayers for the love, fellowship, kindness and food while we were with you. May the good Lord bless and keep you is our prayers.

18th: Motion approved to adjourn, trusting the Lord to permit us to meet again with the Sister Church at Oak Grove in Union County, Tennessee, on Friday before the third Saturday in August, 1989, at 10:30 A.M.

Dismissed in prayer by Elder Joe Bush.

Elder Hugh Brummitt, Moderator
Elder Larry Anderson, Assistant Moderator
Brother Bennie Capps, Clerk
Brother Rina Johnson, Assistant Clerk

SPECIAL ANNOUNCEMENTS

Brantley's Chapel has their second Saturday night services at 7 P.M. every Sunday morning at 10:30 A.M.; Sunday night at 7 P.M. in the summer months and at 6:00 P.M. in the winter months.

The following churches requested the Association for 1989: Black Fox, Brantley Chapel, Gibson Station, Halls, Oak Grove, and Pleasant Hill.

Please make your contributions payable to: Powell Valley Association.

Dates of ordination of the following Elders:

Elder Albert Davis, May 17, 1930
Elder Joe Irving, October 1, 1949
Elder Hugh Brummitt, December 12, 1954
Elder James Branscomb, June 23, 1956
Elder Charles Taylor, April, 1959
Elder Parnick Shelton, December 11, 1960
Elder Claude Rosson, July 4, 1964
Elder Joe Bush, April 27, 1969
Elder Bill Berry, August 27, 1972
Elder Larry Anderson, October 24, 1975
Elder Spurgeon Thompson, December 17, 1976
Elder Bill Rhymer, December 17, 1976
Elder Jerry McBee, April 26, 1981
Elder Nelson Jones, July 17, 1981
Elder Steve Taylor, September 26, 1986
Elder Clearance Hicks, September 26, 1986
Elder Chester Hembree, June 19, 1988

SUMMARY

We are blessed with a fine group of ministers as was illustrated by those who had the opportunity to preach. We regret that time will not permit more of them to preach when we meet with the Association.

Friday night, Elder Joe Bush opened up the services and read from the First Chapter of Genesis and spoke for a few minutes, then Elder Robert Bullion spoke from the second chapter, verse 13, of Second Thessalonians. Both Elders brought a very uplifting sermon. On Saturday morning, Elder Robert Walker spoke on becoming the Sons of God, then Elder Spurgeon Thompson spoke from the 40th chapter of Isaiah, both Elders brought a wonderful message. Saturday night, Elder Parnick Shelton spoke from the second chapter of Genesis and spoke on the River went out of Eden, then Elder Jerry McBee spoke from the 37th chapter of Ezekiel and spoke on the Valley of Dry Bones. Sunday morning Elder John Oliver spoke from the 127th chapter of Psalms on the Lord build the house, then Elder Larry Anderson spoke from the 37th chapter of Ezekiel and spoke concerning the Valley of Dry Bones. All Elders brought very spiritual and uplifting sermons.

CHURCHES AND THEIR DELEGATES

BLACK FOX: Brothers, Dale Capps and Bennie Capps; Sisters, Mary Ruth Capps, Pamela Capps, and Naomi Cabbage.

BRADEN'S CHAPEL: Due to illness of clerk and assistant clerk, the letter did not get in.

BRANTLEY'S CHAPEL: Elder Jerry McBee; Brothers: Robert Welch, Daniel Brantley, David Beason, Richard G. Walker, Everett Brantley, William Beason, Glenn Walker, Rina Johnson, J.R. McBee; Sisters: Blanch Welch, Linda Brantley, Mildred Brantley, Barsha Brantley, Edith Walker, Gaye Lee, Hazel Johnson.

DAVIS CHAPEL: Brothers: Clyde Lynch, O.D. McCarty, Sisters: Pearl Lynch, Mollie McCarty, Ollie Welch.

GETHSEMANE: Brother Tom Carmichael, Sister: June Carmichael

GIBSON STATION: Elders: William Rhymer, Spurgeon Thompson, Brothers: Franklin Jones; Sisters: Karen Rhymer, Fannie Jones, Dorothy Johnson.

HALLS: Elders: Hugh Brummitt, Bill Berry, Parnick Shelton, Brothers: Elwood Evans, Joe Culvahouse, Vance Harmon, Vance Harmon, Jr.; Sisters: Ruby Brummitt, Wilma Shelton, Mildred Evans, Betty Culvahouse, Cookie Harmon, Irene Harmon, Frieda Sharp, and Trula Berry

HEADRICK'S CHAPEL: Elder:Robert Walker, Brother: Clyde Abbott

LENOIR CITY: Elder: Robert Bullion, Brothers: Hubert Spoon, Sisters: Annie Spoon, Vicki Bullion

MEYER'S GROVE. Letter received. No delegate present.

NOETON: Elder: John Oliver, Brothers: Carroll Oliver, Charlie Collins; Sisters: Dora Collins.

OAK GROVE: Letter received. No delegate present.

PLEASANT HILL: Elders: Larry Anderson, Albert Davis.

PLEASANT POINT: No letter received.

ROCKY DALE: Elders: Joe Bush; Brothers: James Boruff, Edward Collett, Josh Stapleton, Glen Johnson, Donald Sharp, Joe Palmer; Sisters: Norma Jean Bush, Saundra Boruff, Fay Collett, Ima Lee Stapleton, Beatrice Johnson, Myrtle Bryant, Dottie Sharp, Dorothy Shelton, Aloha McPhetridge.

MINISTERS DIRECTORY

Elder Larry Anderson, Rt. 3, Box 314-A, Speedwell, TN 869-4635
Elder Johnny Atkins, Bean Station, TN Ph. 767-2397
Elder Buford Doyle Ausmus, Rt. 2, Speedwell, TN ph. 566-0433
Elder William Berry, Rt. 13, Knoxville, TN Ph. 922-9189
Elder LeRoy Braden, 2305 Middlesboro , LaFollette, TN 562-9353
Elder J.H. Branscomb, Speedwell, TN, Ph. 562-6361
Elder Hugh H. Brummitt, 1329 Brown , Knoxville, TN 546-7700
Elder Joe Bush, Rt. 3, Corryton, TN, Ph 687-7018   377 31
Elder Jim Campbell, Louisville, TN, Ph. 983-1654
Elder Noble Clawson, Rt. 4, Speedwell, TN, Ph. 562-2004
Elder Albert Davis, Speedwell, TN, Ph. 869-3596
Elder Joe Irving, Rt.3, Box B101. Middlesboro, KY, Ph. 248-8349
Elder Clarence Hicks, Maryville, TN
Elder Nelson Jones, Rt. 1 - Box 343, Harrogate, TN, Ph. 869-3703
Elder Alvin Graves, 122 Oak Wood Dr., Lenoir City, TN 986-9725
Elder Jerry McBee, 901 Chaparral , Seymour, TN 37865, 577-2669
Elder Sheridan Moore, Rt. 1, Townsend, TN, Ph. 448-6430
Elder J.C. Monday, Speedwell, TN, Ph. 562-3068
Elder John Oliver, Rt. 2, Box 513, Bean Station, TN, Ph. 581-5039
Elder Howard Pippin, 101 Rose Street, Lenoir City, TN, 986-2791
Elder William Rhymer, P.O. Box 12, Shawnee, TN, Ph. 869-3092
Elder Parnick Shelton, 6001 McGinnis , Corryton, TN 687-6142
Elder Charles Taylor, 101 Rose St., Lenoir City, TN 37771
Elder Steve Taylor, Lenoir City, TN
Elder Spurgeon Thompson, P.O. Box 36, Shawnee, TN, 869-8175
Elder Claude Rosson, Rt. 4, New Tazewell, TN Ph. 626-3168
Elder Robert Walker, Sevierville, TN, Ph. 428-1527
Elder Clay Widner, Rt. 1, Tazewell, TN, Ph. 626-3893
Elder Robert Bullion, 101 Rose St., Lenoir City, TN 986-5465
Elder Chester Hembree, Rt. 2, Box 422, Rockford, TN 983-6526

LICENTIATES

Brother Clyde Abbott, Sr., Rt. 7, Sevierville, TN, Ph. 453-2329
Brother Roscoe Branscomb, Speedwell, TN
Brother Odell Carpenter, 812 Brown School Rd., Maryville, TN
37801, Ph. 984-4352
Brother Mark Taylor, Lenoir City, TN
Brother Richard Walker, Rt. 2, Box 430, Rockwood, TN 37853

CIRCULAR LETTER TO
POWELL VALLEY ASSOCIATION

To all the saints in Christ Jesus, which compose the Powell Valley Association of Primitive Baptists.

May God bless the use of the holy scritpures to greet and exhort you as the apostle Paul did at the Church at Philippi. Grace be unto you, and peace from God our Father, and from the Lord Jesus Christ. I thank my God upon every remembrance of you, always in every prayer of mine for you all making request with joy, for your fellowship in the gospel from the first day until now; being confident of this very thing, that he which hath begun a good work in you will perform it until the day of Jesus Christ. The Apostle Paul speaks of the fellowship in the gospel from the first day until now. The gospel that we enjoy is the declaration of Jesus Christ as the son of God, the atonement made by Jesus Christ for the sins of his bride which was given to him by God the Father in the covenant of grace before the world was, the effectual calling of the Holy Spirit, and that all who are regenerated (effectually called) will be finally saved.

The fellowship we enjoy is coming together in one mind, in one accord, in prayer with and for one another. True fellowship comes from deep within the heart that has been cleansed by the power of God. True fellowship is manifested by the outward expression of our love and deeds for God and our brothers and sisters in Christ. True fellowship is blessed and witnessed by the presence of the Holy Spirit.

The fellowship of the gospel that the Apostle Paul and the saints at Philippi enjoyed nearly two thousand years ago can be ours today. Our Lord and Savior said, "Ask, and it shall be given you, seek and ye shall find, knock and it shall be opened unto you. For every one that asketh receiveth; and he that seeketh findeth; and to him that knocketh it shall be opened." (Matt. 7: 7,8)

Beloved of God, may our desire and prayer be as Paul's was for the church at Phillippi. And this I pray, that your love may abound yet more and more in knowledge and in all judgement; That ye may approve things that are excellent; that ye may be sincere and without offence til the day of Christ; Being filled with the fruits of righteousness, which are by Jesus Christ, unto the glory and praise of God. Only let your conversation be as it becometh the gospel of Christ; that whether I come and see you, or else be absent, I may hear of your affairs, that ye stand fast in one spirit, with one mind striving together for the faith of the gospel.

Saints of the Lord and members of the Powell Valley Association, may God bless us to continue to seek for understanding and fellowship. Also, continue to pray that the elders of our association may know the truth of God's word and that they may open their mouth and speak boldly as they should.

Your brother in Christ Elder Bill Berry

RULES OF DECORUM

1. The churches composing the Powell's Valley Association shall not be confined to any set rules as to specific number of Messengers they shall have in the body, but shall have the right to name in their letters as many as they choose, and in addition all orderly members of any of the churches being present be entitled to seats in the body as Messengers fo their respective churches, with all the rights and privileges of the same.

2. The Messengers thus assembled shall be denominated the Powell's Valley Primitive Baptist Church.

3. For the purpose of historical information and statistical edification, the Churches are required to state in letters, the number of members in fellowship, the number received by Baptism, by letter, by confession of Faith, the number dismissed, excluded and dead since last session; also the time of their meeting, their pastoral supply, and the amount of money contributed for ministers and other purposed together with any other information they deem appropriate for the edification of the saints and glory of God.

4. This Association shall have no power to answer queries, give advice, or dictate to the Churches in any case, or to lord it over God's heritage nor any power by which she can directly or indirectly fringe on the internal rights of the church or censure and try any church or member in reference to faith and practice and determine upon validity of gospel ordinances. These things shall rest entirely with the churches; but henceforward our annual meetings shall be only for the purpose of hearing from each other, and for the worship of God and mutual comfort and edification of the Saints. To this end we reserve the privilege annually for Friday before the Third Saturday in August and the two following days or at such other times as may be agreed upon with any church that may invite us having to protect our own standard, while in session, from heresay and disorder to recognize and invite any primitive Baptist minister or any lay brother to worship with us that may deem proper; to request the brethren of our body to visit other churches or bodies in our belief with whom we may desire to culture Christian fellowship; to publish in a minute of our proceedings.

5. Each session of the body shall have a Moderator and Clerk who shall hold office until re-elected.

6. Any order member of any church belonging to this body, when convened, being present shall be eligible to elect on as Moderator and Clerk or to sit on any committee appointed by the same.

7. In all election or questions that may be necessary to determine by vote, the vote shall be taken by churches, each church being entitled to three votes for any number less than one hundred, and one additional vote for every fifty or fraction thereof above the first hundred, but the Messengers of each church may divide their vote as they see proper.

8. All elections or questions coming to vote shall be determined by a majority vote cast, and it shall be the only duty of the minority to acquiesce in the decision thus reached.

9. If new churches desire to be admitted to this union they shall petition by letter and messengers and if voted for and recommended by one or more sister churches for her Presbytery constitutioning them, as orthodox and orderly they shall be received by the vote of the body and manifested by the Moderator giving the Messengers the right hand of fellowship.

10. Any motion or resolution clearly inconsistent with the above rules shall be promptly ruled out of order unless withdrawn by the mover.

11. Any messenger being ruled out of order by the Moderator shall have the right to appeal to the body on the question of order, and if sustained shall be allowed to proceed, but if not take his seat.

12. Our meeting being held in the name of Christ and the worship of God; each Messenger is expected to observe due and proper therein.

13. It will not be considered good for any Messenger whose name has been enrolled as

such to abruptley break off or absent himself from the Association without leave.

14. The Moderator shall be entitled to the same privilege of speech as other members provided the chair is filled.

15. The minutes of the Association shall be read and approved by the body and signed by the Moderator before adjourning.

16. The Association shall be opened and closed by prayer.

17. Amendments to these may be made at any time by a majority of the union voting by churches when they deem it necessary, provide such amendments do not compromise the sovereignty of the churches nor have tendency to give body undue power or jurisdiction over them.

ARTICLES OF FAITH

Article 1. We believe in only one true living God, as He is revealed to us in the Holy Scriptures - Father, Son, and Holy Ghost.

Article 2. We believe that the Scriptures of the old and new Testaments are the words of God and the only rule of all-saving knowledge and obedience.

Article 3. We believe in the doctrine of election according to the foreknowledge of God.

Article 4. We believe in the doctrine of original sin.

Article 5. We believe in man's impotency to rescue himself from the fallen state he is in, by his own will or ability.

Article 6. We believe that sinners are justified in the sight of God only by the imputed righteousness of Jesus Christ.

Article 7. We believe the elect, according to the foreknowledge of God will be called, converted, regenerated, and sanctified by the Holy Spirit.

Article 8. We believe the saints will persevere and never fall finally away.

Article 9. We believe that baptism and the Lord's Supper are ordinances of Jesus Christ, and that true believers are the only subject of these ordinances, and that the true mode of baptism is by immersion. We believe also that feet washing is an example of Jesus Christ and should be kept by his disciples until his second coming.

Article 10. We believe in the Resurrection of the dead and the General Judgement.

Article 11. We believe that the punishment of the wicked will be everlasting and that the joys of the righteous will be eternal.

Article 12. We believe that no minister has the right to administer the ordinances, except those who have been regularly baptized and called of God, and come under the imposition of hands of the presbytery.

483

Obituaries

AUSMUS, FLORA E., 85, of Middlesboro, Kentucky, passed away on July 22, 1988, at the Claiborne County Hospital, Tazewell, Tennessee. She was born in Claiborne County, Tennessee on December 14, 1902, Her parents were Mr. Johnny Housley and the former Rhoda Stinner. She was a member of Brantley's Chapel Primitive Baptist Church.

Her survivors include: two daughters, Vesta Ausmus, Middlesboro, Kentucky and Essie Mae Thomas, New Tazewell, Tennessee; one sister, Callie Lyone, Maryville, Tennessee; eight grandchildren, 15 great grandchildren, 2 great-great grandchildren.

Funeral services were held Sunday night at 8:00 P.M., July 24, 1988 at the Shumate Funeral Home Chapel with the Elder Jerry T. McBee officiating. Burial was Monday, July 25, 1988 in New Salem Cemetery, Claiborne County, Tennessee. Pall-bearers included grandsons and grandsons-in-law.

Sadly missed by family and friends.

AUSMUS, HATTIE CINNAMON of LaFollette, Tenn. was born January 16, 1908. She departed this life April of 1988. She was married to Robert Ausmus while she was quite young and to this union was born 2 daughter, Drexel Ausmus Long Jackson and Irene Ausmus Gilreath. She professed a Hope in Christ and joined Pleasant Hill Primitive Baptist Church and was one of eleven who was baptised in January, 1932 and lived a faithful member until death. She was preceded in death by her husband. She leaves to mourn her passing; 2 daughters, 5 grandchildren and 4 great-grandchildren and other relatives and a host of friends and neighbors. Sadly missed, but God knows best.

CADLE, WILLIAM RILEY, a former member of Brantley's Chapel Primitive Baptist Church. He was born May 11, 1917 and he departed this life June 11, 1988 at Blount Memorial Hospital. He was a member of Broadway Baptist Church, the Rockford Masonic Lodge No. 469 F&M, and a veteran of World War II serving with the 362 Infantry Division in North Africa and Italy. He was a retired employee of ALCOA with 43 years of service. He was preceded in death by; father, James Cadle; mother, Melissa Hurst Cadle; and brother, Alfred Cadle.

Survivors: wife, Edna Johnson Cadle; daughter, Patricia Cadle Craton of Maryville; granddaughter, Leslie Roulette Ledbetter of Maryville; brother, John C. Cadle of New Market; sister, Hazel Cadle Johnson of Maryville.

Funeral services were on June 14, 1988 at 2 p.m. at West Chapel of Smith Mortuary. Rev. L.G. Hutchens and Elder Jerry McBee officiating. Interment Sherwood Memorial Gardens.

The Family - Edna, Patsy and Leslie

COTTES, MARY GODFREY was born October 18, 1896, and died April 13, 1988 at the age of 91. She professed faith in Christ at an early age and was baptised into the church at Headrick's Chapel Primitive Baptist Church and remained a member there until her later years when she joined the Gethsemane Church in Knoxville where she remained until she passed away. To her was born 11 children and she raised 8 children, 3 died in infancy. She leaves 3 children to mourn her passing, Arthur Godfrey, Pauline Brown and June Carmichael. She was very strong in her belief in Christ and she never forgot when and how she was saved and was the first to acknowledge that it was by the Grace of God. She is sadly missed by her family and church, but we know by her testimony here that she has a better home over there in that land of sweet forever.

DYKE, MRS. MOSSIE LEE - age 94, of Knoxville formerly of Sharps Chapel, passed away 3 p.m. Wednesday, Feb. 24, 1988, at Meadowbrook Manor. Member of Oak Grove Primitive Baptist Church. Widow of the late Emit Dyke. Survivors: daughters, Reba Moyers, Knoxville, Vera Sheckles of Wisconsin; sons, Charles Edward Dyke, Knoxville, Frank Dyke of Michigan, Hubert (Pete) Dyke, Sharps Chapel, Willard Dyke of Indiana; 40 grandchildren; several great-grandchildren; a host of nieces and nephews. Funeral service 10:30 a.m. Saturday, Oak Grove Primitive Baptist Church, Elder Jerry McBee, Rev. Greg Sharp officiating. Interment Oak Grove Cemetery. Pallbearers: grandsons. The family will receive friends 7-9 p.m. Friday at Cooke Mortuary, Maynardville.

ELLISON, LELA MAE SHARP, Maryville, Tenn. was born February 7, 1913, and departed this life September 3, 1985, at age 72 years and 7 months. She was preceded in death by her husband, Jefferson Monroe Ellison and infant daughter Rebecca. She was married February 4, 1929, in Union County. She professed faith in Christ Jesus at an early age and was baptised into the Primitive Baptist Church in Union County. After moving to Maryville, she joined Brantley's Chapel Church where she was a Sunday School teacher for many years and an active member until her death. Survivors include son and daughter in law, J.M. and Linda Ellison of Rock Hill, SC; daughters and sons-in-law, Helen and Odell Carpenter, Brenda and Lawrence Adams, all of Maryville; and grandchildren Kim and Shane Ellison of Rock Hill, SC, and Mike, Stephanie and Alison Adams of Maryville, TN. Funeral Services were held at Smith's Mortuary in Maryville. Interment Brantley's Chapel Cemetery. The officiating ministers were Rev. Lawrence Adams and Elder Jerry McBee. She was loved by all who knew her. It can truly be said "The fruits of the spirit were evident in her daily life."

GODFREY, CECIL H. was born May, 1916, died July, 1985, at the age of 69. He joined the Headrick's Chapel as a young boy, later joined Gethsemane Church as a charter member where he remained a faithful member until his death. He leaves to mourn his passing, wife Billie Godfrey and son Charles Godfrey and daughter, Janice Godfrey and several grandchildren. Brother Cecil was a friend to everyone who knew him and he is sadly missed in the little church and we hope to meet him some day over on the other shore where we all can sing God's praises together forever more.

GODFREY, JOHN E., ELDER was born July, 1918, and died Dec. 23, 1987 at the age of 69. He joined the church at Headrick's Chapel and later joined the church at Olivers Chapel in Riverside, California, and at the time of his death he belonged to the Gethsemane Church. Sadly missed by his family, his wife Susan and daughters Nancy, Jeannie and Johnnie of California; brother Arthur Godfrey; sisters Pauline Brown and June Carmichael. He always had felt like one alone in California after Oliver's Chapel Church ceased to be and that he felt he had the Greatest Teacher, The Great God as he had no one, it seemed, in California to fellowship with. We miss him very much but we realize he has went to a wonderful place where Jesus is, and that he will want for nothing any more.

GRAVES, ENMOND, age 89, of Corryton, TN passed away 12:30 a.m. Sunday, Feb. 28, 1988, at Hillcrest Nursing Home. He was a faithful and much loved member and deacon of Rocky Dale Primitive Baptist Church, and a retired barber. Survivors: wife, Grace L. Graves, Corryton; son and daughter-in-law, Lee D. and Vera Graves, Maynardville; daughter and

son-in-law, Elder Parnick and Wilma Shelton, Corryton; grandchildren, Sandra Krebs of Ohio, Douglas Shelton, Corryton; brother, Clay Graves, Toledo, Ohio; several nieces and nephews. Funeral services were at 8 p.m. on Monday at Cooke Mortuary Chapel, Elder Hugh Brummitt, Elder Joe Bush officiating. Interment 11 a.m. on Tuesday in Washington Pike Presbyterian Cemetery. Pallbearers: Charles Bryant, Josh Stapleton, Harry Graves, Harril Edwards, Rev. Joe Sexton, and Arthur Krebs. The family received friends from 6-8 p.m. on Monday evening at Cooke Mortuary, Maynardville. His church seat is empty and he is missed very much but we find comfort in knowing he is with our Jesus whom he loved.

GRAVES, GRACE L. CHESNEY age 89, of Corryton, Tennessee, passed away 7:40 a.m. Wednesday, August 31, 1988 at Hillcrest Central Nursing Home. She was a faithful member of Rocky Dale Primitive Baptist Church and the widow of Enmon D. Graves. Survivors: daughter and son-in-law, Wilma and Elder Parnick Shelton, Corryton; son and daughter-in-law, Lee D. and Vera Graves, Maynardville; granddaughter, Sandra Krebs, Milford, Ohio; grandson, Douglas

Shelton, Corryton; several nieces and nephews. Funeral services were at 8 p.m. Thursday at Cooke Mortuary Chapel, Elder Hugh Brummitt, Elder Joe Bush officiating. Interment was 11 a.m. Friday at Washington Pike Presbyterian Church Cemetery. Pall-bearers: John Edgar Shelton, Avrell Graves, Arthur Krebs, Rev. Joe Sexton, Charles Bryant, and Jack Simmons. The family received friends 6-8 p.m. on Thrusday at Cooke Mortuary, Maynardville. She was a very special little lady, like a mother to her church; and we look forward to seeing her sweet smile again when we meet on that beautiful shore.

Obituaries written by Fay Collett

GRAVES, R.L. - Our dear brother in Christ died on May 21, 1988. Bro. R.L. joined the Lenoir City Church in April 1986. His passing from this life, left with sad hearts, his wife, Dorothy; daughter, Debbie; son, Rodney; grandson, Adam.

He was laid to rest, on May 23, 1988, at the Lenoir City Cemetery.

HEMBREE, ELLEN ALICE, 85, of Maryville, Tennessee, went to meet her Lord On April 7, 1988 at Blount Memorial Hospital after a long illness. She was preceded in death by her husband, John P. Hembree, after a marriage of 60 years. She was born May 6, 1902.

Survivors include: 5 daughters: Mildred Peacock, Mobile, Alabama; Francis Davis of Maryville, Tennessee; Freda Hembree of Knoxville, Tennessee; Edith walker of Rockford, Tennessee; Gaye Lee of Townsend, Tennessee; 4 Sons: Clarence and Hubert of Maryville, Tennessee; Chester of Rockford, Tennessee, and David of Kingston, Tennessee: 28 grandchildren: 39 great grandchildren; 4 great-great grandchildren; sisters: Rosa Hembree of Knoxville, Tenn.; Zora Porter of Ringgold, Georgia.

Sister Hembree was a long time member of the Primitive Baptist Church and a member of Brantley's Chapel Primitive Baptist Church at the time of her death.

The funeral services were held on Sunday, April 19, 1988, at 2 P.M., at the Chapel at Miller's Funeral Home; Maryville, Tennessee, with Elder Jerry T. McBee and her son, Chester Hembree officiating. The music was by The Brantley's Chapel Primitive Baptist Church Quartet. The interment was at Tuckaleechee Primitive Baptist Church Cemetery in Townsend, Tennessee. The grandsons were pallbearers.

Missed by friends and family.

JOHNSON, TILLMAN age 73 of Townsend Tenn., passed away October 29, 1986. He joined Tuckalechee Primitive Baptist Church at an early age and joined Headricks' Chapel Primitive Baptist Church shortly before his death. He is survived by his wife Fannie Nichals Johnson; children, Faye, Ralph, and Ernest. Grandchildren, Sandi, Vernon, and Pamela Ann. Funeral Services were held at Smith Mortuary, Elders Sheridan Moore and Robert Walder officiated.

487

Graveside Services at Bethel conducted by Brother Clyde Abbott, Sr.

LYNCH, ROBERT A. (BOB), 86, of LaFollette, died October 22, 1987. He was a member of Davis Chapel Primitive Baptist Church.

Funeral services were held in LaFollette on October 24 at Walters Funeral Home Chapel, with Elder Leroy Braden officiating. Interment was at Cadillac Memorial Gardens in Westland, Michigan.

Survivors include his wife, Lina Bowman Lynch of LaFollette; sons, Jack and Clinton Lynch of Michigan; sisters, Mamie Parrott of Michigan and Mildred Ellison of LaFollette; brothers, Clyde Lynch of LaFollette and Joseph Lynch of Michigan; seven grandchildren; eight great grandchildren; and one great-great grandson.

OWEN, SARAH VINNIE (JONES) age 80 of Speedwell, passed away Sunday, Nov. 2, 1986 at the LaFollette Medical Center.

She was preceded in death by her husband, James L. "Jim Boy" Owens and one son, Larry Owens.

She was a member of Pleasant Hill Primitive Baptist Church.

Survivors: sons, Vantoy (Rip) Owens, Speedwell, Dewey Owens, Springboro, Ohio, Ralph Owens, Xenia, Ohio, Claude Owens and Marshall Milton Owens, both of Bellbrook, Ohio; daughters: Roxie (Sis) Wilson, LaFollette, Mrs. Kenneth (Annie) Hatmaker, Springboro, Ohio, Mrs. Ralph (Stella) Munday, Lucille Moyers, Mrs. Kelly ((Joyce) Graves, all of Speedwell; sisters: Cecil Edwards, Ada Jones, Bertha Edwards, Hazel Lambert, all of Speedwell; 22 grandchildren and 24 great-grandchildren.

Funeral service Wednesday, Nov. 5 at 1 p.m. at the Pleasant Hill Primitive Baptist Church with Elders Bill Rhymer, James N. Branscomb, and Albert Davis officiating. Music by the Glory Road Boys and the Pleasant Hill Singers. Burial in the Ausmus Cemetery, Speedwell.

Pallbearers: grandsons.

Reece Funeral Home & Valley Chapel in charge.

PARROTT, TILMAN C. age 66 of LaFollette, died Friday, June 26, 1987, at Veterans Administration Medical Center in Nashville. He was of the Baptist faith and a Veteran of World War II. Funeral services were Monday, June 29, 1987, at Walters Funeral Home Chapel with Elders LeRoy Braden and J.L. Thacker officiating. Interment was in Sunrise Cemetery with military honors presented by D.A.V. 105. Preceded in death by his father, O.R. Parrott. Survivors include his wife, Ruby Myers Parrott of LaFollette; a son Martin Parrott; and grandsons Adam and Jason Parrott of Oak Ridge; mother, Mamie Parrott and a sister June Kimberlin both of Monroe, Michigan; brother Carl Parrott of Knoxville; a host of relatives and friends. Our loss is Heaven's gain.

RAICHEL, MILDRED TIPTON age 66, of Speedwell, died Thursday in Dayton, Ohio. Retired employee of General Motors. Member of Braden Chapel Baptist Church. Survivors: husband, Eddie Raichel; sons, Bobby and James Stewart, Vandalia, Ohio; Charles Stewart, Columbus, Ohio; daughter, Patricia Hauna, Vandalia, Ohio; stepsons, Dorse, James, and Larry Raichel, all of Indiana; stepdaughters, Crista Stanley, Patricia Bostic, Joanie Raichel, all of Indiana; sisters: Loretta Cain, West Carrollton, Ohio; Janice Carter, Xenia, Ohio; Elsie Harp of North Carolina; brother, Howard Tipton, Englewood, Ohio; seven grandchildren; six great-grandchildren. Funeral service 2 p.m.

Sunday, Braden Chapel Baptist Church, Elder J.C. Monday officiating. Interment Braden Cemetery.

ROE, MRS. SATRA LOUISE (LIZA) - age 75, of Kokomo, Ind., passed away 9:57 p.m. Friday, Jan. 15, 1988, at St. Vincents Hospital, Indianapolis, Ind. Daughter of the late Bud and Almina Cox Lynch. Widow of Roy Roe. Survivors: daughter, Brenda Fishburn, Maryville; sons, Fred Roe, Seymour, and Jack, Bob and Ken Roe, all of Kokomo, Ind.; ten grandchildren; nine great-grandchildren; ten stepgrandchildren; nine stepgreat-grandchildren; sister, Sequine Robertson, Powell. Funeral service 2 p.m. Tuesday, Oak Grove Primitive Baptist Church, Elder J.C. Monday and Rev. Greg Sharp officiating. Interment church cemetery. The family will receive friends 6-9 p.m. Monday at Cooke Mortuary, Maynardville.

RUSSELL, WALTER LEE JR., (MOONIE) age 35 of Speedwell, TN, passed away Arpil 23rd, 1988. Born June 22, 1952, the son of Walter Lee and Gladys McCreary Russell of Speedwell. He was preceded in death by his father, and was a member of Powell Valley Masonic Lodge #488 and a veteran of the U.S. Army, Signal Corp. Survivors: mother, Gladys Russell; Fiancee, Joan Adams of Cumberland Gap, TN; 4 brothers: Jim, Eddie, Milton, and Harrison, all of Speedwell; 5 sisters: Bobbie Myers, Mary Ann Russell, Katherine Harrison, and Nancy Jessie all of Speedwell, Betty Russell of Maynardville, TN; two special friends: Russ Wilson of Speedwell, and Bill Graves of Maynardville, TN. Elders J.C. Monday and Noble Lee Clawson officiating, music by Bradens Chapel Singers. Burial in the Ausmus Cemetery, Speedwell.

SAEGER, RUTH - Our dear sister in Christ, died March 1, 1988. She joined the Lenoir City Church in November 1947. She had not been in our midst for some years, due to illness and the need to live out of state with her daughter.

She was laid to rest on March 3, 1988, to await the resurrection morning, where her hopes will become reality.

SPARKS, CLARENCE SR. (SLIM) Mr. Clarence Edgar Sparks Sr., 73, died Thursday, January 21, 1988, at Middlesboro Appalachian Regional Hospital. Born in Speedwell, Tenn., January 30, 1914, he was a member of Bradens Chapel Baptist Church, and was the son of the late Leonard (Tip) Sparks and Margaret (Toliver) Sparks. He was preceded in death by two sisters, Pearl Ledford and Lizzy McCarty; and three brothers, James Sparks, and Rev. Bill Sparks, and the Rev. Brad Sparks. Survivors include his wife, Matilda Sparks, Middlesboro; four daughters, Mrs. Ronald (Joyce) Frazier, Mrs. Steve (Delores) Hurst, Mrs. Paul (Sandra) Willis, all of Middlesboro and Mrs. Ricky (Janice) Crockett, Ewing, VA; one son, Clarence Sparks Jr., Pineville; one sister, Mrs. Curtis (Ruby) Sutton, Middlesboro; two brothers, Harrison Sparks, Middlesboro and the Rev. H.M. Sparks, Ewing, VA; 11 grandchildren. Services were to be at 2 p.m. January 23, at West Cumberland Avenue Baptist Church, with the Revs. J.C. Monday, Noble Clawson and David Bullock officiating. Burial was to follow in Sparks Cemetery, with military honors to be presented by the Claiborne County Honor Guard.

SPARKS, HARRISON (RED), age 72, of Noetown passed away Feb. 14, 1988 at his home, Born on July 12,

1915, he was the son of the late Leonard (Tip) Sparks and Margaret Toliver Sparks. He was preceeded in death by four brothers; James Sparks, Rev. Bill Sparks, Rev. Brad Sparks, and Clarence Sparks; two sisters, Pearl Ledford, and Lizzy McCarty. He was a member and deacon of Bradens Chapel Baptist Church. Survivors include his wife, Roberta Braden Sparks, of Middlesboro; six sons: Walter Sparks of Monore, Mich., J.L., Don, David, Roger, and Gary Sparks all of Middlesboro; three daughters: Mrs. John (Wilma) Feketia of Monroe, Mich., Mrs. Albert (Imogene) Wells, and Mrs. Larry (Andrea) Yeary both of Middlesboro. One brother, Rev. H.M. Sparks of Ewing, VA; one sister, Mrs. Curtis (Ruby) Sutton of Middlesboro; 19 grandchildren, 10 great-grandchildren. Burial will be in the Sparks Cemetery.

SPARKS, WALTER LEE, age 52, Woodland Beach, died at 11:10 p.m. Thursday in the Mercy Memorial Hospital intensive care unit. Born Dec. 4, 1935, in Speedwell, Tenn., he was the son of Harrison and Roberta (Braden) Sparks. He was married in October to Retha Kelley. He was a member of Local 723, United Auto Workers. Surviving are his wife; his mother of Middlesboro, KY; two sons, Walter L. Jr. of Dundee and Jeffery H. of Monroe; 4 daughters, Mrs. Michael (Belinda) Heinzerling and Miss Pamela Sparks, both of Monroe, Mrs. Joseph (Nancy) Mathus of Queens, N.Y., and Mrs. Kevin (Dianna) Osborne of Fort Bragg, N.C.; 5 brothers, J.L. of Monore, Donald, David, Roger and Gary, all of Middlesboro; 3 sisters, Mrs. John (Wilma) Feketia of Monore, Mrs. Albert (Imogene) Wells, and Mrs. Larry (Andrea) Yeary, both of Middlesboro; and six grandchildren. He was preceded in death by his father. The

Rev. John Bendewald of Faith Lutheran Church will officiate and burial will be in Northside Cemetery, Maybee.

STIGALL, LILLIE MAE OWENS age 61, died Wednesday May 18, 1988 at Claiborne County Hospital. She was preceded in death by her first husband, Sidney Stigall, two brothers; Dewey and Arthur Owens, one sister, Mary Jane Swangin. She was a member of Gibson Station Primitive Baptist Church.

Survivors are her husband Earl Deweece, California; son and daughter-in-law Clifford and Caroline Stigall, Harrogate, TN; daughter, Fannie Belle Maples, Tazewell, TN; stepsons, Henry, Millard, Carl, John, and Kestrell Stigall; sister, Gladys England, Tipprell, TN. Three grandchildren and one niece Helen Vanover. Services were held at Butchers Gap Baptist Church with Rev. Sam Ayers officiating. Burial was in Arnold Cemetery, Ewing, VA.

WALF, FLOYD LARRY age 60, of Ewing, VA was born March 31, 1927 and passed away November 11, 1987 at his home. He was a member of Gibson Station Primitive Baptist Church. Preceded in death by his parents, Hence and Ginnie Warf, four brothers, Warner, Andrew, Eugene, and Clyde, one son, Raymond Douglas.

Survivors: wife, Nora Ruth Rhymer Warf, Ewing, VA; son, Steve Warf, Ewing, VA; daughters, Betty Jones, Morristown, TN, Audrey Stansberry, New Tazewell, TN, Barbara Hill and Lisa Warf of Ewing, VA; sisters, Marie Russell, Pennington Gap, VA, Fannie Pendleton, Harrogate, TN, Edna Boring, Knoxville, TN; 13 grandchildren and a host of other relatives and friends to mourn his passing. Services were held at Reece Valley Chapel with Elders William Rhymer and Spurgeon

Thompson officiating. He was laid to rest in the Southern Cemetery at Ewing, VA.

WILKERSON, RAYMOND, - This our dear Brother in Christ, died May 16, 1988. He joined the Lenoir City Church in June 1942, where he remained a faithful member until his death.

Brother Raymond leaves to mourn his passing, wife Eliza; daughters, Thelma and Betty; son, Jim; several grandchildren, neices and nephews. Bro. Raymond was laid to rest on May 18, 1988, to await the last trump of God, when we all shall be raised to meet our Lord in the air.

ZWACK, GERTRUDE L. - Mrs. Joseph A. (Gertrude L.) Zwack, 79 died at 4:37 p.m. Saturday in Mercy Memorial Hospital, where she had been for two weeks. She had been in poor health for 20 years and seriously ill since entering the hospital.

Friends may call in the Earle Little Funeral Home where services will be at 11 a.m. Tuesday. Elder Kenneth Wilson of the Monroe Primitive Baptist Church will officiate and burial will be in Roselawn Memorial Park, LaSalle.

Born Feb. 14, 1907, in Claiborne County, Tenn., she was the daughter of James A. and Molly (Day) Drummonds. She married Marshall C. Simmons in January, 1925. He died in November, 1939. She came to Monroe in 1942 from Claiborne County and married Joseph A. Zwack in July, 1944, in Monroe.

She was a member of the Monroe Primitive Baptist Church.

Surviving are her second husband; two daughters, Mrs. Robert (Norma J.) Tabber of Kokomo, Ind., and Mrs. James (Lela) Drummonds of Monroe; three brothers, Carlie Drummonds of Monroe, Virgil Drummonds of Knoxville, Tenn., and Willie Drummonds of Tazewell, Tenn.; a sister, Mrs. Charlie (Dora) Lundy of Monroe; several grandchildren, several great-grandchildren and several great-great-grandchildren.

She was preceded in death by a sister and five sons. A stepson, Marshall O. Simmons, died Sunday.

CHURCH	COUNTY	PASTOR	CLERK	ADDRESS
Black Fox	Grainger	Elder Larry Anderson	Bennie Capps	P.O. Box 91, Maynardville, TN 37807
Braden's Chapel	Union	Elder J.C. Monday Elder Noble Clawson	Linda Bean Phyllis Wilson, Asst.	Speedwell, TN 37870 Speedwell, TN 37870
Brantley's Chapel	Blount	Elder Jerry McBee Elder Chester Hembree	Gaye Lee Mildred Davis, Asst.	Rt. 1, Box 128, Townsend, TN 37882 Rt. 1, Box 344, Townsend, TN 37882
Davis Chapel	Campbell	Elder LeRoy Braden	Katheryn Angel Sondra Wright, Asst.	Rt. 5, Box 170, LaFollette, TN 37766 1256 Middlesboro Hwy., LaFollette, TN 37766
Gethsemane	Knox	Elder Robert Walker	Tom Carmichael	729 Frank St., Knoxville, TN 37919
Gibson Station	Lee, Va.	Elder William Rhymer Eld. Spurgeon Thompson, Asst.	Dorothy Johnson Shirley Sandifur, Asst.	Rt. 2, Box 320, Ewing, VA 24248 Rt. 1, Box 416, Harrogate, TN 37752
Halls	Knox	Elder William Berry Elder Patrick Shelton, Asst.	Alice Powers Sara Jean Harmon, Asst.	7525 Tample Acre Dr., Knoxville 37938 7120 Chermont Cir., Knoxville 37938
Headrick's Chapel	Sevier	Elder Sheridan Moore	Gearldine Abbott	Rt. 6, Box 204A, Sevierville, TN 37862
Lenoir City	Loudon	Elder Robert Bullion	Janice Spoon	1001 Bell Ave. Lenoir City, TN 37771
Meyers' Grove	Claiborne	Elder J.C. Monday Elder Doyle Ausmus, Asst.	Bonnie Miracle Kathy Downes, Asst.	Rt. 2, Box 91, New Tazewell, TN 37825 New Tazewell, TN 37825
Nocton	Grainger	Elder John Oliver	Carroll Oliver Bessie Collins, Asst.	Rt. 2 Box 512, Bean Station, TN 37708 Rt. 5, Morristown, TN 37814
Oak Grove	Union	Elder J.C. Monday Elder Jerry McBee, Astt.	Betty P. Sharp Betty Shoffner, Asst.	Rt. 1, Box 250, Sharps Chapel, TN 37866 Sharps Chapel, TN 37866
Pleasant Hill	Claiborne	Elder William Rhymer Elder Albert Davis, Asst.	William Branscomb Oakien Edwards, Asst.	Speedwell, TN 37870 Speedwell, TN 37870
Rocky Dale	Knox	Elder Hugh Brummitt	Edward Collett Saundra Boruff, Asst.	Rt. 1, Box 17, Luttrell, TN 37779 6916 Weaver Rd., Knoxville, TN

1989 Minutes

POWELL VALLEY ASSOCIATION
OF PRIMITIVE BAPTIST

THE ONE HUNDRED SIXTY-NINTH SESSION
OF THE POWELL VALLEY ASSOCIATION
OF PRIMITIVE BAPTIST
HELD WITH THE SISTER CHURCH AT OAK GROVE
UNION COUNTY, TENNESSEE
AUGUST 18, 19, 20, 1989
NEXT SESSION WILL BE HELD WITH THE SISTER CHURCH
AT PLEASANT HILL, CLAIBORNE COUNTY, TENNESSEE
TO BEGIN ON FRIDAY BEFORE THE THIRD
SATURDAY IN AUGUST, 1990 AT 10:30 A.M.
ELDER WILLIAM BERRY WILL DELIVER
THE INTRODUCTORY SERMON
ELDER JERRY McBEE WILL BE THE ALTERNATE

OFFICERS

ELDER HUGH BRUMMITT   MODERATOR
1329 BROWN AVENUE, KNOXVILLE, TENN., PHONE 546-7700
ELDER LARRY ANDERSON   ASSISTANT MODERATOR
RT. 3, BOX 314-A, SPEEDWELL, TENN., PHONE 869-4635
BENNIE CAPPS   CLERK
P.O. BOX 91, MAYNARDVILLE, TENN., PHONE 992-5571
RINA JOHNSON   ASSISTANT CLERK
1217 BROWN SCHOOL RD., MARYVILLE, TN., PHONE 983-2274

Statistical Table	Printing Minutes	Total Membership	Deceased	Relationship	Dismiss by Letter	Excluded	Baptism	Rec. by Letter	Restored	Regular Meeting Time	Communion Time
Black Fox	$25.00	63	0	0	2	0	0	0	0	Second Sat. Night and Sun. Sunday after Fourth Saturday	Sunday following Second Saturday in June
Braden's Chapel	40.00	147	3	0	5	2	0	0	0	First Saturday Night and Sunday	Sunday following First Saturday in July
Brantley's Chapel	100.00	112	0	0	1	3	2	0	0	Second Saturday Night - Every Sunday and Sunday Night	Sunday Following Second Saturday in July at 10:30 a.m.
Davis Chapel	45.00	83	2	5	0	1	4	0	1	Every Sunday and Sunday Night	Sunday following Third Saturday in June
Gethsemane	35.00	27	0	0	0	0	0	0	0	Second and Fourth Sunday	Fourth Sunday in May and October
Gibson Station	50.00	71	3	0	0	0	2	0	0	First Saturday Night - Every Sunday and Sunday Night	Sunday following First Saturday in June
Halls	100.00	115	2	0	0	0	1	3	0	Every Sunday and Sunday Night	Last Sunday in April
Headrick's Chapel	25.00	109	1	0	0	3	0	0	1	First and Third Sunday of each Month	First Sunday in May and October 11 a.m.
Lenoir City	45.00	100	2	4	1	0	2	0	0	Every Sunday and Sunday Night	Wednesday Night before Easter Sunday
Myers Grove	30.00	79	1	1	0	0	1	1	0	4th Saturday Night & Every Sunday	Sunday following Fourth Saturday in May
Nocton	30.00	38	3	0	0	0	2	0	0	First Sunday - Third Saturday and Sunday of each month	Sunday following Third Saturday in May & September
Oak Grove	35.00	331	2	2	1	0	4	0	0	First Saturday Night and Sunday - Third Sunday	Sunday following the First Saturday in May
Pleasant Hill	45.00	90	1	3	0	0	0	0	0	4th Sat. Morning & Sat. Night Every Sun. and Sun. Night	Sunday following the Fourth Sunday in June at 10:30 a.m.
Rocky Dale	50.00	103	2	3	0	0	9	1	0	Every Sunday Morning	Sunday following Third Saturday in May

1989 Minutes

POWELL VALLEY ASSOCIATION
OF PRIMITIVE BAPTIST

**THE ONE HUNDRED SIXTY-NINTH SESSION
OF THE POWELL VALLEY ASSOCIATION
OF PRIMITIVE BAPTIST
HELD WITH THE SISTER CHURCH AT OAK GROVE
UNION COUNTY, TENNESSEE
AUGUST 18, 19, 20, 1989
NEXT SESSION WILL BE HELD WITH THE SISTER CHURCH
AT PLEASANT HILL, CLAIBORNE COUNTY, TENNESSEE
TO BEGIN ON FRIDAY BEFORE THE THIRD
SATURDAY IN AUGUST, 1990 AT 10:30 A.M.
ELDER WILLIAM BERRY WILL DELIVER
THE INTRODUCTORY SERMON
ELDER JERRY McBEE WILL BE THE ALTERNATE**

OFFICERS

ELDER HUGH BRUMMITT   MODERATOR
1329 BROWN AVENUE, KNOXVILLE, TENN., PHONE 546-7700
ELDER LARRY ANDERSON   ASSISTANT MODERATOR
RT. 3, BOX 314-A, SPEEDWELL, TENN., PHONE 869-4635
BENNIE CAPPS   CLERK
P.O. BOX 91, MAYNARDVILLE, TENN., PHONE 992-5571
RINA JOHNSON   ASSISTANT CLERK
1217 BROWN SCHOOL RD., MARYVILLE, TN., PHONE 983-2274

1990

S	M	T	W	T	F	S
JANUARY						
	1	2	3	4	5	6
7	8	9	10	11	12	13
14	15	16	17	18	19	20
21	22	23	24	25	26	27
28	29	30	31			

S	M	T	W	T	F	S
FEBRUARY						
				1	2	3
4	5	6	7	8	9	10
11	12	13	14	15	16	17
18	19	20	21	22	23	24
25	26	27	28			

S	M	T	W	T	F	S
MARCH						
				1	2	3
4	5	6	7	8	9	10
11	12	13	14	15	16	17
18	19	20	21	22	23	24
25	26	27	28	29	30	31

S	M	T	W	T	F	S
APRIL						
1	2	3	4	5	6	7
8	9	10	11	12	13	14
15	16	17	18	19	20	21
22	23	24	25	26	27	28
29	30					

S	M	T	W	T	F	S
MAY						
		1	2	3	4	5
6	7	8	9	10	11	12
13	14	15	16	17	18	19
20	21	22	23	24	25	26
27	28	29	30	31		

S	M	T	W	T	F	S
JUNE						
					1	2
3	4	5	6	7	8	9
10	11	12	13	14	15	16
17	18	19	20	21	22	23
24	25	26	27	28	29	30

S	M	T	W	T	F	S
JULY						
1	2	3	4	5	6	7
8	9	10	11	12	13	14
15	16	17	18	19	20	21
22	23	24	25	26	27	28
29	30	31				

S	M	T	W	T	F	S
AUGUST						
			1	2	3	4
5	6	7	8	9	10	11
12	13	14	15	16	17	18
19	20	21	22	23	24	25
26	27	28	29	30	31	

S	M	T	W	T	F	S
SEPTEMBER						
						1
2	3	4	5	6	7	8
9	10	11	12	13	14	15
16	17	18	19	20	21	22
23	24	25	26	27	28	29
30						

S	M	T	W	T	F	S
OCTOBER						
	1	2	3	4	5	6
7	8	9	10	11	12	13
14	15	16	17	18	19	20
21	22	23	24	25	26	27
28	29	30	31			

S	M	T	W	T	F	S
NOVEMBER						
				1	2	3
4	5	6	7	8	9	10
11	12	13	14	15	16	17
18	19	20	21	22	23	24
25	26	27	28	29	30	

S	M	T	W	T	F	S
DECEMBER						
						1
2	3	4	5	6	7	8
9	10	11	12	13	14	15
16	17	18	19	20	21	22
23	24	25	26	27	28	29
30	31					

MINUTES OF THE ONE HUNDRED SIXTY-EIGHTH SESSION

Friday, August 18, 1989

The one hundred sixty-nineth session of the Powell Valley Association of Primitive Baptists met with the Sister Church at Rocky Dale in Knox County, Tennessee, on August 18, 19, and 20, 1989.

Elder Bill Berry and Brother Glenn Walker led the congregation in "The Unclouded Day", "There is a Fountain", then the Moderator Elder Hugh Brummitt welcomed the congregation and pleaded for peace and love to abide throughout the entire Association and called for prayer by Elder Albert Davis of Pleasant Hill Church.

Following prayer, Elder John Oliver from Noeton Church delivered the introductory sermon from the 18th. chapter of St. John and the 37th. verse using as his text "Highway of Righteousness", and delivered a very uplifting sermon.

After the introductory sermon, they sang a song and were dismissed in prayer by Brother Richard Walker of Brantley Chapel. The Association was to reconvene after a 15 minute recess.

After recess, the crowd reassembled in the church. Brother Glen Walker led the congregation in singing, and then Moderator Elder Hugh Brummitt read from the 3rd. chapter of Isaiah, then called for prayer by Elder Parnick Shelton from Halls.

The Moderator then asked for the order of business for the following transactions:

1st: Called for letters of the Sister Churches to be presented to the clerk for reading. Thirteen (13) were received.

2nd: The letters were presented and read and motion approved that the delegates be seated.

3rd: The Moderator called for anyone present from any of the Sister Churches not named as delegate who desired to be seated as such to come forward and give the clerk their name and the name of their church. Five came. Ruby Hill, Mildred Ellison, Davis Chapel; Veda Cole, Oak Grove, Brian Brantley, Brantley's Chapel.

4th: Called for petitionary letter if there should be one. None came.

5th: Motion approved that the Association re-elect Elder Hugh Brummitt as Moderator and re-elect Elder Larry Anderson as Assistant Moderator for the ensuing year.

6th: Motion approved that Brother Bennie Capps be re-elected Clerk and Brother Rina Johnson be re-elected Assistant Clerk for the ensuing year.

7th: Motion was appoved that we empower Moderator Elder Brummitt to appoint all the committees to serve this session.

8th: The Moderator, having been empowered to do so, appointed the committees as follows:

Committee on Arrangements:	Brother Carroll L. Oliver
	Brother Clyde Lynch
	Brother Franklin Jones
Committee on Preaching:	Brother Junior McBee
	Brother Mannie Shoffner
	Brother Elwood Evans
Committee on Request:	Brother O.D. McCarty
	Brother Charlie Collins
	Brother Joe Palmer
Committee on Finance:	Elder William Rhymer
	Elder Bill Berry
	Brother Richard Walker

9th: Called for the finances to be turned in to the Finance Committee.

10th: The committees all having been appointed and accepted, the Association moved to adjourn until 10:30 Saturday morning. They sang a song and were dismissed in prayer by Elder William Berry of Halls.

Saturday, August 19, 1989

At the appointed hour of 10:30 Saturday morning and at the sound of singing, the Association reassembled.

After Jerry McBee led the congregation in "I Have Some with Me", "Just a Little Talk with Jesus" and "Sweet Hour of Prayer", the Assistant Moderator Elder Larry Anderson gave a very spiritual and uplifting talk and read from the 1st. chapter 1st. Corinthians, verses 1 - 10, then called for prayer by Elder Doyle Ausmus.

After prayer, the Moderator called the Association to order for the remainder of the business:

1st: Called for any letters from Sister Churches not received on Friday. There was one.

2nd: The letter was presented and read and motion approved that the delegates be seated.

3rd: Called for anyone from any of the churches who were present and desired to be seated as delegate to come forward and give the clerk their name and their church. Lottie Berry, Cleo Berry, from Pleasant Hill; Josh Stapleton, Ima Lee Stapleton, from Rocky Dale, Coram Berry and Twila Berry from Brantley's Chapel.

4th: Called for the report of the Committee on Arrangements who submitted the following report:

Report on Arrangements:

Call for roll call of delegates.
Call for report of Committee on Preaching.
Call for report of Committee on Request.
Call for report of Committee on Finance.

Decide how many minutes we have printed, who shall supervise the printing and delivery of the same, which sister church shall host the next association and who will preach the introductory sermon and who will be the alternate. Who will prepare the Circular Letter.

Respectfully Submitted,
Brother Carroll L. Oliver
Brother Clyde Lynch
Brother Franklin Jones

5th: Motion approved to receive the above report and release the committee.

6th: Called the roll call of delegates of all Sister Churches and check the absentees.

7th: Called for the report of the Committee on Preaching:

Committee on Preaching:

Friday night:	Elder Chester Hembree
	Elder Richard Walker
Saturday morning:	Elder Albert Davis
	Elder Parnick Shelton
Saturday night:	Elder Jerry McBee
	Elder Spurgeon Thompson
Sunday morning:	Elder William Rhymer
	Elder Larry Anderson

Respectfully submitted,
Brother Junior McBee
Brother Mannie Shoffner
Brother Elwood Evans

8th: Motion approved to receive the above report and release the committee.

9th: Called for the report of the Committee on Request, which was given:

We, the Committee on Request, wish to request as follows, that we have 1,100 minutes printed and the clerk supervise the printing and distribution of same and that he recieve $135.00 for his services. We also request that the next session of the Powell Valley Association be held with the Sister Church at Pleasant Hill in Claiborne County to begin on Friday before the third Saturday in August, 1990, at 10:30 A.M. and continue three days. We also request that Elder William Berry preach the introductory sermon and Elder Jerry McBee be the alternate. We also request that Elder Joe Bush write a circular letter for the minutes for 1990.

Respectfully submitted,
Brother O.D. McCarty
Brother Charlie Collins

Brother Joe Palmer
Brother Josh Stapleton

10th: Motion approved to receive the above report and release the committee.

11th: Called for the report of the Committee on Finance, which submitted the following report:

Black Fox	$25.00
Braden's Chapel	40.00
Brantley's Chapel	100.00
Davis Chapel	45.00
Gethsemane	35.00
Gibson Station	50.00
Halls	100.00
Headrick's Chapel	25.00
Lenoir City	45.00
Meyer's Grove	30.00
Noeton	30.00
Oak Grove	35.00
Pleasant Hill	45.00
Rocky Dale	50.00
Total Collection	655.00
Donations	20.00
	675.00
Balance in bank	737.00
	1,412.00
Expenses for 1988	635.00
Balance in bank	777.00

Respectfully Submitted,
Elder Bill Berry
Brother Richard Walker

12th: Motion approved to receive the above report and release the committee.

13th: Motion approved that we grant the request of the committee and have 1,100 minutes printed and the clerk to receive $135.00 for his services.

14th: Motion approved that the next session of the Association be held with the Sister Church at Pleasant Hill to commence on Friday before the third Saturday in August, 1990, at 10:30 A.M.

15th: Motion approved that Elder Joe Bush write the circular letter for the 1990 minutes.

16th: Motion approved that Elder William Berry deliver the introductory sermon and Elder Jerry McBee be the alternate.

17th: Motion approved that the churches of the Powell Valley

Association extend to the church and the people of Oak Grove our heart felt thanks and our prayers for the love, fellowship, kindness and food while we were with you. May the good Lord bless and keep you is our prayers.

18th: Motion approved to adjourn, trusting the Lord to permit us to meet again with the Sister Church at Pleasant Hill in Claiborne County, Tennessee, on Friday before the third Saturday in August, 1990, at 10:30 A.M.

Dismissed in prayer by Elder Charles Taylor.

        Elder Hugh Brummitt, Moderator
        Elder Larry Anderson, Assistant Moderator
        Brother Bennie Capps, Clerk
        Brother Rina Johnson, Assistant Clerk

SPECIAL ANNOUNCEMENTS

Brantley's Chapel has their second Saturday night services at 7 P.M. every Sunday morning at 10:30 A.M.; Sunday night at 7 P.M. in the summer months and at 6:00 P.M. in the winter months.

The following churches requested the Association for 1990: Black Fox, Brantley Chapel, Gibson Station, Halls, Oak Grove, Pleasant Hill, and Lenoir City.

Please make your contributions payable to: Powell Valley Association.

Dates of ordination of the following Elders:
    Elder Albert Davis, May 17, 1930
    Elder Joe Irving, October 1, 1949
    Elder Hugh Brummitt, December 12, 1954
    Elder James Branscomb, June 23, 1956
    Elder Charles Taylor, April, 1959
    Elder Parnick Shelton, December 11, 1960
    Elder Claude Rosson, July 4, 1964
    Elder Joe Bush, April 27, 1969
    Elder Bill Berry, August 27, 1972
    Elder Larry Anderson, October 24, 1975
    Elder Spurgeon Thompson, December 17, 1976
    Elder Bill Rhymer, December 17, 1976
    Elder Jerry McBee, April 26, 1981
    Elder Nelson Jones, July 17, 1981
    Elder Steve Taylor, September 26, 1986
    Elder Clearance Hicks, September 26, 1986
    Elder Chester Hembree, June 19, 1988
    Elder Clyde Abbott, Sr., November 6, 1988

SUMMARY

We are blessed with a fine group of ministers as was illustrated by those who had the opportunity to preach. We regret that time will not permit more of them to preach when we meet with the Association. On Friday night Brother Richard Walker read from the 112th. Psalms brought a very uplifting message concerning being blessed when we are following the Lord, then Elder Chester Hembree spoke for a few minutes on the Will of God. Saturday morning, Elder Albert Davis brought a good message using as his text "The Foundation of God", then Elder Parnick Shelton brought a very uplifting sermon on the Grace and Love of God. Saturday night, Elder Jerry McBee brought a very spiritual message on Camped outside the Walls, the Elder Spurgeon Thomspon preached on being condemned to die but Christ took our place. On Sunday Morning, Elder Larry Anderson preached on Building on the Foundation, and the Elder William Rhymer preached on Nation that know not God, both Elders brought a very uplifting and spiritual message.

CIRCULAR LETTER TO
POWELL VALLEY ASSOCIATION

One of my prayers is and has been for some time that before I leave this old world that I will be able to stand in the stand with another preacher preaching identical words as he is, being fed from the same source on high as Elijah was when he prayed for God to send fire down and consume the alter and prove to this people that He is God and that I am His servant.

Written by Elder Claude Rosson

CHURCHES AND THEIR DELEGATES

BLACK FOX: Brothers: Dale Capps, Bennie Capps; **Sisters:** Mary Ruth Capps, Naomi Cabbage and Sarah Hopson
BRADEN'S CHAPEL: Sisters: Leecy Sparks, Winona Monday
BRANTLEY'S CHAPEL: Elders: Chester Hembree, Jerry McBee; **Brothers:** Richard Walker, Everett Brantley, Rina Johnson, Chester Lee Hembree, Junior McBee, Daniel Brantley, Robert Welch, Glenn Walker, Dan Walker; **Sisters:** Hazel Johnson, Mildred Brantley, Edith Hembree, Blanche Welch, Edith Walker, Barsha Brantley
DAVIS CHAPEL: Brothers: Clyde Lynch, O.D. McCarty, **Sisters:** Pearl Lynch, Mollie McCarty, Ollie White
GETHSEMANE: Bro. Tom Carmichael, Sister June Carmichael

502

GIBSON STATION: Elders: William Rhymer, Spurgeon Thompson, Nelson Jones; **Brothers:** Franklin Jones; **Sisters:** Karen Rhymer, Polly Jones, Evelyn Irving, Fannie Jones, Shirley Sandifur, Amy Sandifur, Dorothy Johnson

HALLS: Elders: Hugh Brummitt, Parnick Shelton, Bill Berry; **Brothers:** Elwood Evans, Joe Culvahouse, Vance Harmon, Vance Harmon, Jr.; **Sisters:** Ruby Brummitt, Mildred Evans, Betty Culvahouse, Irene Harmon, Trula Berry

HEADRICK'S CHAPEL: Elder: Robert Walker

LENOIR CITY: Brother: Hubert Spoon; **Sisters:** Annie Spoon, Ruby Williams

MEYER'S GROVE. Brother: Bill Goods, **Sisters:** Ida Robinson, Velt Muncey

NOETON: Elder: John Oliver, **Brothers:** Carroll Oliver, Charlie Collins, Tim Oliver; **Sisters:** Dora Collins, Mildred Oliver

OAK GROVE: Brother: Mannie Shoffner; **Sisters:** Ruth Shoffner, Frances Eastridge, Alvada Dykes

PLEASANT HILL: Elders: Larry Anderson, Albert Davis; **Sister:** Myra Anderson

ROCKY DALE: Elders: Joe Bush; **Brothers:** Charlie Bryant, Joe Palmer; **Sisters:** Norma Jean Bush, Myrtle Bryant

Elders of the Powell Valley Association

Front row: left to right — Elders Chester Hembree, Spurgeon Thompson, Richard Walker

Back row: left to right — Elders: Larry Anderson, *Asst. Moderator,* Hugh Brummitt, *Moderator,* Claude Rosson, James Henry Branscomb, William Berry, Jerry McBee, Parnick Shelton, Albert Davis and William Rhymer.

MINISTERS DIRECTORY

Elder Larry Anderson, Rt. 3, Box 314-A, Speedwell, TN 869-4635
Elder Johnny Atkins, Bean Station, TN Ph. 767-2397
Elder Buford Doyle Ausmus, Rt. 2, Speedwell, TN Ph. 566-0433
Elder William Berry, Rt. 13, Knoxville, TN Ph. 922-9189
Elder LeRoy Braden, 2305 Middlesboro, LaFollette, TN Ph. 562-9353
Elder J.H. Branscomb, Speedwell, TN Ph. 562-6361
Elder Hugh H. Brummitt, 1329 Brown, Knoxville, TN Ph. 546-7700
Elder Joe Bush, Rt.3, Corryton, TN Ph. 687-7018
Elder Jim Campbell, Louisville, TN Ph. 873-1654
Elder Noble Clawson, Rt. 4, Speedwell, TN Ph. 562-2004
Elder Albert Davis, Speedwell, TN Ph. 869-3596
Elder Clarence Hicks, Maryville, TN
Elder Nelson Jones, Rt. 1 - Box 343, Harrogate, TN Ph. 869-3703
Elder Alvin Graves, 122 Oak Wood Dr., Lenoir City, TN Ph. 986-9725
Elder Jerry McBee, 901 Chapparral, Seymour, TN 37865
                                                    Ph. 577-2669
Elder Sheridan Moore, Rt. 1, Townsend, TN Ph. 448-6430
Elder J.C. Monday, Speedwell, TN Ph. 562-3068
Elder John Oliver, Rt. 2, Box 3482 Bean Station, TN Ph. 581-5039
Elder Howard Pippin, P.O. Box 246, Ider, Ala. 35961
Elder William Rhymer, P.O. Box 12, Shawnee, TN Ph. 869-3092
Elder Parnick Shelton, 6001 McGinnis, Corryton, TN Ph. 687-5070
Elder Charles Taylor, Rt. 9, Box 290, Lenoir City, TN 37771
Elder Steve Taylor, Rt. 4, Box 2375, Tifton, GA 31794
Elder Spurgeon Thompson, P.O. Box 36, Shawnee, TN Ph. 869-8175
Elder Claude Rosson, Rt. 4, New Tazewell, TN Ph. 626-3168
Elder Robert Walker, Sevierville, TN, Ph. 428-1527
Elder Clay Widner, Rt. 1, Tazewell, TN Ph. 626-3893
Elder Robert Bullion, 101 Rose St., Lenoir City, TN Ph. 986-5465
Elder Chester Hembree, Rt. 2, Box 422, Rockford, TN Ph. 983-6526
Elder Clyde Abbott, Sr., Rt. 7, Sevierville, TN Ph. 453-2329

LICENTIATES

Brother Roscoe Branscomb, Speedwell, TN
Brother Odell Carpenter, 812 Brown School Rd.,
                            Maryville, TN 37801, Ph. 984-4352
Brother Mark Taylor, Lenoir City, TN
Brother Richard Walker, Rt. 2, Box 430, Rockwood, TN 37853
                                                    Ph. 977-0414
Brother Ray Walker, Rt. 6, Townsend, TN

RULES OF DECORUM

1. The churches composing the Powell's Valley Association shall not be confined to any set rules as to specific number of Messengers they shall have in the body, but shall have the right to name in their letters as many as they choose, and in addition all orderly members of any of the churches being present be entitled to seats in the body as Messengers fo their respective churches, with all the rights and privileges of the same.

2. The Messengers thus assembled shall be denominated the Powell's Valley Primitive Baptist Church.

3. For the purpose of historical information and statistical edification, the Churches are required to state in letters, the number of members in fellowship, the number received by Baptism, by letter, by confession of Faith, the number dismissed, excluded and dead since last session; also the time of their meeting, their pastoral supply, and the amount of money contributed for ministers and other purposed together with any other information they deem appropriate for the edification of the saints and glory of God.

4. This Association shall have no power to answer queries, give advice, or dictate to the Churches in any case, or to lord it over God's heritage nor any power by which she can directly or indirecily fringe on the internal rights of the church or censure and try any church or member in reference to faith and practice and determine upon validity of gospel ordinances. These things shall rest entirely with the churches; but henceforward our annual meetings shall be only for the purpose of hearing from each other, and for the worship of God and mutual comfort and edification of the Saints. To this end we reserve the privilege annually for Friday before the Third Saturday in August and the two following days or at such other times as may be agreed upon with any church that may invite us having to protect our own standard, while in session, from heresay and disorder to recognize and invite any primitive Baptist minister or any lay brother to worship with us that may deem proper; to request the brethren of our body to visit other churches or bodies in our belief with whom we may desire to culture Christian fellowship; to publish in a minute of our proceedings.

5. Each session of the body shall have a Moderator and Clerk who shall hold office until re-elected.

6. Any order member of any church belonging to this body, when convened, being present shall be eligible to elect on as Moderator and Clerk or to sit on any committee appointed by the same.

7. In all election or questions that may be necessary to determine by vote, the vote shall be taken by churches, each church being entitled to three votes for any number less than one hundred, and one additional vote for every fifty or fraction thereof above the first hundred, but the Messengers of each church may divide their vote as they see proper.

8. All elections or questions coming to vote shall be determined by a majority vote cast, and it shall be the only duty of the minority to acquiesce in the decision thus reached.

9. If new churches desire to be admitted to this union they shall petition by letter and messengers and if voted for and recommended by one or more sister churches for her Presbytery constitutioning them, as orthodox and orderly they shall be received by the vote of the body and manifested by the Moderator giving the Messengers the right hand of fellowship.

10. Any motion or resolution clearly inconsistent with the above rules shall be promptly ruled out of order unless withdrawn by the mover.

11. Any messenger being ruled out of order by the Moderator shall have the right to appeal to the body on the question of order, and if sustained shall be allowed to proceed, but if not take his seat.

12. Our meeting being held in the name of Christ and the worship of God; each Messenger is expected to observe due and proper therein.

13. It will not be considered good for any Messenger whose name has been enrolled as

such to abruptley break off or absent himself from the Association without leave.

14. The Moderator shall be entitled to the same privilege of speech as other members provided the chair is filled.

15. The minutes of the Association shall be read and approved by the body and signed by the Moderator before adjourning.

16. The Association shall be opened and closed by prayer.

17. Amendments to these may be made at any time by a majority of the union voting by churches when they deem it necessary, provide such amendments do not compromise the sovereignty of the churches nor have tendency to give body undue power or jurisdiction over them.

ARTICLES OF FAITH

Article 1. We believe in only one true living God, as He is revealed to us in the Holy Scriptures - Father, Son, and Holy Ghost.

Article 2. We believe that the Scriptures of the old and new Testaments are the words of God and the only rule of all-saving knowledge and obedience.

Article 3. We believe in the doctrine of election according to the foreknowledge of God.

Article 4. We believe in the doctrine of original sin.

Article 5. We believe in man's impotency to rescue himself from the fallen state he is in, by his own will or ability.

Article 6. We believe that sinners are justified in the sight of God only by the imputed righteousness of Jesus Christ.

Article 7. We believe the elect, according to the foreknowledge of God will be called, converted, regenerated, and sanctified by the Holy Spirit.

Article 8. We believe the saints will persevere and never fall finally away.

Article 9. We believe that baptism and the Lord's Supper are ordinances of Jesus Christ, and that true believers are the only subject of these ordinances, and that the true mode of baptism is by immersion. We believe also that feet washing is an example of Jesus Christ and should be kept by his disciples until his second coming.

Article 10. We believe in the Resurrection of the dead and the General Judgement.

Article 11. We believe that the punishment of the wicked will be everlasting and that the joys of the righteous will be eternal.

Article 12. We believe that no minister has the right to administer the ordinances, except those who have been regularly baptized and called of God, and come under the imposition of hands of the presbytery,

506

Obituaries

BALL, PRINCE JAMES, 74, of Rt. 2, Ewing, VA was born January 15, 1915 in Dallas, Texas. He died Tuesday February 2, 1989 at his home. He was a veteran of World War II.

He was preceded in death by four brothers and two sisters. Survivors include his wife, Thelma Virginia Ball, whom he married April 14, 1938, five children, sons, Jack Ball, Napoleon, Ohio, Earnest Ball, Archibald, Ohio. Daughters, Mitzi Miller, Delta Ohio, Patricia Roesch, Morenci, Michigan, Bonita Odham, Marion, Ind.; brother, Curtis Ball, Tazewell, Tn.; sister, Nottie Britain, Gibson Station, Va.; 26 grandchildren and 21 great-grand-children; a host of other family and friends.

Services were conducted at Gibson Station Primitive Baptist Church with Elders Bill Rhymer and Spurgeon Thompson officiating. Burial was in the Southern Cemetery.

BRANTLEY, FERNIE BELL, 79, of Route 1, Bean Station died Nov. 25, 1988 at Jefferson Memorial Hospital. She was a member of Noeton Primitive Baptist Church. She was the grandmother of the late Chilous Brantley, Jr. and Carol Barnes.

Survivors include her husband, Burlis Brantley of Bean Station, sons, Chilous Brantley and James "Buddy" Brantley, both of Bean Station, and Raymond Brantley of Eustis, Florida; sister, Cora Brantley of Knoxville; six grandchildren, two step-grand-children, nine great-grandchildren and several nieces and nephews.

Funeral services were held Nov. 27, 1988 at Neoton Primitive Baptist Church with Elder John Oliver and Elder William Rhymer officiating. Burial was in the church cemetery. Stubblefield Funeral Home of Morristown in charge of arrangements.

CHAMBERLAIN, HENRY, - This dear brother was called home on Nov. 28, 1988. Preceded in death by his wife, Estie Williams Chamberlain, he left these survivors: brothers, John and William; several nieces and nephews. Bro. Henry joined the Lenoir City Primitive Baptist Church in April of 1948 and was ordained as a Deacon on April 19, 1949. He remained a faithful member until his death, although poor health hindered his attendance for several months prior to this time.

COLLINS, BESSIE N. 92, East Morris Boulevard, Morristown, passed away June 30, 1989 at Morristown Hamblen-Hospital. She was a member of Noeton Primitive Baptist Church and had been assistant-clerk of the church since 1954.

She was the widow of Noah Collins. Survivors - daughters: Ruby C. Madgett of Morristown, Mamie McCormack of Powell; sons: Thomas E. Collins of Morristown, Herbert N. Collins of Salisbury, N.C., Charles R. Collins of Strawberry Plains; nine grandchildren and several great-grandchildren and great-great-grandchildren.

Services were 2 P.M. July 2, 1989 at Noeton Primitive Baptist Church

507

with Elder John Oliver Officiating. Burial was in church cemetery. Stubblefield Funeral Home of Morristown in charge of arrangements.

DOSSETT, ORA MAE - 76, of Corryton, passed away Saturday at her home. Member of Halls Primitive Bapist Church. Attended Rocky Dale Baptist Church. Survivors: sisters, Mrs. Dola Webb, Mrs. Maggie Dossett, Mrs. Ruby Brummitt, all of Knoxville; Mrs. Jean Overton, Mrs. Jewell Lewis, both of Tazewell; Mrs. Margie Houser, Mrs. Goldie Langley, both of Maynardville; Mrs. Myrl Nelson, Halls; Mrs. Flora Guy, of Indiana; brother, Jeff W. White, Knoxville. Funeral services were 8 p.m. Sunday, Rose Broadway Chapel, with Hugh Brummitt and Bill Berry officiating. Interment service was at Lynhurst Cemetery.

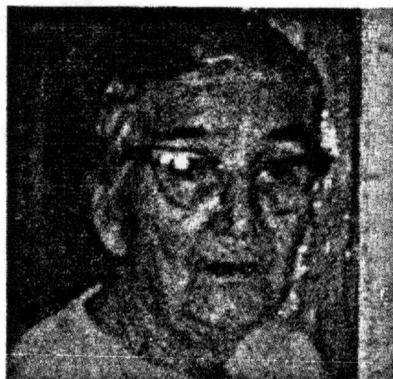

EDWARDS, CECIL GROVES, age 85, of Speedwell, Tennessee died at Laurel Manour Health Care Center Saturday, November 5, 1988. She joined Pleasant Hill Primitive Baptist Church in January 1932 and lived a faithful member until her death. She was preceded in death by her husband Verlin Edwards, 3 sons, 1 daughter, and her parents, 3 sisters, 1 brother. She leaves to mourn her passing: sons: Coy, Condis, Kenneth, Loyd, Austin, Terry, and Carl; daugher Cedilla Edwards Bronscomb; 23 grandchildren, 13 great-grandchildren, 1 great-great-grandson; sisters: Hazel Lambert, Ada Jones, and Bertha Edwards. Services were on Nov. 8, 1988 at Pleasant Hill Church. Elder William Rhymer and Elder James Henry Bronscomb officiating. Burial in the Hunter Cemetery.

We go to sleep so that we may awaken in the morning. If we did not sleep, we would never know the joy of awakening, and if we did not die, we could never live eternally.

JAMES S. HEATHERLY, age 86 years and 10 months, of Route 5, Davis Chapel Community, LaFollette, Tn. passed away on September 9, 1988 at his home. He was a lifelong, faithful member and Trustee of Davis Chapel Primitive Baptist Church. He was preceeded in death by his loving wife, Ruth Ellison Heatherly. "Brother Jim" is survived by a daughter, Trulene Heatherly Nash of La Follette; sons, Arnold of La Follette, and Roy of Knoxville; grandchildren, Sarah Beth Heatherly of LaFollette, Gary Heatherly of Knoxville, and Terri Ann Dolan of Atlanta; daughter-in-law, Polly Heatherly of Knoxville; brother, Homer Heatherly of Dayton, Ohio; sister, Elsie Sutton of Dayton and many, many friends and neighbors.

Funeral services were held at Davis Chapel Primitive Baptist Church with Elders LeRoy Braden and Bill Berry officiating.

HILL, CLUN M. — age 77, of Knoxville, passed away 2 a.m. Sunday at Hillcrest West Nursing Home. Survivors: son and daughter-in-law, Wayne and Joyce Hill; son, Gary Hill; granddaughter, Waynette Hill, all of Knoxville; sister, Mrs. Stella Clapp, Corryton; several nieces and nephews. Funeral services were 10 a.m. Tuesday. Ailor Chapel. Interment Skaggs Cemetery.

HILL, RUSHIA WHITE, age 86, of Route 4, Lafollette, passed away on 12/8/88. She was a member of Davis Chapel Primitive Baptist Church. She was preceeded in death by husband, William Hill; sons, Elmer and Lawrence Hill; and daugher, Florence Hill. She is survived by daughters, Ada Mae Hill and Roxie Johnson; sons, J.T., Robert Dan, and O.D. Hill; 25 grandchildren; 30 great-grandchildren; 2 great-great grandchildren; sisters, Bedie Kitts, Dovie Standford, Mossie Bailey, June Wilhoit, and Trula McFarland; and brothers, Dewey, Conley, and Claude White.

Funeral services were held at Davis Chapel Primitive Baptist Church with Elders LeRoy Braden and Bill Berry officiating.

IRVING, ELDER JOE S., age 84 of Middlesboro, Ky., Rt. 3, died Sunday, Oct. 9, 1988 at the Claiborne County Hospital in Tazewell, Tn. Born May 12, 1904, he was a member of Gibson Station Primitive Baptist Church, Lee Co. Va.

He belonged to Masonic Lodge #546 and Eastern Star Lodge #436. He was a retired coal miner and a machinist at Tecumseh Products in Michigan. United in marriage with Evelyn Gibson Maples on April 29, 1978.

Preceded in death by his parents, John Richard and Susan Ball Irving; two brothers, Tate and John; two sisters, Mary and Angie Irving. Survivors include his wife, Evelyn Maples Irving; stepson, Clyde Maples and wife Hazel; stepdaughers, Virginia Ramsey and Gladys Miracle all of Middlesboro, Ky.; stepgrandson David Maples and step-grand-daughter, Amanda Maples of Tazewell, Tn.; three sisters-in-law: Thelma Irving, Monroe, Mi. and Geneva Hamilton, Pineville, Ky; Lucille Homes, Venice, Fla.; brothers-in-law, James Gibson, Marion, Ohio and Cecil Gibson, Tazewell, Tn.; three nieces: Billie Petree, Clinton, Tn., Glenna Sue Irvin and Evelyn Turner both of Monroe, Mi.; nephew,

Ronald Irvin, Chino, Calif.; other cousins, relatives and friends.

Masonic rites were conducted Tues. night at Reece Funeral Home, Harrogate, Tn. Services were 2 p.m. Wednesday, Oct. 12 at Gibson Station Primitive Baptist Church with Elders Bill Rhymer, Spurgeon Thompson and Bill Berry officiating. Singers were from the Gibson Station Church.

Pallbearers were, Clyde Maples, David Maples, Eugene Petree, Franklin Jones, Claude Sandifur, Wilburn Cottrell, Curtis Ball, and Charles Brittain. Honorary pallbearers: elders of the Powell Valley Association of Primitive Baptists, Shawnee Masonic Lodge and Jack Colson. Laid to rest in Southern Cemetery.

JOHNSON, AUDRY BEATRICE (BORUFF) — of Ridgeview Road, Corryton, Tennessee was born December 11, 1923 and passed away February 2, 1989 at St. Mary's Medical Center in Knoxville, Tennessee. She was preceded in death by her father, James Marion Boruff; mother, Lucy Foust Boruff; sisters, Edith Boruff and Ruth Russell. She was a member of Rocky Dale Primitive Baptist Church and was retired from Standard Knitting Mills. Survivors: husband, Glen R. Johnson; sons and daughters-in-law, Gary Johnson, Larry and Mildred Johnson, all of Corryton, Roy and Delores Johnson, of Knoxville; daugher and son-in-law, Annette and Howard Russell, Knoxville; grandsons, Rodney Russell, Perry Johnson; granddaughter, Jennifer Russell; two step-grandchildren; brother and sister-in-law, James and Saundra Boruff; sisters and brothers-in-law: Fay and Edward Col-lett, Luttrell; Opal and Bill Dickerson, Corryton; Ima Lee and Josh Stapleton, Powell; Christine and Dr. Charles Earl, Rogersville; several nieces and nephews. The funeral service was at 8:30 p.m. Friday, February 3rd., at Mynatt Chapel, Elder Hugh Brummitt and Elder Joe Bush officiating. The family and friends met at the funeral home at 9:45 a.m. on Saturday and proceeded to Highland Memorial Cemetery for graveside services and interment at 10:30 a.m. Pallbearers; Rodney Russell, Perry Johnson, Ronnie and Steve Boruff, Jimmy Russell and Ronnie Bush. The family received friends from 7 - 8:30 p.m. on Friday at Mynatt's Mortuary. Words cannot express how much Rocky Dale Church meant to her during her time of illness. She didn't want to leave the people she loved but was anxious and ready to leave her painful body and be united with her loving Savior.

MAPLES, MRS. NANCY LAY — age 88, of Sharps Chapel, passed away 1:12 p.m. Thursday, Nov. 24, 1988 at Claiborne County Nursing Home after a lingering illness. Member of Oak Grove Primitive Baptist Church. Preceded in death by her husband, John Maples, and son, Earnest Maples. Survivors: daughters, Helen Clark, Monroe, Mich., Ella Franks, Knoxville, Idella Masingo, Sharps Chapel, Ana Lee Roe, Greentown, Ind.; son, Herman Maples, Sharps Chapel; daughter-in-law, Theo Maples, Knoxville; 14 grandchildren; 19 great-grandchildren; several nieces and nephews; a host of other relatives and friends.

RAMSEY, BLANCHE SHOFFNER, age 98 of Harrogate, Tn. was born Dec. 5, 1890. Passed away Jan. 8, 1989 at Claiborne County Hospital.

She was born in Union County, the daughter of the late Hiram and Martha Seals Shoffner. She was a member of the Gibson Station Primitive Baptist Church and at her death was the oldest member.

Preceded in death by her husband Jimmy Ramsey, 7 brothers: Berry, General, Henry, Ike, George, Paris, and Dewey Shoffner; 4 sisters: Roxie Cadle, Vernie Brown, Mossie Cottrell, and Maggie Sandifer; three sons, Spurgeon, Carl and Ewing Ramsey; three daughters: Elverda Ramsey, Pauline Montgomery and Eula Gray Surber; two grandchildren: Arbara and Sandra Ramsey. Survivors: James Ramsey of Harrogate, Paul Ramsey of Shawnee; three grandchildren whom she raised: Don Ramsey, Phyllis Ramsey Russell, Joan Ramsey, Cosby, and 11 other grandchildren; 17 great-grandchildren, sisters: Ada Shoffner Atkinson, brother, Rufus Shoffner, both of Monroe, Mich. Funeral Services were held at Coffey Funeral Home, Tazewell, Tn. with Rev. Ellis Hoskins, Rev. Doug Heaton officiating. Music by Shan Russell. Burial in the Shoffner Cemetery.

RHYMER, HAZEL IRENE — Born June 21, 1909; passed away Dec. 24, 1988.

Funeral Services were held at Gibson Station Primitive Baptist Church Tuesday, Dec. 27, 1988 with Elders Bill Berry and Parnick Shelton officiating.

Music by Pleasant Hill Singers and Elder Spurgeon Thompson. Burial in Southern Cemetery.

Treasured Seasons

For everything there is an appointed season,
and a time for everything under heaven.
A time for sharing, a time for caring,
a time for loving, a time for giving.
A time for remembering, a time for parting.
You have made everything beautiful in it's time,
for everything you do remains forever.

Sadly missed by children, relatives and friends.

ROBINSON, CORA HINES, · age 86, of Lenoir City, Tn. passed from this life on Nov. 6, 1987. She was a member of the Lenoir City Primitive Baptist Church, where she placed her membership in 1971. Preceded in death by her husband, Jack Robinson. These were left to mourn her passing: son, Elden Robinson; grandchildren, John, Mark, and Wade Robinson, Kristi O'Neal, Pheobe Hutson, all of Lenoir City; six great-grandchildren; sisters, Mildred Hines, Maxive Issac; brothers Carl and Kenneth Hines, Lenoir City, and Claude Hines, Loudon; several nieces and nephews.

SHROPSHIRE, MOLLIE, 81, of Montrose Ave., Morristown, passed away Oct. 6, 1988 at St. Mary's Medical Center in Knoxville. She was a member of Noeton Primitive Baptist Church. She is survived by husband, C.L. "Doc" Shropshire; daughters: Mrs. Abraham (Dorothy) Moulton of Morristown, Mrs. Marion (Margie) Hubbard of Jonesborough, Ind., Mrs. Peter (Peggy) Kusnik of Baneburry and Mrs. Cecil (Linda) Moneymaker of Knoxville; 8 grandchildren and 11 great grandchildren.

Services were on Oct. 9, 1988 at Noeton Primitive Baptist Church with Elder John Oliver officiating. Burial in the church cemetery. Mayes Mortuary of Morristown in charge.

SHROPSHIRE, C.L. "Doc", 86, of Montrose Ave., Morristown, passed

away May 7, 1989. He was the widower of Mollie Shropshire. Survivors include his daughters: Mrs. Abraham (Dorothy) Moulton of Morristown, Mrs. Marion (Margie) Hubbard of Jonesborough, Ind. Mrs. Peter (Peggy) Kusnik of Baneberry, Mrs. Cecil (Linda) Moneymaker of Knoxville; 8 grandchildren; 11 great-grandchildren.

Services held May 9, 1989 at Noeton Primitive Baptist Church with Elder John Oliver officiating. Burial in church cemetery. Mayes Mortuary of Morristown in charge.

Mom and Dad, we love and miss you so much.
Your daughters: Dorothy, Margie, Peggy, and Linda

WEBB, MRS. DOLA D. - age 78, formerly of Knoxville, passed away early Friday morning at her home in Andersonville. Member of Halls Primitive Baptist Church. Survivors; husband, Herman R. Webb; daughter and son-in-law, Mary Ruth and Charles A. Hansard; sister, Flora Guy of Indiana, Ruby Brummitt, Knoxville, Jean Overton and Jewell Lewis, both of Tazewell, Margie Houser and Goldie Langley, both of Maynardville, Myrl Peters, Halls, Maggie Dossett, Knoxville; brother, Jeff White, Knoxville; several nieces and nephews. Funeral service 8 p.m. Sunday, Rose Chapel, Elder Bill Berry and Elder Hugh Brummitt officiating. Family and friends will meet at the main entrance to Highland Memorial Cemetery 10:15 a.m. Monday for interment at 10:30 a.m. The family will receive friends 6:30 - 8:00 p.m. Sunday at Rose Mortuary Broadway Chapel.

WILKERSON, ELIZA LEE, - age 76 departed this life on April 14, 1989, at Fort Sanders Hospital. Preceded in death by her husband, Raymond Wilkerson. Survivors; son and daughter-in-law, Jim and Betty Jean Wilkerson, Knoxville; daughters and sons-in-law, Thelma and W.C. Brown, Lenoir City; Betty and Frank Hughes, Knoxville; grandchildren, Frank (Butch) Hughes, and Lisa Shehan, Knoxville; great granddaughter Haley Hughes, Knoxville; brother William S. Lee, Lenoir City; several nieces and nephews. Sister Eliza united with the Lenoir City Primitive Baptist Church in May 1948 where she remained a faithful member until her death. She was laid to rest at the Lakeview Mausoleum to await the final resurrection.

WILLIAMS, MRS. SINDY, 91, of New Tazewell, died Friday, August 5, 1988, at Baptist Hospital after a long illness. She was a member of the Myers Grove Baptist Church. She was the widow of Issac Williams and was the mother of the late Ernest Turner.

Survivors include her daughter, Mrs. Pauline Williams; sons, Oscar and Curtis Williams, all of New Tazewell; stepsons, Charles Williams of Rutledge, Chester Williams of Lincoln Park, Mich.; 19 grandchildren; 26 great-grandchildren; and sister, Mrs. Merniva Fleemon of Monroe, Mich.

Services will be 11 a.m. today at Evans Funeral Home with the Revs. Yadon Howard and Dani Lewis officiating. Burial will be in the Drummonds Cemetery.

CHURCH	COUNTY	PASTOR	CLERK	ADDRESS
Black Fox	Grainger	Elder Larry Anderson	Bennie Capps	P.O. Box 91, Maynardville, TN 37807
Braden's Chapel	Union	Elder J.C. Monday Elder Noble Clawson	Linda Bean Phyllis Wilson, Asst.	Speedwell, TN 37870 Speedwell, TN 37870
Brantley's Chapel	Blount	Elder Jerry McBee Elder Chester Hembree	Gaye Lee Mildred Davis, Asst.	Rt. 1, Box 128, Townsend, TN 37882 Rt. 1, Box 344, Townsend, TN 37882
Davis Chapel	Campbell	Elder LeRoy Braden	Katheryn Angel Sondra Wright, Asst.	Rt. 5, Box 170, LaFollette, TN 37766 1256 Middlesboro Hwy., LaFollette, TN 37766
Gethsemane	Knox	Elder Robert Walker	Tom Carmichael	729 Frank St., Knoxville, TN 37919
Gibson Station	Lee, Va.	Elder William Rhymer Eld. Spurgeon Thompson, Asst. Elder Nelson Jones, Asst.	Dorothy Johnson Shirley Sandifur, Asst.	Rt. 2, Box 320, Ewing, VA 24248 Rt. 1, Box 416, Harrogate, TN 37752
Halls	Knox	Elder William Berry Elder Parnick Shelton, Asst.	Alice Powers Sara Jean Harmon, Asst.	7525 Tample Acre Dr., Knoxville 37938 7120 Chermont Cir., Knoxville 37938
Headrick's Chapel	Sevier	Elder Sheridan Moore Elder Clyde Abbott, Sr. Asst.	Gearldine Abbott	Rt. 6, Box 204A, Sevierville, TN 37862
Lenoir City	Loudon	Elder Robert Bullion	Janice Spoon	1001 Bell Ave. Lenoir City, TN 37771
Meyers' Grove	Claiborne	Elder J.C. Monday	Bonnie Miracle Kathy Downes, Asst.	Rt. 2, Box 91, New Tazewell, TN 37825 New Tazewell, TN 37825, Route 1
Nocton	Grainger	Elder John Oliver	Carroll Oliver	Rt. 2 Box 3480, Bean Station, TN 37708
Oak Grove	Union	Elder J.C. Monday Elder Jerry McBee, Astt.	Betty P. Sharp Betty Shoffner, Asst.	Rt. 1, Box 250, Sharps Chapel, TN 37866 Sharps Chapel, TN 37866, Route 1
Pleasant Hill	Claiborne	Elder William Rhymer Elder Albert Davis, Asst.	William Branscomb Oakien Edwards, Asst.	Speedwell, TN 37870 Speedwell, TN 37870
Rocky Dale	Knox	Elder Hugh Brummitt	Edward Collett Saundra Boruff, Asst.	Rt. 1, Box 17, Luttrell, TN 37779 6916 Weaver Rd., Knoxville, TN

514

1990 Minutes

POWELL VALLEY ASSOCIATION
OF
PRIMITIVE BAPTISTS

THE ONE HUNDRED-SEVENTIETH SESSION
OF THE POWELL VALLEY ASSOCIATION
OF PRIMITIVE BAPTIST
HELD WITH THE SISTER CHURCH AT PLEASANT HILL
CLAIBORNE COUNTY, TENNESSEE
AUGUST 17, 18, 19, 1990
NEXT SESSION WILL BE HELD WITH THE SISTER
CHURCH AT GIBSON STATION, LEE COUNTY, VA.
TO BEGIN ON FRIDAY BEFORE THE THIRD SATURDAY IN
AUGUST, 1991 AT 10:30 A.M.
ELDER JERRY McBEE WILL DELIVER THE
INTRODUCTORY SERMON
ELDER CHESTER HEMBREE WILL BE THE ALTERNATE

OFFICERS

ELDER LARRY ANDERSON,   MODERATOR
RT. 3. BOX 314-A, SPEEDWELL, TENNESSEE, PHONE 869-4635

ELDER JERRY McBEE,   ASSISTANT MODERATOR
P.O. BOX 158, LOUISVILLE, TENNESSEE, PHONE 977-1788

BENNIE CAPPS,   CLERK
P.O. BOX 91, MAYNARDVILLE, TENNESSEE, PHONE 992-5571

RINA JOHNSON,   ASSISTANT CLERK
1217 BROWN SCHOOL ROAD, MARYVILLE, TENNESSEE, PHONE 983-2774

Statistical Table

Statistical Table	Printing Minutes	Total Membership	Deceased	Relationship	Dismiss by Letter	Excluded	Baptism	Res. by Letter	Restored	Regular Meeting Time	Communion Time
Black Fox	$25.00	60	3	0	0	0	0	0	0	Second Sat. Night and Sun. Sunday after Fourth Saturday	Sunday following Second Saturday in June
Braden's Chapel	40.00	146	2	0	1	0	2	0	0	First Saturday Night and Sunday	Sunday following First Saturday in July
Brantley's Chapel	100.00	115	0	0	0	0	2	0	0	Second Saturday Night - Every Sunday and Sunday Night	Sunday Following Second Saturday in July at 10:30 a.m.
Davis Chapel	45.00	94	1	6	0	0	6	0	0	Every Sunday and Sunday Night	Sunday following Third Saturday in June
Gethsemane	35.00	26	1	0	0	0	0	0	0	Second and Fourth Sunday	Fourth Sunday in May and October
Gibson Station	50.00	72	1	0	0	0	2	0	0	First Saturday Night - Every Sunday and Sunday Night	Sunday following First Saturday in June
Halls	100.00	112	1	2	2	0	0	0	0	Every Sunday and Sunday Night	Last Sunday in April
Headrick's Chapel	25.00	110	1	0	0	0	2	0	0	First and Third Sunday of each Month	First Sunday in May and October 11 a.m.
Lenoir City	50.00	107	1	0	0	3	3	0	0	Every Sunday and Sunday Night	Wednesday Night before Easter Sunday
Myers Grove	30.00	88	3	0	0	0	10	2	0	4th Saturday Night & Every Sunday	Sunday following Fourth Saturday in May
Nocton	30.00	41	0	0	0	3	3	0	0	First Sunday - Third Saturday and Sunday of each month	Sunday following Third Saturday in May & September
Oak Grove	35.00	326	4	0	2	1	2	0	0	First Saturday Night and Sunday - Third Sunday	Sunday following the First Saturday in May
Pleasant Hill	45.00	88	3	0	0	0	0	0	0	4th Sat. Morning & Sat. Night Every Sun. and Sun. Night t	Sunday following the Fourth Sunday in June at 10:30 a.m.
Rocky Dale	50.00	100	3	0	0	0	0	0	0	Every Sunday Morning	Sunday following Third Saturday in May

FRIDAY, AUGUST 17, 1990

The One hundred seventieth session of the Powell Valley Association of Primitive Baptist met with the Sister Church at Pleasant Hill in Claiborne County, Tennessee, on August 17, 18, and 19, 1990.

Elder Albert Davis led the congregation in singing "Amazing Grace", then Elder Jerry McBee led "Hold to God's Unchanging Hand" and "Sweet Hour of Prayer"...then Assistant Moderator Larry Anderson welcomed the congregation and pleaded for peace and love to abide through-out the entire Association and called for prayer by Elder John Oliver of Noeton Church.

Following prayer, Elder Bill Berry from Halls delivered the introductory sermon from the 9th. Chapter of Second Samuel using as his text "That I may show him kindness" and preached a very uplifting and spiritual sermon.

After the introductory sermon, they sang a song and were dismissed in prayer by Elder James Branscomb. The Association was to reconvene after a 15 minute recess.

After recess, the crowd reassembled in the church. Elder Jerry McBee led the congregation in singing and the Assistant Moderator, Larry Anderson read from the 14th. Chapter of Romans, Verses 17,18, and 19th., then called for prayer by Elder Chester Hembree from Brantley's Chapel.

The Moderator then asked for the order of business for the following transactions:

1st: Called for letters of the Sister Churches to be presented to the clerk for reading. Thirteen (13) were received.

2nd: The letters were presented and read and motion approved that the delegates be seated.

3rd: The Moderator called for anyone present from any of the Sister Churches not named as delegate who desired to be seated as such come forward and give the clerk their name and the name of their church

church. Three came: Sister Brenda Braden, Davis Chapel; Sister Satre Braden, Davis Chapel; and Brother Coy Edwards, Braden Chapel.

4th: Called for petitionary letter if there should be one. None came.

5th:Motion approved that the Association elect Elder Larry Anderson as Moderator and elect Elder Jerry McBee as Assistant Moderator for the ensuing year.

6th: Motion approved that Brother Bennie Capps be re-elected Clerk and Brother Rina Johnson be re-elected Assistant Clerk for the ensuing year.

7th: Motion Approved that we show our appreciation to Elder Hugh Brummitt for his service to the Powell Valley Association.

8th: Motion was approved that we empower Elder Anderson to appoint all the committees to serve this session.

9th: The Moderator, having been empowered to do so, appointed committees as follows:

Committee on Arrangements: Brother Bill Taylor
Brother O.D. McCarty
Brother Coy Edwards

Committee on Preaching: Brother Carroll L. Oliver
Brother Millard Berry
Brother Everett Brantley

Committee On Request: Elder James Branscomb
Brother Aurell Graves
Brother Charlie Collins

Committee on Finance: Brother Tom Carmichael
Brother Glen Walker
Elder Spurgeon O. Thompson

10th: Called for the finances to be turned in to the Finance Committee.

11th: The Committees all having been appointed and accepted, the Association moved to adjourn until 10:30 Saturday morning. They sang a song and were dismissed in prayer by Elder Spurgeon Thompson of Gibson Station.

Saturday, August 18, 1990

At the appointed hour of 10:30 Saturday morning and at the sound of singing, the Association reassembled. After singing "Send the Light'" "Let My Life be a Light" and "Sweet Hour of Prayer'" Elder Albert Davis stood in the absence of Assistant Moderator Elder Jerry McBee, and quoted the First Chapter of Psalms, then called for prayer by Elder Parnick Shelton from Halls.

After prayer, the Moderator called the Association to order for the remainder of the business:

1st: Called for any letters from Sister Churches not received on Friday. There was one.

2nd: The letter was presented and read and motion approved that the delegates be seated.

3rd: Called for anyone from any of the churches who were present and desired to be seated as delegate to come forward and give the clerk their name and their church. There was none.

4th: Called for the report of the committee on Arrangements who submitted the following report:

518

REPORT ON ARRANGEMENTS:

Call for roll call of delegates.
Call for report of Committee on Preaching.
Call for report of Committee on Request.
Call for report of Committee on Finance.

Decide how many minutes we have printed, who shall supervise the printing and delivery of the same, and what he shall be paid for this service. Which Sister Church shall host the next association and who will preach the introductory sermon and who will be the alternate. Who will prepare the Circular Letter.

Respectfully Submitted,
Brother Bill Taylor
Brother O.D. McCarty
Brother Coy Edwards

5th: Motion approved to receive the above report and release the committee.

6th: Called the roll call of delegates of all Sister Churches and check the absentees.

7th: Called for the report of the Committee on Preaching:

COMMITTEE ON PREACHING:

Friday night: Elder Chester Hembree
Elder James H. Branscomb
Saturday morning: Elder Spurgeon Thompson
Elder Clyde Abbott, Sr.
Saturday night: Elder Nelson Jones
Elder Albert Davis
Sunday morning: Elder William Rhymer
Elder Jerry McBee

Respectfully submitted,
Brother Carroll L. Oliver
Brother Millard Berry
Brother Everett Brantley

8th: Motion approved to receive the above report and release the committee.

9th: Called for the report of the Committee on Request, which was given:

We, the Committee on Request, wish to request as follows, that we have 1,100 minutes printed and the clerk supervise the printing and distribution of same and that he receive $135.00 for his services. We also request that the next session of the Powell Valley Association be held with the Sister Church at Gibson Station in Lee County, Va., to begin on Friday before the third Saturday in August, 1991, at 10:30

A.M. and continue three days. We also request that Elder Jerry McBee preach the introductory sermon and Elder Chester Hembree be the alternate. We also request that Elder Larry Anderson write a circular letter for the minutes for 1991.

Respectfully submitted,
Elder James Branscomb
Brother Avrell Graves
Brother Charlie Collins

10th: Motion approved to receive the above report and release the committee.

11th: Called for the report of the Committee on Finance, which submitted the following report:

Black Fox	$25.00
Braden's Chapel	40.00
Brantley's Chapel	100.00
Davis Chapel	45.00
Gethsemane	35.00
Gibson Station	50.00
Halls	100.00
Headrick's Chapel	25.00
Lenoir City	50.00
Meyer's Grove	30.00
Noeton	30.00
Oak Grove	35.00
Pleasant Hill	45.00
Rocky Dale	50.00
Total Collections	660.00
Donations	20.00
	680.00
Balance in Bank	770.00
	1,457.00
Expenses for 1990	685.00
Balance in Bank	**822.00**

Respectfully Submitted,
Brother Tom Carmichael
Brother Glenn Walker
Elder Spurgeon O. Thompson

12th: Motion approved to receive the above report and release the committee.

13th: Motion approved that we grant the request of the committee and have 1,100 minutes printed and the clerk to receive $135.00 for his services.

14th: Motion approved that the next session of the Association be held with the Sister Church at Gibson Station to commence on Friday before the third Saturday in August , 1991, at 10:30 A.M.

15th: Motion approved that Elder Jerry McBee deliver the introductory sermon and Elder Chester Hembree be the alternate.

17th: Motion approved to remove the names of the following Elders, who left the Association: Jim Campbell, Clarence Hicks, Charles Taylor, Howard Pippin, and Steve Taylor.

18th: Motion approved that the churches of the Powell Valley Association extend to the church and the people of Pleasant Hill heart felt thanks and our prayers for the love, fellowship, kindness, and food while we were with you. May the Good Lord bless and keep you is our prayers.

19th: Motion approved to adjourn, trusting the Lord to permit us to meet again with the Sister Church at Gibson Station, in Lee County, Virginia, on Friday before the third Saturday in August, 1991, at 10:30 A.M.

Dismissed in prayer by Brother O.D. McCarty.

Elder Larry Anderson, Moderator
Elder Jerry McBee, Assistant Moderator
Brother Bennie Capps, Clerk
Brother Rina Johnson, Assistant Clerk

SPECIAL ANNOUNCEMENTS

Brantley's Chapel has their second Saturday night services at 7 P.M.; Sunday morning services at 10:30 A.M.; Sunday night services at 7 P.M. in the summer months ant at 6 P.M. in the winter months.

The following churches requested the Association for 1991: **Black Fox, Brantley Chapel, Gibson Station, Halls, and Lenoir City.**

Please make all contributions payable to: Powell Valley Association.

Dates of ordination of the following Elders:
Elder Alber Davis, May 17, 1930
Elder Hugh Brummitt, December 12, 1954
Elder James Branscomb, June 23, 1956
Elder Parnick Shelton, December 11, 1960
Elder Claude Rosson, July 4, 1964
Elder Joe Bush, April 27, 1969
Elder Bill Berry, August 27, 1972
Elder Larry Anderson, October 24, 1975
Elder Spurgeon Thompson, December 17, 1976
Elder Bill Raymer, December 17, 1976
Elder Jerry McBee, April 26, 1981
Elder Nelson Jones, July 17, 1981
Elder Chester Hembree, June 19, 1988
Elder Clyde Abbott, Sr., November 6, 1988
Elder Robert Walker, October 4, 1970

SUMMARY

We are blessed with a fine group of ministers, as was illustrated by those who had the opportunity to preach. We regret that time will not permit more of them to preach when we meet with the Association. On Saturday morning, Elder Spurgeon Thompson brought a very spiritual and uplifting sermon on "Being About Our Father's Business", the Elder Clyde Abbott, Sr., brought a good message on the "Power of God".

CIRCULAR LETTER TO POWELL VALLEY ASSOCIATION

Dear Brothers and Sisters in Christ, as we were chosen to write this circular letter; I would like to say a few words concerning the church, Jesus said "Upon this Rock I will build my Church and the Gates of Hell shall not prevail against it". I'm glad the Church is built on Christ, because He is the only one it could be built on. The Visible Church we see is not the real church. The real church is within our hearts. The church will be here forever. It can't be destroyed or done away with. Let us put Christ first in our lives, then we shall grow and prosper in the Lord.

Your Brother, Elder Joe C. Bush

CHURCHES AND THEIR DELEGATES

BLACK FOX: Brothers: Dale Capps, Bennie Capps. Sister: Pamela Capps

BRADEN'S CHAPEL: Sisters: Leecy Sparks, Winnona Monday

BRANTLEY'S CHAPEL: Elders: Jerry McBee, Chester Hembree. Brothers: Rina Johnson, Junion McBee, Chester Lee Hembree, Robert Welch, Glenn Walker, Everett Brantley, Richard Walker. Sisters: Hazel Johnson, Blanche Welch, Mildred Brantley.

DAVIS CHAPEL: Brothers: Clyde Lynch, O.D. McCarty. Sisters: Mildred Ellison, Ruby Hill, Pearl Lynch, Mollie McCarty, Ollie White.

GETHSEMANE: Brother: Tom Carmichael. Sisters: Mary Smith, June Carmichael.

GIBSON STATION: Elders: William Rhymer, Spurgeon Thompson, Nelson Jones. Brother: Franklin Jones. Sisters: Karen Rhymer, Polly Jones, Lucille Ball, Dorothy Johnson.

HALLS: Elders: Parnick Shelton, William Berry. Brothers: Elwood Evans, Bill Taylor, Joe Culvahouse, Vance Harmon, Jr., Vance Harmon, Sr.. Sisters: Betty Culvahouse, Cookie Harmon, Irene Harmon, Trula Berry.

HEADRICK'S CHAPEL: Elders: Clyde Abbott, Sr., Robert Walker. Brother: Travis Tipton. Sisters: Margaret Walker, Gearldine Abbott.

LENIOR CITY: Brother: Hubert Spoon. Sisters: Annie Spoon, Ruby Williams.

MYER'S GROVE: Letter Received. No Delegates Listed.

NOETON: Elder: John Oliver. Brothers: Carroll Oliver, Charlie Collins. Sisters: Dora Collins, Mary Atkins.

OAK GROVE: SISTER: Alvada Dykes.

PLEASANT HILL: Elders: James Henry Branscomb, Larry Anderson, Albert Davis. Brothers: Millard Berry, Leo Graves, Glenn Davis. Sisters: Myer Anderson, Audra Davis, Cleo Berry, Ada Jones, Hazel Lambert.

ROCKY DALE: Brothers: Charles Bryant, James Boruff, Josh Stapleton. Sisters: Myrtle Bryant, Saundra Boruff, Ima Lee Stapleton, Fay Collette.

MINISTERS DIRECTORY

Elder Larry Anderson, Rt.3, Box 314-A, Speedwell, TN 869-4635
Elder Johnny Atkins, Bean Station , TN 767-2397
Elder William Berry, Rt. 13, Knoxville, TN 922-9189
Elder LeRoy Braden, 2305 Middlesboro, LaFollette, TN 562-9353
Elder J.H. Branscomb, Speedwell, TN 562-6361
Elder Hugh H. Brummitt, 1329 Brown, Knoxville, TN 546-7700
Elder Joe Bush, 7507 Rodgers Rd, Corryton, TN 687-7018
Elder Noble Clawson, Rt. 4, Speedwell, Tn 562-2004
Elder Albert Davis, Speedwell, Tn 869-3596
Elder Nelson Jones, Rt. 1-Box 343, Harrogate, TN 869-3703
Elder Alvin Graves, 122 Oak Wood Dr., Lenoir City, TN 986-9725
Elder Jerry McBee, Box 158, Louisville, TN 977-1788
Elder J.C. Monday, Speedwell, TN 562-3068
Elder John Oliver, Rt 2, Box 3482, Bean Station, TN 581-5039
Elder William Rymer, Box 12, Shawnee, TN 869-3092
Elder Parnick Shelton, 6001 McGinnis Rd, Corryton, TN 687-5070
Elder Spurgeon Thompson, Box 36, Shawnee, Tn 869-8175
Elder Claude Rosson, Rt. 4, New Tazewell, TN 626-3168
Elder Robert Walker, Severville, TN 428-1527
Elder Clay Widner, Rt. 1, Tazewell, TN 626-3893
Elder Robert Bullion, 101 Rose St., Lenoir City, TN 986-5465
Elder Chester Hembree, Rt. 2, Box 422, Rockford, TN 983-6526
Elder Clyde Abbott, Sr., 3840 Abbott Rd., Severville, TN 453-2329

LICENTIATES

Brother Roscoe Branscomb, Speedwell, TN
Brother Odell Carpenter, 812 Brown School Rd., Maryville, TN
984-4352
Brother Mark Taylor, Lenoir City, TN
Brother Richard Walker, 3627 Rockford St. Rockford, TN 977-0414
Brother Ray Walker, Rt. 6, Townsend TN

RULES OF DECORUM

1. The churches composing the Powell's Valley Association shall not be confined to any set rules as to specific number of Messengers they shall have in the body, but shall have the right to name in their letters as many as they choose, and in addition all orderly members of any of the churches being present be entitled to seats in the body as Messengers fo their respective churches, with all the rights and privileges of the same.

2. The Messengers thus assembled shall be denominated the Powell's Valley Primitive Baptist Church.

3. For the purpose of historical information and statistical edification, the Churches are required to state in letters, the number of members in fellowship, the number received by Baptism, by letter, by confession of Faith, the number dismissed, excluded and dead since last session; also the time of their meeting, their pastoral supply, and the amount of money contributed for ministers and other purposed together with any other information they deem appropriate for the edification of the saints and glory of God.

4. This Association shall have no power to answer queries, give advice, or dictate to the Churches in any case, or to lord it over God's heritage nor any power by which she can directly or indirectly fringe on the internal rights of the church or censure and try any church or member in reference to faith and practice and determine upon validity of gospel ordinances. These things shall rest entirely with the churches; but henceforward our annual meetings shall be only for the purpose of hearing from each other, and for the worship of God and mutual comfort and edification of the Saints. To this end we reserve the privilege annually for Friday before the Third Saturday in August and the two following days or at such other times as may be agreed upon with any church that may invite us having to protect our own standard, while in session, from heresay and disorder to recognize and invite any primitive Baptist minister or any lay brother to worship with us that may deem proper; to request the brethren of our body to visit other churches or bodies in our belief with whom we may desire to culture Christian fellowship; to publish in a minute of our proceedings.

5. Each session of the body shall have a Moderator and Clerk who shall hold office until re-elected.

6. Any order member of any church belonging to this body, when convened, being present shall be eligible to elect on as Moderator and Clerk or to sit on any committee appointed by the same.

7. In all election or questions that may be necessary to determine by vote, the vote shall be taken by churches, each church being entitled to three votes for any number less than one hundred, and one additional vote for every fifty or fraction thereof above the first hundred, but the Messengers of each church may divide their vote as they see proper.

8. All elections or questions coming to vote shall be determined by a majority vote cast, and it shall be the only duty of the minority to acquiesce in the decision thus reached.

9. If new churches desire to be admitted to this union they shall petition by letter and messengers and if voted for and recommended by one or more sister churches for her Presbytery constitutioning them, as orthodox and orderly they shall be received by the vote of the body and manifested by the Moderator giving the Messengers the right hand of fellowship.

10. Any motion or resolution clearly inconsistent with the above rules shall be promptly ruled out of order unless withdrawn by the mover.

11. Any messenger being ruled out of order by the Moderator shall have the right to appeal to the body on the question of order, and if sustained shall be allowed to proceed, but if not take his seat.

12. Our meeting being held in the name of Christ and the worship of God; each Messenger is expected to observe due and proper therein.

13. It will not be considered good for any Messenger whose name has been enrolled as

such to abruptley break off or absent himself from the Association without leave.

14. The Moderator shall be entitled to the same privilege of speech as other members provided the chair is filled.

15. The minutes of the Association shall be read and approved by the body and signed by the Moderator before adjourning.

16. The Association shall be opened and closed by prayer.

17. Amendments to these may be made at any time by a majority of the union voting by churches when they deem it necessary, provide such amendments do not compromise the sovereignty of the churches nor have tendency to give body undue power or jurisdiction over them.

ARTICLES OF FAITH

Article 1. We believe in only one true living God, as He is revealed to us in the Holy Scriptures - Father, Son, and Holy Ghost.

Article 2. We believe that the Scriptures of the old and new Testaments are the words of God and the only rule of all-saving knowledge and obedience.

Article 3. We believe in the doctrine of election according to the foreknowledge of God.

Article 4. We believe in the doctrine of original sin.

Article 5. We believe in man's impotency to rescue himself from the fallen state he is in, by his own will or ability.

Article 6. We believe that sinners are justified in the sight of God only by the imputed righteousness of Jesus Christ.

Article 7. We believe the elect, according to the foreknowledge of God will be called, converted, regenerated, and sanctified by the Holy Spirit.

Article 8. We believe the saints will persevere and never fall finally away.

Article 9. We believe that baptism and the Lord's Supper are ordinances of Jesus Christ, and that true believers are the only subject of these ordinances, and that the true mode of baptism is by immersion. We believe also that feet washing is an example of Jesus Christ and should be kept by his disciples until his second coming.

Article 10. We believe in the Resurrection of the dead and the General Judgement.

Article 11. We believe that the punishment of the wicked will be everlasting and that the joys of the righteous will be eternal.

Article 12. We believe that no minister has the right to administer the ordinances, except those who have been regularly baptized and called of God, and come under the imposition of hands of the presbytery.

Obituaries

ABBOTT, LOUIA H., 82, passed away at Fontana, California, July 21, 1990. He was born February 2, 1908 in Lenoir City, Tennessee. Preceded in death by wife of 33 years, Evelyn (Eva) Walker Abbott, who passed away in 1963, and a son Elder Glenn E.Abbott. Survived by wife Goldie Regina Abbott of Riverside California; Sons, W. Jack Abbott and Fred D. Abbott of Knoxville, Tennessee; J. Raymond and Clarence W. Abbott of Riverside, California; H. Wayne Abbott of Rialto, California; Daughter Wilma J. Greene of Santa Ynez, California; Brothers, Elder Clyde Abbott, Sr. of Sevierville, Tennessee, Walter (Tut) Abbott, of Knoxville, Tennessee; Sister, Myrtle Cook of Sevierville, Tennessee, 16 grandchildren, 17 great-grandchildren and many neices and nephews.

Burial was in Evergreen Cemetery, Riverside California.

He spent most of his early years in and around Blount, Serier and Knox Countys. He moved to Claifornia in 1961. He was the son of Elder D.J. Abbott, Emma Ellen Hembree Abbott, Deceased.

Brother Louia H. Abbott was a long time member of Headricks Chapel Church as well as a deacon. In 1951 he and several members from Headricks Chapel, constituted Gethsemane Church in Knoxville.

We know from the many times we have seen Brother Louia sit and listen to the gospel being preached with tears streaming down his face that he truly had a hope of a better place beyond this veil of tears and we believe he is singing with the Heavenly Host over on the golden shores of glory with Our Lord and Savior Jesus Christ.

BAILEY, ROY, 86 of Maynardville, passed away 12:30 A.M., Friday March 16, 1990 at St. Mary's Medical Center. Preceded in death by wife Roma and son John Bailey. Survivors: daughters, Marie(Polly) Beeler, Rachel Ingle, both of Washburn, Rebon Nicely, Maynardville; sons, Judson and Junior Bailey, both of Maynardville; 12 grandchildren; 13 great-grandchildren; sisters, Hazel Muncey, Nervie Nicely, Maynardville. Funeral service at Black Fox Primitive Baptist Church, of which he was a member for many years, Elder Larry Anderson, Elder Parnick Shelton, Rev. Jimmy Nicely, Rev. Jack Walker officiating. Interment is in Cabbage Cemetry. Grandsons were pallbearers.

BALL, CURTIS, 71, of Tazewell, was born July 14, 1918 and passed away October 29, 1989 at Claiborne County Hospital.

He was a member of Gibson Station

527

Primitive Baptist Church; a member of shawanee masonic lodge and a veteran of world war II.

He was preceded in death by his parents, Robert H. and Mary Robinson Ball, five brothers, two sisters and two sons, Wilburn Henry and Curtis Wayne Ball and one daughter Rosemary Ball.

Survivors: his wife, Lucille Hoskins Ball, Tazewell; three sons Ronnie and his wife, Ocie, LaSalle, Mich.; Douglas, Toledo, Ohio, Gregory, Columbia City, Indiana. Nine grandchildren, six great-grandchildren and one sister, Nattie Britton, Gibson Station, Virginia. Several neices and nephews.

Funeral service was held at Gibson Station Primitive Baptist Church with Elders Bill Berry, Bill Rhymer and Spurgeon Thompson officiating. He was laid to rest in Shoffner Cemetery.

BERRY, NELLIE M., 92, of 6909 Westland Drive, Knoxville, passed away August 8, 1989.

She was preceded in death by her husband, Prior Lee Berry and three daughters, Ruth Berry, Melinda Williamson, Vina Eissenberg. She is survived by one daughter Ethel Dalton, two sons, Grover and Milton Berry. 19 grandchildren and several great-grandchildren, two brothers, George and M.G. Owens. Six sisters, Ellen Marsee, Tilda Hopper, Lottie Evans, Hester Harrison, Mattie Lee Raines, Lena Raines and a host of relatives and friends.

Sister Nellie professed a hope in Christ at an early age and was baptised into Pleasant Hill Primitive Baptist Church and attended regularly as slong as she was able.

She is sadly missed by her church, her family, relatives and friends.

BRADEN, ROY (PETE), 73, of Route 2 Speedwell, passed away Saturday, March 31 at Ft. Sanders Medical Center, Knoxville. He was a member of Braden Chapel Baptist Church. Survivors: wife, Betty Jo Braden, Speedwell; son, Ben Braden, Knoxville; brothers, Ed Braden, Middlesboro, Kentucky, Oscar Braden, Speedwell. Funeral services 2 P.M. Monday April 2 at Braden Chapel Baptist Church. Elder J. C. Monday and Elder Buster Clawson officiating. Interment at Braden Chapel Cemetery.

COLLETT, EDWARD LEE, of Luttrell passed away 11:49 A.M., Wednesday February 21, 1990, at St. Mary's Medical Center. He was a member of Rocky Dale Primitive Baptist Church in Corryton and served as church clerk for 22 years and superintendent of Sunday school for 23 years until bad health forced him to resign. He was a verteran of WW2. He retired from the Union County School System after 47 years, the last 30 years he served as supervisor of attendance. Preceded in death by parents, William and Minnie Collett; sister, Jessie

528

Menges; brother, J. Howard Collett. Survivors: Wife, Fay Boruff Collett; daughter and son-in law, Myra and Joseph White; grand-daughter, April White, all of Luttrell; sister LaVerne DeVault, Blaine; nephews, Rev. John Collett, Clarksville, Steven Collett, Nashville; two grandnephews; two grandneices; special brother-in-law, James Boruff. Service was at 8 P.M. on Friday at Mynatt's Chapel, Elder Hugh Brummitt, Rev. John Collett, Brother Steven Collett officiating, singing by Douglas Earl. Family and friends met at Mynatt's Funeral Home at 10 A.M. Saturday and proceeded to Lynnhurst Cemetery for 10:30 A.M. graveside service and interment. Pallbearers: Roy, Larry and Gary Johnson, Steve Boruff, Jimmy Russell, and Howard Russell. The family received 2-4 and 7-8 P.M. on Friday at Mynatt's Funeral Home.

He worried much about this life, With all it's trouble, grief and strife; He often sang of going Home, To be at peace around God's throne. He loved his Lord, his Church and friends; One day we'll be with him again.

CLAWSON, JAMES RALPH, 73, of Speedwell, died suddenly Tuesday. Prominent farmer. Active board member of ASCS of Claiborne County.

A member of Braden Chapel Church. Survivors: wife, Lucretia Bean Clawson; daughter and son-in-law, Barbara and Bill Haynes, LaFollette; son and daughter-in-law, Bill and Fayetta Clawson, LaFollette; sisters, Mrs. Clarence (Bonnie) Russell, Speedwell, Mrs. Walter (Sara Bet) Brown, LaFollette; brothers, John Clawson, Morristown, Dr. George Clawson, LaFollette; two granddaughters; three grandsons.

Funeral sevice was Friday, June 29 at Speedwell Community Baptist Church, Elder J.C. Monday, Rev. Bill Braden officiating. Interment at Clawson Family Cemetery. Pallbearers: Paul Sowder, Bill Sowder, Jerry Brown, Sam Owens, Ernie Clawson, John Russell.

DRUMMONDS, SILAS THEODORE, 67, of Monroe, Mich. was born August 16, 1922 and passed away December 1, 1989 at his daughter's home.

He was attending Grace Missionary Baptist Church in Monroe, and was a Veteran of World War II, serving in the South Pacific theater.

He was preceded in death by his parents, Silas Washington and Nancy Bunch Drummonds; two brothers and one sister.

Survivors: Daughters, Mrs. Eugene (Bessie) Coker, Monroe; Mrs. Troy (Rosie) Keck; Mrs. Earl (Arlie) Maples, both of Tazewell. Mrs. Michael (Jill Larea) McClure of Milan, Mrs. Leo (Katheryn Faye) Engle, Monroe; Sons, Swanne Drummonds, Union County, and Robert Drummonds of Florida; 25 grandchildren; sister Nona Wilson, Halls; brother Willard Drummonds, Cincinnati, Ohio; several neices and nephews.

Funeral Services was Tuesday December 5, at Meyers Grove Baptist Church. Burial in Drummonds Cemetery. Coffey Funeral Home was in charge.

DUNN, EMMA GRAHAM, 82, was born at Lost Creek, Tennessee on January 14, 1908 and died June 25, 1990 at St. Mary's Medical Center, Knoxville, Tennessee.

Emma was the Daughter of Maston and Belle Petree Dunn. The maternal grandfather was the Rev. Sillus Moss Petree, a prominent minister in the Powell Valley Association.

Emma joined the church at Mossy Springs, Union County at an early age. She became a charter member of Rocky Dale Church at Corryton after the family's move to Knox County. She remained a faithful member until her death.

Emma taught school in Knox Couty for 44 years, 40 of which were spent at the Gibbs Elementary and High Schools. She was a much loved teacher and established life long friendships with her students. The testimonials, tributes, letters, and visits were a source of pleasure to her throughout her life.

She published a number of books dealing with history, geneology and memories. Her last one was published during her long hospital stay, and dealt with the Petree family, which included several ministers in the Powell's Valley Association.

She is survived by sisters: Virgie Collins and Fern Whited; step-brothers Maldon, Palmer and Duke Bridges; four nephews; two neices and several nephews and neices.

Funeral services were held at Gentry-Griffey Mortuary on June 27, 1990 with the Elder Hugh Brummitt and Rev. Hugh Jarrett officiating. The passage of scripture used was from Re. 1: 8-18 (I am Alpha and Omega) which was the text for Sillus Petree's last sermon in 1908. This was read by a beloved niece, Lynn Whited Badgett. Emma was laid to rest in Lynnhurst Cemetery at Knoxville, Tennessee on June 27,1990.

DYKE, VESTIE ELLISON, 88, wife of the late, henry Dyke of Sharps Chapel, passed away Monday, May 28

1990 at the home. Member of Oak Grove Baptist Church. Survivors: sons, Swan and Fate Dyke, Sharps Chapel, Taylor Dyke, Corryton, Dwane, Coy and Aylor Dyke, all of Knoxville; 17 grandchildren; 23 great-grandchildren. Rev. Gordon Dyke, Rev. Johnny Robinson officiating. Grandsons served as pallbearers.
Interment at Ellison-Dyke Cemetery.

MCFARLAND, MARY L. HEATHERLY, 91, of Davis Chapel Community, LaFollette, passed away Tuesday, September 12, 1989, at LaFollette Nursing Home. Member of Davis Chapel Primitive Baptist Church. Preceded in death by husband, John F. M McFarland; son, Clyde W. McFarland. Survivors: daughters and sons-in-law, Hazel and Henry Childs, Betty and Earl Strange, Barbara and George Green, all of LaFollette, Lola Lemons, Indianapolis, Indiana, Carlene Davis, Bossier City, La.; Juanita and Jess Lively, Columbus, Ga., daughter-in-law, Rita McFarland, Corinth, Mississippi; sister, Cynthia E. Heatherly, LaFollette; 16 grandchildren; 9 great-grandchildren; several neices, nephews and cousins.

Funeral Services were at 2 p.m., September 15, 1989, Davis Chapel Primitive Baptist Church, Elder LeRoy Braden officiating. Interment at Davis Chapel Cemetery.

MIRACLE, BILLY G., 88 of Route 2, New Tazewell, born April 5, 1901, departed this life December 29, 1989 at Laurel Manor Nursing Home.

He professed faith in Christ and was a member of Myers Grove Primitive Baptist Church. He was a veteran of World War II.
Survivors: Brother, Andy Miracle, New

Tazewell; Sisters, Rosie Tutle of Crossville, Katie Cupp, Maynardville, Special Nephew, Dane Miracle, New Tazewell; several other nieces and nephews.

Funeral service was held Sunday, December 31, 1989 at 2 P.M. at Coffey Funeral Home Chapel, with Rev. John Robbins, Rev. Buster Clawson officiating. Burial in Drummonds Cemetery.

Singers: Dorothy and Rebecca Miracle.

Pallbearers: Jimmy Miracle, Jeffery Miracle, George DeBusk Jr., Syllus Miracle, Bradley Miracle, Dale Cupp.

MOORE, ELDER SHIRDEN, 81 of Townsend died Sunday, October 29, 1989, at Blount Memorial Hospital.

Survivors included his wife, Virdie Huskey Moore; sons, Harvey Jr. and Wayne S. Moore; daughters, Ada Winters, Idella Walker, Novela Gentry; 10 grandchildern; 8 great-grandchildren; brothers, Harrison and Charlie Moore; and sisters, Jessie Huskey, Josie Walker, Cora Reagan.

Services were at Headricks Chapel Primitive Baptist Church, with Elder Clyde Abbot officiating.

Interment is in Bethel Cemetery, Townsend.

PETREE, CECIL, 86, born October 29, 1903, died April 1, 1990 in South Holland, Illinois. He joined Rocky Dale Primitive Baptist Church by letter August 5, 1922 at the evening service after the church was organized at the morning service. He had remained a member for 68 years but couldn't attend the church because his home was in Illinois. He was preceded in death by his wife, Lynne Petree. Survivors: daughter, Janice Smith; two grandchildren and one great-grandchild; sister, Reva Zachary of Corryton. The funeral was held on Wednesday April 4, 1990 in South Holland, Illinois with burial in Crown Hill Cemetery in Twinburg, Ohio.

PIERCE, SHERMAN, 68, of Speedwell, died Thursday, October 19, at his home. He attended Braden Chapel Baptist Church, Blue Spring Hollow.

Funeral services were Saturday, October 21, at Braden Chapel with Elders Noble Lee Clawson and J. C. Monday officiating.

Interment in Pierce Cemetery, Speedwell. Survivors include his wife, Genese Hunter Pierce; sons, James L. and Donald Pierce, both of Speedwell; daughters, Mildred Pierce of Speedwell and Reba Pierce Crowe of Blairsville, Ga. Four grandchildren and a sister, Sarah Jane (Dollie) Russell of Speedwell.

SHOFFNER, MANNIE J., 68, of Sharps Chapel, passed away suddenly Friday December 1, 1989 at his home. Member and treasurer of Oak Grove Primitive Baptist Church. Member of blazing star lodge 455 f&a m.

Preceded in death by son R. L. Shoffner. Survivors: Wife, Ruth Beason Shoffner, son J. Will Shoffner,

daughers Aretta Walker, Martha Peters, all of Maynardville. Seven grandchildren, one great-grandchild.
Sisters: Belle Moore, Kokomo, Indian;, Nelle Sherritze, New Tazewell; Francis Eastridge, Louisville; several neices and nephews and a host of relatives and friends.
Funeral service was held at 2 P.M. on December 3, 1989. Interment in the Church Cemetery. Elder J.C. Monday, Elder Jerry McBee, Rev. Greg Sharp.
We love and miss him so much...Wife and Family.

RUSSELL, MARY "ANN", 49, of Speedwell. Born March 10, 1941 and passed away April 30, 1990 at the LaFollette Hospital. She was a member of Pleasant Hill Primitive Baptist Church and Powell Valley Chapter #484 Order of the Eastern Star.
She was preceded in death by her father. Walter "Balky" Russell, Sr. and her brother Walter "Mooney" Russell, Jr.
Survivors: husband, Franklin G. "Toppy" Russell; mother, Gladys McCreary Russell; brothers, Jim, Harrison, Eddie and Milt Russell; sisters, Bobbie Myers, Kathern Harrison and Nancy Jessie, all of Speedwell and Betty Graves of Maynardville; serveral neices and nephews, family and friends to mourn her passing.
Funeral services was Wednesday, May 2, 1990, 2 P.M. at Reece Valley Chapel with Elder Bill Rhymer officiating. Music by Donnie Poston. Burial in the Russell Family Cemetery.

WEBB, HERMAN RALPH, 77, of Andersonville, formerly of Powell, passed away at St. Mary's Medical Center. Longtime member of McCalla Avenue Baptist Church. Preceded in death by wife, Dola Webb in August 1989; brother, Earl N. Webb; sister, Mary Catherine Bonner. Survivors: daughter and son-in law, Mary Ruth and Charles A. Hansard, Andersonville; sister, Lucille Nipper, Knoxville; serveral neices and nephews. Funeral service at Rose Broadway Chapel. Elder Bill Berry, Elder Hugh Brummitt officiating. Funeral at Rose Mortuary Broadway Chapel. Interment at Highland Memorial Cemetery.

YORK, NORA-Our dear sister in Christ, Sister Nora York passed from this life to be with the Lord forever on April 2, 1990. She joined the Lenoir City Primitive Baptist Church in May 1948. She is preceded in death by her husband, and leaves to mourn her passing several neices and nephews.

CHURCH	COUNTY	PASTOR	CLERK	ADDRESS
Black Fox	Grainger	Elder Larry Anderson	Bonnie Capps	P.O. Box 91, Maynardville, TN 37807
Braden's Chapel	Union	Elder J.C. Monday Elder Noble Clawson	Pam Goins Phyllis Wilson, Asst.	Speedwell, TN 37870 Speedwell, TN 37870
Brantley's Chapel	Blount	Elder Jerry McBee Elder Chester Hembree	Gaye Lee Beatrice Beason	Rt. 1, Box 128, Townsend, TN 37882 2 Rt. 8, Box 10, Maryville, TN 37804
Davis Chapel	Campbell	Elder LeRoy Braden	Katheryn Angel Sondra Wright, Asst.	Rt. 5, Box 170, LaFollette, TN 37766 1256 Middlesboro Hwy.. LaFollette, TN 37766
Gethsemane	Knox	Elder Robert Walker	Tom Carmichael	729 Frank St., Knoxville, TN 37919
Gibson Station	Lee, Va.	Elder William Rhymer Eld. Spurgeon Thompson, Asst. Elder Nelson Jones, Asst.	Dorothy Johnson Shirley Sandifur, Asst.	Rt. 2, Box 320, Ewing, VA 24248 Rt. 1, Box 416, Harrogate, TN 37752
Halls	Knox	Elder William Berry	Alice Powers Sara Jean Harmon, Asst.	7525 Temple Acre Dr., Knoxville 37938 7120 Chermont Ctr., Knoxville 37938
Headrick's Chapel	Sevier	Elder Clyde Abbott, Sr. Elder Robert Walker, Asst.	Gearldine Abbott	Rt. 6, Box 204A, Sevierville, TN 37862
Lenoir City	Loudon	Elder Robert Bullion	Janice Spoon	1001 Bell Ave. Lenoir City, TN 37771
Meyers' Grove	Claiborne	Elder J.C. Monday	Kathy Downes Bonnie Miracle, Asst.	Rt. 2, Box 91, New Tazewell, TN 37825 Rt. 2, Box 169-A, New Tazewell, TN 37825
Nocton	Grainger	Elder John Oliver	Carroll Oliver Mildred Oliver, Asst.	Rt. 2 Box 3480, Bean Station, TN 37708
Oak Grove	Union	Elder J. C. Monday Elder Noble Lee Clawson, Asst.	Betty P. Sharp Betty Shoffner, Asst.	Rt. 1, Box 250, Sharps Chapel, TN 37866 Sharps Chapel, TN 37866, Route 1
Pleasant Hill	Claiborne	Elder William Rhymer Elder Albert Davis, Asst.	William Branscomb Oakien Edwards, Asst.	Speedwell, TN 37870 Speedwell, TN 37870
Rocky Dale	Knox	Elder Hugh Brummitt	Betty Livingston Saundra Boruff, Asst.	6924 Boruff Road, Corryton, TN 6916 Weaver Rd., Knoxville, TN

1991 Minutes

POWELL VALLEY ASSOCIATION
OF PRIMITIVE BAPTISTS

THE ONE HUNDRED-SEVENTY-FIRST SESSION
OF THE POWELL VALLEY ASSOCIATION
OF PRIMITIVE BAPTIST
HELD WITH THE SISTER CHURCH AT GIBSON
STATION
LEE COUNTY, VIRGINIA
AUGUST 16, 17, 18, 1991
NEXT SESSION WILL BE HELD WITH THE SISTER
CHURCH AT BRANTLEY'S CHAPEL IN BLOUNT
COUNTY, TENNESSEE
TO BEGIN ON FRIDAY BEFORE THE THIRD
SATURDAY IN AUGUST, 1992 AT 10:30 A.M.
ELDER CHESTER HEMBREE WILL DELIVER THE
INTRODUCTORY SERMON
ELDER WILLIAM RHYMER WILL BE THE
ALTERNATE.

Officers

ELDER LARRY ANDERSON, MODERATOR
RT. 3. BOX 314-A, SPEEDWELL, TENNESSEE
PHONE 869-4635
ELDER JERRY McBEE, ASSISTANT MODERATOR
P.O. BOX 158, LOUISVILLE, TENNESSEE,
PHONE 977-1788
BENNY CAPPS, CLERK
P.O. BOX 91, MAYNARDVILLE, TENNESSEE
PHONE 992-5571
RINA JOHNSON, ASSISTANT CLERK
1217 BROWN SCHOOL ROAD,
MARYVILLE, TENNESSEE
PHONE 983-2774

STATISTICAL TABLE	RESTORED	RECEIVED BY LETTER	BAPTISM	EXCLUDED	DISMISSED BY LETTER	RELATIONSHIP	DECEASED	TOTAL MEMBERSHIPS	PRINTING MINUTES	REGULAR MEETING TIME	COMMUNION TIME
Black Fox	0	0	0	0	0	0	1	59	$25.00	Sunday after Second Saturday Sunday after Fourth Saturday	Sunday following Second Saturday in June
Braden's Chapel	0	1	7	0	0	0	1	155	50.00	Every Sunday, second Saturday night	Sunday following first Saturday in July
Branley's Chapel	1	2	5	2	7	2	0	114	100.00	Second Saturday night-every Sunday and Sunday night.	Sunday following second Saturday in July at 10:30 a.m.
Davis Chapel	0	0	1	0	2	0	2	91	40.00	Every Sunday and Sunday night	Sunday following third Saturday in June
Gethsemane	0	0	0	0	0	0	0	27	30.00	Second and Fourth Sunday	Fourth Sunday in May and October
Gibson Station	0	0	0	0	0	0	0	72	50.00	First Saturday night- Every Sunday and Sunday night	Sunday following first Saturday in June
Halls	0	0	0	0	0	0	2	108	100.00	Every Sunday and Sunday night	Last Sunday in April
Headrick's Chapel	0	0	0	1	0	0	3	106	25.00	First and third Sunday of each month	First Sunday in May and October 11:00 a.m.
Lenoir City	0	3	1	2	3	5	1	110	50.00	Every Sunday and Sunday night	Wednesday night before Easter Sunday
Myers Grove	0	0	0	0	0	0	2	86	25.00	4th Saturday night and every Sunday	Sunday following Fourth Saturday in May
Noeton	0	1	1	0	0	0	2	41	30.00	First Sunday-third Saturday and Sunday of each month	Sunday following third Saturday in May and September
Oak Grove	0	0	1	2	0	0	6	319	40.00	First Saturday night and Sunday-third Sunday	Sunday following the first Saturday in May
Pleasant Hill	0	1	1	0	1	1	0	90	45.00	4th Saturday morning and Saturday night. Every Sunday and Sunday night	Sunday following the fourth Sunday in June at 10:30 a.m.
Rocky Dale	0	0	1	5	0	0	4	92	50.00	Every Sunday morning	Sunday following third Saturday in May

MINUTES OF
THE ONE HUNDRED SEVENTY-FIRST SESSION

FRIDAY, AUGUST 16, 1991

The One hundred seventy-first session of the Powell Valley Association of Primitive Baptist met with the Sister Church at Gibson Station in Lee County, Va., on August 16,17,18, 1991.

Elder Albert Davis led the congregation in singing "Amazing Grace", then Elder Jerry McBee led "What a Friend We Have In Jesus"and Bro. Glen Walker led "How Firm A Foundation"then Moderator Larry Anderson welcomed the congregation and pleaded for peace and love to abide through-out the entire Association and called for prayer by Elder Chester Hembree of Lenoir City Church. Following prayer, Elder Jerry McBee from Brantley's delivered the introductory sermon from the16th Chapter of Leviticus using as his text "Having on the Attire, Which are Holy Garments" and preached a very uplifting and spiritual sermon.

After the introductory sermon, they sang a song and were dismissed in prayer by Elder William Berry. The Association was to reconvene after a 15 minute recess.

After recess, the crowd reassembled in the church. Elder William Berry led the congregation in singing and the Moderator,Elder Larry Anderson read from the 2nd Chapter of First Corinthians then called for prayer by Elder Spurgeon Thompson from Gibson Station..

The Moderator then asked for the order of business for the following transactions:

1st: Called for letters of the Sister Churches to be presented to the clerk for reading. Twelve (12) were received.

2nd: The letters were presented and read and motion approved that the delegates be seated.

3rd: The Moderator called for anyone present from any of the Sister Churches not named as delegate who desired to be seated as such come forward and give the clerk their name and the name of their church. One came: Brother Bill Goode, Meyer's Grove.

4th: Called for petitionary letter if there should be one. None came.
5th: Motion approved that the Association Re-elect Elder Larry Anderson as Moderator and Re-elect Elder Jerry McBee as Assistant Moderator for the ensuing year.
 6th: Motion approved that Brother Benny Capps be re-elected Clerk and Brother Rina Johnson be re-elected Assistant Clerk for the ensuing year.
7th: Motion was approved that we empower Elder Anderson to appoint all the committees to serve this session.
8th: The Moderator, having been empowered to do so, appointed committees as follows:

Committee on Arrangements: Brother Carroll L. Oliver
Brother Vance Harmon, Jr
Brother Elwood Evans
Committee on Preaching: Brother Avrell Graves
Brother Millard Berry
Brother Bill Goode
Committee On Request: Brother O. D. McCarty
Brother Everett Brantley
Brother Hubert Spoon
Committee on Finance: Brother J.R.McBee
Brother Charlie Collins
Elder James H. Branscomb

9th: Called for the finances to be turned in to the Finance Committee.
10th: The Committees all having been appointed and accepted, the Association moved to adjourn until 10:30 Saturday morning. They sang a song and were dismissed in prayer by Elder Albert Davis of Pleasant Hill

SATURDAY, AUGUST 17, 1991

At the appointed hour of 10:30 Saturday morning and at the sound of singing, the Association reassembled. Elder Jerry McBee led the Congregation in :"Just A Little Talk With Jesus" and "Victory In Jesus". Elder Jerry McBee opened the service and spoke for a few minutes, then called for prayer by Elder William Berry of Halls.
After prayer, the Moderator called the Association to order for the

remainer of the business.

1st: Called for any letters from Sister Churches not received on Friday. There was two.

2nd: The letter was presented and read and motion approved that the delegates be seated.

3rd: Called for anyone from any of the churches who were present and desired to be seated as delegate to come forward and give the clerk their name and their church. there was two-Brother Coram Berry, Sister Twila Berry of Brantley's Chapel.

4th: Called for the report of the committee on Arrangements who submitted the following report:

REPORT ON ARRANGEMENTS:

CALL FOR ROLL CALL OF DELEGATES.
CALL FOR REPORT OF COMMITTEE ON PREACHING.
CALL FOR REPORT OF COMMITTEE ON REQUEST.
CALL FOR REPORT OF COMMITTEE ON FINANCE.

Decide how many minutes we have printed, who shall supervise the printing and delivery of the same, and what he shall be paid for this service. Which Sister Church shall host the next Association and who will preach the introductory sermon and who will be the alternate. Who will prepare the Circular Letter.

Respectfully Submitted.
Brother Carol Oliver
Brother Vance Harmon, Jr.
Brother Elwood Evans

5th: Motion approved to receive the above report and release the committee.

6th: Called the roll call of delegates of all Sister Churches and check the absentees.

7th: Called for the report of the Committee on Preaching:

COMMITTEE ON PREACHING:

Friday night: Elder Bill Rhymer
Elder Larry Anderson
Saturday morning: Elder Parnick Shelton
Elder Albert Davis
Saturday night: Elder Chester Hembree
Elder Spurgeon Thompson

538

Sunday morning: Elder Bill Berry
Elder John Oliver

Respectfully submitted,
Brother Aurell Graves
Brother Millard Berry
Brother Bill Goode

8th: Motion approved to receive the above report and release the committee.

9th: Called for the report of the Committee on Request, which was given:

We, the Committee on Request, wish to request as follows, that we have 1,100 minutes printed and the clerk supervise the printing and distribution of same and that he receive $135.00 for his services. We also request that the next session of the Powell Valley Association be held with the Sister Church at Brantley's Chapel in Blount County, Tennessee, to begin on Friday before the third Saturday in August, 1992, at 10:30 A.M. and continue three days. We also request that Elder Chester Hembree preach the introductory sermon and Elder William Rhymer be the alternate. We also request that Elder Spurgeon Thompson write a circular letter for the minutes for 1992.

Respectfully submitted,
Brother O.D. McCarty
Brother Everett Brantley
Brother Hubert Spoon

10th: Motion approved to receive the above report and release the committee.

11th: Called for the report of the Committee on Finance, which submitted the following report:

Black Fox	$25.00
Braden's Chapel	50.00
Brantley's Chapel	100.00
Davis Chapel	40.00
Gethsemane	30.00
Gibson Station	50.00

Halls	100.00
Headrick's Chapel	25.00
Lenoir City	50.00
Meyer's Grove	25.00
Noeton	30.00
Oak Grove	40.00
Pleasant Hill	45.00
Rocky Dale	50.00
Total Collections	660.00
Donations	20.00
	680.00
Balance in Bank	822.00
	1,502.00
Expenses for 1990	-735.00
Balance in Bank	767.00

Respectfully Submitted,
Elder James H. Branscomb
Brother Charlie Collins
Brother J.R. McBee

12th: Motion approved to receive the above report and release the committee.

13th: Motion approved that we grant the request of the committee and have 1,100 minutes printed and the clerk to receive $135.00 for his services.

14th: Motion approved that the next session of the Association be held with the Sister Church at Brantley's Chapel to commence on Friday before the third Saturday in August , 1992, at 10:30 A.M.

15th: Motion approved that Elder Chester Hembree deliver the introductory sermon and Elder William Rhymer be the alternate.

16th: Motion approved that Elder Spurgeon Thompson write the circular letter for the 1992 Minutes.

17th: Motion approved that the churches of the Powell Valley Association extend to the church and the people of Gibson Station heart felt thanks and our prayers for the love, fellowship. kindness, and food while we were with you. May the Good Lord bless and keep you is our prayers.

18th: Motion approved to adjourn, trusting the Lord to permit us to meet again with the Sister Church at Brantley's Chapel in Blount County, Tn., on Friday before the third Saturday in August, 1992, at 10:30 A.M.

Dismissed in prayer by Elder John Oliver.

Elder Larry Anderson, Moderator
Elder Jerry McBee, Assistant Moderator
Brother Bennie Capps, Clerk
Brother Rina Johnson, Assistant Clerk

SPECIAL ANNOUNCEMENTS

Brantley's Chapel has their second Saturday night services at 7 P.M.; Sunday morning services at 10:30 A.M.; Sunday night services at 7 P.M. in the summer months and at 6 P.M. in the winter months.

The following churches requested the Association for 1992: Black Fox, Brantley Chapel, Halls, and Lenoir City.

Please make all contributions payable to: Powell Valley Association.

Dates of ordination of the following Elders:

Elder Alber Davis, May 17, 1930
Elder Hugh Brummitt, December 12, 1954
Elder James Branscomb, June 23, 1956
Elder Parnick Shelton, December 11, 1960
Elder Claude Rosson, July 4, 1964
Elder Joe Bush, April 27, 1969
Elder Bill Berry, August 27, 1972
Elder Larry Anderson, October 24, 1975
Elder Spurgeon Thompson, December 17, 1976
Elder Bill Raymer, December 17, 1976
Elder Jerry McBee, April 26, 1981
Elder Nelson Jones, July 17, 1981
Elder Chester Hembree, June 19, 1988
Elder Clyde Abbott, Sr., November 6, 1988
Elder Robert Walker, October 4, 1970
Elder John Oliver, April 15, 1972

SUMMARY

We are blessed with a fine group of ministers, as was illustrated by those who had the opportunity to preach. We regret that time will not permit more of them to preach when we meet with the Association.
On Saturday morning, Elder Parnick Shelton read Proverbs, 23rd chapter and 23rd verse, using as his text, "Buy the Truth". He was then followed by Elder Albert Davis who read from the 2nd chapter of Ephesians, using as his text "For by Grace are ye saved, through faith". On Sunday, Elder William Berry read from the 3rd chapter of Ephesians us as his text "To the Stranger Scattered Abroad". He was then followed by Elder John Oliver reading from the 14th chapter of Job,verse 14, using as his text "If a man die, shall he live again". All of the Elders preached very spiritual and uplifting sermons.

CIRCULAR LETTER TO POWELL VALLEY ASSOCIATION

To all the saints in Christ Jesus, which compose the Powell Valley Association of Primitive Baptists.
I would like to say that each year I look forward to fellowshipping with my brethren of the Powell Valley Association.
In Ephesians 3:9-21, fellowship was hid in God from the beginning and is now manifest to the church as God purposed in Christ Jesus. It is only through the faith of Christ that we can know the love of God. It is with this love, which passeth knowledge, that we can be filled with the fullness of God.
We cannot of our own accord understand the greatness of God, the riches of God, or the fullness of God. If we by faith abide in Christ our Lord, we are rooted and grounded in his love. It is only in this love that we understand with all saints the greatness of God and the fullness of God. True fellowship is when, together we can, through the eye of faith, understand the greatness and fullness of God.
Brethern, may we strive for the fellowship that was hid in God.

Your brother in Christ,
Elder Larry Anderson

CHURCHES AND THEIR DELEGATES

BLACK FOX: Brothers: Dale Capps, Bennie Capps. Sister: Pamela Capps.

BRADEN'S CHAPEL: Sisters: Leecy Sparks, Winona Monday

BRANTLEY'S CHAPEL: Elders: Jerry McBee. Brothers: Glenn Walker, Everett Brantley, Rina Johnson, Junior McBee, Richard Walker, Brian Brantley, Mike Brantley, William Irwin, Tracie McBee, Nathanael McBee. Sisters: Hazel Johnson, Mildred Brantley.

DAVIS CHAPEL: Brother: Johnny Angel. Sisters: Mildred Ellison, Ruby Hill, Stacey Woodward.

GETHSEMANE: Brother: Tom Carmichael. Sister: June Carmichael.

GIBSON STATION: Elders: William Rhymer, Spurgeon Thompson, Nelson Jones. Brothers: Franklin Jones, Claude Sandifur. Sisters: Karen Rhymer, Jean Thompson, Polly Jones, Fannie Jones, Shirley Sandifur, Amy Sandifur, Evelyn Irving, Dorothy Johnson.

HALLS: Elders: Hugh Brummitt, Parnick Shelton, William Berry. Brothers: Vance Harmon, Jr., Vance Harmon, Sr.. Sisters: Ruby Brummitt, Wilma Shelton, Cookie Harmon, Irene Harmon, Trula Berry, Maggie Welch.

HEADRICK'S CHAPEL: Elders: Clyde Abbott, Sr., Robert Walker. Sisters: Margaret Walker, Gearldine Abbott.

LENIOR CITY: Elder Chester Hembree. Brother: Chester Lee Hembree, Hubert Spoon, Tommy Scrabough. Sisters: Edith Hembree, Thelma Brown, Annie Spoon.

MYER'S GROVE: Letter Received. No Delegates Listed.

NOETON: Elder: John Oliver. Brothers: Carroll Oliver, Charlie Collins. Sisters: Eula Atkins, Dora Collins, Mary Atkins.

OAK GROVE: SISTER: Frances Eastridge, Alvada Dykes.

PLEASANT HILL: Elders: James Henry Branscomb, Larry Anderson, Albert Davis. Brothers: Millard Berry, William Branscomb. Sisters: Helen Ruth Branscomb, Audra Davis, Cleo Berry, Mollie McCarty, Lottie Berry.

ROCKY DALE: Brothers: Charles Bryant, James Boruff. Sisters: Myrtle Bryant, Saundra Boruff, Fay Collette.

MINISTERS DIRECTORY

Elder Larry Anderson, Rt.3, Box 314-A, Speedwell, TN 869-4635

Elder William Berry, Rt. 13, Knoxville, TN 922-5070

Elder LeRoy Braden, 2305 Middlesboro, LaFollette, TN 566-4647

Elder J.H. Branscomb, Speedwell, TN 562-6361

Elder Hugh H. Brummitt, 1329 Brown, Knoxville, TN 546-7700

Elder Joe Bush, 7507 Rodgers Rd, Corryton, TN 687-7018

Elder Noble Clawson, Rt. 4, Speedwell, Tn 562-2004

Elder Albert Davis, Rt. 3, Box 320 A Speedwell, Tn 869-3596

Elder Nelson Jones, Rt. 1, Box 263 1/2, Tazewell, Tn 626-8341

Elder Alvin Graves, 122 Oak Wood Dr., Lenoir City, TN 986-9725

Elder Jerry McBee, Box 158, Louisville, TN 977-1788

Elder J.C. Monday, Speedwell, TN 562-3068

Elder John Oliver, Rt 2, Box 3482, Bean Station, TN 581-5039

Elder William Rymer, P.O. Box 374, Harrogate, TN 37752

Elder Parnick Shelton, 6001 McGinnis Rd, Corryton, TN 687-5070

Elder Spurgeon Thompson, Box 36, Shawnee, Tn 869-8175

Elder Claude Rosson, Rt. 4, New Tazewell, TN 626-3168

Elder Robert Walker, Severville, TN 428-1527

Elder Clay Widner, Rt. 1, Tazewell, TN 626-3893

Elder Robert Bullion, 101 Rose St., Lenoir City, TN 986-5465

Elder Chester Hembree, 3604 Rockford Street Rockford, TN 983-6526

Elder Clyde Abbott, Sr., 3840 Abbott Rd., Severville, TN 453-2329

LICENTIATES

Brother Roscoe Branscomb, Speedwell, TN

Brother Odell Carpenter, 812 Brown School Rd., Maryville, TN 984-4352

Brother Mark Taylor, Lenoir City, TN

Brother Richard Walker, 3627 Rockford St. Rockford, TN 977-0414

Brother Ray Walker, Rt. 6, Townsend TN

RULES OF DECORUM

1. The churches composing the Powell's Valley Association shall not be confined to any set rules as to specific number of Messengers they shall have in the body, but shall have the right to name in their letters as many as they choose, and in addition all orderly members of any of the churches being present be entitled to seats in the body as Messengers fo their respective churches, with all the rights and privileges of the same.

2. The Messengers thus assembled shall be denominated the Powell's Valley Primitive Baptist Church.

3. For the purpose of historical information and statistical edification, the Churches are required to state in letters, the number of members in fellowship, the number received by Baptism, by letter, by confession of Faith, the number dismissed, excluded and dead since last session; also the time of their meeting, their pastoral supply, and the amount of money contributed for ministers and other purposed together with any other information they deem appropriate for the edification of the saints and glory of God.

4. This Association shall have no power to answer queries, give advice, or dictate to the Churches in any case, or to lord it over God's heritage nor any power by which she can directly or indirectly fringe on the internal rights of the church or censure and try any church or member in reference to faith and practice and determine upon validity of gospel ordinances. These things shall rest entirely with the churches; but henceforward our annual meetings shall be only for the purpose of hearing from each other, and for the worship of God and mutual comfort and edification of the Saints. To this end we reserve the privilege annually for Friday before the Third Saturday in August and the two following days or at such other times as may be agreed upon with any church that may invite us having to protect our own standard, while in session, from heresay and disorder to recognize and invite any primitive Baptist minister or any lay brother to worship with us that may deem proper; to request the brethren of our body to visit other churches or bodies in our belief with whom we may desire to culture Christian fellowship; to publish in a minute of our proceedings.

5. Each session of the body shall have a Moderator and Clerk who shall hold office until re-elected.

6. Any order member of any church belonging to this body, when convened, being present shall be eligible to elect on as Moderator and Clerk or to sit on any committee appointed by the same.

7. In all election or questions that may be necessary to determine by vote, the vote shall be taken by churches, each church being entitled to three votes for any number less than one hundred, and one additional vote for every fifty or fraction thereof above the first hundred, but the Messengers of each church may divide their vote as they see proper.

8. All elections or questions coming to vote shall be determined by a majority vote cast, and it shall be the only duty of the minority to acquiesce in the decision thus reached.

9. If new churches desire to be admitted to this union they shall petition by letter and messengers and if voted for and recommended by one or more sister churches for her Presbytery constitutioning them, as orthodox and orderly they shall be received by the vote of the body and manifested by the Moderator giving the Messengers the right hand of fellowship.

10. Any motion or resolution clearly inconsistent with the above rules shall be promptly ruled out of order unless withdrawn by the mover.

11. Any messenger being ruled out of order by the Moderator shall have the right to appeal to the body on the question of order, and if sustained shall be allowed to proceed, but if not take his seat.

12. Our meeting being held in the name of Christ and the worship of God; each Messenger is expected to observe due and proper therein.

13. It will not be considered good for any Messenger whose name has been enrolled as

such to abruptley break off or absent himself from the Association without leave.

14. The Moderator shall be entitled to the same privilege of speech as other members provided the chair is filled.

15. The minutes of the Association shall be read and approved by the body and signed by the Moderator before adjourning.

16. The Association shall be opened and closed by prayer.

17. Amendments to these may be made at any time by a majority of the union voting by churches when they deem it necessary, provide such amendments do not compromise the sovereignty of the churches nor have tendency to give body undue power or jurisdiction over them.

ARTICLES OF FAITH

Article 1. We believe in only one true living God, as He is revealed to us in the Holy Scriptures - Father, Son, and Holy Ghost.

Article 2. We believe that the Scriptures of the old and new Testaments are the words of God and the only rule of all-saving knowledge and obedience.

Article 3. We believe in the doctrine of election according to the foreknowledge of God.

Article 4. We believe in the doctrine of original sin.

Article 5. We believe in man's impotency to rescue himself from the fallen state he is in, by his own will or ability.

Article 6. We believe that sinners are justified in the sight of God only by the imputed righteousness of Jesus Christ.

Article 7. We believe the elect, according to the foreknowledge of God will be called, converted, regenerated, and sanctified by the Holy Spirit.

Article 8. We believe the saints will persevere and never fall finally away.

Article 9. We believe that baptism and the Lord's Supper are ordinances of Jesus Christ, and that true believers are the only subject of these ordinances, and that the true mode of baptism is by immersion. We believe also that feet washing is an example of Jesus Christ and should be kept by his disciples until his second coming.

Article 10. We believe in the Resurrection of the dead and the General Judgement.

Article 11. We believe that the punishment of the wicked will be everlasting and that the joys of the righteous will be eternal.

Article 12. We believe that no minister has the right to administer the ordinances, except those who have been regularly baptized and called of God, and come under the imposition of hands of the presbytery.

546

Obituaries

ATKINS, JOHNNY, 85. Born, September 9, 1905, passed away September 11, 1990.

He was a faithful member of Oak Grove Primitive Baptist Church at Sharps Chapel, Tennessee and an Elder in the Powell Valley Association of Primitive Baptists.

He was survived by his wife Hailey Atkins of Bean Station, Tennessee. Funeral Services were held at Noeton Primitive Baptist Church at 2:00 p.m., Friday, September 14, 1990. Elder Fred Oliver and Elder John Oliver officiating. Interment in Head of Richland Cemetery.

Elder Atkins will be sadly missed by his wife, church, and the Powell Valley Association.

ATKINS, GUY ANDERSON, 68, Of 1363 Easley Court, Morristown, passed away January 24, 1991 at Morristown-Hamblen Hospital. He was a retired employee of Morristown-Hamblen Hospital and was a member of Noeton Primitive Baptist Church.

Survivors include his wife, Eula Atkins: son, Steve Atkins of Morristown; foster children, Vivian Wheatley Rose and David Wheatley; grandchildren, Nathan, Lindsey and Keith Atkins; several nieces and nephews.

Services were held at Noeton Primitive Baptist Church with Elder John Oliver and Rev, Ralph Benfield officiating. Burial in Noeton Primitive Cemetery. Westside Chapel Funeral Home in Morristown in charge.

BROWN, WILLIAM C. (BILL), Our dear brother in Christ, departed this life on May 30, 1991, to be forever with Our Precious Redeemer. He was a member and Deacon of the Lenoir City Primitive Baptist Church. His presence will be greatly missed. He leaves to mourn his passing, his loving wife Thelma Wilkerson Brown; parents, Clyde and Katherine Brown; sister, Carol Ann Dennis, all of Lenoir City, and several nieces and nephews.

Funeral services were held on Saturday evening, June 1, at Hawkins Chapel with Elders Chester Hembree and Charles Taylor officiating. Entombment was 2:00 p.m. Sunday at Lakeview Mausoleum.

CAMPBELL, LULA R., 81, of 3410 Lake Drive, Morristown, passed away in Humana Hospital. Member of Black Fox Primitive Baptist Church. Preceded in death by husband, Robert Campbell, in 1967. Survivors: daughters; Mrs. Lucy Gibson, Mrs. Bobbie Stroud, Mary and Marie Campbell, all of Morristown, sons; Wayne and Samuel Campbell, both of Morristown, Coy Campbell, Bulls Gap. Five Granddaughters, two great-grandchildren; one step-grandson; sisters, Mrs. Dolly Helton, Mrs. Kate Lay, Mrs. Iva Davis, all of Washburn, Mrs. Gertrude Grubb, Corryton, several nieces and nephews.

Funeral services at Stubblefield Chapel, Rev. Jack Free, Rev. Elmer Lampkin officiating. Interment at Bethesda Cemetery.

CAPPS, ESTE ALYVE, 78, of Powder Springs, passed away after a lingering illness.

Member of Black Fox Primitive Baptist Church. Preceded in death by husband, Jesse Capps. Survivors: daughter, Maggie Satterfield, Corryton; sons, Dwayne and J.H., both of Powder Springs, Ronnie of Luttrell, Kermit, Ira, and Frank, all of Knoxville, Eugene of Washburn; 34 grandchildren; 38 great-grandchildren; one great-great grandchild; sister Lyra Shipley, Maynardville.

Funeral service was at Mynatt's Chapel, Rev. Fred Atkins and Rev. Bobby Lay officiating. Interment at Doyle Wayne Needham Cemetery, Powder Springs. Grandsons served as pallbearers.

COLE, MRS. FLOY L. SHOFFNER, 79, of Sharps Chapel, passed away on October 20, 1990, at Baptist Hospital. Member of Oak Grove Primitive Baptist Church. Daughter of the late Dave and Lillie Shoffner. Preceded in death by daughter, Brenda Joyce Chittum; two grandchildren; one brother. Survivors: husband, Roy Cole; sons, Bob Cole, Maynardville, Beecher and Bill Cole; daughter, Rose Browning, all of Kokomo, Ind., Ann Sherritze, Galveston, Ind.; 12 grandchildren; 13 great-grandchildren; brothers, Taylor Shoffner, Rutledge, T.W., Gene and Cotton Shoffner, all of Indiana; sisters, Ruth Edwards, New Tazewell, Veda Cole, Sharps Chapel, Arizona Simmons, Kokomo, Ind., June Irwin, Rushville, Ind.; several nieces and nephews.

Funeral Services at Cooke Mortuary Chapel, Elder Jerry McBee, Rev. Greg Sharp Officiating. Interment Shoffner Cemetery. Pallbearers: Clyde Sheckles, Donald Cole and grandsons.

DOTSON, NEVA (BLONDIE), 73, of Route 1, Bean Station, passed away December 5, 1990, at Hillhaven Nursing Home, Jefferson City, Tennessee. She was a member of Noeton Primitive Baptist Church. Survivors include daughter, Janet Jessie; Grand children, Jason and Torie; Nephew, Robert Atkins of

Sister Neva Dotson

Ohio.

Services were held at Stubblefield Funeral Home with Elder John Oliver officiating. Burial in Noeton Primitive Cemetery. Stubblefield Funereal Home in Morristown in charge.

ENGLAND, EDNA MARIE, 73 of Route 4, New Tazewell, was born March 16, 1917 and passed away August 7, 1990 at Claiborne County Hospital.

She was a member of Oak Grove Primitive Baptist Church. She was preceded in death by one son, Robert England Jr.

Survivors: husband, Robert B. England; daughters, Mrs Arthur (Shirley) Tolliver, Mrs Lottie Edna Shoffner, Mrs. Edgar (Ellen) Johnson, all of New Tazewell, Mrs Cecil (Dottie) Braden, Sharps Chapel; sons, Jimmy England, New Tazewell;

son and daughter-in-law, Ellsworth and Janice England, New Tazewell; six grandchildren, and one great granddaughter; brothers, Mitchel Johnson, New Tazewell; several neices and nephews.

Funeral service was August 10, at Oak Grove Primitive Baptist Church with Rev. Greg Sharp and Rev. J.C. Monday officicating. Singers were the Leatherwood Quartet. Burial was in the Oak Grove Cemetery. Nephews were pallbearers.

ENGLAND, ROBERT B., 75, of the Leatherwood Community, New Tazewell, was born February 28, 1915 and passed away August 11, 1990 at his home.

He professed faith in Christ and was a member of Oak Grove Primitive Baptist Church. He was preceded in death by his wife Edna Marie England, on August 7, 1990; also preceded in death by one son, Robert England, Jr.

Survivors: daughters Mrs Arthur (Shirley) Tolliver, Mrs Lottie Edna Shoffner, Mrs. Edgar (Ellen) Johnson, all of New Tazewell, Mrs Cecil (Dottie) Braden, Sharps Chapel; sons, Jimmy England, Ellsworth and wife Janice England, New Tazewell; six grandchildren, and one great-grandchild; sisters, Mrs Dottie Hux, New Market, Mrs Lottie England, Monroe, Mich; brothers, Harding England, Noble England, Odra England, all of Monroe, Mich. and Billy England, New Tazewell; several nieces and nephews.

Funeral service was August 14, at Oak Grove Primitive Baptist Church with Rev. Greg Sharp and Rev. J.C. Monday officiating. Singers were the Leatherwood Singers. Burial was in the Oak Grove Cemetery. Nephews were pallbearers.

HEATHERLY, OLLIE, 81, of Jacksboro, died Thursday April 11, at the LaFollette Medical Center. She was a member of Davis Chapel Primitive Baptist Church.

Funeral services were April 13, at Cross Funeral home, with Brother Carl Bradshaw officiating. Interment was in Sunrise Cemetery.

She was preceded in death by her husband, Raymond Heatherly and her daughter, Mildred Heatherly. Survivors include her brother John Carrol, Jr. LaFollette.

HELTON, MRS DOLLIE M. (GRANNY), 87, of Washburn, passed away Thursday, August 16, 1990 at St. Mays's Medical Center. Member of Black Fox Primitive

Baptist Church. Preceded in death by husband, Lorene Helton; son, Howard Helton. Survivors: daughters and sons-in-law, Fousteen and Vic Bailey, Pauline and Joe Jordan, Iva and Ernest Nicley , all of Washburn, Christine and Cecil Helton, Corryton; sons and daughters-in-law, Ralph and Ethel Helton, Earl and Margie Helton, Washburn, Billy and Shirley helton, Morristown, Don and Teresa Helton, Crossville; daughter-in-law, Stella Moore, Corryton; 22 grandchildren; 31 great-grandchildren; sisters, Kate Lay, Iva Davis, Gertrude Grubb. Funeral Service was at Liberty Hill Baptist Church, Rev. Clyde Helton, Rev. Parnick Shelton, Rev. Grant Vaughn officiating. Interment was at Liberty Hill Cemetery. Grandsons were pallbearers.

LAMBERT, RACHEL FLOY, 78, of Speedwell died September 6 at LaFollette Medical Center. She was a member of Braden's Chapel Baptist Church.

Funeral services were Saturday September 9, at Glade Springs Baptist Church, with the Revs. Don Reynolds and Noble Lee Clawson officiating. Interment was in Ausmus Cemetery.

Preceded in death by a son, Neal James Lambert, survivors include her husband, William Prior Lambert of Speedwell; daughters, Peggy Joyce King, Janice Ann Goins, and Paulette Pebley, all of LaFollette, and Carol Edwards and Martha Matilda Lambert both of Speedwell; sons, Dewitt Lambert of Toledo, Ohio, Herman Lambert of Dothan, Ala., and Lee, Avery Dennis, William Taft, and Brian Keith Lambert, all of LaFollette; 27 grandchildren; 8 great-grandchildren; and sisters, Ruby Hopper and Lassie Mayes, both of Speedwell, Luna Heck of Maryville, and Dona Clawson of Toledo, Ohio.

LAMBERT, WILLIAM PRIOR, 85, of Speedwell, died August 14, at the Lafollette Medical Center. He was born July 27, 1906 in Claiborne County. He was a member of Bradens Baptist Church and Valley Star Masonic Lodge.

Funeral Services were August 17, at Glade Springs Baptist Church, with the Rev. Don Reynolds and Elder Noble Lee Clawson officiating. Interment in Ausmus/Pleasant Hill Cemetery.

He was preceded in death by his wife, Rachel Floy Lambert; son Neal James Lambert. Survivors: Dewitt Lambert of Toledo, Ohio, Herman Lambert of Dothan, Ala., and Lee, Avery Dennis, William Taft, and Brian Keith Lambert, all of LaFollette; daughters, Peggy Joyce King, Janice Ann Goins, and Paulette Pebley, all of LaFollette, and Carol Edwards and Martha Matilda Lambert both of Speedwell;

24 grandchildren and 12 great-grandchildren.

MUNSEY, CORA BELL, 81, Of Halls, passed away August 7th., at her home where she resided with her daughter and son-in-law, Paul and Betty Helton. Member of Black Fox Primitive Church. Preceded in death by husband, Millard Munsey and two infant daughters. Survivors: Dauthers and sons-in law, Rosella and Rev. Clyde helton, Betty and Paul Helton, Vontella and Rev. Donnie Coffman, Pearl Cross, all of Knoxville; son, M.T.; son and daughter-in-law, Charlie and Jean Munsey; 28 grandchildren; 44 Great-grandchildren; three great-great-grandchildren; sisters Flossie Frye, Rhode Bailey; brother, Luther Munsey. Funeral service at Black Fox Primitive Baptist Church, Rev. Andy Vance, Rev. Howard Beeler officiating. Interment in Cabbage Cemetery. Grandsons served as pallbearers.

ROBERTSON SEGUINE LYNCH DAY, 84, of Powell, Born October 1, 1906. Passed away July 14, 1991.
She professed faith in Christ at an early age, joined Oak Grove Primitive Baptist church where she remained a member until death. Survivors: 1 son, Buddy W. Day, Powell; 2 daughters, Mrs Billy Manis, Powell, and Edna Lou Allen, Cincinnati, Ohio. 11 Grandchildren, 28 Great-grandchildren, and 1 great-great-grandchild. Several nieces and Nephews. Funeral services wer July 17, 1991, Elder J.C. Monday officiating. Interment: Oak Grove Cemetery.

TAYLOR, RAYMOND OSCAR, 86, of Knoxville, Tennessee, passed away April 15, 1991 at Knoxville Convalescent Center. He was a member of Halls Primitive Baptist Church of Knoxville (formerly the Kirkwood Primitive Baptist Church), having joined the church Septermber 16, 1945. He was preceded in death by his wife Myrtle Ellen Sharp Taylor.
Survivors: daughter, Joyce Taylor Huffstetler of Knoxville; two grandchildren, James Taylor Huffstetler, Knoxville, and Gwendolyn Kay McClure of Kingston, Tennessee; three great-grandchildren, Jeremiah McClure, Matthew McClure, and Rebekah McClure all of Kingston, Tennessee. Brother Raymond believed deeply in the Primitive Baptist faith and was a devoted member and Deacon of the church. He was Choir Director of the church for more than 30 years as long as he was able, and continued to be elected by his brothers and sisters when he could no longer attend. Brother Raymond touched

many lives when in private business, retired from Sears, and as a member of the Masters Lodge #244 F & AM for 62 years.

Graveside service was held in Lynnhurst Cemetery by Elder Charles Taylor and Elder Bill Berry.

I look back in wonder of the love
  That He gave,
And his belief in the ressurection
  of the last day,
His pillar of strength, never loosing sight
  Will always be with me
Throughout my life.

Joyce

TREECE , MARY, 97, of Port Charolette, Fla., formerly of Knoxville and New Tazewell, was born July 11, 1893 and passed away December 15, 1990 at her home.

She professed faith in Christ and was a member of Meyers Grove Primative Baptist Church. She was preceded in death by her husband Fred Treece.

Survivors: sister, Della Carmony, Middlesboro; brother, Tom Davis, Monroe, Mich.; neice and husband, Pansy and Neal Minton, Port Charlotte, Fla.; nephew and wife Roy and Carolyn Hoskins, Homosassa, Fla.; several other nieces and nephews.

Funeral service was December 19, 1990 at Coffey Funeral Home Chapel with Rev. Lloyd England officiating. Singers Liberty Quartet. Burial was in the Meyers Grove Cemetery.

Pallbearers: Albert Womack, John Price, Hoy Treece, Frank Treece, Jack Treece, and Fayne Davis.

SHELTON, ROSS WILLIAM, 72, passed away at home January 17, 1991. He was a member of Rocky Dale Primitive Baptist Church. A veteran of World War II and a member of Corryton Masonic Lodge. He was a graduate of Knoxville Business Colledge. Prececed in death by parents, W.B. and Lockie Webster Shelton. Survivors: Wife-Dorothy Bailey Shelton; daughter, Peggy Johnson, sons John Edgar and Billy all of Corryton. One grandson, Bryan Christopher Shelton. Also survived by his dear brother, Elder Parnick Shelton of Corryton, Tennessee. Services were held on January 18, 1991 at Mynatt's Chapel. Elders Hugh Brummitt and Joe Bush officiating. Singing was performed by Mrs Trula Berry and Mr. Larry Seivers. Family and friends met at Little Flat Creek Cemetery for graveside services and interment. Pallbearers were nephews. Ross had been a very sick man with many health problems most of his adult life. Thank God Almighty he has a better home now on those

Heavenly shores above. With his eartly trials over, he can rest in unending peace. *Wittten by his wife of 42 years.*

SUTTLES, LINDA FLORENCE SHOFFNER MOZINGO, 85, passed away January 28, 1991. Member of Oak Grove Primitive Baptist Church. Survivors: Sons J.C. Mozingo, Sillus Mozingo both of Sharps Chapel, Tennessee, and Zen Mozingo of Monroe, Michigan; daughter, Mrs. Ula Gray Unsworth, Monroe, Mich. Several grandchildren and great-grandchildren, nieces and nephews.

Funeral services were held at 2 p.m. January 31, 1991 at Cook's Mortuary Chapel, Rev. John Robinson and Rev. Jim Hooper officiating, Interment in Oak Grove Cemetery.

WHITE, WALTER MCHENRY, 84, of LaFollette, died April 6, at the LaFollette Medical Center. Funeral services were Tuesday, April 9, at Martin Chapel, with the Rev. Michael Smith officiating. Interment was in Sunrise Cemetery.

He was preceded in death by his wife, Mrs. Ethel Williamson White; parents, Alfred and Louisa White; daughter Barbara Boatchers. Survivors include his son, Junior White, Barstow, Calif. daughters Tressie Barnes, Sidney, Ohio, Florrine Boshears, Lansing, Ill, Brenda Marlow, LaFollette; Brothers Foster and Clarence White both of LaFollette; sisters Beatrice Nelson and Orabell Miller, both of LaFollette; 22 grandchildren and six great-grandchildren.

WILLS, OPAL M., 81, of Gibson City, Illinois, died on April 23, 1991 at St. Joseph Medical Center, Bloomington. Her funeral was held on April 27, 1991 at Lamb Funeral Home, Gibson City, with the Rev. Gary Johnson officiating. Burial was in Drummer Township Cemetery, Gibson City.

Mrs. Will was born November 28, 1909, in Arrowsmith, a daughter of Marcus and Della Raley Weaver. She married Edgar Wills on January 29, 1944 in Champaign. He died June 7, 1981.

Survivors include one son, Robert Beecher, Madison, Wis.; one stepson, Bill Wills, Bloomington, Il; one stepdaughter, Geraldine Boltz, Vancouver, Wash.; two sisters, Felcie Stroh, Gibson City, and Jessie Finn, Mesa, Ariz.; three grandchildren; one great grandson; six stepgrandchildren; and three stepgreat-grandchildren.

She was preceded in death by one brother and one sister.

Mrs. Wills was a Gibson City resident for seven years and formerly lived in Dandridge and Maynardville, Tennessee. She was a member of Rocky Dale Primitive Baptist Church, Corryton, Tennessee.

WOODBY, ODELL, 70, born October 1, 1920 and departed this life June 9, 1991 at Claiborne County Hospital. She professed faith in Christ at an early age and joined Forge Ridge Baptist Church in October 1935, but had attended Gibson Station and Pleasant Hill Churches for the past several years. Survivors: Daughter and son-in-law, Karen and Elder Bill Rhymer of Shawnee. Son and daughter-in-law William L. and Alta Woodby of Shawnee. Five grandchildren: William Rhymer, U.S. Army, Ft. Riley, Kansas, Steven and Anna Woodby of Shawnee, Teresa and Kathy Woodby of Harrogate. Mother: Ethel Carmac of Tri-State Manor Nursing Home, Shawnee. Sister: Delories West, Hazel Park, Michigan.

Funeral service was June 12 at Coffey Funeral Home Chapel of Harrogate with Elders Bill Rhymer and Bill Berry officiating. Interment in Forge Ridge Cemetery.

"Thy will be done" seems hard to say When one we loved has passed away.
Some day, perhaps we'll understand, When we meet again in that better land.

From our happy home and circle God has taken one we love;

Borne away from sin and sorrow To a better land above.

Only a memory of bygone days, And a sign for a face unseen; But a constant feeling that God alone Knows just what should have been.

MEMORY IS ONE GIFT OF GOD THAT DEATH CANNOT DESTROY!

CHURCH	COUNTY	PASTOR	CLERK	ADDRESS
Black Fox	Grainger	Elder Larry Anderson	Bennie Capps	P.O. Box 91, Maynardville, TN 37807
Braden's Chapel	Union	Elder J.C Monday Elder Noble Clawson	Pam Goins Phyllis Wilson, Asst.	Rt 1, Box 350, LaFollette, TN 37766 Speedwell, TN 37870
Branley's Chapel	Blount	Elder Jerry McBee	Gaye Lee Beatrice Beason	1042 Hembree Hollow Rd. Townsend, TN 37882 1443 E. Brown School Rd.,Maryville, TN 37804
Davis Chapel	Campbell	Elder LeRoy Braden	Katheryn Angel Sondra Wright, Asst.	Rt. 5, Box 170, LaFollette, TN 37766 1256 Middlesboro Hwy., LaFollette, TN 37766
Gethsemane	Knox	Elder Rober Walker	Tom Carmichael	729 Frank Street, Knoxville, TN 37919
Gibson Station	Lee, Va	Elder William Rhymer Elder Nelson Jones, Asst.	Dorothy Johnson Shirley Sandifur, Asst.	Rt.2, Box 320, Ewing, Va 24248 Rt. 1, Box 416, Harrogate, TN 37752
Halls	Knox	Elder William Berry	Alice Powers Helen Branson, Asst	7525 Temple Acre Dr., Knoxville, Tn 37938 4633 Marshall Dr., Knoxville, TN 37938
Headrick's Chapel	Sevier	Elder Clyle Abbott, Sr.	Gearldine Abbott	1780 Alpine Drive, Sevierville, TN 37862
Lenoir City	Loudon	Elder Chester Hembree	Janice Spoon	1001 Bell Ave., Lenoir City, TN 37771
Meyers' Grove	Claiborne	Elder J. C. Monday	Kathy Downes Bonnie Miracle, Asst.	Rt. 2, Box 84, New Tazewell, TN 37825 Rt. 2, Box 169-A, New Tazewell, TN 37825
Noeton	Grainger	Elder John Oliver	Caroll Oliver Mildred Oliver, Asst.	Rt. 2, Box 3480 Bean Station, TN 37708
Oak Grove	Union	Elder J.C. Monday Elder Noble Lee Clawson, Asst.	Betty P. Sharp Betty Shoffner, Asst.	Rt. 1, Box 250, Sharps Chapel, TN 37866 Route 1, Sharps Chapel , TN 37866
Pleasant Hill	Claiborne	Elder William Rhymer Elder Albert Davis, Asst.	William Branscomb Oklen Edwards, Asst.	Speedwell, TN 37870 Speedwell, TN 37870
Rocky Dale	Knox	Elder Hugh Brummitt	Betty Livingston Saundra Boruff, Asst.	6924 Boruff Road, Corryton, TN 37721 6916 Weaver Rd., Knoxville, TN 37721

Elders of the Association

Front Row: Left to Right-Elders, Albert Davis, Parnick Shelton, John Oliver, Nelson Jones, Moderator Larry Anderson, Bill Berry, Spurgeon Thompson.

Back Row. Left to Right-Brothers, William Irwin, O.D. McCarty, Richard Walker. Elders, James H. Branscomb, Claude Rosson, Ass't. Moderator Jerry McBee, William Rhymer.

1992

Minutes

of

the

Powell Valley

Association

of

Primitive Baptists

f

STATISTICAL TABLE

Church	RESTORED	RECEIVED BY LETTER	BAPTISM	EXCLUDED	DISMISSED BY LETTER	RELATIONSHIP	DECEASED	TOTAL MEMBERSHIPS	PRINTING MINUTES	REGULAR MEETING TIME	COMMUNION TIME
Black Fox	0	0	0	0	0	0	1	58	$25.00	Sunday after Second Saturday Sunday after Fourth Saturday	Sunday following Second Saturday in June
Braden's Chapel	0	0	1	0	1	1	1	154	50.00	Every Sunday, second Saturday night	Sunday following first Saturday in July
Brantley's Chapel	1	0	1	0	0	2	2	115	100.00	Second Saturday night-every Sunday and Sunday night.	Sunday following second Saturday in July at 10:30 a.m.
Davis Chapel	0	0	0	0	0	0	1	90	40.00	Every Sunday and Sunday night	Sunday following third Saturday in June
Gethsemane	0	0	0	0	0	0	0	27	35.00	Second and Fourth Sunday	Fourth Sunday in May and October
Gibson Station	0	0	1	10	1	0	4	58	50.00	First Saturday night- Every Sunday and Sunday night	Sunday following first Saturday in June
Halls	0	0	0	0	0	0	2	106	100.00	Every Sunday and Sunday night	Last Sunday in April
Hedrick's Chapel	0	0	0	0	0	0	2	104	25.00	First and third Sunday of each month	First Sunday in May and October 11:00 a.m.
Lenoir City	0	0	0	8	0	1	1	102	50.00	Every Sunday and Sunday night	Wednesday night before Easter Sunday
Myers Grove	0	0	3	0	0	0	0	89	35.00	4th Saturday night and every Sunday	Sunday following Fourth Saturday in May
Norton	0	0	8	0	0	0	0	49	30.00	First Sunday-third Saturday and Sunday of each month	Sunday following third Saturday in May and September
Oak Grove	0	0	0	1	0	3	3	318	40.00	First Saturday night and Sunday-third Sunday	Sunday following the first Saturday in May
Pleasant Hill	0	1	1	0	0	0	1	91	45.00	4th Saturday morning and Saturday night. Every Sunday and Sunday night	Sunday following the fourth Sunday in June at 10:30 a.m.
Rocky Dale	0	0	0	0	2	0	0	94	50.00	Every Sunday morning	Sunday following third Saturday in May

1992 Minutes

POWELL VALLEY ASSOCIATION
OF PRIMITIVE BAPTISTS

THE ONE HUNDRED-SEVENTY-SECOND SESSION
OF THE POWELL VALLEY ASSOCIATION
OF PRIMITIVE BAPTIST
HELD WITH THE SISTER CHURCH AT BRANTLEY'S
CHAPEL
BLOUNT COUNTY, TENNESSEE
AUGUST 14 15, 16, 1992
NEXT SESSION WILL BE HELD WITH THE SISTER
CHURCH AT BLACK FOX IN GRAINGER COUNTY,
TENNESSEE
TO BEGIN ON FRIDAY BEFORE THE THIRD
SATURDAY IN AUGUST, 1993 AT 10:30 A.M.
ELDER WILLIAM RHYMER WILL DELIVER THE
INTRODUCTORY SERMON
ELDER SPURGEON THOMPSON WILL BE THE
ALTERNATE.

Officers

ELDER LARRY ANDERSON, MODERATOR
RT. 3. BOX 314-A, SPEEDWELL, TENNESSEE 37870
PHONE 869-4635
ELDER JERRY McBEE, ASSISTANT MODERATOR
P.O. BOX 158, LOUISVILLE, TENNESSEE 37777
PHONE 977-1788
BENNIE CAPPS, CLERK
P.O. BOX 91, MAYNARDVILLE, TENNESSEE 37807
PHONE 992-5571
RINA JOHNSON, ASSISTANT CLERK
1217 BROWN SCHOOL ROAD,
MARYVILLE, TENNESSEE 37804
PHONE 983-2774

Minutes of
The One Hundred Seventy-Second Session

FRIDAY, AUGUST 14, 1992

The One Hundred Seventy-Second session of the Powell Valley Association of Primitive Baptist met with the Sister Church at Brantley's Chapel in Blount County, Tenn.., on August 14,15,16, 1992.

Elder Jerry McBee led the congregation in singing I'll Be in Glory" and "Lift Me Up Above The Shadows", then Moderator Larry Anderson welcomed the congregation and pleaded for peace and love to abide through-out the entire Association and called for prayer by Elder Hugh Brummitt of Hall's. Following prayer, Elder Chester Hembree of Lenoir City Church delivered the introductory sermon from the 9th Chapter of Hebrews using as his text "The Holy Spirit" and preached a very uplifting and spiritual sermon.

After the introductory sermon, they sang a song and were dismissed in prayer by Elder William Berry. The Association was to reconvene after a 15 minute recess.

After recess, the crowd reassembled in the church. Elder William Berry led the congregation in singing "Amazing Grace", and the Moderator,Elder Larry Anderson read from First John, first chapter,and spoke a few minutes on fellowship and of good things that God has done for us, then called for prayer by Elder John Oliver of Noeton.

The Moderator then asked for the order of business for the following transactions:

1st: Called for letters of the Sister Churches to be presented to the clerk for reading. Fourteen (14) were received.

2nd: The letters were presented and read and motion approved that the delegates be seated.

3rd: The Moderator called for anyone present from any of the Sister Churches not named as delegate who desired to be seated as such come forward and give the clerk their name and the name of their church. One came: Sister Brenda Bowers of Brantley's Chapel.

4th: Called for petitionary letter if there should be one. None came.

5th: Motion approved that the Association Re-elect Elder Larry Anderson as Moderator and Re-elect Elder Jerry McBee as Assistant

561

Moderator for the ensuing year.

6th: Motion approved that Brother BennieCapps be re-elected Clerk and Brother Rina Johnson be re-elected Assistant Clerk for the ensuing year.

7th: Motion was approved that we empower Elder Anderson to appoint all the committees to serve this session.

8th: The Moderator, having been empowered to do so, appointed committees as follows:

Committee on Arrangements: Brother Charlie Collins
Brother Everett Brantley
Brother Tom Carmichael
Committee on Preaching: Brother Hubert Spoon
Brother Vance Harmon
Brother Aurell Graves
Committee On Request: Brother Carroll Oliver
Brother O. D. McCarty
Brother Robert Walker, Sr.
Committee on Finance: Brother Brian Brantley
Elder William Rhymer
Elder Chester Hembree

9th: Called for the finances to be turned in to the Finance Committee.

10th: The Committees all having been appointed and accepted, the Association moved to adjourn until 10:30 Saturday morning. They sang a song and were dismissed in prayer by Elder William Rhymer of Gibson Station.

SATURDAY, AUGUST 15 1992

At the appointed hour of 10:30 Saturday morning and at the sound of singing, the Association reassembled. Brother Glenn Walker led the Congregation in :"Come Unto Me" and "HalleluYAH I'm Going Home" and "Fill My Way With Love". Elder Jerry McBee opened the service and spoke for a few minutes, then called for prayer by Elder William Rhymer of Gibson Station. After prayer, the Moderator called the Association to order for the remainder of the business.

1st: Called for any letters from Sister Churches no received on Friday. There was none

2nd: Called for anyone from any of the churches who were present and desired to be seated as delegate to come forward and give the clerk their name and their church. There was Sisters Alvada Dykes, Bell Moore, Oak Grove; Sister Ruby Hill, Davis Chapel.

3rd: Called for the report of the committee on Arrangements who submitted the following report:

REPORT ON ARRANGEMENTS:

CALL FOR ROLL CALL OF DELEGATES.
CALL FOR REPORT OF COMMITTEE ON PREACHING.
CALL FOR REPORT OF COMMITTEE ON REQUEST.
CALL FOR REPORT OF COMMITTEE ON FINANCE.

Decide how many minutes we have printed, who shall supervise the printing and delivery of the same, and what he shall be paid for this service. Which Sister Church shall host the next Association and who will preach the introductory sermon and who will be the alternate. Who will prepare the Circular Letter.

Respectfully Submitted,
Brother Charlie Collins
Brother Everett Brantley
Brother Tom Carmichael

4th: Motion approved to receive the above report and release the committee.

5th: Called the roll c all of delegates of all Sister Churches and check the absentees.

6th: Called for the report of the Committee on Preaching:

COMMITTEE ON PREACHING:

Friday night: Brother Brian Brantley
Elder William Berry
Saturday morning: Elder Jerry McBee
Elder Hugh Brummitt
Saturday night: Elder Larry Anderson
Elder William Rhymer
Sunday morning: Elder Parnick Shelton
Elder Albert Davis

Respectfully submitted,

Brother Hubert Spoon
Brother Vance Harmon
Brother Averill Graves

7th: Motion approved to receive the above report and release the committee.

8th: Called for the report of the Committee on Request, which was given:

We, the Committee on Request, wish to request as follows, that we have 1,000 minutes printed and the clerk supervise the printing and distribution of same and that he receive $150.00 for his services. We also request that the next session of the Powell Valley Association be held with the Sister Church at Black Fox in Grainger County, Tennessee, to begin on Friday before the third Saturday in August, 1993, at 10:30 A.M. and continue three days. We also request that Elder William Rhymer preach the introductory sermon and Elder Spurgeon Thompson be the alternate. We also request that Elder William Rhymer write a circular letter for the minutes for 1993.

Respectfully submitted,
Brother Caroll Oliver
Brother O.D. McCarty
Elder Robert Walker, Sr.

9th: Motion approved to receive the above report and release the committee.

10th: Called for the report of the Committee on Finance, which submitted the following report:

Black Fox $25.00
Braden's Chapel 50.00
Brantley's Chapel 100.00
Davis Chapel 40.00
Gethsemane 35.00
Gibson Station 50.00
Halls 100.00
Headrick's Chapel..............25.00
Lenoir City 50.00
Meyers Grove 35.00

Noeton 30.00
Oak Grove 40.00
Pleasant Hill 45.00
Rocky Dale 50.00
Total Collections 675.00
Donations 40.00
....715.00
Balance in Bank 767.00
....1,482.00
Expenses for 1992..........-700.00
Balance in Bank 782.00

Respectfully Submitted,
Brother Brian Brantley
Elder William Rhymer
Elder Chester Hembree

11th: Motion approved to receive the above report and release the committee.

12th: Motion approved that we grant the request of the committee and have 1,000 minutes printed and the clerk to receive $150.00 for his services.

13th: Motion approved that the next session of the Association be held with the Sister Church at Black Fox to commence on Friday before the third Saturday in August , 1993, at 10:30 A.M.

14th: Motion approved that Elder William Rhymer deliver the introductory sermon and Elder Spurgeon Thompson be the alternate.

15th: Motion approved that Elder William Rhymer write the circular letter for the 1993 Minutes.

16th: Motion approved that the churches of the Powell Valley Association extend to the church and the people of Brantley's Chapel heart felt thanks and our prayers for the love, fellowship, kindness, and food while we were with you. May the Good Lord bless and keep you is our prayers.

17th: Motion approved to adjourn, trusting the Lord to permit us to meet again with the Sister Church at Black Fox in Grainger County, Tn., on Friday before the third Saturday in August, 1993, at

10:30 A.M. Dismissed in prayer by Elder Parnick Shelton.

Elder Larry Anderson, Moderator
Elder Jerry McBee, Assistant Moderator
Brother Bennie Capps, Clerk
Brother Rina Johnson, Assistant Clerk

Special Announcements

Brantley's Chapel has their second Saturday night services at 7 P.M.; Sunday morning services at 10:30 A.M.; Sunday night services at 7 P.M. in the summer months and at 6 P.M. in the winter months.

The following churches requested the Association for 1993: Black Fox, Brantley Chapel, Halls, and Lenoir City.

Please make all contributions payable to: Powell Valley Association.

Dates of ordination of the following Elders:

Elder Alber Davis, May 17, 1930
Elder Hugh Brummitt, December 12, 1954
Elder James Branscomb, June 23, 1956
Elder Parnick Shelton, December 11, 1960
Elder Claude Rosson, July 4, 1964
Elder Joe Bush, April 27, 1969
Elder Bill Berry, August 27, 1972
Elder Larry Anderson, October 24, 1975
Elder Spurgeon Thompson, December 17, 1976
Elder Bill Raymer, December 17, 1976
Elder Jerry McBee, April 26, 1981
Elder Nelson Jones, July 17, 1981
Elder Chester Hembree, June 19, 1988
Elder Clyde Abbott, Sr., November 6, 1988
Elder Robert Walker, October 4, 1970
Elder John Oliver, April 15, 1972
Elder Richard Walker, March 29, 1992
Elder LeRoy Braden, October 10, 1982
Elder Doyle Ausmus, August 10, 1984
Elder J.C. Monday, February 12, 1958

Summary

We are blessed with a fine group of ministers, as was illustrated by those who had the opportunity to preach. We regret that time will not permit more of them to preach when we meet with the Association. On Saturday morning, Elder Jerry McBee read the 13th. chapter of Joshua, using as his text, "There remaineth yet very much land to be possessed", and preached concerning Joshua inheritance of the land. He was then followed by Elder Albert Davis who read from the 6th chapter of Ephesians, 11th verse, using as his text "Put on the whole armour of God", On Sunday, Elder Parnick Shelton read from the 4th chapter of Hebrews as his text "There remaineth therefore a rest of the people of God", and preached concerning intering into rest for the children of God. He was then followed by Elder Hugh Brummitt reading from the 24th chapter of Joshua, concerning serving God every day of our life and letting our light shine so others might see the good work. All of the Elders preached a very uplifting and spirtual sermons. On Sunday, during the song service, there was great rejoicing in theSpirit of God. The spirit was flowing from breast to breast as was manifisted by the much rejoicing in the Lord.

Circular Letter To Powell Valley Association

Grace be unto you, and peace, from God our Father, and from the Lord Jesus Christ:

As I set here, trying to pen down words for this letter, wondering what I should write and how I should write them, and as aways-relying-on the Good Man from Glory to lead me in everything I undertake to do. The Lord brings to my rememorance the word, "Faith, Hope and Charity, but the greatest of these is Charity."

I love my family, my little church, my brothers and sisters in Christ Jesus, my preaching brethen, the Powell Valley Association, but most of all, a man called Jesus, that first loved me!

We speak of Charity (Love), but our mind just can't comprehend how that the King of Glory, would strip himself of all the privileges of the Godhead, and come unto this unfriendly, cold-hearted world and take upon Himself our sins, and endure all the suffering, sorrow and shame that our Savior took upon himself.(Hebrews: 2:14-18). He laid his life down-that we might have life and have it more abundantly. "A price had to be paid, (we didn't have anything to pay with), but He paid it. He loved us before the foundation of the world because he hath chosen us to himself according to the good pleasure of his will, that we should be holy and without blame before him in love. Brothers and sisters in the fullness of time He will gather all his Elect from the four corners of the world to present us before His Father and I believe we will hear Him say..Father, behold I and the children that thou has given me and not one have I lost.

We speak of Charity (love); to me this is Charity! Let me finish with a line from this song I love..."Because He loved me, my Savior died on the Cross, was Cruified, no greater Love by mortal man has ever been known!"

God Bless each one of you-I love you.

A little shepherd,
Elder Spurgeon O. Thompson

Ministers Directory

Elder Larry Anderson, Rt.3, Box 314-A, Speedwell, TN 869-4635
Elder William Berry, Rt. 13, Knoxville, TN 922-9189
Elder J.H. Branscomb, Speedwell, TN 562-6361
Elder Hugh H. Brummitt, 1329 Brown, Knoxville, TN 546-7700
Elder Joe Bush, 7507 Rodgers Rd, Corryton, TN 687-7018
Elder LeRoy Braden, 2305 Middlesboro, LaFollette, TN 5664647
Elder Albert Davis, Rt. 3, Box 320 A Speedwell, Tn 869-3596
Elder Doyle Ausmus
Elder Alvin Graves, 122 Oak Wood Dr., Lenoir City, TN 986-9725
Elder Jerry McBee, Box 158, Louisville, TN 977-1788
Elder J.C. Monday, Speedwell, TN 562-3068
Elder John Oliver, Rt 2, Box 3482, Bean Station, TN 993-2295
Elder William Rymer, P.O. Box 374, Harrogate, TN 37752
Elder Parnick Shelton, 6001 McGinnis Rd, Corryton, TN 687-5070
Elder Spurgeon Thompson, Box 36, Shawnee, TN 869-8175
Elder Claude Rosson, Rt. 4, New Tazewell, TN 626-3168
Elder Robert Walker, Severville, TN 428-1527
Elder Clay Widner, Rt. 1, Tazewell, TN 626-3893
Elder Richard Walker, 3627 Rockford St., Rockford, TN 977-0414
Elder Chester Hembree, 3604 Rockford Street Rockford, TN 983-6526
Elder Clyde Abbott, Sr., 3840 Abbott Rd., Severville, TN 453-2329
Elder Johnny Ayers, Route 2, Box 97, New Tazewell, Tn. 626-8507

Licentiates

Brother Roscoe Branscomb, Speedwell, TN
Brother Odell Carpenter, 812 Brown School Rd., Maryville, TN 984-4352
Brother Mark Taylor, Lenoir City, TN
Brother Ray Walker, 3029 Jess Wilson Rd, #16, Sevierville, TN 37862 429-5417

Elders Who Wrote the Circular Letter
and
the Church that Hosted the Association

1974 Elder Leonard White————————Lenoir City
1975 Elder Albert Davis————————Kirkwood
1976 Elder Charles Taylor————————Gibson Station
1977 Elder Johnny Atkins ————————Brantley's Chapel
1978 Elder Joe Irving————————Rocky Dale
1979 No Letter Submitted————————Oak Grove
1980 Elder Hugh Brummitt————————Black Fox
1981 Elder James Branscomb————————Pleasant Hill
1982 Elder Noble Clawson————————Lenoir City
1983 Elder J. C. Monday ————————Gibson Station
1984 Elder Walter Lyons————————Brantley's Chapel
1985 Elder Parnick Shelton ————————Black Fox
1986 No Letter Submitted ————————H a l l s
1987 Elder John Oliver————————Lenoir City
1988 Elder William Berry ————————Rocky Dale
1989 Elder Claude Rosson ————————Oak Grove
1990 Elder Joe Bush ————————Pleasant Hill
1991 Elder Larry Anderson————————Gibson Station
1992 Elder Spurgeon Thompson ————Brantley's Chapel

Churches and Their Delegates

BLACK FOX: Brothers: Dale Capps, Bennie Capps. Sisters: Mary Ruth Capps, Pamela Capps.

BRADEN'S CHAPEL: Sisters: Leecy Sparks, Winnona Monday

BRANTLEY'S CHAPEL: Elders: Jerry McBee, Richard Walker. Brothers: Rina Johnson, Robert Welch, Daniel Brantley, Brian Brantley, Glenn Walker, Everett Brantley, Michael Brantley. Sisters: Hazel Johnson, Blanche Welch, Mildred Brantley, Ada McBee.

DAVIS CHAPEL: Brother: Gene Hobbs. Sisters: Mildred Ellison, Ruby Hill.

GETHSEMANE: Brother: Tom Carmichael. Sister: June Carmichael.

GIBSON STATION: Elders: William Rhymer, Spurgeon Thompson,

HALLS: Elders: Hugh Brummitt, Parnick Shelton, William Berry. Brothers: Vance Harmon, Jr., Vance Harmon, Sr.. Sisters: Ruby Brummitt, Wilma Shelton, Betty Culvahouse, Cookie Harmon, Irene Harmon, Trula Berry, Maggie Welch.

HEADRICK'S CHAPEL: Elders: Clyde Abbott, Sr., Robert Walker. Sister: Margaret Walker.

LENIOR CITY: Elder Chester Hembree. Brothers: Hubert Spoon, Tommy Scrabrough. Sisters: Edith Hembree, Marie Scarbrough, Thelma Brown, Annie Spoon.

MYER'S GROVE: Letter Received. No Delegates Listed.

NOETON: Elder: John Oliver. Brothers: Carroll Oliver, Charlie Collins. Sisters: Dora Collins.

OAK GROVE: SISTER: Frances Eastridge, Ruth Shoffner, Mona Rogers.

PLEASANT HILL: Elders: Larry Anderson, Albert Davis. Brother:: Millard Berry. Sisters: Audra Davis, Karen Rhymer, Cleo Berry, Mollie McCarty.

ROCKY DALE: Elder: Joe Bush. Brothers: Charles Bryant, Glen Johnson. Sisters: Norma Jean Bush, Myrtle Bryant, Fay Collette.

Obituaries

BRADEN, ADA BRAY WILLIAMS, age 54 of Lafollette, passed away June 9, 1992, in Baptist Hospital. She was born March 26, 1938, in Claiborne County. She was a resident of Monroe, Mich. for 35 years. And joined the Pleasant Hill Baptist Church at an early age.

She was preceded in death by her father, Abe Williams; Husband, Kenneth V. Braden; and on brother Elvin Williams. Survivors: Mother, Zepher Robinson Williams; sons, Kenneth V. Braden Jr., Lafollette; Ben E. and Deloise Braden, Speedwell, John D. Braden, Joseph W. Braden both of Lafollette; brothers, Bruce Williams, Lake City, Gene Williams, Speedwell, John Williams, Goshen, Ohio, and Jemsey Williams, Speedwell. Sisters: Patsy Williams, Della Mayes, Geneva Cupps, Linda Edwards all of Speedwell, Audie Capps, Forge Ridge and Maxine Miracle, Monroe, Mich.; Granddaughter, Jessica Braden.

Funeral services were Thursday, June 11 in Reece Valley Chapel with Rev. John Robinson officiating. Music by Charlie McDonald and Betty Edwards.

Burial in the Ausmus Cemetery.
Pallbearers: Tim and Hank Williams, Howard Treaday, Doug Capps, Willis and Wendell Edwards.
Reece Funeral Home and Valley Chapel in Charge.

BRADEN, SARAH VENNIE, age 95, of Speedwell died Monday January 6, 1992 at the LaFollette Medical Center. She attended Braden Chapel Baptist Church and was a Christian for 82 years. Funeral services were Thursday, January 9, at Braden Chapel Baptist Church, with Elder J.C. Monday and the Rev. Michael Beal officiating. Interment was in Braden's Chapel Cemetery. Cross Funeral Home was in charge of the arrangements.

Preceded in death by her husband, William Braden and daughter, Ruth Lynch Edwards. Survivors include her son, Willie Braden, Speedwell; daughters, Mrs Roy (Lillie) Bullard, Speedwell, Mrs Clarence (Tilda) Sparks, Middlesboro, Ky., and Mrs. Glenn (Kate) Lynch, LaFollette; Brother, Hubert Clawson, LaFollette; sister, Arletta Leach, Dayton, Ohio; 16 grandchildren; 25 great-grandchildren; one great-great-grandchild.

BRANTLEY, BARSHA ANN OGLE, age 73, of Browns School Road, Maryville, Tn. Passed away Wednesday, July 29, 1992, 12:01 a.m. at Baptist Hospital. Knoxville. She was a faithful member of Brantley's Chapel Primitive Baptist Church. Preceded in death by husband, Elder Clifford Brantley, an Elder of the Powell Valley Association. Survivors include: Sons and daughters-in-law, Daniel and Linda Brantley,

Truman and Deedie Brnatley of Lithia Springs, Ga ; grandchildren, Angela Stafford, of Seymore, Tn., Brian Brantley, Mike Brantley, Tina Brantley, Ginger Brantley, all of Maryville, Gina Brantley of Lithia Springs, Ga. great-grandchild Kyle Palmer; Brothers: Lester Ogle of Maryville, Herman Ogle and Earnest Ogle, all of Maryville, Viva Campbell of Oak Ridge, Tn. and Pauline Jenkins of Chattanooga, Tn.; a host of nieces and nephews. Funeral service was conducted on Friday, July 31, 1992, at Brantley's Chapel Primitive Baptist Church with Elder Jerry McBee, Elder Chester Hembree and Brother Brian Brantley officiating. Interment in the church cemetery. Words cannot express how much Brantley's Chapel Church ment to her during her extended illness.

There's an open gate at the end of the road
Through which each must go alone
and there, in a light we cannot see,
Our Father claims His own;
Beyond the gate our loved one finds happiness
and rest,
And there is comfort in the thought that a Loving
God knows best .

CLAWSON, ELDER NOBLE LEE, age 68, born June 12, 1924, passed away July 20, 1992 at LaFollette Medical Center.

He was a member of Braden's Chapel Church and also assistant pastor of Braden's Chapel and Oak Grove Churches at his passing. He was also pastor of Braden's Chapel and Meyers Grove for several years.

He was preceded in death by his parents, Donnie and Lizzie Clawson, five brothers and two sisters.

Survivors: wife, Helen Edwards Clawson, daughters Mrs. Donald (Patsy) Pierce, Mrs. Marvin (Janice) Bean, both of Speedwell, and Mrs. Kenneth (Pam) Goins of LaFollette, sons, Ernie and Matthew Clawson of Speedwell, 12 grandchildren and 1 grandchild, sisters, Lou Bullard of Speedwell and Nadine Owens of West Carrolton, Ohio, brother, Ray Clawson of Monroe, Michigan, and several nieces and nephews.

Funeral services 2 P.M., July 22 at Braden's Chapel Church with Elder J.C. Monday and Elder LeeRoy Braden officiating. Burial in Braden's Cemetery in Speedwell. Cross Funeral Home in charge.

He will be sadly missed by his family, friends and churches. We feel our loss is heaven's gain. We loved him very much, but God loved him more, called him away to that beautiful shore.
Wife and Children.

CLAWSON, SEBURN, age 74, of Speedwell died November 29, at the LaFollette Medical Center. He was of the Baptist faith and was a retired automotive parts manufacturing employee. Funeral services were Monday, December 2 at Braden Chapel, with Elder J.C. Monday officiating. Intermanet was in Braden Chapel Cemetery.

Survivors include his brother, Hubert Clawason, LaFollette; sister, Sarah Braden, Speedwell, and Arletta Leach, Dayton, Ohio.

COX, ALBIA E., age 78, of Pigeon Forge, formerly of Union County, passed away Thursday morning, October 24, 1991, at Ft. Sanders Hospital, Sevierville. She was of the Baptist faith. Preceded in death by husband, Hughie A. Cox; two step-daughters Eva McMahan and Ruby Welch. Survivors: step-daughter, Ada McBee, Maryville; sister Lodus Ward of Florida; special niece, Retta Blankenship, Maryville; five step-grandchildren; several nieces and nephews. Funeral service was Saturday at 2 p.m. Brantley's Chapel Church, Maryville, Elder Jerry McBee officiating. Interment in church cemetery. Sadly missed by family and friends.

NICLEY, MRS EMMA BORUFF, age 102, of Black Fox Rd., Washburn, passed away 2:50 p.m. Thursday, January 23, 1992 at Claiborne County Hospital. Member of Black Fox Primitive Baptist. Daughter of the late Elder Alfred and Emma (Ellison) Boruff. Also preceded in death by: husband, Eck Nicley; son, Noah Nicly. Survivors: daughters, Bertha and Sarah Nicley, both of Washburn, Zella Washam, Luttrell, Gertie Murphy, Heiskell; sons, Tommy, Cornelius, and Earl Nicley, all of Maynardville; 22 grandchildren; a host of great-grandchildren and great-great-grandchildren; several nieces and nephews. Funeral service at Cooke Mortuary Chapel, Rev. Richard Nicely, Elder Parnick Shelton officiating. Interment at Cabbage Cemetery.

JONES, ELDER NELSON, age 73, of Tazewell, Tennessee was born April 11th, 1918, in Lee County, Va. Son of Milburn & Mattie Vaughn Jones. Passed away April 10, 1992 at Ft. Sanders Hospital. He was the pastor and member of the Gibson Station Primitive Baptist Church. He is survived by his wife Polly Burke Jones, sons: Charles, Bill and Danny Jones. Daughters: Shirley Brasfield and Betty Hatfield. Brother Clay Jones, Sister Lula Williams, (11) grandchildren, (4) great-grandchildren. Funeral Services were conducted at his Home Church by Elder Billy Rhymer and Elder Spurgeon O. Thompson. Brother Jones was laid to rest in Riverview Cemetery til the Resurrection morn. *He shall sleep, but not forever!*

NORTON, LUCY FLORENCE, age 86, of Knoxville, passed away Sunday, May 10, 1992, at Hillcrest Central. Member of Halls Primitive Baptist Church. Widow of M.A. Norton. Survivors: sons, Elbert G. Cheek, Knoxville, Edward O'Neal Cheek, Orlando, Florida, Harold Cheek of Washington; stepson, Jack B. Norton; several grandchildren and great-grandchildren; brother, Ezra Oaks, Jefferson City, sisters, Gladys White of Ohio, Mae Hurst, Halls. Graveside services were conducted by Elder Bill Berry.

PARRIS, MARY (MYRT) COLLINS, born December 10th, 1900, departed this life January 3rd, 1992, to forever be with Our Dear Lord. She was preceded in death by husband, Brother Lee Parris. She leaves a sister, Sallie Anderson, nieces and nephews and a host of friends, to mourn her passing.
Sister Mary united with the Lenoir City Primitive Baptist Church in 1938. She was a faithful and active member, until ill health forced her to enter a nursing home.
Services were held at Click Funeral Home

Chapel with Elder Chester Hembree officiating. Burial was in the Lenoir City Cemetery.

RELFORD, ALFRED G., age 73, of New Tazewell, formerly of Sharp's Chapel, passed away 2:25 a.m., Friday, May 15, 1992 at St. Mary's Medical Center. Member of Oak Grove Baptist Church. U.S. Army veteran of WWII. Preceded in death by brother, Clifton Relford.

Survivors: Mother, Luster Singleton, Sharps Chapel; sons and daughters-in-law, Lowell and Carol Rutherford, Maryville, Lawrence and Betty Rutherford, Corryton; daughter and son-in-law, Irene and Perry Walker, Corryton; special friend, Jean Atkins, New Tazewell, Grandchildren, Steve Michael and Vickie Rutherford, Pamela Rudd, Kristi Walker; five great-grandchildren, Allen, Laura, and Matthew Rutherford; Sonya Dixon and Dannille Rudd.

Funeral services were held at Cooke Funeral Home Chapel, Elder Parnick Shelton officiating. Interment at Oak Grove Cemetery. Pallbearers: Harold Brantley, Lee Berry, C.B. Sharp, Robert Welch, Oris Welch, Ernie Berry, Erwin Berry.

SHARP, FREDA BELLE, age 87, of West Haven Community. Last active Charter Member of the Halls Primitive Baptist Church (she was very proud to hold that title) and member of Knoxville Baptist Tabernacle Senior Saints. Preceded in death by husband, Cyrus Ambrose Sharp; son, J. Victor Sharp. Survivors: son, Donald W. Sharp; daughters, Joyce McFalls, Shirley Bowden; 16 grandchildren; 21 great-grandchildren. Graveside services officiated by Elder Bill Berry, Rev. Benny Miller, Elder Parnick Shelton. Arrangement by Weaver's Cumberland Memorial Chapel.

WHITEHEAD, MARY HELEN, age 41, of 136 Dewberry Drive, Maryville. Survivors include her son and daughter-in-law, Joe and Kim Whitehead; daughter, Tina Whitehead; grandchildren, Britteni and Joey Whitehead; parents, Eskie and Dessie Boruff; sisters, Evelyn Carver, Dorothy Knox, Jean Shinpaugh; Brothers, Doug Boruff, Sam Boruff; all of Maryville; several nieces and nephews. Elder Jerry McBee and the Rev. Sam C. Franklin officiating. Interment in Grandview Cemetery.

Rules of Decorum

1. The churches composing the Powell's Valley Association shall not be confined to any set rules as to specific number of Messengers they shall have in the body, but shall have the right to name in their letters as many as they choose, and in addition all orderly members of any of the churches being present be entitled to seats in the body as Messengers to their respective churches, with all the rights and privileges of the same.

2. The Messengers thus assembled shall be denominated the Powell's Valley Primitive Baptist Church.

3. For the purpose of historical information and statistical edification, the Churches are required to state in letters, the number of members in fellowship, the number received by Baptism, by letter, by confession of Faith, the number dismissed, excluded and dead since last session; also the time of their meeting, their pastoral supply, and the amount of money contributed for ministers and other purposes together with any other information they deem appropriate for the edification of the saints and glory of God.

4. This Association shall have no power to answer queries, give advice, or dictate to the Churches in any case, or to lord it over God's heritage nor any power by which she can directly or indirectly fringe on the internal rights of the church or censure and try any church or member in reference to faith and practice and determine upon validity of gospel ordinances. These things shall rest entirely with the churches; but henceforward our annual meetings shall be only for the purpose of hearing from each other, and for the worship of God and mutual comfort and edification of the Saints. To this end we reserve the privilege annually for Friday before the Third Saturday in August and the two following days or at such other times as may be agreed upon with any church that may invite us having to protect our own standard, while in session, from heresay and disorder to recognize and invite any primitive Baptist minister or any lay brother to worship with us that may deem proper; to request the brethren of our body to visit other churches or bodies in our belief with whom we may desire to culture Christian fellowship; to publish in a minute of our proceedings.

5. Each session of the body shall have a Moderator and Clerk who shall hold office until re-elected.

6. Any order member of any church belonging to this body, when convened, being present shall be eligible to elect on as Moderator and Clerk or to sit on any committee appointed by the same.

7. In all election or questions that may be necessary to determine by vote, the vote shall be taken by churches, each church being entitled to three votes for any number less than one hundred, and one additional vote for every fifty or fraction thereof above the first hundred, but the Messengers of each church may divide their vote as they see proper.

8. All elections or questions coming to vote shall be determined by a majority vote cast, and it shall be the only duty of the minority to acquiesce in the decision thus reached.

9. If new churches desire to be admitted to this union they shall petition by letter and messengers and if voted for and recommended by one or more sister churches for her Presbytery constitutioning them, as orthodox and orderly they shall be received by the vote of the body and manifested by the Moderator giving the Messengers the right hand of fellowship.

10. Any motion or resolution clearly inconsistent with the above rules shall be promptly ruled out of order unless withdrawn by the mover.

11. Any messenger being ruled out of order by the Moderator shall have the right to appeal to the body on the question of order, and if sustained shall be allowed to proceed, but if not take his seat.

12. Our meeting being held in the name of Christ and the worship of God; each Messenger is expected to observe due and proper therein.

13. It will not be considered good for any Messenger whose name has been enrolled as

such to abruptley break off or absent himself from the Association without leave.

14. The Moderator shall be entitled to the same privilege of speech as other members provided the chair is filled.

15. The minutes of the Association shall be read and approved by the body and signed by the Moderator before adjourning.

16. The Association shall be opened and closed by prayer.

17. Amendments to these may be made at any time by a majority of the union voting by churches when they deem it necessary, provide such amendments do not compromise the sovereignty of the churches nor have tendency to give body undue power or jurisdiction over them.

Articles of Faith

Article 1. We believe in only one true living God, as He is revealed to us in the Holy Scriptures - Father, Son, and Holy Ghost.

Article 2. We believe that the Scriptures of the old and new Testaments are the words of God and the only rule of all-saving knowledge and obedience.

Article 3. We believe in the doctrine of election according to the foreknowledge of God.

Article 4. We believe in the doctrine of original sin.

Article 5. We believe in man's impotency to rescue himself from the fallen state he is in, by his own will or ability.

Article 6. We believe that sinners are justified in the sight of God only by the imputed righteousness of Jesus Christ.

Article 7. We believe the elect, according to the foreknowledge of God will be called, converted, regenerated, and sanctified by the Holy Spirit.

Article 8. We believe the saints will persevere and never fall finally away.

Article 9. We believe that baptism and the Lord's Supper are ordinances of Jesus Christ, and that true believers are the only subject of these ordinances, and that the true mode of baptism is by immersion. We believe also that feet washing is an example of Jesus Christ and should be kept by his disciples until his second coming.

Article 10. We believe in the Resurrection of the dead and the General Judgement.

Article 11. We believe that the punishment of the wicked will be everlasting and that the joys of the righteous will be eternal.

Article 12. We believe that no minister has the right to administer the ordinances, except those who have been regularly baptized and called of God, and come under the imposition of hands of the presbytery.

CHURCH	COUNTY	PASTOR	CLERK	ADDRESS
Black Fox	Grainger	Elder Larry Anderson	Bernie Capps-992-5571	P.O.Box 91, Maynardville, TN 37807
Braden's Chapel	Union	Elder J.C. Monday	Pam Goins Janice Bean	Rt. 1, Box 350, LaFollette, TN.37766 Speedwell, TN 37870
Brantley's Chapel	Blount	Elder Jerry McBee	Gaye Lee-448-6392 Beatrice Beason	1042 Hembree Hollow Rd., Townsend, TN 37882 1443 E. Brown School Rd., Maryville, TN 37804
Davis Chapel	Campbell		Katheryn Angel Sondra Wright, Asst.	Rt. 5, Box 170, LaFollette, TN 37766 1256 Middlesboro Hwy., Lafollette, TN 37766
Gethsemane	Knox	Elder Robert Walker	Tom Carmichael	729 Frank Street, Knoxville, TN 37919
Gibson Station	Lee, Va.	Elder Spurgeon Thompson	Dorothy Johnson Shirley Sandifur, Asst.	Rt. 2, Box 320, Ewing, VA 24248 Rt 1, Box 416, Harrogate, TN 37752
Halls	Knox	Elder William Berry	Alice Powers Helen Branson, Asst.	7525 Temple Acres Dr., Knoxville, TN 37938 4633 Marshall Dr., Knoxville, TN 37938
Headrick's Chapel	Sevier	Elder Clyde Abbott, Sr.	Gearldine Abbott	1780 Alpine Drive, Sevierville, TN 37862
Lenoir City	Loudon	Elder Chester Hembree	E.H. Scarbrough-986-3027 Cheri Brown, Asst.-986-3724	270 Hickman St., Lenoir City, TN 37771 500 C. Street, Lenoir City, TN 37771
Meyers' Grove	Claiborne	Elder J. C. Monday	Kathy Downes Gipsy Ayers-626-8507	Rt. 2, Box 84, New Tazewell, TN 37825 Rt. 2, Box 97, New Tazewell, TN 37825
Noeton	Grainger	Elder John Oliver	Caroll Oliver Mildred Oliver, Asst.	Rt. 2, Box 3480, Bean Station, TN 37708
Oak Grove	Union	Elder J. C. Monday Elder William Rhymer, Asst.	Betty P. Sharp Betty Shoffner, Asst	133 Guizzell Ridge Rd., Sharps Chapel, TN 37866 Ledmine Bend Rd, Sharps Chapel, TN 37866
Pleasant Hill	Claiborne	Elder William Rhymer Elder Albert Davis, Asst.	William Branscomb Oklen Edwards, Asst.	Speedwell, TN 37870 Speedwell, TN 37870
Rocky Dale	Knox	Elder Hugh Brummitt	Betty Livingston-688-2352 Saundra Boruff, Asst.-947-7384	6924 Boruff Rd, Corryton, TN 37721 6916 Weaver Rd., Knoxville, TN 37721

ASSOCIATION

93

MINUTES

POWELL VALLEY ASSOCIATION OF PRIMITIVE BAPTISTS

STATISTICAL TABLE	RESTORED	RECEIVED BY LETTER	BAPTISM	EXCLUDED	DISMISSED BY LETTER	RELATIONSHIP	DECEASED	TOTAL MEMBERSHIPS	PRINTING MINUTES	REGULAR MEETING TIME	COMMUNION TIME
Black Fox	0	0	0	0	0	0	1	57	$25.00	Sunday after Second Saturday Sunday after Fourth Saturday	Sunday following Second Saturday in June
Braden's Chapel	0	0	5	0	0	0	1	158	50.00	Every Sunday, second Saturday night	Sunday following first Saturday in July
Brantley's Chapel	1	0	3	1	1	9	1	126	100.00	Second Saturday night-every Sunday and Sunday night	Sunday following second Saturday in July at 10:30 a.m.
Gethsemane	0	0	0	0	0	0	0	27	30.00	Second and Fourth Sunday	Fourth Sunday in May and October
Gibson Station	0	0	0	0	0	0	0	58	50.00	First Saturday night- Every Sunday and Sunday night	Sunday following first Saturday in June
Halls	0	0	0	0	0	0	1	105	100.00	Every Sunday and Sunday night	Last Sunday in April
Headrick's Chapel	0	0	0	1	0	0	0	103	25.00	First and third Sunday of each month	First Sunday in May and October 11:00 a.m.
Lenoir City	0	0	1	1	1	3	2	102	50.00	Every Sunday and Sunday night	Wednesday night before Easter Sunday
Myers Grove	0	0	0	0	0	0	0	89	30.00	4th Saturday night and every Sunday	Sunday following Fourth Saturday in May
Noeton	0	0	0	0	0	0	1	49	30.00	First Sunday-third Saturday and Sunday of each month	Sunday following third Saturday in May and September
Oak Grove	0	0	5	3	1	0	6	318	50.00	First Saturday night andSunday-third Sunday	Sunday following the first Saturday in May
Pleasant Hill	1	1	0	0	0	1	2	90	45.00	4th Saturday morning and Saturday night. Every Sunday and Sunday night	Sunday following the fourth Sunday in June at 10:30 a.m.
Rocky Dale	0	0	0	0	0	0	0	94	50.00	Every Sunday morning	Sunday following third Saturday in May

1993 Minutes

POWELL VALLEY ASSOCIATION
OF PRIMITIVE BAPTISTS

THE ONE HUNDRED-SEVENTY-THIRD SESSION
OF THE POWELL VALLEY ASSOCIATION
OF PRIMITIVE BAPTIST
HELD WITH THE SISTER CHURCH AT
BLACK FOX
GRAINGER COUNTY, TENNESSEE
AUGUST 20, 21, 22, 1993
NEXT SESSION WILL BE HELD WITH THE SISTER
CHURCH AT HALLS IN
KNOX COUNTY, TENNESSEE
TO BEGIN ON FRIDAY BEFORE THE THIRD
SATURDAY IN AUGUST, 1994 AT 10:30 A.M.
ELDER HUGH BRUMMITT WILL DELIVER THE
INTRODUCTORY SERMON
ELDER O.D. McCARTY WILL BE THE ALTERNATE.

Officers

ELDER JERRY McBEE, MODERATOR
P.O. BOX 158, LOUISVILLE, TENNESSEE 37777
PHONE 977-1788

ELDER LARRY ANDERSON, ASSISTANT MODERATOR
RT. 3. BOX 314-A, SPEEDWELL, TENNESSEE 37870
PHONE 869-4635

BENNIE CAPPS, CLERK
P.O. BOX 91, MAYNARDVILLE, TENNESSEE 37807
PHONE 992-5571

RINA JOHNSON, ASSISTANT CLERK
1217 BROWN SCHOOL ROAD,
MARYVILLE, TENNESSEE 37804
PHONE 983-2774

Minutes of
The One Hundred Seventy-Third Session

FRIDAY, AUGUST 20, 1993

The One Hundred Seventy-Third session of the Powell Valley Association of Primitive Baptist met with the Sister Church at Brantley's Chapel in Blount County, Tenn., on August 20, 21, 22, 1993.

Elder Albert Davis led the congregation in singing"Amazing Grace" and Elder Jerry McGhee led, "How Tedious and Tasteless The Hour", then Moderator Larry Anderson welcomed the congregation and pleaded for peace and love to abide through-out the entire Association and called for prayer by Elder Chester Hembree of Lenoir City. Following prayer, Elder Spurgeon Thompson of Gibson Station delivered the introductory sermon from the 24th Chapter of Proverbs. using as his text "Famine in the Land" and preached a very uplifting and spiritual sermon.

After the introductory sermon, they sang a song and were dismissed in prayer by Elder O.D. McCarty. The Association was to reconvene after a 15 minute recess.

After recess, the crowd reassembled in the church. Elder Glenn Walker led the congregation in singing "How Firm a Foundation", and the Moderator, Elder Larry Anderson read from 64th Chapter of Isaiah and spoke a few minutes on being a lump of clay, and being molded to God's will, then called for prayer by Elder Hugh Brummitt of Halls.

The Moderator then asked for the order of business for the following transactions:

1st: Called for letters of the Sister Churches to be presented to the clerk for reading. Eleven (11) were received.

2nd: The letters were presented and read and motion approved that the delegates be seated.

3rd: The Moderator called for anyone present from any of the Sister Churches not named as delegate who desired to be seated as such come forward and give the clerk their name and the name of their church. One came: Sister Dorothy Shelton of Rocky Dale.

4th: Called for petitionary letter if there should be one. None came.
5th: Motion approved that we grant Davis Chapel's request to be dismissed from the association. Any church wiishing to receive members from Davis Chapel can do so by relationship.
6th. Motion approved that the Association Elect Elder Jerry McBee as Moderator and Elect Elder as Larry Anderson Assistant Moderator for the ensuing year.
7th: Motion approved that Brother BennieCapps be re-elected Clerk and Brother Rina Johnson be re-elected Assistant Clerk for the ensuing year.
8th: Motion was approved that we empower Elder McBee to appoint all the committees to serve this session.
9th: The Moderator, having been empowered to do so, appointed committees as follows:

Committee on Arrangements: Brother Carroll Oliver
Brother O.D. McCarty
Brother Everett Brantley
Committee on Preaching: Brother Millard Berry
Brother Aurell Graves
Brother Elwood Evans
Committee On Request: Elder Clyde Abbott, Sr.
Brother Franklin Jones
Brother Charlie Collins
Committee on Finance: Elder Chester Hembree
Brother Joe Culvahouse
Brother Glenn Walker

10th: Called for the finances to be turned in to the Finance Committee.
11th: The Committees all having been appointed and accepted, the Association moved to adjourn until 10:30 Saturday morning. They sang a song and were dismissed in prayer by Elder Albert Davis of Pleasant Hill.

SATURDAY, AUGUST 21, 1993

At the appointed hour of 10:30 Saturday morning and at the sound of singing, the Association reassembled. Brother Glenn Walker led the Congregation in "Old Time Religion" and "There is a Fountain" and

"Amazing Grace". Elder Larry Anderson opened the service and spoke for a few minutes, then called for prayer by Elder James Henry Branscomb of Pleasant Hill. After prayer, the Moderator called the Association to order for the remainder of the business.

1st: Called for any letters from Sister Churches not received on Friday. Two (2) were received.

2nd: Called for anyone from any of the churches who were present and desired to be seated as delegate to come forward and give the clerk their name and their church. There was none.

3rd: Called for the report of the committee on Arrangements who submitted the following report:

REPORT ON ARRANGEMENTS:
CALL FOR ROLL CALL OF DELEGATES.
CALL FOR REPORT OF COMMITTEE ON PREACHING.
CALL FOR REPORT OF COMMITTEE ON REQUEST.
CALL FOR REPORT OF COMMITTEE ON FINANCE.

Decide how many minutes we have printed, who shall supervise the printing and delivery of the same, and what he shall be paid for this service. Which Sister Church shall host the next Association and who will preach the introductory sermon and who will be the alternate. Who will prepare the Circular Letter.

Respectfully Submitted,
Brother Carroll Oliver
Brother Everett Brantley
Elder O.D. McCarty

4th: Motion approved to receive the above report and release the committee.

5th: Called the roll call of delegates of all Sister Churches and check the absentees.

6th: Called for the report of the Committee on Preaching:

COMMITTEE ON PREACHING:
Friday night: Elder Parnick Shelton
Elder Richard Walker
Saturday morning: Elder Chester Hembree
Elder Larry Anderson
Saturday night: Elder O.D. McCarty

Elder Clyde Abbott, Sr.
Sunday morning: Elder Jerry McBee
Elder John Oliver

Respectfully submitted,
Brother Millard Berry
Brother Averill Graves
Brother Elwood Evans

7th: Motion approved to receive the above report and release the committee.

8th: Called for the report of the Committee on Request, which was given:

We, the Committee on Request, wish to request as follows, that we have 1,000 minutes printed and the clerk supervise the printing and distribution of same and that he receive $150.00 for his services. We also request that the next session of the Powell Valley Association be held with the Sister Church at Halls in Knox County, Tennessee, to begin on Friday before the third Saturday in August, 1994, at 10:30 A.M. and continue three days. We also request that Elder Hugh Brummitt preach the introductory sermon and Elder O.D. McCarty be the alternate. We also request that Elder Jerry McBee write a circular letter for the minutes for 1994.

Respectfully submitted,
Elder Clyde Abbott Sr.
Brother Franklin Jones
Brother Charles Collins

9th: Motion approved to receive the above report and release the committee.

10th: Called for the report of the Committee on Finance, which submitted the following report:

Black Fox...$25.00
Braden's Chapel... 50.00
Brantley's Chapel...100.00
Gethsemane.. 30.00
Gibson Station... 50.00

Halls... 100.00
Headrick's Chapel... 25.00
Lenoir City... 50.00
Meyers Grove... 30.00
Noeton... 30.00
Oak Grove.. 50.00
Pleasant Hill.. 45.00
Rocky Dale... 50.00

Total Collections... 605.00
Donations.. 35.00

.... 640.00
Balance in Bank.. 782.00
.... 1,422.00
Expenses for 1993... -800.00
Balance in Bank.. 682.00

Respectfully Submitted,
Brother Joe Culvahouse
Brother Glenn Walker
Elder Chester Hembree

11th: Motion approved to receive the above report and release the committee.

12th: Motion approved that we grant the request of the committee and have 1,000 minutes printed and the clerk to receive $150.00 for his services.

13th: Motion approved that the next session of the Association be held with the Sister Church at Halls to commence on Friday before the third Saturday in August , 1994, at 10:30 A.M.

14th: Motion approved that Elder Hugh Brummitt deliver the introductory sermon and Elder O.D. McCartybe the alternate.

15th: Motion approved that Elder Jerry McBee write the circular letter for the 1994 Minutes.

16th: Motion approved that the churches of the Powell Valley Association extend to the church and the people of Black Fox heart felt thanks and our prayers for the love, fellowship, kindness, and food while we were with you. May the Good Lord bless and keep you is our prayers.

17th: Motion approved to adjourn, trusting the Lord to permit us to meet again with the Sister Church at Halls in Knox County, Tn., on Friday before the third Saturday in August, 1994 at 10:30 A.M. Dismissed in prayer by Elder William Rhymer.

Elder Jerry McBee, Moderator
Elder Larry Anderson, Assistant Moderator
Brother Bennie Capps, Clerk
Brother Rina Johnson, Assistant Clerk

Special Announcements

Brantley's Chapel has their second Saturday night services at 7 P.M.; Sunday morning services at 10:30 A.M.; Sunday night services at 7 P.M. in the summer months and at 6 P.M. in the winter months.

The following churches requested the Association for 1994: Black Fox, Brantley Chapel, Halls, and Lenoir City.

Please make all contributions payable to: **Powell Valley Association.**

Dates of ordination of the following Elders:

Elder Alber Davis, May 17, 1930
Elder Hugh Brummitt, December 12, 1954
Elder James Branscomb, June 23, 1956
Elder Parnick Shelton, December 11, 1960
Elder Claude Rosson, July 4, 1964
Elder Joe Bush, April 27, 1969
Elder Bill Berry, August 27, 1972
Elder Larry Anderson, October 24, 1975
Elder Spurgeon Thompson, December 17, 1976
Elder Bill Raymer, December 17, 1976
Elder Jerry McBee, April 26, 1981
Elder Nelson Jones, July 17, 1981
Elder Chester Hembree, June 19, 1988
Elder Clyde Abbott, Sr., November 6, 1988

Elder Robert Walker, October 4, 1970
Elder John Oliver, April 15, 1972
Elder Richard Walker, March 29, 1992
Elder LeRoy Braden, October 10, 1982
Elder Doyle Ausmus, August 10, 1984
Elder J.C. Monday, February 12, 1958
Elder Clyde Abbott, Jr., July 7, 1979

Summary

We are blessed with a fine group of ministers, as was illustrated by those who had the opportunity to preach. We regret that time will not permit more of them to preach when we meet with the Association. Friday night, Elder Richard Walker read from the First chapter of James using as his text, "Double Minded" and being unstable in all his way. Elder Parnick Shelton used as his text "Election of God's People-Chosen in God before the Foundation".

On Saturday morning, Elder Chester Hembree read from the 8th chapter of Romans, using as his text, "I am the least of All" He was then followed by Elder Larry Anderson who read from the 5th chapter of Second Corinthians, 11th verse, using as his text "Condition of Man", suffering for being out of the will of God". Saturday night, Brother Brian Brantley (in absence of Elder Clyde Abbott, Sr.) preached from the 5th Chapter of Matthew, using as his text "Ye are the salt of the Earth", then Elder O.D. McCarty preached from the First Chapter of Saint John using as his text "All Things are made by Him". On Sunday, Elder Jerry McBee read from the 3rd chapter of Genesis, verses 6-9, using as his terxt "Adam where art thou?" Then Elder John Oliver preached from the 9th Chapter of Romans, using as his text "Except the Lord of the Sabboth had left us a Seed."

All of the Elders preached a very uplifting and spirtual sermons. On Sunday there was much rejoicing in theSpirit of God.

Elder Larry Anderson and members of Black Fox Church wish to extend to the Sister Churches in the Association our heartfelt thanks for helping prepare lunch that was served on Sunday. Please remember our little Church in your prayers.

Circular Letter To Powell Valley Association

Brothers and sisters of the Powell Valley Association: I was chosen by the committee on request in 1992 to write a circular letter for the 1993 minutes.

Let us think about the Articles of Faith that have been written in our minutes of the one hundred seventy-second session.

Let us read them. Let us study them. Let us hold them dear to our heart! I know they were written and taken out of the Holy Words of God.

The first article is "We believe in only one true living God, as He is revealed to us in the Holy Scriptures - Father, Son, and Holy Ghost." I believe the Son was with God when He created man. Genesis 1:26 - "And God said, let us (Father, Son, Holy Spirit) make man in our image." So as God had made man in His image, man was with God, until the fall of man.

God's people fall from God, so Jesus came to save His people. Matthew 1:21 - "Any she SHALL bring forth a son, and they SHALL call his name JESUS, for he SHALL save His people from their sins." Not me, nor anyone, but the name of Jesus. Oh, what a name, a name above the earth, the name of Jesus.

I believe the Articles of Faith. Maybe I don't understand them all, but I believe because they are the Word of God. Not just a people that call themselves "Primitive Baptist", but they are the Word of God.

In Galatians, Paul talked about redemption coming. "But when the fullness of the time was come, God sent forth his Son, made under the law, to redeem them that were under the law...that we might receive the adoption." Galatians 4:4-5.

What does redemption mean? To buy back, or pay the price. That was what Christ did on the cross.

ALL OF GOD'S WORD IS <u>TRUE!</u> AND WILL NEVER PASS AWAY.

Elder William Rhymer

Ministers Directory

Elder Larry Anderson, Rt.3, Box 314-A, Speedwell, TN 869-4635
Elder William Berry, 7607 Mayes Chapel Road, Knoxville,TN 922-9189
Elder J.H. Branscomb, Speedwell, TN 562-6361
Elder Hugh H. Brummitt, 1329 Brown, Knoxville, TN 546-7700
Elder Joe Bush, 7507 Rodgers Rd, Corryton, TN 687-7018
Elder LeRoy Braden, 2305 Middlesboro, LaFollette, TN 5664647
Elder Albert Davis, Rt. 3, Box 320 A Speedwell, Tn 869-3596
Elder Doyle Ausmus
Elder Alvin Graves, 122 Oak Wood Dr., Lenoir City, TN 986-9725
Elder Jerry McBee, Box 158, Louisville, TN 977-1788
Elder J.C. Monday, Speedwell, TN 562-3068
Elder John Oliver, Rt 2, Box 3482, Bean Station, TN 993-2295
Elder William Rymer, P.O. Box 374, Harrogate, TN 37752
Elder Parnick Shelton, 6001 McGinnis Rd. Corryton, TN 687-5070
Elder Spurgeon Thompson, Box 36, Shawnee, TN 869-8175
Elder Claude Rosson, Rt. 4, New Tazewell, TN 626-3168
Elder Robert Walker, Severville, TN 428-1527
Elder Clay Widner, Rt. 1, Tazewell, TN 626-3893
Elder Richard Walker, 3627 Rockford St., Rockford, TN 977-0414
Elder Chester Hembree, 3604 Rockford Street Rockford, TN 983-6526
Elder Clyde Abbott, Sr., 3840 Abbott Rd., Severville, TN 453-2329
Elder Johnny Ayers, Route 2, Box 97, New Tazewell, Tn. 626-8507
Elder Clyde Abbott, Jr., 2628 Old Whites Mill Road, Maryville, TN 37801

Licentiates

Brother Roscoe Branscomb, Speedwell, TN
Brother Odell Carpenter, 812 Brown School Rd., Maryville, TN 984-4352
Brother Mark Taylor, Lenoir City, TN
Brother Ray Walker, 3029 Jess Wilson Rd, #16, Sevierville, TN 37862 429-5417

Elders Who Wrote the Circular Letter
and
the Church that Hosted the Association

1974 Elder Leonard White ———————————Lenoir City
1975 Elder Albert Davis ———————————Kirkwood
1976 Elder Charles Taylor———————————Gibson Station
1977 Elder Johnny Atkins ———————————Brantley's Chapel
1978 Elder Joe Irving ———————————Rocky Dale
1979 No Letter Submitted ———————————Oak Grove
1980 Elder Hugh Brummitt ———————————Black Fox
1981 Elder James Branscomb ———————————Pleasant Hill
1982 Elder Noble Clawson ———————————Lenoir City
1983 Elder J. C. Monday ———————————Gibson Station
1984 Elder Walter Lyons ———————————Brantley's Chapel
1985 Elder Parnick Shelton ———————————Black Fox
1986 No Letter Submitted ———————————H a l l s
1987 Elder John Oliver———————————Lenoir City
1988 Elder William Berry ———————————Rocky Dale
1989 Elder Claude Rosson ———————————Oak Grove
1990 Elder Joe Bush ———————————Pleasant Hill
1991 Elder Larry Anderson———————————Gibson Station
1992 Elder Spurgeon Thompson ———————Brantley's Chapel
1993 Elder William Rhymer ———————————Black Fox

Churches and Their Delegates

BLACK FOX: Brothers: Bennie Capps, Dale Capps. Sisters: Mary Ruth Capps, Pamela Capps, Naomi Cabbage, Sarah Hopson, Sue Atkins, Rachel Ingle, Debbie Sexton.

BRADEN'S CHAPEL: Sisters: Leecy Sparks, Winnona Monday, Helen Clawson.

BRANTLEY'S CHAPEL: Elders: Richard Walker, Jerry McBee, Brothers: Rina Johnson, Brian Brantley, Everett Brantley, Glenn Walker, Robert Welch, Elwood Evans, Cyress McBee. Sisters: Hazel Johnson, Mildred Brantley, Blanche Welch, Mildred Evans.

GETHSEMANE: Brother: Tom Carmichael.

GIBSON STATION: Elders: Spurgeon Thompson, William Rhymer. Brother: Franklin Jones. Sisters: Shirley Sandifur, Amy Sandifur, Fannie Jones, Polly Jones, Dorothy Johnson.

HALLS: Elders: Hugh Brummitt, Parnick Shelton, William Berry. Brothers: Joe Culvahouse, Vance Harmon, Sr.. Sisters: Ruby Brummitt, Wilma Shelton, Betty Culvahouse, Irene Harmon, Trula Berry, Maggie Welch.

HEADRICK'S CHAPEL: Elders: Clyde Abbott, Sr., Robert Walker. Sisters: Gearldine Abbott, Margaret Walker.

LENIOR CITY: Elder Chester Hembree. Brothers: Chester Lee Hembree, Hubert Spoon, Tommy Scarbrough. Sisters: Edith Hembree, Annie Spoon, Nell Anderson, Marie Scarbrough, Thelma Brown, Aileen Watkins.

MYER'S GROVE: Letter Received. No Delegates Listed.

NOETON: Elder: John Oliver. Brothers: Carroll Oliver, Charlie Collins. Sisters: Dora Collins, Mary Atkins.

OAK GROVE: Sisters: Alvada Dykes, Ruth Shoffner,, Monnie Rogers.

PLEASANT HILL: Elders: O.D. McCarty, James Henry Branscomb, Larry Anderson, Albert Davis. Brother:: Millard Berry. Sisters: Helen Ruth Branscomb, Audra Davis, Mollie McCarty, Karen Rhymer, Cleo Berry.

ROCKY DALE: Brothers: Charlie Bryant, Glenn Johnson, James Boruff.. Sisters: Myrtle Bryant, Saundra Boruff.

Rules of Decorum

1. The churches composing the Powell's Valley Association shall not be confined to any set rules as to specific number of Messengers they shall have in the body, but shall have the right to name in their letters as many as they choose, and in addition all orderly members of any of the churches being present be entitled to seats in the body as Messengers fo their respective churches, with all the rights and privileges of the same.

2. The Messengers thus assembled shall be denominated the Powell's Valley Primitive Baptist Church.

3. For the purpose of historical information and statistical edification, the Churches are required to state in letters, the number of members in fellowship, the number received by Baptism, by letter, by confession of Faith, the number dismissed, excluded and dead since last session; also the time of their meeting, their pastoral supply, and the amount of money contributed for ministers and other purposed together with any other information they deem appropriate for the edification of the saints and glory of God.

4. This Association shall have no power to answer queries, give advice, or dictate to the Churches in any case, or to lord it over God's heritage nor any power by which she can directly or indirectly fringe on the internal rights of the church or censure and try any church or member in reference to faith and practice and determine upon validity of gospel ordinances. These things shall rest entirely with the churches; but henceforward our annual meetings shall be only for the purpose of hearing from each other, and for the worship of God and mutual comfort and edification of the Saints. To this end we reserve the privilege annually for Friday before the Third Saturday in August and the two following days or at such other times as may be agreed upon with any church that may invite us having to protect our own standard, while in session, from heresay and disorder to recognize and invite any primitive Baptist minister or any lay brother to worship with us that we may deem proper; to request the brethren of our body to visit other churches or bodies in our belief with whom we may desire to culture Christian fellowship; to publish in a minute of our proceedings.

5. Each session of the body shall have a Moderator and Clerk who shall hold office until re-elected.

6. Any order member of any church belonging to this body, when convened, being present shall be eligible to elect on as Moderator and Clerk or to sit on any committee appointed by the same.

7. In all election or questions that may be necessary to determine by vote, the vote shall be taken by churches, each church being entitled to three votes for any number less than one hundred, and one additional vote for every fifty or fraction thereof above the first hundred, but the Messengers of each church may divide their vote as they see proper.

8. All elections or questions coming to vote shall be determined by a majority vote cast, and it shall be the only duty of the minority to acquiesce in the decision thus reached.

9. If new churches desire to be admitted to this union they shall petition by letter and messengers and if voted for and recommended by one or more sister churches for her Presbytery constitutioning them, as orthodox and orderly they shall be received by the vote of the body and manifested by the Moderator giving the Messengers the right hand of fellowship.

10. Any motion or resolution clearly inconsistent with the above rules shall be promptly ruled out of order unless withdrawn by the mover.

11. Any messenger being ruled out of order by the Moderator shall have the right to appeal to the body on the question of order, and if sustained shall be allowed to proceed, but if not take his seat.

12. Our meeting being held in the name of Christ and the worship of God; each Messenger is expected to observe due and proper therein.

13. It will not be considered good for any Messenger whose name has been enrolled as

such to abruptley break off or absent himself from the Association without leave.

14. The Moderator shall be entitled to the same privilege of speech as other members provided the chair is filled.

15. The minutes of the Association shall be read and approved by the body and signed by the Moderator before adjourning.

16. The Association shall be opened and closed by prayer.

17. Amendments to these may be made at any time by a majority of the union voting by churches when they deem it necessary, provide such amendments do not compromise the sovereignty of the churches nor have tendency to give body undue power or jurisdiction over them.

Articles of Faith

Article 1. We believe in only one true living God, as He is revealed to us in the Holy Scriptures - Father, Son, and Holy Ghost.

Article 2. We believe that the Scriptures of the old and new Testaments are the words of God and the only rule of all-saving knowledge and obedience.

Article 3. We believe in the doctrine of election according to the foreknowledge of God.

Article 4. We believe in the doctrine of original sin.

Article 5. We believe in man's impotency to rescue himself from the fallen state he is in, by his own will or ability.

Article 6. We believe that sinners are justified in the sight of God only by the imputed righteousness of Jesus Christ.

Article 7. We believe the elect, according to the foreknowledge of God will be called, converted, regenerated, and sanctified by the Holy Spirit.

Article 8. We believe the saints will persevere and never fall finally away.

Article 9. We believe that baptism and the Lord's Supper are ordinances of Jesus Christ, and that true believers are the only subject of these ordinances, and that the true mode of baptism is by immersion. We believe also that feet washing is an example of Jesus Christ and should be kept by his disciples until his second coming.

Article 10. We believe in the Resurrection of the dead and the General Judgement.

Article 11. We believe that the punishment of the wicked will be everlasting and that the joys of the righteous will be eternal.

Article 12. We believe that no minister has the right to administer the ordinances, except those who have been regularly baptized and called of God, and come under the imposition of hands of the presbytery.

Ordination for Minister of Deacon

1. MODERATOR OF THE CHURCH WILL CALL THE CHURCH TO ORDER.
2. CALL FOR THE READING OF THE MINUTES OF THE CHURCH AUTHORIZING THE ORDINATION.
3. APPOINT A SPOKESMAN FOR THE CHURCH. HE IS TO STATE IF THE CHURCH IS IN THE SAME MIND AS WHEN THE CANDIDATE WAS ELECTED.
4. THE ELDERS ARE TO ASSEMBLE THEMSELVES TOGETHER FOR THE PURPOSE STATED. (THIS IS DONE BY GATHERING TOGETHER IN A ROOM OR OUTSIDE).
5. THE PRESBYTERS WILL NOW ORGANIZE BY ELECTING A MODERATOR AND CLERK.
6. THE MODERATOR WILL BY CONSENT OF THE PRESBYTERS ASSIGN ONE OF ITS MEMBERS TO QUESTION THE CANDIDATE, ONE MEMBER TO GIVE CHARGE TO THE CANDIDATE, ONE MEMBER TO GIVE CHARGE TO THE CHURCH, AND ONE TO GIVE THE ORDINATION PRAYER.
7. BY MOTION AND SECOND BY THE CHURCH, THE CANDIDATE WILL BE DELIVERED INTO THE HANDS OF THE PRESBYTERY.
8. THE CANDIDATE FOR ORDINATION MUST BE PRESENTED BY THE CHURCH TO THE PRESBYTERS, BEING ESCORTED BY SOME SUITABLE PERSON.
9. QUESTION TO THE CANDIDATE ON OUR ARTICLES OF FAITH.
10. THE CHARGE TO THE CANDIDATE.
11. THE CHARGE TO THE CHURCH.
12. EXAMINATION OF THE CANDIDATE WILL BE GIVEN BY THE OTHER ELDERS AT THIS TIME, FOR ANY QUESTIONS THEY MIGHT HAVE CONCERNING HIS EXPERIENCE, HIS CALL TO THE MINISTRY, OR HIS UNDERSTANDING OF THE DOCTRINE.
13. THE ORDINATION PRAYER, WITH THE LAYING ON OF THE HANDS, BY THE PRESBYTERS.
14. THE RIGHT HAND OF FELLOWSHIP IS EXTENDED TO THE NEWLY ORDAINED MINISTER BY THE PRESBYTERS.
15. THE CANDIDATE, BEING FULLY ORDAINED, IS DELIVERED BACK INTO THE HANDS OF THE CHURCH BY MOTION AND SECOND.
16. BY MOTION AND SECOND, THE CHURCH ACCEPTS AND RECEIVES THE CANDIDATE AS A FULLY ORDAINED MINISTER OF JESUS CHRIST.
17. THE PRESBYTERS BY MOTION AND SECOND IS NOW DISSOLVED.
18. THE RIGHT HAND OF FELLOWSHIP IS NOW EXTENDED TO THE NEWLY ORDAINED MINISTER AND HIS WIFE BY THE OTHER MEMBERS AND FRIENDS OF THE CHURCH.
19. THE CHURCH CONFERENCE MAY THEN BE ADJOURNED AND THE SERVICE CLOSED IN ANY SUITABLE MANNER.

WRITTEN IN ORDER BY
ELDER JERRY T. MCBEE

ATKINS, ALBERTA SPOON (BERTA)-age 67 of 802 Bon Street. Lenoir City, passed away Saturday evening, August 7, 1993 at the home of her daughter. Member of West Broadway Baptist Church; she attended Lenoir City Primitive Baptist Church. Retired from Charles H. Bacon Co. Preceded in death by her husband, John C. (Paddle) Atkins and father Charlie Spoon. Survivors: Daughter and son-in-law, Carolyn and Tommie Bailey of Lenoir City, with whom she made her home for the last nine years; grandchildren, Shane, Casey and Jill Bailey; mother Ruth Spoon; sisters, Mable Brown, Nancy Jenkins, and Judy Hembree; brothers, Hubert Spoon, Bill Spoon, Kenneth Spoon, and Jimmy Spoon, all of Lenoir City; several nieces and nephews; granddaughter-in-law, Greta Bailey. Funeral service was at 7 p.m., Monday, August 9, 1993, Lenoir City Primitive Baptist Church. Elder Chester Hembree and Rev. George Seay officiating. The Family received friend following the funeral. Family and friends gathered at 10 a.m. Tues. for graveside services and interment. Click Funeral Home was in charge.

ALSTON, AGNES LOGAN-age 84 of New Tazewell, was born August 28, 1908 and passed away January 25, 1992 at Claiborne County Hospital. She was a life-long member of Meyers Grove Primitive Baptist Church. She was preceded in death by her husband, James (Jim) Alston.

Survivors: son, Robert T. (Tip) Alston, Edward F. Alston, both of LaSalle, Michigan; daughters, Mrs. Virgil (Helen) Duncan of Tazewell and Phyllis A. Southern of New Tazewell. Funeral services was at 11 a.m., Wednesday, January 29, 1992 in Coffey Funeral Home Chapel with Elder J.C. Monday and Rev. Bill Golden officiating. Singers were J.C. Robertson, Elmore Robertson, and Dixie Gray. Burial was in the Drummonds Cemetery.

Pallbearers were Pete Smith, Dan Atkins, George Logan, Paul Johnson, Carson Honeycutt, and Paul Honeycutt. Honorary pallbearers were Bill Hurst, Tom Ball, Bill DeBusk, Jim DeBusk and Ellis Seals.

Coffey Funeral Home was in Charge.

ATKINS, CHESTER-age 84 of Rutledge, passed away May 5, 1993, at Lakeway Regional Hospital, Morristown. He was preceded in death by daughters; Jean Cannon and Joyce Atkins and one grandchild. He was a member of Noeton Primitive Baptist Church. Survivors include wife, Ina Atkins of Rutledge; sons, Buddy Atkins of Florida, Billy and Hugh Atkins of Morristown, John Atkins of Rutledge, Frank Atkins of Thorn Hill, Steve Atkins of Bean Station; daughters, Mrs. Jim (Sue) Lowery of Russellville, Mrs. Terrell (Sarah) Metcalf of Dandridge, Mrs Jerry (Carolyn) Hixon of Bean Station, Mrs Virgil (Karen) Browser of Morristown; 16 grandchildren; several great grandchildren; brothers, Floyd Atkins of Bean Station, James Collins of Knoxville; sister Sally Evans of Bean Station. Services were held at Smith Funeral Home, Rutledge with Elder John Oliver and Rev. Gary Satterfield officiating. Burial was in Davidson Cemetery in Thorn Hill.

BRANTLEY, DELONA R. (DEL) - Age 59 of Sharps Chapel, passed away suddenly 12:25 p.m. Friday, November 20, 1992, as a result of an automobile accident. He was a member of Oak Grove Primitive Baptist Church and a retired supervisor of Formall Plastics. Preceded in death by father, Kenneth Brantley. Survivors: daughters and son-in-law, Yhona and Roger Jones, of Greenville, Terry and Bob Stewart, and Beth and Robert Stewart, all of Knoxville; sons and daughters-in-law, Jeff and Tonya Brantley, of Sharps Chapel, Rick and Lesley Brantley of Knoxville; seven grandchildren, Kenneth Brantley, Julia Jones, Erick Brantley, Chase Brantley, Catherine Stewart, Taylor Stewart, Hannah Brantley; two step-grandchildren, Denise Cox and T.J. Cox; mother, Sarah (Dossett) Brantley, of Sharps Chapel; sister, Barbara Lamb, of Rockvale, Tenn.; brothers, Wayne Brantley, of Maryville; several nieces and cousins. Funeral service was at Oak Grove Baptist Church, Elder J.C. Monday and Elder Jerry Mcbee, officiating. Interment Oak Grove Cemetery.

BRANTLEY, MISS GNIECE CLEO - age 66 of Sharps Chapel, passed away 6 p.m. Friday, November 20, 1992, at U.T. Medical Center, as a result of an automobile accident. She was a member of Oak Grove Primitive Baptist Church. Preceded in death by father, Kenneth Brantley, Survivors: mother, Sarah (Dossett) Brantley, of Sharps Chapel; sister, Barbara Lamb, of Rockvale,

Tennessee; brother, Wayne Brantley, of Maryville; several nieces and nephews. Funeral service at Oak Grove Baptist Church, Elder J.C. Monday and Elder Jerry McBee, Officiating. Interment Oak Grove Cemetery.

BRANSCOMB, ROSCOE (BUD) - age 94 of Speedwell, Tennessee, born September 14, 1898, passed away October 9, 1992, at LaFollette Nursing Home. Preceded in death by : wife, Sarah Graves Branscomb, sons Abraham and Isaac; daughters, Vestina and Mossie Jane Branscomb; parents, Joe and Rachel Gibbs Branscomb, brother, Newt Branscomb, sisters, Sadie Wilcox and Ellen Branscomb. Survivors: sons and daughter-in-laws, Floyd and Cleo Branscomb, Dayton, Ohio, James Henry and Helen Ruth Branscomb, William and Cedilla Branscomb, daughters and son-in-law, Parsetta and Arvil Braden, Ms. Carrie Branscomb, Ms. Dorothy Branscomb, all of Speedwell; several grandchildren, great-grandchildren, step grandchildren and stepgreat-grandchildren; sister Catherine Jane McGeorge, Pineville, Ky.; sister-in-law, Eva Blanton, New Tazewell; several nieces and nephews; other relative and friends. Funeral services were at Pleasant Hill Primitive Baptist Church, Elder Bill Rhymer and Elder Larry Anderson officiating. Music by Myra Anderson and Church Choir. Interment Hill Cemetery. Pallbearers were grandsons.

CREECH, TISHIE BERRY- age 95 passed away on March 29, 1993 at Laurel Manor Nurs

ing Home in New Tazewell, Tennessee. She was a long time faithful member of Oak Grove Primitive Baptist Church until bad Health over took her. She loved her church very dearly. She was preceded in death by her husband, Felix Arthur Creech. She was survived by her daughters and son-in-law Mildred and Evertt Brantley of Maryville, Tennessee and Lelia and Duke Bridges of Jonesboro, Georgia; Son and daughter-in-law Arthur and Susan Creech of Sharps Chapel and her foster daughter and her husband Mamie and Wayne Brantley of

Maryville, Tennessee. Survivors also include 10 grandchildren, 17 great grandchildren, 5 great great grandchildren, several nieces and nephews.

Funeral services were held on April 1, 1993 at Cooke Funeral Home by Elder Thomas Spurgeon and Elder Gregg Sharp. She was laid to rest in Oak Grove Cemetery.

Our Loss Is Heavens Gain.

DRUMMONS, WILLIE EDWARD

- age 84 of New Tazewell, was born November 3, 1908 and passed away December 28, 1992 at Claiborne County Hospital.

He was a member of Meyers Grove Primitive Baptist Church and a member of Evening Star Lodge #180 Free And Accepted Masons of New Tazewell. he was preceded in death by parents, James Abraham and Mollie Day Drummonds; sisters, Gertrude Zwack, Dora Lundy and Frankie Hayes.

Survivors: wife, Martha Inez Arnold Drummonds; daughter, Billie D. Evans, granddaughter, Lisa R. Martin; great grandson, Daniel Martin, all of New Tazewell; brothers, Carlie Drummonds, Monroe, Michigan and Virgil Drummonds of Knoxville; several nieces and nephews.

Funeral service was December 30, 1992 in Coffey Funeral Home Chapel with Elder J.C. Monday and Rev. John Clark officiating. Singer Bill Duncan. Burial in the Fairview Cemetery.

Pallbearers: Taye Drummonds, Ronnie Hansard, Mike Hansard, Void Hansard, Doyle Hansard, Bobby Drummonds and Bob Shipley.

HALL, CARL COTTON

- age 69 of Speedwell, passed away May 11, 1993 at UT Hospital.

He attended Bradens Chapel Church, as a veteran of World War II and belonged to Linonia-Westlawn Masonic Lodge #586. He was preceded in death by his parents, Tillmon and Maude Harmon Hall; brothers Arnold and Claude Hall.

Survivors: Wife, Ruth Madon Hall, Speedwell, sons, Larry Hall, White Pine. Gary Hall, Speedwell and Howard Hall, New Boston, Michigan, daughters, Betty Hines, Dearborn, Michigan, Barbara Angrrone and Carolyn McEnhill, both of Flat Rock, Michigan. Sister, Irene Duncan, Northwood, Ohio. Thirteen grandchildren.

J. C. Monday, officiating at the funeral. Interment in Beeler Cemetery.

He will be sadly missed by his family, church, and friends.

PARRIS, MABEL GRAVES - age 87 of Lenoir City, passed away at the home of her daughter, Sunday, May 2, 1993. Member of Lenoir City Primitive Baptist Church. Preceded in death by husband, H. Fred Parris Sr. Survivors: daughters and sons-in law, Frankie and A.C. Brown, Marion and Ray Anderson, Lenoir City; sons and daughters-in-law, Fred Jr. and Wanda Parris, Madisonville; grandchildren, Terry and Cheri Brown, Nikki and Steven Bell, Joy Anderson, Tammy and Ismael Delgado, Candi and Ron Blakeslee; eight great-grandchildren; four great-great-grandchildren; brother, Glen Graves, Pulaski, Tennessee; sister, Annie Spoon, Lenoir City. Funeral service was at Lenoir City Primitive Baptist Church, Elder Chester Hembree and Elder Charles Taylor officiating. Burial followed in the Loudon County Memorial Gardens.

PERRY, MOSSIE CHESNEY- age 88 of Washburn, Tennessee, passed away 10:30 a.m. March 7, 1993 at St. Mary's hospital. She was a member of Black Fox Primitive Baptist Church for over 50 years. Preceded in death by two husbands, W.W. Goin and Billy Perry. One daughter, Laura (Goin) Hilton, one son Willard Goin who died in infancy, one sister, five brothers, mother and father, three step children, and two step grand-children.
Survivors: Two daughters, Mrs. Ethel Hilton and Mrs Bonnie Nicely of Washburn. Three grandsons, Gary and Jerry Hilton , & Eddie Nicely of Washburn, and one great grandson Dustin Hilton. Brother Fate Chesney, Maynardville. Sisters Harriet Starnes, Nell Perry, Washburn. Clara Kidwell, Leona Chambell, Mayanrdville, Stella Braden, Halls. Eleven step grand-children.
Funeral service at Black Fox Church, Rev Andy Vance and Elder Parnic Shelton officiating. Internment in Cabbage Cemetery.
Pallbearers, Tom & John Chesney, John Perry, Dale Haynes, Paul Griffin, Calvin Chesney.
Sadly missed by daughters and grandsons.

MONROE, FRANCIE ANN RUSSELL- age 103 Ontario, Canada, died January 26, 1993, at home. Services were at The Chapel of The Roses, Ontario with Rev. Darren Love and Rev. Jared Tenney, officiating. Private vault interment followed at the Evergreen Cemetery, Ontario.

She was born November 23, 1889, at Sharps Chapel, Tennessee. She married H.L. Monroe in 1908. He died in 1963. She live in California for 40 years and for 17 years in Idaho and Oregon. She was a charter member of the Oak Grove Baptist Church of Sharps Chapel. She lived for her family, cooking and gardening.

Survivors include three sons and two daughters-in-law. Thomas Monroe of Ontario, Woodrow and Helen Monroe of Fruitland, and Jeff and Minnie Monroe of Chula Vista, Calif.; a daughter, Winnie Monroe of Ontario; a daughter-in-law, Mrs. James Monroe of Bluejacket, Okla.; four grandchildren, Robert, Jimmy, and Susan of Calif., and Phyllis Marsden of Wilsonville; one great-grandchild, Jimmy Monroe, who is in the U.S. Army in Leesville, La.; three brothers, DenZil Russell of Sharps Chapel, and Milburn and Lloyd Russell of Speedwell, Tenn., one sister, Clemma Raley of Maynardville, Tenn. and many nieces and nephews.

RALEY, CLEMMA JANE - age 87 of Maynardville, passed away February 11, 1993 at Hillcrest Nursing Home. Survivor: Son, Billy Raley of Maynardville; two grandchildren, Karen Nicely, Billy L Raley Jr.; toe great-grandchildren; brothers, Lloyd Russell, Milburn Russell of Sharps Chapel.

Funeral Service was at Ailor Mortuary Chapel, Rev. Dewey Raley and Rev. Clyde Gideon officating. Interment at Milan Cemetery.

RUSSELL, SARAH JANE (DOLLIE) PIERCE -age 74 born October 26, 1918 and passed away on June 20, 1993 at LaFollett Medical Center.

Preceded in death by her parents, Thornie & Susan (Clawson) Pierce, 4 brothers Clyde, Willard, Otis and Sherman, three sisters, Trula, Hallie and Lussie. She professed faith in Christ as a young girl and remained a faithful servant to him: She was a member of Bradens Chapel Baptist Church. She is survived by, her husband, Milburn Russell; son and daughter-in-law, Billy W. and Lucille Russell; two daughters, JoAnn & Christine Russell all of Speedwell. Five grandchildren, one great-grandchild, a host of very special nieces, nephews and friends to mourn her passing.

Funeral Service was at Bradens Chapel Church, Elder J.C. Monday, Elder Jimmy Branscomb, and Elder Michael Beale officiating.

SHARP, ROSIE MAE SHOFFNER - age 78 of Sharps Chapel, passed away March 27, 1993, at Claiborne County Hospital. She was a longtime member of Oak Grove Primitive Baptist Church. Preceded in death by husband, John N. Sharp; daughter, Linda Harrell. Survivors: daughters, Lela Mae Weaver, Polly Sheckels, both of Sharps Chapel, Fay Hicks of Charlotte, N.C., Sue Bailey, of Knoxville; sons, David Sharp, George Sharp, Donald Sharp, and Lee Roy Sharp, all of Sharps Chapel; 26 grandchildren; 21 great-grandchildren; sisters, Macie Freeman, Eliza Presley, both of Sharps Chapel; brother, Dave Shoffner of Luttrell; and a host of friends and relatives.

Funeral services at Cooke Mortuary Chapel, Rev. Johnny Robinson, Rev. Greg Sharp officiating. Interment at Taylors Grove Cemetery. Pallbearers were grandsons: Pick Weaver, Roger Keller, Tim Sharp, Carl Lee Sharp, Danny Harrell, Marty Weaver.

Gone but not forgotten.

TAYLOR, LOU EMMA GRAVES - age 82 of Halls, passed away August 1, 1993 at Knoxville Convalescent Home. Member of Halls Primitive Baptist Church. Survivors: Husband, William H. (Bill) Taylor; daughter and son-in-law, Marylyn and Carroll Cate; granddaughter and husband, Pam and Dan Cosner; sister, Naomi Williams; special friend, Cecelia Turner; several nieces and nephews. Funeral service was at Rose Chapel, with Elder William Berry, Elder Parnick Shelton, Elder Charles Taylor officiating. Interment was at Lynnhurst Cemetery.

CHURCH	COUNTY	PASTOR	CLERK	ADDRESS
Black Fox	Grainger	Elder Larry Anderson	Bennie Capps-992-5571	P.O.Box 91, Maynardville, TN 37807
Braden's Chapel	Union	Elder J.C. Monday Elder LeRoy Braden, Asst.	Pam Goins Janice Bean, Asst.	Rt. 1, Box 350, LaFollette, TN.37766 Speedwell, TN 37870
Brantley's Chapel	Blount	Elder Jerry McBee	Brenda Bowers-977-6623 Gaye Lee, Asst.-448-6392	1042 Hembree Hollow Rd., Townsend, TN 37882 P.O. Box 132, Walland, TN 37886
Gethsemane	Knox	Elder Robert Walker	Tom Carmichael	729 Frank Street, Knoxville, TN 37919
Gibson Station	Lee, Va.	Elder Spurgeon Thompson	Dorothy Johnson Shirley Sandifur, Asst.	Rt. 2, Box 320, Ewing, VA 24248 Rt 1, Box 416, Harrogate, TN 37752
Halls	Knox	Elder William Berry Elder Parnick Shelton, Asst.	Alice Powers Helen Branson, Asst.	7525 Temple Acres Dr., Knoxville, TN 37938 4633 Marshall Dr., Knoxville, TN 37938
Hendrick's Chapel	Sevier	Elder Clyde Abbott, Jr.	Gearldine Abbott	1780 Alpine Drive, Sevierville, TN 37862
Lenoir City	Loudon	Elder Chester Hembree	E.H. Scarbrough-986-3027 Cheri Brown, Asst.-986-3724	270 Hickman St., Lenoir City, TN 37771 500 C. Street, Lenoir City, TN 37771
Meyers' Grove	Claiborne	Elder J. C. Monday Elder Johnny Ayers, Asst.	Wanda Cunningham-626-0271 Rosa Keck-626-7128	Rt. 2, Box 90A-1, New Tazewell, TN 37825 Rt. 2, Box 91, New Tazewell, TN 37825
Nocton	Grainger	Elder John Oliver	Caroll Oliver Mildred Oliver, Asst.	Rt. 2, Box 3480, Bean Station, TN 37708
Oak Grove	Union	Elder J. C. Monday Elder LeRoy Braden, Asst.	Betty P. Sharp Betty Shoffner, Asst	133 Grizzell Ridge Rd, Sharps Chapel, TN 37866 Ledmine Bend Rd, Sharps Chapel, TN 37866
Pleasant Hill	Claiborne	Elder William Rhymer Elder James Branscomb, Asst.	William Branscomb Oklen Edwards, Asst.	Speedwell, TN 37870 Speedwell, TN 37870
Rocky Dale	Knox	Elder Hugh Brummitt	Betty Livingston-688-2352 Saundra Boruff, Asst.-947-7384	6924 Boruff Rd, Corryton, TN 37721 6916 Weaver Rd., Knoxville, TN 37931

94ᵗʰ Minutes

POWELL VALLEY ASSOCIATION OF PRIMITIVE BAPTISTS

STATISTICAL TABLE	PRINTING MINUTES	TOTAL MEMBERSHIPS	DECEASED	RELATIONSHIP	DISMISSED BY LETTER	EXCLUDED	BAPTISM	RECEIVED BY LETTER	RESTORED	REGULAR MEETING TIME	COMMUNION TIME
Black Fox	$25.00	55	2	0	0	0	0	0	0	Sunday after Second Saturday Sunday after Fourth Saturday	Sunday following Second Saturday in June
Braden's Chapel	50.00	156	2	1	1	0	0	0	0	Every Sunday, second Saturday night	Sunday following first Saturday in July
Brantley's Chapel	100.00	131	0	3	0	3	3	0	2	Second Saturday night-every Sunday and Sunday night.	Sunday following second Saturday in July at 10:30 a.m.
Gethsemane	30.00	28	0	0	0	0	1	0	0	Second and Fourth Sunday	Fourth Sunday in May and October
Gibson Station	50.00	59	0	0	0	0	1	0	0	First Saturday night- Every Sunday and Sunday night	Sunday following first Saturday in June
Halls	100.00	103	2	0	0	0	0	0	0	Every Sunday and Sunday night	Last Sunday in April
Headrick's Chapel	25.00	103	0	0	0	0	0	0	0	First and third Sunday of each month	First Sunday in May and October 11:00 a.m.
Lenoir City	50.00	102	2	3	1	1	1	0	0	Every Sunday and Sunday night	First Sunday in May 10:45 A.M.
Myers Grove	30.00	97	1	3	0	0	3	3	0	4th Saturday night and every Sunday	Sunday following Fourth Saturday in May
Noeton	30.00	50	1	0	0	0	1	0	0	First Sunday-third Saturday and Sunday of each month	Sunday following third Saturday in May and September
Oak Grove	50.00	321	1	1	0	0	3	0	0	First Saturday night and Sunday third Sunday	Sunday following the first Saturday in May
Pleasant Hill	50.00	87	4	0	0	0	1	0	0	4th Saturday morning and Saturday night. Every Sunday and Sunday night	Sunday following the fourth Sunday in June at 10:30 a.m.
Rocky Dale	50.00	92	2	0	0	0	0	0	0	Every Sunday morning	Sunday following third Saturday in May

1994 Minutes

POWELL VALLEY ASSOCIATION
OF PRIMITIVE BAPTISTS

THE ONE HUNDRED-SEVENTY-FOURTH SESSION
OF THE POWELL VALLEY ASSOCIATION
OF PRIMITIVE BAPTIST
HELD WITH THE SISTER CHURCH AT
HALLS
KNOX COUNTY, TENNESSEE
AUGUST 19, 20, 21, , 1994
NEXT SESSION WILL BE HELD WITH
THE SISTER CHURCH AT LENOIR CITY IN
LOUDON COUNTY, TENNESSEE
TO BEGIN ON FRIDAY BEFORE THE THIRD
SATURDAY IN AUGUST, 1995 AT 10:30 A.M.
ELDER O.D. McCARTY
WILL DELIVER THE INTRODUCTORY SERMON
ELDER ROBERT WALKER
WILL BE THE ALTERNATE.

. . . .

Officers

ELDER JERRY McBEE, MODERATOR
P.O. BOX 158, LOUISVILLE, TENNESSEE 37777
PHONE 977-1788

ELDER PARNICK SHELTON, ASSISTANT MODERATOR
6001 McGINNIS ROAD, CORRYTON, TENNESSEE 37721
PHONE 687-5070

BENNIE CAPPS, CLERK
P.O. BOX 91, MAYNARDVILLE, TENNESSEE 37807
PHONE 992-5571

RINA JOHNSON, ASSISTANT CLERK
1217 BROWN SCHOOL ROAD,
MARYVILLE, TENNESSEE 37804
PHONE 983-2774

Minutes of
The One Hundred Seventy-Fourth Session

FRIDAY, AUGUST 19, 1994

The One Hundred Seventy-Fourth session of the Powell Valley Association of Primitive Baptist met with the Sister Church at Hall's in Knox County, Tenn., on August 19, 20, 21, 1994. *(On page 3 of the 1993 minutes should have read: "Held with the Sister Church at Black Fox", instead of Brantley's Chapel)*.

Brother Marvin Powers led the congregation in singing"When We All Get to Heaven", "There'll Be Joy", "Victory in Jesus" and "Blessed Assurance", the Moderator Elder Jerry McBee welcomed the congregation and pleaded for peace and love to abide through-out the entire Association and called for prayer by Elder O.C. McCarty of Pleasant Hill Church. Elder Hugh Brummitt delivered the introductory sermon from the 6th Chapter of St. John, using as his text "No man can come to Me except the Father which sent Me draw him". He was then followed by Elder O. D. McCarty who read the 2nd. chapter of Thessolonians, verse 15, and spoke on "Therefore Brethern stand fast holding the tradition which we have been taught". Both Elders brought a very uplifting and spiritual message.

After the introductory sermon, they sang a song and were dismissed in prayer by Elder Parnick Shelton. The Association was to reconvene after a 15 minute recess.

After recess, the crowd reassembled in the church. Brother Marvin Powers led the congregation in singing "Amazing Grace", and the Moderator, Elder Jerry McBee read from 106th Chapter of Psalms, verses 1 and 2 then called for prayer by Elder Richard Walker of Brantley's Chapel..

The Moderator then asked for the order of business for the following transactions:

1st: By move & second, Elder Parnick Shelton , was elected Moderator Pro-tem in the absence of Elder Larry Anderson.

2nd: Called for letters of the Sister Churches to be presented to the clerk for reading. Twelve (12) were received.

3rd: The letters were presented and read and motion approved that the delegates be seated.

4th: The Moderator called for anyone present from any of the Sister Churches not named as delegate who desired to be seated as such come forward and give the clerk their name and the name of their church. One came: Sister Karen Rhymer, of Pleasant Hill.

5th: Called for petitionary letter if there should be one. None came.

6th. Motion approved that the Association Re-Elect Elder Jerry McBee as Moderator and Elect Elder Parnick Shelton Assistant Moderator for the ensuing year.

7th: Motion approved that Brother Bennie Capps be re-elected Clerk and Brother Rina Johnson be re-elected Assistant Clerk for the ensuing year.

8th: Motion was approved that we empower Elder McBee to appoint all the committees to serve this session.

9th: The Moderator, having been empowered to do so, appointed committees as follows:

Committee on Arrangements: Brother Chester Lee Hembree
Brother Glen Walker
Brother Vance Harmon, Jr.

Committee on Preaching: Brother Robert Welch
Brother Hubert Spoon
Brother Millard Berry

Committee on Request: Elder Carroll Oliver
Brother Franklin Jones
Brother Charlie Collins

Committee on Finance: Elder Richard Walker
Brother Marvin Powers
Brother W.H. Taylor

10th: Called for the finances to be turned in to the Finance Committee.

11th: The Committees all having been appointed and accepted, the Association moved to adjourn until 10:30 Saturday morning. They sang a song and were dismissed in prayer by Elder John Oliver of Noeton.

SATURDAY, AUGUST 20, 1994

At the appointed hour of 10:30 Saturday morning and at the sound of singing, the Association reassembled. Brother Marvin Powers led the Congregation in "I'll Fly Away" and "Anywhere is Home" and "The Unclouded Day". Elder Parnick Shelton opened the service and spoke for a few minutes, then called for prayer by Elder James Henry Branscomb of Pleasant Hill. After prayer, the Moderator called the Association to order for the remainder of the business.

1st: Called for any letters from Sister Churches not received on Friday. One (1) was received.

2nd: Called for anyone from any of the churches who were present and desired to be seated as delegate to come forward and give the clerk their name and their church. Eleven came. Sisters: Aileen Watkins, Della Packett, from Lenoir City. Brothers: Glen Walker, Cyrus McBee, Brian Brantley, Sisters: Bernice McBee, Linda Weaver, Amanda Walker, Bobbie Walker, all from Brantley's Chapel. Sister Alice Harvey of Oak Grove. Brother Eddie Sharp of Halls.

3rd: Called for the report of the committee on Arrangements who submitted the following report:

REPORT ON ARRANGEMENTS:

CALL FOR ROLL CALL OF DELEGATES.

CALL FOR REPORT OF COMMITTEE ON PREACHING.

CALL FOR REPORT OF COMMITTEE ON REQUEST.

CALL FOR REPORT OF COMMITTEE ON FINANCE.

Decide how many minutes we have printed, who shall supervise the printing and delivery of the same, and what he shall be paid for this service. Which Sister Church shall host the next Association and who will preach the introductory sermon and who will be the alternate. Who will prepare the Circular Letter.

Respectfully Submitted,
Brother Vance E. Harmon, Jr.
Brother Chester Lee Hembree
Brother Glenn H. Walker

4th: Motion approved to receive the above report and release the committee.

5th: Called the roll call of delegates of all Sister Churches and check the absentees.

6th: Called for the report of the Committee on Preaching:

610

COMMITTEE ON PREACHING:

Friday night: Elder Parnick Shelton
Elder Richard Walker
Saturday morning: Elder William Berry
Elder Chester Hembree
Saturday night: Elder O.D. McCarty
Elder Jerry McBee
Sunday morning: Elder William Rhymer
Elder Spurgeon Thompson

Respectfully submitted,
Brother Millard Berry
Brother Robert V. Welch
Brother Hubert Spoon

7th: Motion approved to receive the above report and release the committee.

8th: Called for the report of the Committee on Request, which was given:

We, the Committee on Request, wish to request as follows, that we have 1,000 minutes printed and the clerk supervise the printing and distribution of same and that he receive $150.00 for his services. We also request that the next session of the Powell Valley Association be held with the Sister Church at Lenoir City in Loudon County, Tennessee, to begin on Friday before the third Saturday in August, 1995, at 10:30 A.M. and continue three days. We also request that Elder O.D. McCarty preach the introductory sermon and Elder Robert Walker be the alternate. We also request that Elder Chester Hembree write a circular letter for the minutes for 1995.

Respectfully submitted,
Elder Carroll Oliver
Brother Franklin Jones
Brother Charles Collins

9th: Motion approved to receive the above report and release the committee.

10th: Called for the report of the Committee on Finance, which submitted the following report:

Black Fox	$25.00
Braden's Chapel	50.00
Brantley's Chapel	100.00
Gethsemane	30.00
Gibson Station	50.00
Halls	100.00
Headrick's Chapel	25.00
Lenoir City	50.00
Meyers Grove	30.00
Noeton	30.00
Oak Grove	50.00
Pleasant Hill	50.00
Rocky Dale	50.00
Total Collections	640.00
Donations	20.00
	660.00
Balance in Bank	682.00
	1,342.00
Expenses for 1994	-800.00
Balance in Bank	542.00

Respectfully Submitted,
Elder Richard Walker
Brother Bill Taylor
Brother Marvin Powers

11th: Motion approved to receive the above report and release the committee.

12th: Motion approved that we grant the request of the committee and have 1,000 minutes printed and the clerk to receive $150.00 for his services.

13th: Motion approved that the next session of the Association be held with the Sister Church at Lenoir City to commence on Friday before the third Saturday in August, 1995, at 10:30 A.M.

14th: Motion approved that Elder O.D. McCarty deliver the introductory sermon and Elder Robert Walker be the alternate.

15th: Motion approved that Elder Chester Hembree write the circular letter for the 1995 Minutes.

16th: Motion approved that the churches of the Powell Valley Association extend to the church and the people of Halls our heart felt thanks and our prayers for the love, fellowship, kindness, and food while we were with you. May the Good Lord bless and keep you is our prayers.

17th: Motion approved to adjourn, trusting the Lord to permit us to meet again with the Sister Church at Lenoir City in Loudon County, Tn., on Friday before the third Saturday in August, 1995 at 10:30 A.M. Dismissed in prayer by Elder Roy Watkins.

Elder Jerry McBee, Moderator

Elder Parnick Shelton, Assistant Moderator

Brother Bennie Capps, Clerk

Brother Rina Johnson, Assistant Clerk

Special Announcements

Brantley's Chapel has their second Saturday night services at 7 P.M.; Sunday morning services at 10:30 A.M.; Sunday night services at 7 P.M. in the summer months and at 6 P.M. in the winter months.

The following churches requested the Association for 1995: Black Fox, Brantley Chapel, Halls, Lenoir City and Pleasant Hill.

Please make all contributions payable to: **Powell Valley Association.**

Dates of ordination of the following Elders:

Elder Alber Davis, May 17, 1930

Elder Hugh Brummitt, December 12, 1954

Elder James Branscomb, June 23, 1956

Elder Parnick Shelton, December 11, 1960

Elder Claude Rosson, July 4, 1964

Elder Joe Bush, April 27, 1969

Elder Bill Berry, August 27, 1972

Elder Larry Anderson, October 24, 1975

Elder Spurgeon Thompson, December 17, 1976
Elder Bill Raymer, December 17, 1976
Elder Jerry McBee, April 26, 1981
Elder Nelson Jones, July 17, 1981
Elder Chester Hembree, June 19, 1988
Elder Clyde Abbott, Sr., November 6, 1988
Elder Robert Walker, October 4, 1970
Elder John Oliver, April 15, 1972
Elder Richard Walker, March 29, 1992
Elder LeRoy Braden, October 10, 1982
Elder Doyle Ausmus, August 10, 1984
Elder J.C. Monday, February 12, 1958
Elder Clyde Abbott, Jr., July 7, 1979
Elder Roy Watkins, August , 1971

Summary

We are blessed with a fine group of ministers, as was illustrated by those who had the opportunity to preach. We regret that time will not permit more of them to preach when we meet with the Association. Brother Marvin Powers led the congregation in singing the old songs of Zion. On Friday night, Elder Richard Walker read the 19th chaper of Exodus using as his text "Moses leading the Children out of Egypt". He was followed by Elder Parnick Shelton reading from the 4th Chapter of First Timothy, verse 8, using as his text "Work out your own salvation".

On Saturday morning, Elder Chester Hembree read from the 17th chapter of Acts, verse 22, using as his text, "Going the way of God" with being a big God and little man. He was then followed by Elder William Berry who read from the 19th chapter of Revelation, first verse, using as his text "The Lord God Reigns". On Saturday night, Elder O.D. McCarty read from the 15th chapter of Saint John using as his text "Abiding in the Vine". He was followed by Elder Jerry McBee who read the 33rd chapter of Exodus, verse 18-23 using as his text "Just a Glimpse".

On Sunday morning, Elder Spurgeon Thompson read from the 22rd chapter of Revelation, verses 16-17, using as his text "Preach the followed by Elder William Rhymer reading from the 3rd chapter of St. John using as his text "Being Born Again". All of the Elders brought a very spiritual and uplifting sermons that was enjoyed by all in attendance.

Circular Letter To Powell Valley Association 1994

Unto the churches of God which make up the The Powell Valley Association of Primitive Baptist, to them that are sanctified in Christ Jesus, called to be saints, with all that in every place call upon the name of Jesus Christ our Lord, both theirs and ours: Grace be unto you, and peace, from God our Father, and from the Lord Jesus Christ.

This introduction was used by Paul when he wrote to the church at Corinth, and even today we still find comfort in his words. It is a great honour for me to write the Circular Letter to the Powell Valley Association for the 1994 minutes. I have a great love for the churches and members who make up this great association.

In my letter to you, I would like to share with you my testimony. Being not ashamed of what God has done for me. On January 12, 1969, the Lord saved my soul at the age of 10, and in the words of John Newton, "I know that it was God's Amazing Grace", that saved me that Sunday morning. On May 8, 1976, at the age of 17, I stood before my church at Brantley's Chapel and announced my calling to preach. On the 23rd day of that same month and year I delivered my first message.

Since that time there has been a lot of joy, and a lot of pain. But I look back over those 18 years of trying to stand for the Lord, and the blessings out-weigh the trials 100 to 1. On August 14, 1994, I stood and delivered a message to the church, and my topic was {I MAY NOT MAKE IT, BUT I MUST TRY}. Even now I am reminded of my favorite scripture in the Bible, Joshua 14:6-15. In verse 12, Caleb said to Joshua, "Now therefore give me this mountain". I know that there is a mountain out there for me. I only pray that God will give me the strengh to climb it {I MAY NOT MAKE IT, BUT I MUST TRY}.

I would like to dedicate this letter to one who has already made that climb, and who's memory will always be with me. My Brother and close friend in Christ, Elder Clifford Brantley.

Your Friend,
Elder Jerry T. McBee

615

Elder Larry Anderson, Rt.3, Box 314-A, Speedwell, TN 869-4635
Elder William Berry, 7607 Mayes Chapel Road, Knoxville,TN 922-9189
Elder J.H. Branscomb, Speedwell, TN 562-6361
Elder Hugh H. Brummitt, 1329 Brown Ave., Knoxville, TN 546-7700
Elder Joe Bush, 7507 Rodgers Rd, Corryton, TN 687-7018
Elder LeRoy Braden, 2305 Middlesboro, LaFollette, TN 566-4647
Elder Albert Davis, Rt. 3, Box 320 A Speedwell, Tn 869-3596
Elder Doyle Ausmus
Elder Alvin Graves, 122 Oak Wood Dr., Lenoir City, TN 986-9725
Elder Jerry McBee, Box 158, Louisville, TN 977-1788
Elder J.C. Monday, 515 Blue Spring Rd., Speedwell, TN 562-3068
Elder John Oliver, Rt 2, Box 3482, Bean Station, TN 993-2295
Elder William Rymer, P.O. Box 374, Harrogate, TN 37752 869-3092
Elder Parnick Shelton, 6001 McGinnis Rd, Corryton, TN 687-5070
Elder Spurgeon Thompson, Box 36, Shawnee, TN 869-8175
Elder Claude Rosson, Rt. 4, New Tazewell, TN 626-3168
Elder Robert Walker, Severville, TN 428-1527
Elder Clay Widner, Rt. 1, Tazewell, TN 626-3893
Elder Richard Walker, 3627 Rockford St., Rockford, TN 977-0414
Elder Chester Hembree, 3604 Rockford Street Rockford, TN 983-6526
Elder Clyde Abbott, Sr., 3840 Abbott Rd., Severville, TN 453-2329
Elder Johnny Ayers, 190 Meyers Grove Rd., New Tazewell, Tn. 626-8507
Elder Clyde Abbott, Jr., 2628 Old Whites Mill Road, Maryville, TN 37801
Elder Roy Watkins, 305 Augusta Ave., Maryville, TN 37804   981-1762

Licentiates

Brother Roscoe Branscomb, Speedwell, TN
Brother Odell Carpenter, 812 Brown School Rd., Maryville, TN 984-4352
Brother Mark Taylor, Lenoir City, TN
Brother Ray Walker, 3029 Jess Wilson Rd, #16, Sevierville, TN 37862 429-5417
Brother Lawrence Adams 810 Brown School Road, Maryville, TN 984-2970
Brother Brian D. Brantley, 3205 Mint Rd., Maryville, TN 982-8349

Elders Who Wrote the Circular Letter
and
the Church that Hosted the Association

1974 Elder Leonard White————————Lenoir City
1975 Elder Albert Davis————————Kirkwood
1976 Elder Charles Taylor————————Gibson Station
1977 Elder Johnny Atkins ————————Brantley's Chapel
1978 Elder Joe Irving————————Rocky Dale
1979 No Letter Submitted————————Oak Grove
1980 Elder Hugh Brummitt————————Black Fox
1981 Elder James Branscomb————————Pleasant Hill
1982 Elder Noble Clawson————————Lenoir City
1983 Elder J. C. Monday————————Gibson Station
1984 Elder Walter Lyons————————Brantley's Chapel
1985 Elder Parnick Shelton ————————Black Fox
1986 No Letter Submitted ————————H a l l s
1987 Elder John Oliver————————Lenoir City
1988 Elder William Berry ————————Rocky Dale
1989 Elder Claude Rosson ————————Oak Grove
1990 Elder Joe Bush ————————Pleasant Hill
1991 Elder Larry Anderson————————Gibson Station
1992 Elder Spurgeon Thompson ————Brantley's Chapel
1993 Elder William Rhymer ————————Black Fox
1994 Elder Jerry McBee————————Halls

Churches and Their Delegates

BLACK FOX: Brothers: Bennie Capps, Dale Capps. Sisters: Mary Ruth Capps, Pamela Capps.

BRADEN'S CHAPEL: Letter Received. No delegate present.

BRANTLEY'S CHAPEL: Elders: Richard Walker, Jerry McBee, Roy Watkins. Brothers: Rina Johnson, Dan Walker, David Beason, Robert Welch, Elwood Evans. Sisters: Hazel Johnson, Mildred Brantley, Blanche Welch, Mildred Evans, Shirley Beason.

GETHSEMANE: Brother: Tom Carmichael. Sister: Mary Carmichael.

GIBSON STATION: Elders: Spurgeon Thompson, William Rhymer. Brother: Franklin Jones. Sisters: Shirley Sandifur, Fannie Jones, Polly Jones, Dorothy Johnson.

HALLS: Elders: Hugh Brummitt, Parnick Shelton, William Berry. Brothers: Joe Culvahouse, Vance Harmon Jr., Vance Harmon, Sr.. Sisters: Ruby Brummitt, Wilma Shelton, Betty Culvahouse, Irene Harmon, Trula Berry, Maggie Welch, Cookie Harmon.

HEADRICK'S CHAPEL: Elders: Clyde Abbott, Sr., Robert Walker. Sisters: Gearldine Abbott, Margaret Walker.

LENIOR CITY: Elder Chester Hembree. Brothers: Chester Lee Hembree, Hubert Spoon, Tommy Scarbrough. Sisters: Edith Hembree, Annie Spoon, Nell Anderson, Marie Scarbrough.

MYER'S GROVE: Letter Received. No Delegates Listed.

NOETON: Elder: John Oliver. Brothers: Carroll Oliver, Charlie Collins. Sisters: Dora Collins, Mary Atkins.

OAK GROVE: Sisters: Alvada Dykes, Ruth Shoffner,, Monnie Rogers, Francis Eastridge.

PLEASANT HILL: Elders: O.D. McCarty, James Henry Branscomb, Albert Davis. Brothers: Millard Berry, Glenn Davis. Sisters: Helen Ruth Branscomb, Mollie McCarty, Cleo Berry.

ROCKY DALE: Brothers: Charlie Bryant, Josh Stapleton. Sisters: Myrtle Bryant, Ima Lee Stapleton, Fay Collett.

Rules of Decorum

1. The churches composing the Powell's Valley Association shall not be confined to any set rules as to specific number of Messengers they shall have in the body, but shall have the right to name in their letters as many as they choose, and in addition all orderly members of any of the churches being present be entitled to seats in the body as Messengers fo their respective churches, with all the rights and privileges of the same.

2. The Messengers thus assembled shall be denominated the Powell's Valley Primitive Baptist Church.

3. For the purpose of historical information and statistical edification, the Churches are required to state in letters, the number of members in fellowship, the number received by Baptism, by letter, by confession of Faith, the number dismissed, excluded and dead since last session; also the time of their meeting, their pastoral supply, and the amount of money contributed for ministers and other purposed together with any other information they deem appropriate for the edification of the saints and glory of God.

4. This Association shall have no power to answer queries, give advice, or dictate to the Churches in any case, or to lord it over God's heritage nor any power by which she can directly or indirectly fringe on the internal rights of the church or censure and try any church or member in reference to faith and practice and determine upon validity of gospel ordinances. These things shall rest entirely with the churches; but henceforward our annual meetings shall be only for the purpose of hearing from each other, and for the worship of God and mutual comfort and edification of the Saints. To this end we reserve the privilege annually for Friday before the Third Saturday in August and the two following days or at such other times as may be agreed upon with any church that may invite us having to protect our own standard, while in session, from heresay and disorder to recognize and invite any primitive Baptist minister or any lay brother to worship with us that may deem proper; to request the brethren of our body to visit other churches or bodies in our belief with whom we may desire to culture Christian fellowship; to publish in a minute of our proceedings.

5. Each session of the body shall have a Moderator and Clerk who shall hold office until re-elected.

6. Any order member of any church belonging to this body, when convened, being present shall be eligible to elect on as Moderator and Clerk or to sit on any committee appointed by the same.

7. In all election or questions that may be necessary to determine by vote, the vote shall be taken by churches, each church being entitled to three votes for any number less than one hundred, and one additional vote for every fifty or fraction thereof above the first hundred, but the Messengers of each church may divide their vote as they see proper.

8. All elections or questions coming to vote shall be determined by a majority vote cast, and it shall be the only duty of the minority to acquiesce in the decision thus reached.

9. If new churches desire to be admitted to this union they shall petition by letter and messengers and if voted for and recommended by one or more sister churches for her Presbytery constitutioning them, as orthodox and orderly they shall be received by the vote of the body and manifested by the Moderator giving the Messengers the right hand of fellowship.

10. Any motion or resolution clearly inconsistent with the above rules shall be promptly ruled out of order unless withdrawn by the mover.

11. Any messenger being ruled out of order by the Moderator shall have the right to appeal to the body on the question of order, and if sustained shall be allowed to proceed, but if not take his seat.

12. Our meeting being held in the name of Christ and the worship of God; each Messenger is expected to observe due and proper therein.

13. It will not be considered good for any Messenger whose name has been enrolled as

such to abruptley break off or absent himself from the Association without leave.

14. The Moderator shall be entitled to the same privilege of speech as other members provided the chair is filled.

15. The minutes of the Association shall be read and approved by the body and signed by the Moderator before adjourning.

16. The Association shall be opened and closed by prayer.

17. Amendments to these may be made at any time by a majority of the union voting by churches when they deem it necessary, provide such amendments do not compromise the sovereignty of the churches nor have tendency to give body undue power or jurisdiction over them.

Articles of Faith

Article 1. We believe in only one true living God, as He is revealed to us in the Holy Scriptures - Father, Son, and Holy Ghost.

Article 2. We believe that the Scriptures of the old and new Testaments are the words of God and the only rule of all-saving knowledge and obedience.

Article 3. We believe in the doctrine of election according to the foreknowledge of God.

Article 4. We believe in the doctrine of original sin.

Article 5. We believe in man's impotency to rescue himself from the fallen state he is in, by his own will or ability.

Article 6. We believe that sinners are justified in the sight of God only by the imputed righteousness of Jesus Christ.

Article 7. We believe the elect, according to the foreknowledge of God will be called, converted, regenerated, and sanctified by the Holy Spirit.

Article 8. We believe the saints will persevere and never fall finally away.

Article 9. We believe that baptism and the Lord's Supper are ordinances of Jesus Christ, and that true believers are the only subject of these ordinances, and that the true mode of baptism is by immersion. We believe also that feet washing is an example of Jesus Christ and should be kept by his disciples until his second coming.

Article 10. We believe in the Resurrection of the dead and the General Judgement.

Article 11. We believe that the punishment of the wicked will be everlasting and that the joys of the righteous will be eternal.

Article 12. We believe that no minister has the right to administer the ordinances, except those who have been regularly baptized and called of God, and come under the imposition of hands of the presbytery.

Ordination for Minister of Deacon

1.   Moderator of the church will call the church to order.
2.   Call for the reading of the minutes of the church authorizing the ordination.
3.   Appoint a spokesman for the church. He is to state if the church is in the same mind as when the candidate was elected.
4.   The elders are to assemble themselves together for the purpose stated. (this is done by gathering together in a room or outside).
5.   The presbyters will now organize by electing a moderator and clerk.
6.   The moderator will by consent of the presbyters assign one of its members to question the candidate, one member to give charge to the candidate, one member to give charge to the church, and one to give the ordination prayer.
7.   By motion and second by the church, the candidate will be delivered into the hands of the presbytery.
8.   The candidate for ordination must be presented by the church to the presbyters, being escorted by some suitable person.
9.   Question to the candidate on our articles of faith.
10. The charge to the candidate.
11. The charge to the church.
12. Examination of the candidate will be given by the other elders at this time, for any questions they might have concerning his experience, his call to the ministry, or his understanding of the doctrine.
13. The ordination prayer, with the laying on of the hands, by the presbyters.
14. The right hand of fellowship is extended to the newly ordained minister by the presbyters.
15. The candidate, being fully ordained, is delivered back into the hands of the church by motion and second.
16. By motion and second, the church accepts and receives the candidate as a fully ordained minister of Jesus Christ.
17. The presbyters by motion and second is now dissolved.
18. The right hand of fellowship is now extended to the newly ordained minister and his wife by the other members and friends of the church.
19. The church conference may then be adjourned and the service closed in any suitable manner.

Written in order by
Elder Jerry T. McBee

Obituaries

AUSTON, DAVID JOHNSON, age 84, of Washburn, was born September 4, 1909 and passed away November 29, 1993 at his home. He was preceeded in death by his first wife, Dosia Mae (McCollough) Johnson; sons, Oral and Dallas Johnson. He was a member, deacon, and assistant song leader of Black Fox Primitive Baptist Church. Survivors; widow, Mary (Hurst) Johnson; sons Basil Johnson, Washburn, and Robert Johnson, Bean Station; daughter, Tracy Hayes, Washburn; sisters, Hila Bullen, Washburn, and Casey Hurst, Morristown; 12 grandchildren and 14 great great grandchildren.

Funeral was at 2 p.m., December 2nd in Coffee Mortuary Chapel. Elder Larry Anderson and Elder John Robbins officiated. Burial was in McGinnis Cemetery.

BRADEN, JOHN "BRICE", age 84, of Speedwell, passed away Monday, December 20, 1993 at LaFollette Hospital.

He was a member of Pleasant Hill Baptist Church and a veteran of World War II. He was preceeded in death by his parents, Fred and Barbara (Cain) Braden; brother, Obie Braden; and sister, Tilda Braden.

Survivors: Lola (Lambert) Braden, Speedwell; daughters Patsy Proffitt, Jacksboro, and Bobbie Sue Hopper, Speedwell; brothers Arvel Braden, Speedwell; Mack Braden, Maynardville, Milton Braden, Lasalle, Mich.; sisters, Vernie Pierce, Betty Braden, and Jane Edwards, all of Speedwell; grandsons, Trevor Proffitt, Derrick Proffitt, Brian Hopper and Todd Hopper; granddaughters, Stefanie Proffitt and Amy Hopper; several nieces and nephews.

Funeral service was held Tuesday, December 21st at 8 p.m. with Elder Bill Rhymer and Elder J.C. Monday officiating. Singers were Charlotte Wilson and Vicky Edwards. Burial Wednesday December 22, at 1 p.m. in the Braden Cemetery. Pallbearers: Billy Braden, Verlin Maddox, Butch Braden, LeRoy Braden and Richard Proffitt. Reece Funeral Home & Valley Chapel was in charge.

BROCK, REBA HELEN WOLFENBARGER, age 82 years, departed this life Friday, June 24, 1994 at Fort Sanders Medical Center. She was born June 2, 1912 and was married to Everett C. Brock on April 20, 1935. She was a member of Rocky Dale Primitive

Brock, Reba Helen Wolfenbarger, continued......

Baptist Church, but had been unable to attend for some years because of arthritis. She was preceded in death by father and mother, James T. and Mary Wolfenbarger, four brothers and one sister, Survivors: husband, Everett Brock of Powell; son and daughter-in-law, Carroll and Marilyn Brock of Knoxville; three sisters - Mildred Hutchinson of Centerville, Ohio; Lorene Berry of Corryton, Tennessee; Trula Berry of Knoxville Tennessee; several nieces and nephews and a host of friends. Funeral services were held at Mynatt's Mortuary on Sunday, June 26, 1994, at 2:30 p.m., Reverend Ralph Cox, Elder H.E. Brummitt, and Elder Bill Berry officiating. Nephews were pallbearers. She was laid to rest in Greenwood Cemetery to await the resurrection morn.

Our beloved sister and loved one was such an inspiration to all her family and friends. Her sweet smile and happy disposition made everyone happy to be around her. She never complained of the pain she suffered and always made everyone happy when they visited her. We miss her so much, but we know God makes no mistakes and she is at rest from all sickness and pain in that beautiful land where we will meet again. Our loss is heaven's gain. *The Family.*

TO MY SISTER
(Reba Brock)
Her sweet voice is now silent
Her face we cannot see
But the sweet memories of her dear
face
Live in our hearts eternally
She's resting now with Jesus
All her battles are now won
She's waiting now to greet us
When Jesus calls us home
Where there'll be no more parting
No more tears will dim our eyes
We'll all be happy with Jesus
Where no one ever dies.
Trula Berry

COOK, DOTTIE LYONS, age 74, of East Knoxville, passed away early Monday, March 7, 1994, at Baptist Medical Center after a lingering illness. She was a member of Halls Primitive Baptist Church. Preceded in death by daughter, Martha Lou

Goddard. Survived by: husband of 52 years, E.P. "Jack" Cook, East Knoxville; son and daughter-in-law, Tommy and Teresa Cook, Pensacola, FL; grandchildren, Stacey Goddard, Dottie Mae Burchfield; Jennifer Cogburn, Kristina Hughes, Tori Lawton, and Tabitha Cook; several nieces and nephews and a host of friends.

Funeral services were held at 8 P.M., Wednesday, March 9, 1994 at Holly Hills South Funeral Home with Elder Bill Berry and Elder Parnick Shelton officiating. Interment was at 10 A.M., Thursday, March 10, at Holly Hills South Cemetery. Sister Dottie is sadly missed by her family and many friends. She was a blessing to all who knew her.

BRADEN, MATILDA SMITH, age 96, of Speedwell, TN, born January 28, 1898, went to be with the Lord February 16, 1994 at LaFollette Medical Center. A member of Braden's Chapel Church, she was preceded in death by her husband, Lauda Braden; parents, Josiah and Martha Clemons Smith; 14 brothers and sisters. Survivors: son, Eugene Braden, Speedwell; daughters, Lorraine Monday, Monroe, MI; Pauline Owens, Lebanon, OH; Jimmie Edwards, Speedwell; 12 grandchildren; 19 great-grandchildren.

Funeral Service was 11:00 A.M. Friday, February 18, 1994, at Braden's Chapel Baptist Church. Elder J.C. Monday and Rev. Bill Braden officiating. Interment in Braden Cemetery.

GRAVES, JESSIE LEO, age 70, of Speedwell, TN passed away Sunday, May 29, 1994 at Claiborne County Hospital.

He was a member and Deacon of Pleasant Hill Primitive Baptist Church. He was born June 27, 1923 in Speedwell, TN. A son of the late McKinley & Mossie Jones Graves. He was also preceded in death by a son Michael Graves, and a brother

Sgt. Lloyd Milton Graves. Survivors: Wife, Clayetta Leach Graves, Speedwell. Sons and daughter-in-laws, Melvin and Betty Graves of Speedwell. Leon and Rhonda Graves of Speedwell. Daughters and sons-in - laws, Judy and Stephen Dunn of Speedwell. Panela and Tim Hanyzwiski of Dayton, Ohio. Melissa Gail Graves of Speedwell. Nine grand children, four step grand children. Brothers Iverson Graves of Speedwell. Kyle Graves and wife Cheryl of Xenia, Ohio. Sister and Brother-in-law Rachael and Kelburn Edwards of Speedwell.

Funeral Services were held at 2 P.M., Wednesday at Pleasant Hill Primitive Baptist Church, with Elders Bill Rhymer, James H. Brascombe and Albert Davis preciding. Singing by Church Choir. Burial in Ausmus Cemetery.

Pallbearers: Chris Riggs, Jason Dunn, Ed Russell, Matthew Russell, Shawn Branham, John Harper.

Reece Funeral Home and Valley Chapel in charge. He is sadly missed by family and friends.

GRAVES, AVRELL HARDING, age 73, of Corryton, passed away Monday, July 11, 1994 at St. Mary's Medical Center. Preceded in death by parents, Elmer and Bessie Cardwell Graves. He was a member of Rocky Dale Primitive Baptist Church, Corryton Masonic Lodge No. 321 and a veteran of WWII. Retired from Ennis Business Forms. He is survived by wife of 47 years, Geneva Hinton Graves; sons and daughters-in-law, Michael Zane and Becky Graves, Joseph Avrell and Debbie Graves; grandsons, Kelly and wife, Micka, Kevin, Gregory; granddaugher, Casey; sisters, Lorene Hubbs, Ruth Clapp, and Alma Clapp, of Corryton, Fern Perrin of Knoxville, Betty Graves of Miami, Fla.; brother, Harry Graves of Corryton; several nieces and nephews. A masonic memorial service was held at 8:30 p.m. Wednesday at Mynatt's Chapel with funeral service following. Elder Parnick Shelton, Elder Bill Berry, and Rev. R.C. Harless officiating. Family and friends met at Rocky Dale Cemetery for interment at 11 a.m., Thursday. Military honors were provided by East Tennessee Veterans Honor Guard. Pallbearers: Marvin Boruff, Butch Chambers, Crosby Drew, Gary Davis, Bill Harless and Landon Lett. Mynatt's was in charge.

LAMBERT, ALBA CLAYTON age 76, of Speedwell, was born August 10, 1917 and passed away November 18, 1993 at Claiborne County Nursing

Home where he had resided for the past 14 years.

He was preceded in death by his parents, Pryor C. and Louvenia "Lou" (Edwards) Lambert; sister, Hettie Morgan, Cassie Braden, Marie Maddox; brother, Walter E. Lambert. He was a veteran of WWII and a member of Pleasant Hill Primitive Baptist Church.

Survivors: wife, Hazel (Graves) Lambert; sons and daughters-in-law, Earl and Peggy Lambert, all of Speedwell; daughter and son-in-law, Debbie and Ben Jolly, Tazewell; grandsons, Ronald Lambert, Justin Jolly, Brandon Lambert and Joey Lambert; sister, Mrs Brice (Lola) Braden, Speedwell, ande Mrs. Milton (Wilma) Braden, Erie, Mich.

Funeral service was at 2 p.m. Sunday November 21st ant Pleasant Hill Primitive Baptist Church with Elders William "Bill" Rhymer, James H. Branscomb, Larry Anderson and Albert Davis officiating. Singing by the church choir. Burial in the Hunter Cemetery. Pallbearers: Verlin Maddox, Vantoy Owens, Bill Braden, Condus Edwards, Kelburn Edwards, and Tom Edwards. Reece Funeral Home & Valley Chapen was in charge.

MUNCEY, LILLIE EMMA WILLIAMS, age 94, passed away November 11, 1993. She was a member of Hall's Primitive Baptist Church. Preceded in death by husband, Thomas Herman Munsey; sons, Luther A. and Edward H. Munsey; daughters, Margaret Faye Brewer and Lucille Munsey.

Survivors: son, Coile C. Munsey, Pigeon Forge; daughters, Edith Long, Pigeon Forge; Eva B. Waggoner and Linda Gail Price, Knoxville; and Ethel Collins, Corryton, TN. Funeral services were held at McCarty Funeral Home, Elder Bill Berry officiating. Interment was at Cabbage Cemetery in Granger County.

MUNSEY, VELTA D., age 92, of Tazewell, was born June 11, 1901 and passed away January 11, 1994 at Claiborne County Hospital.

She was the oldest member of Meyers Grove Primitive Baptist Church. She was the daughter of the late Tandy and Jane (Treece) Drummonds and wife of the late Anderson N. Munsey. Survivors: stepchildren, Whitt Munsey, Jack Munsey, both of New Tazewell, Lourene Munsey, Tazewell; step grandchildren, Marie Davis, Betty Davis, William Munsey, Rita Doss and Jackie Munsey; 10 great step grandchildren; three great-great step grandchildren; several nieces and nephews.

Funeral service was at 11 a.m., Friday, January 14th in the Claiborne Funeral Home Chapel with Elder J.C. Monday and Rev. Eddie Overholt officiating. Music by the Olen Brooks family. Burial was in the Drummonds Cemetery. Pallbearers: Jackie Munsey, William Munsey, Russell Munsey, Kelly Munsey, William Good, Hollis Robinson, kenneth Powell and Billy R. Russell. Claiborne Funeral Home in charge.

PERRY, HERBERT ANDREW, age 75, of Powder Springs, TN, passed away at 11:15 a.m., Wednesday, February 9th 1994 at his home. He was a member and Deacon of Black Fox Primitive Baptist Church. He was preceded in death by his parents, I.N. and Thula Perry; one infant son; and four sisters. He is survived by his wife, Nelle (Chesney) Perry of Powder Springs, sons and daughters-in-law, Alfred and Edna Perry; John and Phyllis Perry, James and Joyce Perry, all of Washburn, Fred and Lillie Perry, Kenneth and Janice Perry, and Bill Perry all of Powder Springs, Kyle Perry of Strawberry Plains; daughter and son-in-law, Dorothy and James Bowlin, of Washburn; 16 grandchildren; 17 great-grandchildren; sisters, Dorothy Wright of Ohio, Dora Donahue of Virginia, Pauline Monroe of Powder Springs. Funeral services were at 2 p.m. Saturday at Ailor's Chapel with Rev. Dennis Johnson and Rev. Willy Nicely officiating. Interment in Cabbage Cemetery. Pallbearers: Jim Greene, Lonnie Bates, Gary Wood, Ralph Bolin, Kermit Carpenter and David Perry. Singers were Florsie and Willard Nicely and Billy Joe and Shirley Nicely. Aiilors Mortuary in charge.

POWERS, ALICE T., age 63, of Halls, passed away Friday, September 24, 1993, at St. Mary's Hospital. She was a member of Halls Primitive Baptist Church. Survivors: husband, Marvin Powers; son, Jeff Powers; daughter and son-in-law, Amy and Rodney Patton; grandchildren, Erica and Whitney Patton, all of Knoxville. Funeral services were held at 2:30 p.m. Sunday, September 26th , at Berry's Chapel, Elder William Berry and Elder Parnick Shelton, officiating. Interment was at Mt. Olive Cemetery.

What words could be found to pay tribute to someone as special as Alice? She exemplified love, faith, and courage in all she did. Singing praises to God when it was so difficult to breath was evidence of her faith and trust in the Lord. We miss her deeply and can only say, "Thank you, God, for al-

lowing her to touch our lives."

RAY, LOCIA MARIE, age 49, of Ray Lane, Sharps Chapel passed away suddenly Sunday morning, March 20th 1994 at her home. She was a member of Oak Grove Primitive Baptist Church. Survivors: husband, Glen Ray; daughters, Anita Louise Ray, Elizabeth Ray, Sandy Michelle Ray, all of Sharps Chapel; sons, Harold Ray of New Tazewell, Darrell Ray of Sharps Chapel; grandchildren, Beverly LeAnn Ray, Bradley Leon Ray, Anthony Andrew Ray; brothers, Everett Wilder of Kansas City, Kansas, Jim Wilder, Tip Wilder, and Chester Wilder, all of Sharps Chapel; several nieces and nephews. Funeral services were at 2 p.m., Wednesday, Oak Grove Primitive Baptist Church, Rev, Johnny Robinson, Rev. Hobart Bailey, Rev. Greg Sharp officiating. Interment Oak Grove Cemetery. Pallbearers: Eugene Holt, Troy Ray, Rick Ray, Leroy Ray, David Ray and Larry McDaniels. The family received friends 7-9 p.m. Tuesday at Cooke Mortuary, Maynardville.

STEWART, ROBERT E. "BUCK", age 75, Straight Branch Road, Speedwell, TN, died Friday, June 3, 1994, at his home.

Born August 6, 1919, in Shelby County, he was the son of Lloyd and Hazel Marie Wooley Stewart. He was married to the former Elizabeth Cox. She survives. Also surviving are a son, Robert Stewart Jr. of Sidney; four daughters, Linda Wade of Sidney, Barbara Conroy of Lakeview; Betty Hatfield of LaFollette, TN, and Mary Murphy of Speedwell, TN.; 14 grandchildren; seven great-grandchildren; a brother, James F. Stewart of Lakeview; and a sister, Beatrice Cox of Powell.

A brother preceded him in death. Funeral services were held Monday at 11 a.m. at the funeral home with the Rev. Norman A. Voltz officiating. Burial was at Fairview Cemetery in Quincy.

The Martin Funeral Home of LaFollette, TN was in charge of arrangements in Tennessee.

CHURCH	COUNTY	PASTOR	CLERK	ADDRESS
Black Fox	Grainger	Elder Larry Anderson	Bennie Capps-992-5571	P.O.Box 91, Maynardville, TN 37807
Braden's Chapel	Union	Elder J.C. Monday	Pam Goins	Rt. 1, Box 350, LaFollette, TN.37766
			Janice Bean, Asst.	Speedwell, TN 37870
Brantley's Chapel	Blount	Elder Jerry McBee	Brenda Beason-982-9426	1445 E. Brown School Rd. Maryville, TN 37804
		Elder Richard Walker, Asst.	Vanessa McBee, Asst.-977-1788	3009 Johnston Rd., Louisville, TN 37777
Gethsemane	Knox	Elder Robert Walker	Tom Carmichael	729 Frank Street, Knoxville, TN 37919
Gibson Station	Lee, Va.	Elder Spurgeon Thompson	Dorothy Johnson	Rt. 2, Box 320, Ewing, VA 24248
			Shirley Sandifur, Asst.	Rt 1, Box 416, Harrogate, TN 37752
Halls	Knox	Elder William Berry	Helen Branson	4633 Marshall Dr., Knoxville, TN 37938
		Elder Parnick Shelton, Asst.	Amy Patton, Asst.	4225 Inisbrook Way, Knoxville, TN 37838
Headrick's Chapel	Sevier	Elder Clyde Abbott, Jr.	Gearldine Abbott	1780 Alpine Drive, Sevierville, TN 37862
Lenoir City	Loudon	Elder Chester Hembree	E.H. Scarbrough-986-3027	270 Hickman St, Lenoir City, TN 37771
			Cheri Brown, Asst.-986-3724	500 C. Street, Lenoir City, TN 37771
Meyers' Grove	Claiborne	Elder Johnny Ayers	Betty Robinson, Asst. 626-4118	530 Cupp Ridge Road, New Tazewell, TN 37825
Noeton	Grainger	Elder John Oliver	Caroll Oliver	Rt. 2, Box 3480, Bean Station, TN 37708
			Mildred Oliver, Asst.	
Oak Grove	Union	Elder J. C. Monday	Betty P. Sharp	133 Grizzell Ridge Rd., Sharps Chapel, TN 37866
		Elder LeRoy Braden, Asst.	Betty Shoffner, Asst	644 Ledmine Bend Rd, Sharps Chapel, TN 37866
Pleasant Hill	Claiborne	Elder William Rhymer	William Branscomb	Rt. I, Russell Lane, Speedwell, TN 37870
		Elder James Branscomb, Asst.	Oklen Edwards, Asst.	Speedwell, TN 37870
Rocky Dale	Knox	Elder Hugh Brummitt	Betty Livingston-688-2352	6924 Boruff Rd, Corryton, TN 37721
			Saundra Boruff, Asst.-947-7384	6916 Weaver Rd., Knoxville, TN 37931

POWELL VALLEY ASSOCIATION OF PRIMITIVE BAPTISTS

STATISTICAL TABLE	RESTORED	RECEIVED BY LETTER	BAPTISM	EXCLUDED	DISMISSED BY LETTER	RELATIONSHIP	DECEASED	TOTAL MEMBERSHIPS	PRINTING MINUTES	REGULAR MEETING TIME	COMMUNION TIME
Black Fox	0	0	0	2	0	0	1	52	$25.00	Sunday after Second Saturday Sunday after Fourth Saturday	Sunday following Second Saturday in June
Braden's Chapel	0	0	2	1	1	2	2	155	50.00	Every Sunday, second Saturday night	Sunday following first Saturday in July
Brantley's Chapel	0	0	8	3	0	4	1	139	100.00	Second Saturday night-every Sunday and Sunday night.	Sunday following second Saturday in July at 10:30 a.m. Fourth Sunday in Jan.
Gethsemane	0	0	0	0	0	0	0	28	35.00	Second and Fourth Sunday	Fourth Sunday in May and October
Gibson Station	0	0	2	0	0	2	2	61	50.00	First Saturday night- Every Sunday and Sunday night	Sunday following first Saturday in June
Halls	0	0	1	0	0	0	7	97	100.00	Every Sunday and Sunday night	Last Sunday in April
Headrick's Chapel	0	0	0	0	0	0	1	102	40.00	First and third Sunday of each month	First Sunday in May and October 11:00 a.m.
Lenoir City	0	0	1	0	2	0	0	101	50.00	Every Sunday and Sunday night	First Sunday in May 10:45 A.M.
Myers Grove	0	2	0	0	2	0	2	95	30.00	4th Saturday night and every Sunday	Sunday following Fourth Saturday in May
Noeton	0	0	0	0	0	0	3	47	30.00	First Sunday-third Saturday and Sunday of each month	Sunday following third Saturday in May and September
Oak Grove	0	0	1	0	1	0	1	320	50.00	First Saturday night and Sunday third Sunday	Sunday following the first Saturday in May
Pleasant Hill	0	0	0	1	0	0	2	85	50.00	4th Saturday morning and Saturday night. Every Sunday and Sunday night	Sunday following the fourth Sunday in June at 10:30 a.m.
Rocky Dale	0	0	0	0	0	0	0	91	50.00	Every Sunday morning	Sunday following third Saturday in May

1995 Minutes

POWELL VALLEY ASSOCIATION
OF PRIMITIVE BAPTISTS

THE ONE HUNDRED-SEVENTY-FIFTH SESSION
OF THE POWELL VALLEY ASSOCIATION
OF PRIMITIVE BAPTIST
HELD WITH THE SISTER CHURCH AT
LENOIR CITY
LOUDON COUNTY, TENNESSEE
AUGUST 18, 19, 20, 1995
NEXT SESSION WILL BE HELD WITH
THE SISTER CHURCH AT ROCKY DALE IN
KNOX COUNTY, TENNESSEE
TO BEGIN ON FRIDAY BEFORE THE THIRD
SATURDAY IN AUGUST, 1996 AT 10:30 A.M.
ELDER ROBERT WALKER
WILL DELIVER THE INTRODUCTORY SERMON
ELDER SPURGEON THOMPSON
WILL BE THE ALTERNATE.

• • • • • • •

Officers

ELDER JERRY McBEE, MODERATOR
P.O. BOX 158, LOUISVILLE, TENNESSEE 37777
PHONE 977-1788

ELDER PARNICK SHELTON, ASSISTANT MODERATOR
6001 McGINNIS ROAD, CORRYTON, TENNESSEE 37721
PHONE 687-5070

BENNIE CAPPS, CLERK
P.O. BOX 91, MAYNARDVILLE, TENNESSEE 37807
PHONE 992-5571

RINA JOHNSON, ASSISTANT CLERK
1217 BROWN SCHOOL ROAD,
MARYVILLE, TENNESSEE 37804
PHONE 983-2774

Minutes of
The One Hundred Seventy-Fifth Session

FRIDAY, AUGUST 18, 1995

The One Hundred Seventy-Fifth session of the Powell Valley Association of Primitive Baptist met with the Sister Church at Lenoir City in Loudon County, Tenn., on August 18, 19, 20, 1995. Brother Ronnie Parris led the congregation in singing "Stand Up for Jesus". "Glory to His Name", "Leaning on the Everlasting Arms", and "Knell at the Cross", then Moderator Elder Jerry McBee welcomed the congregation and pleaded for peace and love to abide through out the entire association and called for prayer by Elder Larry Anderson of Pleasant Hill Church. Elder O. D. McCarty delivered the introductory sermon from the 2nd Chapter of Acts " being in one accord", using as his text "Stand up for Jesus". He brought a very uplifting and spiritual message. Elder Robert Walker was to be the alternate but was absent due to illness.

After the introductory sermon, the congregation sang a song and were dismissed in prayer by Elder William Berry. The association was to reconvene after a 15 minute recess.

After recess, the crowd reassembled in the church. Brother Ronnie Parris led the congregation in "I Know Who Holds Tomorrow", and the Moderator Elder Jerry McBee read from the 4th Chapter of Matthew, verse 18, then called for prayer by Elder Chester Hembree.

The Moderator then asked for the order of business for the following transactions:

1st: Called for letters of the Sister Churches to be presented to the clerk for reading. ELEVEN(11) were received.

2nd: The letters were presented and read and motion approved that the delegates be seated.

3rd: The Moderator called for anyone present from any of the Sister Churches not named as delegate who desired to be seated as such come forward and give the clerk their name and the name of their church. One came: Brother Coram Berry of Brantley's Chapel.

4th: Called for petitionary letter if there should be one. None came.

5th. Motion approved that the Association Re-Elect Elder Jerry McBee

633

as Moderator and Re-Elect Elder Parnick Shelton Assistant Moderator for the ensuing year.

6th: Motion and second Brother Bennie Capps be re-elected Clerk and Brother Don Sharp be elected Assistant Clerk. (Due to the misunderstanding, this motion and second was withdrawn.)

7th: Motion approved that Brother Bennie Capps be re-elected Clerk and Brother Rina Johnson be re-elected Assistant Clerk for the ensuing year.

8th: Motion was approved that we empower Elder McBee to appoint all the committees to serve this session.

9th: The Moderator, having been empowered to do so, appointed committees as follows:

Committee on Arrangements: Brother Chester Lee Hembree
Brother Don Sharp
Brother Robert Welch
Committee on Preaching: Brother Ron Parris
Brother Vance Harmon,Sr.
Brother Daniel Brantley
Committee on Request: Brother Joe Culvahouse
Brother Hubert Spoon
Brother Tommy Scarbrough
Committee on Finance: Brother Nathaniel McBee
Elder Spurgeon Thompson
Brother Elwood Evans

10th: Called for the finances to be turned in to the Finance Committee.

11th: By move and second, the above minutes were approved as read.

12th: The Committees all having been appointed and accepted, the Association moved to adjourn until 10:30 Saturday morning. They sang a song and were dismissed in prayer by Elder Albert Davis of Pleasant Hill.

SATURDAY, AUGUST 19, 1995

At the appointed hour of 10:30 Saturday morning and at the sound of singing, the Association reassembled. Elder Jerry McBee led the Congregation in "Trust and Obey" and "Near the Cross". Elder Parnick Shelton opened the service and spoke for a few minutes, then called for prayer by Elder John Oliver of Noeton. After prayer, the Moderator called the Association to order for the remainder of the business.

1st: Called for any letters from Sister Churches not received on Friday. Two (2) were received.

2nd: The letters were presented and read, and the motion approved that the delegates be seated.

3rd: Called for anyone from any of the churches who were present and desired to be seated as delegate to come forward and give the clerk their name and their church. There were none.

4th: Called for the report of the committee on Arrangements who submitted the following report:

REPORT ON ARRANGEMENTS:

CALL FOR ROLL CALL OF DELEGATES.
CALL FOR REPORT OF COMMITTEE ON PREACHING.
CALL FOR REPORT OF COMMITTEE ON REQUEST.
CALL FOR REPORT OF COMMITTEE ON FINANCE.

Decide how many minutes we have printed, who shall supervise the printing and delivery of the same, and what he shall be paid for this service. Which Sister Church shall host the next Association and who will preach the introductory sermon and who will be the alternate. Who will prepare the Circular Letter.

Respectfully Submitted,
Brother Don Sharp
Brother Chester Lee Hembree
Brother Robert V. Welch

5th: Motion approved to receive the above report and release the committee.

6th: Called the roll call of delegates of all Sister Churches and check the absentees.

7th: Called for the report of the Committee on Preaching:

COMMITTEE ON PREACHING:

Friday night: Elder Bill Berry
Elder Chester Hembree
Saturday morning: Elder Hugh Brummitt
Elder Larry Anderson
Saturday night: Elder Mike Brantley
Brother Brian Brantley

Sunday morning: Elder Spurgeon Thompson
Elder Richard Walker

Respectfully submitted,
Brother Ron Parris
Brother Vance Harmon,Sr.
Brother Daniel Brantley

8th: Motion approved to receive the above report and release the committee.

9th: Called for the report of the Committee on Request, which was given: We, the Committee on Request, wish to request as follows, that we have 1,000 minutes printed and the clerk supervise the printing and distribution of same and that he receive $150.00 for his services. We also request that the next session of the Powell Valley Association be held with the Sister Church at Rocky Dale in Knox County, Tennessee, to begin on Friday before the third Saturday in August, 1996, at 10:30 A.M. and continue three days. We also request that Elder Robert Walker preach the introductory sermon and Elder Spurgeon Thompson be the alternate. We also request that Elder Hugh Brummitt write a circular letter for the minutes for 1996.

Respectfully submitted,
Brother Joe Culvahouse
Brother Hubert Spoon
Brother Tommy Scarbrough

10th: Motion approved to receive the above report and release the committee.

11th: Called for the report of the Committee on Finance, which submitted the following report:

Black Fox $25.00
Braden's Chapel................... 50.00
Brantley's Chapel 100.00
Gethsemane 35.00
Gibson Station 50.00
Halls 100.00
Headrick's Chapel 40.00

Lenoir City 50.00
Meyers Grove........................30.00
Noeton 30.00
Oak Grove 50.00
Pleasant Hill 50.00
Rocky Dale........................... 50.00
Total Collections............................. 660.00
Donations ....
Monroe Primitive Baptist Church.............. 20.00
.... 680.00
Balance in Bank.................. 542.00
.... 1,222.00
Expenses for 1995............. -850.00
Balance in Bank.............................$ 372.00

Respectfully Submitted,
Elder Spurgeon Thompson
Brother Nathaniel McBee
Brother Elwood Evans

12th: Motion approved to receive the above report and release the committee.

13th: Motion approved that we grant the request of the committee and have 1,000 minutes printed and the clerk to receive $150.00 for his services.

14th: Motion approved that the next session of the Association be held with the Sister Church at Rocky Dale to commence on Friday before the third Saturday in August, 1996, at 10:30 A.M.

15th: Motion approved that Elder Robert Walker deliver the introductory sermon and Elder Spurgeon Thompson be the alternate.

16th: Motion approved that Elder Hugh Brummitt write the circular letter for the 1996 Minutes.

17th: Motion approved that the churches of the Powell Valley Association extend to the church and the people of Lenoir City our heart felt thanks and our prayers for the love, fellowship, kindness, and food while we were with you. May the Good Lord bless and keep you is our prayers.

18th:By move and second , the above minutes were approved as read.
19th: Motion approved to adjourn, trusting the Lord to permit us to meet again with the Sister Church at Rocky Dale in Knox County, Tn., on Friday before the third Saturday in August, 1996 at 10:30 A.M. Dismissed in prayer by Elder Robert Walker.

Elder Jerry McBee, Moderator
Elder Parnick Shelton, Assistant Moderator
Brother Bennie Capps, Clerk
Brother Rina Johnson, Assistant Clerk

Special Announcements

Brantley's Chapel has their second Saturday night services at 7 P.M.; Sunday morning services at 10:30 A.M.; Sunday night services at 7 P.M. in the summer months and at 6 P.M. in the winter months.
The following churches requested the Association for 1996: Black Fox, Brantley Chapel, Halls, Lenoir City , Pleasant Hill and Rocky Dale.
Please make all contributions payable to: **Powell Valley Association.**
To those who mail their letters, please mail to clerk of the association.

Dates of Ordination of the Following Elders:

Elder Alber Davis, May 17, 1930
Elder Hugh Brummitt, December 12, 1954
Elder James Branscomb, June 23, 1956
Elder Parnick Shelton, December 11, 1960
Elder Claude Rosson, July 4, 1964
Elder Joe Bush, April 27, 1969
Elder Bill Berry, August 27, 1972
Elder Larry Anderson, October 24, 1975
Elder Spurgeon Thompson, December 17, 1976
Elder Bill Rhymer, December 17, 1976
Elder Jerry McBee, April 26, 1981
Elder Nelson Jones, July 17, 1981

Elder Chester Hembree, June 19, 1988
Elder Clyde Abbott, Sr., November 6, 1988
Elder Robert Walker, October 4, 1970
Elder John Oliver, April 15, 1972
Elder Richard Walker, March 29, 1992
Elder LeRoy Braden, October 10, 1982
Elder Doyle Ausmus, August 10, 1984
Elder J.C. Monday, February 12, 1958
Elder Clyde Abbott, Jr., July 7, 1979
Elder Roy Watkins, August , 1971
Elder O.D. McCarty, March , 1993
Elder Michael Brantley, April 23, 1995

Summary

We are blessed with a fine group of ministers, as was illustrated by those

who had the opportunity to preach. We regret that time will not permit more of them to preach when we meet with the Association.

Brother Ronnie Parris led the congregation in the old songs of Zion. On Friday night, Elder Bill Berry and Elder Chester Hembree brought the message.

On Saturday morning Elder Larry Anderson spoke from the 11th Chapter of Hebrews, verse 1 and 16, using as his text "Being in the Center of God's Will". He was followed by Elder Hugh Brummitt reading from the 26th Chapter of Acts, verse 2, and using as his text "Glorify Our Father".

The Saturday night message was brought by Elder Michael Brantley and Brother Brian Brantley.

On Sunday morning, Elder Richard Walker read from the 4th chapter of Deuteronomy, Verse 24, using as his text "For the Lord thy God is a consuming fire, even a jealous God" He was followed by Elder Spurgeon Thompson who read from First Corinthians, 2nd Chapter, 2nd verse, using as his text "I am Determined".

All of the Elders preached very uplifting and spiritual sermons.

Circular Letter
To Powell Valley Association
1995

To the churches that make up the Powell Valley Association, I send you greetings in the name of the Lord and Savior Jesus Christ.

The honor of writing this letter to the Association, is one of the greatest honors that has ever been given to me.

Paul wrote in one of his letters that we are in constant warfare, it seems that there are times that the war between the flesh and the spirit gets stronger and stronger the older we get, it is then at these times that we realize that the only way we can win this war is to turn back to the one who gives us the strength to fight this war.

We often hear that doctrine will kill the church, but if we do not teach the doctrine which is **" THE TRUTH OF THE SAVING POWER OF JESUS CHRIST"** then we can look for our Association to grow weaker and weaker.

Paul said to "Preach Christ and Him Crucified", this is what we must stand on if we expect to grow stronger. This is meat that we can grow on.

May God Bless You Is My Prayer,

Elder Chester Hembree

Ministers Directory

Elder Larry Anderson, Rt.3, Box 314-A, Speedwell, TN 869-4635
Elder William Berry, 7607 Mayes Chapel Rd, Knoxville,TN 922-9189
Elder J.H. Branscomb, Speedwell, TN 562-6361
Elder Hugh H. Brummitt, 1329 Brown Ave., Knoxville, TN 546-7700
Elder Joe Bush, 7507 Rodgers Rd, Corryton, TN 687-7018
Elder LeRoy Braden, 2305 Middlesboro, LaFollette, TN 566-4647
Elder Albert Davis, Rt. 3, Box 320 A Speedwell, Tn 869-3596
Elder Doyle Ausmus
Elder Alvin Graves, 122 Oak Wood Dr., Lenoir City, TN 986-9725
Elder Jerry McBee, Box 158, Louisville, TN 977-1788
Elder J.C. Monday, 515 Blue Spring Rd., Speedwell, TN 562-3068
Elder John Oliver, Rt 2, Box 3482, Bean Station, TN 993-2295
Elder William Rhymer, P.O. Box 374, Harrogate, TN 37752 869-3092
Elder Parnick Shelton, 6001 McGinnis Rd, Corryton, TN 687-5070
Elder Spurgeon Thompson, Box 36, Shawnee, TN 869-8175
Elder Claude Rosson, Rt. 4, New Tazewell, TN 626-3168
Elder Robert Walker, Severville, TN 428-1527
Elder Clay Widner, Rt. 1, Tazewell, TN 626-3893
Elder Richard Walker, 3627 Rockford St., Rockford, TN 977-0414
Elder Chester Hembree, 3604 Rockford Street Rockford, TN 983-6526
Elder Clyde Abbott, Sr., 3840 Abbott Rd., Severville, TN 453-2329
Elder Johnny Ayers, 190 Meyers Grove Rd., New Tazewell, TN 626-8507
Elder Clyde Abbott, Jr., 2628 Old Whites Mill Road, Maryville, TN 37801
Elder Roy Watkins, 305 Augusta Ave., Maryville, TN 37804 981-1762
Elder O.D. McCarty Rt.5 Box 2100 LaFollette ,TN 37766 562-3850

Licentiates

Brother Roscoe Branscomb, Speedwell, TN
Brother Odell Carpenter, 812 Brown School Rd., Maryville, TN 984-4352
Brother Mark Taylor, Lenoir City, TN
Brother Ray Walker, 3029 Jess Wilson Rd, #16, Sevierville, TN 37862 429-5417
Brother Lawrence Adams 810 Brown School Road, Maryville, TN 984-2970
Brother Brain D.Brantley 806 Brown School Road MaryvilleTN984-3459

Elders Who Wrote the Circular Letter
and
the Church that Hosted the Association

1974 Elder Leonard White ----------------------------------Lenoir City
1975 Elder Albert Davis--Kirkwood
1976 Elder Charles Taylor --------------------------------Gibson Station
1977 Elder Johnny Atkins----------------------------Brantley's Chapel
1978 Elder Joe Irving --------------------------------------Rocky Dale
1979 No Letter Submitted ----------------------------------Oak Grove
1980 Elder Hugh Brummitt ----------------------------------Black Fox
1981 Elder James Branscomb----------------------------Pleasant Hill
1982 Elder Noble Clawson ----------------------------------Lenoir City
1983 Elder J. C. Monday ----------------------------------Gibson Station
1984 Elder Walter Lyons ----------------------------Brantley's Chapel
1985 Elder Parnick Shelton ----------------------------------Black Fox
1986 No Letter Submitted --------------------------------------Halls
1987 Elder John Oliver ------------------------------------Lenoir City
1988 Elder William Berry --------------------------------Rocky Dale
1989 Elder Claude Rosson ------------------------------Oak Grove
1990 Elder Joe Bush --Pleasant Hill
1991 Elder Larry Anderson ----------------------------Gibson Station
1992 Elder Spurgeon Thompson --------------------Brantley's Chapel
1993 Elder William Rhymer----------------------------------Black Fox
1994 Elder Jerry McBee--Halls
1995 Elder Chester Hembree--------------------------------Lenoir City

Churches
and Their Delegates

BLACK FOX: Brothers: Bennie Capps, Dale Capps. Sisters: Mary Ruth Capps, Pamela Capps.

BRADEN'S CHAPEL: Letter Received. No delegate listed.

BRANTLEY'S CHAPEL: Elders:Jerry McBee, Richard Walker, Michael Brantley. Brothers: Daniel Brantley,Brian Brantley, Everett Brantley, David Beason, Rina Johnson,Robert Welch, Elwood Evans, Cyrus McBee,Glenn Walker, Nathanael McBee. Sisters:Shirley Beason, Blanch Welch, Burnice McBee, Carol Wright, Linda Brantley, Mildred Evans, Hazel Johnson, Mildred Brantley.

GETHSEMANE: Brother: Tom Carmichael. Sister: Mary Carmichael.

GIBSON STATION: Elders: Spurgeon Thompson. Brother:Doyle Bolton. Sisters: Dorothy Johnson, Virginia Bolton

HALLS: Elders: Hugh Brummitt, Parnick Shelton, William Berry. Brothers: Joe Culvahouse,Vance Harmon,Sr.. Sisters: Ruby Brummitt, Betty Culvahouse, Irene Harmon.

HEADRICK'S CHAPEL: Elders: Clyde Abbott, Sr., Robert Walker. Sisters: Gearldine Abbott, Margaret Walker.

LENIOR CITY: Elder: Chester Hembree. Brothers: Chester Lee Hembree, Hubert Spoon, Ron Parris, E. H. Scarbrough. Sister: Edith Hembree, Annie Spoons, Aileen Watkins, Della Packett, Thelma Brown, Cheri Brown, Cindy Hembree, Silver Parris, Marie Scarbrough, Dorothy Lowe.

MYER'S GROVE: Letter Received. No Delegates Listed.

NOETON: Elder John Oliver. Borhter: Carroll Oliver.

OAK GROVE: Sister: Francis Eastridge

PLEASANT HILL: Elders: O.D. McCarty, Larry Anderson, Albert Davis. Sisters: Mollie McCarty,Audra Davis, Myra Anderson

ROCKY DALE: Brothers: Charlie Bryant, Don Sharp, Glen Johnson James Boruff. Sisters: Myrtle Bryant, Saundra Boruff, Fay Collett.

Rules of Decorum

1.   The churches composing the Powell's Valley Association shall not be confined to any set rules as to specific number of Messengers they shall have in the body, but shall have the right to name in their letters as many as they choose, and in addition all orderly members of any of the churches being present be entitled to seats in the body as Messengers of their respective churches, with all the rights and privileges of the same.

2.   The Messengers thus assembled shall be denominated the Powell's Valley Primitive Baptist Church.

3.   For the purpose of historical information and statistical edification, the Churches are required to state in letters, the number of members in fellowship, the number received by Baptism, by letter, by confession of Faith, the number dismissed, excluded and dead since last session; also the time of their meeting, their pastoral supply, and the amount of money contributed for ministers and other purposed together with any other information they deem appropriate for the edification of the saints and glory of God.

4.   This Association shall have no power to answer queries, give advice, or dictate to the Churches in any case, or to lord it over God's heritage nor any power by which she can directly or indirectly fringe on the internal rights of the church or censure and try any church or member in reference to faith and practice and determine upon validity of gospel ordinances. These things shall rest entirely with the churches; but henceforeward our annual meetings shall be only for the purpose of hearing from each other, and for the worship of God and mutual comfort and edification of the Saints. To this end we reserve the privilege annually for Friday before the Third Saturday in August and the two following days or at such times as may be agreed upon with any church that may invite us, having to protect our own standard, while in session, from heresay and disorder to recognize and invite any Primitive Baptist minister or any lay brother to worship with us that may deem proper; to request the brethren of our body to visit other churches or bodies in our belief with whom we may desire to culture Christian fellowship; to publish the minutes of our proceedings.

5.   Each session of the body shall have a Moderator and Clerk who shall hold office until re-elected.

6.   Any order member of any church belonging to this body, when convened, being present shall be eligible to election as Moderator and Clerk or to sit on any committee appointed by the same.

7.   In all election or questions that may be necessary to determine by vote, the vote shall be taken by churches, each church being entitled to three votes for any number less than one-hundred, and one additional vote for every fifty of fraction thereof above the first hundred, but the Messengers of each church may divide their vote as they see proper.

8.   All elections or questions coming to vote shall be determined by a majority vote cast, and it shall be the only duty of the minority to acquiesce in the decision thus reached.

9.   If new churches desire to be admitted to this union they shall petition by letter and messengers and if voted for and recommended by one or more sister churches for her Presbytery constitutioning them, as orthodox and orderly they shall be received by the vote of the body and manifested by the Moderator giving the Messengers the right hand of fellowship.

10.   Any motion or resolution clearly inconsistent with the above rules shall be promptly ruled out of order unless withdrawn by the mover.

11.   Any messenger being ruled out of order by the Moderator shall have the right to appeal to the body on the question of order, and if sustained shall be allowed to proceed, but if not take his seat.

12.   Our meeting being held in the name of Christ and the worship of God; each Messenger is expected to observe due and proper therein.

13.   It will not be considered good for any Messenger whose name has been enrolled as such to abruptly break off or absent himself from the Association without leave.

14.   The Moderator shall be entitled to the same privilege of speech as other members

provided the chair is filled.

15.   The minutes of the Association shall be read and approved by the body and signed by the Moderator before adjourning.

16.   The Association shall be opened and closed by prayer.

17.   Amendments to these may be made at any time by a majority of the union voting by churches when they deem it necessary, provide such amendments do not compromise the sovereignty of the churches nor have a tendency to give body undue power or jurisdiction over them.

Articles of Faith

Article 1.   We believe in only one true living God, as He is revealed to us in the Holy Scriptures - Father, Son and Holy Ghost.

Article 2.   We believe that the Scriptures of the old and new Testaments are the words of God and the only rule of all-saving knowledge and obedience.

Article 3.   We believe in the doctrine of election according to the foreknowledge of God.

Article 4.   We believe in the doctrine of original sin.

Article 5.   We believe in man's impotency to rescue himself from the fallen state he is in, by his own will or ability.

Article 6.   We believe that sinners are justified in the sight of God only by the imputed righteousness of Jesus Christ.

Article 7   We believe the elect, according to the foreknowledge of God will be called, converted, regenerated, and sanctified by the Holy Spirit.

Article 8.   We believe the saints will persevere and never fall finally away.

Article 9.   We believe that baptism and the Lord's Supper are ordinances of Jesus Christ, and that the true believers are the only subject of these ordinances, and that the true mode of baptism is by immersion. We believe also that feet washing is an example of Jesus Christ and should be kept by his disciples until his second coming.

Article 10.   We believe in the Resurrection of the dead and the General Judgement.

Article 11.   We believe that the punishment of the wicked will be everlasting and that the joys of the righteous will be eternal.

Article 12.   We believe that no minister has the right to administer the ordinances, except those who have been regularly baptised and called of God, and come under the imposition of hands of the presbytery.

Ordination for Minister or Deacon

1. Moderator of the church will call the church to order.
2. Call for the reading of the minutes of the church authorizing the ordination.
3. Appoint a spokesman for the church. He is to state if the church is in the same mind as when the candidate was elected.
4. The elders are to assemble themselves together for the purpose stated. (this is done by gathering together in a room or outside).
5. The presbyters will now organize by electing a moderator and clerk.
6. The moderator will by consent of the presbyters assign one of its members to question the candidate, one member to give charge to the candidate, one member to give charge to the church, and one to give the ordination prayer.
7. By motion and second by the church, the candidate will be delivered into the hands of the presbytery.
8. The candidate for ordination must be presented by the church to the presbyters, being escorted by a suitable person.
9. Question to the candidate on our articles of faith.
10. The charge to the candidate.
11. The charge to the church.
12. Examination of the candidate will be given by the other elders at this time, for any questions they might have concerning his experience, his call to the ministry, or his understanding of the doctrine.
13. The ordination prayer, with the laying on of the hands, by the presbyters.
14. The right hand of fellowship is extended to the newly ordained minister by the presbyters.
15. The candidate, being fully ordained, is delivered back into the hands of the church by motion and second.
16. By motion and second, the church accepts and receives the candidate as a fully ordained minister of Jesus Christ.
17. The presbyters by motion and second is now dissolved.
18. The right hand of fellowship is now extended to the newly ordained minister and his wife by the other members and friends of the church.
19. The church conference may then be adjourned and the service closed in any suitable manner.

Written in order by

Elder Jerry T. McBee

ATKINSON, EDNA P. age 82, of Monroe, MI, passed away January 31, 1995 in the Mease Countryside Hospital Emergency Room, Safety Harbor, Fl. She was born November 13, 1912 in Harrogate, TN, the daughter of Hiram and Sarah (Braden) Shoffner. She attended Evergreen Acres Missionary Baptist Church in Monroe. She was preceded in death by her husband John J. (Shortie) Atkinson; six brothers, three sisters, three half brothers and four half sisters. Survivors: son, Donald E. Atkinson, Monroe, MI; daughter, Mrs William (Margaret) Krupp of Safety Harbor, Fl; five grandchildren and four great grandchildren. Funeral service was held Friday, February 3rd at 1 p.m. in the Earle Little Funeral Home, Bacarella Chapel in Monroe with Rev. Damon Patterson officiating. She was laid to rest in the Roselawn Memorial Park in LaSalle.

AUSMUS, FLOY ANN, age 95 of Cumberland Gap, passed away Friday, April 21, 1995 at Tri State Manor Nursing Home in Harrogate. She was a member of Pleasant Hill Primitive Baptist Church. She was preceded in death by her husband, Troy Ausmus; parents, Neal and Matilda (Ausmus) Lambert; daughter, Alda Ausmus; brothers, Bill and Charlie Lambert; grandson, Jerry Johnson; sons-in-law, Cecil Keck and George Crawford. Survivors: daughters, Bernice Keck and Colleen Crawford, both of Cumberland Gap; daughters and sons-in-law, Lois and David Johnson of Lakeland Fl and Nila and Johnny Siler of Scottsboro, Al; brother Ben Lambert, Monroe, MI; sisters, Lottie Berry, Audrey Davis, both of Speedwell, Hattie Miracle, Dayon, OH and Etta McCoy, San Diego, CA; 10 grandchildren, 24 great grandchildren, 9 great-great grandchildren; a host of relative and friends.

Funeral service was held 11 a.m. Sunday, April 23 in Pleasant Hill Primitive Baptist Church with Elder Bill Rhymer and Rev. Richard Barnett officiating.. Music by Providence Baptist Church singers. Burial in the Ausmus Cemetery.

Pallbearers: grandsons and great grandsons.

BERRY, HELEN - age 94, of Maryville, died Friday, September 23, 1994 at Asbury

Acres Health Care Center. She was a member of Halls Primitive Baptist Church. Preceded in death by husband, Sillas (Bud) Berry; parents, Will and Ida Welch; five brothers and one sister. Survivors include: daughters and sons-in-law, Ora and R.P. Bridges, Marie and Wayne Weaver, Trula and Edward Alston, all of Maryville; sons and daughters-in-law, Forster and Fronia Berry of Knoxville, Lee and Ruth Berry of Sharps Chapel; 12 grandchildren; one step-grandson and several great-grandchildren; sisters, Luster Singleton and Edythe Helton, both of Knoxville, Bonnie Brantley of Sharps Chapel and Gladys Baker of Tuscon, Arizona. Funeral service was at Oak Grove Primitive Baptist Church, Sharps Chapel. Elders Hugh Brummitt and Bill Berry officiated. Pallbearers; Dale Weaver, Erwin Berry, Ernie Berry, Edwin Berry, Edward Berry, and Corum Berry. Interment in the church cemetery. Elder Hoyle Taylor read scripture and prayed at the visitation on Saturday evening at Smith Mortuary, Maryville.

BRANTLEY, BURLIS (BURKY), 94 of Bean Station, passed away February 17, 1995 at his home. A member of Noeton Primitive Baptist Church, he was preceded in death by wife, Fernie Shelby Brantley. Survivors: sons, Raymond Brantley of Florida, Buddy and Chilors Brantley of Bean Station; brother, Homer Brantley of Greenback. 7 grandchildren, 12 great-grandchildren; a nephew, Carl Miller of Indiana. Funeral service was held at Noeton Primitive Baptist Church with Elders John Oliver and Bill Rhymer officiating. Burial in Church cemetery.

BRITTAIN, SALLY E. 83, born October 8, 1911. Died January 18, 1995 at Emerald Hodgeson Hospital. She was a member of the Gibson Station Primitive Baptist Church. She was survived by a brother Tom Brittain, Ewing VA. Sisters; Mrs Flossie Johnson, Ewing, Va., Clara Sivils, Harrogate, TN, Kate Bays, Middlesboro, KY, also several neices and nephews. Special neice, Mrs Sue Vance,

Tullahoma, TN. Three special great neices, Veronica Wiseman, Tullahoma, TN, Angela Johnson, Winchester, TN, Kimberly Vance, Tullahoma, TN and a very special great-great nephew, Justin Ryan Wisemen, Tullahoma, TN.

Funeral services were at Watson-Gamble Chapel, January 20, 1995 by Rev. Everett Fulmer. Burial was at Watson-Gamble Memorial Park, Winchester, TN.

CLAWSON, ALDA, 65, of Monroe, MI, formerly of Speedwell, TN, passed away February 25, 1995. She attended Steward Road Church of God in Monroe MI. She was preceded in death by parents Jim and Hattie Edwards; husband, P.J. Clawson; and brothers Doyle Edwards and Elmer Brantly. Survivors include stepmother Emma Edwards of Speedwell; Sons, Roger Clawson, Larry Clawson, Phillip Clawson, Randy Clawson, Lee Clawson and Scott Clawson, all of Monroe, MI; Daughters, Brenda Pridemore, Peggy Tyniw, Jody Paul, of Monroe, MI and Sondra Chumley of Speedwell, TN and 16 grandchildren. Brothers, Matthew Edwards, Glen Edwards, Ivo Brantly of Speedwell. Sisters, Helen Clawson, Margie Monday, Alberta Leach, Ruby Bratcher, Mary Whaley, of Speedwell; Betty Jo Clawson of Dayton Ohio, Sue Whaley and Berniece Shepard of Michigan.

Funeral services were Tuesday, February 28, at Bradens Chapel Church with Elder Leroy Braden and Elder J.C. Monday officiating. Interment in Braden Chapel Cemetery.

COOK, EDGBERT F. "JACK" - age 79. of Knoxville, passed away Wednesday evening, December 14, 1994, at Baptist Hospital. He was a member of Halls Primitive Baptist Church. Mr. Cook was a veteran of the U.S. Army (Old Hickory Division) serving in WWII. He also served in the Civilian Conservation Corps. Preceded in death by: wife, Dottie Cook and daughter Martha Lou Goddard. Survivors; son, Thomas Cook of Pensacola, Fl; sisters, Alvilda Shoffner of Andersonville, TN; Lucy Eastridge and Joyce Clark of Sharps Chapel; brothers, Lonnie Cook of Kokomo, IN; Deward and Owen Cook of Sharps Chapel; Glen, Ailor and Taylor Cook, all of Knoxville; grandchildren, Stacey Goddard, Knoxville, Dottie Mae Burchfield and Becky Teaster of Blount County, Tori Lawton and Tabitha Cook of Georgia; one great-granddaughter, two great-grandsons. Family and friends assembled Saturday

December 17, at 11:00 a.m. at Holly Hills South Cemetery for graveside services and interment with full military honors. Elder Panick Shelton and Elder William Berry officiated.

EDWARDS, BERTHA GRAVES, 80, passed away Saturday, March 4, 1995 at Park West Hospital, Knoxville. Born September 23, 1914, in Speedwell, she was a daughter of the late George and Roxie (Williams) Graves. She was a member of the Pleasant Hill Primitive Baptist Church. In addition to her parents, she was preceded in death by her husband, Henry D. Edwards; brother, Johnny Graves; sisters Cecil Edwards, Mossie Graves, Vinnie Owens and Pearl Tinnel. Survivors include her son and daugher-in-law, Johnny Lee and Melissa Ann Edwards, Speedwell; daughter and son-in-law, Nanna Lou and Ozene Meadors, LaFollette, TN; sisters, Ada Jones and Hazel Lambert, Speedwell; six grandchildren, and a host of other relatives and friends. Services wer at Pleasant Hill Primitive Baptist Church with Elders Bill Rhymer and Bill Braden presiding. Burial was in Hunter Cemetery.

GRAVES, JESSIE MAE, Age 72, of Maynardville, passed away Saturday, April 22, 1995 at her home in Maynardville after a short illness. Retired from Alcoa Aluminum Co. with 43 years service and member of 25 Year Club. Member of Oak Grove Baptist Church. Preceded in death by: Father and Mother, Leslie and Anna Jane Dykes Graves; brother, Charlie (Red) Graves. Survivors: sisters, Jean Neely, Loretta Padgett, Bertie Campbell and Pearl Kitts; brothers, Bill, Roy, and Coy Graves all of Maynardville; several nieces and nephews, cousins and friends; three aunts; one uncle; special friend Jake Holloway, Dry Prong, Louisiana. Funeral service conducted by Rev. Leonard Padgett and Rev. Paul Haney. Pallbearers were nephews; Gerald Kitts, Len Padgett, David Campbell, Jeffrey Richardson, Cass and Robbie Graves.

LAMBERT, ALBA C., 76, passed away Thursday, Nov.18, 1993 at the Claiborne County Nursing Home, where he had resided for the past 14 years. He was a WWII Veteran and a member of Pleasant Hill Primitive Baptist Church.
He was preceded in death by his parents, Pryor C. and Louvenia "Lou" (Edwards) Lambert: sisters, Hettie Morgan, Cassie Braden , Marie Maddox:

and a brother, Walter E. Lambert.

Survivors include his wife, Hazel (Graves) Lambert, Speedwell: sons and daughters-in-law, Earl and Peggy Lambert, and Herry and Cathy Lambert, all of Speedwell: daughter and son-in-law, Debbie and Ben Jolly, Tazewell, TN: grandsons, Ronald Lambert, Justin Jolly, Brandson Lambert, and Joey Lambert: sisters Mrs. Brice (Lola) Braden, Speedwell, and Mrs. Milton (Wilma) Braden, Erie, MI. Services were at 2pm Sunday at Pleasant Hill Primitive Baptist church with Elders William "Bill" Rhymer, James H. Branscomb, Larry Anderson and Albert Davis presiding, Music was provided by The Church Choir. Burial was in Hunter Cemetery. Pallbearers were Verlin Maddox, Vantoy Owens, Bill Braden, Condis Edwards, Kelburn Edwards, and Tom Edwards.

LAY, HOMER D. -age 69, of Knoxville, passed away at 8:10 a.m. Monday, Oct.31, 1994 at St. Mary's Hospital. He was a member of Halls Primitive Baptist Church. Survivors: Wife, Bessie Lay; three children, Dwane Lay, Becky Stansberry, Both of Knoxville, Kenny Lay of Georgia; seven grandchildren, Gordy, Randy and Lori Lay, Todd and Ryan Stansbury, all of Knoxville, Joey and Heather Lay of Georgia; brothers, John, Joe, Albert, Ray and Ronnie Lay; sisters, Betty Acuff and Helen Smith; several nieces and nephews. Elder Bill Berry, Rev. E. R. Cooper, and Elder Parnick Shelton officiated. Interment at Lynnhurst Cemetery. Pallbearers: Ralph Turner, Dennis Branson, Joe Culvahouse, Sam Hardman, David Sharp, Floyd Roach, Herbert Loy, Marvin Powers.

MOULTON, ABRAHAM ('Moe"), passed away May 20, 1995 at his home in Morristown, Tn. He was a member of Noeton Primitive Baptist Church. He was baptised June 3, 1990 by Elder John Oliver. Survivors wife, Dorothy; daughters, Judy Mitchell and Margie Hill. 4 Grandsons, 4 brothers and 1 sister.

You were a pillar in our church,
Always lending a helping hand;
Never wanting anything in return.
A vacant seat now stands alone,
Your memory will live on and on;
Just as the fragrance of a flower lingers
after it is gone.

Sadly missed by Church.

OLIVER, SR., THEODORE JAMES (Ted) of Morristown, TN passed away Nov. 6, 1994 at Morristown-Hamblen Hospital.

He was the son of the late Elder Matthew and Ella Long Oliver, he was a member of Noeton Primitive Baptist Church; was a member of Tate Springs Masonic Lodge since 1931 and a member of Carpenters Local Union,No. 50 in Knoxville. Survivors daughters, Dorothy Sams and Donna Hodge of Morristown, Doris Patterson of Virginia, Jerri Southerland of Florida; sons, theodore James Oliver, Jr. of Florida, Donald Oliver of Johnson City: sisters, Vina Haun, Mary McDaniel, and Heddie Keitt all of Morristown, Aileen Childers of Bean Station; brothers, Elder John Oliver and Jack Oliver of Bean Station. 14 grandchildren and 15 great-grandchildren; several nieces and nephews. Rev. Charles Smith officiated. Burial was in the church cemetery.

ROBERTSON, CLIFFORD, age 78 of New Tazewell,passed away Nov.28,1994 at home. He was a member and deacon of Meyers Grove Primitive Baptist Church. He was preceded in death by a daughter, Norma Jean Robertson; parents, Charlie and Maggie (Drummonds) Robertson; brother,Claude Robertson; and sister, Ester Good. Survivors: wife, Mrs. Ida Robertson; son and daughter-in-law, Clifford Lee Jr. and Betty Robertson; daughters, Mrs. Elder Clay (Wanda) Widner, Mrs. Elder Johnny (Gipsy) Ayers, Mrs. Peggy Watson and Mrs. Brad (Kathy) Downes, all of New Tazewell, 16 grandchildren; sister, Mrs. Mattie Holt, Mrs.Eula Gray Good, both of New Tazewell, Mrs.Irene Elliott, Corbin, Ky.; brothers Otis Ray Robertson, New Tazewell, Lawrence Robertson,Detroit MI.;a host of other relatives and friends. Elder J.C. Mundy and Larry Collins Officiated. Singer: Elder Johnny Ayers.

Burial in the Drummonds Cemetery. Pallbearers: Bob Edinger, James Chumley, Beazer Watson, Brad Downes, Jason England, Jimmy Williams.

SHOFFNER, MRS. HETTIE (COX) -age 82, of Maryville, formerly of Sharps Chapel, ;passed away July 13, 1995 at Hillhaven Nursing Home in Maryville. She was a member of Oak grove Primitive Baptist Church. Preceded in death by her husband, Alex Shoffner. Survivors: sons, Alex, Hall, Max, Reed, Austin, Arthur and Billy Shoffner; daughters, Retta Blankenship; 19 grandchildren; brothers, W. D. Cox,Bob Cox; several nieces and nephews. Elder Jerry McBee Officiated.

Our loss is Heaven's Gain...
The Shoffner Family.

SPARKS,ROBERTA ELLA BRADEN, age 78, of Middlesboro, passsed away Dec.31,1994 at her home. Preceded in death by her husband Harrison Red Sparks and one son Walter Lee Sparks, also brothers and sisters, Eli Braden, Dave Braden, Sally Primm, Jane Bussell Voline Cole, Izette Braden. She was a member of the Braden Chapel Church in Bluespring Hollow, Speedwell, TN. Survivors include three daughters, Mrs. John (Wilma) Feketia of Monroe MI, Mrs. Albert (Imogene) Wells of Middlesboro, Mrs Larry (Andrea) Yeary of Middlesboro, Five sons, J.L. Sparks of Monroe, MI; Donald Sparks, David M. Sparks, Roger G. Sparks, And Gary Sparks all of Middlesboro. Sisters and Brothers, Dan Braden, Kyle Braden, and Daris Braden all of Monroe, MI.; Gmma Edwards of Speedwell; Oris Carmon of Tazewell, TN; 18 grandchildren and 20 great-grandchildren. Funeral services were conducted at Shumate Funeral Home Chapel with the Rev. J.C. Monday and Rev. Clarence Lambdins. Burial Was at Sparks Cemetery. Music provided by Kay Carroll, Betty Buell, Margie Waldroop. Pallbearers were her nephews, honorary pallbearers were her grandsons, Travis Hobbs, Donnie Sparks, Chris Sparks, Greg Sparks, Randy McDaniels, Walter Sparks, Jeffery Harrison.

SHARP, EDWARD L. - Age 53 of Halls, passed away Monday, December 26, 1994, at Vanderbilt Hospital, Nashville. He was a member of Halls Primitive Baptist Church and Director of First State Bank of Maynardville. Preceded in death by father, John L. Sharp. Survivors: wife, Kay Rose Sharp; son, Barry Edward Sharp; daughter and son-in-law, Lisa and Brian Childress; grandson, Brian Blake Childress; mother, Evelyn Petree Sharp; brother and sister-in-law, David E. and Virginia Sharp, all of Knoxville; one niece and four nephews; mother and father-in-law, Ed and Alline Rose, Maynardville. Funeral service was at Mynatt's Chapel, Elder William Berry and Elder Parnick Shelton officiating. Interment at Greenfield Memorial Cemetery. Pallbearers were Sonny and Willard Steele, Jimmy Petree, Danny and Jeffery Sharp, Wesley Rose. Honorary pallbearers were the Directors of First State Bank of Maynardville.

Eddie was a faithful church member. He called and visited the sick members of the church regularly and tried to always have a smile. He was very devoted to his mother and family. We miss him very much, but know that he is in a much better place, without pain and suffering, and that we can go to be with him one day.-   *The Family.*

SHARP, MRS EVELYN PETREE, Age 83, of Halls, passed away May 24, 1995, at University of Tennessee Memorial Hospital. She believed strongly in the Primitive Baptist faith and was a faithful charter member (05-07-44) of Halls Primitive Baptist Church (formerly Kirkwood Primitive Baptist Church). Preceded in death by husband, John L. Sharp and son, Edward L. Sharp. Survivors: son and daughter-in-law, David E. and Virginia H. Sharp; daugher-in-law Frances Kay Sharp; sister and brother-in-law, Jessie Mae and Sam Hardman; grandsons, Jeffery D. Sharp and wife Gena; John C. Sharp and wife, Gae; Barry E. Sharp; granddaughters, Lisa Childress and husband ,Brian, Jennifer Gaylor and husband Darren; three great-grandchildren, Jenna and Natali Sharp and Blake Childress. Funeral service at Mynatt's. Elders William Berry and Parnick Shelton officiating.

TAYLOR, WILLIAM H. (BILL)- 88, of Halls, passed away Sunday morning, June 18, 1995 at his home. He was a member of Halls Primitive Baptist Church and served as clerk to the Powell Valley Association for many years. He was retired from the U.S. Postal Service and the Knox County Register of Deeds \office. He was preceded in death by his wife, Lou Emma Taylor. Survivors: daugher and son-io-law, Marilyn and Carroll Cate, Corryton; granddaughter and husband, Pam and Dan Cosner, Seymour; brother, John Taylor, sister Bicy Hodges, both of Maryville, Mae Woods, Dalton, GA, Mary Jackson, Rachel Ausmus, Hassie Callahan, all of Chattsworth, Ga; special family friend, Cecilia Turner, Corryton; several nieces and nephews and a host of friends. Funeral services were at Rose Chapel with Elders Hugh Brummitt and Parnick Shelton officiating. Interment and graveside services were conducted by Elders Hugh Brummitt and Charles Taylor in Lynnhurst Cemetery.

TERRY ARTHUR G. - age 76, of Knoxville, formerly of Washburn, passed away Tuesday evening, April 18, 1995, at his home after a courageous battle with cancer. Member and Deacon of Black Fox Primitive Baptist Church. Preceded in death by first wife, Mary Terry. Survivors include wife, Emma Lee Belitz Terry; daughters, Sue Atkins and Debbie Sexton, both of Washburn; sons,

Stanley Terry of Maynardville, Steve Terry of New Market; step-children, Mary Ruth Capps, Edna Patterson, Walter Turner, all of Knoxville, Angela Maness of Wasburn, Vicki Forowzesh of California, Carl Thomas of Blaine, Several grandchildren, great-grandchildren and step-grandchildren. Special Thanks to ResCare and a very special thank you to Barbara Ferguson. Funeral service at Ailor's Chapel was conducted by Elder Larry Anderson, Elder Parnick Shelton and Pastor A.L. Neubert, Jr. Interment was at Thomas Cemetery. Grandsons were pallbearers.

God looked around His garden and He found an empty place.
He then looked down upon this earth and saw your tired face.
God saw you getting tired, and a cure was not to be,
so He put His arms around you and whispered "Come to Me".
With tearful eyes we watched you suffer and saw you fade away.
Although we loved you dearly, we could not make you stay.
God's garden must be beautiful.
He always takes the best.
He knew that you were suffering, He knew you were in pain.
He always knew in Heaven, you would never hurt again.
He saw the road was getting rough, and the hills harder to climb
so he closed your weary eyelids, and whispered "Peace Be Thine".
A golden heart stopped beating, but you didn't go alone

for a part of us went with you the day God called you home..

WATSON, IRETIS HICKMAN -age 59, of Powell, passed away at her home, Thursday March 30, 1995. Former member of Halls Primitive Baptist Church. Survived by son and daughter-in-law, Sonny and Trish Hickman of Halls; grandson, Zachary Hickman; brother, Paul E. Evans of Halls; stepfather, Millard Elwood Evans; several aunts and uncles. Service was held at Mynatts Chapel, Elder Jerry McBee and Rev. Roy Hammock officiated. Interment in Lynnhurst Cemetery. Pallbearers were Vance Harmon, Jr., Jason Evans, DeWayne Green, Greg Collier, Gregg Simms, Mike Sharp.

WEAVER, LINDA GAIL, 41, of Broadway Towers, Maryville, died at the University of Tennessee Medical Center. She was a member of Brantley's Chapel Primitive Baptist Church. She was preceded in death by mother, Gladys Hall Weaver, and brother, Charles Edward Weaver. Survivors include, father, Charles Weaver of Maryville; stepmother, Bernice Weaver of Maryville; stepsister, Renee' Lindsey Sands and husband Steve Sands of Palmetto, GA; grandfather, Henry Hall of Knoxville; several aunts, uncles and cousins.

Funeral service was in the West Chapel of Smith's Mortuary with the Rev. Chris Burns and Elder Jerry McBee officiating. Interment at Grandview Cemetery.

CHURCH	COUNTY	PASTOR	CLERK	ADDRESS
Black Fox	Grainger	Elder Larry Anderson	Bennie Capps-992-5571	P.O. Box 91, Maynardville, TN 37807
Braden's Chapel	Union	Elder J.C. Monday	Pam Goins Janice Bean, Asst.	Rt. 1, Box 350, LaFollette, TN.37766 Speedwell, TN 37870
Brantley's Chapel	Blount	Elder Jerry McBee Elder Lawrence Adams, Asst.	Brenda Beason-982-9426 Sherry Cable, Asst.-983-8387	619 Brown School Rd. Maryville, TN 37804 P.O. Box 274, Alcoa, TN 37701
Gethsemane	Knox	Elder Robert Walker	Tom Carmichael	729 Frank Street, Knoxville, TN 37919
Gibson Station	Lee, Va.	Elder Spurgeon Thompson	Dorothy Johnson Shirley Sandifur, Asst.	Rt. 2, Box 320, Ewing, VA 24248 Rt 1, Box 416, Harrogate, TN 37752
Halls	Knox	Elder William Berry Elder Parnick Shelton, Asst.	Helen Branson Amy Patton, Asst.	4633 Marshall Dr., Knoxville, TN 37938 4225 Inisbrook Way, Knoxville, TN 37838
Headrick's Chapel	Sevier	Elder Clyde Abbott, Jr.	Gearldine Abbott	1780 Alpine Drive, Sevierville, TN 37876
Lenoir City	Loudon	Elder Chester Hembree	E.H. Scarbrough-986-3027 Cheri Brown, Asst.-986-3724	270 Hickman St, Lenoir City, TN 37771 500 C. Street, Lenoir City, TN 37771
Meyers' Grove	Claiborne	Elder Johnny Ayers	Gloria Hipshire 626-8353 Betty Robinson, Asst. 626-4118	3607 Cave Spring Rd., Tazewell, TN 37879 530 Cupp Ridge Road, New Tazewell, TN 37825
Noeton	Grainger	Elder John Oliver	Caroll Oliver Mildred Oliver, Asst.	Rt. 2, Box 3480, Bean Station, TN 37708
Oak Grove	Union	Elder J. C. Monday Elder Mike Brantley, Asst.	Betty P. Sharp Betty Shoffner, Asst	133 Grizzell Ridge Rd, Sharps Chapel, TN 37866 644 Ledmine Bend Rd, Sharps Chapel, TN 37866
Pleasant Hill	Claiborne	Elder William Rhymer Elder James Branscomb, Asst.	William Branscomb Oklen Edwards, Asst.	Rt. 1, Russell Lane, Speedwell, TN 37870 Speedwell, TN 37870
Rocky Dale	Knox	Elder Hugh Brummitt	Betty Livingston-688-2352 Saundra Boruff, Asst.-947-7384	6924 Boruff Rd, Corryton, TN 37721 6916 Weaver Rd., Knoxville, TN 37931

1996 MINUTES

POWELL VALLEY ASSOCIATION OF PRIMITIVE BAPTISTS

STATISTICAL TABLE

Church	RESTORED	RECEIVED BY LETTER	BAPTISM	EXCLUDED	DISMISSED BY LETTER	RELATIONSHIP	DECEASED	TOTAL MEMBERSHIPS	PRINTING MINUTES	REGULAR MEETING TIME	COMMUNION TIME
Black Fox	0	0	0	0	0	0	0	52	$35.00	Sunday after Second Saturday Sunday after Fourth Saturday	Sunday following Second Saturday in June
Braden's Chapel	0	0	4	0	1	7	2	162	50.00	Every Sunday, second Saturday night	Sunday following first Saturday in July
Brantley's Chapel	0	0	0	3	3	3	1	139	100.00	Second Saturday night-every Sunday and Sunday night.	Sunday following second Saturday in July at 10:30 a.m. Fourth Sunday in Jan.
Gethsemane	0	0	0	0	0	0	0	28	35.00	Second and Fourth Sunday	Fourth Sunday in May and October
Gibson Station	0	0	0	0	0	0	0	61	50.00	First Saturday night- Every Sunday and Sunday night	Sunday following first Saturday in June
Halls	0	0	3	0	0	0	1	98	100.00	Every Sunday and Sunday night	Last Sunday in April
Headrick's Chapel	0	0	0	0	0	0	3	98	40.00	First and third Sunday of each month	First Sunday in May and October 11:00 a.m.
Lenoir City	0	2	0	0	4	0	4	101	50.00	Every Sunday and Sunday night	First Sunday in May 10:45 A.M.
Myers Grove	0	1	2	0	0	0	1	96	30.00	4th Saturday night and every Sunday	Sunday following Fourth Saturday in May
Nocton	0	0	0	0	0	0	4	46	30.00	First Sunday-third Saturday and Sunday day of each month	Sunday following third Saturday in May and September
Oak Grove	0	0	4	0	0	1	6	319	50.00	First Saturday night and Sunday third Sunday	Sunday following the first Saturday in May
Pleasant Hill	0	0	0	0	1	1	1	87	50.00	4th Saturday morning and Saturday night. Every Sunday and Sunday night	Sunday following the fourth Sunday in June at 10:30 a.m.
Rocky Dale	0	0	0	0	0	0	0	91	50.00	Every Sunday morning	Sunday following third Saturday in May

1996 Minutes

POWELL VALLEY ASSOCIATION
OF PRIMITIVE BAPTISTS

THE ONE HUNDRED-SEVENTY-SEVENTH SESSION
OF THE POWELL VALLEY ASSOCIATION
OF PRIMITIVE BAPTIST
HELD WITH THE SISTER CHURCH AT
ROCKY DALE
KNOX COUNTY, TENNESSEE
AUGUST 16, 17, 18, 1996
NEXT SESSION WILL BE HELD WITH
THE SISTER CHURCH AT PLEASANT HILL IN
CLAIBORNE COUNTY, TENNESSEE
TO BEGIN ON FRIDAY BEFORE THE THIRD
SATURDAY IN AUGUST, 1997 AT 10:30 A.M.
ELDER HUGH BRUMMITT
WILL DELIVER THE INTRODUCTORY SERMON
ELDER BILL RHYMER
WILL BE THE ALTERNATE.

• • • • • • •

Officers

ELDER JERRY McBEE, MODERATOR
P.O. BOX 158, LOUISVILLE, TENNESSEE 37777
PHONE 977-1788

ELDER PARNICK SHELTON, ASSISTANT MODERATOR
6001 McGINNIS ROAD, CORRYTON, TENNESSEE 37721
PHONE 687-5070

BENNIE CAPPS, CLERK
P.O. BOX 91, MAYNARDVILLE, TENNESSEE 37807
PHONE 992-5571

DON SHARP, ASSISTANT CLERK
1260 LOVELL VIEW DRIVE,
KNOXVILLE, TENNESSEE 37932
PHONE 966-1896

Minutes of
The One Hundred Seventy-Seventh Session

FRIDAY, AUGUST 16, 1996

The One Hundred Seventy Seventh Session of the Powell Valley Association of Primitive Baptist (due to error in 1976 and 1977 minutes we gained one (1) year) met with Sister Church at Rocky Dale in Knox County, Tenn. on August 16, 17, 18, 1996. Brother Donald Sharp led the congregation in singing "Victory in Jesus", Hold to God's Unchanging Hand", "How Firm a Foundation", "What a Friend We Have In Jesus", "Leaning on the Everlasting Arms", "There is a Fountain", then Moderator Elder Jerry Mcbee welcomed the congregation and pleaded for peace and love to abide through out the entire association and called for prayer by Elder William Rhymer of Gibson Station Church. Elder Robert Walker delivered the introductory sermon from the 23rd Chapter of Psalms using as his text "Heavenly Home". He was then followed by Elder Spurgeon Thompson quoting from the 100th Chapter of Psalms, and also from the 19th Chapter of Revelation using as his text " The Word Was God". Both Elders brought a very uplifting and spiritual sermon.

After the introductory sermon, the congregation sang a song and were dismissed in prayer by Elder John Oliver. The association was to reconvene after a 15 minute recess.

After recess, the crowd reassembled in the church. Brother Don Sharp led the congregation in "Amazing Grace", and the Moderator Elder Jerry McBee read from the 9th Chapter of Ecclesiastes, verses 13-18, then called for prayer by Elder Hugh Brummitt.

The Moderator then asked for the order of business for the following transactions:

1st: Called for letters of the Sister Churches to be presented to the clerk for reading. THIRTEEN(13) were received.

2nd: The letters were presented and read and motion approved that the delegates be seated.

3rd: The Moderator called for anyone present from any of the Sister Churches not named as delegate who desired to be seated as such come forward and give the clerk their name and the name of their church. Three came. Brothers Josh Stapleton, Glenn Johnson, Sister Irma Lee Sapleton from Rocky Dale.

4th: Called for petitionary letter if there should be one. None came.

5th. Motion approved that the Association Re-Elect Elder Jerry McBee as Moderator and Re-Elect Elder Parnick Shelton Assistant Moderator for the ensuing year.

6th: Motion and second Brother Bennie Capps be re-elected Clerk and Brother Don Sharp be elected Assistant Clerk.

7th: By move and second, we show Brother Rina johnson our deep appreciation for his loyal and dedicated service as Assistant Clerk for the last fifteen (15) years. (I consider it a great honor and privilege to work with Brother Rina for the years. The Clerk).

8th: Motion was approved that we empower Elder McBee to appoint all the committees to serve this session.

9th: The Moderator, having been empowered to do so, appointed committees as follows:

Committee on Arrangements: Brother Elwood Evans
Brother Franklin Jones
Brother Millard Berry
Committee on Preaching: Brother Joe Culvahouse
Brother Hubert Spoon
BrotherTommy Scarbrough
Committee on Request: BrotherJosh Stapleton
Elder Spurgeon Thompson
Elder Bill Berry
Committee on Finance: Brother Cyrus T. McBee
Brother Chester Lee Hembree
Brother Charles Bryant

10th: Called for the finances to be turned in to the Finance Committee.

11th: By move and second, the above minutes were approved as read.

12th: The Committees all having been appointed and accepted, the Association moved to adjourn until 10:30 Saturday morning. They sang a song and were dismissed in prayer by Elder O. D. McCarty of Pleasant Hill.

SATURDAY, AUGUST 17 1996

At the appointed hour of 10:30 Saturday morning and at the sound of singing, the Association reassembled. Brother Don Sharp led the Congregation in "God Holds the Future in His Hand" and "There'll Be Joy" and "Brethren We Have Met to Worship". Elder Parnick Shelton opened the service and spoke for a few minutes, then called for prayer by Elder Albert Davis of Pleasant Hill. After prayer, the Moderator called the Association to order for the remainder of the business.

1st: Called for any letters from Sister Churches not received on Friday. There was none.

2nd: The letters were presented and read, and the motion approved that the delegates be seated.

3rd: Called for anyone from any of the churches who were present and desired to be seated as delegate to come forward and give the clerk their name and their church. Sister Polly Jones, of Gibson Station Church.

4th: Called for the report of the committee on Arrangements who submitted the following report:

REPORT ON ARRANGEMENTS:

CALL FOR ROLL CALL OF DELEGATES.
CALL FOR REPORT OF COMMITTEE ON PREACHING.
CALL FOR REPORT OF COMMITTEE ON REQUEST.
CALL FOR REPORT OF COMMITTEE ON FINANCE.

Decide how many minutes we have printed, who shall supervise the printing and delivery of the same, and what he shall be paid for this service. Which Sister Church shall host the next Association and who will preach the introductory sermon and who will be the alternate. Who will prepare the Circular Letter.

Respectfully Submitted,
Brother Elwood Evans
Brother Franklin Jones
Brother Millard Berry

5th: Motion approved to receive the above report and release the committee.

6th: Called the roll call of delegates of all Sister Churches and check the absentees.

7th: Called for the report of the Committee on Preaching:

COMMITTEE ON PREACHING:

Friday night: Elder Richard Walker
Elder Parnick Shelton
Saturday morning: Elder Hugh Brummitt
Elder Bill Rhymer
Saturday night: Elder Brian Brantley
Elder Chester Hembree
Sunday morning: Elder Bill Berry
Elder Jerry McBee

Respectfully submitted,
Brother Joe Culvahouse
Brother Hubert Spoon
Brother Tommy Scarbrough

8th: Motion approved to receive the above report and release the committee.

9th: Called for the report of the Committee on Request, which was given:

We, the Committee on Request, wish to request as follows, that we have 1,000 minutes printed and the clerk supervise the printing and distribution of same and that he receive $150.00 for his services. We also request that the next session of the Powell Valley Association be held with the Sister Church at Pleasant Hill in Claiborne County, Tennessee, to begin on Friday before the third Saturday in August, 1997, at 10:30 A.M. and continue three days. We also request that Elder Hugh Brummitt preach the introductory sermon and Elder Bill Rhymer be the alternate. We also request that Elder Clyde Abott, Sr. write a circular letter for the minutes for 1997.

Respectfully submitted,
Brother Josh Stapleton
Elder Spurgeon Thompson
Elder Bill Berry

10th: Motion approved to receive the above report and release the committee.

11th: Called for the report of the Committee on Finance, which submitted the following report:

Black Fox	$35.00
Braden's Chapel	50.00
Brantley's Chapel	100.00
Gethsemane	35.00
Gibson Station	50.00
Halls	100.00
Headrick's Chapel	40.00
Lenoir City	50.00
Meyers Grove	30.00
Noeton	30.00
Oak Grove	50.00
Pleasant Hill	50.00
Rocky Dale	50.00
Total Collections	670.00
Balance in Bank	372.00
Donations w/Oak Grove letter	5.00
Monroe Primitive Baptist Church	20.00
Collection - Rocky Dale	323.00
Balance in Bank.	1,390.00
Expenses for 1996	-850.00
Balance in Bank	$ 540.00

Respectfully Submitted,
Brother Cyrus T. McBee
Brother Chester Lee Hembree
Brother Charles Bryant

12th: Motion approved to receive the above report and release the committee.

13th: Motion approved that we grant the request of the committee and have 1,000 minutes printed and the clerk to receive $150.00 for his services.

14th: Motion approved that the next session of the Association be held with the Sister Church at Pleasant Hill to commence on Friday before the third Saturday in August, 1997, at 10:30 A.M.

15th: Motion approved that Elder Hugh Brummitt deliver the introductory sermon and Elder Bill Rhymer be the alternate.

16th: Motion approved that Elder Clyde Abbott, Sr. write the circular letter for the 1997 Minutes.

17th: Motion approved that the churches of the Powell Valley Association extend to the church and the people of Rocky Dale our heart felt thanks and our prayers for the love, fellowship, kindness, and food while we were with you. May the Good Lord bless and keep you is our prayers.

18th: By move and second, the above minutes were approved as read.

19th: Motion approved to adjourn, trusting the Lord to permit us to meet again with the Sister Church at Pleasant Hill in Claiborne County, Tn., on Friday before the third Saturday in August, 1997 at 10:30 A.M. Dismissed in prayer by Elder Larry Anderson.

Elder Jerry McBee, Moderator
Elder Parnick Shelton, Assistant Moderator
Brother Bennie Capps, Clerk
Brother Don Sharp, Assistant Clerk

Special Announcements

Brantley's Chapel has their second Saturday night services at 7 P.M.; Sunday morning services at 10:30 A.M.; Sunday night services at 7 P.M. in the summer months and at 6 P.M. in the winter months.

The following churches requested the Association for 1997: Black Fox, Brantley Chapel, Halls, Lenoir City , Pleasant Hill.

Please make all contributions payable to: **Powell Valley Association.** To those who mail their letters, please mail to clerk of the association.

Dates of Ordination of the Following Elders:

Elder Alber Davis, May 17, 1930
Elder Hugh Brummitt, December 12, 1954
Elder James Branscomb, June 23, 1956
Elder J.C. Monday, February 12, 1958
Elder Parnick Shelton, December 11, 1960
Elder Claude Rosson, July 4, 1964
Elder Joe Bush, April 27, 1969
Elder Robert Walker, October 4, 1970
Elder Roy Watkins, August ,1971
Elder John Oliver, April 15, 1972
Elder Bill Berry, August 27, 1972
Elder Larry Anderson, October 24, 1975
Elder Spurgeon Thompson, December 17, 1976
Elder Bill Rhymer, December 17, 1976
Elder Clyde Abbott, Jr., July 7, 1979
Elder Jerry McBee, April 26, 1981
Elder Nelson Jones, July 17, 1981
Elder LeRoy Braden, October 10, 1982
Elder Chester Hembree, June 19, 1988
Elder Clyde Abbott, Sr., November 6, 1988
Elder Richard Walker, March 29, 1992
Elder O.D. McCarty, March , 1993
Elder Michael Brantley, April 23, 1995
Elder Lawrence Adams, September 17, 1995
Elder Brian Brantley, August 4, 1996

Summary

We are blessed with a fine group of ministers, as was illustrated by those who had the opportunity to preach. We regret that time will not permit more of them to preach when we meet with the Association. On Friday night, Elder Richard Walker read from the Second Thessalonians and the Second Chapter using as his text "There Comes a Falling Away"; he was then followed by Elder Parnick

Shelton who read from the First Peter, First Chapter, Second Verse, using as his text "Election and Fore Knowledge of God". On Saturday morning, Elder William Rhymer preached from the 69th Chapter of Psalms using " Hear Me Lord" as his text. He was then followed by Elder Hugh Brummitt who spoke from the book of First Peter using as his text " Blessed Be TheGod, Father of our Lord Jesus Christ". On Saturday night, Elder Bryant Brantley spoke from First Chapter of Isaiah, First Verse, and using as his text "The Vision". He was then followed by Elder Chester Hembree who spoke from the Eighth Chapter of Romans and using as his text "Being in the Wilderness". On Sunday morning, Elder Bill Berry Spoke from the Second Chapter of Revelation,verses 1-6 using as his text "God Had A Plan". Elder Jerry McBee was scheduled but did not take any time. All of the above Elders brought very uplifting and spiritual sermons.

Circular Letter
To Powell Valley Association 1996

To the churches that make up the Powell Valley Association, I send you greetings in the name of the Lord and Savior Jesus Christ.

To write this letter is the way I have to tell my feelings about this Association. I feel it has the most solid foundation that I know. The Articles of Faith that our Elders wrote many years ago are Bible truths and we the Elders, when we were ordained, said before God and the presbyters that we believed them, and would preach accordingly. The Apostle Paul said that we should all give an account unto God for how we had built on the foundation that He had laid.There is nothing that makes me feel better than to hear how great God is and how little man is, and that God only can save the lost sinner. The Gospel only brings life and immortality to light.

It is my wish that our members would get more interested in participation in the Association. May God bless this Association and pray for our ministers.

Your Brother in Christ,

Elder Hugh Brummitt

Ministers Directory

Elder Larry Anderson, Rt.3, Box 314-A, Speedwell, TN 869-4635

Elder William Berry, 7607 Mayes Chapel Rd, Knoxville,TN 922-9189

Elder J.H. Branscomb, Speedwell, TN 562-6361

Elder Hugh H. Brummitt, 1329 Brown Ave., Knoxville, TN 546-7700

Elder Joe Bush, 7507 Rodgers Rd, Corryton, TN 687-7018

Elder LeRoy Braden, 2305 Middlesboro, LaFollette, TN 566-4647

Elder Albert Davis, Rt. 3, Box 320 A Speedwell, Tn 869-3596

Elder Doyle Ausmus, 515 Water St., Speedwell, TN 566-0433

Elder Alvin Graves, 122 Oak Wood Dr., Lenoir City, TN 986-9725

Elder Jerry McBee, Box 158, Louisville, TN 977-1788

Elder J.C. Monday, 515 Blue Spring Rd., Speedwell, TN 562-3068

Elder John Oliver, Rt 2, Box 3482, Bean Station, TN 993-2295

Elder William Rhymer, P.O. Box 374, Harrogate, TN 37752 869-3092

Elder Parnick Shelton, 6001 McGinnis Rd, Corryton, TN 687-5070

Elder Spurgeon Thompson, Box 36, Shawnee, TN 869-8175

Elder Claude Rosson, Rt. 4, New Tazewell, TN 626-3168

Elder Robert Walker, Severville, TN 428-1527

Elder Clay Widner, Rt. 1, Tazewell, TN 626-3893

Elder Richard Walker, 3627 Rockford St., Rockford, TN 977-0414

Elder Chester Hembree, 3604 Rockford Street Rockford, TN 983-6526

Elder Clyde Abbott, Sr., 3840 Abbott Rd., Severville, TN 453-2329

Elder Johnny Ayers, 190 Meyers Grove Rd., New Tazewell, TN 626-8507

Elder Clyde Abbott, Jr., 2628 Old Whites Mill Road, Maryville, TN 37801

Elder Roy Watkins, 305 Augusta Ave., Maryville, TN 37804 981-1762

Elder O.D. McCarty Rt.5 Box 2100 LaFollette ,TN 37766 562-3850

Elder Michael Brantley

Elder Brian Brantley

Elder Lawrence Adams, 810 Brown School Road, Maryville, TN 984-2970

Licenliates

Brother Roscoe Branscomb, Speedwell, TN

Brother Odell Carpenter, 812 Brown School Rd., Maryville, TN 984-4352

Brother Mark Taylor, Lenoir City, TN

Brother Ray Walker, 2281 Douglas Dam Road, Sevierville, TN 37876 429-5417

Elders Who Wrote the Circular Letter
and
the Church that Hosted the Association

1974 Elder Leonard White -----------------------------------Lenoir City
1975 Elder Albert Davis---Kirkwood
1976 Elder Charles Taylor -------------------------------Gibson Station
1977 Elder Johnny Atkins-------------------------------Brantley's Chapel
1978 Elder Joe Irving ---------------------------------------Rocky Dale
1979 No Letter Submitted ----------------------------------Oak Grove
1980 Elder Hugh Brummitt ---------------------------------Black Fox
1981 Elder James Branscomb-------------------------------Pleasant Hill
1982 Elder Noble Clawson-----------------------------------Lenoir City
1983 Elder J. C. Monday ------------------------------Gibson Station
1984 Elder Walter Lyons -----------------------------Brantley's Chapel
1985 Elder Parnick Shelton --------------------------------Black Fox
1986 No Letter Submitted ---Halls
1987 Elder John Oliver ------------------------------------Lenoir City
1988 Elder William Berry --------------------------------Rocky Dale
1989 Elder Claude Rosson ---------------------------------Oak Grove
1990 Elder Joe Bush ---------------------------------------Pleasant Hill
1991 Elder Larry Anderson ---------------------------Gibson Station
1992 Elder Spurgeon Thompson---------------------Brantley's Chapel
1993 Elder William Rhymer--------------------------------Black Fox
1994 Elder Jerry McBee--Halls
1995 Elder Chester Hembree----------------------------Lenoir City
1996 Elder Hugh Brummitt----------------------------Rocky Dale

Churches
and Their Delegates

BLACK FOX: Brothers: Dale Capps, Bennie Capps. Sisters: Mary Ruth Capps, Pamela Capps, Goldie Gose

BRADEN'S CHAPEL: Letter Received. No delegate listed.

BRANTLEY'S CHAPEL: Elders:Jerry McBee, Lawrence Adams, Brothers: Robert Welch, Cyrus McBee, Glenn Walker, Everett Brantley, David Beason, Rina Johnson, Elwood Evans. Sisters:Blanch Welch, Burnice McBee, Mildred Brantley, Mildred Evans, Hazel Johnson, Venessa McBee.

GETHSEMANE: Brother:Tom Carmichael. Sister: June Carmichael.

GIBSON STATION: Elders: Spurgeon Thompson, Bill Rhymer Brother: Franklin Jones. Sisters: Fannie Jones, Virginia Bolton, Dorothy Johnson

HALLS: Elders: Hugh Brummitt, Parnick Shelton, William Berry. Brothers: Joe Culvahouse,Vance Harmon,Sr.,Vance Harmon,Jr., Marvin Powers. Sisters: Ruby Brummitt, Wilma Shelton, Betty Culvahouse, Irene Harmon, Sarah Harmon, Trula Berry, Helen Branson.

HEADRICK'S CHAPEL: Elders: Clyde Abbott, Sr., Robert Walker. Sisters: Gearldine Abbott, Margaret Walker.

LENIOR CITY: Elders: Chester Hembree, Richard Walker. Brothers: Chester Lee Hembree, E. H. Scarbrough, Hubert Spoon. Sisters: Edith Hembree, Marie Scarbrough, Thelma Brown, Aileen Watkins, Della Packett, Nell Anderson

MYER'S GROVE: Letter Received. No Delegates Listed.

NOETON: Elder John Oliver. Borhter: Carroll Oliver, Charlie Collins.

OAK GROVE: Sister: Francis Eastridge, Monnie Rogers

PLEASANT HILL: Elders: James Henry Branscomb, Larry Anderson, Albert Davis O.D. McCarty. Sisters: Helen Ruth Branscomb, .Audry Davis, Mollie McCarty, Karen Rhymer, Cleo Berry.

ROCKY DALE: Brothers:James Boruff, Don Sharp, Charlie Bryant. Sisters: Norma Jean Bush, Fay Collette, Saundra Borruff, Myrtle Bryant.

Rules of Decorum

1.　　　The churches composing the Powell's Valley Association shall not be confined to any set rules as to specific number of Messengers they shall have in the body, but shall have the right to name in their letters as many as they choose, and in addition all orderly members of any of the churches being present be entitled to seats in the body as Messengers of their respective churches, with all the rights and privileges of the same.

2.　　　The Messengers thus assembled shall be denominated the Powell's Valley Primitive Baptist Church.

3.　　　For the purpose of historical information and statistical edification, the Churches are required to state in letters, the number of members in fellowship, the number received by Baptism, by letter, by confession of Faith, the number dismissed, excluded and dead since last session; also the time of their meeting, their pastoral supply, and the amount of money contributed for ministers and other purposed together with any other information they deem appropriate for the edification of the saints and glory of God.

4.　　　This Association shall have no power to answer queries, give advice, or dictate to the Churches in any case, or to lord it over God's heritage nor any power by which she can directly or indirectly fringe on the internal rights of the church or censure and try any church or member in reference to faith and practice and determine upon validity of gospel ordinances. These things shall rest entirely with the churches; but henceforeward our annual meetings shall be only for the purpose of hearing from each other, and for the worship of God and mutual comfort and edification of the Saints. To this end we reserve the privilege annually for Friday before the Third Saturday in August and the two following days or at such times as may be agreed upon with any church that may invite us, having to protect our own standard, while in session, from heresay and disorder to recognize and invite any Primitive Baptist minister or any lay brother to worship with us that may deem proper; to request the brethren of our body to visit other churches or bodies in our belief with whom we may desire to culture Christian fellowship; to publish the minutes of our proceedings.

5.　　　Each session of the body shall have a Moderator and Clerk who shall hold office until re-elected.

6.　　　Any order member of any church belonging to this body, when convened, being present shall be eligible to election as Moderator and Clerk or to sit on any committee appointed by the same.

7.　　　In all election or questions that may be necessary to determine by vote, the vote shall be taken by churches, each church being entitled to three votes for any number less than one-hundred, and one additional vote for every fifty of fraction thereof above the first hundred, but the Messengers of each church may divide their vote as they see proper.

8.　　　All elections or questions coming to vote shall be determined by a majority vote cast, and it shall be the only duty of the minority to acquiesce in the decision thus reached.

9.　　　If new churches desire to be admitted to this union they shall petition by letter and messengers and if voted for and recommended by one or more sister churches for her Presbytery constitutioning them, as orthodox and orderly they shall be received by the vote of the body and manifested by the Moderator giving the Messengers the right hand of fellowship.

10.　　　Any motion or resolution clearly inconsistent with the above rules shall be promptly ruled out of order unless withdrawn by the mover.

11.　　　Any messenger being ruled out of order by the Moderator shall have the right to appeal to the body on the question of order, and if sustained shall be allowed to proceed, but if not take his seat.

12.　　　Our meeting being held in the name of Christ and the worship of God; each Messenger is expected to observe due and proper therein.

13.　　　It will not be considered good for any Messenger whose name has been enrolled as such to abruptly break off or absent himself from the Association without leave.

14.　　　The Moderator shall be entitled to the same privilege of speech as other members provided the chair is filled.

15.   The minutes of the Association shall be read and approved by the body and signed by the Moderator before adjourning.

16.   The Association shall be opened and closed by prayer.

17.   Amendments to these may be made at any time by a majority of the union voting by churches when they deem it necessary, provide such amendments do not compromise the sovereignty of the churches nor have a tendency to give body undue power or jurisdiction over them.

Articles of Faith

Article 1.   We believe in only one true living God, as He is revealed to us in the Holy Scriptures - Father, Son and Holy Ghost.

Article 2.   We believe that the Scriptures of the old and new Testaments are the words of God and the only rule of all-saving knowledge and obedience.

Article 3.   We believe in the doctrine of election according to the foreknowledge of God.

Article 4.   We believe in the doctrine of original sin.

Article 5.   We believe in man's impotency to rescue himself from the fallen state he is in, by his own will or ability.

Article 6.   We believe that sinners are justified in the sight of God only by the imputed righteousness of Jesus Christ.

Article 7.   We believe the elect, according to the foreknowledge of God will be called, converted, regenerated, and sanctified by the Holy Spirit.

Article 8.   We believe the saints will persevere and never fall finally away.

Article 9.   We believe that baptism and the Lord's Supper are ordinances of Jesus Christ, and that the true believers are the only subject of these ordinances, and that the true mode of baptism is by immersion. We believe also that feet washing is an example of Jesus Christ and should be kept by his disciples until his second coming.

Article 10.   We believe in the Resurrection of the dead and the General Judgement.

Article 11.   We believe that the punishment of the wicked will be everlasting and that the joys of the righteous will be eternal.

Article 12.   We believe that no minister has the right to administer the ordinances, except those who have been regularly baptised and called of God, and come under the imposition of hands of the presbytery.

673

Ordination for Minister or Deacon

1. Moderator of the church will call the church to order.
2. Call for the reading of the minutes of the church authorizing the ordination.
3. Appoint a spokesman for the church. He is to state if the church is in the same mind as when the candidate was elected.
4. The elders are to assemble themselves together for the purpose stated. (this is done by gathering together in a room or outside).
5. The presbyters will now organize by electing a moderator and clerk.
6. The moderator will by consent of the presbyters assign one of its members to question the candidate, one member to give charge to the candidate, one member to give charge to the church, and one to give the ordination prayer.
7. By motion and second by the church, the candidate will be delivered into the hands of the presbytery.
8. The candidate for ordination must be presented by the church to the presbyters, being escorted by a suitable person.
9. Question to the candidate on our articles of faith.
10. The charge to the candidate.
11. The charge to the church.
12. Examination of the candidate will be given by the other elders at this time, for any questions they might have concerning his experience, his call to the ministry, or his understanding of the doctrine.
13. The ordination prayer, with the laying on of the hands, by the presbyters.
14. The right hand of fellowship is extended to the newly ordained minister by the presbyters.
15. The candidate, being fully ordained, is delivered back into the hands of the church by motion and second.
16. By motion and second, the church accepts and receives the candidate as a fully ordained minister of Jesus Christ.
17. The presbyters by motion and second is now dissolved.
18. The right hand of fellowship is now extended to the newly ordained minister and his wife by the other members and friends of the church.
19. The church conference may then be adjourned and the service closed in any suitable manner.

Written in order by
Elder Jerry T. McBee

Obituaries

Atkins, Ina Bell Coffey , age 78, of Rutledge, passed away September 23, 1995 at Fort Sanders Medical Center in Knoxville. She was a member of Noeton Primitive Baptist Church. Preceded in death by husband, Chester Atkins, daughters, Jean Cannon and Joyce Atkins and 1 grandchild. Survivors; sons, Buddy Atkins of Florida; Billy, Hugh, & Steve Atkins of Morristown; John Atkins of Rutledge; Frank Atkins of Thorn Hill; daughters, Mrs. Jim (Sue) Lowery of Russellville; Mrs Terrell (Sarah) Metcalf of Dandridge; Mrs. Jerry (Carolyn) Hixon of Bean Station; Mrs. Virgil (Karen) Bowser, Bean Station; 16 grandchildren & several great-grandchildren. Brother, Charlie Jeff Coffey of Ohio; sister, Velva Dalton of Thorn Hill. Funeral services at Smith Funeral Home Chapel of Rutledge with Elder John Oliver and Rev. Gary Satterfield officiating. Burial in Davidson Cemetery of Thorn Hill.

Berry, Elmer L. age 73, of Halls, passed away November 22, 1995. Brother Berry loved and supported Rocky Dale Primitive Baptist Church for years although his membership was at Alder Springs Church. His heart was with his many friends at Rocky Dale and he will be remembered for his faithfulness to the church. He served in W.W. II Battalion No. 825 Tank Destroyer and was actively involved with other veterans. Elmer was the founder and owner of Halls Auto Parts. He was preceded in death by: parents, Harley and Ida Belle Berry; brothers, Elder Everett Berry, Knoxville; Charles and Clyde Berry, Corryton; and Luther Berry, Charlotte N.C.; and sister, Ethel Robinson, Knoxville. He is survived by: wife, Lorene; daughter, Janice George; Knoxville; sons and daughters-in-law, Donald and Shirley Berry, Corryton, Mike and Brenda Berry, David and Nancy Berry, Knoxville; grandchildren, Lisa Whaley, Donna Stansberry, Stacey Berry, Kim Berry, Connie Berry, David Berry, Melanie Hooks, Sheryl Dunsmore, and Amanda George; five great-grandchildren; sisters, Mrs. Hairl (Bertha) Kear, Mrs. Ralph (Jean) Kear, Knoxville; Mrs. Jay (Margie) Lively, Corryton; brothers, Harley, Jr., Ross, Ed, Rev. Wallace (Ronnie), and Rev. Bill Berry, all of Corryton; special friends, Sam Adams, Virgil Duncan and Stephanie Cole, and many military associates. Services were held at 8:30 p.m. Saturday, November 25 at Mynatt's Chapel. Elder Bill Berry, Elder Hugh Brummitt and Rev. Ralph Cox officiated. Interment was at 2 p.m. on Sunday at Clapps Chapel Cemetery. Pallbearers were: Shane Merritt, Gordon Dalton, Larry Severs, Claude Robertson, Doyle Johnson, Don Brantley, Bill Helton, Mike Casey, and Kenny Snow. Honorary pallbearers: Sam Adams and Virgil Duncan.

Clawson, Maxine V., age 67, of West Carrollton, Ohio passed away Monday, January 1, 1996 at Sycamore Hospital. She was a member of Moraine City Baptist Church. She was preceded in death by husband, Roy F. Clawson; father, Timothy P. Walker and son Rickie D. Clawson. She is survived by mother Effie N. Walker of Dayton, Ohio; sons and daughters-in-law Jackie L. & Regina P. Clawson of Farmersville, Ohio, Danny L. and Lois J. Clawson of Moraine, Ohio and Terry A. & Cathy Clawson of West Carrollton, Ohio; brother Malcolm H. Walker of Sharps Chapel, TN; sisters Opal McBride of Sharps Chapel, TN and Hazel Wiggins of Greenfield, Indiana; six grandchildren. Interment was in Evergreen Cemetery. Arrangements by Swart Funeral Home in West Carrollton, Ohio.

Cupp, Denver Roy , age 51, of New Tazewell, was born Aug. 7, 1944 and passed away April 13, 1996 at home. He was a member of Myers Grove Primitive Baptist Church. He was preceded in death by his parents, Frank and Hulda Cupp:two brothers Doyle & Glenn Cupp and one infant sister. Survivors: wife, Roxie Dyer Cupp; daughter and son-in-law Sue and Dennis Massengill; son and daughter-in-law, Jerry and Angie Cupp, all of New Tazewell; sons, Micheal and Wayne Cupp; four grandchildren; brothers, Blaine Cupp of Rutledge, Wade Cupp of New Tazewell; sisters, Lula Keck, New Tazewell, Thelma Collins of Sharps Chapel, Paralee Bolton and Jerree Russell of New Tazewell; many nieces and nephews, and other relatives and friends. Funeral service was held 3 p.m. Monday, April 15 in Coffey Funeral Home Chapel with Rev. Dallas Harrell and Rev. Jerry Epperson officiating. Singers were Rev. Danny and Diana Breeding and Rev. Jerry and Carolyn Epperson. Burial in the Lily Grove Cemetery. Pallbearers: Tony Sutton, Bud Chumley, Mark West, Hubert Brooks, Rodney Dooley, Randy Dooley, Roy Keck and Hoy Keck. Honorary pallbearers: Rev. Hubert Turner, Robert Pressnell, Rev. Johnny England, Rev. Randy Cunningham, Tommy Neely and Randy Widner. Coffey Funeral Home in charge.

Dalton, Leroy age 78, passed away May 23, 1996, at the home of his son in Morristown. He was a member of Noeton Primitive Baptist Church. Preceded in death by his wife, Ethel Bunch Dalton, and brothers, Wilson & Lester Dalton. Survivors, daughter and son-in-law, Dorothy & Charles Beckham of Knoxville; sons &

daughters-in-law, Doyle & Louise Dalton of Morristown; Don & Mary Dalton, Austin, Texas; Freddie & Phyllis Dalton, Nashville, TN; and Jerry Dalton, Talbott, TN. Nine grandchildren, 3 great-grandchildren; sister, Martha Pierce, Durham, N.C., and a host of friends & relatives. Funeral services were held at Westside Chapel Funeral Home of Morristown with Elder John Oliver, Rev. Donnie McNabb, and Rev. Kenny Davis officiating. Burial in Hamblen Memory Gardens, Morristown.

Edwards, Coy L. , age 72, of Speedwell, passed away Tuesday, July 30, 1996 at Baptist Hospital. He was born in Claiborne County, the son of the late Berlin and Cecil (Graves) Edwards. He was a member of Braden Chapel Church and was retired from the Middlesboro Tannery. He liked to fish, whittle and work in the garden. In addition to his parents, he was preceded in death by a sister, Bertha Edwards and four brothers, Arlis Edwards, B.J. Edwards, Lloyd Edwards, and Boyd Edwards. Survivors: wife, Jane Ethel (Braden) Edwards, Speedwell; sons and daughters-in-law, Paul Edwards, Walter and Patsy Edwards, all of Speedwell; daughter and son-in-law, Opal and Harrison Russell of Speedwell; six grandchildren, three great-grandchildren; brothers, Austin Edwards and Condis Edwards, both of Speedwell, Terry Edwards, Dayton, Ohio, Kenneth Edwards, Speedwell, Carl Edwards, LaFollette; sister, Cedilla Branscomb, Speedwell. Funeral Services 2 p.m. Friday at Braden Chapel Primitive Baptist Church with Elders J.C. Monday and Leroy Braden officiating. Music by church singers. Burial in Braden's Cemetery in Union County. Pallbearers: Marvin Bean, Kenny Kidd, Ronnie Dills, James Monday, James Fred Braden, and Doyle Ausmus. Honorary pallbearer: Matthew "Buck" Edwards. Reece Funeral Home & Valley Chapel in charge of arrangements.

Haun, Vina Oliver, age 79, passed away August 7, 1996, at Heritage Center of Morristown. She was a member of Noeton Primitive Baptist Church. Preceded in death by Parents: Elder & Mrs. Matthew Oliver; husband, G. Paul Haun; brother Ted Oliver; sister, Zella Long Patrick. Survivors: daughter, Mrs. Roy (Judy) McClanahan, Morristown; grandsons; Chris, Mark, & Jeff McClanahan, Morristown; 3 great-granddaughters; brothers, Elder John Oliver & Jack Oliver, Bean Station: sisters Mary McDaniel & Heddie Keitt, Morristown; Mrs. Raymond (Aileen) Childers, Bean Station. Funeral services were held at Mayes Mortuary in Morristown with Rev. Hubert Bunch officiating. Burial in Noeton Primitive Baptist Church Cemetery.

Lay, Bessie D., age 70, of Knoxville, passed away at her home November 8, 1995. Sister Lay was a member of Halls Primitive Baptist church. She was preceded in death by her devoted husband, Homer D. Lay. Survivors are: children, Dwane Lay, Becky Lay Stansberry, both of Knoxville; Kenny Lay of Georgia; grandchildren, Gordy, Randy and Lori Lay, Todd and Ryan Stansberry, all of Knoxville, Joey and Heather Lay of Georgia; sisters, Naomi Cabbage, Sarah Hopson, and Jessie Cabbage. Services were held at 2 p.m. on Friday, November 10 at Mynatt's Chapel. Services were conducted by Elder Bill Berry and Elder Parnick Shelton. Pallbearers were: Ralph Turner, Dennis Branson, Joe Culvahouse, David Sharp, Floyd Roach and Herbert Hopson. Interment was at Lynnhurst Cemetery.

Pratt, Relda Ray, age 90, of Oakland Road, Maynardville, passed away 11:30 a.m. Friday, February 16, 1996, at St. Mary's Medical Center. She was a member of Oak Grove Primitive Baptist Church and was baptized June 5, 1920. Preceded in death by her husband, Curtis Pratt. Survivors: daughter Lillie Pratt; son, Ernest Pratt, both of Maynardville; brothers, L.E. Ray, Lowe Ray, both of Sharps Chapel; sisters, Clara Weaver, New Tazewell, Lelia Mills, Indiana; several nieces and nephews. Funeral services 2 p.m. Monday, Cooke Mortuary Chapel, Rev. Johnny Robison officiating. Interment Pleasant View Cemetery. Cooke Funeral Home in charge.

Robinson, Tempa Sexton , age 106, of Lenoir City, passed away Tuesday afternoon, July 23, 1996, at Loudon Hospital. She was Lenoir City's oldest resident. A member of Lenoir City Primitive Baptist Church. Retired from Charles H. Bacon. A member of Eastern Star #188. Preceded in death by husband, Paul A. Robinson; son, Calvin DeWitt Robinson; son-in-law, Jack A. Ratledge Jr. Survivors: son, William H. Robinson, with whom she made her home; daughters and son-in-law, Jennie and Earl Bobo, Polly Ratledge, all of Lenoir City; 11 grandchildren; scores of great and great-great-grandchildren, nieces and nephews; special nephews, Ralph Sexton of Lenoir City, Earl Sexton of Gatlinburg. The family will receive friends 6:30-8 p.m. Thursday, followed by funeral services at 8 p.m. in the Click Funeral Home Chapel. Graveside services 10 a.m. Friday, Loudon County Memorial Gardens. Click Funeral Home, Lenoir City, in charge.

Shoffner, Nora Elnora (Rouse), age 86, of Maynardville, passed away 10:08 p.m. Saturday, November 4, 1995, at Fort Sanders

Medical Center. She was a member of Oak Grove Baptist Church. Preceded in death by seven infant children; three sisters; four brothers; parents; one grandson. Survivors: husband of 71 years, Pettus Shoffner of Maynardville; daughter and son-in-law, Jane and Doyle Bowman of Maynardville; son and daughter-in-law, Bobby and Lillian Shoffner of Halls; brother, R.C. Shoffner of Maynardville; grandchildren, Anthony and Adam Bowman, and Terry Shoffner; four great-grandchildren, Aaron and Andrew Bowman, Autumn and Scott Shoffner. The family received friends 6:30-8:30 p.m. Monday with funeral services following at Ailor's Chapel, Rev. John Holland and Rev. Johnny Robinson officiating. Interment 11 a.m. Tuesday at Monroe Cemetery. Ailor Mortuary, Maynardville, in charge.

Shoffner, Tom P. , age 50, of Sharps, Chapel went to be with the Lord Friday, March 22, 1996. He was an active member and deacon of Oak Grove Primitive Baptist Church. He was preceded in death by loving father, Charlie Schuffner. Survivors: wife, Betty Schuffner of Sharps Chapel; sons and daughters-in-law, Tommy and Penny Schuffner of Luttrell, David and Wilma Barnard of Sharps Chapel; grandsons, Jason and Greg Barnard; granddaughters, Shana and Kayla Schuffner; mother, Edna Schuffner of Sharps Chapel, brothers, J.D., Jack and Steve Schuffner; sisters, Wanda Brown, Glenda Hunley, Ann Williams, Kathy Keck and Donna Flatford; several nieces and nephews. Funeral services were held at Oak Grove Primitive Baptist Church on Monday, March 25, 1996 with Elder J.C. Monday officiating. Interment was in Stiner Cemetery. Pallbearers: Jim Sharp, Jeff Walker, Bob Cole, Gary Cole, Jim Courtney, and Curtis Dyke. Honorary pallbearers were very special friends: Jeff Sharp and Jerry England. Arrangements by Cooke Mortuary of Maynardville.

Shubert, Saranell, age 74, of Lenoir City, passed away Monday April 15, 1996, at her home. She was a retired nurse from Loudon Hospital with 30 years service. A member of Lenoir City Primitive Baptist Church. Preceded in death by husband, John (Jay) Shubert and parents, Joe E. (Buck) and Laura Grace Shubert. Survivors: Daughter and son-in-law, Lana and Don Lee Sr. of Lenoir City; grandchildren, Ginger and Roger Strunk, Sissy and Pete Scoppa, all of Lenoir City and Don Jr. and Debbie Lee of Loudon; great-grandchildren, Olivia and Kimberly Lee, Roger Lee and Devin Strunk, Megan, Morgan and Mallary Scoppa; brothers and sisters-in-law, Edward and Lucille Shubert of Keystone Heights, Fla. and Benny and Fannie Rhea Shubert of Lenoir City; sisters and brothers-in-law, Mary and Kyle Stooksbury and Judy and Wayne Howell, all of Lenoir City; several nieces and nephews. Funeral services were held at Click Funeral Home Chapel with Rev. Mark Gooden and Elder Chester Hembree officiating. The family received friends from 7 to 8 p.m. Graveside services were held at 11 a.m. at Steekee Cemetery. Pallbearers: Donald Lee Jr., Roger Strunk, Pete Scoppa, Lynn Kirby, Ron Lawrence, Wayne Howell and Bobby Russell. Honorary pallbearers: Mark Shubert, Mike Shubert, David Howell, Eddie Shubert, Bobby Shubert, Jamey Oran, Bill Conner, Jim Shubert, Lee Roy Radford, Donny Conner and Tommy Shubert. Click Funeral Home, Lenoir City, in charge.

Singleton, Irene A., age 65, of Bean Station, passed away July 4, 1996, at Ft. Sanders Medical Center in Knoxville. She was a Member of Noeton Primitive

Baptist Church. She was preceded in death by parents; Pate & Katherine Atkins, and sister, Doshia Collins. Survivors: daughter, Lois Jamruz, Knoxville; sons, Larry & Jerry Singleton, Bean Station; 7 grandchildren; sisters Bonnie Hightower, Morristown; Sally Bowlin, Bean Station, several nieces & nephews. Funeral services were held at Mayes Mortuary of Morristown, with Elder John Oliver & Rev. Fred Oliver officiating. Burial in Noeton Primitive Baptist Church Cemetery.

Spoon, Annie , age 83, departed this life on March 28, 1996. She was preceded in death by her son David. She leaves to mourn her passing, her husband of 62 years, Hubert Spoon, two sons, Jerry and Gary, six grandchildren, five great-grandchildren, and two step great-grandchildren. She joined the Lenoir City Primitive Baptist Church in 1938 where she remained a faithful member until her death. Funeral services were held at the Click Funeral Home Chapel at 8:00 p.m. on March 29, with interment in the City Cemetery. It is here that her body sleeps to await that glorious resurrection morning.

Vincil, Oneda Brewer , age 77, of Lenoir City, died Tuesday, May 21, 1996, at her home. She was a member of Lenoir City Primitive Baptist Church and she was preceded in death by her husband, Jess W. Vincil Sr.; parents, Earl and Stella Anderson Brewer; and an infant daughter. She is survived by her children and spouses, Pat and Wayne Gouge of Lenoir City, Geraldine and Phil Bare of Florence, Ala., Bob and Sue Vincil of Cleveland, Wayne and June Vincil of Lenoir City, Jess William "Bill" Vincil Jr. of Lenoir City; 15 grandchildren; six great-grandchildren; brother and sisters-in-law, Gordon and Ruth Brewer of Lenoir City, Hazel Brewer of

Dalton, GA, several nieces ans nephews.Funeral services were held at Click Funeral Home Chapel with the Rev. George Seay and the Rev. Jon Henson officiating. Interment was in Lake View Cemetery.

Walker, Edith Rose, age 60, of Rockford, passed away Friday morning, July 26, 1996, at Blount Memorial Hospital. She was a member of Brantley's Chapel Primitive Baptist Church in Maryville, Tennessee. Preceded in death by parent's, John P. and Ellen Patty Hembree; sister's, Mildred Peacock, Freda Hembree. Survivors: husband, Glenn H. Walker; daughter and son-in-law, Ellen and David Coppinger of Maryville; Daughter, Sharon Blakley of Rockford; sons, Richard G. Walker of Maryville, John D. Walker of Rockford; grandchildren, Jaclyn "Nikki" Walker, Amanda Walker, Bobbi Jo Walker, Stacie Coppinger, Christopher Coppinger, Linda Rose Blakley, John Curtis Walker; sisters, Frances Davis of Maryville, Gaye Lee of Townsend; brothers, Clarence Hembree of Louisville, David Hembree of Kingston, Hubert Hembree of Maryville, Chester Hembree of Rockford; Funeral Services were held at 8 p.m. at Miller Funeral Home Chapel, Elder Chester Hembree, Elder David Hembree, Elder Richard Walker Officiating, Family and Friends met at Bethel Cemetery in Townsend for the Interment Service.

Wiggins, Hazel G. (Walker), age 83 of Greenfield, Indiana passed away April 9, 1996. She was born February 24, 1913 in Sharps Chapel, TN to Tim and Minty (Collins) Walker. She was a nurses aide at Hancock Memorial Hospital before retiring. She was a member of Oak Grove Primitive Baptist Church. Lewisville OES No. 72, Eagles Lodge Ladies Auxiliary and FOP. Survivors: sons Billy P. Wiggins, California and Robert E. Wiggins of Greenfield; daughter Mary Lou Murdoch, California; brother Malcolm Walker and sister Opal McBride both of Sharps Chapel, TN.; seven grandchildren and five great-grandchildren. Services were held on April 12, 1996 at Paco Memorial Mortuary with Dr. J.E. Hail, Jr. officiating. Burial was in the Park Cemetery.

CHURCH	COUNTY	PASTOR	CLERK	ADDRESS
Black Fox	Grainger	Elder Larry Anderson	Bennie Capps-992-5571	P.O. Box 91, Maynardville, TN 37807
Braden's Chapel	Union	Elder J.C. Monday	Pam Goins Janice Bean, Asst.	Rt. 1, Box 350, LaFollette, TN.37766 Speedwell, TN 37870
Brantley's Chapel	Blount	Elder Jerry McBee Elder Lawrence Adams, Asst.	Hobert L. Williams-983-7838 Sherry Cable, Asst.-983-8387	1515 E. Brown Rd. Maryville, TN 37804 P.O. Box 274, Alcoa, TN 37701
Gethsemane	Knox	Elder Robert Walker	Tom Carmichael	729 Frank Street, Knoxville, TN 37919
Gibson Station	Lee, Va.	Elder Spurgeon Thompson	Dorothy Johnson Virginia Bolton, Asst.	Rt. 2, Box 320, Ewing, VA 24248 Rt. 2, Box 394B, Ewing, VA 24248
Halls	Knox	Elder Parnick Shelton Elder William Berry, Asst.	Helen Branson Scott Branson, Asst.	4633 Marshall Dr., Knoxville, TN 37938 4633 Marshall Dr., Knoxville, TN 37838
Headrick's Chapel	Sevier	Elder Clyde Abbott, Jr. Elder Clyde Abbott, Sr., Asst.	Gearldine Abbott	1780 Alpine Drive, Sevierville, TN 37876
Lenoir City	Loudon	Elder Chester Hembree	E.H. Scarbrough-986-3027 Cheri Brown, Asst.-986-3724	270 Hickman St., Lenoir City, TN 37771 500 C. Street, Lenoir City, TN 37771
Meyers' Grove	Claiborne	Elder Johnny Ayers	Gloria Hipshire 626-8353 Betty Robinson, Asst. 626-4118	3607 Cave Spring Rd., Tazewell, TN 37879 530 Cupp Ridge Road, New Tazewell, TN 37825
Nocton	Grainger	Elder John Oliver	Caroll Oliver Mildred Oliver, Asst.	Rt. 2, Box 3480, Bean Station, TN 37708
Oak Grove	Union	Elder J. C. Monday Elder Mike Brantley, Asst.	Betty P. Sharp Betty Shoffner, Asst	133 Grizzell Ridge Rd., Sharps Chapel, TN 37866 644 Leadmine Bend Rd., Sharps Chapel, TN 37866
Pleasant Hill	Claiborne	Elder William Rhymer Elder James Branscomb, Asst.	William Branscomb Oklen Edwards, Asst.	402 Russell Hill Road, Speedwell, TN 37870 Speedwell, TN 37870
Rocky Dale	Knox	Elder Hugh Brummitt	Betty Livingston-922-4332 Saundra Boniff, Asst.-947-7384	4430 Amston Lane, Knoxville, TN 37938 6916 Weaver Rd., Knoxville, TN 37931

www.ingramcontent.com/pod-product-compliance
Lightning Source LLC
Chambersburg PA
CBHW070045030426
42335CB00016B/1808